George Clinton's New York City Residence.

PUBLIC PAPERS

OF

GEORGE CLINTON,

FIRST GOVERNOR OF NEW YORK.

1777–1795—1801–1804.

VOLUME IV.

PUBLISHED BY THE STATE OF NEW YORK

AS APPENDIX " N," THIRD ANNUAL REPORT OF THE STATE HISTORIAN.

ALBANY:
JAMES B. LYON, STATE PRINTER.
1900.

PREFACE TO VOLUME IV.

The contents of Volume IV of the George Clinton papers are of more than passing interest and value. While the grand operations of the war, during the period involved in this volume —September, 1778 to June, 1779—were conducted in other parts of the country, New York occupied a strategic position of great importance and was forced to endure a number of Indian atrocities along her unprotected frontiers, that stand without a parallel in the history of the war. Many of the details now appear for the first time in print and are so largely at variance with generally accepted statements that have stood unchallenged for one hundred years and more, that the historian in the future, will be compelled, in the interest of accuracy and truth, to revise and remodel all of the standard histories so far as those histories touch upon the border wars of New York State.

These were the dark days of American liberty. The British army continued to remain in New York, an unyielding menace to the American cause, ready at any moment, to strike at any opening afforded by the scattered American forces to the East, North or West; our finances were tangled apparently beyond redemption; our debts already under the increased cost of maintaining the war, were swelling alarmingly; the purchasing value of our currency was diminishing; while on the other hand, the prices of the common necessaries of life, were advancing, to ruinous rates; discontent bordering upon mutiny prevailed in the army, a situation that was not mollified by the injudicious bounty system selected by the Congress.

Governor Clinton at this time was compelled to protect his frontiers with the limited means at his command, encounter the problems impinging upon the Vermont imbroglio, cooperate with Congress on one side and with the Legislature of his own State on the other, and act as peacemaker between officers in the army and between statesmen in public life who smarted under grievances real or fancied. Next to the frontier question, the problem of distributing flour and of regulating the distribution gave him the most concern.

In view of all that has come down to us, it is not surprising that Washington, under date of November 27, 1778, should express himself in these words to Joseph Reed: "It is also most devoutly to be wished that faction was at an end and that those to whom everything dear and valuable is entrusted, would lay aside party views and return to first principles. Happy, happy thrice happy country, if such was the government of it!"

And again, March 15, 1779, to Thomas Nelson: "I think there never was a time, when cool and dispassionate reasoning, strict attention and application, great integrity and (if it was in the nature of things, unerring) wisdom were more to be wished for, than the present. Our affairs, according to my judgment, are now come to a crisis and require no small degree of political skill to steer clear of those shelves and rocks which tho' deeply buried may wreck our hopes and throw us upon some inhospitable shore. Unanimity in our Councils, disinterestedness in our pursuits and steady perseverance in our national duty, are the only means to avoid misfortunes. If they come upon us after these, we shall have the consolation of knowing that we have done our best. The rest is with the Gods."

HUGH HASTINGS,

State Historian.

State Capitol, Albany, N. Y., November 5, 1900.

TABLE OF CONTENTS.

MANUSCRIPT VOLUME VII.

iii

CALENDAR FOR THE YEAR 1778.

	Sun.	Mon.	Tues.	Wed.	Thurs.	Fri.	Sat.
Jan.					1	2	3
	4	5	6	7	8	9	10
	11	12	13	14	15	16	17
	18	19	20	21	22	23	24
	25	26	27	28	29	30	31

	Sun.	Mon.	Tues.	Wed.	Thurs.	Fri.	Sat.
Feb.	1	2	3	4	5	6	7
	8	9	10	11	12	13	14
	15	16	17	18	19	20	21
	22	23	24	25	26	27	28

	Sun.	Mon.	Tues.	Wed.	Thurs.	Fri.	Sat.
Mar.	1	2	3	4	5	6	7
	8	9	10	11	12	13	14
	15	16	17	18	19	20	21
	22	23	24	25	26	27	28
	29	30	31				

	Sun.	Mon.	Tues.	Wed.	Thurs.	Fri.	Sat.
April				1	2	3	4
	5	6	7	8	9	10	11
	12	13	14	15	16	17	18
	19	20	21	22	23	24	25
	26	27	28	29	30		

	Sun.	Mon.	Tues.	Wed.	Thurs.	Fri.	Sat.
May						1	2
	3	4	5	6	7	8	9
	10	11	12	13	14	15	16
	17	18	19	20	21	22	23
	24	25	26	27	28	29	30
	31						

	Sun.	Mon.	Tues.	Wed.	Thurs.	Fri.	Sat.
June		1	2	3	4	5	6
	7	8	9	10	11	12	13
	14	15	16	17	18	19	20
	21	22	23	24	25	26	27
	28	29	30				

CALENDAR FOR THE YEAR 1778.

July	Sun.	Mon.	Tues.	Wed.	Thurs.	Fri.	Sat.
				1	2	3	4
	5	6	7	8	9	10	11
	12	13	14	15	16	17	18
	19	20	21	22	23	24	25
	26	27	28	29	30	31	

Aug.	Sun.	Mon.	Tues.	Wed.	Thurs.	Fri.	Sat.
							1
	2	3	4	5	6	7	8
	9	10	11	12	13	14	15
	16	17	18	19	20	21	22
	23	24	25	26	27	28	29
	30	31					

Sept.	Sun.	Mon.	Tues.	Wed.	Thurs.	Fri.	Sat.
			1	2	3	4	5
	6	7	8	9	10	11	12
	13	14	15	16	17	18	19
	20	21	22	23	24	25	26
	27	28	29	30			

Oct.	Sun.	Mon.	Tues.	Wed.	Thurs.	Fri.	Sat.
					1	2	3
	4	5	6	7	8	9	10
	11	12	13	14	15	16	17
	18	19	20	21	22	23	24
	25	26	27	28	29	30	31

Nov.	Sun.	Mon.	Tues.	Wed.	Thurs.	Fri.	Sat.
	1	2	3	4	5	6	7
	8	9	10	11	12	13	14
	15	16	17	18	19	20	21
	22	23	24	25	26	27	28
	29	30					

Dec.	Sun.	Mon.	Tues.	Wed.	Thurs.	Fri.	Sat.
			1	2	3	4	5
	6	7	8	9	10	11	12
	13	14	15	16	17	18	19
	20	21	22	23	24	25	26
	27	28	29	30	31		

1779.

	Sun.	Mon.	Tues.	Wed.	Thurs.	Fri.	Sat.
Jan.						1	2
	3	4	5	6	7	8	9
	10	11	12	13	14	15	16
	17	18	19	20	21	22	23
	24	25	26	27	28	29	30
	31						

	Sun.	Mon.	Tues.	Wed.	Thurs.	Fri.	Sat.
Feb.		1	2	3	4	5	6
	7	8	9	10	11	12	13
	14	15	16	17	18	19	20
	21	22	23	24	25	26	27
	28						

	Sun.	Mon.	Tues.	Wed.	Thurs.	Fri.	Sat.
Mar.		1	2	3	4	5	6
	7	8	9	10	11	12	13
	14	15	16	17	18	19	20
	21	22	23	24	25	26	27
	28	29	30	31			

	Sun.	Mon.	Tues.	Wed.	Thurs.	Fri.	Sat.
April					1	2	3
	4	5	6	7	8	9	10
	11	12	13	14	15	16	17
	18	19	20	21	22	23	24
	25	26	27	28	29	30	

	Sun.	Mon.	Tues.	Wed.	Thurs.	Fri.	Sat.
May							1
	2	3	4	5	6	7	8
	9	10	11	12	13	14	15
	16	17	18	19	20	21	22
	23	24	25	26	27	28	29
	30	31					

	Sun.	Mon.	Tues.	Wed.	Thurs.	Fri.	Sat.
June			1	2	3	4	5
	6	7	8	9	10	11	12
	13	14	15	16	17	18	19
	20	21	22	23	24	25	26
	27	28	29	30			

CALENDAR FOR THE YEAR 1779.

July	Sun.	Mon.	Tues.	Wed.	Thurs.	Fri.	Sat.
					1	2	3
	4	5	6	7	8	9	10
	11	12	13	14	15	16	17
	18	19	20	21	22	23	24
	25	26	27	28	29	30	31

Aug.	Sun.	Mon.	Tues.	Wed.	Thurs.	Fri.	Sat.
	1	2	3	4	5	6	7
	8	9	10	11	12	13	14
	15	16	17	18	19	20	21
	22	23	24	25	26	27	28
	29	30	31				

Sept.	Sun.	Mon.	Tues.	Wed.	Thurs.	Fri.	Sat.
				1	2	3	4
	5	6	7	8	9	10	11
	12	13	14	15	16	17	18
	19	20	21	22	23	24	25
	26	27	28	29	30		

Oct.	Sun.	Mon.	Tues.	Wed.	Thurs.	Fri.	Sat.
						1	2
	3	4	5	6	7	8	9
	10	11	12	13	14	15	16
	17	18	19	20	21	22	23
	24	25	26	27	28	29	30
	31						

Nov.	Sun.	Mon.	Tues.	Wed.	Thurs.	Fri.	Sat.
		1	2	3	4	5	6
	7	8	9	10	11	12	13
	14	15	16	17	18	19	20
	21	22	23	24	25	26	27
	28	29	30				

Dec.	Sun.	Mon.	Tues.	Wed.	Thurs.	Fri.	Sat.
				1	2	3	4
	5	6	7	8	9	10	11
	12	13	14	15	16	17	18
	19	20	21	22	23	24	25
	26	27	28	29	30	31	

ILLUSTRATIONS.

Public Papers of George Clinton.

Mss. Volume VI (Continued).

MANUSCRIPT VOL. VI.

(CONTINUED).

[No. 1737.]

A DELICATE PROPOSITION.

The Appointment of State Officers to Continental Regiments—The Reorganization of the Fourth New York Line—Its Officers.

Dear Sir, By the Request of the Committee of Congress, now Setting in Camp for the arrang't of the Officers of the army, I Send you the within inclosed List, which is a Coppy of one given to the Said Committee, Last Feb'y at Valley Forge, by Colonel Livingston, few alterations Excepted, which have happened Since, by the Resignation of Several officers, then Included in that List, which names, I thought not necessary to incert, as they are no more, in the Regim't. I have Coppied it, with as less partiality as possible, I have had the Greatest regard for their former Ranks, to place them in this according to the new arrangem't. But Captain Samuel Sackett, Captain Johnatan Titus, Lieut. Norton and Lieut. Benschoten, which Colonel Livingston Chose to be left out, or not to recommend in his arrangem't, which as I am ignorant of the Cause for which he Left them, I have left them out, yet in this not to appear partial by his absence or disoblige him, only if they are Left, I recommand them to you to Be reinplaced in some of the other Regts., if there is possibility, as I am a witness of their having served well, and it would be a pity to turn them out at this Juncture, without some reward.

Also John Franks, paymaster which Colonel Livingston had recommanded for the 6th Captain upon his List, which Recommadion is now refused, by the Committee, as a paymaster had no Rank in the Line of officers, and it would have been superceding all the Lieuts. of the Regt. & create more Discontentement.

And, as there is, by this arrangem't if it takes place, ten vancancies to be filled up, and refered to your Excellency for Recommendations I Beg you would recommand, John Franks for the Lieutenancy vacant. Likewise, Azariah Tuthill, sergt. major in the Regt., Andrew Hartness, Qr. master sergt., & Samuel Talmage also sergt., and Brother to Major Talmage, of Colo. Sheldon's Dragoons, if you think proper to recommand them to the Committee of arrangem't for Ensiegncies. I am with Respect of your Excellency the most ob't serv't

P. Regnier Lt. Col. 4th N. York.

Camp White Plains August 31st 1778.

His Excellency Governor George Clinton.

Poughkeepsie 7th Sep'r 1778.

Sir, I am favoured with your Letter of the 31st Ultimo inclosing a List of the Officers of the 4th New York Regiment, as arranged by the Committee of Congress & containing a Recomendation of several Gentlemen to fill the Vacancies in the same. I some Time since, informed the Committee of Congress that no Mode was pointed out, either by the Constitution or any Law of this State, for the Appointment of Officers to our Continental Regiments. The next Session of the Legislature is to commence on the first of next Month, when I mean to recomend some suitable Provission to be made for this Purpose; till this shall be effected, I can give no other Answer to your Letter than that I have great Reason to believe such Persons of Merit as are recommended to fill the Vacant Offices will be appointed. I am Sir with great Respect Your most Obed't Serv't

Geo. Clinton.

Lieut. Colo. Regnier, 4th New York Regiment.

RANK ROLL OF THE OFFICERS, YET PRESENT IN THE FOURTH N. YORK REGT. AS ARRANGED BY THE CONVENTION OF THE STATE, PRESENTED TO THE COM'TEE OF CONGRESS.

Dates of Comissions and Late Promotions	Names of Officers	Ranks	Recommanded to what	Casualties & Observations
Nov'ber 21st 1776	Henry B. Livingston	Colonel	As before	On Furlough
Jun. 12th Do	Pierre Regnier	Lieut. Col.	Do Do	
	Staff Officers			
April 10th 1777	John Franks	Pay master		On furlough
Feby. Do	John F. Vashee	Surgeon	Do Do	
	Captains			
Nov'ber 21st 1776	Samuel Sackett	1st Captain	1st Captain	Sick at Horse Neck
Do	John Daviss	2d Captain	2d Captain	Dispute Rank with Sackett
Do	Nathan Strong	3d Captain	3d Captain	On furlough
Do	Benjamin Walker	4th Captain	4th Captain	Aide de camp to Baron Steuben
Do	Israel Smith	5th Captain		On Command at Valley Forge
Do	Jonathan Titus	6th Captain		
	1st Lieutenants			
Do	Nathaniel Norton	1st Lieut.	5th Captain	
Do	Theodoricus Fowler	2d Lt.	6th Captain	
Do	Edward Dunscomb	3d Lieut.	Capt. Lieut.	
March 13th 1777	Silas Grey	4th Lieut.	1st Lieut.	
Sep'ber 2d Do	Peter Ellsworth	5th Lieut.	2d Lieut.	
Nov'ber 8th Do	Silvanus Conkling	6th Lieut.		
Do 9th Do	Peter Van Benschoten	7th Lieut.		
	2d Lieutenants			
Nov'ber 31st 1776	Thomas Hunt	1st Lieut.	3d Lieut.	On Command at Valley Forge
Do	Abraham Hyatt	2d Lieut.	4th Lieut.	
March 13th 1777	Rodolphus Van Howenburg	3d Lieut.	5th Lieut.	
Sep'ber 2d Do	Joseph Frylock	4th Lieut.	6th Lieutenant	
Nov'ber 8th Do	James Barrett	5th Lieut.	7th Lieut.	

N. B. Joseph McCraken as the oldest Captain of the state is to fill up the majority vacant by Genl. Washington's Recommandation.

And the Committee of Congress desire your Excellency would let them know his intentions upon the within arrangem't and give the Recommandation as soon as possible.

P. Regnier Lt. Col.

[No. 1738.]

Colonel Hathorn and His Exempts.

Warwick 7th September 1778.

Sir, Inclosed I transmit the Honourable the Council of appointment, the Recommendation of the principal Number of the Exempts of my Regiment,* a variety of Circumstances hath prevented my Compliance with that part of the Militia Law, respecting the Association of the Exempts Untill this time. I have the Honour to be your Excel'ys and the Council most Obt. Servant

John Hathorn.

His Excellency Governor Clinton.

[No. 1739.]

HISTORIAN SMITH DEMANDS HIS SERVANTS.

Governor Clinton Condemns the Proposition as Unjust and Unreasonable.

Poughkeepsie 7th Sep'r 1778.

Dear Sir, I have received your Excellency's Letters of the 27th of last Month & 1st Instant. I am greatly concerned for the Unhappy Fate of Van Tassel, who I am informed always maintained a good Charecter & his Family have afforded many Proofs of their Attachment to the Cause of their Country in which some of them have been great Sufferers. At the same Time as Capt. Colson has already Quit the Army Until It can be discovered to what Place he is gone I think it will be most prudent to make as little stir about the Matter as possible. When this is the Case, if your Excellency's aid in securing him shall be necessary, I will take the Liberty of asking it. In the mean Time your Excellency will please to accept my warmest acknowledgments for the Regard you have paid to the Rights of the Civil Authority.

* See pages 734–735, Vol. III.

Before Mr. Smith left the Country, he applied to me concerning his Male Servants,* which the Commissioners did not conceive themselves authorized to permit him to take with him as they might be imployed to fight against their Country. The Slaves he might have sold if he had pleased. The white Servants he mentions in his Letter to your Excellency, tho they are hardy Scotch Hierlings in whom he has no Property, yet I promised to send them into him in Exchange for any Two subjects of this State in the Power of the Enemy which he shoud procure to be sent out for that Purpose. This being the Case I cant help thinking Mr. Smith's Letter to your Excellency complaining of Injustice in the Commissioners as well as his Request of having his Servants sent into him not only exceptionable but very unjust & unreasonable. I am with the highest Respect Your Excellency's Most Obed't Serv't

G. C.

His Excellency Genl. Washington.

[No. 1740.]

Colonel Malcom Denounces Captain Van Allen and Tories Generally.

Fort Clinton Sep'r 7 1778.

D'r Sir, Capt. Vanallen, who commands the Flagg Sloop, it seems has been making friends with the mammon of unrighteousness. One of my soldiers, (a lad of veracity), who went as Servant to Major Stagg—overheard him giving the Officers of the man of war an account of this Garrison & the Comparative value of our paper mony &c. From his Character, as Disafected, I am amazed that he was permited to have such an opportunity. And I shoud have sent him in Irons to Poughkeepsie if I had the least reason to expect that any notice woud have been taken of him.

*See pages 484-487, Vol. II.

Your Commiss's to Defeat or rather to encourage Conspiracies would have thought me a fool for noticing so triffling a matter as it certainly would appear to them.

Inclosed is a Copy of one of their adjudications—which I shall hand to several men who I suppose will not thank them for their services—the face of the judgement I am sure will raise your Indignation. Shall a Villain be allowed to hire another to bear the punish't of his Guilt. This is carrying the practice of substitution a great Length. Surely as the first magistrate of the State, you will correct these things or point out the defects in our Constitution that restrains your power—that the people at Large may not be imposed on any Longer.

The Day is not far off when there will be another Tribunal to handle these parricides & their abettors.

I have hoped to see you here this week past & must break out & come to you as I want to see you much, being D'r Sir most respectfully yrs.

W. Malcom.

I shall [ ] the soldier up if Vanallen is detained to answer for his Delinquency.

[To Gov. George Clinton.]

[No. 1741.]

Captain John Copp Petitions Governor Clinton for a Commission.

May it please your Excellency, Hearing that I was left out of the Arrangement of Colonel Goose Van Schaick's Regiment for the new Establishment, in Justice to myself I take the Liberty to lay the inclosed Copies of Letters,* (which were sent to the Commissioners) before you, being informed with what gives me much Satisfaction, that the Arrangement is to receive your Ap-

---

*See pages 722–724, Vol. III, and page 26 in this volume.

probation before it takes Place. I am at a Loss to know how to inform your Excellency of the Reason of my being neglected, as Colonel Van Schaick who solely recommended his Officers & was the Occasion of my being left out, never accused me with the least Fault in any Respect, and has to the great Astonishment of all that have heard it, promoted two Subalterns to Companies. Give me Leave to assure your Excellency, I have no other Views at Heart, by wishing to continue in Service than an ardent Ambition to become serviceable to my Country, and a Solicitude to preserve what 'though apparently trifling to my Colonel, is of the last Importance to me, my Reputation.

Should any farther Recommendations prove necessary, I flatter myself that I can easily procure what will be satisfactory from a Number of respectable Gentlemen in the Army. I have the Honor to be with the greatest Respect your Excellency's most obedient humble Servant.

John Copp.

Camp, White Plains Sept'r 7th '78.
His Excellency Governor Clinton.

[No. 1742.]

Association of Exempts for Albany County.

Albany 8th Sept. 1778.

Sir, The enclosed association was a few days ago delivered me with a request to forward it to your Excellency. I told the Gentleman that delivered it, as there was another association going about, and as the Council of Appointment were not met, to wait and get the whole together when Signed and then recommend their Officers and make a Return to your Excellency, but he rather chose it in the way it is.

In this association your Excellency will observe that the three Persons first on the list are those who have been chosen for Officers. I have the Honor to be with the greatest Respect Your Excellency's Most Obt. Serv't

Mat: Visscher.

His Excellency, George Clinton, Esqr. Governor of the State of New York &c.

———

Whearas in and by an Act of the Legislature of the State of New York entiteled, an act for Regulating the Melitia of the State of New York, it is Declaired that the Persons under the Age of Fifty five yeares, who have held Cevil or Melitary Commissions, and are not or should not be Reappointed to there Respecktive Rancks of Office, and all other Persons between the age of Fifty and Fifty five yeares who had not associated and Elected their officers and should associate them Selves in the manner in the said act mentioned, Should be Exempted from serving as part of the Enroled Melitia, We, the Subscribers do, therefore, in persuance of the said act hereby Promise and Engage, that we will Severally on all occations, obey the orders of our Respective Commanding Officers, and will Severally in case of Invasion of Incursions of the Enemey or Insurrections march to repell the Enemy or Suppress Such Insurrections in the Like manner as the Enrolled Melitia are Compelled to do as witness Our hands.

Capt. Corn's Van Santvoordt, Let. David Groesbeeck, 2d Marte Mynderse.

Teunis Bradt, Isaac Van Aernam, John Roseboom, Jur, Saml. Pruyn, Paul Hogstrasser, William Verplanck, Jon. James Abbet, John Cluet, Jun'r, Anthony E. Bratt, John J: Bleecker, Casparus Pruyn, Jellis Winne, Wouter Deforest, Jno. Van Ness, William

Dewitt, R. Visscher, Isaac Verplanck, Hendrick Bogert, Dirck Roseboom, Jacob Cuyler, Richard Lush.

[No. 1743.]

Governor Clinton Promises His Good Offices in Behalf of Mr. Tallmadge.

Poughkeepsie 8th Sep'r 1778.

Sir, I am favoured with your Letter of the 3d Instant. I am not Ignorant of the Charecter of your Familly, or the Merrit of your Brother, and you may rest assured, that if his being properly provided for in the Regiment in which he has served, depends on my good Offices they shant be wanting. At present we have no Mode established, Either by the Constitution or any Law of this State, for the Appointment of Officers to our Continental Battalions. It is probable some Provision will be made for this Purpose by the Legislature at their next Session which is to con‧vene the 1st of next Month. I am Sir Your Most Obed't Serv't

[G. C.]

To Major Benjamin Tallmadge.

[No. 1744.]

Governor Clinton Diplomatically Attempts to Harmonize the Differences Between Colonel Butler and the Commissioners.

Poughkeepsie Sept'r 8th 1778.

Gentlemen, I have rec'd your Letter of the 1st Inst. with the enclosure.

I commend your Conduct in the exercise of your Office with respect to the Cattle taken by Colo. Butler's Troops, & fully agree with you in Sentiment that it would be very dangerous to

encourage the Soldiery to plunder the farms of the Inhabitants
on the frontiers.   I am not authorized to make any Decision relative to the Disposal of the monies arising from the Sale of the
Cattle alluded to in your Letter, but at the same time (considering the critical Situation of our Western Frontiers & the necessity
of keeping in good humour the Troops stationed for their Protection), I cannot but approve of the mode addopted by you & Colo.
Butler as the most prudent untill the matter can by proper authority be finally determined.   The Service of those employed on
the frontiers is naturally Hazardous & fatiguing & they undoubtedly are entitled to all reasonable Encouragem't, but I could wish
that this might be given them in some other way.   I am with
great Esteem Gentlemen Yr. most Obed't Serv't

Geo: Clinton.

Myndert Roseboom Floris Bancker Esqrs, Commiss'rs of
Sequestration in the County of Albany.

[No. 1745.]

GEORGE CLINTON DISCREDITS JOHN STARK.

*Commends the Aggressive Policy of Colonel Butler—The Confiscated
Cattle Question Not Decided.*

Poughkeepsie Sept'r 8th 1778.

Dear Sir, I have received your two Letters of the 13th & 31st
Ultimo (both which came to hand much about the same time) &
thank you for the Intelligence they contain.   In answer to that
part of your last Letter, which respects the Cattle bro't in by
your Scouts I have to inform you that I am not authorized to
make any Decision respecting them and altho' I agree with you,
that the Troops should have all reasonable encouragem't given

them for any extraordinary Exertion; yet I am not without my fears that a Reward arising in this way among the most virtuous Soldiery, might be productive of dangerous Consequences by lead'g them (on the principle of encreasing their Reward) to acts highly prejudicial to the well affected Inhabitants in preference to that of destroying the Enemies of the Country. By the Affidavits which I inclosed you in my Letter of the 6th Inst., w'th respect to the murder of Dumond & the plundering of several of the well affected Inhabitants who were removing with their Effects from the Delaware, I am confirmed in this Opinion. I do not however mean to disapprove of the mode you & the Commiss'rs have agreed upon of selling the Cattle & detain'g the monies aris'g from the sale until the Disposition thereof shall be properly determined.

I am more then ever convinced, that offensive Operations ag't the Savages & Tories is absolutely necessary, & could, therefore, have wished that the plan by you proposed to Genl. Starke had been carried into execution, especially as (if I know the man) it must have been much better than any he can devise.

Some short time ago our Guards stationed on the Delaware in Ulster County destroyed the Grain &c. to prevent its falling into the hands of the Enemy, since which a small Party of Indians & Tories who stole past our Guards burnt 3 or 4 Houses & Barns near Rochester, killed two men & carried off another. I have received no Intelligence from the southern or eastern Quarter lately. I remain with great Esteem D'r Sir Your most Obed't Serv't

Geo: Clinton.

Colo. Butler.

[No. 1746.]

Governor Clinton Chafes Under the Congressional Resolutions Relating to the Loss of the Forts in the Highlands.

Poughkeepsie Sept'r 9th 1778.

Dear Sir, I have rec'd your favor of the 18th Ulto. I have not as yet been able to hear of a trusty Person coming this way from the Southw'd to bring forward the Cash you mention. If no oppertunity should offer for this purpose before the meeting of the Legislature, (which is to be on the first of next month for the purpose of mak'g the annual Election of Delegates to Congress & other Business) I shall recommend it to them to take the proper measures for getting the money into the Treasury.

As I do not conceive myself left in the most agreable Situation by the Resolution of Congress respect'g the Loss of the Posts in the Highlands, I have written to the President* requesting certified Copies of the Proceed'gs of the Court of Enquiry &c. in Order that I may be enabled to evince the Propriety of my own Conduct on that Occassion.

I have inclosed in a Letter to you & your Brethren Copies of sundry Papers respect'g the Conduct of the usurped Gov't of the People on the Grants towards some of the Subjects of this State to which I am persuaded you will pay due attention.

Capt. Smith the bearer, hereof, who formerly saild out of New York & has suffered much in the Contest bears the Character of a very deserving man & well qualified for the naval Department; he is lately arrived from on board the French fleet in which he went in Character of a Pilot from Sandy Hook & continued on

---

*Under date of September first Governor Clinton had written to Congress demanding an investigation into his conduct as commander of the Forts at the Highlands. He followed this letter up with the above letter to William Duer September 21. Congress "ordered that Governor Clinton be furnished with copies of the papers desired and that the president inform him that Congress are well satisfied of the propriety of his conduct as commander of the forts on Hudson's River."—STATE HISTORIAN.

board until their arrival at Boston. I should be happy if he could meet with some public Employment on board some of the Continental vessels by which he may have an Opportunity of serving the public & acquiring a Livelyhood. I believe Mr. Lewis is acquainted with his Character better than I am. I remain with great Esteem D'r Sir Yrs. &c.

[G. C.]

The hon'ble Wm. Duer Esqr.

[No. 1747.]

Governor Clinton Requests that Abraham Hammon, a Prisoner be Forwarded to Poughkeepsie.

Sept'r 9th 1778.

S'r, I thank you for your Letter inclosing a List of the Prisoners of this State & for the attention you have p'd to that Business.

The friends of Ab'm Hammon, one of the Prisoners, mentioned in the List are desirous of his being permitted to return to this State & Capt. Scott, w'th whom you have placed him, giv'g him a good Character, I have, therefore, to request that you will put him on his Parole, to repair directly to this Place and appear before the Commiss'rs for Conspiracies & receive their further Order respect'g him. I am Sir Yrs.

Geo: Clinton.

Ezekiel Williams Esqr. D'y Commis'y Prisoners at Hartford.

[No. 1748.]

Lieutenant Colonel Staats Reports to General Ten Broeck that Brant is Contemplating Another Raid.

Cherry Valey 9th Sep'r 1778.

" Dear General, This afternoon arrived our Scout from the Unindilla, Commanded by Capt. McCeen & have brought three Prisoners from there, which he has taken in the night of the 7th

Instant; the one is an Inhabitant of that Place; he saith that Brant has issued Orders for a meeting on the 8th of this Instant, in order to draw ammunition; that there was an Expedition agoing on in short, but Could not tell which way, their number he says is Reported to be Two Thousand men; the other two Prisoners are from Col. Quackenboss's Regt., their names are Andries Ostrande & Joachim Van Alstyn, who was Tryed at the Genl. Court martial. They tell one Story. They say that they had been down 9 days at Unindilla, that Frederick Oliver & Gerrit Sixbee, Persuaded them to go along & that Oliver was taken also with them, but made his Escape, but is Supposed to be Dead as they fired Several shot at him, Van Alstyn & Ostrande say as the former Relating to the Expedition & the ammunition but differ in the number; their account is between 400 & 600 men as they have heard, but have not seen more than 100 which were at the Unindilla the others where at Ochquaga."

The above is Extract of a letter from Lt. Col. Staats* to General Ten Broeck.

[No. 1749.]

EXCITING TIMES ON THE DELAWARE FRONTIER.

Colonel Cantine's Report to Governor Clinton of an Encounter Between Settlers and Indians.

Marbletown 9th Sept. 1778.

Sir, The Day after I came from Paghkataghkan to this Place, I received Intelligence that the Enemy had burnt three Barns or Barracks, Viz. of Andries Shurker, Peter Millar and Jacob Baker, The two first they have killed and scalped, Baker and a Boy of Millar are not found, therefore think they have taken them along. I came to Hunk last Saturday at two O'Clock After Noon, as the

*See page 31.

Mischief had been committed that morning about Break of Day. Capt. Telford with the advice of the Neighbours had ordered a Party to go upon the Papacton Road, and waylay them, when they should return under the Command of John Graham, who acted in the Station of a Lieut. The Party consisted of fourteen; they went up the Road about seventeen miles, it being then late in the Afternoon, they intended to stay there, as there was no Tract. From whence they concluded they were ahead of them if they intended to return that way. But what could have induced them to choose a place so disadvantegeous to themselves I cannot account for. The place in my Opinion was neither calculated for Defence, or to save a Retreat. They had been there about half an hour, and heard the Enemy coming. An Indian came about thirty Yards before the rest, and when he came opposite to them, he perceived them as they were in ꟻo way properly concealed. The Indian on seeing them squatted, and then Abraham Vancamp shot at him. Several of the others came within forty Yards of our Men, who then discharg'd their Pieces upon them, but believe, did Little or no Execution, at Least I could see no Signs thereof; It appears to me that the greater part of our Men then endeavoured to make their Escape, but the Enemy was between them and the Inhabitants, & our Men between them and the Indian Country, or else probably the greater Part of both parties would have fled. In Justice to Mr. Graham and Ens'n McBride, I must say they were the Last who left the Ground, as I am informed. They were obliged to go up a Hill as steep as the Roof of a House, which was just back of them. Had the Enemy pursued with Vigour, I have reason to believe from the Situation of the Ground, that few of them would have escaped. Mr. Graham, Robert Temple and Adam Ambler were killed and scalped in this Fray, the Remainder are all safe returned. The Enemy consisted as near as I can learn between seventeen and Twenty four. When I found that Mr. Graham's Party was so small and not provided with Provisions to pursue them far, I immediately ordered five Days Provisions to be made ready for fifty two Men, which was the whole fit for such a Journey, who march'd early the Morning following under the Command of Capt. Clark, to pursue them as far as where the Middaghs Live, unless apprized of a superior Number of the Enemy to be there, for which purpose I directed them to send a Spy to that Place when they should come to Pappacton.

The Inclosed is a Copy of the Orders I gave to Capts. Nichols* and Vankeuren, when they went to Delaware. When they returned, they told me they had brought off the Effects of Burch, who was gone to the Enemy, and of several others. They ask'd me whether I would admit the Men to have it as plunder, I told them it was not in my power to give, thought it my Duty to write to one of the Commissioners of Sequestration, informing them that the Guard who had been to Papacton, had brought off some Cattle, Horses &c. Capt. Vankeuren took the Letter to him. Colo. Pawling desired my Coming down the same Day to go and look to the Post at Shandekan, which I did. When I returned to Hunk, they had sold Part there, and some was carried over the mountain. Capt. Vankeuren also was gone home. I enquired whether the Commissioners had given them Leave to sell. I was told by Capt. Nichols they had; I then thought I had discharged my Duty, if I have erred in applying to the wrong Person, I confess it has been for want of Judgement, for I directly thought I was in the Line of my Duty.

---

*See page 626, Vol. III.

The twelve Men, which were last, had no other Orders than to fetch down John Middagh, Hendrick Bush and Nathan Parks. I promised them a Reward (for each of them) of Fifteen pounds and as much more as I could collect, and to destroy the Grain on the River. Before they return'd, I had Information of Dumond's being shot at Paghkataghkan, and that five hundred Indians & Tories were at that Place. I then went to Paghkataghkan, and before I return'd, they were come and had sold what they brought. The greater Part of these twelve men did not belong to my Detachment, and went voluntarily for the above Reward promised by my Self & Coll. Pawling to them, so that it will be impossible for me to correct what is past. For the future I will endeavour to prevent it, for I am well satisfied it will not answer a good End. I am equally of Opinion with your Excellency, that our frontiers will not have peace, till the places where they harbour are destroyed. But it is my humble Opinion, that so long a rait cannot be taken without pack horses to carry provisions to subsist on, especially with a number of men sufficient to subdue that place. I have also received a Letter from Coll. Pawling, who says he has been informed, that there are many Indians, who are our friends, at Oquago. The Villains who disturb us are at Cokehouse and Delaware. I have, heretofore, given my Opinion of the Post at Laghewack; if you judge best that the Guard should occupy that place, I will immediately remove there. And in the mean Time remain, Your Excellency's Most humble & obed't Serv't

John Cantine.

P. S. The fifty two Men are not yet returned, expect them next Day after tomorrow.

His Excellency, George Clinton, Esq're.

[No. 1750.]

SERIOUS CHARGE AGAINST JOHN STARK.

Accused of Encouraging Seizure of Cattle, the Proceeds of Whose Sale Were to be Distributed Among the Troops Capturing Them.

Albany 10th Sept'r 1778.

Sir, We beg leave to inclose your Excellency Copy of an Affidavit of Mr. Isaac Bogert, from which you will perceive that General Stark has given Orders, (or at least his Sanction), for the Sale of a Number of Cattle the Property of several of the Subjects of this State and intends to have the Amount distributed among the Troops.

From the best Information we have been able to collect, we cannot learn that the People from whom the Cattle were taken have acted such a Part as to forfeit their Property.

The Spirit of plundering is so apparent among the Troops on the Frontiers, particularly those at Cherry Valley, that unless some Steps are soon taken to put a Stop thereto, our Frontiers will be ruined; we have had Persons sent down by them upon Pretence of being Guilty of Treason, but suspect in fact that the motive proceeded only from having a better Oppertunity to appropiate their Effects for the above Purposes.

We are with Respect your Excellencies Hum'e Servants.

John M: Beeckman, Mat: Visscher, Isaac D. Fonda.

His Excellency George Clinton, Esq.

Governor of the State of New York.

Isaac Bogart of the City of Albany being duly sworn, deposeth, and saith that he was lately at Cherry Valley, where he was informed by Capt. Robert McKeen, that he went on a Scout with

Captain Ballard of Colo. Alden's Regiment, and that while on their way they proposed to Capt. Ballard to proceed on in Order to take Prisoners, and Brant in particular; that Ballard answered he did not desire to see Brant nor to fight with him as his Orders from General Stark were to bring off the Cattle from the Butter Nuts and other Places which amounted to upwards of an hundred besides Horses and Sheep; that several other Persons gave him much the same Information, and the Deponent further says that from the best account he could obtain, there then were at Cherry Valley of the Cattle &c. brought in by Capt. Ballard from the Butter Nuts &c., forty two Head of neat Cattle, four at Goose Van Alstyne's ten Horses, twenty nine Sheep and one Iron Shod waggon; that Capt. Ballard and Party killed and made use of nine or ten Sheep on their way to Cherry Valley. And this Deponent further says, that he was informed by Weter Johnson, Deputy Commissary of Purchase, that of the Cattle so brought in as aforesaid, seven Head weighing 1715 wt. and three or four Sheep had been killed at Cherry Valley by Order of the Commanding Officer, and this Deponent further says, that the said Ballard informed him that General Stark had or would give Orders for the Sale of the Cattle so taken and brought in, and for the Division of the Proceeds of such Sale among the Party that brought in the Cattle &c. And this Deponent further says that the General talk at Cherry Valley was that the Cattle &c. was to be sold for the use of the Troops.

Isaac Bogert.

Sworn before me 10th Sept'r 1778.

John M. Beekman Justice.

a true Copy from the Original.

Leon. Gansevoort, Jun'r, secy. to the Commissioners of Conspiracies.

[No. 1751.]

FORAGE SCARCE AND DEAR.

Washington Requested to Call Upon the Eastern States to Cooperate with the Quartermaster General to Supply the Army at Reasonable Prices.

Camp White Plains, 10th Sept'r 1778.

Sir, The Scarcity of Forage, and the Reluctance with which the Farmers part with what they have to Spare, has, for some Time past, filled me with more Alarming apprehensions than I have felt on acc't of any other branch of the Quarter Master's Department. The necessary Comsumption of Forage not only in and about the Army, but for the numerous Teams employed in the inland Transportation of Provisions and Stores, has so far exhausted the Resourses of former Crops, that every Farmer in the middle States discerns that the Demand for Grain is equal, if not more than equal, to all that can possibly be furnished, and of course that the Purchasers, whether for publick or private use, must of necessity pay whatever Price shall be insisted on. The Discretion of each Individual is, therefore, the only Boundary to the Price Demanded. Hence we find it impossible without the Interposition of legislative Authority, to adhere Steadily to any fixed Price, and at the same Time obtain the necessary Supplies. For altho' many of the better disposed among the Farmers would be willing to sell their Forage at the Present Current Prices, if they were not apprehensive their most avaricious neighbours would obtain a higher Price for theirs, yet while they see Prices constantly rising and unbounded, they are unwilling to preclude themselves from the Advantages which Experience has taught them may be obtained by withholding their Commodities from the present Market. This increases the Avidity of the Demand, and of course obliges the Purchaser to submit to the Terms imposed by the Seller. The enormous increase of the Publick Exditures, tho' perhaps the greatest, is but one of the Evils which must attend the permitting the Prices of Grain to continue rising without any other Limitation than the capricious Discretion of the Sellers of it. The mischief is increased both in Size and Velocity by every Step it advances, and must, if permitted to continue, produce the most pernicious consequences. On the other Hand, if the Legislatures of the respective States will give us their Aid, by fixing a Table of Prices between Individuals and the Publick, and establishing a legal Mode as well for the obtaining at such Prices what each Individual can spare, as for ascertaining the Quantity which may be taken in Case of Dispute, I imagine the Quantity of Grain in the Country will be found more adequate to the demand than present Appearances indicate.

From the Scarcity, whether real or artificial, which we now feel, and have for some Time past experienced in the States northward of Chesapeak Bay, we have been under a necessity of drawing considerable Quantities of Grain from Virginia, Maryland and Delaware; the Transportation of which, not only enhances the Price, but, by employing more Teams in the publick Service, increases the Consumption. If, therefore, the Inhabitants of the States more contiguous to the Army could be induced to deliver, in a short Time, what they can with Propriety spare, it would not only enable us to form our Magazines in due Season, but might authorize us to relax our Demand on the distant Places from whence Supplies are transported at so great an Expence.

I take the Liberty of troubling your Excellency with these Facts and observations, together with a Letter from Col. Biddle, Com'y Gen. of Forage, which is inclosed herewith, on a Confidence that a Representation of the Matter from your Excellency to the Legislatures of the respective States, either immediately or thro' Congress, will be the most likely way to have the Business speedily and effectually attended to, and to procure it that dispatch which its Importance demands. I have the Honour to be, with the greatest Respect, Your Excellency's most obedient & most humble Servant

                                    Cha. Pettit, A. Q. M. G.
His Excellency General Washington.

                    (Copy.)

                    ———

                    Camp White Plains Sep'r 6th 1778.

Dear Sir, The consumption of Forage is so great & from the distance it is brought, subject to so many delays, & disappointments, that I wish to fall on every method that will be most likely to answer a certain & regular supply; at this time we draw considerable quantities of Corn & Oats from Virginia & Maryland by the way of the Head of Elk to Trenton & thence by land to this Camp. The same from the Delaware state & these supplies must be continued as long as the Season will permit, the middle States being much drained.

However I think much more might be drawn from Penns'a, Jersey, New York & Connecticut, if the Legislatures of those States would take effectual measures to bring out their Hay & Grain for the use of the Army. And we shall have occasion for all that can possibly be spared from each of those States to subsist our Horses. At present N: Jersey cannot furnish a sufficiency to Forage the great number of Teams passing through there, altho' the Gentleman imployed in that State has as much

Interest & Industry as any one in it. He complains of the great Prices demanded; the same complaints from my Agents in Penns'a, N: York & Connecticut; & all agree that from various causes the Forage is not brought to Market. The absence of the Militia in service in some places has been one cause of their not threshing & in many the expectation of a rising Price induces them to keep it back—some measures are necessary to bring them to thresh & deliver all that can be spared for the use of the Army. The limitting a generous Price beyond which they would not have an expectation of a rise would have a good effect & they should deliver it at the Seasons in which it is most wanted: Viz. Fall, Winter & Spring; therefore, I would propose that his Excell'y Genl. Washington, should be informed of this, & be requested to write to the different Legislatures to take the most effectual means to assist my Agents in the different districts in the Collection of Forage by limitting the Prices & enforcing a Delivery of the Hay & Grain that can be spared at stated Periods, also in furnishing Carriages to hawl the same in their respective States to such places as it may be wanted at.

If the Prices should be limitted from Penna. to Connecticut inclusive, it may be necessary to make an application to the Legislatures of Delaware, Maryland & Virginia on the same occasion, as the conveniency of water carriage & from the great abundance of Corn & Oats in those States as well as the insufficiency of Grain in the other States will make it necessary to draw regularly from them. The proposition you made of a number of Ox Teams would be a great relief if they could be procured, as the Oxen could be subsisted on Grass and a very little Hay. In the winter a small quantity of Grain would be necessary.

I submit it to you lay such part of this as you may think necessary before the General & am D'r Sir Your most Obedient servant

Clement Biddle, C. G. F.

(Copy)

P. S. There is so little Grain threshed in this & the adjoining
States & our present situation requiring immediate supplies there
is no time to be lost in adopting some method to get the Farmers
to work.

To Colonel Charles Pettit, A. Q. M. Genl.

(Copy)

[No. 1752.]

*Governor Clinton Declines to Commit Himself to the Case of Captain
Copp.**

Poughkeepsie Sept'r 11th 1778.

Sir, I have rec'd your Letter of the 7th Inst. with the enclosure.
I have never heard of your having acted unbecoming the Character of an Officer; and the Letters from the Gentlemen (of whom
I have the best Opinion) in your favor, convince me that you
have acted with Propriety. Neither the Constitution or any Law
of this State has made Provision for the Appointment of Officers
to the Cont'l Regts. raised under the Direction of this State. If,
therefore, the Arrangem't of the Committee of Congress is to be
submitted to me for my approbation, I am at pres't Ignorant of
the principle on which it is to be done. But, if this should be
the Case & the Legislature should also authorize me thereto I shall
endeavor to do ample Justice to the merit of the Diff't Officers.
I am &c.

Geo: Clinton.

Capt. Copp.

---

*See pages 722-724, Volume III, and pages 8-9 in this volume.

[No. 1753.]

ALBANY UTTERS A VIGOROUS PROTEST.

Against Billeting Two Thousand Troops in that City—And the Mayor Gives His Reason.

Albany 11th September 1778.

Sir, A Report that 2,000 Troops are to be stationed here the ensuing winter renders it our indispensible duty in behalf of the Inhabitants of this City and its Suburbs, to write to your Excellency on the Subject and to request your directions in the Premisses, to which End we deem it necessary to observe:

That this City (from the Nature of its Situation) has been, during the present war, a Magazine of Stores and Provisions, and the Place for Confinement of disaffected Persons, both from the Northern and western Parts of the State and as such always was a Capital object by the Enemy to be subdued. In Consequence of which, it has for upwards of three years past undergone innumerable distresses and Inconveniences necessarily attending the operations of war.

The Inhabitants of this City were some of the first who stepped forth in the Cause of their Country and took an active Part in the Contest. They have from time to time, endeavored to conciliate the affection of the Indians and to their utmost furnished arms, Blankets, Ammunition, Camp Equipage, Intrenching Tools and Provisions, and Specie in exchange for Continental Currency to supply the wants and necessities of the Northern army.

This County (exclusive of the Manors), includes a large Quantity of Lands setteled of late, Chiefly by Emigrants from Europe, as well as from other American States and the Southern Counties of this State; that from the Tenure under which many hold their Lands, and the Monies due on Mortgages from others, together with their necessitous Circumstances they have by these means been more open to Seduction by the disaffected, and more readily induced to distress the well affected by Robberies, Plots and Conspiracies against the State; besides the well affected among us, in subduing and apprehending the Tories and in rendering other public Services to their Country have so wasted their Time and Substance, that many of them are now reduced to the utmost necessitous Circumstances.

The Inhabitants of this City were usually supplied with many of the necessities of Life as well as food for their Cattle from small inclosed Lotts of Ground within the Bounds of this City, the Fences whereof were last Fall & winter burnt and destroyed by the Continental Troops, which Lotts by means thereof have been thrown into Commons, and have ever since lain waste, which together with the great Drought of the Summer has greatly diminished the necessities of Life among the Citizens.

There is also a greater Scarcity of Firewood here than ever was known in this City, owing to the Consumption thereof by the Troops that were last winter billetted on the Inhabitants, who supplied them therewith and for which no recompence has been made.

From this State of Facts we beg leave to inform your Excellency, that however willing we have always been and still are to risk our all in supporting the Freedom and Independance of our bleeding Country, yet it is our earnest request (and we deem it no more than reasonable) that in the distribution of the Troops for winter Quarters, a due respect may be had to the former distresses and present sufferings of the Inhabitants of Albany and its Suburbs. And, as there are Barracks in this Place which may contain about 400 Troops, exclusive of an Hospital which will contain 800, tho we presume the latter will be appropriated for the use of the Sick, we would deem it equitable that no more Troops may be allotted to us than the Barracks and Hospital (if not used as such) may contain. That the strictest orders be issued against Pilfering and stealing from and insulting the Inhabitants and that the Officers be enjoined in punishing the refractory and disobedient. We have the Honor to be Your Excellency's most Obt. & most Hum'e Serv'ts

By order of Common Council.　　　John Barclay, Mayor.

His Excellency, George Clinton, Esqr. Governor of the State of New York &c.

[No. 1754.]

Three More Tories Who Refuse to Take the Oath of Allegiance.

State of New York Ss,

To his Excellency George Clinton Esquire Governor of the State of New York, General and Commander in chief of all the militia, and admiral of the navy of the same.

In pursuance of an act of the Legislature of this State Entitled " an act more " effectually to prevent the mischiefs arising from the Influence and Example of " persons of equivocal and suspected Characters in this State," We do hereby notify your Excellency that, Joseph Mabbet, Benjamin Lapham and Richard Bartlett, all of Dutchess County, having severally appeared before us, and being respectively by us tendered the Oath, in the said act contained did severally refuse to take the same, and that unless your Excellency shall think proper to detain them, for the purpose of exchanging them for any of the Subjects of this State, in the power of the Enemy, we shall Cause them respectively to be removed to some place within the Enemy's lines.

　　　　　　Peter Cantine, Jur., Robt. Harpur, Egb't Benson, Commissioners.*

Poughkeepsie 12th September 1778.

---

*By accounts from Fort Clinton, on Hudson River, we learn that the magistracy of the State of New York send their disaffected inhabitants into that place, from whence they are transmitted in vessels, under a flag of truce, to New York city. These persons are discriminated by their refusal to make attestations of their allegiance to the State, and to renounce the tyrant of Britain. It appears that the highest characters are not winked at. The Honorable William Smith, Esq., formerly of the royal council under the former government, and author of the History of New York, &c., forced out of his inglorious neutrality, has been lately brought to the test, and refusing the oath, was about four or five weeks since delivered to the enemy through this channel. His Majesty of Britain will be difficulted to provide for his faithful adherents, and may think in earnest of selling Hanover and his other German dominions to raise a fund equal to their expectations. Where, then, will such as Mr. Smith, who are justly despised both by royalists and Americans, find shelter and relief?—Pennsylvania Packet, September 17.

[No. 1755.]

Returns of Colonel Van Schaick's regiment at White Plains.

A RETURN OF THE FIRST NEW YORK REGIMENT COMMANDED BY GOOSE VAN SCHAICK ESQR. COLONEL

Camp White Plains Sep'r 13.	Field			Commissioned				Staff					Non Commissioned						
	Colonel	Lt. Colonel	Major	Captains	1st Lieutenants	2d Lieutenants	Ensigns	Adjutant	Pay master	Qu'r master	Surgeon	Mate	Serjt. Major	Qr. Mr. Serjt.	Drum major	Fife major	Serjeants	Drum & Fifers	Rank & File
8 Companies																			
Total	1	1	1	6	7	7	5	1	1	1	1	1	1	1	1	1	29	12	392

N. B.   100 men not fit for duty for want of Cloths

PETER B. TEARSE *Adjt.*
G. V SCHAICK *Coll.*

[No. 1756.]

General Ten Broeck Forwards Correspondence to Governor Clinton.

Albany 13th Sep'r 1778.

Sir, I inclose your Excellency, Copy of a letter from Joseph Brant* to Colonel Jacob Klock & Extract of a letter from Lieut. Colonel Staats† to me & am with great Respect Your Excellency's most Obedient Humble Servant

Ab'm Ten Broeck.

His Excellency George Clinton Esqr.

[No. 1757.]

Marbletown Exempts.

Marbletown 14th Sep'r 1778.

Sir, As there was an Act or Resolve passed, that all such persons as were exempt from doing military Duty, should associate themselves by such a certain Day, as in the said Act or Resolve was prescribed.

I have, therefore, thought proper herein, to inform your Excellency, that on the Last Day of said Limited Time, this Number of Exempts (herein inclosed) of Marbletown assembled & associated themselves, according as the said Act or Resolve prescribed. Some Time after, I went to Col. Cantine, and shewed him the said List of Exempts. Col. Cantine apprehensive that there might perhaps be some who had no Notice, notified them by Advertisements, that they should associate on the 1st of Aug't Last past, otherwise that he would enrol them along with the Militia. I Remain at the same Time Sir, Your Excellency's Most Obt. & humble serv't

John Broadhead.

[Endorsed: "Agreed to & Entred Nov'r 4th, 1778."]

---

* Brant's letter not found.
† See page 15.

That the Associators will Severally on all Occasions, obey the
Orders of there Respective Commanding Officers, and will in
Casses of invasions, or Incursions of the Enemy, or Insurrections,
march to Repel the Enemy, or suppress sutch Insurrections, in
the Like manner as the Enrolled militia are Compelled to do:
so that they shall not, when Called out in Detachments, be annexed to any other Regiment or Company, or be under the Immediate Command of any Other then there Own Officers;

We the subscribers being the magoritey of the Companey of
associated Exempts inrolled on this Paper do Hearby Recommend to the Honorable the Councel of Appointment for Officers
for said Company. Witness our Hands.

Frederick Shurter, Wilhelmus Roosa, Benjamin Louw, Jur,
John Brodhead, Jacob Gn. Louw, Gradus Hardenbergh, Tobias
Dubois, Johannes Vendermark, Abraham Catine, Jacob Snyder,
Isack Davis, Cornalus Bogart, Thomas Eltenge, John C. Dewitt,
William Arnold, Oswald Dewald, Jonas Smith, Thos. Brinckle,
Mortynus Oosterhout.

John Broadhead, first in Command; Garardus Hardenbergh,
Second in Command; Tobias Dubois, third in Command.

[No. 1758.]

*Four of Colonel Ludinton's Captains Refuse to Accept Their
Commissions.*

Fishkills Septem'r 14th 1778.

D S'r, Inclosed you have a Letter I Reciv'd of Col. Ludinton
acquainting me that, Foure of his Capts. had Refused to Except
of theire Commissions and the Consequence was That he Cou'd
not Turn out the Fourth man agreeable to his orders—and De-
siares I Sou'd acqaint his Excellency Theire with. I Live the

matter with his Excellency to act as he Shall Think most proper in the premises. If I can be of any Service I am at his Excellency's Command. I am with Due Respect his Excell'ys most Humbl. Sarvant

Jacob's Swartwout.

His Excellency George Clinton.

Sir, I have Had my offisars together in order to give out the Commisons and there is fore of the Capts. Refuses to take them to wit: John Haight, John Crane, David Waterbery and Nathaniel Scribner which Renders it imposable for me to turn out my Coto of men; therefore, Shall Exspect, Sir, that you will acquaint His Excelency of the Diferculty that atends me on that acount in order that the abov mentind Capt. Be Brought Before His Excelency to Shew Cause why they Did not Exsept of their Commisions and Likewise to Enable me to Comply with your orders which I am Disposed to do as Soon as the Diferculty is Removed and, am, Sir, your verry Humble Servant

Henry Ludinton.

Fredrecksburg Sept. 8th 1778.

to Colo'll Comedant Jacobes Swoughought.

[No. 1759.]

HARVEST BEFORE MILITARY DUTY.

List of Men in Colonel Peter R. Livingston's Regiment Who Refused to Go to West Point when Ordered.

Manor Livingston ye 15th Sep'r 1778.

D'r Sir, Agreeable to orders Rec'd from Brig'r General Ten Broek, I have now ordered the 7 & 8 Clases of our Regement a Second time, to march Down to Fourt Arnald, and find that it

3

is only Lost Labour to order out any part of our Regement any more without the Delinquents are punished, as there Semes to be No dread of any Such thing.   I have been under the Necessity of takeing those few who where willing To go, to drive the waggons which where required from This Destrict, as no Suficiant Nomber of drivers Could be procured, and I understood the waggons where very Necessaryly waunted to remove Contenental Stores, which Lay much Exposed to the Enemy; it is at present a very Pressing time with the farmers in this quarter, as they are mostly Imployed at present in Sowing There wheat & rye, Some Say they are willing to Go as Sune as they have done Sowing and that They are partly Rewned (ruined) if they must go Now.   Inclosed you have a list of the above mentioned Classes belonging to our Regement, I hope his Excellency the Governor will do as he in his wisdum Shall thinck proper in this Case, I am Sir Your Frind & Sar't

Samll. Ten Broeck, Major.

P. S. Those who are gone as Drivers out of those Clases you will find it mentioned opposit there Names on the List.

To Colo. Robt. Banson.

A List of the 7 and 8 Clases belonging to Colo. Peter R. Livingston's Regement ordered to go Down to Fourt Arnald in the Highlands Under the Command of Capt. Tiel Rockafeller, Sep'r 11th 1778.

Capt Tiel Rockafeller,	Thomas Bayley,
Leut. Jacob Haugedorn,	George Leaman,
Coenradt Patrie Cor:, waggoner,	Duncan Mac Intire, Sar't,,
	Nickolus Traver,
Samuel Rosaman, waggoner,	Handrick Schut, waggoner,

Patrick Mac: Fall,

Thomas Denels,

John Silvernail,

Mikle Jorgh,

Will'm Morrisson,

John Shats Sar't,

Peter Shaver,

Robt. Mac: Fall,

Coenradt Cris'r Patrie,

Teunis Sower,

John Cor's Dacker, waggoner,

Coenradt Ham, Jun'r,

Johan's Wiest, Sar't,

Siemon Mighael, waggoner,

Coenradt Rosaman, Jun'r,

David Mincaler, Sar't,

Jacobus J. Dacker,

Andries Gardner,

Josiah Minckaler,

Barnard Sipperley, Cor.,

Henry Shultis,

John Salbaugh,

Marks Lasher,

John Pierce, waggoner,

Saml. Snyder,

Henry Dick,

Phillip Ringsdorph,

Barnard Albertie,

Johan Jost Donspaugh, wag-
    goner,

Wandle Pulver,

William Frts, waggoner,

Zachariah Ray,

Asa Holams, Cor.,

Arthor Mac: Arthor,

Johan's Loot, Cor.,,

Abrham Van Deusen,

Fredrick Schut,

Antony Kline,

Wilhalmus Vielie, waggoner,

Johan's Nicko's Brusie, Do,

Martin Wash Burn,   Do,

Abraham Frayr,

Casparus Lantman, Jun'r,,

Jacob L. Dacker,

Peter Crine,

William Siemon, Cor.,

Andries Reghter,

Johan's Pulver,

Johan's Kilmer,

Peter Colwell, waggoner,

William Merryfield, waggoner,

Johan's Denius, waggoner,

Johan's Miller,

Handrick Heysradt,

Phillip Duff, waggoner,

Cristayan Denius,

Johan Adam Denius,

Michael Wauters, waggoner,

Handrick Baner, Sar't,

Hand'k Best, waggoner,

William P. Linck, Cor.,

Banjamin Dacker,

Adam Frease,

Jurry Coen,

William Livingston,

Harmen Snyder, Sar't,

Peter Berenger,

Hand'k Teus. Klum, waggoner,

David Bosarune,

William Linck,

Joseph Bayley,

Jacob Finger,

Minderd Schut, Jun'r,,

Harme Taylor,

John Finger, Jun'r,

Emrigh Dacker,

John Harris,

Adam Mincaler,

Handrick Rypenbergher,

Jacob Saulpaugh, Sar't,

Johan's Shaver,

Jacob Aligh, Cor.,

Petrus Brusie, Jun'r,

Winesan Brusie,

Peter Proper,

Handrick Proper,

William Ackerman,

Daniel Rypenbergher, waggoner,

Johan's Niver,   Do,

Cristophel Niver,   Do,

James Boucher,   Do,

Peter Showerman,   Do.

[No. 1760.]

General Ten Broeck Appeals to Private Secretary Benson for More Light on Court Martial Punishment.

Albany 16th Septem'r 1778.

Sir, Your favour of the 10th Instant I have Received & as I am Still not Clear on the Subject matter to which your letter Referrs I would beg leave again to state the same as I conceive more fully; I am under no doubt but that all Capital offences Cognizable before a General Court martial & Capitally found, I mean that of Death, ought & must have the approbation or Disapprobation of the Commander in Chief, but my Doubt is whether, if a militia General Court martial Trying a man for Desertion & Sentence him to Receive a Corporal Punishment of whipping or a fine in Commutation thereof, is a matter that Requires the approbation or Disapprobation of the Commander in Chief or whether I, as Brigadier General of the militia of this County, who ordered this Court martial can officially approve or Disapprove any Sentence above mentioned & under that of Death. I am led to believe I can, & that from his Excellency the Governor's letter to me of the 1st Instant, in which he advises me to Remitt the Punishments Sentenced by the Court martial against the Delinquents of Kings District lately Referred to him, which was Corporal Punishment or a Commutation by paying a fine, this I have done in Conformity to his Excellency's desire; Please to set me Right in this with his Excellency's opinion as soon as Possible. I am the more Pressing as I have order'd two new Courts martial to Try every Delinquent in my Brigade that can be brought before them for Trial with all Possible dispatch. I Expect their Report in a few days & I shall think my self not at liberty to approve or disapprove their Sentences untill I am better Informed, whether I am to send them for his Excellency's approbation or not.

I am much averse to Corporal Punishment in the first Instance, (in the field it may be Perfectly Right), & I hope the Legislature at their next meeting will Judge it Expedient to amend that Part at least of the militia Law, & Instead of Corporal Punishment, lay a fine to be Levyed on the Goods & Chattels of the offenders, in default of which Imprisonment; this I humbly Conceive will answer better Purposes then Corporal Punishment; the Sentences of the Court are gone forth & I do not know but some of the yeomanry of Kinderhook & Claverack have before now been Tyed up to the Post; this I must Confess (Refractory as they are) Disquiets me much; the fine, many Cannot pay from their Indigent

Circumstances; I cannot be Supposed to be acquainted with the abilities of every Person in my Brigade, but Conceive the Court to be from their Personal knowledge and, therefore, (with Respect to the Quantum), I have Confirmed their Several Sentences & have order'd them to be put into Execution; from their obstinacy or Ignorance, not one application for Pardon or Remission (safe that of Kings-District) has been made to me.   We Expect Important news from below, such as you have will at all times be gratefully Received by Sir Your Most Obedient Humble Servant

Ab'm Ten Broeck.

Robert Benson Esqr. at Poughkeepsie.

— ——

[No. 1761.]

Governor Clinton Resorts to Retaliatory Measures.

Poughkeepsie Sept'r 16th 1778.

Gentlemen, His Excellency the Governor being informed by the Officer who conducted the last flag, that the Enemy at New York have determined to suffer no more flags to come down by water untill a flag with notice thereof be previously sent in by hand, & their consent for the purpose obtained, supposes the sending down those Persons who refuse to take the Oath is become rather disagreeable to them & that they, therefore, mean to retard this Business as much as possible.   He is, therefore, determined for this as well as for other Reasons to detain Messrs. Fletcher Matthews & Thomas Bull for exchange & directed me to inform you of this & to request that you will cause them to be confined in Goal accordingly; where it is his Pleasure they receive similar treatment w'th that of our friends who have been confined in the Provost Goal at New York untill they can effect their Exchange. This letter deliv'd to the Sharif will be a suff't warr't to him for receiving the Prisoners into his Custody & confin'g them accordingly. I am &c.

Robt. Benson, P. Secy.

To the Commiss'rs for detect'g Conspiracies &c. Orange County. Similar letter to the Albany Commissioners.

[No. 1762.]

ANOTHER FORAY IN THE MOHAWK VALLEY.

Colonel Bellinger Sounds the Alarm and Colonel Klock Promptly Rallies to His Relief.

Palentine September 16th 1778.

Sir, This Evening came John Helmer one of the Nine Men of the Rangers which we sent out on Monday last; they was attacked at Major Edmerson's place and only one has escaped, the said (John Helmer); what is become of the rest he cannot tell. The Enemy after he making his Escape, passed by him in the Bush; about two O'Clock this afternoon about Nine Miles from the German Flats he laid behind a Tree and counted about 200 Men, but he thinks that he did not count above half and as we expect them this Night or at farthest to Morrow Morning now is the Time for you to assist us. Therefore, I humbly beg for God sake to assist us all that lays in your power and let your people travel all Night for our assistance. I am yours

(Copy of Collo. Bellinger's Letter.)

You are hereby Ordered to march up to the German Flats immediately with your Regiment without a moment's loss of Time with three Days' provision. I have Ordered the rest of the Regiments to march on immediately. I am Sir your humble Serv't

Jacob Klock, Collo.

To Collo. Fisher.

[No. 1763.]

Ensign Pendleton a Prisoner on Long Island Asks Governor Clinton for Authority to Allow Nicholas Cowenhoven to Advance Him Money.

To His Exelency George Clinton Esqr. Governor of the State of New York &c.

Sir, I beg leave to inform your Exelency, that I have received no other money, or supply from without these lines, then that your Exelency was pleased to send me last winter in conjunction with the other Officers Captivated at Forts Clinton, and Montgomery: the reasons are to me unknown. The former marks of favour your Exelency has been pleased to show the Officers Captivated as above, Imboldens me to beg, that your Exelency will favour me, with your request to Nickoles Covenhoven, Esqr., living about a mile from my present station, in the same township; that he will furnish me with hard money to answer my present nesessetys; or such a Certain sum as your Excelency shall think proper. Mr. Covenhoven will readily comply with the request, and take pleasure in serving your Exelency, or any prisoner at your request nor does he want his money; but will patiantly wait till futer events shall put it in our power to make a return: If your Exelency, after due consideration shall think proper to send directions to Mr. Covenhoven as above, and should not think it prudent to send in plain words by way of the Office, sumthing like the following words in a Letter to me will answer the same purpose and come unsuspected which I think the most prudent,— Tell the man you mentioned to deliver you that money proposed) who I am confident will take my word for the rest. I should have mentioned some other Officers wants besides my own; but know of no other so nesesseated as myself, as I have had less supplys then any one Captivated with me by far, without Exception; I therefore leave your Exelency to Judge of the rest. The sooner your Exelency will pleas to answer me the better, as events are very uncertain here, for present security against uncertain events untill my enlargement, my wagers, and subsistance are at your Exelency's servis for the favour proposed, which is twice the sum I shall think of spending during my Captivity; unless a great alteration of times should Justifie me in making more fredom with economy than at present. The prisoners are generally in good helth. Mrs. Godwin is here, by whome I shall take the fredom to write to your Exelency at her departure, which I expect will be in about ten days. This Letter goes out by a safe, trusty hand, who is exchanged; so that I remain sure that it will be inspected by none, till it reaches your Exelency. I have the honer to be Your Exelency's most obedient and very humble servant

                                    Solomon Pendleton.

New Utrecht Long-Island Sept'm 16th 1778.

P. S. I hope your Exelency will pardon my freedom, after considering that nesessety is the Soul cause.

[No. 1764.]

The subject matter under documents 1764 to 1767 inclusive, will be found subjoined to document 1807, to which it was originally attached.

                                    STATE HISTORIAN.

[No. 1768.]

Colonel Malcom Ridicules the Appearance of Militia Officers.

Dear Sir, Capt. Lewis has Occassion for an anchor & Cable which he says is on board the sloop Com'dd by Cap. Benson—and as that vessell is not imediately to be employd I beg your Excellency will be pleased to give him orders for it & for any other articles at Poughkeepsie which he wants—About 300 of the militia are come in—pardon me for saying that as a Subject of the State I am ashamed of their officers—do pray call down & look at us. I hear the Doctor is recovering—are the Torys coming down—woud it do to inlist any of them if so I w'd let Albert come up—is the Substitute Law in force if so can I derive any benefit from it. I can get the men. My respects to your Lady & family—& believe me to be with the greatest regard & respect Your Excellency's much obligd & most Hble. Serv't

W. Malcom.

Fort Clinton Sep. 16 1778.

[To Gen. George Clinton.]

———

Poukeepsie 17th Sep'r 1778.

D'r Sir, I have rec'd your Letter of yesterday by Capt. Lewis. Whether the Sloop commanded by Capt. Benson is the Property of the State or the Continent I cant determine, She was purchased & fitted by the Committee of Convention who formerly had the Management of obstructing the navigation of the River & I believe tho' never formally delivered up by them is charged in their account ag't the Continent. I dont chuse, therefore, to give any Order for the removal or Disposition of any of her Stores; but I will readilly consent that the Qu'r Master Genl. take the Sloop & all that belongs to her giving his Receipt to the State for the same & then he can dispose of her & her Stores as shall to him seem best for the public Service. I have no doubt even as Matters now stand Capt. Benson will deliver up the Anchor & Cable or any Part of the Sloop's Stores to the Q'r Master's Orders.

I am not in the least surprised at your Feelings on account of our Militia Officers. We are at best scan of proper Materials but better might perhaps have been found had we not been oblidged to pay defference to former Rank founded upon the Choice of the People which in too many Instances was influenced by a Dram Shop Interest & had almost ruined our Militia. The Tories will be forwarded to you as they come in; unless the Whiggs prevent it. In the Case mentioned in your last Letter the Com'rs were influenced to depart from the Plan I had advised (to wit an absolute Confinement & hard Labour till the Meeting of the Legislature who alone have Power to pardon Treason) by the Importunity of a Whigg neighbourhood in Behalf of the Culprit who it seems is a Black Smith & they wanted one.

The Legislature is to meet the first of next Month. I am perswaded it woud be for the Interest of the State to put your Regt. & part of Colo. Lamb's on the same Footing with Respect to recruiting at least with the 5 N. York Regts. (which is not the Case at present); and I will chearfully render any aid in my Power to effect it shoud any application for this Purpose be made. I wish you had confined Van Allen. I consider every Person on Board a Flagg subject to Military Authority. Mrs. Clinton joins in best Respects to yourself & Mrs. Malcom, with D'r Sir Your Most Obed't Serv't

G: Clinton.

I cant promise myself the Pleasure of seeing you at the Fort till the End of next Session at soonest.

Colo. Malcom.

[No. 1769.]

THE CASE OF ROBERT C. LIVINGSTON.

James Duane Vouches for Him—Governor Clinton, General Stark and the Vermont Controversy.

Manour Livingston 14th Septem'r 1778.

Sir, I have examined Mr. Rob. C. Livingston's Case with Impartiality and attention. From all his Conversation he appears to me to be a firm Friend to our Cause. The Enemy looked upon him in this Light. They have treated him as Prisoner, exacting a Parol that he shall return within their Lines when required, tho' they forgot to seal his Lips. It is consistent with the Knowledge of hundreds that he went from hence in 1775, by the advice of his Phycisians, in a very low State of Health; supposed to be in a deep decline. The Council of Safety gave him a Pass & Testimonial in the words following—

" Committee of Safety for the Colony of New York during the Recess of the provincial Congress.

City of New York September 9th 1775.

Robert C. Livingston, of this City Esqr. several days ago informed this Committee of his Intention to go to Brittain for the Recovery of his Health at present very much impaird. The Committee firmly perswaded of his attachment to the Liberties of this Country, approve of his intended Voyage, wish him the Restoration of his Health & a happy Return to his native Country."

By order

John Haring, Chairman.

Attest   John McKesson, Robt. Benson, Secrys.

He returned at the Request of his Father & because his Finances were nearly exhausted in an expensive Excursion of three years. His Health in my Opinion very little betterd, not-withstanding the benefit of the air & waters of France where he has chiefly resided.

The only thing Questionable in his Case, is, why he did not return by the way of France? To this he answers that he was in a bad State of Health; that the Risk of Capture by the English Cruizers was very great—that if he had been taken he must have been thrown into a Goal & have perished as he was utterly unable to bear Hardships. That, on the other hand, if he had been taken by an American Cruizer he had no doubt of being able to vindi-cate himself and of being treated with Kindness.

I may be partial to a Friend of whose Honour & Integrity I have the highest Opinion; but really this Justification appears to me sufficient; & I think Mr. Livingston may be permitted to stay with his Friends, as long as the Enemy will suffer him. Under-standing it was your Excellency's wish that he shoud consult with me I have stated these facts & submit them to Consideration.

If Mr. Livingston understood your Excellency right, it is your wish to see me about the time of the Legislature's assembling. Shoud they reelect me as a Delegate, I shall think it my duty to set out immediately afterwards to relieve Mr. Duer, & to wait on you & them for your Commands. This I suppose to be what your Excellency woud advise. If I err I shoud be glad of the Honour of a Line to set me right; indeed it woud be very accept-able at all Events as we are out of the way of Intelligence. With most respectful Complim' to your Lady and the highest Respect

I am Sir Your Excellency's most Obed't hum'e Serv't

Jas. Duane.

P. S. The Fever has left me & I gain strength daily.
His Excellency, Governour Clinton.

Poughkeepsie 18th Sep'r 1778.

D'r Sir, I am favoured with your Letter of the 14th Instant. I have not the least Objection to Mr. Robt. C. Livingston's continuing with his Friends at the Manor if you think it adviseable. I mentioned (with great Freedom) to Mr. Livingston the Reasons which occassioned some Difficulties in my Mind on this Subject. I considered this due to the Friendship I owe to himself and the Familly. Knowing you to be not only his Relation but his most cordial Friend & placing the greatest Confidence in your Prudence, I desired him to repeat to you what had passed between us & to govern himself by your good advice.

The Hurry of Business & Want of a Convenient Opportunity have prevented my answering your Letter of the 29th Ultimo before this. I perfectly agree with you in Sentiments respecting Genl. Schuyler; when he was at Poughkeepsie on his Way to Camp I expressed mine to him freely. I mentioned in a former Letter his Intentions to proceed from Camp to Congress if his Tryal was not likely soon to take Place. I ommitted to add it only was in order to expedite his Tryal.

Last Sessions I mentioned as well by public Message as privately to several Members of the Legislature the Propriety or rather the necessity of the State's raising Men & erecting Posts for the Defence of our Western Frontiers. It was however in great Measure neglected & I fear will till it is too late. I shoud not be surprized to hear that Genl. Stark & the Green Mountain Boys claim the whole Western Country by Right of Conquest if they Shoud take it in their Heads to go scouting that Way & kill one Tory or Indian it woud go far tow'ds establishing their Title. I mean at the ensuing Session to submit this Matter a second Time to the Legislature & as I am desirous of doing it in a manner equal to its Importance, I should be happy in having your advice & assistance on this as well as other public Business. I am with best Respects to Mrs. Duane in which Mrs. Clinton Joins me, with great Regard Your Most Obed't Serv't

[G. C.]

[To James Duane.]

[Nos. 1770-1771.]

DESTRUCTION OF GERMAN FLATS.

The Enemy's Blighting Foray—Heavy Losses of the Settlers in Property—Colonel Bellinger's Report.

Caugnawaga Sept. the 18th 1778.

Sir, I just now received an Express from Collo. Klock* that the Enemy have destroyed the whole German Flats and also the South Side of the River and took with them all the Cattel; went up this week—also the Cattel of the Inhabitants of the German Flats. Collo. Klock is marched last Night to Charivaley [Cherry Valley] in order to cut off the Enemy's Retreat, and as soon as the lower part of my Regiment comes up I am to march to the aforesaid place. Sir, I am Your humble Serv't

Fred'k Fisher.

P. S. The Enemy left the German Flats yesterday about Noon. To Collo. Wemple.

Colonel Bellinger's Report to Governor Clinton.

German Flatts, Sept'r the 19th 1778.

May it please Your Excellence. I humbly beg to lay our Distresses open to Your Excellency. On Thursday the 17th instant, about six in the morning, the Enemy attacked Fort Dayton, on the north side of the German Flatts and Burned and Destroy'd all the

Houses, Barns, and Grain, and drove a great number of Horses, and horned Cattle away with them. The Church, Fort, together with two houses, is all that is left on that side, and they had two men kill'd and one wounded, The enemy tried to take Fort Day- ton, but they kept them off. On the south side the River, they began about six miles above Fort Herkimer, and Burn'd all the Houses, Barns, and Grain quite down to the Church; at Fort Herkimer they tried to set fire to the Barn, but we sallied out with what men we could spare and kept them from Destroying any more houses.

We have Built in our District four Garrisons, and have none but my Regiment to Guard them, and a few Rangers. I sent out a scout of the Rangers, nine men, three days before this happen'd. They met the Enemy, at Major Edmonston's place, at the head Branch of Tunadella River, the enemy attack'd them, and drove them into the River, they have kill'd two of the Rangers, and scattered the rest. One of them came in, the night before the Flatts was attacked. And immediately I wrote pr. Express to Col. Klock, and another to be sign'd by him, to be sent, to the nearest place for Assistance, as the enemy was within 9 miles of Us, when the Rangers saw them last. In my letter to Col. Klock, I beg'd him for God's sake to assist us with men, and if he had march'd his men on directly, he might have been at the Flatts before we was attacked, and if he had sent 200 men, we might in all Probability, have saved a great many houses, and a great deal of Grain, and Creatures. But alas, we could get no assist- ance. Several times this Summer we have intelligence that they intended to Destroy this place, and I have wrote to General Starks in Albany for assistance, but could get none, and once I wrote to Your Excellency, but I imagine You did not receive it.

Our Case is really very hard, as the Enemy threatens us yet. Therefore, I am oblig'd to be thus troublesom to Your Excellency, to desire the Favour of a Reinforcement, otherwise I cannot pretend to keep the Inhabitants here any longer. I have given Orders to the A. D. C. of Issues at Fort Dayton, to supply those who have lost their Effects with Provision, as they was Crying to me for Bread. But if Your Excellency does not approve of it, I hope You'll send me Orders how I must behave in the said Affair. After the enemy had finish'd the destruction of the Flatts, they went off about Noon. In the afternoon I sent an Express again to Col. Klock, desiring him to send to Col. Alden at Cherry Valley, that if he would turn out with about 400 men, and strike across to the Creek at Tunadella, where I was certain they would come up with the Enemy they might have recover'd most part of the Plunder again, but as far as I can learn, they did not mind it.

I have had a great deal of Trouble I can assure Your Excellency to keep the inhabitants from moving off, on the account of having no Assistance. I was oblig'd to threaten them, that I would take their Effects from them. But as the Place is mostly Destroy'd, I have prevail'd on them to wait till I have Orders from Your Excellency how to Behave in our Distressed Circumstances, But if there is no Reinforcement comes up, I shall not be able to hinder them from moving off.

I here send Your Excellency an Account of the Damage done by the Enemy on both sides of the River. They Burn'd Sixty three Dwelling houses, Fifty seven Barns, with Grain and Fother, Three Grist mills, One Saw Mill, and they have taken away with them, Two Hundred Thirty five Horses, Two hundred Twenty nine horned Cattle, Two hundred Sixty nine Sheep, and they kill'd and Destroy'd a great number of Hogs, and they have Burn'd a great many Out houses.

4

I humbly hope Your Excellency will take our Circumstances into Consideration, and grant us a reinforcement sufficient to hinder the enemy from utterly ruining of us. So relying entirely on Your Excellency,

I Beg leave to Subscribe myself, Your Excellencies most Obedient, humble Servant

Peter Bellinger, Colo.

To His Excellency, George Clinton, Esqr.

[No. 1772.]

THE CASE OF HAMMELL AND GEAKE.

Governor Clinton Suggests to Washington a Court Martial for the Former.

Poughkeepsie Sept'r 19th 1778.

D'r Sir, By the last flag which arrived from N. York I received Certificates from the Commiss'y Genl. of Prisoners there with Proposals for exchang'g Stephen Lush, (late my Brigade Major & taken at Fort Montgomerie) for Henry Cuyler—Corn's Van Tassel for Alex'r White & James Dole for Ab'm Maybie. As I conceive the Exchanges advantageous, I mean to agree to the Proposals & to direct the Persons (who are all confined in Albany), together with a few more Exiles to be sent down to Posts in Fishkill there to wait till further Orders. I am, therefore, again under the necessity of request'g your Excellency (if you shall deem it expedient) to appoint an Officer to conduct them with a Flagg to the Enemy's Lines.

On my arrival from headq'rs Major Hamel was put in close confinement in consequence of the Information of Gakes [Samuel Geake]* who was tried & convicted at Fort Schuyler. He had

---

*Samuel Geake was an American soldier, who while a prisoner in New York, met Major Hammell, who had been captured when Forts Clinton and Montgomery fell. Both yielded to British temptation, forsook the American cause and joined the English

previous thereto confessed that he was sent out for the purpose of discovering what effect the conciliatory Bills had on the minds of the People, but alleged that tho he had consented to the Measure to obtain his Liberty he never attempted or meant to execute the Business. As Major Hammell at the Time of his being made Prisoner was Brigade Major to my Brother & subject to the Articles of War, I humbly conceive his case is properly cognizable before a Court Martial. If your Excellency is in Sentiment with me I could wish how soon as convenient that he be brought to Tryal.* I am &c.

Geo: Clinton.

P. S. I forgot to mention that the Officer who conducted the last Flag informed the Commiss'rs that the Enemy declared they would receive no more flags by water unless previous notice thereof was sent in by land for their approbation.

His Excellency Genl. Washington.

[No. 1773.]

Marbletown Asks for a Guard to Protect Its Western Border.

To his Excellency George Clinton, Esquire, Governor of the State of New York General and Commander in Chief of all the Militia and Admiral of the Navy of the same.

The Petition of the Subscribers Inhabitants of the Township

---

army. Geake accompanied Hammell to Poughkeepsie where they joined Captain Abraham Swartwout's Company, and were subsequently ordered to Fort Schuyler as part of General Gansevoort's command. Both men were acting under instructions from Sir Henry Clinton, with the ultimate object of betraying the American forces. As early as June, 1778, Colonel Varick notified Gansevoort that he suspected Geake of being a confederate with Major Hammell, and of attempting to corrupt American soldiers and encouraging them to desert.

Geake was promptly arrested, as he was on the point of deserting to join the British army in Philadelphia. He admitted he was sent by an aide-de-camp of Sir Henry Clinton's, as a spy for the purpose of enlisting Irishmen from the American army. He was tried by a general Court Martial, where he made a full confession, in which he declared that Hammell had been promised by the English authorities, the Colonelcy of the new Irish regiment, and he himself a commission as Lieutenant. He was sentenced to death, but Washington spared his life in order to use his testimony against Major Hammell.—STATE HISTORIAN.

*See page 624, Vol. II.

of Marble Town, in the County of Ulster, in Said State Humbly Sheweth,

That your Petitioners chiefly preside on the Western Borders of Said Township. That from the late incursions of the enemy in these quarters, your Petitioners from their Situations conceive themselves in eminent danger from the like depredations especially as from a deficiency in Guards a communication is left open from the Westward to this Town, from which circumstance your Petitioners are induced to apprehend that a Speedy attack will be made upon the Western Parts thereof. That a number of the Inhabitants of Said Town especially at and in the Vicinity where the danger is apprehended are now Called upon to turn out their Classes which are to compose the Guard for the Western frontiers and which from the present disposition, thereof, adds nothing to their immediate Security.

Your Petitioners, therefore, humbly pray that your Excellency will be pleased to order, That a sufficient Guard may be Stationed on the Western borders of This Town, to Scout along the Same, North & South, in such manner as the commanding officer on this Station Shall think most conducive to the Security, thereof, and your Petitioners as in duty bound Shall ever pray. Marble Town Sept'r 15 1778.

Matthew Cantine, Andrew Davis, Jacob S. Freer, Benoni Mulks, William Leggett, Peter Hodler, Salomon Hodler, John Anthony, Johnnes Middgh, William Cantine, Falter Smith, Abr'h Sailer, Wilhelmus Roosa, Isaiah Robeson, Frederick Shurter, Willim Tees, John Cushnichan, Joseph Chambers, Arie Tack, Cornelus Enst, Thomas Vandemerken, Aldert Rosa, Thomas Smith, Simon Krom, Johanis W. Rosa, Epreim Chambers, Dirck Chambers, Jacob Chambers, Thomas Chambers, Petras Smith, Henry Boghart, John Connor, John Connor, Jun'r, Thomas Schoonmaker, Jr. Simon Van Wagenen, Jr. Salomon Van Wagenen, Charles W. Brodhead.

Poukeepsie 19th Sep'r 1778.

Gentlemen, I have received a Petition dated the 15th Instant subscribed by you and other Inhabitants of the Marble Town praying " That a Guard may be stationed on the Western Borders of the Town to Scout along the same north & South in such manner as the Commanding officer on that Station shall think most conducive to the Security thereof," In Answer to which I can assure you that Colo. Cantine has my Orders to take such Posts on the Western Frontiers & make such Disposition of the Detachment under his Command as will give the greatest & most equal Security to the Inhabitants, Which as I have the greatest confidence in his Zeal for the Service & general Knowledge of the Frontier Country, I have Reason to believe, will be faithfully executed, & if, therefore, stationing a Guard in the Manner you desire is consistent with the Genl. safety & the number of Men he has under his Command will admit of, it will be done. I am with great Respect &c.

[G. C.]

To Messrs. Mathew Cantine Solomon Van Wagenen & Chas. W. Brodhead.

[No. 1774.]

GOVERNOR HEARS OF THE GERMAN FLATS DISASTER.

And Admonishes General Ten Broeck on the Necessity of Maintaining Full Quotas of the Militia at All Times.

Albany 18th Sep'r 1778 3 P. M.

Sir, I think it my Duty to Inclose your Excellency Copies of letters I Rec'd, the one from Collonell Bellinger giving an account of the approach of the Enemy I Received this morning at 1 O'Clock; the other from Colonel Fisher giving the melancholy account of the Enemy having destroyed the Settlement at the German Flatts I Received this moment. Colonel Wemple's Regiment is already on their march to that Quarter & on the Receipt of the first letter, I Immediately Issued my Orders for Col. Schuyler's & Colonel Van Schoonhoven's Regiments without one moment's loss of time also to march thither. With great Regard I Remain Your Excellency's Most Obed't Hum'le Servant

Ab'm Ten Broeck.

P. S. The Cattle alluded to in Col. Fisher's letter is about 100 Head destined for Fort Schuyler.

His Excellency George Clinton Esqr.

Poughkeepsie 20th Sep'r 1778.

Sir, I have received your Letter of the 18th Instant & am exceedingly distressed by the Melancholly Account it contains of the Desolation of the German Flatts and what adds to my Unhappiness on this Occassion is that I observe by the Returns which you have from Time to Time transmitted me, not half of the Number of the Militia Ordered for the Protection of the Frontiers have been at any Time actually out on that Service. You will perceive by this Event how dangerous it is to be lulled into a State of Security by favourable appearances & of Course how extreamly wrong it woud have been to have consented that the last Class of Militia for this Service might not be oblidged to march. A sufficient Number of the Militia to afford Security to the Frotiers must at all Events be brought into actual Service & statedly kep out for that Purpose. Had this hitherto been the Case, much Misschief & Distress woud have been prevented, and I am perswaded even the Duty of the Militia woud not have been equal to what it has been in the present imperfect Way of doing Business.   For when any Disaster takes Place, the whole Country is alarmed & All march when it is too late to prevent, & indeed at a Time when the least Danger is to be apprehended from the Enemy, who having accomplished their ends may not be expected to return suddenly & when we are prepared to receive them.

I cannot account for Genl. Stark's Conduct.   It does not appear to me that he pays the least Attention to the safety of the Frontiers.   Can you tell me where Alden's Regt. is stationed & how it was employed at the Time of this Disaster, As I wish to give his Excellency Genl. Washington, to whom I mean immediately to forward the Intelligence received, the most perfect account of the Situation of our Frontiers & the Measures pursued for their Defence that he may be enabled to correct whatever may be wrong in the Management of this Business.   I have only to add that I cant learn any Part of the 3 Regts. of your Brigade who were destined for the Posts in the Highlands have marched thither & to desire that you shall esteem it necessary alter their Destination to the Frontiers giving me notice thereof.   I am your Most Obed't Serv't

Geo: Clinton.

Brig'r Genl. Ten Broeck.

[No. 1775.]

REFRACTORY SOLDIERS TO BE STERNLY HANDLED.

Captain Talmadge of the Rangers Ordered to Arrest the Ringleaders.

Poughkeepsie Sept'r 20th 1778.

D'r Major, I have rec'd your Letter with the enclosure & shewn it to his Exellency the Gov'r who has directed me to inform you that Capt. Tamage with a party of his Rangers will be directed to repair to the Manor and apprehend some of the Delinquents

of your Regt. & bring them down.   He will call on you for your
advice & his Excellency requests you to point out to him some of
the most refractory who will be made examples of.   His Exellency further directs me to inform you that unless the Officers
of your Regt. exert themselves & cause the Regt. to do their proportion of Duty he will be under the necessity (however disagreable the measure) of breaking up the Regt. & subjoining it to the
adjacent Regts. of Claverack & Rhinebeck.   You'l be pleased to
communicate this Letter to the other field officers.   I am D'r
Major Your most Obed't Serv't

                                        Robt. Benson.
Major Ten Broeck.

———

Genl. Orders Poughkeepsie Sept. 21st 1778.

Capt. Tamage will immediately repair with as many of his
Company of Rangers as can be spared to the Manor of Livingston
& cause to be apprehended & bro't down to this Place such of
the Delinquents of Colo. Peter R. Livingston's Regt., of militia
as have refused or neglected to march agreable to Orders for that
purpose issued.   Capt. Tamage will call on Major Ten Broeck,
for a List of the Delinquents to be apprehended & take his advice
in the prosecution of this Business.   And in Case such Part of
Capt. Tamage's Company as can be spared for this Service may
not be sufficiently strong to carry this Order into Execution, he
is to call on the Commanding Officer of the Company of Rangers
raised in Colo. Van Ness's Regt. who are hereby commanded with
his Company to assist him therein.

———

                                        Sept. 21st.

Sir, A most Disobedient & refractory Spirit prevails in Colo.
Livingston's Regiment in the Manor of Livingston, in so much

that they will not submit to any Military Duty & it does not appear that there is a sufficient Number of Well affected Subjects among them to cause the Refractory to be brought to due Punishment & thereby to a proper Sense of their Duty.   Influenced by these Considerations, his Excellency, the Governor, has thought proper to issue the inclosed Order which I am directed to transmit to you & to request that you will carry the same into Execution without the least Delay.   I am &c.

R. Benson.

Capt. Talmage.

[No. 1776.]

Major Lush Ordered " to Forward " Henry Cuyler Without Delay.

Poughkeepsie Sept'r 20th 1778.

D'r Major, By his Excellency's Direction I send you the inclosed extraordinary Letter* which was forwarded to our Office this morn'g by Mr. Adams Dep. Commiss'y Genl. of Prisoners, at White Plains.   His Excellency is at a Loss to account for the Cause; but supposes it to arise from perfidy in the Enemy or some Deception on the part of Mr. Cuyler.   You'l, therefore, get the Commiss'rs to forward Mr. Cuyler & the others down without Delay.   You'l also endeavour to possess yourself of the original Certificate of which Mr. Cuyler only sent us a Copy & come down with Mr. Cuyler to this Place yourself in order that this matter may be inquired into & adjusted.   His Excellency directs me to assure you that he will do every Thing on his Part that may be necessary to Procure you ample Justice.   Yrs. &c.

Robt. Benson.

Major Lush.

------

*Not found.

[No. 1777.]

Governor Clinton Mildly Rebukes the Albany Conspiracy Commissioners.

Poukeepsie 20th Sep'r 1778.

Gentlemen, I some Time since received a Letter subscribed by Leonard Gansevoort, Jun'r, as Secretary to the Com'rs at Albany & said to be wrote by their Order, Dated the 5th Instant, notifying me that David Vanschaak & Seven other Persons therein mentioned had refused to take the Oath prescribed in the Act of the Legislature to be administered to Persons of an equivocal & neutral Charecter that I might detain such of them as I thought proper to Exchange. I am now surprized to find that those Persons were sent down to Fishkill under the Care of Colo. Fisher to be forwarded within the Enemy's Lines, and that your Warrant to him for this Purpose is dated the 7th being only two Days after the Date of your Secretary's Letter on the Subject, of Course not affording you a possibillity of receiving an Answer.

How you will be able to Account for this extraordinary Proceedure so contrary to the Spirit of the Law under which you act, I am unable to determine. The good Oppinion I Entertain of you induces me to believe it must have been occassioned by some Misstake. The Flaggs passing my Quarters to Fishkill with an Intention to have proceeded to the Enemy's Lines without my Orders is not unexceptionable which a little Reflection will discover to you.

I wrote to you the 16th Instant directing the Persons referred to be detained & confined for Exchange which I expect will be complied with as they are ordered back for that Purpose. I am yours &c.

Geo. Clinton.

To the Commiss'rs for detect'g Conspiracies &c. Albany.

[No. 1778.]

Returns of the Militia at Schoharie Under Lieutenant Colonel Philip Van Alstyne.

Sep'r 20th 1778.

Regiments.	Officers Present fit for Duty									Rank & File						
	Field		Commission			Staff		Non Comm's.								
	Lieut. Col.	Majors	Captains	Lieutenants	Ensigns	Adjutants	Qr. Masters	Serjeants	Drum & Fifers	Present fit for duty	Sick Present	Sick Absent	Absent with Leave	Absent without Leave	On Command	Total
Col. Van Alstyn's	1															1
Col. Lansingh's			1	2		1	1	4	1	11						21
Col. Philip Schuyler's		1	1	2	1			4	1	34	1				1	46
Col. Rensselaer's			1	1				3		11						16
Col. Van Bergen's			1	1				3		10	1					16
Col. Quackenboss			1	1	1			3		12						18
Col. Wemple's			1			1		4		31						37
C Stephen Schuyler's				1	1			2		22						26
Col. Vroman's			1	2				3	2	33					3	44
Total	1	1	7	10	3	2	1	26	4	164	2				4	225

Philip Van Alstyne Lt. Colonel.

A True Copy.

[No. 1779.]

George Clinton Reports the German Flats Disaster to the Commander-in-Chief.

Poukeepsie 20th Sep'r 1778.

Dear Sir, By the inclosed Copies of Letters which were forwarded to me by Genl. Ten Broek & came to Hand this Forenoon, your Excellency will receive the Disagreable Intelligence of the Destruction of the valuable Settlements of the German Flatts by the Enemy & the Loss of 100 Head of Cattle which were destined for Fort Schuyler.

I have not received any Accounts of this affair or of the Disposition of the Troops on the Frontiers from Genl. Stark & I am not able to inform your Excellency whether it is

probable that the Militia who are said to have been on their
March to cut off the Retreat of the Enemy, will be able to effect
it, or whether Alden's Regiment is so situated as to afford them
any Assistance. I am with great Esteem Your Excellency's Most
Obed't Serv't

Geo. Clinton.

His Excellency Genl. Washington.

[No. 1780.]

ALBANY AS A MILITARY POST.

*Governor Clinton Disagrees with the Citizens of That City on the
Question of Billeting 2,000 Troops.*

Poughkeepsie 20th Sept'r 1778.

Sir, I am honored with the Rec't of your Letter, (wrote by Order
of the Common Council of the City of Albany), of the 11th Inst.
It contains the only intimation I have rec'd of an Intention to
station a body of Troops in your City the ensuing winter.   If this
is really to be the Case, I presume it must have originated as well
from your Letters to Genl. Gates & Genl. Starks of the 20th &
21st of May last, setting forth the importance of the public Stores
&c. &c. deposited there, the weak state of the militia to guard
them & the great Danger of their being destroyed, if the Continental Troops should be withdrawn from that Quarter, as from a
Desire of having a proper Force conveniently situated for carrying on offensive Operations ag't the Enemy on our western frontier early next Spring—a Measure of the utmost moment to this
State & therefore earnestly to be wished for.

From sad Experience, it is found impracticable to secure the
frontier Settlements while acting on the Defensive only from the
Depredations of a Savage Enemy; & with the utmost Exertions

we have not hitherto been able to collect a sufficient Force from the Militia to carry the war into the Enemy's Country. I am, therefore, lead to consider the stationing a Body of Troops in the Vicinity of Albany as a very favorable Circumstance, which may in the End be productive of the most salutary Consequences and I trust when considered by the Citizens of Albany in this Point of View, they will (as usual) afford every Encouragem't to a measure so evidently calculated for the good of the public Service & the Safety of this State in Particular.

I cannot entertain a Doubt that the Commander in Chief, who has always discovered the strictest attention & regard to the Rights of the Citizens of this State, will issue such orders for the good Goverm't of the Troops in winter q'rs as to prevent all cause of Complaint arising from any disorderly behavior in the Soldiery. You will readily perceive the Impropriety of my dictating to him, or of interfering in the Disposition of the Troops under his Command. If, however, the citizens of Albany receive any Injury from the military for which they may not be able to obtain Redress in the Courts of Justice in the ordinary way, you may rest assured that the authority of Gov't will be cheerfully exerted for this Purpose. I am with great Respect Sir Your most Obed't Serv't

Geo: Clinton.

The worshipfull Jno. Barclay Esqr. Mayor of the City of Albany.

[No. 1781.]

Exempts of South East Precinct.

South East precinct Septem'r 21st 1778.

The Subscribers of the inclosed association To his Excellency George Clinton Esqr. Governor of the State of New York.

May it please your Excellency. We beg leave to transmit to your Excellency a Copy of our association, to which we have ordered our names annexed, if we have err'd in matter or manner we wish to be hon'd with your instructions, & assure your Excellency we only mean to render ourselves as Serviceable as possible upon every Emergency. We yet Expect a respectable addition to the Company, but as it is at present rather small, we have elected only one Lieut. the officers Chosen by ballot are: Alexander Kidd, Capt'n, Charles Cullen, Lieut. William Calkin, Ensign, and whom we beg to recommend to your Excellency for Commissions; the Bearer Lieut. Tubbs will await any Commands your Excellency may have for Sir with Great respect y'r Excellency's most Obed't & most Hum'le Ser'ts

Signed By desire & in behalf of the Company

Char's Cullen Clk.

Dutchess County State of New York Sept. 15th 1778.

We, the subscribers, being disposed to form ourselves into an associated Company of militia, (agreeable to a Clause in the Last Act of Assembly for regulating the militia of this State wherein all persons under the age of Fifty five years who have formerly held Civil or military Commissions and are not or shall not be reappointed & all persons between the ages of Fifty & Fifty five years who Shall associate themselves shall be Exempted from Serving as part of the enroll'd militia), Do, hereby, bind ourselves each to the Other and Severally to the State at large, that from and after the appointment of Proper officers, Commissioned by his Excellency the Governor of this State, & by us recommended, we will Obey the orders of our Commanding Officer upon all Occasions, and will in Cases of Invasion or Incursions of the Enemy or

Insurrections march to repel the Enemy in like manner as the enrolled militia are Compell'd to do, so that we may not when Call'd out in detachments be annexed to any Other Regiment or be under the immediate Command of any Other than our own officers.

(Signed)

Eben'r Gage, Isai'h Bennett, Jabez Chase, Daniel Ketchum, John Warring, Thom's Hinkley, Caleb Fowler, David Crosby, Jun'r, Jon'n Parish, Simeon Ellis, William Palmer, Jr., Thom's Burgis, Abra'm Birsdell, Malcom Morison, William Calkin, Jerem'h Sabin, Jun'r, John Salmon, Rowlin Russell, Saml. Dickinson, Theod's Crosby, David Akin, Moss Kent, Char's Cullen, Elijah Oakley, Isaac Ellwell, Phinehas Baker, Seth Nickerson, Joshua Conklin, Alex'r Kidd.

A true copy.

[No. 1782.]

The Governor Issues Stringent Orders to Colonel Van Alstine.

Kinderhook 18th Sept. 1778.

Sir, I Re'd order from General Tenbroeck for one fourth of my Rigment to march to Fort Arnel properly officered, & to make a Retorn of them to your Exselencie; after a grat dell pans taken to gat the men to march, it gaves me the gratest unesnis to tell yor Exselency that I, with all the asastance of my officers, Could not gat moor then Six or Seven presend to march, which I have ordered to march under the Command of Cap'n Trusdel, who will make you a retorn of the men under his Command & there to Recive your Exselencice's forther Commend. I am sir with Respect your humble servent

Abr'm J. Vanalstine, Coll.

His Exelencie Gorge Clinton Esqr.

Poughkeepsie Sept. 21st 1778.

Sir, His Excellency the Governor directs me to acknowledge the rec't of your favor of the 18th Inst. by Capt. Trusdel. As it can answer no good Purpose to send down a Capt. with so few men His Excellency has directed the Capt. to Return. It being absolutely necessary that severe Examples should be made of the Delinquents, his Excellency requests that you'l imploy Capt. Trusdel with his men & cause the Delinquents to be apprehended and immediately taken before the Court martial which we are informed is now sitting in your neighbourhood, to be tried and punished with the utmost rigor of the Law.

If, in the mean time, you should receive Gen'l Ten Broeck's order for the Detachm't of your Regt., which were ordered to Fort Arnold in the Highlands to march to the western frontiers, you will, as they become sensible of their Duty, by the Examples which may be made, cause them to march accordingly; but if that should not be the Case, you'l cause them to march to Fort Arnold agreable to the former Orders, even tho' you should be obliged to use the whole strength of your Regt. to bring them down in Custody. I am &ca.

Robt. Benson, A. D. C.

Colo. Van Alstyne.

[No. 1783.]

ONE HUNDRED DOLLARS REWARD.

For the Arrest of Parks and the Middaghs—Colonel Cantine's Troubles.

Hunk Sept'r 18th 1778.

Dear Sir, Not Withstanding my frequent applycations to the Commanding officers of ye Different Regim't of Ulster & Orange Countys to Send up there men, Still are great Deficiancecys,

Espesially Collo. Wodhul's, Who for a Considerable time past has had None at all, and if there Be any Now of his Regim't, it is But of Late they are Come; one of ye Classes of Collo. McCloughree's Regim't time, was Expired Day Before yesterday and there Reliefe is Not yet Come, But Hear they Where to march this morning; the Classes Not marching in time makes the Numbers at the Different posts often Very Defitient; Where they all fited for ye Soldier, I think we might preform the Duty Which Could be Exsected of us, But many of ye men are But poorly Equipt, other wanting Shose; Where it Not for a few active I Could under my present Circumstances Exspect Little Else But Sensure & Blame, from those whome I Endeavour to Serve, for it is Nateral for every man to Be for his own Safety and whould Be fond of haveing a guard at his own Door. Beside this, there are many passes Now known Which heretofore I Never have heard of. But this I am Satisfyed of, that there are more then I am able to guard so as to prevent the Enemy of Snatching one a Way By times. Where my Number much Larger then it is at present; I whould to God that it was in our Power to Do the Work affectually. I mean to go with a Number Suffitent to Distroy their habitations. I am Willing to Be one of them, tho Whould be glad to See the Command put in an ableer hand then I am of Sir with Esteem Your most Hum'e Ser't

John Cantine.

His Excellency George Clinton Esq.

Sept'r 21st 1778.

D'r Sir, I have rec'd your favor of the 18th Inst. & in consequence, thereof, I have issued the enclosed Orders, which if duly executed will remove the difficulties you complain of. I have rec'd a Petition of some of the Inhabitants of Marble Town, pray'g that a Guard may be stationed on the frontiers of that Town to scout north & south &c. &c. I have answered it by reciting to them the Substance of that part of the enclosed orders, which respects the tak'g Post & stationing the men & that I doubt not that you will, from your zeal for the Service & knowledge of the Country, comply w'th their Request, if the Genl. Safety of the frontiers & the number of men under your Command will admit of it. For your own Information & to prevent your being censured by those People, I would advise you to avail yourself of the advice of Judge Pawling & the other principal Inhabitants of the neighbourhood.

I should be happy to (know) that an Expedition could be carried on ag't Ooghquaga & would, therefore, wish to have your Opinion what number of militia would be adequate for such Service. I have only to add that I have great Reason to believe the greatest mischiefs arise thro' the agency of the two Middaghs & Parks, & you have, therefore, my consent to Offer a Reward of 100 Dollars for the apprehend'g of them or either of them—this matter should be so far kept a Secret as only to be communicated to the Party who most likely to fall in with them. I am &c.

                                              Geo: Clinton.
Colo. Cantine.

[No. 1784.]
JAMES DUANE WRITES DESPONDENTLY.

Indian Raids have Destroyed Crops, Terrified the People and Desolated the Frontier—Exorbitant Charges for Meat.

                    Manour Livingston 22d September 1778.

Dear Sir, I am honour'd with your Excellency's obliging favour of the 18th Instant, and beg you'l accept my Thanks for the friendly Sentiments you express for this Family, as well as for myself. Mr. R. C. Livingston is now at Ancram where he expects to remain, chiefly, as he thinks the air of that place agrees best with his feeble Constitution. He is really in a poor way after all the Trouble and Expence he has encounter'd for the Recovery of his Health. I shall communicate to him the very kind manner in which your Excellency consents to his remaining with his Friends.

I never doubted, but that your Excellency sensibly felt the Indignity, as well as Calamities, which our unfortunate State suffers from the barbarous Incursions of a few Indians & Tories—few, Compared to our own strength, I must call it, if their number shoud be 1000, which by the way I have no Reason to believe. I flatter myself your Exertions on this important Subject will be more attended to & have greater weight, the ensuing, than at the last, Sessions. The Destruction of our western frontier, is the Destruction of our Granary, & will be severly felt; and what is worse the Inhabitants, finding they are not protected, will loose Confidence in the present Government, and the Spirit of Disaffection encrease, at a period when it ought to be extinguished.

I feel with your Excellency, disgust and anxiety, that when we have so many brave officers & Troops belonging to our own State, our Frontiers shoud be defended by our Neighbours, who know little or nothing of Geography of the Country, and who do not love us, or value our Interest, with all the Cordiality that coud be wished. I do not mean, however, to censure any part of the past Conduct of the Troops to the Northward. They were too few to undertake any Expedition into the Indian Settlements, and every thing else is vain and absurd. We may as well hunt

the Eagles of the air as Indians in the woods. They have only
two points in war—an ambush, and the nimbleness of their
Heels; to the Efficacy of the latter of which a perfect Knowledge
of our extensive Forests greatly contributes; One other Eminent
advantage they enjoy, which depends upon ourselves and is,
therefore, much more to be lamented, and that is the unmanly
Dread which our militia in general, and the low Dutch more
especially, entertain of these Savages. Dastardly as they un-
questionably are,—a Detachment of the Continental Forces will
be necessary to subdue them effectually, but if they coud be
spared from the grand army, I fear, with your Excellency, that
the Season is passed for carrying on any decisive Expedition
against those perfidious Murtherers this Campaign. They might,
by suiteable Reinforcements, properly station'd, be overawd and
frightend into Retreat or Inactivity, and that itself woud be
of great Consequence: for If the German Flatts are really cut
off, as reported, & there should be no further Succour, I shall
not be surprised if our western Borders shoud be abandoned
by all who do not make peace with the Enemy and accept of
their Protection.

It will give me infinite Pleasure to serve my Country, or to
afford any assistance to the Executive at this critical Juncture,
when the war seems to center, and to be about spending all its
Fury within the Circle of my native State. I shoud, therefore,
most chearfully repair to Poghkeepsie by the first day of the
Sessions was I not strongly restraind by the feeling of Delicacy.
I will not, whatever becomes of my private Fortune, or whatever
I suffer in being separated from my Friends & Family, decline the
Office of Delegate during the war; But I cannot reconcile it to
myself to appear as If I Sought that or any other Office: But

the Moment I hear that the Election of Delegates is made, I shall repair to Poghkeepsie and be at your Excellency's Service; whether I am reappointed or not. As that must necessarily be the first business to prevent the Loss of Representation in Congress, the little Delay will not produce any Inconvenience.

I cannot conclude without mentioning to your Excellency the pain I feel at the excessive and unaccountable Rise of Bread & Meat. I cannot but ascribe it to the secret arts & Practices of conceald agents of our Enemies, who take this last Method, since their arms are like to fail, to ruin our Affairs. Surely it is impossible that the Friends of America, however mercenary, can deliberately promote such detestible Extortion. How Sir, in the name of Heaven, can an army be supported on Beef at £60 for a mean Ox, and Flower at £6 to 8 a hundred & daily rising? A Remedy must be provided, at all Events, for this destructive Mischief or—:but I need not enlarge to your Excellency who so clearly foresees the consequences.

Mrs. Duane Joins me in respectful Compliments to yourself & Mrs. Clinton—with the greatest Esteem & Regard I have the Honour to be Sir Your Excellency's most Obed't & very hum'e ser't

                                                    Jas. Duane.
His Excellency, Governour Clinton.

not forwarded for want of Opportunity till the 1st of October.

[No. 1785.]

Commissary Fisher Makes a Financial Statement in Regard to Flour.

Fishkill Sept'r 22d 1778.

D'r Sir, I rec'd your favour of the 19th Inst; had not rec'd a Line from you, before this, since I had the Pleasure of paying you

£207—0—0 on Acct. of his Excellency; must alow there may be a Ballance due his Excellency on Acct. of the Casks, as I mentioned to you when paying the Money; am at present out of Cash but expect a Supply very shortly, when I shall wait on his Excellency for a final Settlement, the old Com'y Department is indebted to me for all Moneys I advanced which keeps me so short of Cash. I am, Sir, with due Respect, Your most obd. Ser't

George Fisher.

Robt. Benson Esqr.

[No. 1786.]

John Tayler Requests That a Bill for Rum Be Settled.

May it please Your Excellency The bearer, Mr. Blair & myself, purchased Jointly a parcel of rum, which he took to Fort Montgomery in May 1777 and disposed of a part of the same to Mr. Waterbury, the Commissary, for the use of that Garrison, taking his bill for the amount on Elisha Avery, Esq. Mr. Avery Refer'd him to the Commissary General, that Post not being in Mr. Avery's department—the Bill remain'd in my hands until after the taking of Fort Montgomery, I then sent it to Mr. Trumbull, who answerd he could not pay any of Waterbury's accounts, until he had an order from Congress for that purpose. I am informed the most of those accounts are Setled, as you Commanded Fort Montgomery at that time, Mr. Blair waits on you for your direction in this affair; any assistance that you will please to give him will be Gratefully acknowledged by Your Excellency's most obed't Humble Serv.

John Tayler.

Albany 22d Sept. 1778.

Governor Clinton.

[No. 1787.]

Order for Musket Cartridges.

Poughkeepsie Sept. 22d 1778.

Sir, Please to deliver to the Commiss'rs for Conspiracies &c. at Poughkeepsie or their Order 1000 musket Cartridges filled of diff't Sizes for the Use of the Militia appointed to Guard the State Prisoners under their direction.

Geo: Clinton.

To Colo. Lasher, Commiss'r of military Stores.

[No. 1788.]

Scarcity of Shoes and Stockings—Colonel Curtenius on Exempting Certain Workmen from Military Duty.

Wall Kill Sept. 22d 1778.

May it please your Excellency, Inclosed is a list* of the persons names, who are willing to work at the Soldiers Clothes & Shoes, provided they can be exempted from Militia duty during the time they are at work. Your Excellency will be pleased to send the Exemptions by the bearer, Mr. Abraham Vangelder, who I have desiered to wait for them until they can be got ready.

I have Received as yet, but 14 p Shoes & 18 pr. Stockings from the supervisors, & by what I can learn, but few more will come in. I have wrote to the supervisors & advertized it in the public papers, to bring in the Shoes & Stockings agreeable to act, but to little purpose; the reason of their backwardness is owing I understand to the supervisors not getting the act until after the time appointed for their meeting was Expiered, after which they say, it would have been to no purpose to lay the assesment, because the fine could not have been recovered if the persons had refused that were asses'd, If this is so it will be·necessary to have the

---

* Not found.

act Reviv'd, It would also be necessary that the counties should provide blankets, as there are none in store, neither have I orders to purchace any. I remain with great Respect Your Excell'ys most Obed't Serv't

Peter T. Curtenius.

His Excell'y Geo. Clinton Esqr.

[No. 1789.]

Joost Garrison Refuses to Take the Oath of Allegiance.

State of New York Ss,

To his Excellency George Clinton Esquire Governor of the State of New York, General and commander in chief, of all the militia, and admiral of the navy of the same.

In pursuance of an act of the Legislature of this State Entitled " an act more efect- " ually to prevent the mischiefs arising from the Influence and example of persons of " equivocal and suspected Characters in this State " we do hereby notify your Excel- lency that Joost Garrison of Charlotte precinct in Dutchess County, having appeared before us, and being by us Tendered the Oath in the said act contained, did refuse to take the same, and that unless your Excellency shall think proper to detain him for the purpose of exchanging him for any of the subjects of this State, in the power of the Enemy, we shall cause him to be removed within the Enemy's Lines.

Peter Cantine, Jur., Robt. Harpur, Egb't Benson, Commissioners.

Poughkeepsie September 23d 1778.

[No. 1790.]

Robert Benson for the Governor on the Authority of General Officers in Courts Martial Sentences.

Poughkeepsie Sept'r 23d 1778.

Sir, I had the honor of receiving your favor of the 16th Inst. yesterday & agreable to your Request shall endeavor to answer agreable to his Excellency's Opinion on the Subject, the questions you have stated. By the Militia Law " a refusal or neglect to march " is declared Desertion & of Course a Capital Crime & altho' a Court martial may in some Cases think proper to sentence the Criminal to Death & in others to lesser Punishments, yet this by no means can alter the nature of the Crime; Circumstances may justify the Court in ordering a Punishm't of an Inferior nature to that of Death. By the usage of our army every Genl. Officer having a seperate & distinct Command is supposed to be authorized to approve or disapprove the Sentences of all C'ts martial within his Departm't, & to order the same to be carried into execution &, therefore, the Proceed'g are always reported to him for that purpose. In this light is to be considered your command at present, as having the Direction of the Defence for the western frontiers & order'g out the militia for that purpose, altho' subject to the controul and orders of the Commander in Chief. It was on this principal, that his Excellency instead of ordering, only recommended, it to you, to suspend the Sentences (which were then already reported to & approved by you) respect'g the Delinquents in Colo. Whiting's Regt. However, notwithstanding, what has been said, Doubts may arise whether in Cases where the Sentence extends to deprive the Criminal of Life, this Line of Conduct would be prudent or adviseable. I think not, &, therefore, that the Proceedings in such cases had better be reported to the Commander in Chief for his approbation or reversal.

We have not a word of news. I supose before this reaches you you will have heard that our main army is withdrawn from the White Plains; & a part of them occupy the Posts in the Highl'ds; another part of them the eastern Parts of Westchester County, & the remainder are encamped towards Fredricksburgh, where Genl. Washington has his headq'rs. I am &c.

                                                        Robt. Benson.
The hon'ble Brig'r Genl. Ten Broeck, Albany.

[No. 1791.]

The Albany Conspiracy Commission Apologize for the Slight to Governor Clinton.

                                        Albany 23rd Sept'r 1778.

Sir, We yesterday rec'd your Excellency's Letter of the 20th Instant.

In answer to which we beg leave to observe, that on the 24th August in the afternoon, and but a few Minutes before we adjourned, we ordered our Secretary to furnish your Excellency with the names of Henry Van Schaack and the seven other Persons referred to. The next Morning he received orders from us to go to Claverack to take the examination of a number of Persons there confined. The business he was ordered upon, being very urgent, and the hurry he was in, in preparing himself for the Journey, we presume was the Cause of his omitting to notify your Excellency in due Season agreeable to our order. He did not return untill the 3rd Instant, and as we were led to suppose from the positiveness of the order and the attention he usually paid to our business, that our order was complied with, we made no further enquiry respecting it, but on the day when the warrant was Signed for the removal of those Persons, he informed us that the notice had not been transmitted to your Excellency till the 5th Inst. Finding then that between the Time of the notice and the day fixed for their removal (to wit the 9th) there were but four days, and being aware of the Impropriety of this measure, we ordered Coll. Visscher, whom we had appointed to Superintend their Removal, not to leave Kinderhook (the Place they were to set off from) untill the 13th with a view, in Case your Excellency should determine to detain them, that we might order accordingly.

The Flags passing your Excellency's Quarters, was owing to a Report made to us, by Colo. Visscher, that when he called upon your Excellency with the former Flag, you had been pleased to say there was no necessity for his stopping at your Quarters, and that for the future we should send the Persons to be removed on to Fish Kill.

We return your Excellency our thanks for entertaining the good opinion of us, whereby you are induced to believe that it must have been occasioned by some Mistake, which was really the Case, and shall endeavour to prevent the like in future.

The Persons referred to in yours of the 16th and your last Letter, shall be confined for exchange agreeable to your directions. We are with the greatest respect Your Excellency's Most Obt. Serv'ts

Mat: Visscher, Isaac D. Fonda, John M. Beeckman.

His Excellency, Governor Clinton.

[No. 1792.]

ROBERT R. LIVINGSTON DEFENDS THE MANOR.

Governor Clinton, However, Corrects Several Discrepancies— Movements of the Commander-in-Chief.

Clermonnt 23d Sep'r 1778.

Dear Sir, Mr. Albertie will deliver this to your Excellency. The Convention at Kingston at my request, let him purchase on their acct., 200 hides to be tanned for the halves on acct. of the State; they are now finished, & he waits upon your Excellency to take your direction about them. He is a good whig, & a man of a very good character; if your Excellency sh'd have any proposal to make for further business of this sort I dare say he would execute it honestly.

I find the Manor ag'n called upon for waggons & upon the principle of their having done little duty I am perswaded that your Excellency has been greatly deceived by misrepresentations on this head. No part of the state has suffered half so much by the oppressions of quarter masters & Commissaries, or done more duty, they, having been freequently called upon for a quota of men to go to the norward, & another the Southerd besides large

demands for waggons. At a time when every fourth man was
called down, every sixth was summoned by Genl. Ten Brock to
go to the Norward. Of the whole number of waggons in the Mannor which does not exceed 200, I will undertake to prove the 30
were lost last campaign to the norward & near one hundred
horses for which no compensation has been allowed.

They sh'd certainly be considered as belonging to one County or
the other & not obliged to do the duty of both. And some care
sh'd be taken that justice was done them; when they did serve no
wages having ever yet been rec'd. I mention this, because I am
informed that the quartermaster upon this last requisition shew'd
no warrant from your Excellency, but talked of procuring the
waggons by his sword: a language that ought not to be spoken
in a free country. I know that your Excellency can not at the distance you now are, know the true state of this country, where the
people are so incapable of representing their grievances, and upon
that principle I am satisfied that your Excellency will be pleased
at the liberty I have taken to mention facts that have arissen within my own knowledge.

We have various accts. of the movement of the enemy & our
own army—none of which can be depended on—if any thing sh'd
have turned up of consequence I sh'd be obliged to your Excellency for a line by the bearer. I am, D'r Sir, Your Excellency's
Most Obt. Hum: Serv't

                                        Robt. R. Livingston.
To His Excellency Gov'r Clinton.

                                    P. 23d Sep'r 1778.

D'r Sir, I am favoured with your Letter by Mr. Albertie; if any
Thing shoud turn up in which I can save him I will do it with
great Pleasure.

I am far from approving of the Quarter Master's Conduct towards the Inhabitants of the Manor. He has indeed no Warrant from me nor have I ever issued one to any of them for the Purpose. By the Law, (except on special Occassions), Impresses are to be made by Warrant from the Justices of the District & as there is not any Quallified in that this may have induced the Quarter Master to think himself Justifiable in proceeding as formerly with respect to that manor.

I have been most grossly deceived if the Manor Regiment has been overcharged with duty. It is true in the Spring, they received thro' Misstake my Orders for marching one fourth of the Regt., to reinforce the Posts in the Highlands & at the same Time they had Genl. Ten Broeck's Orders to march an Eighth or Sixth to the Western Frontier. This was rectified immediately, but neither order [was] ever complied with, and if I may credit Genl. Ten Broeck's Returns to me, every Order he has issued to that Regiment has been imperfectly obeyed or totally disregarded by them; it appears it has not in any one Instance, furnished half its Quota & in some Times not a Man. This is the Case to my certain Knowledge at this present Time.

The Army has left the Plains & are now posted along the Mountains from Danbury to West Point, Head Quarters at Jno. Kain's at Fredricksburgh, for which Place Genl. Washington after having visited the Forts, passed thro Fishkill on Sunday last. I am not informed of the Occassion of this Movement. I can but conjecture & mine are not worth Communicating. I am D'r Sir Yours sincerely,

[G. C.]

[To Robert R. Livingston.]

[No. 1793.]

GEORGE CLINTON TO WASHINGTON.

Fear of Losing All the Settlements on the Mohawk River—Stark Regarded More as a Politician Than a Soldier.

Poukeepsie 24th Sep'r 1778.

D'r Sir, I wrote your Excellency on the 20th Instant inclosing an Account of the Destruction of the German Flatts on the Mohawk River. Since I have been favoured with a Letter from Colo. Bellinger of which the inclosed is a Copy giving the particulars of that unhappy Affair. Colo. Bellinger's Letter was handed to me by Mr. Herkimer, Brother to the late General Herkimer, who, (as he is well acquainted with the Situation of that Country & the distresses of the Inhabitants), I have prevailed upon to be the Bearer of this, that he may afford your Excellency the fullest Information.

From the first Appearance of Danger in that Quarter, the Commanding Officers of the Militia of Albany & Tryon Counties have had my most positive Orders to keep out one fourth Part of their Commands on the Frontiers, and tho I am sensible my Orders have not been fully complied with, yet from the Returns made me it appear that a Considerable Force has been constantly out on that Service, and I entertained Hopes that with the assistance of Weston's Regiment they would have been able to have afforded some Security to the Frontier Inhabitants; but the Extensive Country to be guarded, & the want of Judgment in not fixing on the most advantageous Station, with some other Causes, has rendered the Measures hitherto pursued, innefectual & I fear will End in the Total Loss of the many valuable Settlements on the River. Shoud this be the Case, besides the Distresses which will be experienced by Individuals, we will find it Extreamly difficult to get the Necessary Supplies to Fort Schuyler & of Course that Important Post very insecure.

I have been favoured with two Letters from Genl. Stark on the subject of his Command last Spring one, & the other the later Part of Summer, neither of any Consequence & if I may Judge from this & the Common Report of the Inhabitants, corroborated by the Complaints of a Civil Officer of the State, I may reasonably conclude that he has paid a greater share of attention to the support & Encouragement of the disafected Subjects of this State on the Grants, in establishing their usurped Government, than to the Defence of the Western Frontier & Protection of its Inhabitants.   I am, Sir, with the highest Esteem & Respect Your Excellency's most Obed't Serv't

[G. C.]

His Excellency Genl. Washington.

[No. 1794.]

SKELETON MILITIA REGIMENTS.

General Ten Broeck Dwells Upon the Difficulties of His Position— The Losses at German Flats.

Albany 24th Septem'r 1778.

Sir, Your Excellency's letter of the 20th Instant by the Returning Express I have Rec'd.   I am very Unhappy that so few of the militia Ordered for the Protection of the Frontiers have been at any time actually on that Service; at the very time when I desired your Excellency's Opinion Relative to the keeping back the last Class, (& I wrote purely to Gratify the Officers who in behalf of their men dayly applyed to me), I pressed them & Urged the necessity of sending on their full Proportion of men to Relieve in due time those then in Service.

In the last alarm I only Ordered Colonel Wemple's, Schuyler's & Van Schoonhoven's Regts; the two later did not march, I having Countermanded the Order, when I was Informed that the Enemy had gone off; Col. Wemple's did march but Returned soon home.

Colonell Alden's Regiment is Stationed at Cherry Valey, I am Informed that he sent part of his Regt. to Intercept the Enemy, who it is said took their Rout back by the same way they came to Unindillo; what Success they have had or whether they are Returned I have not learnt. Colonel Klock was on his march, as he Informs me, with about 300 men of his militia; when within ab't 4 miles of Cherry Valey an Express overtook him Informing him that the Enemy was in full march & near Canajohary, which Obliged him to march back on the Cherry Valey Road to the River; on his arrival there, he found there was no truth in the Information & then Ordered his men to follow him to Cherry Valey, but could Prevail only on about 60 men to go with him, with whom he arrived at Cherry Valey on Fryday noon, when Colonel Alden told him he came too late; his men were so farr gone that it would be Impossible to Overtake them; then he Returned & dismissed the militia; Inclosed I send Copy of Col. Fisher's letter to Col. Wemple & Copy of Col. Wemple's letter to me. Major Rensselaer Informs me that about 40 men of Col. Rensselaer's Regiment went by water some days since to Fort Arnold, Lieut. Col. Livingston tells me some of Col. Livingston's men have marched but Cannot say how many, I am told only 4 or 5 of Col. Van Alstine's are march'd to Fort Arnold. I have, therefore, Ordered one fourth part of his Regiment to march Immediately this way.

Colonel Whiting has only about 20 men & Col. Van Ness about

the same number at Cherry Valey, I inclose your Excellency Copy of a Return I have Rec'd from Schohary. I have wrote to the Colonels & Informed them of the great Deficiency & have Ordered them without one moment's delay to Compleat the number, being one fourth part of their Respective Regiments.

Two General Courts Martial are now setting, one in the Manor of Livingston & one at this place, to Try the Delinquents.

General Stark called upon me yesterday & Requested me to Order one fourth part of Colonell Van Schoonhoven's Regiment to Canajohary in Tryon County which I have done.

One fourth part of all Except the three northern Regiments of my Brigade have long since been Ordered into actual Service to be Relieved monthly, & I shall do my Utmost Endeavours to bring them into actual Service & Statedly keep them out, to Protect the Frontiers; if your Excellency should Judge the number Ordered out Insufficient you will please to Signify if to me. The men of Course are Stationed where General Stark Orders them. He yesterday Informed me that he has Rec'd Intelligence that a Body of the Enemy Intend soon to make an attack on our northern Frontiers, of this I have apprized the Colonels of the four northern Regiments & have directed them to Order their men to be in perfect Readiness so as to be able to march at a moment's notice.

I inclose a list of the number of Houses &c., Burned & destroyed by the Enemy at German Flatts on the 17th Instant; Mr. Herkhimer who lives at the Flatts went down to your Excellency two or three days ago; he is able to give a more Particular account. I Remain with great Regard Your Excellency's most Obedient Humble Servant

                                        Ab'm Ten Broeck.

His Excell'y George Clinton Esqr.

Copy.

Brimstone Hill Sep'r 19 1778.

Sir, I was within 3 miles from Chere Vallie where I met Col. Clock, and he Dismiss'd us all.   Col. Alden sent out yesterday a party to cut off the Enemies Retreat if the were able.   Alden told Clock that his party were too farr to overtake them, that it was not worth wile for the Militia to pursue.   Sir I am yours &c.

Fred'k Fisher.

P. S.   Sir, I now go to the Germin Flatts to see how it is with them.

To Col. Ab'm Wemple.

Caughnewaga Sep'r 20 1778.

Hono'd Sir, To my great Sirprise this morning, I received Inteligence from Col. Vischer, that the Tryon County Militia are all Dismis'd; none gone in persuit of the Enemy; only about 200 of Col. Alden's troops & militia from Cherevallie are gone after them; not one of these Militia that I can understand are even stayed at Charevallie to guard that place, till they see the Event of those that are gone after the Enemy; now I am much at a stand what to do; but I have upon the whole Concluded to stay at the Nose or Van Alstyn's, till I here the Event of those that are gone after the Enemy, and if I dont find it necessary to Proceed, shall Return home, without I receive your Orders to the Contrary.   I am Dear General Your Humble Serv't

Ab'm Wemple.

To General Ten Broeck.

THE LOSS AT GERMAN FLATS.

Houses	63
Barns	57
Grist mills	3
Saw mill	1
Horses	235
Horned Cattle	229
Sheep	269

The above Buildings at the German Flatts are Burned & the Cattle taken off by the Enemy the 17th day of September 1778.

2 white & a negroe man Inhabitants Killed.

A man a son of Mrs. Magin, who has for some time been deprived of his Senses was Burned in a house.

———

[No. 1795.]

Peter Colt Asks the Governor's Assistance in Purchasing Supplies for the Eastern Department and the French Fleet.

Hartford Sept. 25 1778.

May it please y'r Excellency, Being informed that considerable Quantities of wheat yet remains, of the old Crops, in the hands of disaffected persons, & such others as refuse to sell to the Commissaries for the use of the army,—for paper Money—& being called on for larger Supplies of Flour for the use of the Eastern Department & French Fleet, than can Supply, unless the Farmers sell without reserve; must request the aid and assistance of Goverment in procuring this necessary article. I have directed my assistants in your State, to apply to your Excellency (in case they cannot obtain the wheat & Flour otherways) for a warrant to seize all goods so unreasonably withheld. I am unacquainted with the Laws of your State—dont know what provisions they have made in such Cases—however dont doubt but the powers of Goverment will be properly exerted in maintaining & Supporting this just & necessary Contest. Mr. Philip Leak purchases under me in West Chester County, Maj. Henry Schenk of Fishkill, Mr. Paul Schenk of Poughkepsee, David Van Ness Esq. of Redhook & Capt. James Reed of Amenia precint in Dutches County. If either of those Gentlemen should apply to your Excellency for advice & assistance, must request you to consider them as Persons in public service—any aid afforded them will be gratfully acknowledged by Your Excellency's most respectful humble Servant

Peter Colt D. C. G. Purchases.

His Excellency Go. Clinton Esquire.

[No. 1796.]

General Ten Broeck Ordered to Protect the Western Frontier.

Poughkeepsie Sept'r 25th 1778.

Sir, By order of his Excellency, the Governor, I inclose you the Copy of a Letter from Colo. Bellinger; which is not meant to inform you of the particulars of the Ravages of the Enemy at the German Flatts of which you are fully acquainted, but to shew you the Sense of the Inhabitants in that Quarter & the necessity of immediate Reinforcem'ts being sent thither, not only to prevent the Inhabitants coming away & leaving that Country entirely open to the Enemy, but to secure the Communication for the transportation of Provisions &c. to Fort Schuyler; which, if neglected, may render the situation of that Post very precarious. His Excellency, therefore, most earnestly request you to exert yourself to the utmost in rousing the militia to a Sense of their Duty & to cause one full fourth part of them forthwith to march to the relief of the suffering Inhabitants on the Western Frontiers & that they be so stationed as to afford the most equal & perfect Security to all the frontier Settlements.

His Excellency further directs me to inform you, that he is not authorized to appoint a Pay Master in Albany, & therefore advises that the Pay Rolls &c. should be sent down by an officer to the Auditor Genl. & that immediately on their being audited a warrant will issue for the Paym't of them. This may be done without any great Inconvenience. I have the honor to be &c.

Robt. Benson, A. D. C.

The hon'ble Brig'r Genl. Ten Broeck.

His Excellency (from Genl. Washington's Letter in answer to his, contain'g a Representation of the Distresses of the frontier Settlem'ts) has Reason to expect some small Succour (however illy to be spared) from the main army; but as some time must elapse before they can possibly arrive, the utmost Exertions of the militia are in the meantime absolutely necessary.

[No. 1797.]

Governor Clinton Reminds Colonel Klock of Previous Orders That Have Been Neglected, Concerning the Frontier.

Poughkeepsie Sept'r 25th 1778.

Sir, By my Orders to you of the 6th April last, you was directed to raise two Companies of sixty men each, including non Commissioned Officers, from the Militia of Tryon County to be stationed on the Western Frontier for the Protection of the Inhabitants ag't the Incursions & Ravages of the Enemy &ca. And by my subsequent Orders, you was directed to Call into actual Service and constantly keep out one fourth Part of the Militia for the same Purpose, & similar Orders to the last were also issued at the same Time to the Commanding Officers of the Militia of Albany County. But, as I have not been favoured with a Line from you on that Subject, or any Return of the Men you may have had in Service in Consequence of these Orders, I am altogether ignorant whether they have been complied with by you. The daily Depredations committed by the Enemy on the Frontier

Inhabitants & particularly the late mellancholly one at the Flatts, leads me to believe they have not, as I am perswaded had my Orders been fully & faithfully carried into Execution most of the Distresses experienced by those Unhappy People might have been prevented. I am, therefore, again to repeat my above Orders to you, & the absolute necessity of their being faithfully & without Delay carried into Execution; & it is my further Orders that the Militia for this Service be so stationed as to afford the most equal & perfect Security to all the Frontier Settlements & that you make Returns to me from Time to Time of the Numbers you have out, where stationed &c. I have Reason (from his Excell'cy Genl. Washington's Letter in answer to mine contain'g a Representation of the Distresses of the frontier Inhabitants) to expect some small Succour, (however illy to be spared), from the main army; but as some time must elapse before they can arrive the utmost exertions of the militia are absolutely necessary. I am Sir Your most Obed't

G. C.

To Colo. Clock.

[No. 1798.]

A Cry of Alarm from Harington Township.

Harington Township September 25th 1778.

Dear Sir, As we expect that Col. Hay has left home by this time, on his way to Genl. Washington, we address this letter to you and acquaint you that from good authority we inform you that the enemy have already Seventeen field pieces at the liberty pole, they daily receive reinforcements from Newyork and have actually part of their army near the New Bridge; their intention is to march thro' this place your way. this Intelligence or the Chief part thereof we have from a Creditable woman who has been among the enemy, she has seen the above number of field pieces.

We beg of you to forward this Intelligence and in the strongest Terms to press for assistance; you will inform the General Officers that unless they send us Speedy relief they will not have Occasion to send or give any, on our account, as it is not worth while for us to think of maintaining our Ground much longer. We are of Opinion that our Governor ought to be acquainted with our Scituation and, therefore, request of you to send him a true account thereof and beg his assistance, We are Sir Your Humble Servants.

John Haring

Gilb't Cooper.

P. S. This moment some women and Children are coming up the road and Give an alarm; they say the enemy take women and Children and Commenced their old practice of burning.

J. H.

8 O'Clock in the Evening.

To Thos. Smith, Esquire at Haverstraw.

[No. 1799.]

DISTRESS AT GERMAN FLATS.

An Appeal to Be Made to the Legislature for the Alleviation of the Sufferers.

Poukeepsie 26th Sep'r 1778.

Sir, Two Days before the Receipt of your Letter of the 19th Inst. by Mr. Herkimer, I had the Mellancholly News of the Destruction of the German Flatts, and tho my Accounts of that Unhappy Affair were not so perfect as by your Letter I immediately communicated them to his Excellency Genl. Washington, by Express, as I have since the particulars as received from you. I need not mention to you how great my Concern is for the Distresses of the Frontier Inhabitants & particularly for those of your Neighborhood who have suffered most by this last Unhappy Affair. I have, however, this Consolation that my utmost endeavours for their Protection & Security have in no Instance been wanting and I am perswaded had my Orders been faithfully executed much Injury & Distress might have been prevented. The inclosed Copy of a Letter which I have forwarded to Colo. Clock will discover to you what my Orders to him were & that similar Orders has also issued to Genl. Ten Broeck. You will also observe, that besides again repeating my former Orders to those Gentlemen I have directed that the Militia ordered out, be stationed so to give the most perfect & equal Security to all the Frontier Settlements. As I dont possess any Authority over the Continental Troops you will readily perceive that the only Relief or assistance I am of myself able to afford you, must be by the Militia, and that this much depends on the Exertions of the subordinate Officers who are charged with the Execution of my Orders. I am lead to hope however from his Excellency Genl. Washington's Letter to me of yesterday, in Answer two Letters I had the Honor of writing him on this Subject that however illy able to spare it, he will afford you some small Succour from his Army, but till they can arrive in your Neighbourhood which will naturally take some Time, your safety will depend on the Exertions of the Militia.

The Inhabitants of the Flatts who are deprived of the Nessaries of Life by the late unhappy Event, are in a particular Manner to be commiserated, & I sincerely wish it was in my

Power in some Measure to alleviate their Distresses by ordering the Commissary of Issues to dispense to them a Temporary supply of Provisions, but as the Stores belong to the Continent my Orders on them as Governor of a particular State woud be improper. The only proper Measure I can pursue in their Favour, is to represent their Case to the Legislature & this you may rest assured shall be faithfully done at their next meeting, which is to be as early as Thursday next, & I have not the least reason to doubt that as it merrits it will engage their first attention. I am Sir Your most Obed't Serv't

G. C.

Colo. Bellinger.

[No. 1800.]

THE DIFFICULTY IN PROCURING FLOUR.

Governor Clinton Questions the Charge that Tories Are Holding up the Cereal for an Advance in Price.

Sir, I take the liberty to lay before your Excellency the inclosed extracts of letters from Mr. Jacob Cuyler,, D. C. G. of Purchases at Albany. At the same time, I must mention some of the difficulties that attend getting supplies of flour adequate to the wants of this army.

The purchasing Comisaries complain, that the greatest part of the old wheat now in this state, is in the possession of men so far disaffected to the measures of America as to be unwilling to dispose of their commodities for continental bills. Another complaint is, that those men who do not object to the currency are induced to withold their grain from the public purchasers, in an expectation that they can have a much higher price from private persons. They not only expect this; but the buyers are continually among them and make encouraging offers. To remedy these evils, I must request your Excellency to grant such warrants to the purchasers as will empower them to obtain the wheat if the proprietors will not voluntarily sell it at the current price.   I have directed Mr. Jacob Cuyler, D. C. G. of Purchases to consult your Excellency on this occasion.   Mr. Peter Colt,, D. C. G. Purchases in whose district are included the counties of Dutchess and West Chester will also make application for some assistance.

It was an unfortunate Circumstance for the public purchasers that the Superintendent of the French Fleet made a Contract with Mr. Price of Boston for a large quantity of flour.   Mr. Vandurhuyden, I suppose is now buying flour to fulfil that contract.. Congress had ordered the Com'y General to furnish the provisions for the Fleet & preperations were actually making to procure them.   I cannot conceive that Mr. Price's Contract will be acceptable to Congress.   The evil consequences of such measures are easily known to your Excellency.

The magazines of Flour are so nearly exhausted at the eastward, that I fear we should be much distressed for bread to feed a considerable army in that quarter.   Our Dependance must be on this state.   General Schuyler informs me that very large quantities may be had with proper exertions.

It was not known to me till lately that these difficulties were in the way.   I must repeat my request for your interposition in such a manner as will be most likely to enable the purchasers to obtain Flour for the Army.   I have the honor to be Your Excellency's most obed't & hbl. Srvt.

                    Royal Flint Ast. C. G. of Purchases.
Camp Fredericksburgh Sept. 25: 1778.
His Ex'y Gov. Clinton.

*Extract of a Letter Dated Albany Sept. 18th 1778.

Mr. Jacob Van Derheyden, of Great Barrington, has Purchased a Considerable Quanty of Flour in this City for five Pounds Currency pr ct., which so much exceeds what I have given, that it must prove very detrimental to the Public Service; since his Purchase I have been Inform'd he has a License from Governor Clinton to Export it out of this State and it was Obtaind by the Board of War at Boston for a Suply towards the French Fleet. If it is so, and the practice Continued, It must work a very great Evil.

I give you this Information as I conceive it a matter worth Inquiring into through what Channel Mr. Van Derheyden Obtained his Licence.

Another Dated Sept. 20th 1778.

I have been informed, and believe it to be true, that Mr. Van Derheyden has got persons in every part of the County to buy wheat Either for paper Currency or Specie. If this Contract is not stopt I dont know where the Evil will End.

I am in hast tho with much Respect & esteem Your most humble Serv't

Jacob Cuyler D. C. G. P.

Royal Flint Esquire.

————

P. 26th Sep'r 1778.

Sir, I have received your Letter of yesterday. The Difficulties complained of in procuring proper Supplies of Flour for the army do not arise from the disafected Inhabitants withholding that Article from Sale as mentioned by you for tho we have a Proportion of them among us, there are but few of them so firmly at-

---

*These extracts from Colonel Cuyler's letters and Governor Clinton's response were made a separate document (No. 1804) by the editor of the mss. The present editor attached them to document 1800 to which they manifestly belong.

tached to any Principle as to make so great sacrafise to it. Such disinterested Conduct even in a bad Cause is too much like Virtue to be practiced by Tories. Ignorance, Fear & Interest are the Parents of Toryism. The two latter have taught their Children long since to dispose of the Produce of their Farms for Continental Currency & those of the former have little to sell. Difficulties are in a great Measure owing to your Assistants in this Quarter having neglected to purchase when they might at a moderate Price have got all the Flour the Farmers coud spare. This was the Case in the Months of July & Aug't last. I at the Time inquired of some of them the Cause. They informed me such was their Orders.

The Legislature of this State as early as last Fall laid an Embargo on Flour prohibiting the Exportation of that Article out of the State except on special Occasions. They were influenced to this Measure tho manifestly ag't the Interest of their Constituents in order that the army might have a plentiful Supply & at a moderate Price. This Law is yet in Force but under a pretence of supplying the Eastern Troops the French Fleet &ca. it is evaded by the Trader notwithstanding the utmost vigilance of the Magistrate. The Price is thereby become exhorbitant & I am sorry to add a real Scarcity is likely to be the Consequence. What you mention of the Measures pursuing to supply the French Fleet is too true & I am perswaded will be attended with bad Consequences if permits to export large Quantities for this Purpose are granted them & this tho' disagreable now coud not be refused. The Legislature is to meet next week your Letter will be submitted to their Consideration.

.[G. C.]

[To Royal Flint.]

[No. 1801.]

CONGRESS ESTABLISHES THE TREASURY.

Officers, How Appointed, Their Oaths of Office and Forms to Be Used in the Transaction of Public Business.

IN CONGRESS,

SEPTEMBER 26, 1778.

Resolved, That a house be provided at the city or place where Congress shall sit, wherein shall be held the several Offices of the Treasury:

That there be the following offices, viz. the Comptroller's, Auditor's, Treasurer's, and two Chambers of Accounts:

That each Chamber of Accounts consist of three Commissioners and two Clerks, to be appointed by Congress:

That in the Treasurer's office there be a Treasurer annually appointed by Congress, and one Clerk appointed by the Treasurer:

That in the Auditor's office there be an Auditor annually appointed by Congress, and two Clerks appointed by the Auditor:

That in the Comptroller's office there be a Comptroller annually appointed by Congress, and two Clerks appointed by the Comptroller:

That the Auditor, Treasurer and Comptroller shall not be appointed unless by the voice of nine states; and that they be accountable for the conduct of their Clerks respectively:

That the Auditor shall receive all accounts brought against the United States for money lent, expended, or advanced; goods sold or purchased; services performed, or work done; with the vouchers; and shall refer them to one of the chambers of accounts; indorsing them in the manner marked A:

That the Commissioners of the chamber to whom an account shall be referred, shall deliver the same to their Clerks to be properly stated:

That the Clerks shall state the accounts referred to them by the Commissioners, number and arrange the vouchers, examine the castings, and make necessary copies:

That the Clerks to whom an account shall be delivered, after they have compleated the same, shall indorse it in the manner marked B:

That the Commissioners to whom an account is referred as aforesaid, shall carefully examine the authenticity of the vouchers (rejecting such as shall not appear good,) compare them with the articles to which they relate, and determine whether they support the charges: That they shall reduce such articles as are over charged, and reject such as are improper; and shall indorse the accounts in the manner marked C, and transmit them, with the vouchers, to the Auditor, and cause an entry to be made of the ballance passed:

That the Auditor shall receive the vouchers and accounts from the Commissioners to whom he referred them, and cause them to be examined by his Clerks. He shall compare the several articles with the vouchers, and if the parties concerned shall appeal from the judgment of the Commissioners, he shall call before him the Commissioners and the party, and hear them, and then make determination, from whence no appeal shall lie, unless to Congress. That after a careful examination of the account as aforesaid, he shall indorse it in the manner marked D; of which indorsement he shall send a duplicate, to be filed in the same chamber of accounts, and shall transmit the account and vouchers to the Comptroller:

That the Comptroller shall keep the treasury books and seal, and shall file the accounts and vouchers on which the accounts in the said books are founded, and shall direct the manner of stating and keeping the public accounts. He shall draw bills under the said seal on the Treasurer for such sums as shall be due by the United States on accounts audited, which, previous to the payment, shall be countersigned by the Auditor; and also for such sums as may from time to time be ordered by Resolutions of Congress, which, previous to the payment, shall be countersigned by the Secretary of Congress, in the form marked E: That when monies are due to the United States on accounts audited, he shall notify the debtor, (and after hearing him, if he shall desire to be heard,) fix a day for payment, according to the circumstances of the case, not exceeding ninety days, of which he shall give notice to the Auditor in writing, in the form marked F:

That it be the duty of the Treasurer to receive and keep the monies of the United States, and to issue them on bills drawn by the Comptroller as aforesaid, filing duplicates thereof with the Auditor day by day as he shall make payment: That on receipt of monies he shall give a receipt therefor, and transmit the same to the Comptroller; and that he shall draw out and settle his accounts quarterly, giving the same in to the Auditor for examination by one of the Chambers of Accounts, to be from thence transmitted through the Auditor to the Comptroller, who shall compare the same with the treasury books, ascertain the ballance, and return a copy of the same to Congress:

That the Comptroller shall receive from the Treasurer all receipts by him signed, and after making due entry thereof by charging the Treasurer and crediting the proper accounts, he shall indorse the same in the manner marked G, and deliver them to the

party who made payment. That he shall every quarter of a year
cause a list of the ballances on the treasury-books, to be made out
by his Clerks, and lay it before Congress. That where any person hath received public monies which remain unaccounted for,
or shall be otherwise indebted to the United States, or have an
unsettled account with them, he shall issue a summons in the
form marked H, in which a reasonable time shall be given for
the appearance of the party according to the distance of his place
of residence from the treasury, of which he shall notify the
Auditor:

That in case a party summoned to account shall not appear,
nor make good essoign, the Auditor on proof made of service in
due time, or other sufficient notice, shall make out a requisition in
the form marked I, which he shall send to the Comptroller's office,
where the same shall be sealed; and then it shall be sent to the
executive authority of the state in which the party shall reside.

That it be recommended to the several states to enact laws for
the taking of such persons, and also to seize the property of persons who being indebted to the United States shall neglect or
refuse to pay the same. Notice whereof shall be given by the
Auditor to the executive authority of the respective states in the
form marked K, under the treasury seal:

That the several officers of the treasury do, before they take
upon them the execution of their offices respectively, before the
President of Congress, for the time being, make and subscribe
the following oath; viz.

" I A. B.   in the treasury of the United States, do
solemnly and sincerely swear, promise and declare in the presence of Almighty God, that I will diligently and faithfully according to the best of my skill and understanding in all things

do my duty as a   as aforesaid, without fear, favour, affection or partiality."

A. Account between the United States and   with the vouchers, referred to   Commissioners of accounts, the day of   in the year &c.

B. The within account hath been stated, the castings examined, and the vouchers arranged, by   C. D. } Clerks of
                                                        E. F. } accounts.

C. The within account stated by   and   Clerks of accounts, between the United States and   hath been examined and settled, and a ballance of   found to be due to   by

G. H. }
I. K. } Commissioners of accounts.
L. M. }

D. Audited the account between the United States and   , stated by   and   Clerks of accounts, and examined by   and   Commissioners of Accounts, for a ballance of   due to   Done the   day of   in the year, &c.   A. B. Auditor.

(L. S.) E. To the Treasurer of the United States, Greeting. You are required to pay the sum of   to   or his order, according to (say either account audited, &c. or a resolution of Congress, &c.) whereof entry is made the   day of   in the year &c.

N. O. Comptroller.

F. Day is given to   until the   day of   next, for the sum of   by his assent. Whereof taken notice. Given the   day of   in the year, &c.

N. O. Comptroller.

G. Entered in the treasury-books the   day of   in
the year, &c.   N. O. Comptroller.

H. To   Greeting. You are required on or before
the   day of   next, to appear before the Auditor in
the Treasury-office of the United States, at   , then and
there to adjust and settle your accounts. Whereof take notice.
Given   the   day of   in the year, &c.
                                             N. O. Comptroller.

(L. S.) I. To   Greeting. The United States having
summoned   to account, the which he hath neglected to do,
it is their request that you cause to be taken and sent the
said   to be before them on the   day of   next,
before the Auditor in their treasury at   then and there
to account, that justice may in this behalf be done. Given
the   day of &c.
                                             Witness A. B. Auditor.

(L. S.) K. The United States to   Greeting. Whereas
            hath been before us in our treasury found to be in-
debted in the sum of   the which sum was by his assent
to be paid before the   day of   in the year, &c. but is
not yet paid, or in any manner satisfied. These therefore are
thereof to notify you: To the end that you according to the
powers and authorities unto you given, may of the estate of the
said   cause to be made the sum aforesaid with the costs
and charges which may accrue: And of your proceedings in the
premises you are desired to certify us in our said treasury with
all convenient speed. Given at   on the   day of &c.
                                             Witness, A. B. Auditor.

That in the blanks of the forms above written, no figures be
used either for dates or sums, but that the same be distinctly

and plainly set in words at length, and without erazures or inter-lineations.

Extracts from the Minutes,

CHARLES THOMSON, Secretary.

[No. 1802.]

GEORGE CLINTON VINDICATED.

Congress Absolves Him from Responsibility in the Loss of the Forts in the Highlands.

Philadelphia 27th Septem. 1778.

Sir, On the 21st I had the honor of receiving & presenting to Congress your Excellency's favor of the 9th Inst. and in answer, I herewith transmit an Act of Congress of the 21st, duplicate of the Act of the 17th, & Copies of the sundry Papers which your Excellency desired to be furnished with. In these I trust will be found no deficiency & I intreat, Sir, you will be assured, the late omission of which you have justly complained, was not the effect of inattention on my part.

All our public Offices which have hitherto been conducted as well, I presume, as circumstances in an Infant State would admit of, now call for inspection & improvement & none more than the Secretary's Office, from whence alone according to the present mode, I derive subject for every public Letter.

The Act of the 21st signifies the entire approbation by Congress of your Excellency's conduct as Commander of the Forts on Hudson's River which I repeat with great pleasure in obedience to the order of Congress & from that sincere respect & esteem for your Excellency's character, with which I have the honor to be Sir Your Excellency's Most obedient & Most humble serv't

Henry Laurens, President of Congress.

His Excellency Governor Clinton New York.

[No. 1803.]

POLITICS IN BESTOWING COMMISSIONS.

Ethan Allen's Commission of Colonel Held Up by Governeur Morris.

Phila: 27th Sep'r 1778.

Sir, I write this short note to your Excellency to suggest the Hint of sending a Committee to confer with the Legislature of New Hampshire on the Affairs of Vermont. You are not to learn that these new States men have debauched some of the Western Townships of New Hampshire. The temper of Congress in this Business from what passed lately, seems to be if possible to keep matters quiet untill the Enemy leave us, when the Forces of the whole Continent may be turned to reduce them if refractory to the Resolutions of that Body. Application was made for a Commission of Colo. to Ethan Allen which I opposed. When he was redeemed I moved a Brevet Rank for him which was granted, and he would certainly have had the Commission if I had not learnt that he hath lately interfered in Opposition to the authority of the State of New York.

I am with Respect Your Excellency's most obedient & humble Servant

Gouv. Morris.

As Mr. Duer intends [to leave] soon for the State I have not written at large. Should he delay I shall be more full and more particular on our private Affairs. I mean those of the State as distinct from the Continent. I have the Pleasure to tell you that at Length with infinite Pains and many Disappointments we have got an arrangement for our Treasury which promises the best Consequences, We are now to be employed in Finance. A proper System is before Congress. But will they adopt it?

His Excellency George Clinton Esqr.

[No. 1804.]*

———

[No. 1805.]

A Report that the Enemy are Moving up the West Side of the Hudson.

Sir, This moment I Received the Inclosed by Express; in addition to this Intelligence I am to inform you, that I Returned from below Tappan yesterday morning at the Instance of the Inhab'ts, to solicit assistance from General Putnam, but cannot as yet find that any Troops are ordered over, tho' he by letter to Col. Hay gave him assurances of Troops being sent to his aid yesterday morning. Last night Col. Hay at the Instance of his Officers and Mr. Herring Returned and is gone forward to General Washington to Procure Troops but I fear they will come too late.

Col. Hay's Regt., Consisting of about 250 men, now lie two miles below Tappan on the Road leading to Scraulingburgh Church; they have Drove off the Cattle from below to Clarks Town, but I much fear the Enemy will overtake them before the can be Drove further as they have about 200 Light Horse with them. I am D'r Governor Your most humble serv't

Thos. Smith.

Saturday morning 5 Clock.

P. S. The Enemy have thrown up some works at the Tena Fly near the Liberty Pole; we hear nothing of the Jersey militia or General Maxwell's Troops and suspect the Enemy have moved to N. Jersey from Staten Island to keep back every assistance from that Quarter while Cornwallis who it is said Commands below pushes into this County. We beg all the assistance in your Power.

To His Excellency Governor Clinton.

———

*See foot note page 91.

Poughkeepsie Sept'r 27th 1778.

Sir, His Excellency the Gov'r directs me to send you the enclosed Copies of Intelligence which he rec'd last night. As this is the only acct. he hath rec'd of the matter 'tis impossible for him to judge of the Enemy's Strength or intentions & of course difficult for him to give such particular Orders respect'g the matter as he could wish, but as you will have an opportunity getting fuller Information he, therefore, requests that you will without delay consult the other Officers command'g Regts. & cause as great a part of the militia immediately to march, as may be judged suffic't, to check the progress of the Enemy & protect the Inhabitants. The moment his Excellency receives further Information, the militia of Dutchess & Ulster will be ordered out if necessary. I am with great Respect Sir Your most Obdt. Serv't

R. Benson.

Colo. Woodhull.

[No. 1806.]

Colonel Malcom Reluctant to Use a Flag—Asks for Furloughs for His Men.

Fort Clinton Sep'r 27 1778.

D'r Sir, I had Mrs. McGlaghery & Mrs. Forman with me last night. I have sent them over to the good old general [Putnam] on the other side, who perhaps will get over some difficultys, that are too mighty for me. I will render them every Service in my power, but without the approbation of the Commander in Chief, cannot have any agency in forw'dg a flag at this crisis. If General Put. refuses them, I shall write their case to the General.

This goes by Mr. Lawrence, Ast. Ad. General, to the garrison, who will tell your Excellency, Haight's case which I apprehend is a bad one—he will also take Charge of a few Strong Torys, if your Commissioner see their way clear, or dare, put them to hard Labour. We can get a very considerable number of recruits if we coud take the Substitutes. As Comand'r in Chief, would your Excellency indulge us with furloughs, or exemptions or any thing that woud prevent those men who procure them from being calld out untill the pleasure of your Legislature can be obtained. Major Pawling will attend when they meet on the Subject. I most respectfully am D'r Sir Y'r mo. Ob. serv't

W. Malcom.

[To Gov. George Clinton.]

[No. 1807.]

THE DEATH OF COLONEL DUMON.

Colonel William Butler Furnishes Affidavits Producing Many Facts Bearing on the Case.

May it please your Excellency, Yours of the 6th & 8th Instant I received with the Affidavits concerning the death of Demon.

It gives me much pain to find the affair represented to your Excellency in so Black a light to the Injury of the party. By your letter you imagined the party was Commanded by Coll. Harper, But I must inform your Excellency it was Commanded by Major Posey an Officer whose Conduct both a Gentleman & Soldier has ever remained unquestionable.

In my Opinion Coll. Cantine shou'd have Acquainted me with his intentions of coming to Pachkatagten & given me the Character of Demon & any others who he knew to be Friends & were employd by him in giving intelligence as he must have had every reason to believe my Scouts wou'd be often in that Quarter & it is very Happy that Coll. Cantine's party had returned before mine arrived at that place, otherwise there might have been Blood Spilt through mistake as we did not expect any of our Friends were in that Quarter.

I have made the strictest inquiry with regard to Plundering the Inhabitants which was a matter I never suspected until I rece'd your Excellency's letter, & on Examination find my troops are in some degree Blamable. I have Ordered a Search and found some things which I have delivered to the persons you directed & I imagine the residue of the things mentioned in the list which those men produced, were taken by the party from Esopus, or by one Inhabitant from another which is customary.

The Cattle Brought in from that & other places was brought in by my Orders that they might not fall into the Enemy's Hands.

The Soldiers who Kill'd Demon Belong to a militia Company under the Command of Cap'n Harper who with his men some time ago left this place, But agreable to your Excellency's directions I will make them Prisoners & deliver them to whom your Excellency shall Order, at the same time it is my Humble Opinion the men did their duty as good Soldiers & think those who Kill'd Service & Smith equally Blamable.

I inclose your Excellency some depositions relative to the matter & Major Posey has also wrote you on that Subject.

A few days ago four of my men who were out as Spys returned with three prisoners which they had taken at Unandilla who give accounts that the Enemy at Unandilla are 300, 400 at Achquaga and a party at Chamong their Number they coud not ascertain, I came here a few days ago with Hopes of procuring Necessaries for a Body of Troops in advancing on the Enemy But found not the most trivial thing provided. I have consulted Genl. Stark & we have agreed to detach 150 Chosen troops to destroy Unandilla which I have great hopes of their doing with Success, & have

procured a few Bags & intended impressing some Horses for conveying provisions with them.   On their return I will inform your
Excellency of their success.

I suppose you have heard of the Enemy's have Burned the German Flats, my distance being so great from that place, I cannot
tell the particulars.   I am Yr. Excellency's Hble. Serv't

Wm. Butler.

Albany Sept'r 27th 1778.

His Excellency Gov. Clinton.

DEPOSITION OF CAPTAIN LONG.

Aug't 26th '78.   Being on a Scout with Major Posey at Paughkataughen where I saw two men, one of whom I examined (his
name I have since been Informed was Burrow) I ask'd him where
he was going, he said to Esopus.   I then ask'd him if he
had seen any of the Kings men, he answered not lately.   I ask'd
him if he assisted them, he said he did.   I ask'd him in what way
he assisted them, he Said in letting them have a Cow.   I ask'd
him if he did it willingly, he said he did.   I then ask'd him if that
was all he had assisted them in, he said he had no more.   I further ask'd him if he was willing to assist them again in any thing
he was able, he answered he was willing, at which time him and
the other was delivered to a Guard whilst the party went through
the Settlement of Paughkataughen; they both attempted to make
their escape; one was shot and the other escaped; while we were in
the above settlement some of the men plundered different houses
and all that could be found at that time among the men were
given up by order of Major Posey to the owners; but after our
arrival at camp found several other articles which were plundered
at the same time which have been Restored also.

Gab. Long Capt. in the Rifle Regt.

Personable appeard before me a Justice for the County of Albany in the state of New York Capt. Gab'l Long & made oath that the fore going was the Truth according to the Best of his Knowledge. Sept'r 16th 1778.

Jonas Vroman Justices for the County of Albany.

Deposition of Major Posey.

In Pursuance of Orders Delivered me by Lt. Coll. Butler, I set out from Schohary 24th August early in the morning, Reach'd Poughkataghten on the 26th of the same month. This place being pointed out to me to be chiefly inhabited by Tories & People who had Actually been in Arms against the Country, I made use of Precautions with regard to the Command of my party (after being made Acquainted with the People that Inhabited that Quarter) as being in an Enemies Country; when I arrived the first Houses my Scouts came to, they found to be evacuated upon which they came & inform'd me. I immediately sent out another small Scout in order to reconnoiter, while I Penetrated thro' the Settlement, in some short time I came to a House wherein I found some women. I made a Halt for some short time & inquired of the Women what had Become of the People; they told me there had been a Scout which had taken them and what Stock they had into the Settlement. I did not take up much time in Questioning the Women But march'd on & within the distance of Half a mile in a piece of Woods met two men, one driving a Waggon, the other Riding on Horse Back & leading another Horse with a Gun Slung to his Back. I Halted my Party & upon examination found the man with the Waggon to be one Demon. I ask'd him where he was driving his Waggon; he said he was moving his Goods into the Settlement, that a Scout had been from Esopus which had taken all the Stock & chief of the Inhabitants. I ask'd him if there had been any Scouting parties from Unandilla lately or whether Butler & Brandt frequently sent Scouting Parties into this Settlement; he said they had sent Scouting Parties at different times; I ask'd him (the said Demon) whether he had assisted the Enemy, he answered he had Assisted his King in whatever he was able to do; he had given them Beef, Cattle & such Assistance as he cou'd from time to time. After I had ask'd him such Questions as I thought proper, I ordered Capt'n Harper of the militia to set three of his men as a Guard over Demon & the man who was with him, who I understand since is one Burrow, Burrow was examined at the same time by Capt'n Long of the Rifle Corps & upon examination was found to have Assisted the Enemy in cattle. He (the said Burrow) had a Gun with him which some of the party took from him. The Guard took them (the said Demon, & Burrow) into their custody & was ordered to take particular care of them. I Pursued with all possible expedition down the Delaware, thinking as those men had demonstrated themselves Enemies to the country by the confession they had made, that they only intended imposing on me with regard to moving into Esopus that perhaps it might be a party of the Enemy which had been there. When I got near the lower end of the Settlement (which was about 6 miles) I was told the Guard which had the Prisoners in charge had come up without them; upon which I Ordered them to be Brought to me & ask'd them where the Prisoners were; they told me they (the Guard) had taken the Horses out of Waggon, mounted the two Prisoners on a Horse & each of them (the Guard) riding on the other Horses follow'd me; that after riding some distance the two Prisoners rode off to try to make their escape, upon which they (the Guard) immediately pursued & finding they (the Prisoners) were likely to get off thro' the Woods one of the Guard Fired upon them & miss'd; they (the Prisoners) then dismounted one of them making his escape thro' the Woods the other kept the road. After pursuing near a mile the one who continued the road was fired upon & Shot, who proved to be Demon; they (the Guard) left him in a House & made their way as Quiet as possible to the Party.

After my excurions down the Delaware in which I Gathered what Stock I possibly cou'd, which amounted to few, being chiefly drove off by the other party, I returned to the House that I had conversed with the Women before mentioned in which I found Demon the person who was Shot by the Guard, I ask'd him his reason for Running from the Guard; his excuse was that he thought we were some of Brandt's or Butler's men. I asked him how he cou'd think so when I, upon meeting him, ask'd him If any of Butler's or Brandt's parties had been in this Neighbourhood lately, upon which you reply'd there had & that you had Assisted Brandt & Butler in Beef. I ask'd him If he cou'd deny what he had said to me, upon meeting me first, he said no that he acknowledged he said what I asserted, & said he really had assisted the King. After which I left him & march'd on towards Schohary.

Thomas Posey, Capt. Commdt. Rifle Regi't.

Several Things the Soldiers might have taken in the settlement without my Knowledge, But I made them Give up & return several things which I discoverd them to take,

Personable appeard before me a Justice for the County Albany in the State of New York, Thomas Posey & declared the Purport of the Foregoing to Be Facts according to the Best of his Knowledge.

Given under my Hand this 16th Sept'r in the yeare of our Lord one thousand seven Hundred & seventy Eight.

Jonas Vroman, Justice.

DEPOSITION OF LIEUT. ALEX'R RAMSAY OF THE RIFLES.

Beeing on Command by order of Lieutenant Colonel William Butler & under the immeadiate Command of Major Posey August 26th 1778:

We went into Paughtaughen, stoped at a house belonging to Simon Van Wagonner which was the Second house we came to in the Setelment; I heard Captain Harper ask a women, which I Understood was the landlady of said house & the said Captain Harper asked her If she was as Great a Torry as she formerly was. She answered she was not a Torry and If he did not believe her he might Enquire of Hermanus Demung who was a Torry. We then pursued our Rout about half a mile, where we met said Demung with his waggon & Horses, and another man Rideing one horse and leading another loaded with goods; Said Demung beeing stoped by the party, Captain Harper Came forward to the waggon and asked said Hermanus Demung his name who answered that his name was Demung; the said Capt. Harper asked him If he was as good a man for the king as he used to be; he answered yes; what have you Don for the king or his party in this Countery and how many Cattle did you give Brant's party; he answered I gave four head of Cattle & suplyed them with all the provision that lay in my Power; Harper asked him again Will you Suply them with any more; he answered he would; but the Rebils had Carried them all to Esopus, meaning his Chattels & provision, as I Understood him, with my Famely. Harper then asked the man that was with Demung how many Cattle he had given to Brant; he said one; I Believe Replyed Harper that you are a Churlish Fellow; the answ'r I Did not heare, But Harper Replyed that he was a poore man & had but one Cow left.

On our Return out of said settelment Major Posey stoped his Command & ordered the soldiers to be serched, & all the Cloathing or other necessarys belonging to the Inhabitance to be Returned; allso myself Colected the Goods that the musqetree had to be Collected when we Came to Camp & Returned which was don and left at Maj'r Churches marquee.

Alex'r Ramsay, Lt. 4th P. R.

Sworn before me this 16th day of Sept. 1778.

Jonas Vroman Justices in the County of Albany

in the Staet of New York.

DEPOSITION OF CAPT. ALEXANDER HARPER.

Being on a Scout to Paughcutaughen with a Party under Command of Major Posey on Wednesday Aug't the 26th 1778:

We Stoped at a House belonging to Simon Van Waggoner which was the Second. I asked the Woman of the House if She was as Great a Tory as She Us'd to be, She Answer'd she was not a Tory, and if I Did not believe her, I might Enquire of Hermanus Demong who was a Tory. We then Proceeded about half a Mile, when we met said Demong with his Waggon and horses, and another Man with Two Horses; (they being Stopp'd by the front of the Party) I came up and Ask'd him his Name, he Replyed Demong? Are you as Good a Man for the King as you Used to be? Yes. What Did you ever do for the King, and how many Cattle Did you give to Brant's Party? I gave four Cattle and Supply'd them with all the Provision that lay in my Power. Will you Supply them with any more? I would but the Rebels have Carried them all to Esopus with my Family. I think you Look like a Rebel and I believe you are one—he Reply'd no by God I am no Rebel.

I then asked the Man that was with him how Many Cattle he had given to Brant, he said One, I believe you are a Churlish fellow for not giving more; he Reply'd it was all he had excepting one Milks Cow.

And said Deponent, Capt'n Harper, further saith, that he heard Major Posey, Repeatedly forbid the Party of Plundering the Women of any thing belong to their apparel for Necessaries Whatever, Except the Horses, and Caused a Search to be made that if any thing had been taken, It might be given back if found among the Party.

Alexander Harper.

Personable appeard before me a Justice for the County of Albany & State of New York Capt. Alexander Harper & made Oath that the fore going is the Truth to the Best of His Knowledge. 16th Sept'r 1778.

Jonas Vroman, Justices for the County of Albany.

[No. 1808.]

Officers of the Company of Exempts of Rumbout Patent.

At a Meeting of the Associated Exempts in the district assigned to Abraham Schenck by Coll: Jas. Swartwout, on Monday the 28th of Sept'r 1778, at John McBride's Tavern in Rumbouts precinct, the following Gentlemen where Recommended by a Plurality of voices as proper persons to be Field Officers of the Regiment of Voluntary Associated Exempts in Dutchess County Viz: Jacobus Swartwout, Esqr., Colonel; Zepheniah Platt, Esqr., Lieutenant Colonel; Israel Thompson, Major.

As also the following Gentlemen where Recommended for Officers of Said District, Viz: Abraham Schenck, Captain; William Boerum, Esq., 1st Lieutenant; Daniel Rapelje, 2nd Lieutenant.

[No. 1809.]

The Parole of Alexander White, James Dole and Henry Cuyler, as Made by the Commissioners of Conspiracies.

Albany 28th Sept. 1778.

Sir, Inclosed your Excellency will find Copy of a Parole entered into by Messrs. Henry Cuyler, James Dole and Alexander White at the Time they were liberated from Confinement and hope the same will meet with your Excellencies approbation.

Captain Willet who has the Command of the vessel they are going with, is a Gentlemen whose attachment to the Cause cannot be doubted, and we have directed him to wait upon your Excellency for Directions—and you may be assured, that all the Dispatch necessary has been used to get them off sooner. We are with the greatest Respect Your Excellencies Most Obed't Servants: John M. Beeckman, Isaac D. Fonda, Mat. Visscher.

His Excellency, Gov'r Clinton.

We Henry Cuyler and James Dole and Alexander White do severally promise and engage on the word and Faith of a Gentleman that we shall severally proceed from hence to Poughkeepsie, to be from there sent in to New York agreeable to Exchange whenever the Commissioners for detecting Conspiracies &ca. shall so direct and that we shall and will not hold (during our Stay in the

City of Albany and until our Arrival at Poughkeepsie) any Correspondence upon political Matters with any Person or Persons whatsoever and that we severally will not say or do any thing by which
any Hurt or Detriment may come to the Measures pursued by the
United States of America or either of them and that we shall
severally upon our arrival at Poughkeepsie follow the Directions
of his Excellency Governor Clinton.   Given under our Hands at
Albany this 19th Day of September 1778.

           Alexander White, James Dole, Henry Cuyler.

A true Copy from the Original.

                    Leon: Gansevoort, Jun'r, secy.

[No. 1810.]

BRANT ON THE WAR PATH.

A Report that His Objective Point is Rochester, Ulster County.

               Marbletown 28th Sept'r 1778.

Sir, Inclosed I Send you an Affidavit of Robert McGinnis who
Came in at Great Shandeken the 25th Instant with Negro man,
whose master Lives at New York; the Negro man I have Sent to
Johannis Sleght one of the Commissioners of Sequestration.

By Thos. Kyte from Pienpack I have been Informed that one
Briant Cain who formerly Lived at Coschecton Came in at Pienpack the 22d Instant and was to Come this way but is not yet
arived.   This Cain left Aquago the 14th Instant, and Says that
Brant was gone to the German Flats with four hundred & fifty
men, And McGinnes who told me, That they Said their Party
was four hundred But thinks there was no more at Unidela than
Two hundred, as is mentioned in the Affidavit.   They both agree
that on their Return they would then make a Push Some where on
this Quarter.

8

I think it would be advisable to have men out as Spys as far back as Delaware, So that I might have timely notice of their Comeing, But the men I have Under my Command are Unacquainted with these woods and Cannot Answer for that Purpose. I would be glad if your Excelency Should think it Proper To have Liberty to Engage one or Two Persons for that purpose on whose fidelity I may Rely.

As for the Number of Militia Adequate to Carry into Execution an Expedition against Anaquago is to me Very Uncertain. I think it would be advisable to go there with Six or Seven hundred men were they Chosen men, But as my Regt. now Stands, it is not in my Power to undertake an Expedition of that nature as the Reliefs are a going and Comeing Every week in the month, I have Consulted with Judge Pawling But he thinks it will not answer with militia as they are Called out in Classes, as many of them are men you Cannot Depend on, Unless the number be Greater then what I mentioned, McGinnes & Kain Both agree that Butler is gone to Niagara. Kain Says that Brant's Party Consists of Six or Seven hundred Chosen men. I Remain with Due Esteem Your Excelency's Most Obedient Friend & Serv't

John Cantine.

His Excellency George Clinton Esqr.

Poughkeepsie Sept. 29th 1778.

Sir, I have rec'd your favor of yesterday. I have no particular authority to direct the employ'g & keeping out of Spies. But as I think the measure adviseable & necessary, I have not the least doubt that the Expences attending it will be allowed in your acct. I should be glad to know the Distance from Rochester to Coolitie & to Oghquago, the nature of the Road, &c. &c. & how many cont'l Troops, joined with your militia, would be a Compentent force to carry an Expedition thither with a prospect of Success. As it appears from McGinnis acct. that the Enemy have it in view to visit the frontiers of Rochester, I must recommend it to you to be extremely vigilant in keeping out the militia & using every means in your Power to prevent a surprise.   I am &c.

                                                        Geo. Clinton.
Colo. Cantine.

———

Robert McGinnis, of Sixty Nine Years of age, being duly sworn saith that he Lived at the Unindilly; that on Saturday, being the 19th Instant, he was taken Prisoner, with his Two sons, one Tygart & Three other men by a number of Onida Indians; the Deponant saith, that said Tygart had been taken Prisoner some time before, by Brant's Party, on the Mohawck River, & brought to the Deponant's house, & there Left.   After the Deponant had been the Prisoner some short time he was set at Liberty on account of his Great age, his sons with Tygart & the other three, were Carryed of by said Indians; the Next day being Sunday, Capt. Joseph Brant with his party Came to the Settlement his party Consisting, the Deponant thinks, of about Two hundred men, Indians and Torys; the Deponant says, they Came from Germain Flatts, & were on thier way Down to onoughquawga; the Deponant Further saith, that he was stript of every thing he had, meaning all his Goods, Excepting what he had previously Concaled; the Deponant Further adds, that Brant had a very Large Number of Cattle with him; he Likewise understood by some of the party, that they intend to Make their Next Stroke Some where back of Esopus, but he the Deponant Conjectures, From what he could learn, that it was some part of Rochester they Intended, & further Saith Not.

Robert McGinnis.

Marbletown Sept'r 27th 1778.

Sworn before me Jacob DeLametter.

[No. 1811.]

Richard Varick Asks Governor Clinton to Intercede for His Father,
a Prisoner in New York City.

Fredericksburg Sept. 28 1778.

Sir, Already five weeks have elapsed since Your Excellency was kind enough, at my request, to give Mr. Peter Van Schaack Leave, to procure my father's Enlargement from a distressing Captivity, in Exchange for himself; which I believe he has not done as Yet, & fear (thro want of Influence in his Family Connections of late) he will not be able to effect; Especially as I have Cause to think That my father is held up as a very obnoxious Character & detain'd at the Instance of some of his Neighbours, probably of near Connection to him, who are, or have affected to shew themselves, Friends & Abettors to the Enemies of their Country.

I am just inform'd by Mr. Jeremiah Van Rensselaer, that a Mr. Cummins, a Scotch Gentleman of Katts Kill, now confin'd at Albany & Subject to an Exchange is from his Interest & Connections in Engl'd, a man of pretty considerable Influence with the Enemy & that it is very likely he will be able to effect an Exchange for my father.

It gives me Pain to become so troublesome to Your Excellency, but filial Duty to an affectionate, Indulgent Parent, who has suffered the most cavalier Treatment from an imbitter'd Enemy; whom, when nearly expir'g of a very dangerous Dissentery (on his

Giving Bail) they have vouchsaf'd a temporary Enlargement from Provoost & confind to a House, where still labouring under his Indisposition, unless soon relieved, he will in all Probability end his Days, constrains me to exert my little Efforts for his release & makes me exceedingly anxious for his speedy Exchange.

If Mr. Cummins is not already Exchanged, I shall esteem it the greatest favor, if Your Excellency will permit him to be exchang'd for my Father who, if he recovers from his Illness, has no other Prospect, than that of an immediate return to a loathsome Provoo. Goal, or the disagreeable Alternative of continuing under Obligations to a relation, a worthless man, who took advantage of his extream Illness & attempts to make a merit of the act of becoming his Bail.

I have the Honor to be Sir, with every Respectful Sentiment Your Excellency's Most Obed't serv't

Rich'd Varick.

His Excelleny, Gov'r Clinton.

[No. 1812.]

TRYON COUNTY ASKS FOR ASSISTANCE.

Small Reliance to be Placed Upon the Militia—The Enemy Preparing for Another Raid.

Canijohary Tryon County Sept. 28th 1778.

Sir, We beg leave to represent to your Excellency the most deplorable Situation of this County. The Enemy have from Time to Time desolated and destroyed the Settlements of Springfield; Andrews Town and the German Flatts, by which at least one hundred and fifty Families are reduced to Misery and Distress. People who before were in flourishing Circumstances are thus by our wanton Act brought to Poverty.

Notwithstanding we have repeatedly wrote our Situation down and asked Relief, we have obtained none except Colo. Alden's Regiment, which is stationed at Cherry Valley where they remain in Garrison. Woeful Experience teaches us, that the Troops in Cherry Valley are by no means a Defence for any other Part of the Country. We should long e'er now have desisted from requesting any farther Support were we not convinced that unless we obtain Relief, the Enemy are strong enough and we fear will in short make another Attempt to lay waste this Country.

Strange as it may appear to your Excellency, it is no less true, that our Militia by Desertion to the Enemy and by Enlistments into our Service, are reduced to less than seven hundred Men. Indeed if these 700 would do their Duty and act like Men, we might perhaps give the Enemy a Check, so as to give Time to the Militia from below to come up, but, Sir, they are actuated by such an ungovernable Spirit that it is out of the Power of any Officer in this County to command them with any Credit to himself— for notwithstan'g the utmost Exertion the Officers have nothing but Blame in Return.

From the Information we are able to collect from Prisoners and otherwise, we learn that the Enemy, when at the German Flatts were 500 or upwards strong commanded by a Capt. Caldwell. That they intended soon to make another Incursion, and that a Reinforcement of 5 or 600 were on its March from the western Nations of Indians to join the Enemy, Indians being frequently seen and our People fired upon, seems in our opinion to indicate a speedy Return of the Enemy.

We have, therefore, now to request of your Excellency, to order up a sufficient Force, in order to make a vigorous Impression on

the Enemy's Quarters, and to drive those murdering Villains out
of our Country, Your Excellency may be assured that we shall
exert every Nerve to collect what Men we possibly can.

We send the Bearers, Colo. Fisher and Peter S. Deygert, Esq.
to give your Excellency what farther Information you may desire
to know, and to join us in supplicating your Excellency to afford
us immediate Succour.   We have the Honor to be Sir Your Excellency's most Obedient and very Hble. servants

Jacob Klock, Saml. Campbell, Pieter Weizger, Saml. Clyde, Christopher W. Fox, John Hess, Jacob Defendorff, Christ Stofel Fox.
Gov'r Clinton.

[No. 1813.]

*The Question of Clothing for the Troops and Officers and Returns
for the Five Regiments Furnished.*

Wall Kill Sept. 28th 1778.

May it please Your Excellency, as the Hono'bl House of Assembly will meet in a few days I thought it my duty to give your
Excell'y an accout of what cloathing is still deficient to complete
our 5 Regiments, particulars of which may be seen by the Inclosed Return.   If the House see no prospect to draw the deficiencies out of the Continental cloathing Store, I should be glad
to have orders in time from them to purchase, & I beg, If your
Excell'y should think proper to Recomend this matter to the
House, that your Excellency would put them in mind not to stint
me to a Certain sum as was the case the last time, but give me
orders what quantity of Each Arti'e I must purchace & give me
a Credit on the Treasury to draw for such sums as I shall from
time to time want to complete any orders I may receive,   If it is
not done in this way the business will be only half done.

I have also to acquaint your Excellency that our officers complain much that no cloathing is provided for them, in the same manner the other states provide for their officers. I remain with due Respect, Your Excell'y most Obed't Serv't

Peter T. Curtenius.

To His Excellency, George Clinton, Esqr.

	Shirts	Coats	Vests	Breeches	Stockings	Shoes	Hatts	Blankets	Hunt'g Shirts	Overhauls
Drawn for Genl. Clinton's Brig'd	2059	1006	1006	1006	2588	2588	1006	1006	2588	2452
Ditto in fav'r of Colo. Gansewort	279	119	390	424	518	269	376	298		
	2338	1125	1396	1430	3106	2857	1382	1304	2588	2452
Purchac'd by P. T. C. & Rec'd from Supervisors	464	1014	1014	1074	22	18				
Deficient	1874	111	382	1356	3084	2839	1382	1304	2588	2452

N. B. The officers who came to the Store for cloathing Infor'd me that the above demand was for the deficiencies of last year, that on the 21th Novem'r next the men were entitled to one suit pr. man more.

A True return Sept. 28, 1778.

Peter T. Curtenius Commiss'y of cloath'g to the State of N. Yorke.

What Mr. Henry has in store I cant say but believe it is but trifeling.

[No. 1814.]

Petition for Pardon of Bartholomew Hess.

To the Honorable the Judges and Justices of a Coart of Oyer and Termener and general goal Delivery to be held at the City Hall of the city of Albany on the 29th Day of September 1778.

A Humble Petietion

That whereas Bartholomew Hass Being undoutly gilty of Sunderys felonys in Robbing and Being Lead there to by the Instagation of the Divel Contrary to the will or knowledge of his parants But always heretofore having had an unblammished Carracter until verry Latly as also his Parants Being poor but Perfactly Honnest and well grounded in prinsepals of Religion.

We your Petietioners therefore Humbley Pray that the Said Bartholomew Hass now a prisoner may be permitted and allowed to be a States or Congress Evedence.

[Here follows the names of 182 persons.]

[Note on back of No. 1814.]

There was also a Counter Petition to this signed by some persons assigning Reasons ag't this, charging Hess with want of principles and stealing &ca. privately—but it is at present mislaid or at the Board of Commissioners & it was signed by a few persons.

[No. 1815.]

Cornelius Taylor Offers to Turn States Evidence.

To the Honorable John Jay Esquire Chief Justice, and Robert Yates & John Sloss Hobart Esquires Puisne Judges and their Associates Justices of the Court of Oyer & Terminer and General Goal Delivery held in & for the City & County of Albany.

The Petition of Cornelius Taylor Most humbly Sheweth That your Petitioner is now in close Confinement in this Goal, for haveing bcen guilty of some misdemeanors which may cause his Life to be brought in Danger for the preservation of which; he is willing to become a States Evidence, and Devulge many matters that may be of more Service to the State & the good People thereof than the takeing his Life by an Ignomenious Death, can be.

Your Petitioner therefore humbly Prays; that he may be admitted to Serve his Injured Country in that Particular, your Honours granting him that Previledge will cause your Petitioner (as in duty bound) Ever to Pray &c.

                                                        Cornelius Taylor.
Albany Goal September 29th 1778.

[No. 1816.]

General Ten Broeck Orders One Fourth of the Men of Certain Regiments to Tryon County.

                                        Albany 29th Septem'r 1778.

Sir, I did my self the Honor to write your Excellency the 24th Instant; yesterday I Received Colonel Benson's letter of the 25th Instant. I shall Continue to Exert my self to the Utmost in Rousing the militia under my Command to a sense of their duty. Being Informed that such of the militia of Collonel Rensselaer's & Livingston's Regiment as were at Fort Arnold are Dismissed, I have this day Ordered one full fourth part of said Regiments Immediately to march to the Mohawk River to the Relief of the Suffering Inhabitants on that Frontier. I have the honor to be with great Respect Your Excellency's Most Obedient Humble Servant

                                        Ab'm Ten Broeck.
His Excellency George Clinton Esqr.

[No. 1817.]

COLONEL MOSES PHILLIPS COMPLAINS

And Meets with a Reproof from Governor Clinton—Colonel Cantine Sustained.

May it Pleas youre Excelency. I take the liberty to offer you the Reasons why a Part of Oure Rigiment are defisiant in Send-

ing out there Clases; the greater part of four Companys lif
Oposite Bashes land, where there is no guard kept for 15 miles
& which was, heretofore, the Indeans Usual way Into the Country. Repeated application has been made to Coll. Cantine for a
Guard to be Stationed in that Quarter, which he Evades by Saying he has no Authority to Alter the present Station of the
Guards, which with Other things has So Allarmed the Inhabetants, that for Some time they have kept a Special Guard Exclusive of their Clases & lately many Refuse to turn out in theire
Clases & leave there familys Exsposed to go and guard Others,
Unless there is a guard allowed in their frontier; Many have
moved into the Interior part Of the Country & I take the liberty
of giving it as my Opinion that they will be followed by most of
the Inhabetents of three Companys, the Consiquense of which is
Obveous. I hope, therefore, your Excelency will take the matter
into Consideration & grant Such Relief as you Shall think Best.
I am youre Ecelency's most obed't Hum'l Serv'nt

Moses Phillips.

Walkill Sep'r 29 1778.

To his Excellency George Clinton Esqr.

Poughkeepsie 30th Sep'r 1778.

Sir, I have received your Letter of yesterday. The Reasons
assigned for not furnishing your Quota of Men are by no means
sattisfactory, & such as I coud not have expected from an Officer
of whom I have always entertained so good an Oppinion. The
Field Officers of Ulster & Orange Counties were summoned to
meet at the Paltz to determine on the Number of Men necessary
for the Defence of the Frontiers, and on the Station most proper
to be occupied for this Purpose; many of them attended accordingly & the Advise was taken & have been strictly pursued. You

did not attend, as you ought to have done, & now because the Guards are not stationed agreeable to your Oppinion & that of some your Men, they refuse or at best neglect to obey orders & threaten to leave the Country exposed unless they are gratified. I wish to give the Frontier Inhabitants the most equal & perfect protecton. Such is my Orders to Colo. Cantine & he has (with the advice of the other Field Officers on the Frontier) authority specially given to him, to change the Stations assigned him by my ordes from Time to Time so as best to answer the Purpose. Reasoning upon the Subject will convince you, the General safety of the Frontier Inhabitants must depend on the guards being stationed some Distance in the Rear of the Settlements and in such Force as to deter the Enemy from passing in between them, which cannot be the Case if the men ordered for this Service are thus withheld by each Neighbourhood confining their Views to the guarding their own immediate Settlement. I have only to add that your Regiment as well several others have not furnished their Quota of men exclusive of the Frontier Companies. If the whole number ordered out were actually in Service I have not the least Doubt that Colo. Cantine woud place a guard at the Place you mention as the want of Men only prevents it. I am Sir Your most Humble Serv't

[G. C.]

[To Moses Phillips.]

[No. 1818.]

THE GOVERNOR COMMENDS COLONEL DRAKE

And Honors His Requisition for 9,000 Cartridges for His Regiment.

Peeks Kill Sept. 28th 1778.

Deir Sir, Since The Removing of our troops from the County, the Enemy tak from Every person without any Exception, Leving

nither Clothing, provisions or forage.   Our Infentery is Retreaed
up to Capt. Lyons & the Church in North Castel; the County lying
open; no gaurds from our Infentery to the River; the Horses air
Carred of from the Inhabtence Every Night; in order to put a Stop
I Have ordred out, Agreeable to the milia act, 3 first Classes of my
Regiment for two days, with thair provision; Shall order them
Releved with the next 3 Classes in Rotation Every 2 days if thay
Shold be needed; in order to guard from Croten Brid to the ferry
and Indever to driv those Robers that have Deserted from New
York,* who air Concealed By the Inhabitants, with arms Ready
for to Rob and Steal the Horses; if not Stoped will Sun Cary of
all the fat Catel in this County and Duches; they air Harboured
by Persons Living from Pines Bridg to the mouth at Croten fery,
which for the Safty of the people, thair Houses ought to Be Destroyed; your Direction will Be very Nesery, the Regiment having No Powder nor Ball.   I have Sent my Quart. master for your
order to State Store for Nine Thusand Cartridges; if thair Shuld
be No Cartridges to get powder & Ball.   I Remain your very
obliden Sarvent

                                             Samll. Drake.
To His Excelency Gorge Clinton.

---

*Early this morning, [September 16] Lieutenant-Colonel Simcoe, with the Queen's
Rangers, Lieutenant-Colonel Emmerick, with the chasseurs, and a detachment of the
second battalion of General De Lancey's brigade, Lieutenant-Colonel Tarleton, with
the dragoons of the legion, and one troop of Colonel Emmerick's, and the Hessian
Jagers, moved from their respective encampments near King's Bridge. Lieutenant-
Colonels Simcoe and Emmerick marched undiscovered between two rebel pickets, and
got one mile and a half in the rear of a body of two hundred and thirty select Virginia riflemen, strongly posted in front on Babcock's Heights, under the command
of Colonel Gist. Lieutenant-Colonel Tarleton marched to Colonel Philip's farm. About
six in the morning, Lieutenant-Colonel Emmerick, with the detachment of De Lancey's,
attacked the rebels, and though discovered when going to attack, killed three on the
spot, wounded several, and took thirty-five prisoners, among which are three officers.
The rebels were so briskly charged, that many of them forgot their arms, &c., and
fled with the utmost precipitation; their colonel in particular, scampering off without
his breeches or boots, and 'tis thought he was wounded in his flight. At the same
time, Lieutenant-Colonel Tarleton, with the dragoons, charged a body of rebels posted
on Valentine's Hill, but as the enemy were near a very thick wood, they took
shelter where the horse could not possibly act, which prevented their sustaining any
other loss than the capture of a few of their number. The only loss sustained by his
Majesty's troops in both attacks, was one horse of Emmerick's killed.—Gaine's Mercury
September 21, 1778.

Poukeepsie, 30th Sep'r 1778.

Sir, I have received your Letter of the 28th Instant. I approve of your conduct in calling into actual Service such Part of your Regiment as may be necessary for the Protection of the Inhabitants & their Effects. I presume Genl. Morris will attend to his Duty in the County at the Critical Conjucture & make the best Use of his Brigade. It is an unpardonable Neglect, not to have seen that your Militia were properly provided with Ammunition agreeable to the Militia Law before this; And it gives me great Pain to find that even now your Quarter Master is without an Ammunition Return for your Regt. & your Order on the Commissioner of Military Stores for the same, as without this, the ammunition cannot be issued. I have, therefore, directed your Quarter Master to return without Delay for the necessary Return & with your order thereon which I will back with my Warrant the Moment I receive it. I am &c

[G. C.]

[To Col. Drake.]

[No. 1819.]

Exempts of Hanover, Ulster County.

A Majority of Capt. William Simrall's associated Company of Exempts (of Coll. Haasbrouck's Regiment) in Hanover Precinct Ulster County beg leave to Recommend to the honorable the Council of Appointment the following promotions to take place in the said Company vizt:

Isaac Rosa, 1st Lieut. vice John Graham deceased; James Huey, 2d Lieut. vice Isaac Rosa promoted; John Shaver, Ensign vice James Huey promoted; Hanover Precinct 30th Sept'r 1778.

William Simrall, Capt., Isaac Rosa, William Stephens, Yonatan Decker, John Comfort, Hendrekus Terwillegen, James Douglass,

Jacob his X mark Teers, Samuel Barkley, John Shaffer, Thomas Mott, John Barkley, William Simrell, James McCurdy, Daniel his X mark Anderson, James Gillespy, James Huey, Hugh his X mark Dougherty, Thomas Turner, Crist his X mark Miller, John Luts, Peter Pencel, Jost Henrich Theis, ——— ———, Stephen his X mark Carney, Henrey his X mark Crance, John Yeamons, ——— ———, Jacob Selts, James Mchugh, Joshua his X mark Smedes.

[No. 1820.]

Lieutenant Pendleton Renews His Application for Cash.

To His Exelency George Clinton Esqr. Governor of the State of New York &c.

Sir, I took the liberty on the 16th Instant of addressing your Exelency on the subject of my want and the manner in which it might be relieved. I beg leave to asure your Exelency that the proposition wants nothing but your approbation and directions to make it successful. If your Exelency will please to send me an answer by Mrs. McCloughry or Mrs. Furman who are shortly expected here it will much oblige your humble servant. I am Confident your Exelency would pardon my freedom if acquainted with the Circumstances which would be imprudential in me to perticularise at this time. I am with due respect Your Exelency's most obediant and very humble servant

Solomon Pendleton.

New Utrecht Long Island Sept'm 30th 1778.

P. S. I Expect your Exelency will shortly see the bearer Mrs. Godwin who will give an account of the helth and sittuation of our Officers Prisoners here.

[No. 1821.]

Three Exchanged Tories Protest Against Restrictions Imposed Upon Them.

Albany 25 August 1778.

Gentlemen, Your having refused to take the oath tendered you by us, renders it our indispensible duty to inform you, that we have fixed upon Wednesday the ninth day of September next for your removal—At which time you will be prepared with fourteen days Provisions & such of your respective Families as may chuse to accompany you (Persons capable of bearing arms excepted.) You are also permited to take with you all your Cloathing & Household furniture—and as the Charges of Transportation must be borne by yourselves, you can hire a Vessel at Kinderhook & set off from there. We shall send a person from here to attend you down. You will also observe that Security is to be given for the return of the sloop which is to convey you to the Enemies Lines. You will be pleased to acquaint us by the bearer whether you can get a sloop at Kinderhook or whether one must be sent from here. we are Your Humb. Servants

Mat. Visscher, John M: Beekman, Jer'h V Renselaer, Commissioners.

To Messrs. Henry Van Schaack David Van Schaack Mathew Goes Jun'r &c.

Permission is hereby granted to Henry Van Schaack, David Van Schaack & Mathew Goes Jur. prisoners to the State of New York, to pass to the British Lines in exchange for Messrs. Smith, Philips & Wheeler who are come out, & to take with them their wearing apparel. They are to take such Rout as shall be assigned them by any commanding officer upon the Lines or elsewhere. Given under my hand the 23d of Decem'r 1780.

Philip Pell Jun'r Com: Prisoners State of New York.

Whom it may concern.

If the commissioners had a right to grant us the indulgences, within mentioned, we know of no power Mr. Pell has to deprive us of having the benefit of those Effects. If it was a matter of favor, others in the same predicament, have been indulged to a greater degree and we flatter ourselves your Excellency will not discriminate us. It would seem hard to curtail us in any indulgence when it is considered how much more we have suffered than others and that through us three subjects, faithful to this State, have been liberated.

Upon the whole, we cannot but flatter ourselves but that your Excellency will be pleased to grant us leave to carry with us, for the present, not only our wearing apparel, but our Bedding, and other necessaries, so as to Load two Sleas or Waggons as the Season may be and suffer the remainder of our furniture &c. to go down with our families in the Spring by water.

All which, however, is submitted to your Excellency's consideration by Your Excellency's most Obedient humble Servants

H. V. Schaack, Mathew Goes, Jur., David V. Schaack.

[No. 1822.]

Colonel Udny Hay Complains Against Persons Who Fail to Qualify as Justices of the Peace.

Fish Kill 1st Oct. 1778.

Sir, I will not attempt to apologize for the frequent occasions I am oblidged to make of troubling you, as it arises from a real desire to serve the people of this State in particular, as well as the public in general, I am certain no excuse will be demanded by you.

As there are many Gentlemen in this State who have been nominated for justices of the Peace, but have not yett qualified, which neglect is a hurt to the Country in general, should be much obligded to you for a return of those Gentlemen's names, and particular places of abode, that I might have it in my power to order their waggons out in a particular manner, through whose fault it is that we are obligded to call in a military force to execute a law, which ought and very easily might be executed by civil authority only. I have the honour to be w'h much esteem, Sir, Your most obed. humble Se't,

Udny Hay.

[To Gov. George Clinton.]

[No. 1823.]

Certificate of Refusal by Sundry Tories of the Oath of Allegiance.

State of New York Ss.

To his Excellency George Clinton Esquire Governor of the State of New York, General and Commander in chief of all the militia, and admiral of the navy of the same.

In pursuance of an act of the Legislature of this State Entitled " an act more effectually to prevent the mischiefs arising from the Influence and example of persons of equivocal and suspected Characters in this State " we do hereby notify your Excellency that Samuel Washburn, Samuel Dickinson and Samuel Peters all of Fredricksburgh precinct in Dutchess County, having severally appeared before us and being respectively by us tendered the oath in the said act Contained, did respectively refuse to take the same, and that unless your Excellency Shall think proper to detain them or either of them for the purpose of exchanging them for any of the subjects of this State, in the power of the Enemy, we shall cause them respectively to be removed to some place within the Enemy's Lines.

Peter Cantine, Jur. Robt. Harpur, Egb't Benson, Commissioners.
Poughkeepsie October 1st 1778.

[No. 1824.]

On the Advice of Three Members of the Legislature the Governor Assents to Sending 250 Barrels of Flour to Boston.

To his Excellency Governor Clinton of the State of New York.

Council Chamber September 5th 1778.

The Council of the State of Massachusetts Bay would represent to your Honor that the Inhabitants of this State are in great

9

want of Flour for their own Consumption & would, therefore, recommend Thomas Russel a respectable Inhabitant of this State for your Honor's Permission, by his agent Peter R. Livingston, Esqr., to purchase & bring to the Market here two hundred and fifty Barrels of Flour for the use of the Inhabitants.

True Copy.   attest: John Avery D'y Secry.

State of New York Ss:

The within named Peter R. Livingston in Behalf of Thomas Russell, Esqr. having applied to us in order to obtain Permission to export two hundred and fifty Barrels of Flour out of this State for the use as above recommended by the Council of the Massachusetts Bay, we do hereby advise his Excellency the Governor to permit the said Quantity of Flour to be exported out of this State for the use aforesaid.

October 2d 1778.

Walter Livingston, Leonard Gansevoort, John Tayler,
                                          Members of Assembly.

I have no Objection to the Exportation of two hundred & fifty Barrels of Flour out of this State agreable to the above advice on the use therein specified.

[G. C.]

[No. 1825.]

FRIENDLY ONEIDAS AND TUSCARORAS.

They Bring Nine Captives to Fort Schuyler and Declare their Loyalty to the American Cause.

Albany October 2th 1778.

Sir, I Inclose you a Speech of the Oneida and Tuscorora Indians delivered to Major Cochran at Fort Schuyler.

Sir, I am in Great distress for the article of Salt; as that Can best be purchas'd for flower to the Eastward I Beg your Excellency will grant me a pass to Boston or to any of the Easteren Stats for Eight Barrels of flower, which will make a Cart Load and your Excellency will Oblige your most Hum'e Serv't

                                        Volckert P. Douw.
To his Excellency Governor Clinton.

Fort Schuyler Sept. 28 1778.

Gentlemen, On Fryday last arrived here the sachems & Warriors of the Oneida & Tuscarora Nations, their number upwards of One hundrd. After the usual formalities, they Delivered themselves nearly as follows (Being badly off for an Interpreter Mr. Dean having been absent a long time).

Brothers, we have now Taken The hatchet and burnt Unendello & a place called the Butter Nuts; we have Brought five Prisoners from Each of the above places. Our Warriors were Particular that no hurt should be Done to Women & Children; we Left four old men Behind who were no more able to go to War. We have retaken Wm. Dygert, who was taken about nine weeks agoe by Brant on the Fall hill; we now Deliver him to you so that he may return to his Friends. Last year we took up The Hatchet at Stillwater and we will now Continue it in our hands. The Grass Hopper, one of Oneida Chiefs, took to himself one of the Prisoners to Live with him in his own Family; his name is Wm. Lull and has adopted him as his Son. Brothers, we deliver you six Prisoners, with whom you are to act as you Please. Brothers, you had a man scalped here sometime agoe. The Oneidas & Tuscaroras have taken revenge & have Brought you some Slaves. We do not take Scalps. We hope you are now Convinced of our

Friendship towards you & your great Cause. The Warriors detain two of the Prisoners till tomorrow morning. The Conasarangas have one more Prisoner in their Possession, taken at the same Time; they will bring him tomorrow or next day.

Then the Conference ended. Accordingly the next morning they Delivered me the Prisoner mentioned in their speech the Evening before. I have them all in the Guard House here & allow them a Pound of Beef & a Pound of Bread Pr Man Pr day. At foot, hereof, you have Their Names:

Rechard McGinnis Inlisted among Butler's Rangers in January last and was at Wioming last Summer with Coll. Butler at their head; Capt. Gilbert Tise came from Neagara a few days Before the party set out with Brant to Distroy the German Flatts; he had 33 Indians with him mostly Mohawks and Conajoharry Indians. Brant whole party that Destroyed The Flatts was 300 Tories & 152 Indians. There were no Regular Troops among them.

The Indians that were here Behaved with the greatest Openness that I could have Wished. I thanked them for their Services at this Time. I fed 'em & gave them a hearty drink of Rum. I promiss'd that I would Communicate this affair as well to the General as to the Commissioners of Indian affairs at Albany. With the above Indians arrived also Eight Princepal Indians from Caughnawaga in Canada. They have Important intilligence to Communicate to us, in regard to Canada affairs which are in our favour, by what I have yet Learn'd. But as I heard last night that Mr. Dean is beetween here & Schonectady on his way for this place I have Deferred saying any thing particular to the Coughnawagas. I have victulled them for six Days and they are returned to Oneida with The Sachems & the moment Mr. Dean arrives here they will know it next day & Came immediately. The Intilligence they give will doubtless be Communicated by Mr. Dean without loss of Time. The 24th about sun Setting, 7 of our men being out towards the sluice, were fired on by Indians and returned the fire. I sent off a party Immediatly to support them, who pursued the Indians over the sluces, and returned. No harm was done. I am Gentleman with respect Your Most Hum. Sevent

Robt. Cachran.

Prisoners Names—William Lull, Rechard McGinnis, John Mc-Ginnis, Jno. Harrison, Michael Stopplopen, Barry Loghlin, Moses Thurston, Caleb Lull, Benjamin Lull.

[No. 1826.]

The Officers of Glover's Brigade Petition for Flour for their Own Use.

The Humble Petition of the Officers in the Brigade commanded by Brigadier General Glover:

Sheweth That we your Excellency's Petitioners, having Families, (some of them at a great distance from us), and the Crops of Grain in this State turning out in general very light, beg leave to sollicit your Excellency's permission for the Bearer, Mr. John Braddish, to purchase such quantitys of Flour annex'd to our Names for their use; and to have liberty to Transport it out of the State of New York. Your Excellency's compliance to this will lay your Petitioners under a lasting obligation who will be in duty bound to every pray.

Providence October 3d 1778.

His Excellency Governor Clinton.

Moses Ashley, Capt. 3 Barrels; Orringh Stoddard, Capt. 3 Barrels; Geo. Smith, Capt. 3 Barrels; Robert Davis, Capt. 3 do;

Jeremiah Miller, do 3 do; T. Hollister, Lieut, 3 Do; John Grace, Lt. 3 Do; Thomas Smart, R. P. M. 3 Barrels; Abra: Tinkerman, Capt. 3 Barrels; Alex'r Orr, Lt. 5 Bar'ls; Belcher Hancock, Lieut. 3 Barrells; Fran's Green, Lt. 4 Barrells; Oliver Hunt, Lt. 4 Barrells; James Webb, Ens'n 5 Barrels; Abra'm Hunt, Capt. 4 Barrells; Nathaniel Nason, Lt. 5 Barrells; George Jacobs, Lt. 4 Barrells; Eben'r Williams, Lieut. 4 Barrells; Abner Dow, Lieut. 5 Barrels; James E. Finley, Surgeon 4 Barrels; Joseph Fisk, 4 Barrels; Leb's Ball, Maj'r, 6 Barrels; E. Whittelsey, B. Q. M., 6 Barrels; S. Larned, Adjt., 6 Barrels; Benj'm Wells, Ens'n, 3 Do; Joseph Hodgkins, Capt., 4 Bar'l; Silv's Smith, Capt., 4 Barrels; Adam Mortin, Capt., 4 Barr'l; Moses Roberts, Lt., 4 Barels; Joseph Brown, En., 4 Barrels; Archelaus Lewis, adgt., 6 Barel; Ivory Hovey, Surgeon 6 Bar'l.

[No. 1827.]

Colonel Malcom Desires to have His Regiment Transferred to the Regular Establishment.

Fort Clinton Oc'r 4 1778.

Sir, I have already presented two memorals to the Legislature, solliciting them to patronise my Regiment. Many of the members have promised me their influence, & acknowledged my request reasonable. Major Pawling comes on purpose to obtain their determination on the Subject. And I take the Liberty to Request that you would bring on the affair by a message, or part of one which will certainly bring it to issue.

If they refuse, the General will think that in their judgment, he has made a wrong choice in this state when he know that other States in which he appointed officers on our Establishment

have all given to them equall encouragement as their particular
Quota Troops. I most respectfully am Sir your very H'ble Serv't

W. Malcom.
[To Gov. George Clinton.]

———

[No. 1828.]

Assistant Commissary Flint Asserts that Causes and Incidentally
Want of Cash, are Responsible for the Wheat and Flour Famine.

Sir, Your Excellency will please to accept of my thanks for
your early attention to my letter of the 25th ultimo. I must
again take the liberty to trouble you with a few remarks on the
circumstances of our department.

In justice to the Assistants, to whom you have attributed the
blame of our present wants, I must observe that the scantiness
of their supplies, is owing to causes which very probably have
escaped your notice. There was flour enough actually contracted
for, to have carried us plentifuly through the campaigne. But
unluckily they were not seasonably furnished with cash to make
good their contracts. By this means, when they were called
to collect their supplies, they found the farmers had disposed
of their wheat to private persons for an higher price than they
engaged to pay. Several thousand bbls. of flour have been lost
to the public by such practices. None of the purchasers in this
state, except those in Dutchess and W. Chester Counties ever
had orders to discontinue buying. And had cash been timely
received, to pay for what was agreed for, in those counties, our
magazines would not now have so empty. The blame, if properly
fixed, would fall on causes, which I choose to mention with
delicacy; and without too critically tracing the evils to their
true origin, I had rather invigorate the measures to releve them.

It would ill become me to suggest how far it is expedient to extend the indulgence of granting permits to export flour. If those permits are granted except in cases of absolute necessity, I much fear the consequences will prove hurtful & perhaps prevent the purchasers from being able to obtain supplies suitable for the purposes of the army.

I am still of the opinion that there are considerable quantities of wheat both in this state & Connecticut that is the property of men who are scrupulous of taking Continental money—and others who are not influenced by this consideration keep their grain for an higher price. I should suppose that the legislative body could frame an act to appoint assessors to rate every farmer to supply a certain quantity of wheat in a limited time. The particular mode of executing such a scheme, could be better determined by your assembly than by me.

Unless something uncommon should happen to prevent, I will wait on your Excellency sometime this week & know your sentiments of this proposal. In the mean time I am with much respect & esteem Your Excellency's most obed't & hbl. Ser't

Royal Flint, A. C. G. P.

Fredericksburgh Octo. 4th 1778.

His Excellency Gov. Clinton.

[No. 1829.]

Returns of Colonel Samuel Drake's regiment.

RETURN OF YE —TH REGIMENT IN GENL MORRIS'S BRIGADE OF MILITIA COMMANDED BY SAMUEL DRAKE COLL.

	Officers Present — Commissioned									Non Comis'd						and for what Exempted
	Coll.	Lieut. Coll.	Major	Captains	1st Lieuts	2nd Lieuts.	Ensigns	Adjutant	Qr. Master	Serjeants	Corporals	Drums & fifes	Rank & File	Total	Exempts	
Field Officers																
Coll Drake	1															
Lieut. Coll. Hyatt		1														
Maj. Delavan			1													
Capt. Kronkhite				9	6	8	7	1	1	26	36	0	464	571	7	4 Cripples 1 Subject to Fits 1 impediment in his Speech 1 Lost one Eye
Capt. Delevan					1	1	1			4	4	0	63			
Capt. Tallor					1	1	1			4	4	0	40		12	9 Quakers 3 Cripples
Capt. Laurence					1	1	1			4	4	0	31		11	1 Quaker 8 Contin'l Certif'e 2 Sickly and weakly
Capt. Haight					1	1	1			4	4	0	77			
Capt. Drake					1	1	1			4	4	0	58			
Capt. Lockwood					1	1	1			4	4	0	54			
Capt. Boyd					1	1	1			4	4	0	47			
Capt. Strang					1	1				4	4	0	51			
Total	1	1	1	9	6	8	7	1	1	36	36	0	464	571		

ROTATION OF DUTY FOR EACH OFFICER AND SOLDIER BELONGING COLL. SAMUEL DRAKE'S REGIMENT.

	Capts.	1st Lieuts.	2nd Lieuts.	Ensigns	Classes No.	Kronkhite Men	Delavan	Tailor	Laurence	Haight	Drake	Lockwood	Boyd	Strang	Total
1st on duty	Strang	Keelor	Gordeneer	Carman	1	9	7	6	5	10	8	8	6	7	66
2nd	Laurence	Benedict	McKeel	Porter	2	9	6	6	5	11	9	8	9	8	69
3rd	Kronkhite	Cudney	Danl Purdy	Drake	3	9	6	6	4	11	11	8	8	8	71
4th	Lockwood	Murtine	Veal	Vermiller	4	9	6	6	5	11	12	8	7	8	72
5th	Tailor	Dyckman	Sol'm Purdy	Rogers	5	9	7	6	5	11	7	8	7	7	67
6th	Haight		Ferriss	Clark	6	9	6	6	5	10	6	7	7	7	63
7th	Delavan	Delavan on duty	Reynolds	Benedict	7	8	6	6	5	11	7	8	5	7	65
8th	Boyd		V'n Wart		8	9	7	6	5	10	6	7	6	7	68
9th	Drake on duty														
Total						71	51	48	39	85	66	62	55	59	536

Octo'br 5th Day, 1778.

SAMLL DRAKE Colo.

[No. 1830.]

Flour for the French Fleet.

I do Certify, That The Thousands Barils of flour Bought by Mr. de Matigny are destin'd for The use of The French fleet Commanded by The Count D'Estaing & I do beg The Government of New York would be pleas'd to permit These provisions past unmolested for The Service of The Said fleet.

Boston The 5th october 1778.

Signed The Chev. de Borda, major General of The fleet.

Translated from The French.

[No. 1831.]

GOVERNOR CLINTON EXONERATES MAJOR POSEY.

But Believes Captain Harper was Responsible for the Error that Cost Colonel Dumon his Life.

Schohary, Middle Fort 23d Sept'r 1778.

May it Please your Excellency,

I make Free to Trouble you with a Few Lines Respecting a Command which I was ordered on by Colo. Butler to Paughataughton, I Can ashure you, I really am unhappy to find you have that matter Painted to you in so Black a Light as I understand you have, for be ashurd, That on that Expedition, for which I am Culpable, I took as many precautions as Lay in my Power; you must be sensible in what manner a man is to act when Possitively Told to be in an Enemies Country, as its Evident the moost of those Frontier settlements have actualy been in arms against us, or assisted the Enemy in Provition, & I have had the fortune to se & Know a Good Deal about the Disaffected People in this Countery in Genl. & I Can scarcely se any of them, be them the Greatest Villians, But what has some one to speek in there behalf.

My affidavits, with those of the officers under me upon that Expedition, Colo. Butler informs me he will send inclosd to you for your Perusial. I am with Esteem Your Obed't Hum'le ser't

Thomas Posey.

P. S. I am Informd there is a number of People throughout the Frontier settlements, which Can Prove Dumond's Carrector to be Exceeding Bad. Youl se his own Confesion in the affidavits of the officers.

His Excellency Governor Clinton.

————

Pokeepsie 5th October 1778.

Sir, I am favoured with your Letters of the 27th & Major Posey's of the 23d Ultimo with several Affidavits accompanying the same respecting the Death of Dumond. I never understood from the Complaints made to me of that Unhappy Affair, the least Intention of charging any of your Officers with Misconduct, and Please to assure Major Posey that I entertain too good an Oppinion of him to doubt the Propriety of his Behavour on that Occassion. It is not, however, so clear to me that Mr. Harper Judging from his own Account, did not make Use of some Deception which might have betrayed a better Man than Dumond into Imprudent Expressions in his Situation which if so is wrong. The Soldiery who had Dumond in Charge, were Right in obeying Orders even tho at the Expence of his Life, as he was wrong in attempting to Escape out of their Custody. And tho' it is my Duty to guard the Rights of the Subjects of the State, I shoud be sorry were they to suffer for doing their Duty. Please to offer my best Re-

spects to Major Posey & believe me your Friend & most Obed't
Servant

Geo. Clinton.
Colo. Butler.

[No. 1832.]

CONGRESS CONTINUES THE EMBARGO ON PROVISIONS.

*And Passes an Act to Exchange Bills of Credit Emitted by States
for Continental Currency under Certain Conditions.*

Philadelphia 7th October 1778.

Sir, Since my last of the 27th Ulto. I have not been honored
with a Letter from your Excellency.

Within the present Inclosure will be found two acts of Congress viz.

1—of the 2d Instant for continuing the present Embargo on
Provision until the last day of January 1779 and for divers other
purposes therein mentioned.

2—An Act of the 5th for exchanging with Continental Currency
such local Bills of Credit as have been received in the Loan Office
of each State respectively.

I have the honor to be, With the highest Respect Sir Your
Excellency's Obedient & most humble servant

Henry Laurens, President of Congress.
His Excellency George Clinton Esquire Governor of New York.

In Congress, Oct'r 2d 1778.

Whereas the scantiness of crops of wheat & other grain in the
States of New York, New Jersey, Pensylvania, Delaware, Maryland & Virginia & the wicked acts of speculators, forestallers, &

engrossers, who infest every quarter of the country & are indus-
triously purchasing up grain & flour at the most exorbitant prices,
render it impracticable to obtain timely & sufficient supplies for
the operations of the army & navy, unless the most vigorous
measures are without delay adopted to restrain practices so destructive of the public Weal:

Resolved, That it be earnestly recommended to the legislative
or where vested with sufficient power to the executive authorities
of the States above mentioned, to authorise & direct any civil
magistrate within their respective jurisdictions on an information given by the commissary or quarter master general, or by the
deputy commissary or quarter master general of the respective
districts of any extraordinary quantity of grain or flour being purchased & in the possession of individuals, forthwith to issue his
warrant impowering the informant to seize the same for the
public use paying for the same such price, as may to the respective legislatures appear proper to prevent the practice of engrossing those articles in future not exceeding six dollars per hundred
for flour & in proportion for grain, which may be found in the
hands of engrossers.

And whereas the facilitating the supply of the army which
was one of the principal objects in laying the embargo, has been
defeated by individuals purchasing grain & flour with a view of
exporting the same at the expiration of the term for which the
embargo is laid in the respective States;

Resolved, That the embargo on provisions, which by the resolution of the 8th day of June last was laid until the 15th of November next, be continued in force subject to such exceptions as are
recommended by the resolution of the 2d Sept'r till the last day
of January 1779 or until such time as Congress shall give notice

to the respective States that sufficient supplies have been obtained for the operations of the army & for the French Squadron and that it be recommended to the respective States to take the most effectual measures for carrying this resolution into effect.

Resolved, That it be farther recommended to the legislatures of the several States to pass laws for the seizure & forfeiture of all grain & flour purchased up or engrossed, with such exceptions & under such limitations & restrictions as they may think most expedient.

And, whereas, there is reason to believe that the end proposed by Congress, in recommending an exemption from embargo by their resolution of 2d Sept'r, may not only be defeated by private purchasers enhancing prices or by captains making false protests & bearing away to foreign ports, but in cases where vessels may actually arrive in some parts of the eastern States the cargoes may be engrossed by individuals at an extravagant rate, with a view of preying upon the public; to guard against which evils,

Resolved, That it be earnestly recommended to the legislative & executive authorities of the respective States not to grant any exemptions from embargo to any vessels whatever unless, in addition to the former security recommended, the persons applying for the same, comply with the following stipulations, to wit:

1st. That the shipper or shippers of the cargo solemnly make oath that no part of the flour or grain proposed to be shipt has been purchased or contracted for since 10 day of Octo'r 1778.

2d. That the shipper and every man on board of the said vessels whether seamen or passengers solomnly swear, that they will not directly or indirectly be privy to or concerned in any measure whatsoever which may tend to defeat the arrival of the vessel at some safe port in one of the Eastern States, but that they will without any deception, mental reservation or equivocation whatever take every measure to carry into effect the intention of the license granted:

3d. That the shipper shall first agree with the commissary genl. or person by him duly authorized, for such purpose on the price for which the flour shipt shall be delivered at one of the ports in the Eastern States for the public use.

Resolved, That the exemption from the embargo as recommended by the resolution of Congress of the 2d Sept'r be extended to vessels belonging to the middle & southern as well as those of the Eastern States under the restrictions & stipulations above mentioned.

Extract from the minutes.

Chas. Thomson secy.

In Congress 5th Oct'r 1778.

Whereas, it is represented by several commissioners of the continental loan offices, that they have received for loan office certificates & lottery tickets of the United States, considerable sums in bills of credit emitted by States, who by acts of their respective legislatures have stopped the circulation of such bills:

Resolved, That it be recommended to the said States, to direct their treasurers to receive such bills of credit from the said commissioners respectively, & deliver in exchange continental currency to the amount thereof; the said commissioners declaring on oath if required, that such bills were received by them in virtue of their office.

Extract from the minutes.

Chas. Thomson secy.

[No. 1833.]

A Petition to Procure the Exchange of Edward Covenhoven.

We, your Excellencies humble Petitioners, take the Liberty to represent the unhappy fate of one of our Friends & Acquaintances to your Excellencies attention & Consideration, Edward Covenhoven, a worthy & zealous friend to his Country, who, after having lost his all, which was very Considerable, has unluckily fallen into the hands of our Common Enemy at Tarry-Town, & in Consequence, thereof, has left numerous, destitute & distressed family among us. We, therefore, your Excellencies Petitioners humbly pray that your Excellency will be pleas'd, if there is any medium for an Exchange, that the first & wou'd wish a speedy oppertunity may be improved, that the distresses of the family may in some measure be relieved.

And we your Excellencies Petitioners shall ever pray.

Flats in Rhine-Beck, Oct'r 7 1778.

Stephen Van Voorhees, Robt. R. Livingston, Everardus Bogardus, Jacobus Kip, Isaac Kip, Leonard Kip, Hans Kiersteade, Cornelius Bradford, Wm. Radclift, William Skepmus, P. D'Witt.

To his Excellency George Clinton Esqr.

[No. 1834 and 1836.]*

MAJOR NATHANIEL STRONG MURDERED.

A Serious Charge Against Colonel Woodhull—Verdict of the Coroner's Inquest.

Blooming Grove 7th 8b: 1778.

Sir, We lament having it in our power to furnish you with a fresh instance of the villainy of Claudius Smith and his Comrades.

---

* To make this story consecutive, documents 1834 and 1836 have been consolidated under one heading.—STATE HISTORIAN.

Last night, at midnight, Claudius with six others came to Capt. Woodhull's, Stole several valuable articles—the Capt. was gone to Clarks Town; some of the villians swore they would soon have him dead, or alive—immediately after they went to Major Strong's, broke open his door, and his windows—he coming in the room was shot down and immediately expired—two shot enter'd his face, one in his neck and one in the breast—three men fired at him as is said.

Such conduct is truely alarming. All our Militia are below the mountains, which these beings undoubtedly knew, for we have reason to believe that the whole of David Smith's tribe are concerned in assisting them. In short we have not thought ourselves secure for a long time. We live so scattered that they can come in the dead of the night to any one family & do what they please.

You, sir, may, with propriety, say that we have men enough when the Militia are at home to take, kill, or drive them away—'tis true, but what can we do when those to whom we have given power screens the villians from Justice. 'Tis not our wish to injure Characters, but when it becomes necessary for the good of the Community to describe the conduct which opens a door to such actions as above, we think it our duty to deliver ourselves with freedom.

Coll'n Woodhull as a Senator should endeavour to have removed every evil the People justly complain of—he is Coll' of our Regt., frequent applications have been made to him; those villains still range at large. We are informed and believe it true, That he has endeavoured to screen from Justice a part of Claudius his Gang. We shall not add further than to beg your Excellency to use your endeavour, in such way as you think best, to have

removed this Smith Gang without leaving the Executive part to
Coll'n Woodhull. We are with respect Your Excellency's Most
Obed't Humb'e Serv'ts,

Henry Brewster, Israel Seely, Ebenezer S. Burling, John Brewster, Joshua Hobart, Jos: Sackett, jun., William Bradley.
His Excellency George Clinton Esq.

                                    Poukeepsie 8th October 1778.

Gentlemen, I have received your Letter of the 7th Instant containing the Melancholly Account of the Murder of Major Strong
& the Roberies committed by Claudius Smith & his Confederates
in your Neighbourhood which gave me real Concern. I have by
the Bearer issued such Orders as if vigorously executed trust will
put a stop to these Outrages in Future. I am Your Most Obed't
Serv't
                                                        G. C.

To Henry Brewster &c.

PROCEEDINGS BEFORE THE CORONER.

                                    Goshen October ye 8th 1778.

Honoured Sir, Inclosed I send you a coppy of an Inquisition
taken yesterday upon view of the Body of the worthy Nethaniel
Strong. I send it you to Confirm the mischiefs Practised by the
Notorious Claudeus Smith and his party hopeing sum Measures
may be taken to stop his Coreer.

Excuse hast as the opertunity wates. I am with Regard your
Excelency moste obedient Humble Servant
                                        Wm. Holly, Coroner.

Blooming Grove Oct'r 7th 1778.

Orange County.

Mrs. Woodhull being Duly Sworen Saith that on the Night of the Sixt of this Instant, Claudius Smith and a party of armed Men Came to hur House about Twelve Oclock, and Did Rob hur and wished hur Husband was at Home for he would have him Ded or a Live.

Sworn to before me   Wm. Holly, Coroner.

Mrs. Strong Sath that about One OClock She heerd Sum men Knocking at the Dore and Braken in the windows, on which hur Husband got Up and askt who was there; they answered a Friend; on which they ordered him to Lay Down his arms and open the Dore and they would not Hurt him; he answered he would if he Could, but that they had so broake it he Did not know if the Could; they Told him to lay Down his Gun; he Said he had; on which he Stept Forred and was Shot by the party that had attackted the House and further She Heared hur Husband Say it was Claudious Smith.

Sworn before Wm. Holly, Coroner.

These Depositions wer onely taken hear so fur as thay Respected Claudeus Smith and his party.

Orange County New Cornwell Precent, State of New York.

Inquisition Indented taken at the house of Major Nathaniel Strong the seventh Day of october in the year of our Lord Christ, one thousand seven hundred and seventy Eight, and in the third year of Independency upon View of the Body of the said Nathaniel Strong, then and there lying Dead by the oath of Daniel Colman, Benjaman Gale, John Wood, Coe Gale, Ebenezer Burling, Patrick McLaughlin, William Williams, Elija Heddy, William Bradly, Sail Colman, Jonathan Deboys, William Tuthill, &

Samuel Bartly, good and Lawfull Men of Said county, Being Duely Sworn and charged Before William Holly, one of the Coroners for said county, to inquire in behalf of the good People of said State, when, where, how and after what Manner, the said Nathaniel Strong hath came by his Death, do say upon their oath, that on the Night of the Sixth of this insta. betwen one and two oclock as it is made appear to us by the Evidence of the wife of the Deceased, A cumpany of armed men one of them supposed to be Claudeus Smith, broak into the house fiered hir husband and Killed him; that so and Not other ways the said Nathaniel Strong is came by his death; to this Inquisition as well the Coroner as the Juriors Do set their hands and seals.

Wm. Holly Coroner; seal, Daniel Colman, Benjaman Gale, Capt. John Wood, Coe Gale, Ebenezer Burling, Patrick McLaughlen, William William, Elija Heddy, Wiliam Bradly, Sail Colman, Jonathan Deboys, William Tuthill, Samuel Bartly.

a Trew Coppy Exammined by William Holly, Coroner.

You shall Delijently inquire and trew presentmant make, in behalf of the good People of this State, when, where, how, and after what manner, Nathiniel Strong, hear Lying Dead, came by his Death, and of all such other matter Respecting the same as shall cum to your Knowledg; So help you God.

[No. 1835.]

The Flag Boat Reports for Cuyler Dole and White.

Poghkeepsie Oct'r 8 1778.

Sir, Henry Cuyler, James Dole & Alex'r White being duly exchanged for Major Lush & Messrs. Vantassel & Maybe of this State, I gave them with their Families & effects Permission to pass to N. York with a Flag on Tuesday with the Officer to command the Flag to be appointed by the Commanding Officer at W. Point.

I am this Moment favored with a Line from Genl. Washington informing me that a Boat with a Flag coming up from the Enemy for Mr. Cuyler & his Family is stopped below the Fort. I am extremely happy this Caution is taken, for tho Mr. Cuyler & the other Persons are completely exchanged and I have no Objection ag't their passing to N. York with their Families & Effects as soon as convenient, yet I have Reason to believe the Enemy must have other views in send'g up the Flag than barely for Mr. Cuyler, as Mr. Cuyler informed me on his Return lately from N. York where he had been to perfect his Exchange, that he had Permission to proceed to New York with the sloop engaged here for that Purpose. I am Sir Your most obed't serv't

[G. C.]

[To Gen. Putnam.]

[No. 1836.]*

[No. 1837.]

William Palfrey Asks for a Permit to Export Flour.

Fish Kills October 9 1778.

Sir, My Errand to this place was to purchase a few barrels of Flour for the use of my family the ensuing Winter, which I find I cannot export from the State without a special Licence for that purpose.

Nothing less than absolute necessity could induce me to trouble your Excellency on such an Occasion, but I know your goodness and humanity are such, that you would not wish to see the fami-

---

* See footnote page 145.

lies of those engaged in the public Service suffer for want of Bread, which is really the Case with mine. Mrs. Palfrey writes me word she cannot purchase Flour, or Grain of any kind for Money.

You will, therefore, oblige me exceedingly by sending me a Permit to convey out of the State, Eight barrels of Flour, which I assure you upon my honor, is intended solely for the use of my family, of which I have nine in number, exclusive of myself and a Servant that is with me. You will please to inclose the permit in a Letter by the Post, directed to me at General Washington's Head Quarters.

I have the honor to be with the greatest Respect Your Excellency's most obed't humble Servant

Wm. Palfrey.

His Excellency Governor Clinton.

[No. 1838.]*

[No. 1839.]

A Postal Thief Steals the Governor's Mail.

Weathersfield Oct'r 12th 1778.

Sir, We have Procur'd a few Sheets of Parchment, beg your Excellency will be Pleas'd to accept of one half of the Roll and deliver the other half to Thomas Tredwell, Esqr. I am for Mr. Platt & self Your Excellency's most obed. Hbe. Serv't

Samuel Broome.

His Excellency, Gov'r Clinton.

Fairfield 13th October 1778.

S'r, No Doupt you will be Surprised to find that this Letter has been broke open; the occation was this: Mr. Peet, the post

---

Rider, came to a publick house in this town and hung his horse
under a Shed Just in ye Dusk of ye Evening and went into the
house to Deliver his Newspapers and Letters—and within ten
minutes after, the above mention'd Rool of Parchment was Stole
and taken from off his horse and the thief got off undiscovered.
Mr. Peet being Exceedingly uneasy and Concern'd for fear it
might be of great Value and importance applyed to us, the Subscribers to for our advice, whether as it was Reasonable to
suppose that this Letter would give full information of the
Contents of ye Rool, it would not be prudent to open it, that
if it was a matter of great Value & importance, measure to Recover ye Same and take ye thief might be taken accordingly;
upon mature Consideration of the matter we thought it prudent
on the whole to open ye Letter, and shall use all possible means
to Recover the Same and bring the thief to Justice, and we dont
Doupt as we acted for your Interest you will Justify us in the
measures we have Taken., we are with great Respect S'r your
most obedient Humble ser't

Saml. Bradley, Justice Pe.

George Burr, Just. Peace.

To his Exelency Gov'r Glinton.

<hr>

[No. 1840.]

Schaghticoke Exempts.

To his Excellancy Governor George Clinton General and Commander in Chief of all the Militia and admiral of the State
of New York.

We the Subscribers inhabitants of Schacktekock assotiated
in Pursuencence of an Act of the People of the State of New
York represented in Senate and Assembly, Passed the 3 Day
of April 1778, Do humbly Hereby Certify that we have Elected

for Capt, Cornelius W. Van Den Berg; for first Liut. James Kip; for Second Liut. Jacob Fort; for Ensign Richard Van Veghten and we hereby Engage that we will Severally and on all occations obey the orders of our Respective officers and in all cases of invasion or Incurtions of the Enemy or insurrections march to repel the Enemy or Suppress Such insurrection in Like manner as the enrolled Militia are Compelled to Do as witness our Hands the Twelvth day of October 1778.

Wouter N. Groesbeck, Gerret Winne, Leuwes Vele, Tunis L. Velan, Henrich Möller, Weynant Van den Bergh, John J. Viele, Peter Benaewa, Johns N. Groesback, Lawies H. Viele, Gilbert Giles, Hendrick Mandevil, Peter P. Winne, Jacob Herman, Conradt Herman, Goseph Gadwin, Charls Tol, Luas P. Vyele, Harma Quackanbus, Luas Vanantwarpn, Lowyes G. Viele, John Velan, Wendel Overacker, John Roos, Willem Klum, John Slay, Laurans Stansalor, Wylem Mestes, Magiel Sisko, Jams Lyans, Nycklas Becker.

[Agreed & Entred Nov. 5 1778.]

[No. 1841.]

*Petition for the Pardon of Isaac Scouten.**

[No. 1842.]

THE GOVERNOR HOLDS OFFICERS TO BLAME.

Informs Colonel Klock that had His Orders Been Obeyed, the Country Would not Have Been Injured to the Extent it Was.

Poghkeepsing Oct'r 12th 1778.

Gentlemen, I have received your Letter of the 27th ult but have not seen either Colo. Lush or Mr. Dygert whom you mention

---
* Omitted.

as the Bearers and to whom you refer me for more particular Information.

When we are acquainted that W. Chester, Orange, Ulster & Albany & Charlotte Counties are equally exposed to the Ravages of the Enemy with yourselves and that the Militia of Dutchess which is the only remaining County have been during the Summer frequently called to strengthen the Posts in the Highlands, you will readily perceive that your Safety must in a great Measure depend upon your own Exertions & the aid which can be afforded you by the County of Albany. Upon the first appearance of Hostilities in your Quarter, I represented your exposed Situation to his Excellency Genl. Washington and in Consequence of my application, Alden's Regiment was continued on and another Regt. sent to the western Frontier. If these are improperly stationed so as not to afford the Settlements there the Protection that might be expected, it is the Fault of the Commanding Officer at Albany and not in my Power to correct. With Respect to the Militia, 2 Companies of Rangers were directed to be raised in Tryon County & 1 small Company at Schoharry for Albany; as early as last winter the $\frac{1}{4}$ of the Militia upon the first Intimation of Danger were ordered upon the Frontiers of both those Counties to be stationed by the Command'g Officers at such Places as would give the most equal & perfect Protection to the different Settlements. And, had these Orders been obeyed, the Country I am persuaded would not have experienced the Injuries which have been committed upon it by the Enemy. These Orders are yet in Force & I am extremely sorry, if have it not in my Power at present to give you any further aid than what you can derive from carrying them into Execution.

I will, however, make it my Business to lay your distressed Situation before the Legislature, and I wo'd fain hope that they will put it in my Power to raise a sufficient Body of men to carry on offensive operations ag't the Enemy & thereby give more Security to the Frontier Settlements in future. It is not for me to determine whether it is from the refractory spirit of the men, or neglect of the Officers, that my orders have not been executed. No Returns have been made to me by any of the officers in Consequence of my repeated orders; neither does it appear to me that Courts Martial have been held upon the Conduct of the refractory & disobedient. In these Instances the officers are certainly to blame & merit all the Censure they have received. I am &c.

[G. C.]

[To Col. Klock.]

THE GOVERNOR'S LEGISLATIVE SPEECH.

A Brief Account of the Movements of the Enemy and of the Condition of the State at that Time.

*Gentlemen of the Senate and Assembly,

The Enemy, by the Evacuation of Philadelphia, and their Removal to the City of New-York, have again made this State the principal Seat of War. I am happy, however, to inform you, that instead of effecting the Conquest of the United States of America, their Main Army, after several fruitless Campaigns, on their Part barbarously and cruelly conducted, is at length, through the Vigilance of his Excellency General Washington, and the Spirit and Bravery of the Troops under his Command, confined

---

*By proclamation the Governor, on September 1st, 1778, directed the Legislature to meet at Poughkeepsie on the 1st day of October following, but the number of members being insufficient for the transaction of public business, an adjournment was effected from day to day, until October 13, when they assembled in the Senate Chamber, where Governor Clinton made the above speech.—STATE HISTORIAN.

to defensive Operations only; and there is the greatest Reason to hope, that, with the Blessing of a kind Providence, we shall be enabled, speedily, to bring the War to a happy Conclusion, and perfectly establish our Freedom and Independence.

Our Northern Frontier has, this Season, remained in a State of Tranquility, and the Inhabitants thereby been favoured with an Opportunity of recovering, in some Measure, from the extreme Distress to which they were reduced by the Operations of the last Campaign.

I am, at the same Time, Gentlemen, unhappy to inform you of the Ravages committed on the Western Frontier, and the Destruction and Desolation of several valuable Settlements in the Counties, of Tryon, Albany, and Ulster, by the Savages, in Conjunction with the disaffected Subjects of this and the neighbouring States: On the first Appearance of Hostilities in that Quarter, I ordered, into actual Service, a considerable Part of the Militia for the protection of the exposed Inhabitants; but every Exertion I have been able to make for their Security, though burthensome to the Militia, and very expensive to the Public, has (owing to the Extent of Country to be guarded, against an Enemy carrying on a desultory War) proved ineffectual.

The Disaffection and turbulent Conduct of many of the Inhabitants of the Northeastern District of this State, will claim your Attention, and call for such Measures, as Justice, the public Good, and the Honour of the State may demand.

Gentlemen of the Legislature,

As the Terms for which the present Delegates in Congress, and the Members of the Council of Appointment for this State, were elected, are expired; it will, of Course, be your first Business to proceed to the Election of proper Persons to fill those important Offices.

The continued Depreciation of the Paper Currency, is a Circumstance of the most alarming Nature. Temporary Expedients, such as, Laws for the Reduction of Prices, though they may serve for a Time to palliate, will, in the End, be found to increase the Evil. The only effectual Remedy is, that of reducing the Quantity of circulating Currency, by Taxation; a Measure which I would wish to recommend to your particular and early Attention: For, exclusive of every other Consideration, no Time can be more proper than the present, for paying off our public Debts by Taxes, when the staple Commodities of the State command the most advanced Prices.

By the 35th Section of our Constitution, the Laws of this State are necessarily become complicate; and, as every Member of Society is materially interested in the Knowledge of the Laws by which he is governed, I am induced to believe, a careful Revision of the Laws of this State, would be an acceptable Service to your Constituents, and attended with the most salutary Effects.

In the Course of the War, this State has frequently been charged by Congress with the Superintendence and Management of various Kinds of public Business; in the Prosecution of which, large Disbursements have been occasionally made, and, notwithstanding the Advances by Congress, I am informed a very considerable Balance remains due to this State; and, as new Accounts are daily accruing, some proper and permanent Mode, for the Liquidation and Settlement of the public Accounts of this State, is become necessary.

You will readily perceive, from the Nature of the Service, it is not in my Power to render you an Account to any fixed Period, of the Expenditures made in the Payment and Subsistance of the Militia, who have been employed on the Frontiers: I have

great Reason to believe that they far exceed the Sum allowed by
the Legislature for this Purpose, and have therefore to recommend, that Provision be made, not only for Discharging the extra
Debts that may have been contracted for this Service, but also,
for enabling me to execute more effectual Measures for the Defence of the Frontier Settlements, against the Depredations of a
savage Enemy in future.

Gentlemen,

There are many other Matters worthy of the Deliberation of the
Legislature, which in the Course of the Session, I shall occasionally take proper Opportunities of laying before you.

Your Zeal for the public Welfare, as well as the Duty you owe
to your Constituents, will, I am persuaded, induce you to prosecute the Business of the present Session with that Unanimity and
Firmness which become the Representatives of a free and virtuous People; and the Necessity there is (during the unsettled
State of our public Affairs) for your Presence in the several
Counties in which you reside, will equally excite you to Dispatch.

                                            Geo. Clinton.
Poughkeepsie, October 13, 1778.

[No. 1843.]

COLONEL HAWKES HAY ASKS FOR REINFORCEMENTS.

*Governor Clinton Orders Captain Bell's Company to Protect the
Southern Part of Orange County.*

                                    Clarkstown Octo'r 9 1778.

Dear Sir, I hope your Excelency will be good enough to excuse
my not writing to you before; but can assure you, that it is owing
to the distresst Confusion we have been in, and the hurry of

---
*From Journals of the Legislature.

business, On the first alarm we gott of the Enemy, I imediately imbodied my Regt. and marched down two or three miles in New Jersey to oppose the Enemy, but soon found to our Sorrow that we had not one Twentieth part of strength enough and if two Deserters had not come in to us and given us Intelligence we all would have been cut off. My malitia which is very few, have behaved Extraodinary well, but they are now, very much distressed and fatigued, and am very apprehensive I shall not be able to keep them together much longer; many of them have not sowen any winter Grain this Season, and none have cut their Buckwheat, which is now spoiling. I do, therefore, request that you will be so kind as to order us some assistance and relieve a poor distrest People, who have never yett rec'd any assistance from any of their neighbours, or the army Except from Col. Marvin who is down with about one Hundred men including Officers. We raised a Company for Col. Graham's Regt. which was to be imployed for the defence of this State and they are now imployed in New Jersey. I beg leave to request that you will be so kind as to order that Company here; they may be of great Service to us as they are well acquainted with the Ground; I am Dear Sir Your Excellency's most Obt. Serv't

A. Hawkes Hay.

N. B. I am informed that Lt. Col. Wisener of Warwick is on his march with Eighty men.

His Excellency Governor Clinton.

Poghkeepsie Oct'r 13th 1778.

D'r Sir, By the acct's which prevailed here for some Days past and which I credited the more from my not having any application for assistance from your Quarter, I was led to believe that the Enemy had left you, until I was undeceived by your Letter of the 9th this Day received. I am sorry to learn that my orders to the Militia of your County on the North Side of the Mountains, which was to march as great a Proportion as could be spared consistent with the Safety of the Frontiers, has afforded you so little aid. I have sent an Order to Capt. Bell to join you in the Protection of the Inhabitants in your Part of the Country & take his further Orders from you or other officer command'g the militia being superior to him in Rank. You may rest assured that every other possible Exertion shall be made to give you Succor. In the mean Time let me intreat you to continue your own laudable Exertions. I am &c.

[G. C.]

[To Col. Hay.]

Poughkeepsie Oct'r 13th 1778.

Gentlemen, Upon the first Intimation I had from Mr. Smith of the Enemy's being in your Quarter, I issued my orders to the Commanding Officer of the Militia in your County on the N. Side of the Mountain to call into actual Service and march to your assistance as great a Proportion of their respective Regiments as could be spared consistent with the safety of the Frontiers. I am extremely sorry to find that these orders contrary to my Expectation have afforded you so little assistance. From the accounts which prevailed here, I had been induced to hope that the Enemy had left your Part of the Country, as they were so well authenticated as to be commonly credited, and I was confirmed in this by receiving no applications from you for further aid. I send you inclosed an Order for Capt. Bell's Company to join the Militia in your Defence, and you may rest assured that every other Exertion in my Power shall be made to give you succour as well by application to Genl. Washington for Continental Troops as by the Militia. Let me intreat you in the mean Time to continue your own Endeavors. I am &c.

[G. C.]

[To the Committee from the Southern Part of Orange County.]*

Capt. Bell's Company raised for Defence of this State will immediately upon Receipt hereof march & join the Militia of Colo. Hay's Regt. in the Defence & Protection of the Inhabitants of the Southern Part of Orange County ag't the Ravages of the Enemy and take his further Orders from Colo. Hay or the Officer command'g the Militia, being his superior in Rank.†

---

*This letter in mss. is addressed to no one. It is evidently intended as an answer to the petition from the residents of the southern part of Orange County. The dates have no doubt been confused. See pages 169-172.—STATE HISTORIAN.

†The British commander at New York having information that seven hundred rebel militia were cantoned in the neighborhood of Hackensack, New Jersey, a little after eleven o'clock last night, ordered the troops to march. The second battalion of light infantry led the column, supported by the 2d regiment of grenadiers, with the 33d and 64th regiments, these commanded by Major-General Gray. Between one and two this morning they arrived at the rebel cantonments; Major Straubenzee had been detached with six companies of the same battalion of light infantry; the other six under the Honorable Major Maitland, kept the road, by which manoeuvres the enemy's patrol, consisting of a sergeant and about a dozen men, was entirely cut off. Major Straubenzee moved on with the 71st light company, and in a small village surprised a party of Virginia cavalry, styled Mrs. Washington's Guards, consisting of more than one hundred, commanded by Lieutenant-Colonel Baylor, who, with Major McLeod and two other officers, upon forcing the door of a house, attempted to get up a large Dutch chimney; the two former were mortally wounded, the third killed, and the fourth made prisoner. Upon entering the house, one of the rebel officers, demanding the name of the corps which had attacked them, was answered, " The Britsh light infantry," on which he exclaimed, " Then we shall all be cut off."

From hence a part of Sir James Baird's company was detached to a barn where sixteen privates were lodged, who, discharging ten or twelve pistols, and striking at the troops *sans effet* with their broadswords, nine of them were instantly bayoneted, and seven received quarter. Major Maitland's force coming up at that time, attacked the remainder of the rebel detachment, lodged in several other barns, with such alertness as prevented all but three privates from making their escape. The troops lay on their arms till daybreak, when moving forward, the light infantry fell in with a volunteer company of militia in a very thick wood and swamp; these gave one fire, which the 40th company, commanded by Captain Montgomery, returned and drove them off, leaving six dead, but afterwards scampering across a road in front of a company of our grenadiers, three more were killed by them. The light infantry in pursuing them up to Tappan, where they were entirely dispersed, took five prisoners, all of them wounded. The whole loss of the British, on this occasion, was one private of second battalion light infantry killed.—Rivington's Royal Gazette, October 3, 1778.

[No. 1844.]

Nathaniel Gorham Requests a Permit to Export Flour to Massachusetts.

To his Excellency Governor Clinton of the State of New York.

Council Chamber October 14th 1778.

The Council of the State of Massachusetts Bay would represent to your Honor that the Inhabitants of this State are in great
want of Flour for their own Consumption and would, therefore,
recommend Nathaniel Gorham, Esqr. a respectable Inhabitant of
this State, for your Honor's Permission to purchase and bring to
the Market here a Quantity of Flour for the Use of the Inhabitants.

A true Copy.   Attest Jno. Avery, D'y Secy.

––––––

Boston Oct. 15 1778.

Sir, The great want of Bread in these parts and the great distress into which many people, the poor especially, are thereby
involved is truly alarming. I have, therefore, been induced to
attempt the bringing a quantity of flour from your State into
this, and having applied to Councill desiring them to take some
measures for facilitating the plan, they have furnished me with
the within recommendation to your Excellency; but my avocations in the Assembly & at the Board of Warr are such as renders
it impossible for me to pay my respects to your Excellency in
person. Mr. William Stimpson the bearer of this will, therefore,
wait upon you as he is connected with me in the affair, and if it
is by any means possible to permit him to transport a quantity of
flour from your place to this, it will be an act of the greatest
humanity and benevolence and treating a sister state in that way
and manner which I have no doubt your Excellency will be glad

to do is possible. I am, with the greatest respect, your Excellency's most obedient Humble servant, &c.

Nathaniel Gorham.

[To Gov. George Clinton.]

———

[No. 1845.]

THE INCEPTION OF THE SULLIVAN EXPEDITION.

Governor Clinton Calls Washington's Attention to the Necessity of Destroying an Indian Settlement.

Poukeepsie 15th October 1778.

D'r Sir, I am unhappy in being again obliged to trouble your Excellency with the further disagreable Intelligence from our Western Frontier contained in the inclosed Copies of Letters which I have just now received from Colo. Cantine & Colo. Thustin.

I find it impossible to secure the Frontier Settlements ag't the Depredations of the Enemy by the utmost exertions I am able to make with the Militia, & I am lead to fear that unless some effectual Check can be given to their Opperations, exclusive of the Distresses which they bring on Individuals, who more immediately suffer by them they will sensibly affect the public, as the last Settlements they have destroyed usually afforded greater supplies of Grain than any other of equal Extent in this State.

I have hitherto entertained some Hopes that Colo. Butler's & Alden's Regiments, joined by the Militia who were ordered into Service on the Frontiers & posted abjacent to the Places at which they are stationed, would have been imployed in some Offensive Opperations ag't the Enemy at Anaquaga. This Place is a considerable Indian Settlement not far distant from our Frontier Settlements, nor (for light Troops) difficult of access, and is the Principal Place of Rendevouz for the Enemy, and I am perswaded

unless it can be destroyed & the Enemy thereby oblidged to retire farther Back into the Country that no Force however formidable will be able to protect us ag't their practices. Besides the
Enemy by occupying that Post, will soon acquire a very considerable accession in strength & Numbers. Many of the Militia of
Ulster & Orange Counties are desirous of Joining in Expedition
ag't the Enemy at that Post, & if they coud obtain the Assistance
of one Continental Regt., only, with a Proper officer to take the
Command, I am perswaded the Measures woud be attended with
Success & the most salutary Consequences. I inclose your Excellency a Copy of a Letter I lately received from Colo. Cantine
on the Subject giving the Distance & Route to Anaquago. I have
only to add that if your Excellency shoud approve of the Measure
I will exert myself in rendering every Assistance in my Power
towards executing it & as the Season is quickly advanced the
sooner it is entered upon the more practicable it will be.

[G. C.]

[To Gen. Washington.]

[No. 1846.]

Captain Jeremiah Snyder Asks for Ammunition for His Command
at Shandaken.

Little Schondeacon Octbr. 15 1778.

Sir, I think proper to let you know that upon my taking the
Command at this Place I found that the Company was in a bad
posture of Defence in Regard to Ammunition. I, therefore,
would be glad you would endeavour to send a fresh Supply as
soon as possible, that we may be able to make some Resistance
in case the enemy should make an excursion upon this Settlement; but we have at Present no Intelligence of there being near
this Place.

The Company now Consists of Forty-one Private, besides Serjeants & Corporals, and these I can not Suply with three Cartirages a peice; from this you may Judge what Defence we can make. My Request is, therefore, you will Send a Supply as soon Possible and you'll oblidge, Sir, Your Most Hble Serv't

Jeremiah Snyder, Capt.

[To Gov. George Clinton.]

___

[No. 1847.]

A Proposition to Exchange Edward Covenhoven for John Cummings.

Dear Sir, I have the Pleasure to inform you that a Certificate accompanys this Letter by Mr. Willet's Flag, under Cover, to Governor Clinton, of which I send you a Copy herein inclosed, expressing that Mr. Covenhoven (a Gentleman of Influence in the neighbourhood of Tarry Town), who was lately taken in Arms at that Place, will be sent out the Instant that you shall make your appearance at our Lines, and I hope there remains at this Hour no further Obstructions to your Release. That it may be so and that I may have the Pleasure of seeing you soon at this Place is the sincere wish of, D'r sir, Your very hum'e Serv't

Arch'd Campbell Lieut. Colo. 71st Regiment.

New York Oct. 15th 1778.

(Transcript)

Governor Clinton.   New York Oct. 14th 1778.

In Consequence of your Letter to Mr. John Cumming now a Prisoner of war in Albany Goal, I make you a tender of Mr. Edward Covenhoven taken at or near Tarry Town on the 28th Sept. last in Exchange for him and have the Honour to be with due Respect Your most &c.

Jos. Lowring.

[No. 1848.]

Colonel Newkerk's Guards Attacked.

New Hurly, Octo'r 16th 1778.

D'r S'r, I make no doupt before this Comes to hand your Hon'r will be Inform'd of the depretation made by the Enimy at Pepack and all the particulars of it.

I, however, thought it my duty to Lett your Honn'r know that on Tuesday night about 11 oClock, I Rece'd an Express from Capt. Cross, from Poughkanisink, who teld me, that he had that moment Rece'd an Express from Collo. Newkerk, at peen-pack, that the Gards of that place had been attacked about 11 oClock that morning & before night had Retreated; that Collo. Newkerk thought the whole Gards along the frontier to Marble-town whould be attac'd the next morning, I, thereupon, Issued orders to seven Comp's of Collo. Hasbrouk's Regt., Immediately to march to Mamecotting & Left the four River Comp'ys till fur-ther orders; (but ordered them under arms); I went myself to Mamecotting next morning, in order [to] act In conjunction with Collo. Cantine, but at my Coming there I found the Enemy had Gon of. I thought it best to dismiss part of the men but Left a Sufficient Gard untill Cantine & his Gard should Return. I am with much Esteem Honn'd S'r Your Verry Hum. Serv't

Joh's Hardenbergh, Jr. Lt. Collo.

To his Excel'y G. Clinton.

A Company of Rangers for Ulster County's Western Frontier.

[To the Legislature:]* Gentlemen, I Take this Method of pre-senting to the Legislature, for their Consideration, the Memo-rial of John Beebe, Philip Frisbie, and others, in Behalf of them-selves and their Associates, Inhabitants of King's District, in the County of Albany, with a State of their Cause to which it refers.

---

*From Journal of the Legislature.

And also, a Paper, signed by a Number of the Inhabitants of Peinpack, on the Western Frontier of Ulster County, and requesting that a Company of Rangers be raised for their Protection; together with Copies of two Letters which I have received, giving an Account of some late Depredations committed by the Enemy in that Quarter.

Geo. Clinton.

Poughkeepsie, October 17, 1778.

[No. 1849.]

Washington Orders General Scott to Detail Small Parties to Protect Farmers in the Field.

(Copy)   Head Quarters October 17 1778.

Sir, You will give Orders to the Commissary of your Corps to Supply such small Parties of Militia with Provisons as Genl. Morris shall think Necessary for the Protection of the Farmers, who by their Situation are Liable to be Interrupted in their farming business, and you will Second the Militia in this Duty as much as circumstances will allow by the Disposition of your Patrolls contributing all in your Power to the Security of the Country People. I am Sir Your most ob. Servant

Geo. Washington.

Brigadier Genl. Scott near Bedford.

[No. 1850.]

PLANNING AN EXPEDITION AGAINST INDIANS.

Governor Clinton Submits a Project to the Commander-in-Chief with Rochester as the Base.

Poghkeepsie 17 Oct'r 1778.

Sir, I am favored with your Excellency's Letter of yesterday. Anaquaga lies on the Susquehanah about a West Course from

Kingston in Ulster County different Routes may be taken to it—
the first by the way of Peenpack or Minisink which is situate
on the Delaware about 40 miles west of New Windsor, the second is from Rochester 25 miles S. W. of Kingston as described
in Colo. Cantine's Letter Copy of which I inclosed in my last
to your IExcell'y. The 3d is from Schohary, which is at the
Distance of 35 or 40 miles S. W. of Albany, being the Place
at which Colo. Butler was stationed; this last Route is by the
way of Cobus Kill & Unadilla & I am informed is the shortest
and most practicable and Troops marching from thence ag't
Anaquaga may be join'd by those from Cherry Valley at Cobus
Kill or Unadilla. There are many Reasons which induce me,
however, to prefer Rochester as the Place of Rendevous for
the Troops which are now intended for the Frontier Service.
A greater Number of the Militia in that Part of the Country
may be obtained to assist in the Expedition; they are more to
be relied on than those at the other Places & the Inhabitants
in general will chearfully give every assistance in their Power.
Supplies also of Provision & Forage can be easier provided for,
and as this Place abounds in good Teams, there will be no Difficulty in convey'g any Stores than may [be] necessary from
the Land'g at Kingston (to which Place they ought to be forwarded), to the Frontier Settlem't at Rochester, and the Troops
from this & the other Posts may co-operate together by forming
Junction with much perseverance at Papachton on the East
Branch of Delaware.

Besides, by the Troops occupying 3 different Stations the principal Frontier Settlements will in some measure be guarded ag't
the Depredations of the Enemy whilst the Preparations requisite for the Expedition are making.

Your Excellency will observe that by Colo. Cantine's Letter, the Route from Rochester to Anaquaga is particularly described and that the greatest Part of it is not passable with Carriages but by Pack Horses only. A Number of Horses, tho' I think not a Sufficiency, may be procured in the Neighbourhood upon the Principles mentioned in Colo Cantine's Letter. Pack saddles & some Horses will, however, be necessary—as the Season is far advanced—it will not admit of any very formal Preparations for the Expedition, nor indeed do I conceive them to be of Consequence, as the Success of the Enterprize will in some measure depend upon its being carried suddenly into Execution. If Anaquaga was Colo. Butler's Object, as I suppose it was, Unadilla, the only intermediate Settlement being destroyed before he marched, he must have arrived at Anaquaga at the time when the Enemy were at Peenpack & of Course has been able to destroy it with little or no Opposition—but I fear the Force he had with him was not formidable enough to render it prudent to venture so far into the Country without knowing the Force there was to oppose him. If anything further occurs to me on the Subject I shall take the earliest Opportunity of transmitting it to your Excellency. I am &c.

[G. C.]

[To Gen. George Washington.]

[No. 1851.]

ORANGE COUNTY PROTESTS.

Troops Raised for that District Ordered Elsewhere—The Frontier Unprotected.

To his Excelency George Clinton Esqr. Governor and Commander in Chief of the State of New York.

The Petition of the Subscrbers Freeholders and Inhabitants of Orange County and State of New York.

Humbly Sheweth That your petitioners conceive it to be their duty to inform your Excelency that on the 23d Ulto. the Enemy Landed a large body of Troops at Paulus Hook and marched to Hackensack Bridge and Scralenburg; that the Inhabitants imediately turn'd out in Coll. Hays Regt., to oppose them and gave Information to Genl. Putnam of the Strength and Situation of the Enemy and Required assistance, and tho' we were assur'd by Letter from him of imediate help, yet he has since given us to understand that we are not to expect any from him.

That upon application to his Excelency Genl. Washington, Genl. Woodford's Brigade of 700 men was sent over to our assistance, and marched as far as the New City Court House, where they lay for a Short time and then were drawn off to New Jersey, and Coll. Hays Regt. alone left to protect the property of the Inhabitants of this State.

That the men raised by the South part of this County for the Express purpose of Defending this State and put under the Command of Major Fell has also been Stationed in New Jersey tho' raised at a great expence by the Inhabitants of this State.

That the malitia under Coll. Hay has been upon actual Service since the first appearance of the Enemy, and are worn out by the hard duty they have been obliged to perform, that many of them have not put any Winter Grain in the Ground and their Buckwheat now suffer for want of Hands to cut it; that the whole Shore from Sneden's to Kings Ferry Remains open to the Enemy, who have Several times appeared in the River with their Shiping; that Coll. Hathorn's Regt., march'd into New Jersey and after some stay there, just made their appearance at Kackeate and returned home, that the only assistance your petitioners have had from the State is about 90 men under Coll. Marvin; that the

Enemy having Plunder'd the Inhabitants in the English Neighbourhood and carried of their Grain and fforage and are now Extending their Ravages into this State, and on Monday the 29th Ulto. made their appearance at Tappan with a large Body Commanded by Cornwallis in Person, and after Butchering in a most inhuman manner a number of the Light Horse and malitia who had Surenderd themselves prisners, they turn'd their Cruelties to Women and Old men, whome they treated with every kind of Bruteality their Perfidiousness could invent; and from thence Extended their Depradations within a quarter of a mile of Clarkstown, and have Continued every day since to display in and about this State the most wanton Sceenes of Cruelty; and knowing the small number of our whole force we have every reason to expect we must unless imediately Relieved fall a Sacrifise to the Enemy, ard as we have every reason to believe that no aid will be afforded from the Continental Army.

In this Distressed Situation your petitioners think it their duty to apply to your Excelency for Relief, and to Intreat your utmost Exertions in their behalf; and Humbly pray, that imediate assistance may be given in such way as to your Excelency may seem best, and that you would use your Influence with Genl. Washington for that purpose as we cannot but Consider our selves and property in the utmost danger of being entirely Destroyed unless imediately Supported.

And your petitioners shall ever pray &c.

Andris Onderdonck, Johannes Blauvelt, Thomas Blauvelt, Cornelius Blauvelt, Abraham Blavvelt, Uyldrick Brouwer, Derick Vanderbilt, Daniel Martine, Johannis Vanderbielt, David Smith, John Coleman, William Sickels, Walter his X mark Vanorder, Jacob Onderdonck, ——— ———, Johannis Blauvelt, Abraham

Blawfelt, David Pye, Jacob Cole J. P., G. Jones, John Stagg, Sen'r, John Farrand, John D. Haring, Wm. Heyer, Martines Hogenkamp, Abraham Lamater, Barent Nangle, David his X mark Demeray, Yan Nagel, John J. Bogert, Richard Blauvelt, Thomas Cregier, Andrew Thompson, James Emmens, Henry Broadwell, Roulof Onderdunck, William Stephens, William his X mark Slutt, Jhon Poulhemeus, Handrick Poulhamous, Joseph D. his X mark Clarck, Yohannis Nagel, Resalvirt Striegansen, Gerret Onderdunck, John Montanye, Edward Salyer, James Quackinbush, Nicholas Cox, Isaac Blauvelt, Peter De his X mark pue, Andris Onderdonck, Yohanis Myer, Joseph Seaman, David Van Sickel, Aart Polhemeus, Andrew Cole, Johannes J. Blauvelt, Capt., John Hoogland, David Vanhouta, his X mark, Joseph Johnson, John Hallsed, Stephen Canpell, Jacobus de Clerck. Roger Osborn, Abram Derunder, Garret Van Cleft, Abr'm W. Van Deursen, Peter Vandervoort, Jacob King, William Nagel, William Christie, Cornelius Blauvelt, John Tinkie, John Gardner, Daniel Haring, Jacobus Ver Veelen, Tobies Derunder, John Blavelt, Gilbirt Hunt, John Onderdunck, Samuel Knapp, William Conklin, Daniel Phillips, Eli Phillips, Gibbart Phillips, Richard Dickens, Corn's C K his mark Cooper, Hendrick his X mark Derunder, Peter his X mark Crum, Gilbert his X mark Williams, Rulof Stephens, John Stagg, John his X mark Conkling, Joseph his X mark Conkling, Wiam his X mark Tilt, Francis his X mark Gurnee, Lukus his X mark Degraw, Edward his X mark Smith, John Smith, Jack Campbell, A. L. Haring, John Myer, Johannis Vandalfsen, Corn's C. Roosevelt, Jacob Arden Jun'r, John Suffern.

Oct'r 18 1778.

[No. 1852.]

Petition for the Pardon of Andrew Bois,* aged 16 years.

[No. 1853.]

Petition for the Pardon of Cornelius Tayler.*

CLINTON AND WASHINGTON COMMENDED.

Patriotic Answer of Both Branches of the Legislature to the Governor's Speech—The Governor's Replies.

†The Answer of the Senate of the State of New-York, to the Speech of his Excellency George Clinton, Esquire, Governor of the said State, General and Commander in Chief of all the Militia, and Admiral of the Navy of the same:

Sir, Distressed as we are to see this State, once more, the principal Seat of War, yet we cannot sufficiently admire and applaud the distinguished Conduct of his Excellency General Washington, and the Bravery of the Troops under his Command, in not only obliging the Enemy to adandon the State of Pennsylvania, and with it the Idea of conquering the United States of America, but also in compelling them to desist from offensive Operations, and seek Security in their strong Holds; We are happy in agreeing with your Excellency, that there is the greatest Reason to hope that this War (which a merciless Enemy have pursued with more than savage Cruelty) will be soon brought to an honorable and happy Conclusion, and the Freedom and Independence of our Country established upon a secure and permanent Basis.

Having felt, most sensibly, the Distresses of our Bretheren on the Northen Frontier of this State, we enjoy particular Satisfac-

---
* Omitted.
† From the Senate Journal.

tion in your Excellency's Assurances, that the Tranquility in that Quarter, this Season, has enabled them, in some Measure, to surmount the Evils they suffered from the last Campaign.

The Condition of the Western Frontier is truly distressing: We highly approve of the Measures your Excellency has taken for the Security of its Inhabitants, and are extremely sorry they have not been more adequate to your good Intention. But from late Information, that his Excellency General Washington intends to send Troops into that Quarter, and your known Zeal in applying the Strength of the Militia, we flatter ourselves with a Prospect of greater Security to that Part of the State.

We view, with the greatest Concern, the turbulent Conduct of many of the Inhabitants of the Northeastern Parts of this State: Convinced that a decisive Interposition by Congress, would have effectually checked it, we are surprised they have so long delayed thus to interpose: We are clearly, however, of Opinion, that should they much longer omit it, the Honour of this State, and the Safety of the Thirteen United States, will call upon us to concur in Measures to secure the Obedience of those disorderly Subjects of this State: We say the Safety of the United States, clearly foreseeing should such Practices be permitted to pass unopposed, they will stand as Precedents for turbulent and unruly Dispositions to perpetrate the like Offences in any or all of the other States; thereby gratify our inveterate Enemies by creating internal Divisions, and render the Confederation a mere dead Letter.

We are extremely happy in agreeing with your Excellency, that the properest Time for discharging our public Debts, is when the staple Commodities of this State are at the highest Prices, and that the most effectual Method to put a Stop to the encreasing

Depreciation of our Paper Currency, is a Diminution of its Quantity by Taxation: We shall, therefore, with the greatest Cheerfulness, concur with the other Branch of the Legislature in a Bill for that Purpose.

The Senate will contribute its utmost Endeavours for a Revision of the Laws of this State, and the Liquidation of the public Accounts, as Matters of the highest Concernment.

We are convinced of your Excellency's Prudence in the Public Expenditures for the Militia Service, and will cheerfully unite with the Honorable the House of Assembly in making a further legal Provision, suitable to the Nature of that Service.

Anxious for the Welfare of the State, we assure your Excellency, we shall zealously and firmly pursue the public Business, and give it all the Dispatch in our Power, consistent with its Importance.

Ordered, That the same be signed by the President.

THE GOVERNOR'S RESPONSE.

* Gentlemen, The polite Terms in which you have been pleased to express your Approbation of my Conduct, and the Confidence you repose in my Attention to the public Interest, demand my warmest Acknowledgments.

Give me Leave to assure you, that my Endeavours shall not be wanting to give Vigor and Success to every Measure for promoting the Honor and Prosperity of the State, and that I entertain the fullest Persuasion that these great Objects will invariably have their due Weight in all your Deliberations.

Geo. Clinton.

Poughkeepsie, October 22, 1778.

---

*From the Senate Journal.

THE ASSEMBLY CONGRATULATES THE GOVERNOR.

*To his Excellency George Clinton, Esquire, Governor of the State of New-York, General of all the Militia, and Admiral of the Navy of the same.

The respectful Address of the Assembly of the said State, in Answer to his Excellency's Speech, at the opening of the Session. May it please your Excellency,

We the Representatives in Assembly, of the State of New-York, beg Leave in Return, to congratulate your Excellency, on the pleasing Prospect, that, from the reduced Condition of the Enemy, the War will be speedily and honorably terminated; and consequently that our Freedom and Independence, will soon be perfectly established: And while we humbly acknowledge this Instance of the Divine Goodness, we cannot sufficiently admire and applaud the Vigilance and good Conduct of the General, and the Valour and Perseverance of the Army, who have been the happy Means of effecting these important Purposes.

With your Excellency, we sincerely lament the late Devastations on our Western Frontiers; we have Confidence, however, Sir, that you have not been wanting in your Endeavours to protect those exposed Settlements; and your Excellency may be assured, that as far as the present Circumstances of the State will admit, we will readily make further Provision for their future Safety and Defence.

It is with the greatest Concern, we learn from your Excellency, that Disorders still prevail in the North-Eastern Parts of the State—We hoped that the Inhabitants, in that Part of the Country, after the present Government of this State, had so evidently testified a Disposition to satisfy every Claim, consistent with

---

*From the Assembly Journal.

Justice; would at least have made Overtures towards an Accommodation—That from a Consciousness that they might safely have confided in us for a Redress of their Grievances, they would have relinquished the Scheme of separating from us; a Scheme so unjust with Respect to the rest of the Community, so subversive of all Government, so peculiarly injurious at this Crisis, to the common Cause of America; and if persisted in, so ruinous and destructive to themselves; for we solemnly assure your Excellency, that tho' we are willing, and we conceive we speak the general Sense of our Constituents, that the Controversy, relative to the Right of Soil, should be determined upon the most enlarged Principles; yet that we are resolved, at every Hazard, to maintain the Jurisdiction of the State, throughout the whole of its Territory—Little will avail our Resistance to a Foreign Enemy and Domination; unless we can, by inforcing a due Subordination to Government, establish Peace and good Order among ourselves.

We entirely agree with your Excellency, that the Depreciation of the Paper Currency, is a Circumstance of an alarming Nature; and that Taxation is the only effectual, and rational Remedy— From this Conviction therefore, we shall embrace every Opportunity for carrying into Execution so salutary a Measure.

The other Matters recommended by your Excellency, will receive from us that Degree of Attention, which they justly merit; and in deliberating on them, together with the other Business of the Session, we shall be influenced by a due Regard to the Interest and Honor of our Constituents, and the general Peace and Prosperity of the whole Confederation.

By Order of the Assembly of the State of New-York.

Walter Livingston, Speaker.

Assembly Chamber, October 15, 1778.

12

THE GOVERNOR'S REPLY.

*Gentlemen, I thank you for this Address; confiding in the Wisdom and Justice of the Assembly, permit me to assure you, that it shall be my constant Endeavour, effectually to carry into Execution, every Measure which may be found best calculated to promote the Interest and Prosperity of the State.

Geo. Clinton.

Poughkeepsie, October 16, 1778.

The Governor Again Addresses the Legislature.

*Gentlemen of the Legislature,

With this Message I supmit to your Consideration, the copy of a Letter† from his Excellency General Washington, dated Fredericksburgh, September 22, 1778, representing the Difficulties that attend the obtaining of a sufficient Quantity of Forage for the Use of the Army; together with Copies of two Letters, dated the 6th and 10th of the same Month, from Colonel Biddle, Commissary of Forage, and Charles Pettit, Assistant Quarter-Master General, on the same Subject; and a Representative of Royal Flint,‡ Assistant Commissary General of Purchases, containing a State of the public Magazines, and the Difficulties he labours under in procuring the necessary Supplies of Flour and Wheat, for the Consumption of the Army, together with the Copy of a Letter from the Common Council of the City of Albany, setting forth the Distresses that threaten the Inhabitants of that City, from the Conduct of Engrossers and Monopolizers of Flour and Wheat.

Geo. Clinton.

Poughkeepsie, 16th October, 1778.

---

*From the Assembly Journal.
† Not found.
‡See pages 89 and 135.

The Governor Notifies the Legislature that Congress has Advanced One Hundred Thousand Dollars.

*Gentlemen,

You will receive with this Message, an Extract of a Letter from the Honorable William Duer and Gouverneur Morris Esquires, two of the Delegates of this State, informing that they have obtained from Congress, an Advance of One Hundred Thousand Dollars,† for the Use of this State, and for which it is to be accountable. This Money, for Want of a safe Opportunity of conveying it to the Treasury, remains in the Hands of the Delegates; and it appears to me necessary that a Method should be devised for having it brought forward, or that some other proper Disposition be made of it.

For the Information of the Legislature, you will herewith also receive the Returns of Clothing,‡ now in the public Stores of this State, and of the late Issues, and the Deficiencies; with a Copy of a Letter from Peter T. Curtenius, Esquire, one of the Commissaries, which, as it points out the Inexpediency of the present Mode of obtaining Supplies, merits the early Attention of the Legislature.

A Copy of a Resolution of Congress of the 8th of September, 1778, respecting the Clothing of the Army, will also be herewith delivered you.

Geo. Clinton.

Poughkeepsie, October 17, 1778.

[No. 1854.]

General Greene Proposes an Enumeration of all the Grain in the State.

Fish Kills Oct. 21 1778.

Sir, Your Excellency is sensible how necessary it is for a General to know the resources of a Country in which he means to

---

*From the Assembly Journal.
†See Volume III, pages 460-461, 500-501, 567-570, 648, and Volume IV pages 294 and 321.
‡See page 119.

canton his Troops. I was mentioning to His Excellency General Washington the necessity of haveing an account of all the Grain taken in this State and that the best mode to effect it would be to get your Excellency to appoint proper Persons for the purpose in every Town. The General promised me he would write your Excellency upon the subject; and that he would engage the expences to be defrayed by the Public. If it meets with your Excellency's approbation I wish it may be executed as soon as possible. It is a very interesting question to the quarter master's department. In takeing the account there must be no dependance upon the information of the Proprietors; but the Persons must see and examin for themselves. All kinds of Grain should be taken into the account that will answer either for bread or Forage.

I am well perswaded from the feeble influence of money that both the Commisaries and quarter masters department will stand in need of the aid of Civil Government to procure sufficient supplies for the Army.

However, this is a question that will come upon the carpet hereafter.

The Enemy appear to be preparing for a general evacuation of New York;* and most people think they are all going off, but I cannot help thinking they will leave a Garrison. However if they should we must endeavor to serve them as they did us, drive them out by Force.

---

*The British, at New York, have embarked ten full regiments, and the vessels have fell down with them to the Hook. We have information by deserters this day that the enemy have evacuated Paulus Hook and Hoobuck; if so, they have no fort left in Jersey. They were also evacuating Fort Washington and Fort Independence; their other works without King's Bridge they had abandoned some days ago. We observed them moving off from their encampment nearest us on Staten Island this morning, whether with intent to leave the island, or settle down on some other part of it, is yet uncertain.—New Jersey Gazette, October 21, 1778.

I beg your Excellency to make my most respectful compliments to Mrs. Clinton. I am with great respect Your Excellency's Most Obedient humble Serv't

Nath Greene,* Q. M. G.

His Excellency Governor Clinton.

[No. 1855.]

Tarrytown and its Neighborhood Harassed by the Enemy.

Oct'r 21st 1778—Pokeepsie.

Sir, The Inhabitants of Tarry Town and the adjacent neighbourhood complain that they are greatly exposed to the Incursions of the Enemy, which are very frequent and distressing to them on these occasions; you will observe by the Militia Law that it is your Duty without waiting for Orders, to call into Service a sufficient Proportion of your Brigade to expel the Enemy & protect the Inhabitants, and this I expect you immediately will do, unless you can obtain from General Scott a Body of light Troops, competent for this Purpose, which I am persuaded he will readily grant you, if it can be done consistent with the good of the public Service. I am D'r Sir with great Regard Your most obed't serv't

[G. C.]

Genl. Morris.

[No. 1856.]

Governor Clinton Prepares Colonel Cantine for the Contemplated Movement Against the Indians.

Poughkeepsie 21st October 1778.

Sir, The inclosed Copy of a Letter from Mr. Deane our Indian Interpreter at Onida, I just now received by Express from his

---

*March 2, 1778, General Greene was appointed quartermaster-general by Congress and was permitted to retain his rank of major-general of the line.—STATE HISTORIAN.

Excellency Genl. Washington. The Account it contains of the Hostile Intentions of the Senecas & other Tribes of Savages, perfectly agreeing with those transmitted by Colo. Hartly from the Frontiers of Pensylvania to Congress & other Intelligence, may be relied on, and of Course we have the greatest reason to apprehend some Capital Stroke ag't our Frontier which it is our Duty by all Means to guard against. Colo. Cortlandt's Regiment are now on their March from Peeks Kill for Rochester, and I have Reason to expect my Brother's whole Brigade, which as Van Schaak's is ordered to relieve the Garrison of Fort Schuyler now consists of but 3 Regts. for the Frontier Service. It will, however, be some Time before even Cortland's Regiment can possibly reach the Frontier Settlements. I have thought it adviseable in the Mean Time, to call into actual Service on the Frontier a greater Proportion of the Militia, agreable to the inclosed Orders, Copies of which you will immediately forward by Express to the several Officers commanding Regiments of Militia in the Counties of Ulster & Orange & press their Complyance with them without the least Delay. From the inclosed Accounts Minisinck appears to me to be in the most iminent Danger & you will of Course pay particular Attention to its Safety. I have submitted your Letter respecting Provisions to the Legislature & I have every Reason to believe they will remove all Difficulties on that Score. In a little Time you will be properly supplied by Continental Commissaries. I am your most Obed't Serv't

                                                            [G. C.]
Colo. Cantine.

I have forwarded Copies of the inclosed Orders to the Comman'g Officer of the 3 Regts. of Orange County myself.

[No. 1857.]

Major Pawling Instructed by Governor Clinton to See to it that Mr.
Hake Smuggles no Goods.

Instructions for Major Pawling:

Major Pawling will proceed with Mr. Samuel Hake (who is lately come out of New York with the Flag Schooner, " Janet ") to Peeks Kill. Mr. Hake was taken on Board of a vessel coming from England to New York and had my Permission with General Washington's Pass to go into New York for the Purpose of securing his Books and accounts in the Hands of Cary Ludlow, Esqr., with such articles of Furniture as he represented were left at New York when he went Home to England. Mr. Hake is lately returned from New York with the Schooner above mentioned, in which there are Reasons founded upon his own Confession to believe, there is considerable Quantity of Merchandize which he intends to dispose off in the Country and so under Pretext of the above Indulgence make a trading voyage. Wherefore, Major Pawling, is to see that no Goods be brought by Mr. Hake from on Board the said Schooner but his Furniture, Books & accounts, together with his wearing apparel, & for this Purpose is to examine all suspected Packages & compare the Packages with the Invoice, and if it appears that any goods have been taken out, he is to make Report thereof to me and cause the Flag to be detained until my farther orders shall be received by him. But if nothing has been taken out, then after the Furniture, Books, accounts & wearing apparel aforesaid are on shore, Mr. Hake will return with the Major without being permitted thereafter to go on Board the said Schooner & strict orders be given to the Centinels to prevent any thing from being landed. And, further, Mrs. Lupton with her Servants (except male ones capable of bearing arms), is to be suffered to go on Board the said Schooner, agreeable to her Permission, and the Flag is then without the least Delay to return to New York. One Lewis who is on Board the Flag is not to be permitted to come on Shore but to return.

By orders of his Excellency Gov'r Clinton

Stephen Lush A. D. C.

Oct'r 22d 1778, Poghkeepsie.

Congress in the Cause of Good Morals.

*Gentlemen, This Message is accompanied with a Copy of a Resolution of Congress, of the 12th Instant, which, as it is intended for the Encouragement of Religion and good Morals, cannot fail engaging the particular Attention of the Legislature.

Geo. Clinton.

Poughkeepsie, October 22, 1778.

In Congress Oct'r 12 1778.

†Whereas true religion and good morals are the only solid foundations of public liberty and happiness

Resolved, That it be and it is hereby earnestly recommended to the several States, to take the most effectual measures for the encouragement thereof, and for the suppressing of theatrical entertainments, horse racing, gaming and such other diversions as are productive of idleness, dissipation and a general depravity of principles & manners.

Extract from the minutes.

Chas. Thomson secy.

---

*From Journals of the Legislature.

†This message to the Legislature is not found in the Clinton MSS. The resolution of Congress is numbered in the MSS. collection as document 1838. For the sake of unity it is subjoined to the Governor's message.—STATE HISTORIAN.

[No. 1858.]

Depositions of William Thomson and Henry Main, Relative to Colonel Butler's Expedition.

October the 22th 1778, Apeared Before me, Jochen Schonmaker, Esqr., one of the Justices of the peace for the County of Ulster, in the State of New York, one William Thomson and Henry Main Being Sworn Upon the holy Evengilist of almigty [God] Deposeth and Saith:

That on the 25th Day of Sept'r Last, they was Commanded to march from Schohary to Unidille, Under the Command of Coll. Wm. Butler, and from that to an Indian Settlement Called Auchquago, and from that to Tuskarora, which Latter they Destroyed, after which they Returned to Auchquago and Burnt and Destroyed that; from that to Unidilla which Sheared the Same fate; these Deponents further Saith that after they left Unidilla about 35 miles, they was ordered out to look for horses, and when they Returned the party they Belonged to was gone of; from thence they Whent on to Schohary Kill, Where they where informed By an officer of the Rifel men that the Company they Belonged to and two other Companies was gone Down to a place Called Cokehose, and from thence Down to the Minissings, which said Officer Ordered them to make the Best of their way to Minissing to Joyn their Company. And farther these Deponents Saith not.

The above affidavids was takeing By Request of Coll. John Contine.

                                        Jochem Schoonmaker.

To his Excellency, Gorge Clinton, Pochkepsy.

[No. 1859.]

A Proposition to Exchange Prisoners Confined at Albany.

Peekskill 22nd Oct. 1778.

Gent, Having received Orders to send into New York all the British officers, Prisoners of war, as well as the officers belonging to the New Levies now in our Possession, for which Purport have taken the Liberty of Inclosing a Return of five now residing at Albany; should there be more in your Parts either British or New Levies to have them collected, adding their Names to the Return with the Cores they belong to; a Parole I have inclosed for them to sign, which please get them to do, with the Rank they hold & Regiment; it will be necessary that they discharge their Board, and what other Debts they may have contracted, and that in hard Specie, before you send them off; when accomplished let them be ordered of immediately to Fish Kill under the Care of a proper Person to whom you'll give your Letter to be forwarded to Head Quarters; on his arrival there direct it for Colo. Beatty Commissary General of Prisoners Head Quarters or to myself as I shall then know what Rout they will be ordered in—your immediate Compliance will singularly oblige, as our own Officers are suffering in Captivity for want of theirs being sent in. I, am with much Respect Gent, Your most Obedient hum: Serv't

John Adams, D. C. of Prisoners.

N. B. their Paroles and Return don't omit inclosing. I set out to Day for Head Quarters at Fredericksburgh & shall endeavour to be if possible at Fish Kill by the Time I expect them down.

A Return of five Officers in the British Service belonging to the

New Levies taken Summer 1777 up the Mohawk River and at Saratoga and now residing at Albany.

Peter Ten Broeck, Captain, William Bowen, Lieut., Sir John Johnson's Corps;

William Schermerhorn, Capt. Coll. Jessup's Core Loyal Americans;

Peter Drummond Capt., William McCrea, McAlpin's Corps.

[No. 1860.]

*Petition for the Pardon of Bartholomew Hess.**

[No. 1861.]

OCTOBER OYER AND TERMINER.

The Judges' Report to Governor Clinton—Together With the Evidence in the Ducalon Case.

Albany October 23d 1778.

Sir, During the sitting of a Court of Oyer and Terminer and General Goal Delivery in the County of Albany the following persons have been tryed convicted and sentenced, and their Execution ordered on the sixth day of November next to wit:

Cornlius Taylor. On an Indict't for robbing Rutger Vanden Bergh. On an Ind't for stealing of him a Black Gelding; On an Ind't for robbing Cornelius Vanden Bergh; On an Ind't for robbing George White Isaac Sheldon & Abner Pease; On an Ind't for stealing three Geldings of the same persons; On an Ind't for robbing Henry Van Rensselaer; Each of these convictions were on the fullest proof.

Isaac Scouten. On Indictm't for stealing a roan Horse, and Bay mare of Isaac Fonda—upon his own confession.

Andrew Buys. On an Indict't for the same felony as last above mentioned—upon his own confession. He stands also convicted on two other Indictments, the one for stealing a Harnass & the other for stealing a woodsleigh, both within Clergy.

Bartholomew Hess. On an Indictment for robbing Harmen Coons. On an Ind't for Burglary in the House of Hend'k Mesick. On an Ind't for Burglary in the House of George Philip—Upon full proof.

Nathaniel Morgan alias John Morgan. On an Ind't for robbing Henry Van Rensselaer. On an Ind't for Burglary in theHouse of Hendrick Mesick. On an Ind't for robbing Harmen Coon. Upon full proof.

Of this number we beg leave to recommend Andrew Buys for a pardon. Because he is a Lad under seventeen years, and appears ignorant harmless and undesigning, and probably has been seduced by Isaac Scouten. His mother who is a widow in indigent circumstances, and depends on him for support.

Altho' Bartholomew Hess has been convicted for several Robberies and Burglaries, there are several Circumstances in his conduct, which operate with us in favour of mercy. We shall however only mention those circumstances, and leave it with your Excellency to determine whether he is a proper object for a pardon.

Upon his Examination at Claverack, he confessed every Robbery in which he had been concerned, and with great candor discovered his accomplices, and the persons who harboured and con-

cealed them.   Many of the unhappy sufferers, thro' his means, got
a great part of their Effects again.   Many persons there testifyed
in favour of his humanity.   That he had been instrumental in
restraining his Companions from committing greater Excesses.
We have the honour to be with the greatest Respect Your Excellency's most obt. and humble servants

Robert Yates,

Ab'm Ten Broeck,

John Barclay.

To his Excellency George Clinton Esqr.

---

*See Volume III pages 665 and 701, and Volume IV page 237.

The People of the State &c. vs. Stephen Ducalon; On Trial.

Jan V. Schaack proves the Robbery on Saturday night before easter Sunday of a small Trunk with Hard money—about 50 silver Dollars or upwards in it—800 Doll'rs Continental money, Quantities of cloathing—and sundry arms—value, and persons in the House as per Indictm't.

William Bartow, sworn, says that upwards of a week before the Robbery of Arent V. Schaack, S. Ducalon bo't a pistol of him for 5 Dollars & promised to pay him in a few days. About two hours after he bo't the pistol he returned to the House with Robt. Youngs. Youngs proposed to buy a Higland Broad sword. That he declined selling it & said he might incur blame. Ducalon urged him to sell the sword as he had other arms enough. Ducalon agreed with him for the sword for himself as he said. The price also 5 Doll'rs. At Ducalon's request he went with them to receive the money for the pistol.

Ducalon called him upstairs into his Doctor's Shop. Ducalon proposed to tell him of something would be a great Benefit to him as he was a poor man, & perhaps would be the making of him—but laid him under the most Solemn & Strict engagements not to discover it. That by many persuasions he engaged to keep the Secret. Ducalon then told him a party intended to cross the River to Philip Van Alstyne's to take his hard cash, and wanted him to steer the Batteau. That he made objections—asked who they were—that Ducalon answered that man below (meaning Youngs) would be one of them. That Ducalon urged him much on the subject, told him he need not leave the Batteau or go up from the river, only wait and bring the party back—he would receive a full share—it would be worth his going. As it blew very hard he objected, the difficulty & hard wind. Ducalon said it would be nothing to poll her up ag't the wind. That he declined to go. Ducalon paid him 5 Dollars for the pistol. They came out of the House, & Youngs with them. That Deponent said it blows hard. Youngs answered rather too fresh; that next day he saw two men well dressed go to Doct'r Ducalon's. Deponent went there soon after. Each of the two men had a pistol slung by a strap or Garter under their coats. That these two men he has since known to be John Sloss & Robert Sloss. That John Sloss wore the pistol which Depon't sold to Ducalon. That Deponent told him he knew that Pistol. That he was induced to go to Ducalon's, after saw the said two men go there as he suspected they were Continental Officers or persons in some continental employm't; that as he was coming away Elizabeth Ducalon was at the Door—he observed to her that these two men answered the Descriptions of the two men whom the people on the other side of the River were searching for. That the said Eliz. Ducalon charged him for his life not to tell that he had seen such men there.

That aftwards and about a week or some days before the Robbery of V. Schaack, Robt. Sloss about dusk one Evening, came to him armed near his the depon'ts House and ordered to go in and get his arms—swore he should get them & threatned him, —he got his arms, when he came out, five others came up armed. They ordered him to shew them the House of John L. Bronk. He went with them a part of the way—attempted to alarm them by informing them that Bronck's family were numerous & well armed. That the Dogs would alarm them. Some of them threatened to shoot the first man who drew back. That afterwards spoke to Roeloff Vander Kar one of the party whom he knew in the same manner. Vander Kar was alarmed. They stopped & conferred together, then suffered him to come up to them. Morgan spoke of getting more men. They charged him at his peril not to mention what had passed among them—they returned & separated—and Robt. Youngs and Morgan went to Step. Ducalon's.

That on the Friday Evening before Easter Sunday, he went across to the East side of Hudson's River to a smith & for some Hay. The wind [blew] so hard he did not return until Saturday Evening. Saw some of Penman's family—was desired to send word to Ducalon that his mare had been sick—it was dark when depon't got home. That some time in the night two or three Hours after he came home Robt. Sloss came to him armed & desired him put him s'd Sloss and some others over the River. Depon't fatigued & unwilling. Sloss promised to pay him well if he went & threatned him if he refused. He put on his shoes &c. went to the River Side—there came to them Stephen Ducalon the other Sloss Youngs and Morgan.

Ducalon told him these men had been to his house to be ferried over, but that he refused unless deponent with him—being asked which way they came to him at the canoe, says they came from the southward or southwestward and along a path which was the most direct road from A. V. Schaak's—and that the prisoner's house is to the northward from there & from the deponent's house.

That they put several Guns and some Bundles of Cloathing into the canoe. That he ferried them across the River.

That this was on Saturday night before Easter Sunday. That on landing he wanted his pay. One of the company ordered to give him seven Dollars. That another of them gave him immediately a Bill & told him it was a seven Dollar Bill, (but it was only a four dollar Bill and that he kept it until he shewed it to the Commissioners at Albany who said it was a good Bill). That he proposed to return home, but Ducalon insisted on going up to the House of Alexander Penman and that he would soon return with him. That he went with Ducalon to Penman's. The others remained at the Boat. That Ducalon called. Penman awaked & answered & let them in. Ducalon asked for a Candle, Penman said he had none—by Information of one of the women a piece of candle was found & alighted. That at Ducalon's desire he went to the party at the Boat & told them that Doctor Ducalon desired them to come to the House. They bro't up two large Bundles, appeared to be Cloathing—five Guns—& one of bro't a small Trunk under his arm. Ducalon with the candle went with them into the Cordwainer's shop. That Morgan in the shop had a small Trunk in his hand. That Ducalon come out and told him to go farther off from the shop—on the deponent asking the reason, Ducalon said, lest he would see more than he ought to see. Ducalon went into the shop & shut the door. Deponent heard pounding & breaking, sounded as if on the Trunk; heard ratling & Jingling like silver or hard money. Ducalon came out to him, gave him a silver Dollar—told him the company gave him that for his Trouble. Ducalon went into the shop again; some time after came out & bro't him a Gun—told him they gave him that for a fowling piece. That he refused, saying he had a good Gun but Ducalon insited on his taking & he took it. Ducalon bid him take good care of it. That Ducalon asked him to pilot the men to and over the Creek towards Meesick's & they would pay him for it—he peremptorily refused. Ducalon desired to ask Penman to pilot them. Deponent asked Penman & he refused to arise or pilot them. That they came out of the shop with several Bundles. That when they could get no pilot one of them said he could find the way himself. That some of them spoke of taking Horses. That Ducalon advised them to the contrary, & damned them and asked them would they take Horses there & make a disturbance at that side of the River also. That Ducalon had a Gun which he said he would keep; one of the company took a fowling piece & said he would take that with him—that the Deponent had one which Ducalon before bro't to him.

That there were two other Guns, which the party refused to take with them—they then offered them to the depon't, he refused them. They then said that he and Ducalon must take them & if they would not keep them they must throw them in the River. That when they were gone off, not chusing to throw the Guns in the River or carry them home, he proposed to Ducalon to conceal the four Guns, to which Ducalon agreed—they accordingly hid them under a fallen Tree on a hill in the woods. They then returned to Penman's & went into the House, and S. Ducalon told Penman that if any person enquired about his having been there, Penman should say that he came about his mare that was sick. Penman said he would give that answer. That in crossing the River homward, Ducalon told him that he believed he could find another Gun which those men had thrown away in a Slough. That he said to Ducalon he wondered where they had been. Ducalon answered a little way back here. That the next day being Easter Sunday he the deponent went again to the East Side of the River with some women. That he went alone to the Guns immediately; knew the Gun which Ducalon had the night before taken to himself to be the Gun which Jan Van Schaack shot a Goose with at the house of —— the Xtmas preceeding, and also thought that the other three belonged to Van Schaack's Family. That he removed all the four Guns and hid them in a Brush Fence. That he told Penman he had hid some Guns safely in one of his Brush Fences, but did not tell him the place.

That on the next Sunday after Easter Sunday, Ducalon came to the deponent's House. That the deponent told him that the Gun which he had hid away for himself over the River was the Gun of Jan Van Schaack with which he had Shot the Goose last Xtmas. That Ducalon replied it is the very same. That the Deponent then mentioned and also afterwards mentioned the Gun which he had said was thrown into a Slough, and proposed at each Time of mentioning that they should go together & search for it; but that the prisoner did not to that make him any answer.

That the prisoner on that day told the deponent that they would put the Guns they had hid away into a hollow log or piece of Timber and bury the Stick with the Guns in it. That the deponent did not inform the prisoner that he had removed the Guns from where they were at first secreted. That he soon after discovered the said Guns to the Committee and the said four Guns were delivered to the Committee.

Jan Van Schaak. Further examined says that the said four Guns delivered to the Committee were taken away at the time of the Robbery and have been returned to his Father & the Family. And that one of them was the Gun with which he shot the said Goose at the preceeding Xtmas.

Alexander Penman—sworn, says that Ducalon had a Horse & mare at his Farm—he was to maintain them some time & use them in his Plow. That the mare got sick. That on the Saturday afternoon preceeding Easter Sunday, he saw Wm. Bartow at Jacob Moors and desired him to tell Ducalon that his mare was sick. That he found the mare the better for riding and had that day rode to the mill with a little Grain and returned home when the sun was an hour high. That in the night Ducalon & Bartow came to his door. Ducalon called to him—he let them—Ducalon asked for a Candle. That he told him he had none. That Ducalon insisted he must have a Candle. That by the Information of one of the women a piece of candle was found for him. That the deponent alighted the Candle & gave it to Ducalon. That Ducalon went out with the Candle & ordered the Deponent not to come out of his house until he Ducalon came in again. That the deponent went to bed again.

Being asked what time of the night it was he says he does not know. That he wrought at his Trade with candle Light that night an hour and half or two Hours until he had no more candle that he knew of. That he was up some time afterwards but cant tell how long he had slept. That he heard some pounding or striking in his shop and that he afterwards heard some Jingling or noise—but did not then much attend to it as Ducalon had wagon Giers & Tacklin in the shop. That some time after Bartow called to him & asked if he would pilot four men to the Creek or over the Creek and that they said they would pay him. That he refused. That some time after S. Ducalon & Bartow came into the House. That Ducalon desired him if any person should enquire if he had been over there to say that he came to see his mare which was sick. Deponent promised to give that answer if it should be enquired about. That some time the next afternoon Wm. Bartow came to deponent's house. Enquired of Depon't if he intended to burn any of his Brush fences soon. Dep't said no, not this spring. Bartow said its very well as it is Sunday. I have hid some Guns in one of them—but gave depon't no other information. That s'd Guns were afterwards delivered to the Committee.

John Sloss. Sworn, proves the Robbery fully & perfectly—that the prisoner planned it—was their guide—that each of the company had on a division of the silver nine dollars (except Ducalon who had but eight because he had refused to go into the House but only to stand sentry) and that a silver Dollar was sent out by Ducalon to Bartow.

See Sloss Examination of the 17th August before J. M. Beekman Esqr. page 1669, & his affidavit taken by Grand Jury the 7th Instant.

On Behalf of the Prisoner at the Bar:

Johannes Spore. Sworn, asked as to prisoner's general Character & reputation says " That before this Robbery he never heard that the prisoner robbed or stole."

Matthias Goes—sworn, says the very same words.

Peter Bronk—sworn, asked as above, was about to mention some former particular charges ag't the prisoner but being prevented and enquired of as to his general reputation says " it is & has been but very indifferent." That " before this Robbery he never heard of his having robbed or stolen from any of the neighbours in the neighbourhood where he lately dwelt."

Peter Conine—sworn, says That the prisoner since he grew up to manhood lived most of his Time somewhere in the Bounds of Claverack at the west side of the River. That he did not hear of his doing any hurt in the Deponent's neighbourhood before this Robbery.

Elizabeth Ducalon—Sworn—Says that she is sister in Law to the Prisoner at the Bar. That she knows nothing of the Robbery of V. Schaak. That Ducalon was at home the Evening it is said to have happened, to wit the Saturday Evening before Easter Sunday. That Ducalon went to go over the River to see his mare some time before sundown & returned before dark. That he eat supper with his Family—went upstairs to go to bed; it was then early, it was hardly dusk—eat supper with daylight. That she went to bed soon after—she did not hear him go out again.

Being interrogated says there was another passage out of the House above, without his coming down stairs again, but then he must have gone thro a room where another woman slept—names the other woman.

N. B. This other woman subpoenad but is not attending. She says the other woman refused to attend. Says Robt. Youngs was not at Ducalon's that Evening. Says she never saw any but one Sloss there and only once. Says she does not remember to have told Bartow for his Life not to mention the Sloss's being there.

Wm. Bartow—further Examined says this Eliz. Ducalon is the woman gave him the charge above mentioned &ca. & confirms his former Testimony.

Alex'r Penman—That he returned from mill with Ducalon's mare on the Saturday afternoon before Easter Sunday about an hour before sunset—was not from his house afterwards—did not see Ducalon there nor hear he had been there until Ducalon waked him in the night as before mentioned.

John Sloss—knows the witness Eliz., has seen her at Ducalon's—says Ducalon came to them in the woods near his house about Dusk—piloted the company to Van Schaak's &ca.

Observed to the Jury—Eliz. Ducalon's Testimony reconcilable to the witnesses for the people. Ducalon might have gone out of the door of the upper house. The woman who slept in that room has refused to attend. Eliz. Ducalon prisoner's sister in Law & if the Testimony is not reconcilable she is contradicted by three witnesses as to parts of her Testimony.

Nathaniel Morgan being duly sworn the 6th of October 1778.

For Morgan's testimony see Volume III page 701.

The above is a part of the Deposition of Nathaniel Morgan wrote by William Ludlow, subscribed & Sworn to by the said Morgan before Hezekia Van Orden Esqr. one of the Justices &ca. and the same is a true Copy of part of the said Deposition or affidavit.

John McKesson.

[No. 1862.]

PUTNAM SNUBS COLONEL MALCOM.

The Colonel Appeals to the Governor and Insists upon His Rights.

Fort Clinton Oct. 23rd 1778.

Sir, Notwithstanding General Putnam thought proper to take the direction of your flag out of my hands, I hoped nothing w'd have happened to lay me under the necessity of troubling your Excellency on the Subject.

However the Vessell is returned; what went ashore below the fort I know not, but there is still a Considerable cargo remains—a number of women—Mr. Van Schaack &c. and a considerable quantity of goods. I send an Inventory of the whole as complete as possible, but as an examination on board has not been made, I doubt it is not all. I detain the whole here for your orders. Genl. Clinton is with me & joins me in opinion that these women shoud be sent back. Every kind of Policy urges the doing so. I have got all the newspapers &c. & send them. Willet has by no means followd your orders— which were to take the flag officer from me,—& Genl. Putnam orderd him off, contrary to directions I had from the Commander in Chieff—" to allow no flags to pass without his knowledge." This I know would have been got (as it was from you) on asking—but still I coud not dispense w'h the Ceremony. I send Major Stag who will relate to you the whole process. The Enemy are fond of send'g persons out, if only to disperse their papers—which I should have burnt only, that I thought it right to send them to you. Genl. Clinton thinks these people ought to be sent by the Vessel Hake came in—whether to send them at all—by Willet or w'h Hake's Sloop is for your Excellency to pronounce.

13

If I am to command at this post I insist on having the direction of flaggs. You know what I mean. You recollect the correspondence of old times. I wish not to suffer as much by it as you did. I am with the greatest Respect Your Excellency's mo. ob. serv't

W. Malcom.

[To Gov. George Clinton.]

———

[No. 1863.]

Major Paine Seizes Flour as Contraband of War—The Governor's Position.

Oct'r 23th Day 1778.

Sir, As I was Returning home I was Informd of a quantity of flower being about to be Exported out of this state; on this Information I went after said flower and found it on the Road betwen Backmens presinct and Connecticut, and Seisd said flower; the Baror Shoes an agreament betwen him self and one Mr. Wing, that Lives in this state on the Edge of Connecticut, I shall wait Your Excellency's order in the matter. I am Your Verry Humble Serv'nt

Brinton Paine.

To His Excellency, George Clinton, Esqr.

———

Poukeepsie Oct'r 24th 1778.

Sir, In answer to your Letter of yesterday, his Excellency the Governor directs me to inform you, that he has no Instructions to give you, (in consequence of the joint Resolutions of the Senate & Assembly), other than those contained in his Letter to you, accord'g to which you'l govern yourself and do what is proper on the Occasion. I am &c.

R. Benson.

Major Brinton Paine.

[No. 1864.]

MR. WILLETT EXCEEDS HIS AUTHORITY.

The Governor's Stringent Orders to Colonel Malcom in Regard to Flags.

Poukeepsie 24th October 1778.

Sir, I have received your Letter of yesterday. The inclosed Abstract of a Letter from his Excellency Genl. Washington, Copy of my Letter in Consequence thereof to Genl. Putnam, together with the Original Pass or Flagg which you can see in the Hands of Mr. Willett, will fully inform you of the Business for which the Flagg was sent into New York with the Cautions that were taken on my Part that the same shoud be carefully & properly conducted. You will observe, that it was the Commanding Officer at West Point whom I intrusted with the Appointment of an Officer to take Charge of the Flagg, & that his Excellency Genl. Washington's Permission for its passing down was previously obtained. Mr. Willett had my most positive Directions not to bring any Person on his Sloop on his Return from New York but such as coud produce my Permission to come into the Country or such of our Friends as might be exchanged. He, likewise, was forbid to bring up the least Article of Merchandize & all. Letters which he was possessed of containing Orders for that Purpose were kept back. Mr. Willett indeed, who was to be paid by Mr. Cuyler for the Service of himself and Sloop, had my Consent to receive from Mr. Cuyler in Part pay, some few Articles for his own private Use only; which I presume are those mentioned in the Certificate granted to Cuyler. Considering the Precautions which I had taken, I am much surprized to find this Flagg so basely prostituted, and am determined to have a thorough Inquiry made into this Matter;

for this Purpose Major Lush will accompany Major Stagg to your Post, & assist in collecting the necessary Evidence of the different Facts respecting this Matter, who I have directed to consult you on the Subject, & to cause all the Persons on Boat to be returned by the Flagg, except such as you shall determine ought to remain in the Country, which brought Hake up. I am Sir Your most Obed. Ser't

[G. C.]

I shall always approve of the strictest Measures you shall take in Transactions of this Nature.

[To Col. Malcom.]

[No. 1865.]

THE DISPUTE BETWEEN NEW YORK AND VERMONT.

The New York Legislature Willing to Submit the Matter to Congress for Arbitrament.

State of New York.   In Assembly Octob 24th 1778.

Whereas, the Senate and Assembly of this State did by concurrent Resolutions, passed the twenty first day of February last, propose certain Overtures with respect to the controverted Lands in the North Eastern parts of the County of Albany, and certain parts of the Counties of Cumberland, Charlotte and Glouster, in order to quiet the Disorders prevailing in that part of the State,   And, whereas, the said Resolutions have been misunderstood by some and misrepresented by others, & are deemed, not to apply to the Cases of many Persons entituled to relief, by reason whereof apprehensions still remain on the minds of many of the Inhabitants in that part of the State, and they have not in consequence, thereof, returned to their allegiance to this State within the time for that purpose in the said Resolu-

tions limited, in Order, therefore, more effectually to remove
such apprehensions and more fully to explain the said Resolutions and manifest the equitable intentions of the Legislature,

Resolved, Nem: Con: that with respect to all such Lands which
have, heretofore, been granted by the Governments of Hampshire
or Massechusets Bay and have not since been granted by the
Goverment of New York, that all such Grants under New Hampshire or Massechusets Bay shall be confirmed and declared good,
valid, and effectual to all intents and purposes, as if the same
had been made by the Goverment of New York, & shall not be
deemed null or void by reason of the nonperformance of any
Condition contained in the same.

And whereas it is impossible to establish any general principle
for the determination of all disputes that may arise between
Persons claiming under New Hampshire or Massachusets
Bay on the one and New York on the other part but each case
must be determined according to its particular merits,

Resolved, therefore Nem: Con: that in all cases of Disputes
arising between Persons claiming under New Hampshire or Massachusets Bay on the one, and New York on the other part,
for the same Lands (besides confirming such Possessions as were
made under New Hampshire or Massachusetts Bay prior to any
Grants for the same Lands under New York) the Legisature will
submit the determination thereof, to Such Persons as the Congress of the United States of America, shall elect or appoint
for that purpose, to be determined according to equity and justice without adhering to the Strict rules of Law, and will also
provide that where Persons claiming under New Hampshire,
Massachusetts Bay, or New York, shall by any such determina-
tions, or where any Person claiming under New York, shall by

reason of such Confirmations to Settlers under New Hampshire
or Massachusetts Bay be deprived of property, such Persons
shall be compensated for such Loss by Grants of other Lands,
or money in lieu thereof, according to the Equity arising out of
each particular case; Provided always, that nothing in these
Overtures contained, shall deprive any Person actually possessing Lands under New York of the Lands so by them severally actually possessed, but such persons shall be Confirmed
in their respective possessions, and the Persons claiming such
Lands under Massachusetts Bay or New Hampshire and having
equitable right to the same shall be compensated for the Lands
they may be deprived of, in consequence of Such Confirmations to
Occupants under New York in like manner as is above Specified.

Resolved, that nothing contained either in the above mentioned
or these Resolutions, shall be construed to effect any Disputes
that may arise between any Persons independent of a Claim under New Hampshire or Massachusetts Bay on the one & New
York on the other part.

Resolved, that all persons shall be intitled to the benefit of
the above mentioned or these Resolutions, notwithstanding they
may have withheld their allegiance from and been in opposition
to the Government of this state Since the first day of May last.

Provided, that no Person shall be intitled to such benefit who
shall have committed Treason against this State by adhering to
the King of Great Britain.

Ordered, that Mr. L'Hommedieu and Mr. E. Clarke carry a
Copy of the above Resolutions to the Honorable the Senate and
request their Concurrence to the same.

A true copy from the minutes.

John J. Myers, D. Clk.

[No. 1866.]

Bold Robberies in Eastern Long Island.

Poukeepsie 25th Dec'r 1778.

Dear Sir, I am favoured with your Letter of the 22d Inst. with the Representation it inclosed of abuses committed on the Inhabitants of Long Island. I have always been opposed to the Measure of sending small Parties on Long Island, (except on particular Occassions, & then under the Conduct of a discreet Officer), from a Perswasion, that our Friends were some Times plunderd by them & frequently suffered in other Respects by their Impudence. You will please to observe, that the few Commissions granted by this State, authorizes the Persons to whom they are given to exercize in the Sound only & they are not possessed of any Instruction extending the authority granted by their Commissions. Capt. Scudder has been recommended to me as a brave honnest Man by a Number of Gentlemen of Charecter & among them I think by yourself and as such I have no Doubt but he will not only meet with Justice but every Indulgence which can be given him by you, consistent with the good of the Service.

The Deposit of Money in our Treasury will not discharge a Debt due in Great Britain. The Law providing, only in Cases where the Creditor has gone over to the Enemy or being an Inhabitant of the State have volluntarilly remained with the Enemy. I am D'r Sir Your most obed't serv't

[G. C.]

Genl. Parsons.

––––––

Oct. 23d 1778 at 1 or 2 o'Clock A. M.

There came to the House of Arthur Dingee, Simeon Crossman, Isaiah Whitman and carried out of the House by Force, in hard

money £52—7—10, besides small cash, taken out of a Chest un-
known to me how much; three Dollars in congress money—at the
Same Time a pr. of Silver Knee Buckles; one pr. of Cloth
Breeches; a Hat; a peice of Bearskin; two & one half papers of
Pins; 6 Knives & forks, new; a cannister with 1½ Lb. Tea; 1 foul-
ing Peice; a p't of a Bag of Shott; Powder Horns & Powder; 2
Pocket Books, one a Leather, wrote in the double, Zophar
Wheeler.

Arthur Dingee.

Huntington South on Long Island.

Copy

Nehemiah Heart Jr. & Philip Platt both of Huntington say
that Oct'r 22d 1778, at Night, between the Hours of 11 & 12, the
House of Nehemiah Heart was besett by Eleazer Whitman &
Simeon Crossman & order me to open the Door or they would
Have it open; & then I opend the Door & then they came in &
plunderd the House of Cash & Goods to the Value of 300 or 400£
and carried them out of the Door, & was going of with them, but
found that they were known by P. Platt & Timothy Abbott; they
brought the Goods & Cash back & returnd it to me again; &
then Wm. Sammis came into the House as one of their Company,
& said their were more out of Doors, and they staid till between
the Hours of 1 & 2 o'Clock and then went off.

Nehemiah Heart.

Copy.

[No. 1867.]

THE PUTNAM-MALCOM MISUNDERSTANDING.

The Latter Places All the Correspondence Before Governor Clinton.

Fort Clinton Oct. 25 1778.

Sir, The arrival of Major Lush last evening, I imagine saved me
from an arrest by General Putnam,—The major came up to the

Flag sloop last night armed with a pass & orders to proceed to Poughkepsie from his father. For your amusement I send by Major Lush a Copy of our Correspondence.

You will observe that I endeavor'd to keep the old Gentleman from engaging in a dispute which would have added to his disgrace. I thought it was prudent and I dare hope that you will approve of my doing so. By his letters &c. it appears that he mistooke your Excellency's meaning, as well as the General's. The Greatest part of the passengers were put on shore ere the vessell got to Peeks Kill and there are very extraordinary reports on that account. Some we have dissmissd & others are returnd with Mrs. Lupton. I consider Mr. Vanschaack as a very dangerous man and indeed wish he were sent by Land to York even without an exchange, if none can be speedily got for him. I believe he is made use of as a Mercury.

I got from on board another cargo of papers & Proclamation which I have burnt. I shoud have seized the goods on board, only for the reputation of the Country & my own. I wish I had your orders concerning such Civil matters of that or any kind which may be supposed to come in my way, while on my present duty.

Major Lush has heard the storys that prevail concerning the whole Transaction but as he has not time to waite for a proper enquiry I shall write again if any of consequence are supported to deserve your notice.

I take leave to Congratulate you on the Increase of your family and am with much Respect Your Excellency's most ob. & very Hble. serv't

W. Malcom.

His Excellency Governor Clinton.

(Copy)

Mandevils 23rd Octob'r 1778.

Sir, I should be glad to know by what authority you stop the Flagg, which his Excellency Governor Clinton ordered to New York, and which was to make her Return to the Governor. His Excellency Genl. Washington ordered and Governor Clinton desired me, to give a Flagg for the Sloop to go to New York, and to put an Officer on board to conduct it down. This I did, and on her Return gave a Pass for her to proceed to Poughkeepsie and make her Report to the Governor.

If you, Sir, have not particular Orders either from Genl. Washington or Governor Clinton to stop the sloop I desire that she may have Permission to proceed. I am Sir Your hum'le Serv't

Israel Putnam.

Col. Malcom.

———

(Copy of the Answer)

October 23rd 1778.

Sir, I had no kind of intention to offend you by detaining the Flag Sloop. I nevertheless think myself justifiable in doing so and know that I must answer the consequence if I do wrong.

I have sent all the Papers, Proclamations, Letters and Passports to his Excellency the Governor and expect his Orders in the morning. I am with due Respect Sir &c.

W. Malcom.

Genl. Putnam.

———

(Copy)

Flagg Sloop 24th October.

Sir, Inclosed, I send you an Order I have just receiv'd from Genl. Putnam directing me to proceed immediately to Governor Clinton with the Sloop, that I went as a Flagg in to New York.

I consider this passport as sufficient, unless you absolutely forbid me to proceed. In that case, I think this question will remain to be solved "Whether as Commanding Officer of the Garrison at West Point, your authority is sufficient to detain a Vessel that has the Pass of a Major Genl. and positive Instructions to proceed immediately to the Governor."

I shall be glad if you will return the Instructions that I have inclosed you. I am with respect Sir Your most Obed't Serv't

D. Putnam.

Col. Malcom.

_____

(The answer)

October 24th 1778.

Sir, I every moment expect the Governor's Orders concerning the Flag Sloop which will probably decide the matter without any trouble, either to Genl. Putnam or me. However, sir, if you are unwilling to wait this evening for that purpose, you shall have my answer to your demand by the return of your next messenger. I submit the Choice to your prudence and am with respect S'r Y'r mo. Ob. Serv't

W. Malcom.

To Major Putnam on board the Flag Sloop at Fort Clinton.

_____

(Copy)

7 O'Clock P. M.

Sir, I am this moment favor'd with y'r Letter. I wish that orders from the Gov'r concerning the Flagg may arrive soon, as it is verry disagreeable for the Passengers to wait here longer than is absolutely necessary. The Wind is now fair and the Tide will serve some time this Night for us to proceed. I shall give you my Honor that nothing shall be landed from the sloop till I make a report to his Excel'y of every particular. These things all consider'd and the prospect of a Northerly Wind at this season of the year, added to our having lost our Cable & anchor in the last storm, I think will justify our proceeding when the Tide will serve. I am told that a Mrs. Davis who came up in the Flagg has reported that I landed a woman with *sealed* Letters on my way up. I think I ought in Justice to my own Reputation say, that it is an infamous Falsehood as every Person on board is willing to say upon Oath, that there was no Letters of any kind went on Shore. The woman was a poor distressed Creature who has been shut up in New York & whose Children are all in the Country—this and this only is the ground from w'h that Woman has made such a false representation. I am with great Respect Sir Your most Obed't

D. Putnam.

P. S. The Husband of the woman above mentioned is now confined in New York and is as hearty a friend as any there.

D. P.

(True Copy)

The bearer Major Putnam my Aid De Camp has Permission to pass under sanction of a flag to New York, for the purpose of conducting thither the Families & Effects of Henry Cuyler, Mr. Dole & Mr. White. He will also take under his care the British flag now in the River and Conduct that to the first British post on the North River.

Given &c. 9th Octob'r 1778.

Israel Putnam, M. G.

(A true Copy)

Sir, You will immediately proceed to Poughkeepsie and make y'r Report to Governor Clinton of your proceedings at New York during the time you were at New York under the protection of the Flag sent in at the Request of Gov'r Clinton and this shall be y'r sufficient passport.

Israel Putnam, M. G.

Highlands 24th Oct. 1778.

To Major Putnam.

[No. 1868.]

GEORGE CLINTON'S OLD SOLDIERS APPEAL.

Exchanged Troops Captured at Fort Montgomery Ask for Arms, Wages and Rations Due Them.

To his Excellency George Clinton Esq. Governour &c of the State of New York.

Worthy Sir, We the Subscribers hereof, being of the Number of those who had the Misfortune to be taken Prisoners at Fort Montgomery, and lost our arms at that fatal Time, which renders us unfit for the further Service of our Country, now when we are return'd, And, therefore, have presumed in this manner to apply to your Excellency that we may be supply'd with Arms; and also receive our Wages, Rations, due. And we trust your Excellency will take our Case into your Consideration, and grant such relief in the Premises, as to your Excellency may seem meet. We conclude in the most profound respect, Worthy Sir,

Your most Obed't Humble Serv'ts

John Darcos, Serjt.,	Andrew Willson,
Cornelius Slote, Serjt.,	Eliphant Seers,
William Humphrey,	John Vanorsdall,
George Humphrey,	Robert Cooper,
James Humphrey,	Robert Wool,
William Stinson,	James Wood,
Robert Henry,	James Miller,
John Blakeny Carmichael,	John McMullen,
Moses Contine,	William Scoat.

Of and belonging to Coll. James McClaghry's Regt. of Militia
foot, in Ulster County, who was taken Prisoners of War at Fort
Montgomery, who was exchanged by Cartel, at New York, August
6th, 1778:
26th October 1778.

John Darcos, Serjt. Cornelius Slote, Serjt. William Humphrey,
George Humphrey, James Humphrey, William Stinson, Robert
Henry, John Blakeney Carmichael, Moses Cantine, Andrew Willson, Eliphant Seers, John Vanorsdal, Robert Cooper, Robert
Wool, James Wood, James Miller, John McMullen and William
Scot, Privates all of Colo. McClaughry's Regiment of Militia being made Prisoners at the taking of Forts Montgomery & Clinton
by the Enemy, and having there lost all their arms, & since
suffered a long Imprisonm't, and being now unprovided with
arms, and not having received their Pay and Rations for their
Services, are to be exempted from ordinary Militia Drafts until
steps can be taken to provide them with arms and their Pay
and Rations rec'd for their past Services.   Given at Poghkepsie
Oct'r 27th 1778.

By order Stephen Lush.

[No. 1869.]

Leniency to be Shown Prisoners for the Time Being.

Gentlemen, This will be handed to you by Mr. Van Schaack
who is returned from New York, without having been able to
affect an Exchange for himself and the other Gentlemen confined
at Albany.   I am informed, however, and have Reason to believe,
that our State Prisoners are not now treated with the same Degree of rigor which they formerly experienced, and as it is not
my Desire to increase the Distresses of Individuals by Close &

rigorous Confinement, only when it may become necessary by Way of Retaliation, which is a Rule I mean strictly to adhere to, I have, therefore, to request that you will cause Mr. Van Schaak with the other Prisoners for Exchange, to be placed in such Mild Confinement, either by Parole to a certain limitted District, not being their former Place of Residence, or to a Room as you shall judge most consistent with Prudence & safety, until their Exchange can be effected, or Contrary Usage to our Friends in New York may render different Treatment necessary & Justifiable. I am &c.

[G. C.]

I, Henry Van Schaack, Esqr., Prisoner, do promise that I will proceed immediately to Albany, and deliver myself up to the Commissioners for detecting Conspiracies, &c., there, and abide their farther order.

Given under my Hand at Poghkeepsie Oct'r 26th 1778.

H. V Schaack.

Test:

[No. 1870.]

The Alleged Infractions of the Saratoga Convention.

Albany October 26th 1778.

Sir, Upon my Return to Town, this Evening, I found Mr. Swart had procured Major Frey to give an Account of the Enemy's procedure respecting the Conventionists. His Affidavit* I do myself the Honor to inclose.

Several persons who are now in the Neighbourhood of Stilwater, and who have recently left Canada can corroborate Major Frey's Information, but apprehensive of being committed, they will with Difficulty be persuaded to make Depositions. Mr. Swart

*Not found.

will take Measures to induce them to meet him and I propose to go up on Monday to assist in taking their Affidavits, which will be transmitted to your Excellency as soon as possible.   I have the Honor to be Respectfully Sir Your most obedient & very hble. Servant

                                                  J. Lansing, Jun'r.
His Excellency, Governor Clinton &c.

[No. 1871.]

Associated Exempts in Albany County.

                                    Albany the 27 Octob'r 1778.

Sir, The Association alledged to in Mr. Visscher's Letter in-closing your Excellency an association in which we ware recommended as Officers has been compleated, and the associators have also Elected Us as their Officers.   A Recommendation of as many of them as ware in Town and could Conveniently meet, Your Excellency will find inclosed together with a Return of those that have associated.

We beg your Excellency will forward our Commissions as soon as Conveniently may be.

We have the Hon'r to be y'r Excellency's most Obed't Serv'ts Corn's Van Santvoordt, David Groesbeeck, Marte Myndertse.
To His Excellency George Clinton, Commander in Chief of the State of New York, Poghkeepsie.

A Return of the Associated Company in the City of Albany Commanded by Capt Corn's Van Santvoordt.

Capt.	Lieuts.	Sergt.	Corp'ls	Privates	Total
1	2	4	4	41	52

Albany the 8 Octo'r 1778.

Corn's Van Santvoordt, Capt. David Groesbeeck, Lieut. Marte Myndertse, Lieut.

We, the Subscribers, having agreeable to an Act of the Legislature of this State for regulating the Militia thereof, associated ourselves and having Elected the following Gent., to be our Officers, to wit Corn's Van Santvoordt Capt., David Groesbeeck & Marte Myndertse Lieuts., do hereby Recommand them to be Commissioned accordingly; and we do hereby farther request our said Officers to transmit this our Recommandation together with a return of our said Company to his Excellency Governor Cinton with all Convenient speed.

William Verplanck, Wouter Deforest, Anthony E. Bratt, Saml. Pruyn, Teunis Bradt, Jellis Winne, Paul Hogstrasser, Isaac Van Aernam, Isaac Verplanck, Jacob Bleecker, John Roseboom, Jr. Casparus Pruyn, John J: Bleecker, Henry Merselis, Jocghem Js. Staats, Thomas Lansingh, Thomas Barrett, Isaac Freyer, Johannis L. Reddli, B. Visscher, Jonathan Pettet.

[No. 1872.]

Major John Frey Makes a Brief Affidavit Relative to the Breach of the Saratoga Convention.

Albany 27th Oct'r 1778.

I am directed to enclose to your Excellency Extracts of the Indictments whereon Andrew Buys was lately convicted and sentenced—also a Copy of one of his Examinations.* Some other papers and extracts relative to the other prisoners lately convicted and sentenced are also enclosed.

Major John Frey of Tryon County arrived here yesterday and tarried in Town about two Hours—he was in great Haste however I obtained a short affidavit of him before the mayor, in substance that after the Resolutions of Congress preventing the

---

* Omitted.

14

Embarkation of Gen. Burgoyne's Army, General Carlton published a proclamation requiring all persons who had been included in that Convention to join their respective Corps and Regiments and hold themselves no longer bound by the Convention. Major Frey said he read a Copy of the proclamation frequently, & bro't a printed Copy into New England.

Major Lansing last Evening took the affidavit, informed me he was directed to procure proof that nature, and would transmit it to your Excellency. I have sent for it repeatedly this morning and hope to detain the Bearer until it may be obtained & sent to you by him.

I wish you Joy of a son—my most respectful compliments wait on Mrs. Clinton. I have the Honor to be Sir Your most obedient humble Serv't

John McKesson.

His Excellency Governor Clinton.

[No. 1873.]

An Indian Uprising Reported from Rochester.

Sir, Major Wynkoop just arrived here, from Rochester informs me that the Inhabitants on the Frontier are greatly alarmed by accounts of the approach of a considerable Body of the Enemy under Brandt, who have advanced as far as Coshicting and expect a Reinforcement there from the Seneca Indians. If it is possible you will, therefore, cause your Regiment to be marched there without Delay where as Major Wyncoop acquaints me they will be provided with Shoes and Stocking by the Inhabitants.

Your Compliance with this Request will greatly oblige the Country as it will probably tend to the Safety and Protection of a most valuable Part of it. I am &c.

[G. C.]

Oct. 27th 1778.

Colo. Cortlandt.

Edm Burke.

[No. 1874.]

Militia Reported to be Short of Ammunition—The Governor's Quick Response.

Kingston, Oct'r 27th 1778.

Sir, It is with concern that we are reduced to the necessity of representing to your Excellency a matter which ought to flow from a Different Quarter—and as we are daily allarmed with accounts of the Enemies approach towards our Froniers, we conceive it our duty to inform your Excellency that it has been represented to us that the militia late Ordered out are destitute of ammunition, particularly that Detachment now lying at Shandaken have, as we are informed, sent down for a Supply of that necessary article, and have not been able to procure more than about three Pounds of Cartrages, which has provoked the Men stationed there, to such a Degree, that they openly declare that they will quit that post whenever the Enemy shall appear.

This, Sir, is a matter that gives us such concern, that we hope it will require your attention, which will be greatfully acknowledged by Sir Your most Obed't Humb'e Serv'ts

Christopher Tappen in behalf of the Trustees of Kingston.

His Excell'y Gov'r Clinton.

———

Oct'r 28 1778.

Gentlemen, It gives me great Pain to find that a scandalous Neglect of the Officers whose Duty it is to see that the Militia is properly provided with ammunition shoud have occassioned you the Trouble of addressing me on that Subject. I have now issued an order in Favour of Colo. Snyder's Regt. on the Commissary of Military Stores & I am determined to prevent you the like Trouble in Future by calling the Delinquents to a most severe account. I am &c.

[G. C.]

To the Trustees of Kingston.

[Nos. 1875–1877–1880.*]

THE DISPUTE WITH VERMONT.

Further Legislative Deliberation on the Subject—The Governor Directed to Issue a Proclamation.

State of New York.   In Senate Oct'r 27th 1778.

The Senate proceeded to the consideration of the Resolutions of the Honorable the House of Assembly of the 24th Instant respecting the Disorders in the north eastern Parts of this State. The first of the said Resolutions being read and the question put whether this Senate do Concur therein, it was carried in the affirmative:

Resolved, therefore, that this Senate do concur with the Hon'e the House of Assembly in the first of their said Resolutions.

The second of the said Resolutions being read & the question put thereon it was carried in the negative.

Resolved, therefore, that this Senate do not concur with the Honorable the House of Assembly in the second of their said Resolutions.

The third of the said Resolutions being read and the question put, thereon, it was carried in the affirmative.

Resolved, therefore, that this Senate do concur with the Honorable the House of Assembly in the third of their said Resolutions.

The fourth or last of the said resolutions being read and the question put thereon it was carried in the negative.

Resolved, therefore, that this Senate do not concur with the Honorable the House of Assembly in the fourth or last of their said Resolutions.

Ordered, that Mr. Scott and Sir, James Jay, be a committee to prepare and bring in Resolutions to be substituted in the stead of those, of the above mentioned Resolutions of the Honorable the House of Assembly, in which this Senate do not concur.

---

*For the purpose of making a consecutive chapter, documents 1877 and 1880 are consolidated with document 1875.

Oct'r 28th P. M.

Mr. Scott from the Committee for the Purpose appointed reported the following resolutions (to be substituted in the stead of those of the Hon'e the House of Assembly of the 24th Instant in which this Senate do not concur) which were read and agreed to viz.

"And, whereas, it is impossible to establish any general Principle for the Determination of all Disputes that may arise between Persons claiming under New Hampshire or Massachusets Bay on the one and New York on the other part But each case must be determined according to its particular Merits.

Resolved, therefore, if the Honorable the House of Assembly concur herein, that in all cases of Disputes arising between Persons claiming under New Hampshire or Massachusets Bay on the one, and New York on the other Part for the same Lands, besides confirming such Possessions as were made under New Hampshire or Massachusets Bay prior to any Grants for the same under New York, the Legislature will submit the Determination thereof to such Persons as the Congress of the United States shall elect or appoint for that purpose to be determined according to Equity and Justice without adhering to the strict Rules of Law. Provided always that nothing in these overtures contained shall deprive any persons actually Possessing Lands under New York of the Lands so by them severally actually possessed but such Persons shall be confirmed in their respective Possessions.

Resolved, in case of the like Concurrence that all Persons shall be entitled to the benefit of the above mentioned and these resolutions and those of the hon'ble the House of Assembly of the 24th Instant wherein this Senate has concurred notwithstanding they may have withheld their allegiance from and been in opposition to the Government of this State since the first Day of May last Provided that no Person shall be entitled to such Benefit who shall have committed Treason against this State by adhering to the King of Great Britain.

Ordered, that Sir James Jay, carry a Copy of the aforegoing Resolutions together with a Copy of the proceedings of this Senate (of the 27th Instant) on the Resolutions of the Hon'ble the House of Assembly of the 24th Instant, to the hon'ble the House of Assembly.

A true Copy from the minutes. Robt. Benson, Clk.

A true copy from the minutes. John J. Myers, D. C'k.

State of New York.   In Assembly October 30th 1778.

The House proceeded to the consideration of the two Resolutions of the Honorable the Senate of the 28th Inst. respecting the disorders prevailing in the North Eastern parts of this State, thereupon

Resolved, that this House do concur with the Honorable the Senate in the said two Resolutions:

Resolved, (if the Honorable the Senate shall concur herein), that his Excellency the Governor be requested to Issue his Proclamation, to Contain the substance of the Concurrent Resolutions of both Houses, passed in this present Session, relative to the Disorders prevailing in the North Eastern parts of this State, and to cause such proclamation to be published & distributed throughout those part of the State, and employ Persons for that purpose; and that the Legislature will defray the Expense thereof, and that his Excellency in such Proclamation be authorized to pledge the Faith of the Legislature of this State for the faithfull Performance of the several matters contained in the said concurrent Resolutions, and require all Persons to take notice thereof, and to Govern themselves Accordingly.

Ordered that Mr. Honeywell & Mr. Baker carry the above Resolutions to the Honorable the Senate.

A true copy from the minutes.

John J. Myers D. Clk.

State of New York.   In Assembly Octob: 31st 1778.

A message from the Hon'ble the Senate by Mr. Smith was read, and is in the words following, to wit,

" State of New York.   In Senate Octob. 31st 1778.

" Resolved that this Senate do concur with the Hon'ble the House of Assembly in their Resolution of Yesterday requesting his Excellency the Governor to issue his Proclamation to contain the Substance of the concurrent Resolutions of both Houses passed in this present session relative to the Disorders prevailing in the Northeastern parts of this state and to cause such Proclamations to be published & distributed throughout those parts of the State and employ Persons for that purpose and that the Legislature will defray the Expence thereof, And that his Excellency in such Proclamation be authorized to pledge the Faith of the Legislature of this state for the faithful performance of the several matters contained in the said concurrent Resolutions & require all Persons to take notice thereof & to govern themselves accordingly.

" Ordered that Mr. Smith carry a Copy of the aforegoing Resolution to the Hon'ble the House of Assembly.

"A true Copy from the minutes.

" Robt. Benson, Clk."

A true Copy from the minutes.

John J. Myers D. Clk.

[No. 1876.]

Petition for the Pardon of Stephen Ducalon. *

[No. 1877.]†

[No. 1878.]

Returns of Major Fonda's Corps of Militia at Schoharie.

A WEEKLY STATE OF THE MILITIA AT SCHOHARY UNDER THE COMMAND OF MAJOR JOHN FONDA 30TH OCT'R 1778.

Regiments	Officers present fit for Duty								Rank & File							
	Field	Commiss'd			Staff		Non Commiss'd									
	Major	Captains	Lieutenants	Ensigns	Adjutants	Q Master	Serjeants	Drum & Fifer	Present fit for duty	Sick Present	Sick absent	Absent with leave	Absent without leave	Confin'd at the middle fort	On. Command	Total
Col. Stephen Schuyler's	1	1		1			2		14							14
Col. Philip Schuyler's		1	1				4		26				1		1	28
Col. Lansing's		1			1	1	3	2	24			1			2	27
Col. Rensselaer's		1	2				4		12	1						13
Col. Quackenboss		1					2		14							14
Col. Wempel's		1	1		1		4		33						2	35
Col. Vroman's		1	1				3	2	34					1	3	38
Total	1	5	7	2	2	1	22	4	157	1	—	1	1	1	8	169

Lieut. Phlemsburgh of Col. Quackenbush Regiment abs't with leave.

John J. Fonda Major.

[No. 1879.]

The Albany Conspiracy Commissioners Decline a Peculiar Request.

Albany 30th Oct. 1778.

Sir, Mr. Volckert P. Douw, Mr. Harmon Gansevoort and six other Gentlemen applied to us this Day in Behalf of theselves

*Omitted.
†See page 212.

and several other Gentlemen of this City, to permit Mr. Henry Van Dyck and the other Persons, late Inhabitants of this City, by us removed within the Enemies Lines, to return to their respective Places of Abode, under such Restrictions as we might think proper, except taking the oath prescribed for neutral Characters; upon their being informed that were we even inclined thereto, no such Power was vested in us, and that their application ought to be to the Legislature, they requested us to lay such their application before your Excellency, which we have hereby the Honour of doing.

Those Gentlemen further requested, in Case Mr. Van Dyck could not be permitted to return that Mrs. Van Dyck and her Sister Miss Rachel Douw might be permitted to go in and see him and return. We have the Honor to be Your Excellency's most Ob't Serv'ts: Mat Visscher, Isaac D. Fonda, John M: Beeckman. His Excellency Gov'r Clinton.

[No. 1880.]*

More Money Required for the Five Continental Battalions.

†Gentlemen, As the Monies, heretofore granted by the Legislature for supplying the five Continental Battalions, raised under the Direction of this State, with Necessaries, are nearly expended; I have to recommend that a further Provision be made for this Service: A Letter from Mr. Currie, on this Subject, will be herewith delivered to you for your better Information.

I also, with this Message, refer to the Consideration of the Legislature, sundry Pay-Rolls for Services performed by the

*See page 212.
† From Journal of the Legislature.

Militia, at the Request of the Civil Magistrate, which, however, reasonable they may appear to be, I do not conceive myself authorised by Law to discharge.

Geo. Clinton.

Poughkeepsie, October 31, 1778.

———

[No. 1881.]

Contractor Lewis Appeals to Governor Clinton Because Lumber Dealers have Doubled their Price.

Albany 28th Octo'r 1778.

I am under the Necessity of Troubling your Excellency on a Subject, which tho disagreeable, of sufficient importance to justify my application. Some few weeks since I received orders from the Quarter Master Genl., to purchase all the Boards that could be procured within my Department, for the purpose of Building Barracks at Fish Kill for the Reception of the Soldiery. When I first entered upon this Piece of Business the Proprietors sold their Boards to my agent at two Shillings and their Plank at Three, delivered at the Mills. But soon as they discovered the Great Demand these articles were in, and the Necessity I was under of Purchasing them, they took a base advantage of the Necessities of the Public, and at a meeting held for the Particular purpose, advanced immediately One Hundred P Cent on the Prices afore mentioned, Vizt.: four Shillings for Boards, & Six for Plank. By advice of the Quarter Master General, I have offered them Three Shillings and four Shillings & Six Pence, imagining that fifty P Cent advance at one Step was a Generous allowance, and sufficent to satisfy any Reasonable person. Buf they have absolutely refused to accept of it, and thereby put me under the Necessity of requesting your Excellency to lay the

Matter before the Legislature who I am Satisfied will do Justice to all Parties. I am With sentiments of Esteem & Respect Your Excellency's Most Obt. Serv't

M. Lewis.

His Excellency Geo. Clinton.

Pokeepsie Nov'r 1st 1778.

Sir, I rec'd your Letter of the 28th Ult. but as the Legislature are now preparing to adjourn it will answer no End to lay your application before them. The Practices you complain of, in the Proprietors of Board &c. meet'g together & confederating to secure their Prices are certainly unjust and injurious to the Public but I know of no Method at present, you can adopt, but that of agreeing with them for their Boards at the lowest Rate you can obtain them for. They are Merchants and as the Demand for their Commodities increases so will their Price. I am &c.

[G. C.]

[To Col. Lewis.]

[No. 1882.]

Tribulations of Numerous Tories—The Albany Commissioners to Governor Clinton.

Albany 2nd Nov'r 1778.

Sir, We yesterday received a Letter from Mr. Adam, Deputy Commissary of Prisoners, inclosing a Return of Five Officers of the New Levies confined in Goal and in and about this City; a Copy of the Letter and Return your Excellency will find inclosed.

As the Persons mentioned in the Return are in a peculiar Situation we think it our Duty before we send them down to state their Situation to your Excellency and to wait your Directions on the Subject.

Peter Ten Broeck is an Inhabitant of Tyron County and did go over and join the Enemy after the Declaration of Independance.

William Bowen the same.

William Schermerhorn is an Inhabitant of this County and in the spring 1777 enlisted several Persons for Howeston's Regiment and in the Summer carried Intelligence to and from Burgoyne's Army.

Peter Drummond came over from Scotland in 1774 lived with Capt. McAlpine at Saragtoga Lake, and with him in the Spring 1777, went over to and joined the Enemy; he and McAlpin enlisted divers of the Subjects of this State and took them to Crown Point.

William McCrea is an Inhabitant of this County and in the summer 1777 when General Burgoyne came to Fort Miller, he went over to and joined his Army and has since been indicted for high Treason.

Besides those above mentioned we have in Goal a certain Zadock Wright; his Situation will appear from the inclosed Copy of an Order of the Council of Massachusetts Bay we think it necessary to observe to your Excellency that the Removal of this Mr. Wright from Northampton to this Place has cost us £36—0 and should be happy to be informed in Case of an Exchange whether he or the continent is to pay the Expence.

We also inclose your Excellency a List of Persons that have applied to us for Leave to go to New York, their Situation we have pointed out opposite their Names.

Mr. John Cumming has most earnestly requested us to be permitted to go to Fish Kill where he will remain until such Time as his Exchange is effected. The Reason he assigned for this application is the advanced Season and the Difficulty that may arise in getting his Family down in about a Fortnight's Time; he has also requested us to transmit to your Excellency Copy of a Letter he has received from Lieut. Colo. Campbell and a Transcript of his Exchange.

Mr. Robert Adams has also most earnestly entreated us to write to your Excellency to permit his Daughter Mrs. Mulligan to come out of New York and if that could not be granted to permit him to send in her Cloaths. We have the Honour to be Your Excellencies most Hum: Servants,

Mat: Visscher, Isaac D. Fonda, John M. Beeckman.

His Excellency, Gov'r Clinton.

[No. 1883.]

Jane Blauvelt Applies for a Pass for Three Blauvelt Men in New York.

Tappan, Novmbr 2d 1778.

To his Excelliancey, Governor Clinton:

S'r, Thier has bin Information made To me by Some of the Prisinor Relived, their is now Left in the City of New York three men, Daniel Blauvilt, Son of John Blauvilt, Daniel Blauvilt, Son Abraham Blauvilt, Handrick Blauvilt, Son of Abraham Blauvilt, who has Bin Deluded away By the Enemy; Do Humbly Pirtion to your Excellancey for Pardon, to Return To their Respect'd Home, In Tappan, To their Parent; Do Begg the Grant of a Pass By the Barrer, If it is your Excellencey Pleasure To.

Jane Blauvilt.

Tappan Noumbr 2d 1778.

The Humble Pertion of Margret Blauvit:

To His Excellencey Governor Clinton: S'r A Child if mine has bin Taken away of Six Years Old by Abraham Lent, for which

Effection Obligates me to Begg of your Excellencey for a Pass
to Git Reliefe for my Child to his Respect'd home at Tappan.

John Bell Capt.

[No. 1884.]

Governor Trumbull of Connecticut Asks for Flour for His Troops.

Stanford November 2d 1778.

Sir, Inclos'd I Send your Excelency a Letter* from his Excellency Govenor Trumble, To Beg the Favour that you will give me
a permit To Bring out the within Mentioned flower & Wheat as
the Troops are in Great Distress for it,   Should have waited
upon your Excellency my Self, but the Malitia are Comeing in So
fast to the Sawpitts, it is out of my power to Leave home,   I
Trust your Excellency will Send the permit by the Bearer, Mr.
Jonathan Weed, as Readily as if I was there my Self,   Should he
Not Obtain a permit, the Troops must Return home.   Your Excellency's Compliance with the Above Request will Greatly
Oblige the Publick & your humble Servant.   I am with Respect
Your Excellency's most Obedient Humble servant

Daniel Gray, D. C. P.

To Governor Clinton in New York State.

[No. 1885.]

WILLIAM BUTLER'S SUCCESSFUL EXPEDITION.

*His Destruction of Two Indian Settlements—His Interesting Account
from His Journal Filed with Governor Clinton.*

May it please your Excellency, The 16th Instant, I returned
from my expedition against the Indian Settlements, & shoud
before have acquainted your Excellency with the event of it, but
have been exceedingly Indisposed ever since, and conceive you

----

*Not found.

must have heard of it from Genl. Stark. I have inclosed your Excellency an Account extracted from my Journal, & Hope it will meet with your Excellency's Approbation; as I am well convinced that it has sufficiently secured these Frontiers from any further disturbances from the Savages at least this Winter; and it will be ever, hereafter, difficult for them to distress these parts, By reason of their having no Settlements near. But I imagine that the Frontiers of Jersey & Pennsylvania will be more liable to be annoyed by them. The Naked situation of my troops, with the Badness of the weather on our march & a scarcity of Provitions occasioned the march to be very difficult & disagreeable.

As perhaps some things worth remarking, may have escaped my memory, I refer your Excellency to the Bearer, the Rev. Doctor Jones, who was with me on the Expedition.

I have enclosed your Excellency a return of the Troops at this place, with also one of those Troops I had with me at Onoghquaga. I remain Y'r Excellency's very H'ble Serv't

                                                    Wm. Butler.
Schohara, Octob'r 28th 1778.

N. B. Two Families which I let remain at the Unadilla Settlement in Consequence of their having engaged to attend at this place, the 25th Instant, came in agreeable to their Engagements, But have heard nothing of the Enemy since.

                                                    W. B.

                Extracts from Lt. Col. Butler's Journal.*
Date
1778.   Day
        October 1st: As I intended Marching the next day, I dispatched Lieut. Stevens with 12 men & a Sub., and 16 of the Militia to the frontiers of the Settlement to guard the Roads and Passes to the Enemy, to prevent any Intelligence being carried them.

---

* Colonel Butler's Journal was printed by order of Congress.—STATE HISTORIAN.

Oct'r 2nd: I marched the Troops consisting of the Rifle Chore, 4th Pensylv'a Regt., and 20 Rangers, with 6 days Provision on their back and 5 days Provision on Pack Horses. March'dt this day 12 miles to one Maticus, nothing material happening.

October 3rd: March'd early this morning; arrived at Mr. Sawyer's on the Head of Delaware, being 15 miles; Rainy, Disagreeable, W'r and very bad Roads.

October 4th: The W'r being clear about 10 o'Clock marched to Cawlys down the Delaware 10 miles.

October 5th: Proceeded down the Delaware 15 miles then leaving the Delaware struck across the Mountains for the Susquehanna this day march'd 18 miles.

October 6th: Marched early this Morning; at Dusk arrived within 8 miles of the Unidilla settlement. I then detach'd Lieuts. Stevens and Long with small Parties to make Prisoners of some of the Inhabitants who liv'd within 4 miles of the Unidilla. I then continued my march in the Night, in order to lay conceal'd, within a small distance of the Settlem't & make the attack early in the Morning, but after having March'd about 7 miles, met the Parties, who I had detach'd with one Prisoner; he told me that the Enemy had left that place some days before and were gone for Anohoghkwage which is about 30 miles lower, this day march'd 25 miles.

Oct'r 7th: Early this Morning I detach'd Lieut't Stevens, with a few men to Unidilla to make Prisoner of one Glasford, who I intended shou'd guide me to Anohaghkwage; this he effected, & after the Troops had cook'd their Provisions, & refresh'd themselves a little, I march'd 5 miles beyond Brandt's Camp—having cross'd the Susquhanna 3 times,—about 2 miles below the Castle, at the Mouth of the Unidilla, which is the third crossing, my ad-

vanc'd Party discovered a fresh Tract of a Man, who I imagin'd
had been left by the Enemy, to give them the earliest intelligence
of any of our Movements. I immediately sent out three Runners
who follow'd the Track about 8 miles, when Night coming on they
were obliged to Return. I then order'd off Lieut't Stevens about
10 o'Clock at Night, to Recontroitre the Country ab't Anahaghkwage, and meet me the next day with accounts.

Oct'r 8th: About 2 o'Clock this Morning there came on a very
heavy rain which put me in a very horrid Situation, being in the
Woods without any Possibility of the Men's keeping their arms or
Ammunition secure—you'l judge my fear of the River's rising, so
as to hinder my advancing or retreating; about 8 o'Clock A. M.,
the weather cleared, and having the Arms clean'd, I continued my
March; about 3 or 4 miles from Anahaghkwage I met Lt. Stevens,
who gave me as good a description of the Place as he was able,
from the adjacent Mountains to discover—the Susquehanna being
between me and Anahaghkwage; I thought it more proper to
cross in the Night & attack the Town—As I had every reason to
Expect they wou'd ambuscade me in crossing, where they had
great advantage of me; the River 250 yds. wide, and almost to the
armpits of the Men; we had a Hill a mile long to ascend, thick
Woods and Logs; I for that purpose ordered the 2 Companies of
Rifle Men, to March in front & attack the Flanks, with the Musquetry, with fixt Bayonents charge the Centre; in this order I
cross'd the River and took Possession of the Town about 11
o'Clock at Night without interruption; the Enemy having that day
left the Town, in the greatest Confusion, & at least 2000 Bush'ls
of Corn, a Number of Horses, Cattle, Poultry; their Dogs, houshold furniture, &c. &c. It was the finest Indian Town I ever saw;
on both sides the River; there was about 40 good houses, Square

logs, Shingles & stone Chimneys, good Floors, glass windows &c. &c. On my taking Possession of the Town, I order'd a large Number of fires to be made, in order to make my little Party, loom as large as Possible; lay on our Arms and at daybreak, had my Bugle Horn blown, when all got under Arms.

October 9th: Major Church with a Party went over the River, as part of their Settlements are on both sides, and burnt that Part of the Settlement, consisting of 10 good Houses, and a large Quantity of Corn, & brought off some Cattle, Some of the Pack horses having stray'd some distance from the Town, the Keepers went in quest of them, & contrary to my Positive orders, went without their Arms, on going about ½ Mile from the Party, they were fired on, & one of them was Shot through the Side & through the Brains; yet liv'd till we brought him within 40 miles of this Place, As soon as I heard the Discharge of the Guns, I march't my whole Party to the Place, with all my horses and Baggage in the Rear, as if I intended marching right down the River & I am well convinc'd, Brandt & all his Forces were not far from me. I judg'd by their Manuver, it woud carry of all their Spies & Scouts, which I believe had the desir'd effect for we was not disturb'd on our Retreat; while I lay with the Main Body conceal'd in the Woods, about 2 Miles below the Town, expecting they wou'd attack me, while I sent Capt. Par & 30 men, 3 miles lower to burn a Castle, which he affected and brought off some Stock. I then march'd off from the left, in fine order, 3 o'Clock P. M., having sett Fire to the whole Town, except one house, which belong'd to a friend Indian now with the Onidos. As we march'd from the left, the Musquetry was in front, and I much expected to be attacked in recrossing the River, & had 2 Miles of a very dangerous defile; order'd Capt. Scull in front, with his

Granadier Company, with fixt Bayonets, and at all events to force the ford, which he affected, and the whole cross'd in good order; then burnt a small Village and some Corn. March'd till 11 o'Clock at Night, bad roads and much hinder'd with the Wounded Man, this day 13 miles to a Town called Callacrunty.

Oct'r 10th: About 1 o'Clock this Morning, came on a very heavy rain which Continued all Day—at day break march'd, it raining excessive hard, & the Creeks rising very fast, after marching about 10 Miles came to a Creek that was high, the Pack horses was oblig'd to Swim, and the greatest difficulty; got the Troops over by falling Trees, & upon coming to the crossing of the Susquehanna, it was so high, that, unless on such an Occasion, it would be thought impracticable to cross it. But our Provision being almost Expended, it render'd our Case desperate. I, therefore, had every Horse collected, and in about 20 Trips, of such Horses as was able to cross, got over the Troops, part of the Way swiming with 2 Men on a Horse; no lives lost; 7 Muskets & some Ammunition Baggage and some Provision lost, We then Proceeded on our March across the Mountains, avoided crossing it twice more, which I would otherwise been Oblig'd to do; Burnt all the Houses on the South side of Susquehanna in the Unidilla Settlement, except Glassford's, which I let remain for the Service he had done me, also burnt a Saw & Grist Mill being the only Grist Mill in that Country; march'd 7 miles from the Unidilla this day, 23 miles.

October 11th: This day order'd the Troops to dress and clean there arms, and Prepared a Raft to transport some Men over the Susquehanna to burn the other Part of the Unidilla Settlement. Lieut. Long with one Private went over on the Raft, & burnt all the Houses. According to my Computation, I think there was upwards of 4000 bushels Grain burnt at Anohaghwage and the Unidilla. March'd about 12 Miles; Waters very high.

October 12th: March'd this day 25 Miles; found it impossible to cross the Delaware, & by the Negligence of our Guides, in attempting to evade the River, lost the Whole Party in the Woods; we went at least 6.Miles in the Dark Expecting to Come to Cawley's which is

October 13th: The first Inhabitant, having been 2 days without Provision; lay in the Mountain this Night.

October 14th: With some Difficulty crossing the Mountains got to Cawley's, being the first Inhabitants on the frontier settlements between there & Unidilla; March'd this day to Mr. Sawyer's about 16 Miles.

Octob'r 15th: Note: All I could furnish for my Men was an Ear of Corn pr Man which they Parch'd—March'd this day to Mattius.

October 16th: About 2 o'Clock the Troops return'd to this Place, where I order'd 13 Rounds of Cannon & a feu de joy to be fired as a Compliment, which I thought due to the Brave Troops who with the greatest Fortitude surmounted such difficulties.

A RETURN OF THE DETACHMENT OF FOOT COMMANDED BY WM. 'BUTLER ESQR. LT. COL. COMM'DT AT SCHOHARRY.

State	Regiments	Field: Cols.	Lt. Cols.	Majors	Commiss'd: Captains	Lieuts.	Ensigns	Staff: Chaplains	Adjutants	Pay Masters	Qr. Masters	Surgeons	Mates	Non com: Serjt. Majors	Qr. Mr. Serjts.	Drum Majors	Fife Majors	Trumpeters	Serjeants	Drums & Fifes	R&F: Pres't fit for Duty	Sick Present	Sick absent	On Command	On Furlough	Total	Wanting: Serjants	Drums & Files	Rank & File	Alt: Deserted	Join'd R. & File
	4th Pennsa. Regiment		1	1	4	6	2	2	1	1	1	1	1	1	1		1	1	23	14	127	9	9	43	8	185	1	3	265	2	1
	Rifle Corps			1	1	4	1			1	1			1	1				9		84	15	8	8	3	122					
	Lt. Deitz's Rangers					1													2	2	10		4	4		18					
	Upper fort Militia			1	1	1			1										6		53	1				54					
	Lower Fort Militia				2	2	1		1										10	2	65		1			67					
	Middle Fort Militia				1	3	1												3		30			2		30					
	Total		1	3	9	20	5	1	4	2	2	1	1	2	2	1	1	1	53	18	369	25	22	56	11	476	1	3	265	2	1

Places Where

Places Where		
Valley Forge	13	1
Brunswick	10	3
Chester County	1	1
Albany	1	3
Eastown	3	2
Yellow Springs	2	2
Trenton	4	3
Princetown	3	3
Caryll's Ferry	3	5
Kingston	1	1
Reading	1	2
Lancaster	2	
Englishtown	2	1
Pequea	1	1
Radnor	1	2
Sick in the country	2	
	56	15

Waggoners — Valley Forge
Waiting on Capt Fishbourn
Waggoners in the Army
With the Commissary in Jersey
On Scout
On Com'd present

N. B. 1 Serjt. Sick Albany
1 Do at Radnor
1 Serjt. Discharged

Abs't Offi'rs Names — Reasons for — Time of absence

Abs't Offi'rs Names	Reasons for	Time of absence
4th Pennsa. Regt.	A.D.C. to Gen. Wayne	17th February 1778
Capt. Fishbourn	Recruiting	13th April
Lieut. Campbell	Sick abs't	29th June
Lieut. Dover	Prisoner of War	4th Oct'r 1777
Lieut. Blewer		
Rifle Corps		
Capt. Long	Resigned since last Return	

NAMES OF THE MILITIA OFFICERS AND THE REGIMENTS THEY BELONG TO.

Names	Rank	Regts. they belong to	Major	Capts	Lieuts	Ens's	Serjts.	D's & Fifes.	Rank & File
Jacob Hager	Capt.	Col. Vrooman's Regt.		1	1	1	2	2	24
Wm. Kneaskern	Lieut.								
Peter Vanatvorp	Ensign								
Walter Vrooman	Capt.	Col. Wemple's Regt.		1	1		4		29
Jilles Funda	Lieut.								
George Passage	Adjt.								
John Funda	Major	Col. S. Schuyler's Regt.	1	1			1		12
John Grott	Capt.								
Levi Vanacker	Lieut.	Col. Philip Schuyler's Regt.		1	1	1	4	1	27
Isaac Lansing	Lieut.								
Wm. Grossoeck	Lieut.	Col. Jacob Lansing's Regt.			1		4	1	19
Doruva Funda	Adjt.								
Johnathan Nailles	Lieut.	Col. Renselars Regt.			1		1		7
— — Staats	Capt.	Col. Vrooman's		1	2		3		30
— — Ostrander	Lt.								
— — Vanenwerpen	Lt.								

A RETURN OF THE DETATCHMENT OF FOOT THAT WAS AT ONOHOGWAGE UNDER THE COM'D OF WM. BUTLER, ESQR. LT. COL. SCHOHARY. [October, 1778]

Regiments	Colonels	Lt. Colonels	Majors	Capt'ns	Lieuts.	Ensigns	Chaplains	Adjutants	Qr. Masters	Surgeons	Mates	Serjeant Majors	Qr. Mr. Serjeants	Drum Majors	Fife Majors	Serjeants	Drums & Fifes	Trumpeters	Rank & File
4th Pennsa. Regiment		1	1	4	5	2	1	1	1	1		1	1			20	2		122
Rifle Corps			1	1	4	1		1	1				1			8		1	56
Lieut't Deitz's Comp'y Rangers				1	1											2			18
Militia, Guides, & Packhorsemen																			7
Total		1	2	6	10	3	1	2	2	1		1	2			30	2	1	203

GOVERNOR CLINTON'S REPLY TO COLONEL BUTLER'S LETTER.

Pokeepsie 3d Nov'r 1778.

D'r Sir, I am this Moment honored with your obliging Letter of
the 27th Ultimo inclosing a Copy of the Journal of your Expedition ag't Unidilla & Anaquaga, for which I thank you as well as
for the Services you have rendered your Country by the Destruction of those Places which have hitherto harboured & fed the Villians who have so much distressed our Frontier Settlements.
The Rev'd Mr. Jones, who was kind enough to call upon me &
deliver your Letter, informed me that you have never received
my answer to your Letter of the 27th Sep't. I was not a Little
surprized at this Information, as I immediately wrote an answer
& forwarded it with other public Dispatches to Albany. I now
inclose a Copy of what I then wrote and am with much Esteem
Your most Obed't Serv't

Geo. Clinton.

Colo. Butler.

————

The Case of Samuel Hake.

*Gentlemen, In Compliance with the Request contained in
your Resolution of the first Instant, communicated to me by the
Honorable John Morin Scott, Esq; and Sir James Jay, two of
your Members, I now communicate to you all the official Information I have received, respecting the Subject of your Enquiry:
General Reports, resting only on the Evidence of common Fame,
I presume, make no Part of the Information requested of me.

In September last, Samuel Hake, a Prisoner, taken in a Vessel
bound from Britain to New-York, obtained a Flag from his Excellency General Washington, with my Consent, to go to New-
York, for the Purpose of removing his Books, Papers and House-

*From the Senate Journal.

hold Furniture from thence to the interior Part of this State. While in New-York, he put a Quantity of Goods and Merchandises on Board a Sloop, which had been sent with a Flag to New-York with a Number of Tories, and was then returning: These Goods were landed at or near Rhynebeck, but to whom they were consigned, or how disposed of, I have no Information, except Hearsay and Common Report.

In October last, the said Samuel Hake, being still in the City of New-York, put another Parcel of Goods and Merchandises on Board a Vessel, which was coming up the River with a Flag from the Enemy, in which he came Passenger: On the Arrival of this Vessel at King's Ferry, I made Mr. Hake a Prisoner, and confined him on his Parole: I stationed an Officer on Board the Vessel, with Orders not to permit the Goods to be landed, and gave Directions that the Vessel should return with them to New-York.

There have also been several Instances of Persons in New-York having sent out small Quantities of different Articles to their Families and Friends in the Country by the Return of Flags: This Practice cannot be effectually prevented, without a proper Law for the Purpose.

As to Seizures made by Virtue of the Embargo-Law; the Magistrates, authorized to make these Seizures, are not directed by Law to make Returns, or give me any Information respecting them: I can, therefore, communicate to you, no other Intelligence on this Subject, than what arises from Reports, the Credit of which is not yet ascertained: From these Reports, however, there is Reason to suspect, that the Embargo-Law has, in many Instances, been violated, and that a proper and full Enquiry into these Abuses may be of public Utility.

Geo. Clinton.

Poughkeepsie, November 2, 1778.

[No. 1886.]

*Commissary Flint Approves of the Act of the Legislature Relative
to Subsistence for the Army.*

Sir, I have seen the act, of your Legislature, passed for the purpose of subsisting the army. It appears to me adequate to the
occasion for which it was requested.

A quantity of salt is ordered to be distributed in the various
parts of this state, to render the law easy & agreeable to the
farmers.

Philip Leek Esq., is a Purchaser at Bedford. His business will
not permit of his absence. I take the liberty to mention him to
your Excellency as an honest, attentive person; and will esteem
a favor of your Excellency to send me an approbation of his appointment as an assistant Comisary of purchases. I have the
honor to be with great respect Your Excellency's most obed't &
hb. Ser't

                                        Royal Flint, A. C. G. P.
Fred'g Nov. 4 1778.

His Ex'y, Gov. Clinton.

[No. 1887.]

Associated Exempts of Poughkeepsie District.

                              Poghkeepsie June 12th 1778.

Sir, From the Inclosed orders, you will observe that I have
divided the County into five districts, that you are appointed to
superintend the association in one of them, and that all persons
entitled to associate and resident within the District are to apply
to you for that purpose. You will make Return to me as soon as
possible of the associators within your District, and call a meeting of them to determine upon the persons they would recommend for the Officers in the District whose names you will also

return to me, that I may communicate them to the Council of Appointment and have the Commissions made out. Inclosed you have also the form of the association which the associators are to subscribe and the form of a certificate, you are thereupon to give each person; as his Excellency the Governor has in General orders, declared his Intentions of speedily calling out the whole Corps you will give the necessary Directions for every man to hold himself in readiness to march at a moment's warning. The associators should be directed to produce their Certificates as soon as they have received them, to the Captain of the militia Beat where they reside, to the end that their names may be struck off the militia Roll.

Jacobus Swartwout, Col.

[To Andrew Billings.]

———

Persons names who sign'd the first associated list within the Precinct of Poughkeepsie and the beat of Capt. John Van Benschoten's company in Rumbout, agreeable to the Roll given me by Capt. John Schenk.

Zepheniah Platt, John Bailey, Jr., Andrew Billings, Gilbert Livingston, Peter Tappen, Zepheniah Platt, Jr., Moses Degraft, Richard Lewis, Henry Mott, Timothy Babcock, Austin Lawrance, James Brisbin, Gideon Van Veler, Isaac Cole, Morris Hazard, Samll. Dodge, Thomas Crabb, Peter A. Lansing, Paul Schenck, John Burger, Lankister Burling, Davis Hunt, Samll. Tuder, Stephen Seamans, Alexander L. Miller, Geo. Smart, Jacobis Degraft, Guilean Ockerman, Thomas Cannan, Elias Van Benschoten, Cornelius Westervelt, Charles Hoffman, John Fort, Peleg Seamans, James Gibson, Cornelius Brower, Nicholas Anthony, Isaac Vandusen, William Hamilton, John Miller, Henry Livingston, Jr., Thos. B ———, Thomas Anderson.

At a meeting of the Associated Exempts in Poghkeepsie & the District of Capt. John Van Bunschoten in Rumbout prec't on the 28th day of September, 1778, the following Gentlemen were by a plurality of Voices, agreed to be Recommended to the Hon'le Council of Appointment, as officers in the said Company.

Viz: Elias E. Van Bunschoten Capt., Zephaniah Platt, Jun'r. 1st Leut., Ezekiel Cooper, 2 Do.

Gilbert Livingston, Jno. Burger, Abraham Sleght, Thos. Hendeson, Jacobus Sleght, Jonas Riley, Henry Mott, Gideon Vervelin, Richard Lewis, John Bailey, Jun'r.

I Certify that the above persons were nominated for officers as they Stand, by a number of the associated Exempts of Poughkeepsie precinct, and the District of Capt. John Van Benschoten's company in Rumbout precinct, agreeable to the orders given me by Col. Jacobus Swartout.

                                        Andrew Billings.

Dutchess County.

We, the Subscribers being persons either under the age of Fifty five years, who have held civil or militaryCommissions and have not been reappointed to our respective Ranks of Office or being between the ages of fifty and fifty-five years, do hereby assosiate, agreeable to the act for regulating the militia of this State, and do hereby severally promise that we will severally on all Occasions, obey the Orders of our respective Commanding Officers, and will in Cases of Invasion or Incursions of the Enemy or Insurrection, march to repel the Enemy or suppress such Insurrection in like manner as the enrolled Militia are compelled to do, so as that we shall not when called out in Detachments be annexed to any other Regiment or Company or be under the immediate Command of any other than our own officers.

Jacobus Sleght, Jacob V. Bunschoten, Matthew Van Keuren, Jr., James Cumpten, Francis his X mark Jacoks, Coorod Philips, Hezekiah Collins, Benjamin Westervelt, Zachariah Ferdon, Wilhelmnus Ploegh, Jonas Riley, Elias E. V'Bunschoten, Ezekiel Cooper.

———

[No. 1888.]

Judge Robert Yates Notifies the Governor that Dr. Ducalon has been Sentenced to Death.

Albany Nov'r 4th 1778.

Sir, During the sitting of the last Supreme Court, the following persons have been capitally convicted:

Stephen Ducalon*—On an Indictment for the Robbery of Arent Van Schaack. Upon his arraignment he stood mute; and altho' an act of the Legislature of this State authorized the Court to proceed to tryal in the same manner, as if he had plead not guilty and put himself upon the Country, yet as there were appearances that the Prisoner was rendered speechless by sickness, it was judged most advisable to take an Inquest to determine whether he stood maliciously and obstinately mute, or by the Providence and act of God. It appeared in proof by the concurrent testimony of five Physicians that the Prisoner laboured under a paralitic lateral complaint, which at least impaired the motion of one half of his Body, and that his organs of speech were thereby affected, tho' not in so great a degree, as to deprive him of articulation. It also appeared that the Prisoner had attempted a few days before the

———

*See Volume II pages 655 and 701 and Volume IV pages 189-192.

sitting of the Court, by a mercurial ointment, applyed near his throat to bring on a salivation, and probably for the purpose of postponing his tryal; the effects of which had however ceased at the time of this examination.

Upon these circumstances the Jury found, that he obstinately and wilfully stood mute, and a day was fixed for his tryal of which he was informed. The Clerk of the Court was thereupon furnished in behalf of the Prisoner with a List of the names of witnesses he wanted on his defence, and process issued to bring them in, and all but one or two appeared, and were called upon to give testimony in favour of the Prisoner's character, in addition whereto one of them swore, that the prisoner was at home at or near the Time when this robbery was committed.

The principal proof whereon his conviction is grounded was the testimony of John Sloss, which was full and pointed, and stood corroberated by two other witnesses who declared they saw the Prisoner on the very night of the Robbery in company with the rest of the Gang, having in possession many of the Effects of Arent Van Schaack.

Philip Shiffer stands convicted, upon his own confession in writing and subscribed by him before a majestrate, for robbing two unknown Persons on the High way. I have respited passing sentence until January Term, in order to have an opportunity in the mean while of consulting my Brethren on the doubts which have arisen in my mind upon the Evidence, which altho' it proved the robbery sufficiently, yet was defective in ascertaining its having been committed on or near a high way, and the only Statute which takes away Clergy from robberies, wheresoever committed is the 3 & 4 of W & M, C 9, which I am doubtful whether it extends, or has ever been practised on.

When Stephen Ducalon on the last day of the Term was set to the Bar, he was asked what he had to say why sentence of death should not pass against him. He then spoke, tho' not very distinctly, yet so as to be understood. He avowed his Innocence, and declared he would give any thing to have his Life spared. As nothing legally was offered in arrest of Judgment sentence of death was pronounced, and his execution ordered on the twenty seventh day of November.

As this tryal was attended with uncommon circumstances I thought it my duty to lay them before your Excellency. I have the honor to be with the greatest Respect Your Excellency's most obedient & humble serv't

Robert Yates.

His Excellency George Clinton Esqr.

Governor of the State of New York,

Poughkeepsie.

[No. 1889.]

Associated Exempts of Albany County.

Wee, the Subscribers under the age of fifty five years, who have held civil or Military Commissions and have not been reappointed to our Respective Ranks of office or being between the ages of fifty & fifty five years, Do hereby Severally Engage, that wee will Respectively, on all occassions, obey the orders of our Respective Commanding officers, & will In Case of Invasion or Incursion of the Enemy or Insurrections, march to Repell the Enemy or suppress Such Insurretions in the like manner as the Enroled Millitia are Compelled to Do, so as wee shall not when Called out in Detachments, be annexed to any other Ridgement or Company or be under the Immediate Command of any other then our own officers. Witness our hands this Day.

July ye 21 1778 James Saxton; July ye 21 Jedediah Darrow; July ye 21 Ashbel Goff; July ye 22 Roger Kinne; July ye 23 Benjamin Chittendoen; July ye 24 Jonathan Davenport; July ye 26 Joel Pratt; July ye 26 Nehemiah Spencer; July ye 26 Nathaniel Kinne; July ye 26 Samll. Foot; July ye 27 John Stedman; July ye 28 Ithmer Spencer; July ye 28 Eli Reynolds; July th 28 Thomas Brown; July ye 28 Solomon Hutchinson; July 28 Isaac Clark; July 28 Gideon Potts; July 28 Richard Holdridg; July 28 Jonathan Dean; July 31 Jonathan Chittenden; Agust 3d Samuel Andrus; August ye 6 Ephreham Widbeck; August ye 6 Jeremiah Chapman; August ye 8 James Spencer; August ye 8 Ambrus Vinson; August 9 Jonathan Dudley; August 10 Wm. Powers, Surgeon; August the 12 Elias Delong; Elijah Smith, Samll. Dean, Edword Cadman, Matthew Scott.

Wee, the Subscribers, being a Majority of the Company of associated Exempts Enroled on the other part of this sheet of paper Do hereby Recommed to the Honourable the Council of Appointment:

Roger Kinne, to be Captain; Benj'm Chittenden, to be first Lieut; Nehemiah Spencer, to be Second Lieut; and Samll. Dean, to be Ensign of said Company. Witness our hands this —— Day of —— 1778.

James Saxon, Jedediah Darrow, Ashbel Goff, Jonathan Davenport, Samll. Foot, John Stedman, Joel Pratt, Nathaniel Kinne, Iithmer Spencer, Eli Reynolds, Thomas Brown, Solomon Hutchinson, Gideon Potts, Isaac Clark, Richard Holdridg, Jonathan Dean, Jonathan Chittenden, Samuel Andrus, Ephreham Widbeck, Jeremiah Chapman, Ambrus Vinson, Jonathan Dudley, Wm. Powers, Surgeon, Elias Delong, Elijah Smith, Edword Cadman, Matthew Scott.

[No. 1890.]

Associated Exempts of Albany City.

Whereas, in and by an act of the Legislature of the State of New York, entitled "An act for regulating the Militia of the State of New York," it is declared that all Persons under the age of fifty five years who have held civil or Military Commissions, and are not or should not be reappointed to their respective Ranks of office, and all other Persons between the ages of fifty and fifty five years who had not associated and Elected their officers and should associate themselves in the manner in the said act mentioned, should be exempted from serving as part of the enrolled Militia;

We, the subscribers, do, therefore, in pursuance of the said act, hereby promise and engage, that we will severally on all occasions, obey the orders of our respective Commanding officers, and will severally in Cases of Invasion or Incursions of the Enemy or Insurrections, march to repel the Enemy, or suppress such Insurrection, in the like manner as the enrolled Militia are compelled to do; as Witness our Hands.

Capt. Bastejan T. Vischer, Lucas Van Veghten, Johannes Marsselus, Edward Davis, David his DF mark Fearo, Willem ——, Abraham L. Witbeck, Peter Levensen, Fraric Reef, Samuel Anthoney, First Lt. Derick Heemstrate, Alexander Chesney, Philip Van Veghten, John Van Woert, Simon Van ——, 2d Lt. Chris A. Yates, John Harbark, Hendrick Lyker, Staats Van Santvoort, John Tillman, Jun'r, Carl Hanstrott, Ewert Van den Bergh, John Pattersson, Jacob D. Fonda, Peter Quackenbos, Abr'm N. Cuyler, Frederik Dampf, Gerret H. Visscher, Comrade Ruby, Henderick Gerdener,

Bastian Visscher, Capt; Dirck Heemstraat, first Lt; Christo: Adam Yates, Second Lt. "Agreed & Entred Nov'r 5th 1778."

[No. 1891.]

The Problem of Proper Treatment of Military Prisoners.

Pokeepsie Nov'r 5" 1778.

Gent., I have received your Letters of the 30" ult. & 2d Inst. I would very willingly oblige Mr. Douw & the other Gentleman in their Request, requesting Mrs. Van Dyck, Mrs. Douw, if it co'd be done consistent with my Duty, but it would appear very strange to the Public, if this Indulgence should be granted to the Ladies whose Husbands are in N. York, when the Enemy within a very short Time refused to allow the wives of some of the principal Officers taken at Fort Montgomery to visit those Gentlemen unless they would consent to remain there.

With Respect to the other application contained in your Letter of the 30" Oct'r, I do not conceive it my Duty to lay it before the Legislature, as they might consider it an Impropriety from me whose particular Business it is to see the Law faithfully Executed; if it is proper, it ought to have been made in the first Instance by the Petitioners themselves. The Legislature will adjourn to Day and, therefore, cannot now take it into Consideration, and if they could a Regard to your public Characters, as well as my own, wo'd prevent me from interfering. The Petitioners, if they think proper, may prepare a Petition and lay it before the Legislature at their next meeting—will be on the 2d of Jan'y next.

I have not received the Original Certificate from the Commissary of Prisoners alluded to in Colo. Campbell's Letter, but I am resolved not to exchange Mr. Cummings until the Enemy shall consent to receive Mr. Van Schaack & the other State Prisoners, for such of the subjects of this state as are now confined in New York, and I also have a Right previously of insisting that Mr.

Menier & others who were suffered to go in upon their Parole be either exchanged or returned. This you will please to notify to Mr. Cummings & the other Gentlemen, and to inform them that I am acquainted, that some of the Prisoners in N. York belong'g to this state, are closely confined and unless an Exchange is speedily effected, I shall conceive myself obliged to order similar Treatment to the Prisoners in our Hands.

As to the military Prisoners which Mr. Adams applies for, I do not conceive myself authorized to give any Directions, and, considering their peculiar situation, I cannot even advise. You must, therefore, in this Instance act for yourselves and take such measures as you may determine proper and justifiable.

I inclose the List of Persons applying to go N. York with the answers subjoined by which you will please to govern yourselves. I am &c.

[G. C.]

[To Commissioners of Conspiracies at Albany.]

[No. 1892.]

Captain Smith Addresses a Note to a Superior Officer Whose Name is not Given.

May it please your Honour; This Moment arrived a person, who was taken on the 1st Inst. and carried to Crown Point, where there was an Incampment of the Enemy, (as he says), of three or four Hundred and determined for three Different Routs, One to Otter Creek and One to Skeensborough, and one to this place—supposed to Distress the Inhabitants.

I have sent out three different Scouts, and, if from them, I receive any thing Meterial, shall give your Honour the earliest Intelligence.

I have wrote to the Colonels of the Millitia at Saratoga & White Creek, to hold themselves in readiness, agreeable to Genl. Stark's Orders. Sir I wate your further Orders. I am with due Respect Your Honour's most Obedient Servant,

                                   Simeon Smith, Capt. Comdg.
Fort Starks Nov'r 5th 1778.

·[No. 1893.]
McDOUGALL DISPARAGES GATES.
He Speculates Upon the Movements of the Enemy—Protection of Private Property by Troops on the March—Question of Rank Settled.

Camp, Second Hills 3 miles from New-Milford 5th Nov'r '78.

My dear Sir, I had the Honor to address you before I marched from Fredericsburgh, and then informed you of the reasons, which caused my march. Two days after the orders of the Commander in chief reach[ed] me here to halt till farther orders, as the Troops said to have sailed remained in York Harbour the 23d Ultimo, vizt. Twelve British and six regiments of new Levies. Those which sailed and caused the movement were only the invalids, and the officers of Broken regiments taken to fill up others. General Gates reached Hartford; I am still in a state of disagreeable suspence; out of the route of Post; and every intelligence which can be relied on; and with no great society, Generals Parsons and Huntington not being with their Brigades. This is the more disagreeable, as Mrs. McDougall has been very ill at Hartford. The resignation of personal Liberty, is not the least sacrafice which a man makes, by becoming a soldier.

General Gates I understand is gone to command at Boston. I know he was exceedingly impatient under command. And from his known temper, I suspect, he prefers being the first man of a vilage, to the second in Rome. He has but litle to do there; but the service will not suffer, by his being at a Post of ease and security. I could hardly believe he was so extreamly credulous; as I found him to be. He is the most so, in his profession of any man I ever knew, who had seen so much service. He has the weakest mind to combine circumstances, to form a judgment of any man I ever knew, of his plausible, and specious appearance. In short sir, he [is] as weak as water. His whole Fort lies, in a litle Rotine of detail, of duty, & a perfect knowledge of the English corrupt Nobility. The Lord of Hosts have Mercy on that Army, whose movements must depend on his combination of Military demonstrations of an Enemy. God avert so great a Judgement to America; as his having the chief command of her Armies. It's fortunate for America Gen. Burgoyne was so rash as to put himself in the Position he did; and that there was no other route, for him to Albany, but the one he took, or he would not have been an American Prisoner.

It is unquestionable the Enemy have, or are about making, large detachments of their Army from New York, which many in the Army and the country consider as certain evidences of an evacuation. The Tories, and whigs in the city draw the same conclution. The one from Fear, the other from sanguine hope. But I cannot flatter myself that desireable event will take place soon. New York is the last post in the United States they will quit. Newport will first be evacuated, the Hospital will be shipt, and the Merchants will pack and ship their Goods. Neither of these was done by the last intelligence from those places; where can the Enemies fleet be so secure from the French line of Batle ships as in N. York? What Position can they hold so well situated as N. York, to harass our Trade? Where can they get so much subsistance, of various articles so securly, as from that, Long and Staten Islands? Where can they so much Embarass America, and increase our expence by Land Carriage as by remaining there? Can it enter into the mind of any man of sense that are not well acquainted with our country and the difficulties they subject us to, by holding the Key of our Contry? It cannot.

It is true they cannot hold their West India Islands, and those they have in possesion of ours, one or the other they must part with, and I think it will be the Latter. When they receive the advice of the Loss of Dominica, a national system of defence will be formed, against France and us, for she cannot carry on offensive operations against both. But as the officers here in the Navy and Army cannot now act on the loss of that Island without orders, it will be the Latter end of December probably before the effect of the new system to be taken, can reach New York. Then, and not till [then] will it be evacuated.

You are fully acquainted with the great difficulties which the unsetled state of rank has occationed in the Army. To prevent this for the future, the committe of Congress at the Plains, desired a Board of General officers to take up principles and report on them; the result you have inclosed approved by the committe; so that the rule of Rank is now setled. Concluding it might be of use to you and the Council of appointment I have caused it to be transcribed from the orders and examined it. It was the opinion of the Board and the committe that the American Army is composed of Thirteen Armies, one belonging to each independant state, forming one joint Army. Upon this principle, they have determined, and this seems to have been the Idea & determination of Congress, by the Resolutions, which directed the raising the present Army.

I had almost forgot to inform you of a matter, which I know will be entertaining. The destruction of property on the march has always given me great pain and concern. I was, therefore, determined to prevent it if Posible; and, therefore, I issued very particular and severe orders for the March. The Division is composed of three New England Brigades, vizt: Nixon's from the Bay, Parsons' and Huntington's from Connecticut. In a course of Conversation with the officers of the Latter, they observed with grave Face, the orders of march were exceedingly proper and necessary, and they must be obeyed. For they were going among their people who would think the Devil had got into the army, if those prudent orders were violated. You may be sure I concured with them in opinion, and added that I would have no trouble with Transgressors; for I should give them over to the civil authority; and let them deal with them.

The consequence has been, that not a single Pannel of Fence has been burnt, on the march; or Since we encamped. The truth of the matter is, they are much in awe of their authority; and fear their reputations at Home. Their country men would indeed conclude the Devil was in them, if they had conducted, as they have done with the Army, and in other places. It is however agreeable to find men's conduct regulated from those considerations. But I think a regard for their state; influence this, and produce this circumspection. I wish the other motives governed them abroad, with more tenderness for other men's property. I confess, however, that the officers who have charge of Brigades and Divisions are much to blame for the Destruction of Fence. Much of it is done thro' wantonness in the Troops and carelessness in their officers. There has been line on line, and precept on precept in General orders, but hitherto to no purpose. The

officers are not sufficiently attentive to orders or their duty. The
Troops at Hartford being scarce of Flour, and obliged to scoute
for Private property or want, in the Course of this service, they
collected on Connecticut River in one day 200 Barrels belonging
to the Eastern engrossers and other Jobbers.   And, I am informed, there are great quantities of that Article in the vicinity
of that River and the roads from your state. The General was
at a loss how to dispose of the Army, when I left head Quarters
for the winter. It is feared the state of New York will not be
able to subsist the whole of it, in the winter. If not a great
part of that article for his and the Eastern Armies, infantry as
well as navy must come from Virginia which must render their
support very uncertain. For these reasons I have advised, if the
Enemy detach Ten full regiments, to quarter one third of our
army in Jersey, including what is now there. If another Considerable detachment is made from thence, then to quarter half
our Army, there, that is, the moiety of what we marched from
the Plains, including Maxwell's Brigade. What do you think of
it? Is it not too dangerous an experiment, to Hazard the want
of subsistence for the Army?

You may remember, when I was at Poughkeepsie, I took the
Liberty, to apply for the office of the Town Clerk of the City of
New York Mr. Lawrence my son in Law. I have been informed
to-day by mere accident, that office has been promised twelve
months since, to Lieut. Col. Livingston. If this was done, I am
perswaded you did not know it, or you would have mentioned it.
As some officers have been already appointed for that City, I
think there is no impropriety in my applying in Form, which I
have taken the Liberty to do, in the Letter which accompanies
this.   I have early and Long contended for the rights of this

people at the expence of my fortune and constitution, when our affairs were in suspence; before the union was formed, when the Livingstons kept at an aweful distance, and rather looked for offices from another Quarter, than from the people. But I would not plead this to induce my country to make an improper appointment, of a person unqualified for the office—Let his connection be ever so near to me. For I know besides the wicked-[ness] of such a request, the disposes of the Honors and offices of the Public, have, or ought not to have, favors to Grant. The person I apply for, is industrious, and has preserved his Morals in the Army; and the Gentlemen of the Law inform me who were at His Examination, that he made a respectable one. I have by this time tired your patience, and shall, therefore, no longer trespass on it, than by requesting my respectful Compliments to be made to Mrs. Clinton; and my best wishes to Mr. McKesson. I am my dear Sir, Your affectionate Hble. Servant

Alex'r McDougall.

Governor Clinton.

[No. 1894.]

FLAG COURTESIES SUSPENDED.

Governor Clinton Explains Why He Cannot Pass Tory Women to New York—The Legislature Adjourns.

Clermount 4th Nov'r 1778.

Dear Sir, I have just rec'd a very melancholy Letter from Mrs. Van Dyck, the wife of Doct'r Van Dyck, entreating me to apply to your Excellency for permission for & her sister Miss Dowe to go to New York, to her husband, whom she represents as in the greatest distress.

I am led to conclude from this Letter that H. Van Schaack has not given her the most favourable representation of the

State of affairs at New York, & that the Tories begin to find that they have no resourse but the Clementcy of the whigs.   Notwithstanding the injuries I have rec'd I must own I pity them. How far it may be prudent to suffer Mrs. Vandyck to go down, your Excellency is best able to judge.   For my own part I believe the more they see of it in its present state, the less they will be pleased with the part they have taken.   I am D'r Sir With the greatest respect Your Excellency's Most Obt. Hum: Serv't

Robt. R. Livingston.

His Excellency Gov'r Clinton Poughkeepsie.

Poukeepsie 6th Nov'r 1778.

Dear Sir, I am honored with the Receipt of your Letter of the 4th Instant.   I am unhappy in not being able to comply with your Request in Favour of Mrs. Vandyck & Miss Dowe.   The latest Accounts I have had from the Army give me Reason to believe the Enemy will not receive any Flaggs at present, but if this was not the Case I cannot with Propriety & without giving great Disattisfaction, consent to grant these Ladies an Indulgence which not many Days since was refused by the Enemy to the Wives of the Principal Officers taken at Fort Montgomery. They had my Permission to go to New York to vissit their Husbands who have been upwards of a year in Captivity & after being detained, they proceeded to Elizabeth Town, for 3 Weeks amused with incouraging Promises, were at length informed they coud not be gratified, unless they woud consent to continue with their Husbands & so were oblidged to return Home greatly mortified.

The Legislature adjourned this afternoon till the 2d Tuesday in Jan'y next.   The Tax Bill losst in the Assembly on being Returned with objections ag't one very exceptionable Clause only. The Chief Justice is elected an Extra Delegate. The Delegates allowed £4 pr Diem; Both Houses have entered Resolves asserting their Right of originating Monied Bills but no steps taken for determining the Point.

Mrs. Clinton beggs her best Respects to the old Gentlewoman & to offer her Thanks for her oblidging Letter which she is not yet so far recovered as to be able to answer, & joins in my best Compliments to Mrs. Livingston & the young Ladies. I am D'r Sir Yours Sincerely

Geo. Clinton.

[To Robert R. Livingston.]

[No. 1895.]

Joshua Green Requests a Permit to Export Flour from this State to Massachusetts.

Westfield Nov'r 6th 1778.

May it please your Excellency, Inclosed is a recommendation from the honorable Council of this State to your Excellency in order to obtain a permission to purchase flour in the State of New York as therein mention'd, & which I sho'd have had the honor of presenting myself did not bodily indisposition prevent. Whether having been driven by the enemy (as I was early this war from Boston) so near to your Government, or from any other reasons that I am recommended is not for me to say, my chief concern is to make the application to your Excellency in the most speedy & proper manner I can, for which purpose I have engaged Samuel Fowler Esqr. of this place to wait on your Excellency, & who will be able to represent the necessity of the case, nor is doubted that your Excellency's inclination will lead you to grant the necessary assistance in your power: if in the permission which it may please your Excellency to grant, you sho'd think proper to order Mr. Fowler's name to be inserted with mine, it may be a means of facilitating the business. In hopes of a favorable return, I beg leave to subscribe With the greatest respect Your Excellency's most obedient & most humble serv't

Joshua Green.

His Excellency Gov'r Clinton, Poughkeepsie.

[No. 1896.]

The Final Cargo of Tories to be Despatched to New York.

Poughkeepsie Nov'r 7th 1778.

Sir, About two weeks hence the Commiss'rs will be ready (as they have informed me) to send off the last Cargo of Persons who have refused to take the Oath of allegiance, as prescribed by Law, to this State & are sentenced to be banished within the Enemy's Lines.

I have, therefore, to request that your Excell'cy will be pleased to direct the Commanding Officer at W't Point to furnish an Officer to take the vessel in Charge on her arrival there & to conduct her to New York.* The necessary Instructions & the Flag will be forwarded to Colo. Malcom. I have the honor to be with the greatest Respect. Yrs. &c.

Geo. Clinton.

His Excellency Genl. Washington.

---

* The intelligence to-day, that may be depended upon, is, that the British have made a very considerable embarkation, supposed already to amount to near ten thousand, on board one hundred and fifty sail of transports, which, at different times, have fallen down from New York to Sandy Hook and the watering place, and were every moment expected to sail. There are different rumors as to their destination; some say to Boston, others to South Carolina. But it is generally believed, considering all circumstances, that the West Indies are the object. The embarkation still seems to be going on, which leads to a conclusion that a total evacuation of New York will ensue; concerning this, however, opinions are much divided. There is a report in New York that Jamaica is taken, and it is said that rum and molasses have had a very extraordinary rise in consequence.—New York Journal, November 9, 1778.

[No. 1897.]

Dr. Ducalon's Fight for Freedom Interrupted by John McKesson.

Albany 8th Nov'r 1778.

May it please your Excellency, Stephen Ducalon a prisoner in the Gaol at Albany was after many indulgences & frivilous Delays tried & Convicted of a Robbery and has received Sentence. On proceeding to his Trial, some Jurors were set aside at their own request because they alledged they were (tho distantly) connected to him by marriages. The prisoner challenged twenty Jurors peremptorily, and long persisted in his challenge to a twenty first, tho' he said he could not give any other reason than that he did not like him.

Since his Trial, his Relations (as I am informed) have procured affidavits of one Skinkle, a Brother in Law of Ducalon's, now in the Gaol, and of one Owens, a particular Friend of Ducalon's long in the Gaol for grand Larceny, (for which he has not been tried by occasion of the Indisposition of the witnesses) and of other prisoners in the Gaol to discredit the Testimony of the witnesses on the part of the People. These affidavits I am informed are to be transmitted to your Excellency.

I believe neither the Court or the Country had the least doubt of the Truth of the Testimony given in the present Case.

I have observed more attempts of late in this County to discourage the making of Discoveries & giving Testimony than I have seen elsewhere. I wish I could correct the evil.

I have taken the Liberty to enclose you such notes copys and Extracts of the Evidence in the Cause as will I imagine fully satisfy you of the Truth of it, & the justice of the Sentence, if you should chuse to take the Trouble of perusing them. I have the Honor to be your Excellency's most Obedient humble Servant

John McKesson.

[To Gen. Clinton.]

[No. 1898.]

GENERAL HAND SUCCEEDS STARK AT ALBANY.

*Discrepancy of Pay between State and Federal Troops—
Depredations of Tories and Indians.*

Albany 8th November 1778.

Sir, Your Excellency's favor of the 22d Ultimo Pr General
Hand I have Rec'd, I am Satisfied his taking the Command here
is truely acceptable to the Citizens, I shall on my part give Particular attention to him as an Officer & Gentleman.

A small party of the Enemy 8 or 10 in number, Indians &
Tories, at break of day last Tuesday near Tribes Hill, in Tryon
County a few miles from Johnstown, came to the House of Peter
Hansen & took him & his Servant Prisoners, directed his wife &
Children to take every thing out of the House, & then put Fire
thereto, & to the Barn which are both Consumed, they sett the
women & Children at liberty & took Hansen & the Servant with
them to Canada as is said; Col. Fisher writes me he sent a Party
of his militia in Pursuit of the enemy.

It is said that last week, five men (who were Hunting Deer)
where taken Prisoners on Lake George. It is also Reported in
Town, that a Body of 4 or 500 of the Enemy have been seen on
Lake Champlain some Distance on this side of Crown Point; a
letter from the Commanding Officer at Fort Edward is Forwarded
to General Hand, who last Monday morning sett out for Schohary
& Cherry Valey; his Return is momently Expected; whether
this Letter Contains this or any other Intelligence I don't know.

I inclose your Excell'cy the latest Returns I have Received of
the militia of my Brigade now on the Frontiers; the number is
greatly short of that Ordered into actual Service; it being ¼ part
of all my Brigade Except the three northern Regts. I am aston-
ished at it.

A Draft of a Pay & Subsistance Roll of the members Compos-
ing the General Court martial of which Colonel Robert Van
Rensselaer was President, has been shewed to me, by which I
find the Officers have charged Continental Pay & Rations, according to their Respective Ranks; the Judge advocate charges 40/
Pr day.

I also Inclose your Excellency Copy of a Petition Signed by
Col. Van Alstine, President of a General Court martial, now setting by my Order at Claverack; the Court now setting in this
City Expect I believe the same allowance these ask for, I must
beg your Excellency to let me know as soon as Possible what Pay
& Rations these Officers are Entitled to; if your Excellency approves of it, I will pay them out of the monies I Receive as Fines
laid by the Genl. Courts martial on delinquents. I am with
great Esteem Your Excellency's most Obedient Humble Servant

Ab'm Ten Broeck.

His Excellency George Clinton Esqr.

[No. 1899.]

CLINTON, MORRIS AND JAY.

*The Latter Carries a Letter from the Former to Morris with an
Explanation.*

Nov'r 8th 1778.

Sir, I am indebted to you for several Letters. I have been
oblidged to pay attention to public Business occasioned by the
Meeting of the Legislature & as well the want of Opportunity
of Conveyance has prevented my answering before this Time—
and as our Friend the Chief Justice* who is appointed a special
Delegate for the Vermont Business, will deliver this, it is needless
to be particular, for, by him, you will be able to learn the Situation

---

*John Jay.

of our public affairs here and every other Matter that you wo'd be anxious to know more fully than I can communicate to you on Paper.

I sent you by Mr. Duane who left this yesterday Morning for Congress an Exemplification of the Delegates Commission from which however I expect but little Credit as the Inaccuracies of another Person may probably be attributed to me.

The Legislature who were to have met on the 3d of last month, did not form a Quorum before the 14th, and after hav'g elected Delegates, a Council of appointment passed a few Laws & joined Issue on the disputed Right of originating Money Bills, which the Assembly claim as their exclusive Priviledge, adjourned to the 2d Tuesday in Jan'y next.   In this Recess I may have some more Leisure which I will endeavor to employ, in writing you a Line as opportunity offers, and shall be happy to hear as often as the important Concerns in which you are engaged will admit, being &c.

[G. C.]

[To Gouverneur Morris.]

[No. 1900.]

Governor Clinton Refuses to Give a Pass to Mr. Douw for Mrs. Van Dyck.

Nov'r 8" 1778 Pokeepsie.

Sir, It is some Time since I rec'd your Letter containing Major Cochran's account respect'g Indian affairs and thank you for the Information contained in it.   The Hurry of Business attend'g the meeting of the Legislature neecessarily prevented my answering your Letter on the Receipt of it.

I should have applied agreeably to the Directions of the act to 2 members of the Legislature for their advice to enable me to grant you Permission for exchang'g a Quantity of Flour for Salt for the use of your Family but many applications for similar Purposes hav'g been previously made without Effect I esteemed it more prudent not to apply. If you can still obtain such advice from any two Members it will give me Pleasure to comply with your Request in granting a Permission.

The present situation of our public affairs and the Procedure of the Enemy in a similar Case prevented my granting an Indulgence to Mrs. Vandyck & Miss Douw which I would be happy in grant'g if it could be done consistent with my Duty as a public Officer. Be assured, Sir, whenever I can serve you or your Family, an opportunity of doing it, will be pleasure, being &c.

[G. C.]

[To Volkert P. Douw.]

[No. 1901.]

THE FLOUR SHIPPING ABUSE QUESTION.

Commissary Colt Protests Against General Sullivan's Arbitrary Procedure.

Hartford Nov'r 9, 1778.

May it please y'r Excellency, This Serves to inclose an extraordinary warrant, given by the Honourable M'r General Sullivan to Messrs. Clark & Nightengale of Providence, in order to enable them to furnish his Troops with Provisions &c. The supposed occasion for his taking a Measure so directly against the Laws of this & your State & repugnant to the general system, adopted by Congress, for subsisting their armies, was his being nearly out of Flour. Indeed, suppose some part of his Troops had no Bread for 3 or 4 Days. This was owing to several Causes—their not keeping me regularly informed of their daily expenditures—& the state of their Magazines—partly to the urgent Demand for Flour for the Fleet at Boston—to the late Excurtion of the Enemy

17

into Jersey, which interupt'd the supplies coming on from Pen-
silvania—& partly to the agents for the Fleet, & private Jobbers
biding the Flour out of the hands of my assistants in your State.
By these various causes, the Magazine of Flour, designed to feed
the Troops in State Rode Island, was unequal to their wants, &
they were reduced to a few Days distress. But the Department
was not neglected & as soon as I knew their Distress I turned my
whole attention to relieve them & am now, by help of ye spirited
Measures of your State, in a fair way of properly supplying them—
this will be greatly facilitated, by marching the Troops of convention to the Southard & having no further demand to feed the
French Squadron. But the Business of my Department will be
greatly injurd & delayd & my supplies rendered altogether precarious, if Genl. Sullivan persists in his present plan. I have
appoint'd a sufficient number of trusty Men to purchase Flour in
that part of your State which is within my Department viz. Mr.
Philip Leak in West Chester County, Maj. Henry Schenk, Mr. Paul
Schenk, Dav. Van Ness Esq. & Capt. James Reed in Dutchess
County; believe they are able to secure the whole for the use of
the army, except private persons are sufferd to transport it out
of the state.

Mr. Mumford is now gone into some part of your State to make
large purchases for Clark & Nightengale; suppose he will apply
to your Excellency for a permit to transport it out of the State.
Tho he may honestly deliver to ye use of the Army all the Flour
he may buy, in consequence of this Com's (of which however
there is no assurance) yet it will be very unadvised to permit his
buying & exporting it. It will put it out of the power of my
people to regulate the Price, as Mr. Mumford is under no controul
or limited to any price, he must give what the Farmer asks. As

he is a stranger & from home at great Expence, it wont do for
him to stand for a price—this will occasion a Vendue of the wheat
& Flour; which tho not at first view, prejudicial to your State;
yet is so to the United States.   To shew you that they are not
under any immediate necessity for the Flour, assure your Excellency, that within Ten days past I have shiped to Norwich, for
the purpose of supplying Gen. Sullivan, 220 bbs. Flour; also sent
him by land 130 bbs. & this day am shiping 150 more—we expect
at this post from Sharon & Fishkills 1500 bar's in the cours of
ten days, 1000 of which shall send to Providence, except the
Troops now here, march eastward.   This being a true representation of the Affair, cannot but believe your Excellency will agree
with me in oppinion, that it will be of dangerous Consequence to
permit Mr. Mumford, or any other private person, or agent to
any private Merchants to transport the Flour out of the State, tho
for the purpose of feeding any part of the Armies of the United
States, when proper Measures are taken by public Officers to feed
them.

In consequence of your Excellency's request to Mr. Flint, I am
sending Salt into your State to barter for Flour—suppose Mr.
Cuyler & myself shall be able to supply 4000 bushels for that
purpose.   I have the honour to be with due Esteem your Excellency's most obdt. hum'e Servant

                              Peter Colt D. C. G. P. East Department.
    [To Gen. Clinton.]

                              ————

[No. 1902.]

AN APPEAL FROM CHERRY VALLEY.

*Prominent Citizens Ask General Hand to Protect Them from Their
Enemies.*

To Genl. Hand: The humble petition of us the Subscribers Inhabitants of Cherry Valley, In behalf of Ourselves and other fel-

low sufferers in this and other Frontier Towns, in Tryon County,
Humbly sheweth,

That there has been and still are, men yet remaining in our
Neighbourhood, and betwixt us and the Saviges and their associats, that have been frequently keeping up a Corrispondance,
and assisting our Enemies, with Rations and in plundering and
robing us of our Cattle, and secreting them, for the Enemies
use; and Some of these Villans have been apprahended at ye
Butternuts and Elsewhere on our Frontiers Since Col. Alden
came amongst us & by his means, who has acted with great activity & prudence in Subduing these Rebbels to the States; and
that they might be used according to their Conduct; they were
sent to Albany to be secured from further harming us, and that
they might be treated according to ye demerite of their Crimes;
Now, by some means or other, these our Enemies, are set at
liberty and tolerated to return with their passes to come again
amongst us; now for God's Sake and for ye Sake of ye states,
and ye sake of us who have & still are willing & ready to venture our lives and our all for the Common Good of ye states,
Let Speedy methods be taken to apprahend and Carry off these
Notorious Villans that are known to have been our Enemies,
and still have some of their frainds, Relations and associats with
Brant & Butler's party and some of w'ch yt were sent to Albany
and are now at liberty & to walk at large, it can be proven have
aided Brant in his way of burning & Slaughter, and some of these
men we are mentioning, have been seen with our Savige Enemies
at ye distruction of Kobiskill, Springfield, Andrewstown, & the
Jerman Flats and by whom we have still reason to fear receaving
a stroak, and be made to fall a pray Into the hands of our Enemies, and to have this quarter of the state ruined; to prevent

w'ch & to dissapoint our fears, O Genl. let a sufficient number of Troops be alowed us, & if possible those we now have under Col. Alden, as they now are acquaint with our country & the Roads & Haunts of our Enemies, so that by their means we may be screaned from Slaughter & Devastation and this Quarter from Ruine & Disstress &c. And your aid we now Implore, & your Care in this is the Earnest desire & Request of,

Yours whilst —— —— ——

Will'm Johnston, v. d. m.; Saml. Campbell, Colo.; Will'm Johnston, Justice; Saml. Forguson; Jas. Cannan, adjt.; Will'm Wills, Lt. Col.; James Willson, Capt.; Saml. Campbell, Lieut.; Saml. Clyde, Lt. Coll.; John Campbell, Leut.; James Scott, Capt.; Samuel Willson, James Rickey, William Tomson, Richerd Jonston, Pat'k Deavison, William McConnal, Hugh Mitchal, Robert McKeon, Capt.; Robert McKown.

Cherry Valley 9br 7th 1778.

[To General Hand.]

———

[No. 1903.]

Congress Strives to Brace Up the Commissary and Quartermaster's Departments.

In Congress 10th Novem'er 1778.

Whereas, it hath become necessary not only that speedy & vigorous measures should be taken to regulate the commissary's & quarter master's departments, but also that a constant attention should be paid to those departments

Resolved, That Mr. Scudder, Mr. G. Morris & Mr. Whipple be a committee to superintend the same departments, and that they or any two of them be empowered to take such steps relating to the same as they shall think most for the public service.

Extract from the minutes.

Chas. Thomson secy.

[No. 1904.]

PETER LIVINGSTON IMPORTUNES THE GOVERNOR,

And Obtains Permission to Transport Two Hundred Barrels of Flour for Boston.

Manor Livingston 4 Nov'r '78.

Dear sir, I Inclose you a Letter to his Excellency concerning the Permit for 250 Barr's of flour (and also the Certificate of the Council of Boston). Have beg'd the fav'r of the Gov'r to Reconsider the Matter, as my Situation is very disagreable. When I tendered the Certificate to the Gov'r last Sep'r he told me if the Members of the Legislature would advise his signing of it he would. As soon as I obtained their advise I immediately set about buying the flour and sending it towards the line, relying upon the Govenor's word to obtain his Consent, as I had already the Consent of three members of the Legislature, and advised my friend in Boston of it. Have acquainted the Gov'r I returned the Certificate to you and beg you'll offer it to him with my Letter, as I know not what to do unless he is so kind as to grant me his permission, by your endeavours for me. If notwithstanding all, I cannot git the Govenor's Signature, please again to return it to me with a line by some safe Conveyance as quick as you can. I beg you'll look for the Exempt list of our furnace men in your office. I sent it in a letter to the Gov'r some time ago and several of them are now fined by the Court Martial it must be among the Govenor's papers. Beg a line. Your Very Hu'e ser't

Peter R. Livingston.

I expect daily 10 or 12 teams in from Boston with Salt &c. that I have engaged to load back with flour on the prospect I had of gitting the permit, which if I do not, must pay them £60 a piece

for going back empty.   Beg you'll represent this to the Gov'r and
endeavour all in your power to assist me.

To Major Lush Secretary to his Excellency Govenor Clinton,
     Poughkeepsie.

LIVINGSTON'S LETTER TO THE GOVERNOR.

Manor Livingston 3d November 1778.

May it Please your Excellency, My Brother Inclosed me your
fav'r of the 31 Octo'r, together with the Certificate of the Council
of the Massachusetts Bay, signed by the three members of our
Legislature advising your Excellency to sign the same.   When
I tendered the Certificate last September to your Excellency, you
then told me, that as the certificate mentioned only for the use
of the Inhabitants of the town of Boston, he did not think any
of the Members of the Legislature would advise him to admit
the flour to be exported but if they did, he would sign it.   I told
the Govenor I would try some of the Members and if they did
would again wait upon him with it.   On the first, and second of
October, three Members did sign it, upon which haveing the
promise of the Govenor, I immediately proceeded to purchase and
send on my flour from the River towards the line thinking, I
could when ready, wait on the Govenor and obtain his signature,
relying upon the recommendation of the members of Assembly
according to Law, and the Govenor's kindness in promising me
to grant the Permission upon said advice.   If any circumstances
has turned up since I obtained the advice of the members of the
Legislature, think it hard it should opperate ag't me.   I cannot
think the Govenor would let me suffer, as I looked upon all
obsticles removed when the three Members signed it, having the
Governor's word.

1 must Beg the Govenor to Reconsider the Matter; it will be an essential Injury to me. Haveing advised my friend some time since that the Permission would be granted, as three Members had signed it, and the Govenor had promissed me if they advised it, he would give his Consent. I Beg your Excellency to excuse my importunity, and to grant me your Signature. Have sent the Certificate to Major Lush and must again intreat the Govenor to help me out of the Difficulty. Am with great Esteem Your Excellencey's Very Hu'e ser't

Peter R. Livingston.

[To Gen. Clinton.]

AIDE-DE-CAMP LUSH'S RESPONSE TO PETER LIVINGSTON.

Nov'r 11" 1778.

Sir, I rec'd your Letter of the 4" Inst. and delivered the Inclosure to his Excellency. After a long search I have found the List for Exemptions to which you allude; it was mislaid by Mr. Benson who had forgot that it had ever been received. I now return it with Exemptions for 39 Persons being all whom he conceives himself authorized by the Militia Law to exempt.

He desires me to inform you that he is surprized, you should found your Expectation of obtain'g his Permission for the Exportation of the 250 Barrels of Flour upon a Promise that he wo'd grant it, if two Members wo'd advise it, when at the Time he mentioned that by the Cert: from the Council of Boston, the Flour you wanted to export was for the use of the Inhabitants of Boston, or rather for the ordinary Business of Trade, and, therefore, not being warranted by Law that no two Members wo'd be found to advise it, adding that similar applications being frequently made to him & had always been refused, that you must readily perceive that such a Promise wo'd therefore be absurd in its Nature, as it would seem to imply that he was willing to violate the Law, if two Members of the Legislature could be found to advise it when his real Intention was to discourage an application that he could not consistent with his duty however willing to oblige you comply with.   He further directs me to inform you, that even if he had made such a Promise, which he does not admit, yet two Members of the Legislature did not at the Time your Cert: was delivered to him to advise the Exportation by signing the Certificate who had recommended it find'g the army distressed for want of Flour thro' the conduct of Monopolizers & Traders in that article, a Circumstance not known to them before earnestly requested the Governor not to add his Permission in Consequence of their hav'g signed the same.

[Stephen Lush.]

[To Peter R. Livingston.]

[No. 1905.]

Samuel Hake Again—Asks for an Extension of His Parole.

Red Hook, 13th Nov'r 1778.

Sir, As the parole which your Excellency was pleased to take from me, deprives me the pleasure of seeing many of my Friends that I have about in the Country, & as I flatter myself your Excellency will not refuse any indulgence which has been granted to other Gentlemen, in a similar situation, I take the liberty to request my Parole may be so far enlarged as your Excellency shall not deem improper. I have lately been informed, it has been asserted, that I shoud have taken an inimical part to these States while in England, which I take this opportunity most solemnly to deny, & doubt not but this disavowing will gain Credit with your Excellency, at least till some proof is adduced to the contrary, more especially as I can confirm it by assertion by Letters which I have in my possession & by others which have been received by Gentlemen in this Country prior to my arrival.

The Goods I purchas'd in N. York & brought up in the Flag, which I obtaind, & being such as Blankets & other articles which the Country & army I judge to be in absolute want of, was doing this State an essential service. Your Excellency will be pleased to remark, that I took no cash or any kind of Produce with me to N. York. If I had the least Idea of giving offence or meeting with the least difficulty, I shoud not have attempted to have come up in so public manner, or to have risqued a shilling prop-erty. I am with the greatest respect Your Excellency's most Obedient Servant

Saml. Hake.

His Excellency Geo: Clinton.

———

[No. 1906.]

ALARMING NEWS FROM THE NORTH AND WEST.

Cherry Valley Again Reported Attacked—Depredations Along Lake Champlain.

Albany 13 Novem'r 1778.

Sir, I had the Honor to write your Excell'cy the 8th Instant, since which I have Rec'd a letter from Col. Van Woert dated at Cambridge the 7th Informing me, that he had Rec'd a letter from Major Armstrong dated at White Creek, the 6th Instant, ac-quainting him that Lake George was full of Boats with Regu-lars, Tories & Indians, Requesting him to come on with his whole Regt; he Informs me he accordingly marched with his Regt., but Returned again in a day or two, the Intelligence not Proving True. General Hand Returned to this place last Tues-day morning; the letter alluded to in mine of the 8th Informed

him that a Person who was made Prisoner & made his Escape
from the Enemy at Crown Point said that there was an Encamp-
m't at that place of about 300 men.   While the General was at
Cherry Valey, Col. Alden Rec'd an Express from Col. Gansevoort
acquainting him that he had Rec'd Information from two Oneida
Indians that at a Council held by the Enemy at Tieoga, it was Determined to fall upon Cherry Valey.   Yestarday morning General
Hand was Informed by letter from Col. Klock that the Enemy
had attacked Col. Alden at Cherry Valey; the General Immediately sett out for that place & at noon Col. Van Schaick's Regt.
marched, I have not as yet heard how the attack has Terminated,or what devestations have been done by the Enemy, save
that Mr. Willis's House & barn which stood near the Fort was
Burned. I Expect momently to hear. At General Hand's Request I Ordered the Regts. of Cols. Lansingh, Schuyler & Quackenboss to Schohary to Reinforce that Post.

Last Evening I Rec'd a letter from Colonel Van Woert Containing the Intelligence of which the Inclosed is Copy, He Informs
me he Immediately marched with his Regt; the other three
northern Regts., viz. Col. McCrea's, Yates's & Schoonhoven's have
had my Orders Sometime past to be in Readiness to march at a
Moment's notice, When I Rec'd Col. Van Woert's letter of the
7th Instant I informed them of its Contents & directed the Col.
nearest to Fort Edward to send an Express to the Commanding
Officer there for Information & to let him know that they were
ready to march to his assistance & to give me the Earliest notice
of their doings & the Discovery motions & Strength of the Enemy.
I have Rec'd no accts. from that Quarter.   I Remain with great
Esteem Your Excellency's most obedient Humble Servant

Ab'm Ten Broeck.

His Excellency George Clinton Esqr.

Cambridge Nov'r 11 1778.

Genl. Ten Broeck,

Hon'd sir, I have Just now rec'd an express from Colo. Webster, dated Charlotte County and the words are as follows,   .

Black Creek Nov'r 10th 1778.

To Colo. Van Woert: This moment have rec'd an express from Skeensbourough that the enemy are burning on both sides of the Lake all the houses & taking all the men prisoners, Striping all the women &. Children the way they go, killing all the Cattle; these are therefore to beg your Immediate assistance as we are on our march—Pray-forward this to the next Colo. or Command'g Officer Send an express to Genl. Ten Broeck. Tell him to send an express to his Excellency the Governour that he may act accordingly from Your hum: Servant

Alexander Webster, Lt. Colo.

The above is a True Copy.

[No. 1907.]

Governor Clinton Offers to Assist in the Search for Cary, who Uttered Counterfeit Money.

Providence State of Rhode Island Novmr. 14 1778.

Sir, One George Cary, of Plainfield, in the State of Connecticut, was lately apprehended hear, on suspicion of his having passed a quantity of Counterfitt Continel Thirty Dollar Bills of Novmr. 2 1776, also Twenty Dollar Notes Emitted by this State baring Date Feb. 1777. But the Evidence not being full against him he was permitted to go at large to collect Evidence of his having taken the Money in fair Trading &c. He has not surrender'd himself according to his promise, but has departed from his Dwelling, and tis supposed he is now in your State at or about Pekepsey, at the House of his Brother Doct'r Ebenezer Carys; he is a likely fair spoken young Man of about Twenty two years of

Age, weirs his own Hair &c.   I most earnestly Request that your Excellency will give Orders that dilligent search be made for the said George Cary.   That he be apprehended and sent in safe Costody to Hartford, or to this place.   If he is strictly Examined, I make no doubt but he can discover Numbers in your State concerned in this Nefarious scheeme.   Your Early attention to this matter will Oblige the publick, and your Excellency's Obedient Humb. Servant.

Jabez Bowen Dep. Gov'r State of Rhode Island &c.

Governor Clinton.

Poukeepsie 19th Nov'r 1778.

Sir, I am honored with your Letter of 14th Novem'r.   Immediate Attention will be paid to the Business it recommends.   I have not the least Doubt if George Cary is at his Brother, the Doct'rs, who lives about 24 Miles from here, or in the Neighbourhood of this Place, he will be apprehended & secured, until he can be forwarded to your state or Hartford.   I am Sir

[G. C.]

Gov'r Bowen.

[No. 1908.]

COURTS MARTIAL PENALTIES.

Governor Clinton Believes in Leniency as Productive of Better Results from the Militia.

Warwick 7th November 1778.

Sir, Agreeable to a General Order of the 21st of September last. I have the honour to transmit your Excellency the proceedings or rather the verdicts of a Court Martial held in my Regiment from the Continued movements of the Regiment, was prevented from Transmitting it Earlier.

I take the liberty of Submitting to your Excellency the Particular situation of John Monger & John Newberry, two of the Inclosed delinquents, whose fines run pretty high; the former was not at home when the Regiment marched; was moving his family to or near New Windsor, and when the Court sat, he had not the Oppertunity of mak'g his defence, not being apprised, of the Court's sitting; the latter has abundantly sattisfied me that he is an infirm person seldom capable of marching or undergoing the least fatigue; therefore, would hope their fines may be lessened or mitigated.

I would thank your Excellency for your direction in Collecting the fines inflicted by Regimental Courts Martial, as don't find any way pointed out by the Militia Law, for that purpose, I think it too great a burthen on Either Adjutant or Serjents, to collect so many fines without being rewarded; the Militia I assure your Excellency, are almost weary even of welldoing; the time that consequently must be spent in obtaining such serious sums of money must be considerable. Neither do I find any provision made to pay the Court Martial for their service, which is an Intollerable Burthen on the Officers.

I send a person with this and hope your Excellency may not be so much engaged in other Business as to prevent your determination on the within proceedings, that return may come back by the bearer, as Immediate Examples are Realy necessary.

I am happy in being at liberty to Transmit this proceedings; the time is Elapsed since I received a message from the Industrious Col. Newkirk, that on my noncompliance to his Special order, given under his hand, I was to be put under an arrest, I have not complyed with the order. I could not think myself Justified in doing it. I consider myself, however unfit to be honoured with the care of a Regiment, therefore, not Subject to the Controul of any Inferior Officer, the Dignity of my Commission I am determined not to lessen, It is my duty and I have made it my Study, to invariably, Execute, every order, of your Excell., as well as other Superior officer. I cant concieve I am vested with power by any Law or order, to make any person go into service; the Militia Law points a punnishment for delinquents by Courts Martial which I had put in practise, previous to the Recieval of your Excellency's Orders, or the Orders of Lieut. Col. Newkerk.

Being Conscious that his* orders was not Complied with, in any of the Neighbouring Regiments no more than mine, I feel myself as willing to endure the Censure of a Court Martial, as to be threatned with it; I think my Conduct will stand the strictest enquiry of a Court Martial; am therefore prepared for defence.

I shall be obliged to continue Courts Martial unless otherwise ordered by your Excellency. I wish it was in my power to recall, and Establish that publick virtue in the minds of every Individual, of my Rgt. Which is apparently lost, it would stimulate to duty, and would Supercede the Necessity of Courts Martial. I have the Honour to be with the Greatest Regard Your Excellencyes most Obedient Servant

John Hathorn.

N. B. Pardon my imperfect Letter being in hast.

His Excell'y Governor Clinton Poughkepsey.

———

At a Regimental Court Martial Held at Warwick in the County of Orange, for the Trial of Sundry delinqu'ts of Col. Hathorn's Regiment of Militia, Commencing the 12th of October and Con-

*Col. Newkerk.

tinued by adjournments unto the Thirty first of the same month 1778; Whereof Capt. Andrew Miller was President, Lieuts. Benjamin Cooley Nathaniel Ketchum and James Right, & Ensigns John Wood & Henry Bartolf Members: the following Persons were fined the several Sums annexed to their names for disobeying orders to march in the late Class Service at Minisink & General Alarm to Parramas:

Andrew Wood £5; Phinehas Tompkins 8; Colvil Bradner Jun'r 40; Abraham Osburn 24; Joseph Todd 5; William Clerk 10; Andrew Christie 5; James Demorest 40; David Demorest 40; Philip Reddick 20; John Newberry 40; John Robinson 24; John Miller 5; Garret Decker 4; John Tebow 40; Smith Wesner 5; Joseph McCane 12; John Coster 5; John Sandford 24; Isaac Winings 5; James Bennedict, Jun'r 12; Anthony Bramer 10; Thaddeus Scott 4; Thomas Allenton 5; Cornelious Decker 2; Samuel Hamanway 5; Joshua Hallack 8; Justice Odle 5; Henry Allison 8; James Tidd 24; Jesse Mullocks 12; James Arsball 5; James Reder 5; Stephen Wood 12; Henry Clerk 20; George Hamilton 8; Isaac Jennings 5; George Wood 5; John Monger 16; Samuel Raner 20; Samuel Raner Jun'r 40; Richard Clerk 5; Timothy Clerk Jun. 6; Henry Jackson 8; John Low 16; Isaac Decker 8; Nathaniel Davies 16; Thomas Welling Jun'r 5; John Welling 5; William Helmes 12; John Kelly 12; Oliver Baley 2.   £687 0.

A Coppy

GOVERNOR CLINTON'S REPLY TO COLONEL HATHORN.

Poukeepsie 14th Nov'r 1778.

Sir, I have received your Letter of the 7th Instant with a Copy of the Proceedings of the Court Martial ag't several Persons for Disobedience of Orders; such of them as you think are hardly dealt with, you will please either to mitigate or remit their Punishment as you may Judge, most conducive to the good of the Service. The Privates tried by a Court Martial are suposed to be in actual Custody & not released till the Fine is paid; an allowance, therefore, for the Collection of them is not provided for by Law. With Respect to the Officers serving on Courts Martial I think it perfectly just & reasonable they should receive pay & Rations as if out on actual service, but I doubt whether the Law as it now stands will warrant my ordering them Payment & I mean, therefore, to apply to the Legislature at their next meeting to have this matter properly explained. On the Complaint of the Frontier Inhabitants I issued my Orders to Lieut. Colo. Newkerk who commands on the Frontier to demand of the different Regts. their respective Proportions. I am ignorant how he has executed my Order as he has not reported his Proceedings to me & he may as well have exceeded his Orders as been uncomplaisant in the Execution of them. I am far however from agreeing that there were great deficiencies in the Militia ordered out for their Protection.

That you are not vested with Power to compell the refractory to do their Share of Duty when ordered into actual Service, they are Subject to Martial Law in its full Extent, & are not only subject to Tryal & Military Punishment for Disobedience of Orders in the first Instance, but are also liable to be forced out & punished for Desertion shoud they quit the Service before properly discharged. I wish however as little Severity may be used as possible, as the milder the means to induce the Militia to perform their Duty if effectual, the better. I am fully perswaded you will always exert yourself in the Execution of your office & am &c.

[G. C.]

[To Col. Hathorn.]

18

[No. 1909.]

The Clove Asks to Become a Permanent Military Post.

Novem'r 14, 1778.

To His Excellency George Clinton Esqr. Governor of the State of
New York.

The Humble Petition and Representation of the Subscribers
Inhabitants of Orange County in Smith's Clove

Humbly Sheweth, That for a Considerable time past, a great
part of that County hath been infested by a Banditti of Villains,
who have Committ'd many Robberies, & Murder, and that at this
time notwithstanding some exertion to suppress them, they continue in Numbers to the great terror of the peacable Inhabitants
as well as danger to Travellers through the Country:

That if some Spirited measure is not Speedily pursued to apprehend their principals, and shorly to reduce the Gang, your
Petitioners are perswaded that the most dangerous Consequence,
may be expected, to the public, as well as certain Ruin to the
Country where they harbour. Deserters already are Collecting to
them and as they are favoured by the Mountanious Situation of
the Country, as well as by too many of the Inhabitants, and also
have an easy communication with New York it's feared that in
a short space of time they will be formidable.

Your Petitioners confess that Colo. Malcom at their Request,
hath for Two Months past kept a party of Troops on duty at the
Clove for their Protection, but for reasons which we cannot dis-
approve of, he has lately called them to the Garrison, so that the
Country is now exposed to the insults, and depredation of those
Lawless banditti.

Your Petitioners therefore moved by their wish for the Public
good, as well as their own safety, most humble intreat your

Excellency will be pleased to Sollicet the Commander in Chief, to Establiss a Post, in the Clove this Winter, which, we are perswaded will have a salutary effect, If conducted by a Judicious Officer or such other means as your Excellency shall judge most proper, for the Public good & their Production and as in duty bound

Your Petitioners Shall ever Pray &c.

Adam Gilchrist, David June, William Miller, Sen., David Miller, Zebert June, David Phillips, Thomas Smith, Benjamin Prindle, David Prindle, Ittiel June, Roger McManus, Peter Reynolds, Thos. Couper, James Runels, Abner Thorp, Silas Reynolds, Chever Devenport, Thomas Devenport, Robert Devenport, John Woolly, John Wygand, Andrew Thorp, John Waygant, Jun., Cloudes Reynolds, Wm. Miller, Abraham Smethen, John Johnston, James Tuthill, Abraham Butler, Francis Smith, John Floranc, Thomas Lemerix, James Galiway, Henry Reynolds, Eseri Earles, John Earles, Sen., William Reynolds, Solomon Lewis, Johnathan Earll, James Lewis, Peter Earll, John Brooks, Samuel Earll, David Reynolds, Daniel Reynolds, Andrw Reynolds, John Lamoureux, Jun'r, John Demerest, Jacob Compton, sen'r, Jacob Compton, Jun'r, Wm. Compton, James Lewis, Jun'r, Samuel Lewis, Fracis Miller, Wm. Clark, Morris Pilgrim, Wm. Bell.

[No. 1910.]

Judge Marvin Requests a Special Commission of Oyer and Terminer be Issued for Orange County.

Goshen 14th November 1778.

May it please your Excellency, At the Court of General Sessions of the Peace holden here this Week, the Grand Jury has found several Bills of Indictment, amongst which are three Bills for High Treason, four for misprison of Treason, several for Horse Stealing, Larceny and other Felonious Crimes—most of the culprits are confined in the Goal in this Town, with several others who will no doubt be Indicted and most probably convicted when a proper court can sit to hear and determin upon their cases.

The Court has, therefore, desired me to request your Excellency that a Commission of Oyer and Terminer may Issue as soon as posible for this County (if it has not Issued already) in order that those Villains may be speedily brought to Trial, least by some means they should make their Escape, the consequence of which might prove fatal to several very valuable members of society, as the implacable nature of those Enemies of Mankind knows no relief but in Revenge. I am with Esteem your Excellencies most obedient Humble Servant

Elihu Marvin.

Governor Clinton.

[No. 1911.]

Count Pulaski Stationed at Minisink.

Rochester Nov'r 15th 1778.

Dear Sir, Upon the Receipt of your Excellency's Letter I went to Minisink in Company of Colo. Cantine. I found about 150 men at that post, 40 of which I Sent Under the Command of Capt. Cuddiback to the assistance of Colo. Sowers who was gone to Keshecton, and by accounts which I collected from Some persons who had left him, I was led to believe he wanted assistance to Cross the Mingoup Kill. Various and uncertain are the accounts from that Quarter; however, I am not apprehensive of the Enemy attempting any thing further this Season. Upon my return I found orders from his Excellency Genl. Washington to Remain here, where I have taken post accordingly and shall guard

as far as Lunen Kill. Count Polasky is to take post at the Minisinks, and then I should Immagine the militia may be Discharged,
it being too far advanced in the Season to attempt doing much in
the Expidition way this Fall. Shall be glad your Excellency will
please to give Directions with Respect to the Militia am with all
Respect yr. obd. Hum'e Servant

Philip Cortlandt.

[To Gov. Clinton.]

[No. 1912.]

Governor Clinton Approves General Ten Broeck's Dispositions.

Nov'r 15" 1778 Poghkeepsie.

Sir, I this moment rec'd yours of the 13" Inst. pr. Express.
Colo. Cortlandt's Regiment, Contin' Troops, the one half of the
militia of Ulster and Orange Countys, the ¼ of this, are now on the
Western Frontier of Orange & Ulster and his Excellency General
Washington has ordered Count Pulaski's new raised Legion
(which is also some accession of Force) to Minisink.

I much approve of the steps you have taken in the ordering out
of the Militia of your Brigade for the Defence of the Frontiers and
in assisting General Hand as occasion required.

Your attention to the Northern Frontier also receives my approbation. I would wish equal Care to be used for the safety and
Protection of the Inhabitants there, as of those on the western
Frontier. You will continue to give Genl. Hand every assistance
in your Power and to transmit me by Express such accounts as
you esteem of any Importance. Be assured that my Endeavors
shall not be wanting to render you occasionally every aid I can
obtain or command for your Relief.

[G. C.]

[To Gen. Ten Broeck.]

[No. 1913.]

GOVERNOR CLINTON DECLINES.

Sheriff Nicoll of Orange County Fails to Obtain a Small Militia Guard for the Goshen Gaol.

Goshen Nov'r 14 1778.

May it please your Excellency, There is a number of persons In Goal here aganste whome the Grand Jury have found Bills of a high nature, and a number of Others who will no doubt be found guilty when properly Charged, and it is beyon a peradventure with me, that they will endevor to make their Escape, and I am afraid will affect it unless a Better Guard is allowed then at present; the Militia Guards in General are very remiss, especily when neare home; and those at the Court House, are Such as Live in Goshen; it tis the Opinion of the Court, that a Subaltern's Guard aught to be kept, untill Such time as the Court of Oyer & Terminer Sets, and I Should be glad if a Militia Guard is Continued that it might be Ordered out of Coll. Hathorn's Redgment.

I am with Due Respect your Excellency's Most Obedient and Humble Servent

Isaac Nicoll.

To His Excellency George Clinton.

The Governor's Answer.

[November ——, 1778.]

Sir, I have rec'd yours of the 14" Inst. yesterday. I do not think any Militia Guard will be a sufficient Check upon the Prisoners unless they are in the Custody of a good Gaoler and properly secured with Irons. We have Claudius Smith, Austin Smith and severall other Capital Offenders in Prison here. They are well secured with Irons and added to this the principal People of the Place to the Number of 30 have voluntarily divided themselves into Parties of 6 each Night. They sit in the Court Room and visit the Prisoners every Hour and mean to continue this Duty until the Gaol is discharged. Let me, therefore, recommend similar Measures to be pursued by the Inhabitants of Goshen who I trust have at least equal Zeal for the public Security. It will keep your Prisoners safe and ease the ordinary militia of a Share of Duty that does not properly belong to them.

By the Bearer Mr. Barclay, you will receive a Precept for a Court of Oyer & Terminer & Genl. gaol Delivery signed by Mr. Justice Hubbart. I have directed Barclay to go by the way of the New Paltz and to get Judge Marvin who is attend'g a Court martial at that Place also to sign it, and you will on the Receipt of it, either immediately go yourself or send a trusty deputy and get Judge Haring or Judge Cooper to sign it or both if any accident prevents Mr. Marvin from signing it as it must be signed by three of the Judges at least. This Business must not be delayed as there must be at least 15 Days between the Receipt of it properly executed by three of the Judges & the Day of its Return which is on Tuesday the 15th of December next. I am Sir

[G. C.]

[To Isaac Nicoll.]

[No. 1914.]

President Laurens Keeps in Touch with New York State.

Philadelphia 16th November 1778.

Sir, My last address to your Excellency was under the 16th Ultimo by Messenger Brown, since which I have not received any of your favors.

I now have the honor of inclosing herewith two Copies of the undermentioned acts of Congress viz.

An act of the 26th August 1776 for establishing a provision for Soldiers and Seamen maimed or disabled in the service of the United States—to which is subjoined a supplementary act of the 25th September 1778 for the benefit of maimed or disabled Volunteers in the service of the States antecedent to the date of the first above-mentioned act.

An act of the 26th September for organizing the public Treasury* and for providing an House for the several offices of Treasury.

You will likewise receive an act of Congress for holding a general Thanksgiving throughout these States on Wednesday the 30th December next—and three Copies of the Treaty of Amity and Commerce and of Alliance eventual and defensive between His Most Christian Majesty and these United States for the information and use of the State of New York. I have the honor to be with the highest Respect & Esteem Sir Your Excellency's Most obedient & Most humble servant.

Henry Laurens, President of Congress.

His Excellency George Clinton Esquire Governor of New York.

[No. 1915.]

CAPTAIN SWARTWOUT CASHIERED.

Failure of His Charges Against Colonel Frear, who is Vindicated by a Court Martial.

At a Brigade Court Martial held on Monday the 16th Day of November 1778 at the House of Wm. Haskin at New Hackinsack, in Rombouts Precinct, for the Trial of such Commissioned officers as were ordered to appear before said Court by order of Colo. Comdt. Jacobus Swartwout of the Militia of the County of Dutches, of which Court was

Colo. Abraham Brinckerhoff President:

Members:

Lieut. Colo., Jacob Griffen,	Capt., John V. Bunschooten,
Maj'r, Andrew Hill,	Capt., Hugh Van Kleeck,
Capt., George Brinckerhoff,	Capt., John Brinckerhoff,
Capt., John Van Kleeck,	Capt., Isaac Van Wyck,
Capt., Matthew V. Bunschooten,	Capt., Thomas Storm,
Capt., Johannes Scutt,	Capt., Lemuel Concklin,

Hend'k Wyckoff to act as Judge Advocate.

---

* See page 93.

The President and Members being Duly sworn by the Judge Advocate, and the Judge Advocate by the President, according to Order Proceeded upon Buisiness.

A Charge against Lieut. Finch of Colo. Hopkins Regt. being sent by Colo. Comdt. Swartwout and laid before said Court being as follows,

A Charge against Leut. Finch of Colo. Hopkins Regt. for taking Thirty Dollars from Elisha Latimore who lives at the City, for Receiving a Boy under Size in the place of a Militia Man to serve the last Tour at Fort Clinton.

Sign'd—Elisha Latimore Lieut.

Oct'r 29th 1778.

Lieut. Finch not appearing before said Court, the Court have thought proper to acquaint the Colo. Comdt., as soon as possible of the Non appearance of Lt. Finch.

A Charge was laid before said Court by Colo. John Frear against Capt. Barnardus Swartwout of his Regt. whom Colo. Frear had put under arrest, the Charge being as follows,

Charge against Capt. Barnardus Swartwout of my Regt. for Disobedience of orders and behaving unbecoming as an Officer.

Poughkeepsie (October) 1778. John Frear Colo.

Capt. Barnardus Swartwout appearing before said Court pleads not Guilty.

David Cypher, a private of Capt. Barnardus Swartwout's Company, Colo. Frear's Regt., appearing before said Court as an Evidence and being Duly sworn saith, that he heard Colo. John Frear tell Capt. Barnardus Swartwout on the Road, not to go to the Fort, that he was not wanted there, that he the Colo., had got another man in Capt. Swartwout's Room, and that Colo. Frear told Capt. Swartwout farther to turn out such men as Could be best spared, single men and such as were hired and not men of families and Distress their Families.

Lieut. Abraham Fort of Capt. Barnardus Swartwout's Company in said Regt. appearing before said Court as an Evidence and being Duly Sworn saith, That he himself Delivered a warrant of Colo. John Frear to Capt. Barnardus Swartwout—the warrant being produced to the Court by Capt. Swartwout Read as follows,

Poughkeepsie Sept'r 24th 1778.
Sir, You are hereby Required and Commanded to turn out Six men from the fourth Class of your Company Immeadiately, in Order to Guard the Governor's and the Court House who are to serve for one Month unless sooner Discharged, You are likewise Required to Releive the Men weekly. Fail not at your Peril.

John Frear, Colo.

N. B. You are likewise Commanded to turn out your first Lieutenant to Command the Guard.

After the Deponent had Delivered the warrant to Capt. Swartwout and having Read it he (Capt. Swartwout) got the Deponent to write an answer to said warrant to Colo. Frear which Letter Capt. Swartwout Signed himself (a Copy of the Letter being produced Read as follows),

Wappens Creek Sept'r 24th 1778.
Sir, Whereas I Received Orders from you this morning to turn out Six Men out of the fourth Class of my Company which I think ungenerous and not Consistent with the Laws of our Assembly to turn out any of the fourth Class, before the third Class has done their Tour of Duty, so I dont Intend to send any of the fourth Class untill the third Class has done their Tour, as the weekly Releif of the Third Class is going up this Day, and as each man has served only one fortnight, their Tour will not be out untill the 24th of next month; after that time is Expired if it is then Required, I will send men out of the fourth Class.

N. B. You also Command me to order my first Lieutenant to take the Command of the Guard which belongs to the Fourth Class, which I will not order 'till the Lieuts. of the Third Class has done their Tour.

B. Swartwout.

After the Letter was wrote and Capt. Swartwout had put his name to it, he Desired the Deponent to Deliver the Letter to Colo. Frear; the Deponent made an apology, that if he Carried the Letter and Delivered it to Colo. Frear, that Colo. Frear would order him to take the Command of the Guard, Capt. Swartwout answered, that he might do as he pleased, but if he did not take the Command of the Guard after being thereunto Commanded by Colo. Frear, that he (Capt. Swartwout) would stand between him and all harm, upon which the Deponent Carried the Letter and Delivered it to Colo. Frear, who after Reading it, Commanded the Deponent to take the Command of the Guard and send a warrant to the Corporal of the fourth Class, to warn six men out of the fourth Class During the term of one month, both which the Deponent obeyed and sent a warrant to the Corporal. Two Days afterwards Capt. Swartwout, saw the Deponent and shewed the Deponent the same warrant which he sent to the Corporal, and asked the

Deponent if it was his Hand writing; he answered Capt. Swartwout, it was his Hand writing; then Capt. Swartwout Immeadiately ordered the Deponent under arrest for Disobeying his orders, and said, he, (Capt. Swartwout) had taken the warrant away from the Corporal himself—farther saith, that Colo. Frear ordered him (the Deponent) to send the serjeant of the Third Class then with the Guard with the above warrant, to the Corporal and told the Serjt., that he need not Return again as the Guard of the fourth Class was Coming to Releive him—farther saith not.

The Court after Due Deliberation are of opinion and agree that Capt. Barnardus Swartwout is Guilty of the Charge alledged against him, and, therefore, unfit of Holding a Commission and ought to be Cashiered.

Colo. John Frear appearing before said Court for trial, being ordered under arrest by Colo. Comdt. Jacobus Swartwout, upon Complaint of Capt. Bernardus Swartwout.

Capt. Barnardus Swartwout appearing before said Court brought three Charges against Colo. John Frear which being Laid before said Court and were Read as follows—

1st Charge, against Colo. Frear, Commanding me to turn out more than the fourth man which is against the Governor's orders.

Oct'r 31st 1778.   Barnardus Swartwout.

2nd Charge, Commanding the Fourth Class on Duty or Command a fortnight before it fell to them by Ballot and Discharging the Third Class from Duty a fortnight before their time was Expired by Ballot.

Oct'r 31st 1778.   Barnardus Swartwout.

3rd Charge, against Colo. Frear, for neglect to give or Render a just account of all the Delinquents monies which was Collected and the assess money of his Regt. from the 6th of August 1777 untill the first Day of Oct'r 1778.

Oct'r 31st 1778.   Barnardus Swartwout.

Colo. John Frear Pleads, not Guilty.

Lieut. Stephen Hendrickson of Capt. Hugh Van Kleeck's Company, Colo. Frear's Regt., appearing before said Court as an Evidence, and being Duly sworn saith, that Capt. Barnardus Swartwout came to his House and Desired him to go with him to his Excellency's the Gov'r that the Deponent having an Errand there himself accordingly went with Capt. Swartwout. Upon the way Capt. Swartwout told the Deponent his Buisiness; that his Company was abused &c; that he was going to Complain upon Coming to the Governor's. His Excellency came out; Capt. Swartwout laid his Grievance before his Excellency, who answered that it was Impossible for him to Enter into the Details of the Companies; that if his Company was abused he must apply to the Commandant; if the Commandant would not see him Righted he would, and farther said that he Commanded no more than one fourth part of the Militia out into actual service. What Discourse passed farther between his Excellency and Capt. Swartwout the Deponent does not Remember—farther saith not.

The Court after Due Deliberation are of opinion and agree that the first and second Charges or Crimes alledged against Colo. John Frear not being supported, that Colo. Frear is not Guilty.

Concerning the Third Charge against Colo. Jno..Frear, the Court are of opinion and Judge, that it does not Belong to this Court to Call Colo. Frear to Render an account of the assess money of his Regt., and that it is out of the Power of this Court to Meddle with the same; and this Court, therefore, are of Opinion that Colo. John Frear ought to be Discharged from his arrestment with Honour.

                                              Abr'm Brinckerhoff President.

New Hackinsack Nov'r 16th 1778.
        A true Copy from the Original.
                Hend'k Wyckoff.

                                    Poughkeepsie th 24th August 1778.
Sir, You are hereby ordered to send six men out of your Company to Poughkeepsie to keep gard on his Excelencies Request well acquiped and accutered to Be in Sarvices for the space of one fortenite and then to Releaved By others. You may fix your for one week if you Like or any other Convenant manner the whole gard will Consist of 24 men under the Command of one Lutennant the men are to Be Thare on Tuesday att 12 o'Clock if possible and if you Can not get them Ready the 27 in the Morning. Given under my hand.

                                              John Frear, Col.

Capt. Barnardus Swartwout.

Poughkeepsie the 31 August 1778.

Sir, In Consequans of orders Receaved of His Excelencey Requesting the Forth part of the Mallitia to gard the post and pass in the Highlands att Fort Arnold, you are therefore Commanded to order that part of your Companey which Have Sarved part of there Time, to Sarve one month Including the time Thay Have alereadey Sarved, Then to Be Releaved By the Next Class. Theay are to be well acquiped and accotered if posable. You will also Hold the Rest of your Companey In parfect Readyness to March on the Shortest Notice if Requiered. Hereof Fail Not att your peril. Given under my hand.

John Frear, Coll.

Capt. Swartwout.

N. B. Thay to march Saterday next or Shuner if posable.

Fort Clinton September ye 23 1778.

Capt. Swartwout is dismiss with his Compny—permitt them to Cross the River.

James V D Burgh.

Samuel Concklin—1; 1 Liet. Stephen Hendricks 1; 2d Liet. John Johnson; Ensign Abraham Van Keuren. Officers that are to Go with the first Class.

Second Class: B. Swartwout, Capt; Eliphelet Platt 1 Liet; Elias Frayr 2 Lie; Henry Kip Ensign.

Third Class: John Van Kleek, Capt. Jacobus Frayr, 1 Liet,. Simon Leroy, 2 Liet. Phelix Lewis, Ensig.

Fourth Class: Hugh Van Kleek, Capt; Abraham Fort, 1 Lie; Simon Lawson, 2 Liet; Jacobus Van Debogert.

A List of those men in my Compeny that is not Able to Buy Guns: Matthew Duboys, John French, Levy Quimby, Isaac Piet. Lawson, John Henrick Mires, Thomas Duboys, George Ames, Jeremiah Duboys, Isaac Forgeson.

Fort Arnold July 18, 1778.

Capt. Swartwout, with the Company of Militia under his Command from the State of New York, have General Glover's thanks for their services at this post, & are permitted to pass from hence to their respective places of abode, by the General's Commad.

Thomas Fosdick, Major Brigade.

[No. 1916.]

Mr. Hillhouse's Permit to Export Flour Threatened.

Amenia 16th Nov'r 1778.

Sir, Lieut. Doty waits on your Excellency with a Letter from Mr. Colt which I Conclude is to Indeavour to Put a Stop to Particular Persons Purchasing Large Quantities of Flour Under Pretence of Purchasing For the Eastern State Troops. Great abuses have been Committed in that way, Especially by one Hillhouse, who is Purchasing Large Quantities in my District Part of which he Pays in hard Money what he pays in Paper Money he Pays at an Advans't Price from the Resident Purchasers.

I Could wish No Permits might be Given to Such People as it only Tends to Raise the Price and is a Violation of a Rule of Congress which forbids Purchasers Interfearing into other Districts. I am S'r Your Humb. Serv't

James Reed, A. C. P.

His Excellency Gov. Clinton Esq. Poughkeepsie.

Poukeepsie 17th Nov'r 1778.

Sir, I have received your Letter of the 16th Instant. You may rest assured that no Person shall have my Permission to export any Quantity of Flour out of the State until the army is supplied. Mr. Hillhouse procured a Permit to export 50 Ton on the Recommendation of Gov'r Trumbull but as I have good Reason to believe he has abused the Indulgence by already exporting a greater Quantity, if this is the Case & I think you may easily prove it, his Permit [should be revoked]. I am Sir your most Obed't Serv't

Geo. Clinton.

[To James Reed Esq.]

[No. 1917.]

DESTRUCTION OF CHERRY VALLEY.

Reports from Subordinate Officers Transmitted Through Governor Clinton to General Washington.

Schenectady 15th Nov'r 1778.

D'r Sir, Upon Information that the Enemy on the Evening of the 12th Inst. had left Cherry Valley after having destroyed the Village and put a Number of the Inhabitants together with Colo. Alden and some of the Garrison to the Sword, the Number of which cannot as yet be particularly ascertained, I recommended it to Colo. Clock who had collected about three hundred of the Militia to pursue them, if he found it practicable; but a want of a sufficient supply of Provisions & ammunition added to a Persuasion that the Enemy had gone too far to be overtaken induced the Colo. to lay aside all Thoughts of a pursuit and disband his Regt. I, therefore, left Cocknawaga yesterday and arrived last evening at this Place, where I had not been many Hours before I was sur-

prised with the disagreable Intelligence of the Enemy having
returned yesterday Morning and at 12 O'Clock took the Garrison
of Fort Alden by Storm.   Colo. Van Scaak's Regt. was advanced
as far as Fort Johnson this Morning, and pushing forward with
all possible Dispatch for Fort Plank, which, you will see by the
inclosed Letters, is reported to be likewise attacked.   I shall
leave this immediately for aforesaid Place and use every Means
in my Power to check the further Approaches of these Savages.
Time will not admit of my writing to his Excellency Genl. Washington; shall therefore be much obliged to you, sir, to forward
him the Intelligence.   I am sir with esteem Your most Obt. Serv't

Edw'd Hand.

His Exc'y Geo. Clinton.

GENERAL TEN BROECK TO GENERAL HAND.

Albany 12" Nov'r 1778 5 P. M.

Sir, Agreable to your request I immediately ordered Colo. Lansing's, Schuyler's & Col. Quackenbosh Regts. to Schohary & I
desired Capt. Sprout who travelled with you to desire you to
give Orders to Col. Wemple who commands the Schonectady
militia.

The inclosed is a copy of a Letter I just this moment received
from Colonel Van Woert of my Brigade, Before I rec'd this I had
determined to sett out early in the morning presence.   I now wish
to receive your directions.   Some days ago I sent orders to the
Colonels of my four northern Regt. to hold their Regts. ready at
a moment's notice, & directed Col. Van Vegten who lives at
Saratoga, to send an Express to Fort Edward to know from the
commanding officer there whether the Intelligence he received
made it necessary for them to march but have not yet heard from

that Quarter. I remain with esteem Sir Your most humb. servant

                                              Ab'm Ten Broeck.
    The Honble. Genl. Hand.

MAJOR WHITING TO GENERAL HAND.

Fort Alden Cherry Valley Nov. 13, 1778.

Hon'd Sir, I embrace the earliest opportunity the present situation of our affairs would admit of, to inform you of the state of the Garrison. On the 11" ins. the Enemy, notwithstanding all our endeavours to the contrary, surprised us, having taken a scout of Sergt. & 8 of ours & took one & compelled him to pilot them to the officers Quarters. They push'd vigorously for the fort and had it not been for great activity & alertness of the Troops they had rushed within the lines. The Colonel fell in attempting geting to the Fort; the Lt. Col. Stacy was made prisoner, together with one Lt., one Ens., the Surgeon's mate & a few privates. We had about 6 or 8 of the Regt. killed, some missing. The enemy was very numerous; burnt all the buildings in the settlement, killed a great number of the inhabitants, men women & Children, carryed off many prisoners; some few that hid in the woods have got into the Fort. They collected all the cattle, horses & Sheep they could and drove off; they paid us a second visit yesterday, but nothing of them has been discovered this day. Notwithstanding the earliest & repeated dispatches to the river have had no reinforcement from there. When we were first attacked, we had not a pound of bread pr man in garrison; had it not been for a barrel of powder & half a box of Catridges belonging to the Town, our ammunition would have failed us. One Scout, a Sergt. & 8 men that went by the Butternuts has not been heard off yet. I am with due respect Sir Your very humb. servant

Daniel Whiting.

Genl. Hand Schonec'd.

P. S. We have a Soldier with his leg broken, that's necessary to be amputated; the Surg. has no Instruments; request a case to be sent if possible.

———

COLONEL GORDON TO COLONEL GOOSE VAN SCHAICK.

Fort Plank 14" Nov'r 1778.

D. sir, Colonel Clyde is this moment arrived from Cherry Valley & brings the melancholy news that the Fort at that place was taken by Storm this day about 12 O'clock, He was out with a party burying the dead and collecting the few effects the Indians had left, when he heard three cannon fire at the Fort. He immediately ran towards it and did not see any one in the outside, but heard dreadfull yells of Indians and cries of murder in the inside. You will, therefore, no doubt think it necessary to march your Regt. up as quick as possible, and get them in this side of the River, to be ready to assist us in case they should come towards the river in the morning. Yours in haste

James Gordon Lt. Col.

Colonel Goose V. Schaick.

———

JELLES FONDA TO COLONEL VAN SCHAICK.

1778 Nov. 14" at 11 O'clock at night.

Sir, Just now John Ryckman Jun'r came to my house who was sent from Anthony V. Vegten, Esqr. by Col. Fred'k Pellenger & says that Fort Plank is attacked and that Col. Pellenger heard the Cannon fire as also did the Bearer the Express. Pray come on with all speed with your Regt. He will inform you further about it. I am your very Hum. servant

Jelles Fonda.

To Col. G. V. Schaick.

In his absence to the next Commanding Officer.

COLONEL VAN SCHAICK FORWARDS THE LETTERS TO GENERAL HAND.

Mount Johnson Sunday morning 2 O'clock.

Sir, The inclosed letters this moment came to hand I have sent forward for your information. I shall march my Regt. for Canajohary as soon as the daylight appears. I am with respect Your very Humble servant

Goose Van Schaick Colo.

General Hand.

AND GENERAL HAND SENDS COPIES TO GOVERNOR CLINTON.

Sir, I am requested by the Honble. General Hand to send the inclosed copies of Letters to you by Express. I am with respect Your Excellency most Obed. Humb. servant

Henry Glen.

Schen. Nov'r 15th 1778.

To His Excellency G. Clinton, Poughkeepsie.

GOVERNOR CLINTON TRANSMITS THEM TO GENERAL WASHINGTON.

Poukeepsie 17th Nov'r 1778.

Dear Sir, I am this Moment honored with yours of the 15th Instant with the very disagreeable Accounts from Cherry Valley which according to your Request I have forwarded to his Excellency Genl. Washington. If I do not hear that Enemy have left the Frontier & nothing extraordinary happens to prevent me I mean to set out for Albany Tomorrow or next Day at farthest that I may be the better able to render you assistance. I am with great Regard your most Obed't Serv't

[G. C.]

[To Gen. Hand.]

[No. 1918.]

AN AGGRESSIVE MOVEMENT NECESSARY.

Governor Clinton's Suggestions to John Jay—Cherry Valley the Seventh Valuable Settlement Destroyed in this State.

Nov'r 17" 1778 Pokepsie.

D'r Sir, I have this moment received the Letters & Papers of which the inclosed are Copies, giving the very disagreeable account of the Destruction of Cherry Valley by the Enemy & of their having surprized & taken Fort Alden at that Place by Storm, which I begg you to lay before Congress for their Information. Fatal Experience has more than sufficiently taught us the Impracticability of defending our extensive Frontiers by the Militia of the County & the small Proportion of regular Troops imployed in that service against an Enemy acting upon a desultory Plan. There are so many Passes leading into the Different important Settlements to the Northward & westward which equally claim attention, that when the present Force is distributed for their Defence it becomes too weak to resist the united strength of the Enemy employed against any particular Point. Cherry Valley was occupied by Colo. Alden's Regt. and was, therefore, esteemed to be most secure; but even here the Enemy have proved too strong for us. This is the 7th valuable settlement in the state which this season has been destroyed exclusive the Injuries & Distresses experienced by Individuals. The Public have losst by the Destruc-

19

tion of these settlements some of the principal Granaries in this State from whence alone the army might have drawn supplies sufficient, at least to have prevented their present want.

It is of the utmost Importance that some more effectual Measures than have hitherto been pursued be adopted for the Defence of the Frontiers & I am perswaded this can only be effected by Offensive Opperations, thereby carrying the War into the Enemy's Country, For which Purpose a proper Force ought to be imployed, I might say raised for, unless the Enemy at N. Y. leave us I can't think a Competent Force can be detached from the Main Army without leaving it too Weak. If the Enemy are suffered to continue their Depredations much longer the Consequence may be fatal, as this state will be disabled from furnishing any supplies to the army & hitherto they have depended upon it for Bread.   I am Sir,

                                                              [G. C.]

[To John Jay Esq.]

[No. 1919.]

"WANTON DESTRUCTION AND HORRID MURDERS."
Course of the Enemy at Cherry Valley—False Rumor Regarding Fort Alden.

Head Quarters, Schohary November 17th 1778.

Sir, In my last which I had the Honor to address you from Albany, I informed you that I had ordered three Regiments to the assistance of this post, and on Friday last set out for this place where I arrived on Saturday, and it gives me pain to add, that of the three Regiments ordered, but about 100 of Colo. Lansing's and 60 of Colo. Schuyler's Regiments arrived with me, and about 50 of Colo. Quackenboss's Regiment are just come.   Upon my arrival here I found that Colo. Butler had marched with his

Regt. of Continental Troops and the Corps of Riflemen to the relief of the Garrison of Fort Alden at Cherry Valley, and that this Post was left to the Detachment of Militia who had been here for some Time, consisting, by the returns, of about 90 men.   On Sunday about 12 O'Clock Colo. Butler returned, who informed me he had been within seven Miles of Fort Alden, that he there received a Letter from Major Whiting (who commands that Fort) informing him that the Enemy had left Cherry Valley, on the 12th Instant, and that they had march'd twenty Miles before Evening.   On the afternoon of the 15th, I received a Letter from General Hand, dated the same day at Schonectady, acquainting an Express had come to him, with an account that the Enemy had carried Fort Alden by Storm on the 14th and had attack'd Fort Plank; that previous, thereto, he had discharged Colo. Wemple's Regt. of Militia and that Colonels Klock and Fisher upon arriving at Cherry Valley and finding the Enemy were returned had dismiss'd their Militia, and concluded by requesting that Colo. Butler and myself would move all the Force we could spare from the immediate defence of this place towards the Enemy.   In this State of public affairs, I deemed it expedient to call a Council of the officers, as well Continental as militia, before whom I laid the Letter from Genl. Hand, and they unanimously determined that no Troops could be spared from the Defence of this post, without leaving the settlement exposed to the ravages of the Enemy, tho' there were more perhaps than were necessary for the sole defence of the Fort; but as the protection of the Settlement was an object of the first Consideration they esteem'd it unadvisable to detach any part of them.   Of this I informed General Hand by Express; and yesterday received another Letter from him, dated at Caughnawaga, containing the happy Tidings that Fort Alden was still in our possession and that the Intimation he had received respecting its being taken, was groundless, and requested me not to march the Troops as he had desired in his former Letter.

I have now with me of Colo. Lansing's Regiment about 150 men, and of Colo. Schuyler's ab't 160. The latter is stationed with his Regiment at the lower Fort, and the former in the vicinity of the middle Fort, there being no covering for the Men in the Fort or Lines. Colo. Quackenboss I have ordered to take post at the upper Fort to join part of the Schohary Militia who are at that post.

As this is the fifth Day since the Enemy commenc'd their retreat, and having no Tidings of them from our Scouts who are kept out constantly, I flatter myself they do not mean to attempt the Destruction of this settlement at this Time; and the season being so far advanc'd leads me to think they will hardly return from their Holes, to renew an Expedition replete with Fatigue and Danger. Our Scouts tell us there is twelve Inches of Snow in the woods.

By the above Letter from Major Whiting to Colo. Butler, we learn that Colo. Alden is killed, and Colo. Stacey made Prisoner; the Scout from Colo. Alden's Regiment, consisting of two Subalterns and 12 privates, were taken or killed, which was the cause of the surprize. The most wanton destruction and horrid murders have been committed by the Enemy. The Settlement of Cherry Valley is entirely destroyed and about thirty men women and Children were massacred. By the best accounts we have been able to get of the Enemy's strength, they are about 600 Indians, 150 Tories, 50 British Troops and four British officers. I remain with great Esteem Your Excellency's most humble Servant,

Ab'm Ten Broeck.

His Excellency, George Clinton Esqr. &c.

[No. 1920.]

MILITIA NOT TO BE DISCHARGED.

In Consequence of the Startling News from Cherry and the Mohawk Valleys.

Nov'r 18, 1778 Pokepsie.

Sir, On the 17" Inst. I received a Letter from Genl. Hand of the 15th, inclosing Copies of several Papers & Letters, giving the following accounts: that on the 13" Instant Cherry Valley was destroyed by the Enemy, all the Buildings burnt, a Number of the Inhabitants, Men, women & Children barbarously murdered, Colo. Alden & some of his Regiment put to the Sword, and his Lt. Colo. (Stacy) some Officers & a few Privates and Inhabitants made Prisoners; that on the 14" Inst. after the Enemy were supposed to have gone off & the Militia was disbanded Fort Alden (in Cherry Valley) was taken by storm and from every Circumstance the Garrison cruelly murdered—& that on the same Day Fort Plank (lying on the Mohawk River) was attacked. Colo. Van Schaack was on his March for the Relief of Fort Plank and the Militia of Albany & Schenectady are ordered to cover the Frontiers and act as occasion requires. The Party of savages & Tories who have committed these Depredations are numerous, & from the best Intelligence I have received collected at the Tioga Branch of the Susquehanah, I suppose at Chemung, & are command'd by Brandt & young Butler & it is said there are some British Troops with them. I do not, therefore, think it wo'd be adviseable to discharge the Militia as suggested in your Letter of the 15", till we have the most certain accounts of the Enemy's hav'g left the Frontier; and in the mean Time it wo'd be proper that strong Reconnoiting Parties be kept out towards the Delaware. You'l please to forward a Copy of this to Count Pulaski for his Information. I am &c.

[G. C.]

[To Col. Cortlandt.]

[Nos. 1921, 1926.]

FOR MONEY AND PROTECTION.

Clinton Delegates Two Agents to Obtain the One Hundred Thousand Dollars from Congress—Continental Troops Required on the Frontier.

Nov'r 18" 1778.

Gentlemen, This will be delivered to you by Ab'm B. Bancker, Esqr. or Mr. Peter Wyncoop* whom in Pursuance of an act of the Legislature passed at their last Meeting I have employed to bring forward to our Treasury the 100,000 Dollars advanced by Congress in Favor of this State. These Gentlemen will produce you a certified Extract of the act with an order to warrant the Delivery of the Money to them, and as they will be accompanied by a Guard which will be attended with Expence I have to request that they may meet with as little Delay at Philadelphia as possible.

I wrote to Mr. Jay yesterday, giving him the disagreable acct. of the Destruction of Cherry Valley and the Loss of Fort Alden at that Place, with Copies of several Papers respecting our affairs in that Quarter, which as Mr. Jay was to set out this Day or Tomorrow for Philadelphia must reach you before this can. I have only to add Copies of two Papers which I had not rec'd at my writing to Mr. Jay as they were not transmitted me by Express.

I need not repeat to you, Gentlemen, the impracticabillity of defending our Extensive Frontiers by the Militia of the Country & the necessity there is of some more effectual Measures being speedilly taken by Congress for this Purpose, which if neglected will end in the total Desolation of the most valuable Parts of this state. I am sensible, Offensive Opperations only can give

---

*See page 321.

us Security and that the season is too far advanced to attempt any Thing formidable at present; but it is of the utmost Importance that Preparations shoud be made again the opening of the spring; & in the Mean Time the Troops which are to be employed in this Service shoud be stationed on the Frontiers, which woud not only give spirit to the Inhabitants & prevent the Desertion of their Settlements, but enable us to carry the war into the Enemy's Country as early as practicable.

[G. C.]

[To New York Delegates in Congress.]

---

*Copy of an Extract from an Act entitled "An act for the Payment of the several Sums, and for other purposes therein mentioned."

WHEREAS the Congress of the United States of America have Advanced to this State the Sum of One hundred thousand Dollars, Be it therefore further enacted by the Authority aforesaid that his Excellency the Governor be and he is hereby Authorized to send for the said Monies in such manner as he shall think most proper and to cause the same to be deposited into the Treasury of this State and that the Legislature will provide for the Expence attending the same.

A true Copy.

Abr'm B. Bancker D. Secretary.

To the Delegates of the State of New York in Congress of the United States of America and to the Honble. William Duer Esqr.

Please to Deliver to Messrs. Abraham B. Banker & Peter Wynkoop or either of them One hundred thousand Dollars advanced

---

*Mr. George W. Clinton numbered this matter as document 1926. It is a part of and properly belongs with document 1921. Hence the transfer.—STATE HISTORIAN.

by Congress to this State whom I have appointed agreable to an act of the Legislature of which the above is an Extract to bring forward & deposit the same in the Treasury of this State taking their Receipt. Given at Poukeepsie this 18th Day of Nov'r 1778.

G. C.

Attest

Instructions to Messrs. Abraham B. Bancker & Peter Wyncoop.

Gentlemen, As you are intrusted with the important Charge of bringing from Philadelphia to the Treasury of this State 100,000 Dollars advanced by Congress I have directed Capt. Salisbury of Ulster County to provide you a Guard of a serjt & 4 Men from his Company of Light Horse properly armed and accoutred to be ready at such Time & Place as you may appoint. It is my Desire that you set out as early in the Beginning of next week as may be convenient to you and your own Prudence will dictate the Propriety of keeping the Nature of your Business a secret as if it was publickly known it might induce evil minded Persons to waylay you and rob you of your Charge. In going down you'l make yourselves acquainted with the best affected Neighbourhoods in which you will lodge upon your Return where you will keep nightly Guards at least of two at a Time but this ought to be done in such a manner as to create the least possible suspicion of the Importance of your Business. The Letter accompanying this directed to the Delegates is to apprize them of your Commission & give you Dispatch. You'l receive also with this an Extract of the act authorizing me to execute this Business with my order thereon warrant'g the Payment of the money to you. I have only to add that you will be as expeditious as possible keeping an exact acct. of the Expences attend'g the same which will be paid. On Paym't of the money to the Treasurer you will of Course take his Receipt & transmit the same to me. I am &c.

[G. C.]

[No. 1922.]

The Unprotected Westchester Frontier.

Sir, I just now rec'd the enclosed Petition,* setting forth the distressed situation of the Subscribers and others the Inhabitants on the Frontiers of West Chester County. I have therefore to request that you will immediately upon the Receipt hereof order out such a Proportion of the Militia of your Brigade as will give them the best Protection their Situation and your Strenghth will admit of. I have been favored with your Letter of 26" ult. & by the Letter it enclosed from Genl. Washington to you I entertained Hopes that a Party of Continental Troops had been employed in that Service which I am sorry to learn is not the Case. I am &c.

Nov'r 18 1778.   [G. C.]

[To Gen. Morris.]

[No. 1923.]

GENERAL HAND AFTER WEALTHY MISERS.

Opulent Tryon County Citizens Sell Provisions to the Commissary and Draw Rations from Him at Public Expense.

Albany 18th Nov'r 1778.

Sir, I am happy to be able to contradict the alarming accts. transmitted your Excellency the 15th. Col. Clyde's Letter to Col. Fisher a Coppy* of which is inclosed in Genl. Washington's Packet will unravel the Mistery. I leave the General's Packet

----

*Not found.

Open that your Excellency may peruse the Contents if you have time & Curiosity to do it.

I must request you will be pleased to write to the Commander in Cheif on the Subject & give him your Opinion as to the Quartering of Gansevort's Regiment & the future disposition of the Men at Cherry Valley.

Altho my Letter of the 13th & General Tenbrook's of the 16th give no great Credit to the Militia in General, I think it my Duty to acquaint your Excellency that Col. Wemple's Schenectady Militia, (a very respectable Body of Men) turned out with much Chearfulness, tho the remoteness of their Situation prevented their answering the wished for purposes.

Indeed it is not to be wondered at that the Militia of any District Harrased, as they are by repeated alarms, cannot be Collected in time to oppose a sudden Invasion.

Your Excellency will See, by the Inclosed Petition* of the Inhabitants of Cherry Valley, preferr'd previous to their late Unhappy Fate, that the out-cry against the Tories remaining in Trion County is General. You will, therefore, please to take such notice of it as you think it Merits; after perusing the General's Packet please to close and forward it by this Express.

The Commissary at the Garman Flatts has Represented to me, that much imposition is practised in drawing Provision for the Inhabitants. He says that many who are very Opulent & have Provision of their Own to sell to the Commissary, are permitted to draw the same from him as Rations, at the Public Expence.

As I apprehend this Indulgence was meant to relieve the Distressed who had no other means of support, and not to fill the Coffers of wealthy misers I have given them a Hint that, unless

*See page 259.

these abuses are rectified, the whole supply will be Cut off, & will be Obliged to your Excellency, if you will write to Colonel Bellinger or some other leading Man in that Settlement on the Subject. I am Sir with much Respect Your Excell'y most Obed't & most Humble Servant

Edw'd Hand.

His Excell'y Gov'r Clinton.

[No. 1924.]

A Sergeant and a Squad of Men Detailed to Escort the State's Financial Agents.

Poukeepsie 18th Nov'r 1778.

Sir, I have occassion to send Abraham B. Bancker Esqr. Deputy Secretary & Mr. Peter Wynkoop abroad on public Business which will take them about twelve Days to perform. It will be necessary that they have a Guard of Trusty Men with them. You are, therefore, to furnish for this Service, a Serjant and four Privates, to rendezvous at such Day & Place as either of the above Gentlemen shall appoint, properly armed & provided, to proceed on the above Service. I am Your most Obed't Serv't

Geo. Clinton.

Capt. Salisburry, Kingston Light Horse.

[No. 1925.]

Captain Swartwout Appeals to Governor Clinton, Unaware of the Court Martial Verdict.

Wappings Creek Nov'r 18th 1778.

May it please your Excellency, As a Court Martial was held on Monday last* to whom I Referred several Charges against Col. Frear, and being apprehensive the Court will pass them over in Silence or Neglect, I am under the necessaty of applying to your

*See page 282.

Excellency, whose Commands I ever study, to obey as well as the Laws of our Legislature, on which the Charges against Col. Frear are found, not to suffer a Faithfull Friend to his Country to suffer the Reproach of a Court, when all his actions and the orders he gave where agreable to the Militia Act—would beg leave to Mention the Charges against Col. Frear which I can support by his own handwriting.

Charge the 1st, against Col. Frear Commanding me to turn out more than the fourth man, which is against the Governor's orders.

The 2nd Charge, Commanding the Fourth Class on Duty a fortnight before it fell to them by Ballot, and Discharging the third Class a fortnight before their time was Expired by Ballot.

The 3d Charge, Against Col. Frear for neglect to give or render a just account of all the Delinquent Moneys which was Collected & assesed out of his Regt. from the Sixth of August 1777 untill the First Day of October 1778. I Remain with the utmost Esteem Your Excellency most Devoted and very Humble Servant

Barnardus Swartwout.
[To G. C.]

———

[No. 1926.]*

———

[No. 1927.]

John Jay Presents Two Cases to Washington Showing Abuse in the Purchase of Commissary Stores.

New Windsor 19 Nov. 1778.

Sir, Capt. Bedlow of this Place (whom I have long known to be an exceeding good man) tells me, that Coll. Freer near Poughkeepsie, lately assured him that Morris Hazard of that Place had purchased of him, for Publick use expresly, a Quantity of Flower, which in a few days afterwards he sold at an advance of between four and five hundred pounds.

Capt. Bedlow further tells me that Col. Palmer of Newborough, informed him lately, that one of the Commissary's agents purchased a pair of Cattle in this way. The Seller offered them for forty Pounds; the agent thereupon told him that he would give him forty two pounds, if the seller woud sign a Receipt for fifty pounds; the Seller agreed. Coll. Palmer told Capt. Bedlow that this fact coud be fully proved. I have the honor to be with the greatest Esteem & Respect

John Jay.

His Excell'y Gen. Washington.

(Copy)

[No. 1928.]

Colonel Malcom Writes a Facetious Letter Regarding Tories Assigned to Work on the Fortifications.

Fort Clinton, Nov. 20 1778.

Sir, Last night I rec'd a fine Reinforcement of Torys, from Peeks Kill and this morning they are at work. From the information of Lt. Connelly who brought them in, I expect a world of Sollicitations in their favor, and I imagine they will apply to your Excellency. I expect the more so, because I am tormented with the Orange County Justices, whenever any miscreants are brought in from the mountains.

Now, as I only want to get a whiles worth out of them, and as it is the very least attonement they can make for their crimes, I request that your Excellency will evade the Interest that I know will be made for them; by boobies as bad as they. I have never kept any of those fellows above Three months & then give them a discharge and Certificate that they are white wash'd. This serves the States, the State, & in fact them also, as they will not be troubled, I am pretty sure with such a credential, and also if you think fit, the State may draw pay for them; we give them none. However, only amuse your stupid Justices that they may not torment me with their foolish demands & we shall make you a Good Fort by & by.

I beg my respects to your Lady and am most respectfully Your Excellency's most obd. and very Hble. Serv't

W. Malcom.

[To G. C.]

Torys rec'd by Lt. Connelly Nov. 19:

Jordan Norris, Crompond; deserted from the Enemy; has not take ye O. of A; [oath of allegiance;] Robert Craig, Robinson's Stores; employd as a Guide with the Enemy 12 mo's; no O. of All'gce; Stephen Currie, Peekkill; a great offender. went of March '77; refuses to take the O. of A; Hen. Traverse, Bar. Traverse, Manor of Cortlandt; were in the Enemy's Service & refuses to take ye oath; Peter Hervy, Robinson's Stores; was in the Enemy's Service & refuses ye O; Peter Angevine, John Angevine, Queen's Ranger; refuses to take ye oath; charged w't murder, theft &c.; refuses the Oath; Jacob Badeaux; enemy's Service; refuses the Oath; John Francis Do Gilbert Barlow Do Do.

I have about a dozen more.

[No. 1929.]

FLOUR NOT SO SCARCE AS REPRESENTED.

Commissary Wadsworth Explains Methods of Attaining Wealth by Enterprising Citizens.

Frederocksburg Nov. 20th 1778.

Sir, This is the first moment of leisure I have been master of since my late arrival in Camp, and I eagerly embrace it to thank

Your Excellency for your attention to my department; and the representations by my assistant in my absence. The great pains taken by the People of New England to procure flower in this State and transport it out, is not oweing to so great and distressing a scarcity as represented; flower may be bought in all the New England States at a high price; this acknowledged by every person who has applied to me for Permits; my purchasing Commissaries have lately purchased 15 Tons of flower in Norwich and as much in Providence.

The purchasers of flower from the Eastward are, many of them, those who have amassed much wealth by a disgracefull inland trade; and the inhabitants of the New England States in general have neglected the cultivation of wheat and turned their attention to trade and never will return to cultivation till necessity oblidges them.

When the Enemy evacuated Philadelphia, their remained great quantities of every kind of European and India goods in that Citty, persons who not ever been friendly to the United States were generally possessed of them. A great number of professed Whigs (whose friendly disposition is only known by their eagerness to grow rich) rushed into the Citty and purchased the articles wanted by the Publick, and the well affected inhabitants of these States. Many of those wretches, who have ever been with the Enemy and never had an expectation of being worth a thousand pounds, are become immensely rich, and are now treated as good subjects to the United States, I trouble your Excellency with this representation, believing that persons are gone into the Citty of New York with traid and will avail themselves of the evacuation (if it happens) to do as they have done at Philadelphia. I have the honor to be your Excell'cys most Obedt: and much oblidged hum'e Servant

Jere'h Wadsworth, Com. Gen. P.

His Excell'y Gov'r Clinton.

[No. 1930.]

Governor Clinton Corrects the Errors Contained in the First Reports from Cherry Valley.

Poughkeepsie Nov'r 21st 1778.

Gentlemen, I wrote you on the 18th Inst. by Mr. Bancker* giving an acct. of the Depredations committed by the Enemy on the frontiers & the loss of Fort Alden since which I have received a Letter from Genl. Hand† enclosing the Copy of a Letter containing an acct. contradictory to the above as far as it respects the Loss of Fort Alden. A Copy of which I take this earliest Oppertunity of enclos'g to you. I am &c.

Geo. Clinton.

The hon'ble the Delegates of the State of New York, in Congress.

———

[No. 1931.]

Destitution at German Flats.

German Flatts, Nov'r the 22nd 1778.

Sir, Agreeable to the Orders I receiv'd from his Excellency Governor Clinton, inclos'd I send you a return of the inhabitants of this Place, who have suffered by the Enemy. I must beg leave to inform you, that the poor distressed inhabitants has been without Provision, now for fourteen Days, not having any Flour to serve them. If the inclos'd Return is not proper, I beg you'll let me know, That I may alter it. I am Sir Your most Obedient Hum'le Serv't

Peter Bellinger, Colo.

To The Hon'ble General Hands Commander of the Northern Department, Albany.

---

*See page 294.
†See page 297.

[No. 1932.]

Reducing the Militia Along the Delaware River Frontier.

Poukeepsie 22d Nov'r 1778.

D'r Sir, Colo. Cortlandt by his Letter to me just now received, mention as his advises that the Militia in actual Service on the Frontiers of Ulster County, North of Pienpack, may for the present be safely dismissed, except about 70 to be stationed as follows: 2 Officers & 25 Men at Shandacon; 1 Do & 10 at Yaugh's, Crepple Bush; 1 Do & 10 at Luren's Kill; 2 Do & 20 at Mamcotten.

And, as I am extreamly desirous of making their Duty as little Burthensome as may be consistent with the safety of the Frontier Settlements, it is, therefore, my desire that you dismiss for the present, all but the above Number, which you will station in the above, or such other Manner, as you & Colo. Cortlandt shall on Consultation judge best.   At the same Time you will advise with Genl. Hand on the Propriety of dismissing those at Pienpack & Minisinck, which if judged prudent, I desire may also be immediately done.   I am &c.

[G. C.]

To Colo. Cantine.

[No. 1933.]

A Small Supply of Commissary Stores.

Oswago 24 Nov'r 1778.

Sir, I have sent By the Bearer one ton hay and twenty Bushels of Corn In Behalf of Wm. Boland A. C. F.   Please to send a Rec't for the same By the Bearer.

Benj. Tobey.

To His Exalency Govounur Clinton att Poughkeepsie.

[No. 1934.]

Governor Clinton Vetoes a Suggestion for a Respite for Dr. Ducalon from Judge Robert Yates.

Claverack Nov'r 22d 1778.

Sir, At the close of the last Supream Court I stated to your Excellency the proceedings on the tryal of Stephen Ducalon, and as no favourable circumstances appeared to induce me to recommend him as an object of mercy, I ordered his Execution on the 27" instant.

Many of his Friends and Relations have since the sitting of the Court represented to me the bad characters of Sloss and Battoe, the two principal witnesses against him, and offered to make out in proof that no credit ought to be given to their Testimony, and in consequence thereof have beg'd me to recommend him for a pardon. Altho' I do not conceive myself justifyed on this representation to grant their request, yet I would submit it to your Excellency's consideration, whether it would not be advisable to respite the Execution for a few weeks, in order to give them in the meanwhile an opportunity of laying before your Excellency such matters they may judge favourable to the prisoner. I am with the greatest respect, Your Excellency's most obt. hum. Serv't

Robert Yates.

To his Excellency George Clinton Esqr. Governor.

———

Poukeepsie 24th Nov'r 1778.

D'r Sir, I am honored with your Letter of the 22d Inst. Some Days since a personal Application was made to me for a Pardon to Dr. Ducalong accompanied by a Petition signed by a Number of the Inhabitants of your District & some Affidavits, the Run of

COL. ISAAC BARRÉ

Isaac Barré

which was to shew that the Testimony of Sloss, on whose Evidence alone it was alledged Ducalong was convicted, ought not to be regarded.

I was possessed of the Testimony delivered in Court ag't him & I thought fully convinced his Friends that I coud not consistently pardon him, & least they shoud be troublesome to you living in the Neighbourhood. I informed them that even your Certificate in his Favour woud not avail any Thing. I am perswaded they can procure no Testimony to alter my oppinion & a respite, therefore, woud answer no good purpose. I am &c.

[G. C.]

[To Robert Yates.]

[No. 1935.]

More Recalcitrant Tories.

New Perth Charlotte County Nov'r 25 1778.

Sir, By Virtue of the Act of the 30 Jun, We, as Commissioners, have Ordred, Seth Chase of the County of Albany, Archbald Livingston & James Mount of this County, persons who refused to take the Oath as prescribed by the aforsaid Act, We, therefore, Agreable to said Act, Inform your Excellency that we are about to remove the above Named Dissaffected persons within the Enemies Lines. We only waite your Excellency's Answer, as to what you do or direct us, as to their Exchange for any of the Subjects of this State that May be in the hands of the Enemy.

We are Sorry that So many of the disaffected have been sent to Canady, as they have such oppertunitys to put their hellish plots in Execution. We are your Very obt. & Humble Serv'ts

Alex'r Webster, Alex'd McNitt, Eben Clark Commiss'rs.
His Excellency Gov'r Clinton.

[No. 1936.]

ATROCITIES ALONG LAKE CHAMPLAIN.

Colonel Webster Makes Report of a Daring Indian Movement and of the Sufferings of Patriots.

Black Creek Novr 26th 1778.

D'r Govenor,* I received by Express from the Command't at Fort Edward Information, that by a person (says he) Just arrived who made his Escape from the Enemy at Crown Point; this was a man that was taken prisoner the first Instant at Lake George a hunting, & says he, their is of the Enemy Encamped at Crown Point 500, who is to divide them Selves in to three parties to Destroy the Inhabitants upon this Information I Imediately Issued Orders to the Deffrent Capts. to hold them Selves in readieness & their Companies to march at a minut's warning. This I received the 6th Inst. Next Morning Verbally Came a report that the Lakes was full of the Enemy's boats. I Imediatly sent of a scout to Skeensborrough to know the Truth & ordred the militia to Embodie which they readly did at my Howse; my Scout returned & reportd that they Could not here of any Enemy; this was on Saturday, then I Ordred that the men should go home and keep themselves in readiness to march at the shortest Notice; on Munday Night following I receved an Express from Skeensborrough that the Enemy was burning on both sides of the Lake & begged for Imediate assistance. I Imediately Ordred out the Militia and Sent an Express to Cambridge and I must praise the Militia for their readieness in Turning out. We Marched to Skeensborrough. I had above 200 with me. The Company that Lay above Fort Edward I Ordred to Cooperate with Collo. Warner if their was

---

*For Governor Clinton's answer see page 375.

need; otherways to Join me at Skeensb'h. I Sent of a scout to Crown Point to bring Sure Intilligence of the motions of the Enemy. The Scout was out four days and brought Sure Intilligence that the Enemy was gone off & had burned Six (6) Townships mostly on the Grants. The Men they took prisoners; the women & children they stript, and sent into the Country, Many of them wanting shoes & stockings, among Snow three or four Inches Deep, and only two old men with them, which they did not Choice to take with them—these Miscreants Behaved in this way—the most of the Creaters they Collected into the howses & Sett them on fire and burned them. Others they Cut Large pesses out of and Let them run alive.

I talked with Several of the women that Escaped. They say they herd them talk much of Skeensborrough & it is thought that if we had not been their that they would Certainly a Come. One Capt. Allan was at Crown Point when my Scout was their, and he found two Hessians that had Deserted from the Enemy; they had been Eight Days wanting Vitles & they give Much the Same account about the Enemies behaviour & say that the hellish band was about Six hundred in number & that their is three regiments in Canada & that the Enemy talked of penetrating further Into the Country; they say that St. Johns is Strongly fortifyed & the Isle of Noix.

One of Collo. Warner's Scouts took two Ingians at the half way brook near Lake George; they said they were hunting Indians and Came with a flag. I herd Last Night by a person that Came from Fort Edward, that these Indians said that they knew where the party of Indians was that took the Hunters at Lake George & if they Could have a party of men they would bring them prisoners. Accordingly it was agred, that one of the Indians should be kept as an hostage, and a party Sent with the other, which was accordingly Done & that they took four days provision & that the party had been out ten Days & no word of them.

If more men is not stationed on our frontiers for the Ensuring Campain then has been this, I do not belive any of the Inhabitants will stay, as the Enemy Intends the most Cruel usage for us. I am with Great respect your Excellency's Very obidt. & Humble Serv't

Alex'r Webster.*

P. S.   Just now a person from Fort Edward brings Information that the Scout is returned & brought in with them, four Indians; they give Account that a number of Indians was about 40 mils back of them and that they would Either take or kill them if they had a large party to go with them.

To His Excellency George Clinton Governor of the State of New York.

———

[No. 1937.]

Governor Clinton Utters a Complaint.

Nov'r 26 1778.

D'r Sir, It gives me Pain to trouble your Ex'y with the inclosed Complaint against some Gentlemen in the Military Line and agreable to the Law of this State for regulating Impresses of

---

* Alexander Webster was born in Scotland, came to this country in 1772 and settled at Black creek, Charlotte, now Washington county. For years he was one of the most influential men in the northern part of the State of New York. He served through the Revolutionary War, advancing from the rank of captain to Colonel in command of his regiment. He served in the Provincial Congress as a member of the Committee of Safety, and in the State Senate from the first session in 1777, continuously to 1785, and from 1789 to 1794, having been elected to the Assembly for the sessions of 1788-1789. He acted as County Judge of Washington County—from June 3, 1786 to March 17, 1788. While a member of the Senate he was a member of the Council of Appointment for several years. He died in 1810.—STATE HISTORIAN.

Forage &c. to request that the Offender be delivered over to the Civil Magistrate.*

[G. C.]

[To Gen. Washington.]

[Nos. 1938–1939.]

ABUSES OF FLAGS OF TRUCE.

Lieutenant Smith Brings the Subject to the Attention of Governor Clinton who Promises to Make an Investigation.

Fort Clinton Nov. 27 1778.

Sir, The inclosed copy of a letter from Lt. Smith, to the Baron de Kalbe will give your Excellency some extraordinary information. I have consider'd as my duty to bring the matter before you, and Request your Orders. Mr. Smith's letter is so full on the Subject that I have occassion to say nothing, but that by many accounts it appears to be true, and that the Vessell was never intended to appear publickly.

I have rec'd your Excellency's letter concerning Maps. Be assured, Sir, that I will not do any thing to forfeit the good opinion which I flatter myself your Excellency entertains off me. I really have not time to aquaint you with the particulars of that affair, but from what I know of it, am sure you have not been well informed—all shall be done as you direct when Capt. Sanford arrives. Genl. Clinton, if he is at Poughkeepsie, can tell you how it was, because a trial was before him, but proper Examinations shall be taken on oath & sent to you without delay. I have the Honor to be with great Respect Your Excellency's most ob. & Hb. serv.

W. Malcom.

---

*Draft letter to General Washington, Nov. 25, inclosing original letter from Major Strang of complaints against Major Lee's Corps of Light Horse for abuses committed in Westchester County. Indorsement on back.

I have wrote to the Baron that this affair is yours & that I expect to follow your orders concerning it.   W. M.

His Excellency Gover. Clinton.

(Copy.)   LIEUTENANT SMITH'S COMPLAINT.

Sir, Agreeable to your Order, I have been stationed here for these five days for the purpose of receiving a Flag, with Stores for the Convention Army w'h arrived yesterday; and was dispatched by the evening.   Likewise another Flag with the following Articles on board, with directions to call at Haverstraw and there apply to Col. Hay of the Militia for Directions, Vizt: Forty-five Bush: of Salt in two Casks; Two p's of Sheeting; Fifteen & half yds. of Broad Cloth; Twenty pounds of Bohea Tea & Six pounds Green do., with two small Bundles, the Contents unknown.

This Flag without any ceremony run up along side one of the Wharves at Haverstraw, and then by Col. Hay's permission, the Crew went on shore, and one of them went into the Country. The Commander of the Boat says, they were to procure Permission from the Governor of the state, to exchange their Cargo for Wheat; he also says all the Papers belonging to the Flag, excepting the within pass, were delivered to Col. Hay who has gone to the Governor with them.   Now, sir, under the above Circumstances, I have thought proper to detain her untill I receive your orders.   Untill then I shall Remain yours &c.

Jas. Smith, Lieut. Officer of the Guard.

Kings Ferry 25th Nov'r '78.

N. B.   The Cargo of the last Flag was to be disposed of by Col. Hay, who was to send them Wheat in the place of it.   J. S.

[To Baron De Kalbe.]

LIEUTENANT SMITH FILES HIS REPORT WITH THE GOVERNOR.

Sir, You No dout have before this seen Coll. Hay, with the papers belonging to a Flag of truse that arrivd at Haverstraw the 24th Ult. with a Cargo of Salt, Linen, Cloaths, Tee &c. for the perpose of bartering it for Grain with the above Col., who the Neighbours of this place acquaints me, has a suspistious Carrecter as to his wigesim. [Whigism.]

This morning arrivd here anothe flag with the within papers of which I require your directions what to do with, as well as the former one & the pasengers of the Latter & Untill then I will remain yours

Jas. Smith, Lt. of the 4th M. R. Offi'r of the Guard.

Kings Ferry 27th Nov'r 1778.

N. B. The first flag I had brought here the Morning of the 25th.

J. S.

His Excellency Govener Clinton.

———

THE GOVERNOR PROMISES TO INVESTIGATE THE CHARGES.

Sir, I am favoured with your Letter of yesterday, informing me of the arival at Kings Ferry of two Sloops under the Sanction of Flaggs from the Enemy. The first which appears by your Account transmitted to Baron De Calb, a Copy of which was forwarded to me, to be a prostitution of a Flagg, to the Business of Trade, I have ordered under the Care of Colo. Malcom who commands at West Point, and requested him to cause a proper Inquiry to be made respecting that Matter. With respect to the last, I desire she may also be put under the Charge of Colo. Malcom, to whom I have wrote by the Bearer on the Subject, till I can have Time to make the proper Inquiries concerning the Business she is sent out upon. You will please to forward the Flagg papers which I now return you the Letters excepted to Colo. Malcom. I am Sir your most Obed't Serv't

Geo. Clinton.

[To Lieut. Jas. Smith.]

———

[Nos. 1940—1941—1942.]

COLONEL HAY CALLED UPON FOR EXPLANATIONS.

Governor Clinton Desires Information Concerning Flags of Truce and Historian Smith's Effects.

Nov'r 26 1778.

Sir, I am informed a Sloop is arrived opposite your Place, said to be under the Sanction of a Flag from the Enemy at New York in order to transport the remaining Effects of William Smith, Esqr., who was lately sent by this State within the Enemy's Lines & that this Sloop is not under the Direction of any Officer, as is usual in those Cases, & the Permission for coming out signed only by a Person stiling himself, aid de camp to Lieut. Genl. Sir H. Clinton. You will, therefore, be careful that no abuse be committed thro' the medium of this Flag & for this Purpose keep an officer on Board till the Time of her Departure. And you will cause to be put on Board of her, such of the Furniture & Effects of Mr. Smith as is in your Custody or Care, provided, the same do not consist of Provision, Forrage, Arms or Military Stores, & Order the Sloop back to New York, & by his Return, inform the Commander in New York that no such informal Flags will be received in Future.

[G. C.]

[To Col. A. Hawkes Hay.]

THE CASE OF THE HAVERSTRAW SLOOP.

Poukeepsie 28th Nov'r 1778.

Sir, I have this Morning received the inclosed Information of Lieut. Smith as transmitted by him to Baron De Calb respecting the Flag which lately arived in your Neighbourhood & which by my Orders to you of the 26th Instant was put under your Charge. You will readilly perceive, that Lieut. Smith's Account respecting the Business of this Flagg &c. differs so very materially from that I received from you, as to make it my Duty, to cause the Sloop Hands & whatever is on Board, untill due inquiry can be made concerning this Matter, to be taken into Custody. And I have, accordingly, directed Colo. Malcom to take them under his Care & to cause such Inquiry to be made & the Result thereof to be reported to me. If it shall be found that the sole Business of this Flag, is to carry the Effects of Mr. Smith to New York, Colo. Malcom has my orders to suffer them to be loaded on Board, subject to the Instructions contd in my orders to you, & the sloop to proceed with them to New York. I am, Sir, your most Obed't Serv't,

G. C.

Colo. Hay.

THE GOVERNOR ISSUES INSTRUCTIONS TO COLONEL MALCOM.

Poukeepsie 28th Nov'r 1778.

Dear Sir, Since I wrote you this Morning I have received a Letter from Lieut. Smith at Kings Ferry, informing me of the Arival of another Sloop with a Flagg at that Place, whose Business it appears by the Papers forwarded to me is to bring up the several Persons on Board & to take down to New York the Famillies &

Effects of Saml. Mabit, & Thos. Thom two Exiles under the late Act. I have ret'd the Papers to Lieut. Smith & directed him to transmit them to you. And I must request that you will receive with them the Charge of this Sloop untill she can be properly dispatched. It does not appear from Lieut. Smith's account or the Papers, that she is on a Trading Voyage; but it is not clear to me, however, that it is good Policy to receive Flags in this loose way, and to Return them, without accomplishing their Business on which they come, might Answer a good Purpose. I do not know any of the Persons mentioned in the Papers, except Mrs. Dole who cannot have my Permission to proceed to Albany. If the others are Friends to the State, which you may know as they appear to be Citizens, let them pass into the Country. Is not Mrs. Tom & Child of your Family. As soon as I can possibly determine with Respect to this last Flagg you shall hear from me. I am &c.

[G. C.]

Colo. Malcom.

GOVERNOR CLINTON SENDS INSTRUCTIONS TO COLONEL MALCOM REGARDING MR. SMITH'S EFFECTS AND INCLOSES HIS LETTER TO COLONEL HAY.

Poukeepsie 28th Nov'r 1778.

Sir, I am this Morning favoured with your Letter of the 27th Instant inclosing the Information transmitted by Luten't Smith to Baron De Calb respecting the Conduct of a Flag lately arived at Haverstraw. Previous to the Receipt of your Letter, Colo. Hay waited upon me (as mentioned in Leut. Smith's Account) & informed me of the Arival of this Flagg for the Purpose of transporting the Effects of William Smith, Esquire, to New York agreable to my Permit formerly given to Lieut. Colo. Burr for this

Purpose, whereupon I gave Colo. Hay the Order, whereof I now inclose you a Copy, which I had reason to hope would not only have prevented any Abuses being committed through the Medium of this extraordinary Flag, but also prevented the Enemy from attempting to trouble us with the like in Future. I am sorry to find the Account of Leut. Smith differing so very matterially from that I received from Colo. Hay, as to make it my Duty to request (which I now do) that you will Take this Flag with the Hands, & whatever is on Board the Sloop, under your Care & that you will please to cause due Inquiry to be made respecting this Business & transmit the Result to me. I would only add, that If on such Inquiry, you find that the Business of this Flag was not Trade, but for the Purpose only of carrying the Effects of Mr. Wm. Smith to New York you will in that Case, suffer them, subject nevertheless to the Restriction ment'd in my Orders to Col. Hay, to be put on Board & the Sloop to proceed to New York. I inclose you a letter to Colo. Hay, on this Subject for your Perusal, which when you have read, you'l be pleased to seal and forw'd to him. I am, with great Regard, Your Most Obed't Serv't,

Geo. Clinton.

Colo. Malcom.

[No. 1943.]

John Doremus Writes for the Restoration of His Horses and Cash.

Paramas November the 29th 1778.

To the Hon'ble George Clintin, E'rs, Govenor and Chief Commander of the Province of New York.

Sir, Haveing meet with an Oppertunyty the 17th of April in the year 1777, to have Some Conversation with Judge Morris, and he was kind to write a few Lines to your Excelency, and I wold have

been up with your Excelency about the Same time, but my wife
Laid very bad with the Consomtion, and have had the misfourtune
of Loseing her; after that I was taken with the Rumatics, so that
I was Not Able to wake without Crotch, So I have been Detaind
till this time: & Now haveing meet with An Oppertunity to Send
it to you: and I hope to have the favour of you to See the money
and horses Returned. This is, Sir, from Your Humble Serveat

John Doremus.

[No. 1944.]

Again the Question of Contraband Wheat.

Poughkeepsie Nov'r 30th 1778.

S'r, I am directed by his Excell'cy, Gov'r Clinfon, to send you
the enclosed Letter & affid't & to inform you that on the 4th Nov'r
last a Permission was given to Jon'a Fitch, or his agent Danl.
Gray, to export (under the direction of the Commiss'y Genl. of
Purchases or one of his assis'ts) for the use of the Troops stationed on the Coast of Connecticut, One hundred & fifty bar'ls of
flour, & five hundred Bush'ls of wheat, which by a Certificate of
Mr. Flint, was directed to be exported under the Direction of Mr.
Philip Leake. Upon the application of the Person now apply'g,
the enclosed Letter & affidavit, is sent you for your Information.
His Excellency, therefore, requests that you'l make the necessary
Enquiry, & if you find the Facts as stated therein to be true,
which you may discover by Examin'g Mr. Leake, & the Persons
from whom the wheat was taken, his Ex'cy has the highest Confidence that you will do that which is Right. I am &c.

R. Benson.

Peter Lions, Esqr. Westchester County.

[No. 1945.]

Connecticut Relies Upon New York for Bread.

New London, Nov'r 30th 1778.

Sir, Inclos'd is a letter from Goven'r Trumbull Requesting that you would Grant me Liberty to purchase and bring out of your State Two hundred Barrells of Flower.

This is Just to Inform you that I have Imploy'd Mr. John Blagg to purchase the above Flower for the use of this States Ships. I am Sir Your moast Obed't Hum'e Serv't

Nath'l Shaw.

His Excellency Gov'r Clinton.

State of Connecticut. Lebanon 25th Novem'r 1778.

Sir, The Oliver Cromwell, and Defence, two Ships belonging to this State are now lying in port at New London. I have this minute received a Letter from Capt. Nath'el Shaw, of that place, informing that it is impossible to purchase flour in this State, to make bread for the said Ships and desiring that I would write to your Excellency for liberty to purchase in N. York State a quantity sufficient for that end.

I must, therefore, in behalf of Capt. Shaw, request your Excellency to grant Licence to him, or his order, for purchasing about two hundred Barrels, which is thought to be sufficient to answer the present exigence—& to transport the same into this State. I am, with great Esteem & Regard Sir your most obedient hble Servant

Jon'th Trumbull, Gov'r.

His Excellency Gov'r Clinton.

[No. 1946.]

WILLIAM MILLER'S EARNEST APPEAL.

Tories Permitted to Drive Cattle to New York—Connecticut and Eastern Westchester County's Defenceless Condition.

May it Please your Excelency; With Reluctance I Trouble you with these my Imperfect Lines, though I have Two motives that Induces me To Undertake, First, your Excellency's Permission to write If the Letter to General Morris had not the Desired effect, and Secondly, the Love of my Countery and All those who hath Put their Lives and fortunes in Jaeperdy for its Defence. As to the Letter, it had no Appearent effect; Genneral Morris Saith there is no Provision and, therefore, will not Call the militia. As to the State of our Army, I am not knowing And if they are Like to Disband for want of Provision, Gen'rl Morris's giving Permission for So many Hundred Cattle & Hogs to go Down, and nine Tenths of Them to People that has During the Contest been our Inviterate Enemies, is at Least bad Policy. As to the good People they are now Left naked. The Smal Piquets are Call'd in and wee hear the Infantry are ordered to Leave Bedford, the good People are now left without any one to Leade Them fourth in their own Defence, Like Sheep not having any Shephard. I being one, they formerly Placed Some Confidence in, many applys To me with Gastly Countenances, Saying, what Shall wee Do, which Intirely Confounds me, I not knowing what To Advise. O that the good People of West Chester County Could be Together, and Circumstances would admit your Presence among them, if it were but one Hour, For the Late Petitioners, when I informed them that you had taken up Their Petition on Receipt and had Set about To Do all in your Power for their Security, they express'd great Joy, and I now have their order To Return you their

Hearty thanks. And Shall Conclude my Counteries Devoted Friend, And your Excelencies Very Humble Servant

Wm. Miller.
Francis Nashes, Township of Greenwich.

State of Conecticut December ye 1st 1778.

P. S. While writing this, 10 Tories from below has Pass'd by to go to Bedford for Permits to Drive Cattle. The Numbers mention, is Taken from Common fame, as I have not been an Eye witness to So many Cattle & hogs Drove, but have Seen many and fame as above Says Hundreds.

[No. 1947.]

NEW YORK, VERMONT AND CONGRESS.

Opinions of Our Delegates—Ethan Allen's Subterfuge—New York Receives One Hundred Thousand Dollars—The Treaty with France.

Philadelphia, 1st Decemb'r 1778.

Sir, We are now to acknowledge the Honour of your Excellency's Dispatches of the 18th and 21st Ult. by Messrs. Bancker and Wynkoop* for whose return we made the necessary Preparations without delay. This day will be spent in counting and paying the money, a Trouble which will fall on Mr. Duer who has charged himself hitherto with the Care of it.

We had the good Luck to recover the Copies of the Constitution of our State which were printed, and on our retiring to York Town, left in this City. They are forwarded by this Conveyance: part of the Expence of the Press was defray'd by Mr. Duer; & the remainder by Mr. Lewis which with the advance of 1000 Dollars for each of the present Delegates will be deducted out of the money granted by Congress.

*See page 294.

It gives us particular Pleasure that we are at Liberty to transmit to your Excellency several Copies of the Treaties of Amity and Commerce between his most Christian Majesty and the United States.† Your Excellency will see how totally groundless have been the suspicions propagated by our Enemies respecting these Treaties. They will appear to be founded on perfect Equality, and in every Respect liberal and reciprocally beneficial. It is the Direction of Congress that no Impression of them be made untill their further order.

We have not yet the Pleasure of Mr. Jay's Company. Mr. Ethan Allen has lately presented a Paper to Congress, as an act of what they call the Assembly of the State of Vermont. It is calculated to shew that the New Hampshire Towns on the East side of Connecticut River which Joind in the Revolt had retracted and seperated from the Towns on the west side. The Design of this flimsy artifice is obvious: but it was a little unreasonable for the Projectors that only two days after the Production of this Paper, Lieut. Col. Wheelock presented a Remonstrance from the Revolted Towns on the East side of the River, complaining that Allen had no authority to make the before mentioned Declaration; that they utterly renounced it and adherd to their Revolt from New Hampshire. This Incident renders ridiculous the Plan which Allen and his adherents boasted of as decisive. When Mr. Jay arrives we hope this important Subject will be taken up, notwithstanding Congress is pressed by a variety of Objects which call for attention and Dispatch.

While we lament the reiterated sufferings of our Fellow Citizens from the Depredations of the savages and disaffected, we agree with your Excellency that every defensive system in a

---

† See Volume III, pages 230-231, and foot note on pages 308-309.

predatory war must prove vain and Chimerical and that a vigorous Irruption into the Enemy's Country can alone promise advantage and Safety. To this great object we shall extend our Views and endeavour to have it carried into Effect as soon as the Season will permit. In the mean time, if the whole of the New York Brigade which is orderd to march for the Defence of our Frontiers is not thought a sufficient Force, be pleased to inform us, and it shall be our Care to obtain the aid you may require and to promote any measures which may be recommended for the immediate Protection and future Security of the State we represent.

We have the Honour to be, with the utmost respect, Sir, Your Excellency's most Obedient humble Servants

Jas. Duane,

Fra' Lewis,

Gouv'r Morris.

His Excellency Governour Clinton.

[No. 1948.]

LIVING EXPENSES OF A DELEGATE TO CONGRESS.

Gouverneur Morris Forwards Facts and Figures to Governor Clinton.

Phila. 1st Dec'r 1778.

Sir, The Legislature of our State having at Length complied with my ardent wishes in sending for the money which was long since obtained, and which I did hope, would have reached their Treasury many months ago. I cannot omit the first Opportunity of testifying to you my Joy on that Occasion. Money matters are, of all others, those which I wish to have least concern in. Many Reasons may be assigned for this, which your Delicacy will catch at a Glance. But among that many, there is not one which did not give me Solicitude while so considerable a Deposit remained with us. I say, with us, for altho I did not personally touch or take Charge of it, yet in the minds of my Constituents I was doubtless considered as one of those who was accountable for any accidents which might happen.

My time being continually occupied, even to a minute, insomuch that I am under a necessity of borrowing large Portions from my Slumbers, I have not seen the act you allude to in your Letter. I am told however that an advance is made to each of the Delegates of 1000 Dollars. I am also told that in Consideration of the Expences which must necessarily have accrued by living in this Town, the Legislature have directed the additional Sum of three Dollars pr Day, to be paid since our arrival in this City. I pray you, Sir, on the first convenient Opportunity to make the proper Returns on my Part for this equitable Provision. Since I am on the Subject of money, which I think will not be an object in many of my Letters, I am to observe that considering the high Trust with which I am honored by my Constituents, I determined to support the Character to the Extent of what would be afforded from my private Fortune. Whether the State would make Retribution rested indeed with their Generosity, but this was by no means a bad Foundation. At any Rate I knew the worst and after certain Expenditures, I should inevitably have quitted a station the Dignity of which I could no longer support. My Expences have been by no means small.

Before I left New York, an advance was made to me, but how much I cannot at present ascertain, for as the Receipt &ca., were of Record, I took no memorandum. In order that my account may be adjusted, I am to request, that I be considered in the Public Service as from the 25th of Dec'r 1778,* True it is I left the

---

*This palpably is an error. The correct date, as Morris desired it, was December 25, 1775.—State Historian.

State much earlier, but I staid a considerable Time among my Friends in New Jersey, wherefore, counting the Days I was really on my Journey, back from the Time I Came to Congress, will bring it to that Period. In addition to what I received there, I have had of Mr. Duer 2000 Dollars, which he will I suppose charge in his accounts. I shall also receive now the 1000 Dollars before mentioned in advance. The auditor will find no Difficulty from these Data to make out a proper account which I hope may be done.

I must again intreat that your Excellency will urge to the Legislature the Necessity of adjusting the public accounts so that Congress may finally settle the Ballance. I have the Pleasure to say that after many earnest Efforts the Treasury Board is at Length organized and I hope to see my Labors on this Occasion productive of some good Consequences to my Country. Hoping this greatest Reward I have the Honor to be your Excellency's most obedient & humble Servant

Gouv. Morris.

His Excellency Governor Clinton.

[No. 1949.]

COLONEL MALCOM DISCREDITS COLONEL HAY.

Governor Clinton, However, Indulgent—Salt as a Contraband of War.

Fort Clinton Dec'r 1st 1778.

Sir, Both the flag Vessells are now in Charge of my Guards. Your Excellency's letter hath been handed to Col. Hay but he has not appeared to give an Explanation of his Conduct. My Opinion is that Both Vessells ought to be sent down the river under the Care of a guard with a whale boat, to see them near the Enemy's Lines. Altho' I am also of opinion that the property ought to be seized (I mean the Salt &c. on board Mr. Smith's Vessel) yet I am not fond of that kind of bussiness. Nevertheless, if your Excellency shall order it to be done, I will cause the Q. Master of the Garrison do it. Mrs. Tom is "a child of my family". Being confident that I fully comprehend what your Excellency wishes to be done in such cases, I have taken her on shore & she is with her husband in my Quarters, I suppose receiving her back Rations. Doctor Vandycke & Mrs. Cole as also Lowndes ought to be sent back & I dare say you will order it.

With respect to Col. Hay I imagine he will answer for his Conduct before your Excellency. The Country are Loud in their complaints & many are offended with the freedoms he has taken with your name to give Sanction to his proceedings in this affair. As the sooner these Vessels can be sent off, the better, because they are an incumbrance to us. I beg to have your orders to morrow. Please send them to Col. Hay who will send to me instantly.

With the greatest Respect I have the Honor to be Your Excellencys mo. ob. & very Hb. serv?

W. Malcom.

His Excellency Governor Clinton Pokepsie.

GOVERNOR CLINTON WILL GIVE ADVICE BUT WILL NOT ISSUE ORDERS.

Poukeepsie 1st Dec'r 1778.

Dear Sir, I am favoured with your Letter of this Date. By the Papers you will observe it appears that the last Flagg has on Board the Effects of the Revered Mr. Freligh, a Dutch Refugee Parson from Long Island, who is a sound Whig & has sustained great Losses by the Present War. These were sent out through the Influence of Bardsly, a Torry Parson, late of this Place on

my Certificate that Mr. Freligh shoud be permitted to send in
Bardsly's Effects in Exchange for them.   Both Honor & Justice
are, therefore, concerned not to dismiss that Vessel, until Mr.
Freligh can have an opportunity of receiving his Effects & fulfill-
ing his Promise founded on my Certificate.   This cannot be
effected in less than three or four Days.   It is our Interest also,
that Mabit & Thom's Famillys, go down with this Flagg, as it
will make Room for better People, & save us from many Troublesome applications from them in future.   I have, accordingly,
signified to them that they will have my Permission to depart,
which I expect they will accept.   I am surprized, Colo. Hay has
not been with you, if it was only to put on Board Mr. Smith's
Effects, which you will observe by my orders he is permitted to
do, but more so to learn that he attempts to Justify any Misscon-
duct of his by my orders.   They are written & speak for themselves.   You have a Copy.   I care not how soon this Flagg is
ordered down, tho I believe it may be as well to detain her, (if
not too Troublesome) till both go together as by this Time our
Flagg may be clear of the Enemy & on her way up.   I agree with
you in oppinion the Salt & other Things ought to be taken from
on Board her & carefully deposited, to be applied as shall be hereafter directed by the Legislature of the State; but as our Laws
are silent as to such Seizures I woud rather wish to advise than
give any positive orders on the Occassion.   I impute the whole of
this affair to the wickedness of my old Master, who under the
Colour of serving Colo. Hay, has lead him into this Difficulty.
Hay, I have charity to believe, is honest tho Imprudent, & the
War rendered necessitous, for this Reason I coud wish how little
he might suffer.   I am &c.

                                        Geo. Clinton.
Colo. Malcom.

P. S. Mr. Van Dycke & the other Persons mentioned in your Letter, must by all means be sent back with the flag & not suffered to put foot on shore.

[No. 1950.]

SETTLING DIFFERENCES IN RANK.

Congress at Last Takes Action on this Long Disputed Matter—Simplifying the Forage Question.

Philadelphia 2nd December 1778.

Sir, On the 16th November I had the honor of addressing your Excellency by Messenger Dodd, since which I have not received any of your favors.

Under the present Cover will be found two Acts of Congress viz.

1. Six Copies of an Act of the 24th November for arranging the Army.

2. An Act of the 30th for obtaining Forage for the Army of these United States.

I have the honor to be With the highest Esteem & Respect Sir Your Excellency's Obedient humble servant

Henry Laurens, President of Congress.

His Excellency George Clinton Esquire Governor of New York.

In Congress, November 24, 1778.

Congress took into consideration the Report of the Committee of Arrangement, and thereupon came to the following resolutions.

Whereas the settlement of rank in the army of the United States has been attended with much difficulty and delay, inasmuch as no general principles have been adopted and uniformly pursued; RESOLVED, THEREFORE, That upon any dispute of rank the following rules shall hereafter be observed:

1. For determining rank in the continental line between all Colonels and inferior officers of different States, between like officers of infantry and those of horse and artillery, appointed under the authority of Congress by virtue of a resolve of the 16th of September, 1776, or by virtue of any subsequent resolution prior to the first of January, 1777, all such officers shall be deemed to have their commissions dated on the day last mentioned, and their relative rank, with respect to each other in the continental line of the army, shall be determined by their rank prior to the 16th day of September, 1776. This rule shall not be considered to affect the rank of the line within any State, or within the corps of artillery, horse, or among the sixteen additional battalions, where the rank hath been settled; but shall be the rule to determine the relative rank within the particular line of artillery, so far as the rank remains unsettled.

2. In the second instance, preference shall be given to commissions in the new levies and flying camp.

3. In determining rank between continental officers, in other respects equal, proper respect shall be had to their commissions in the militia, where they have served in the continental army for the space of one month.

4. All Colonels and inferior officers, appointed to vacancies since the 5th day of January, 1777, shall take rank from the right of succession to such vacancies.

5. In all cases where the rank between the officers of different States is equal, or between an officer of State troops and one of cavalry, artillery, or of the additional battalions, the precedence is to be determined by lot.

6. All officers who have been prisoners with the enemy, being appointed by their State, and again enter into the service, shall do it agreeably to the above rule; that is to say, all of the rank of Captains, and under, shall enter into the same regiment to which they formerly belonged, and if such regiment is dissolved or otherwise reduced, they shall be intitled to the first vacancy in any regiment of the State in their proper rank, after the officers belonging to such regiment have been provided for.

7. The rules of rank above laid down between officers of different States, are to govern between officers of the same State, except in cases where the State may have laid down a different rule, or already settled their rank.

8. A resignation shall preclude any claim of benefit from former rank under a new appointment.

Whereas, from the alteration of the establishment and other causes, many valuable officers have been and may be omitted in the new arrangement, as being supernumerary, who, from their conduct and services, are intitled to the honourable notice of Congress, and to a suitable provision, until they can return to civil life with advantage.

Resolved, therefore, that Congress gratefully acknowledge the faithful services of such officers, and that all supernumerary officers be intitled to one year's pay of their commissions respectively, to be computed from the time such officers had leave of absence from the Commander in Chief on this account. And Congress do earnestly recommend to the several States to which such officers belong, to make such farther provision for them as their respective circumstances and merits intitle them to.

Whereas it will be for the benefit of the service, that some rule for promotions be established:

Therefore, Resolved, that it be recommended to the several States, to provide that in all future promotions officers rise regimentally to the rank of Captain, and thence in the line of the State to the rank of Colonel, except in cases where a preference may be given on account of distinguished merit.

Resolved, That all officers who have been in the service, and, having been prisoners with the enemy, now are or hereafter may be exchanged, or otherwise released, shall, if appointed by the authority of the State, be intitled, in case of vacancy, to enter into the service of their respective State, in such rank as they would have had if they had never been captured; provided always that every such officer do, within one month after his exchange or release, signify, to the authority of the State to which he belongs, his release, and his desire to enter again into the military service.

Resolved, That every officer so released, and giving notice as aforesaid, shall, until entry into actual service, be allowed half pay of the commission, to which, by the foregoing resolve, he stands intitled; provided always, that in case of his receiving any civil office of profit, such half pay shall thenceforth cease.

Resolved, That no brevets be for the future granted, except to officers in the line, or in case of very eminent services.

Resolved, That Pay-Masters, not being of the rank of Captains, Quarter-Masters and Adjutants, be intitled to receive *Twenty Dollars per* month, subsistence money, in lieu of rations.

Resolved, That all officers and persons employed on the Staff shall receive, for subsistence money, *One-Third of a Dollar* for each extra ration heretofore allowed them.

Resolved, That Adjutants, Pay-Masters and Quarter-Masters, taken from the line, be again admitted into the rank they would have been intitled to. had they continued in the line. And such

Adjutants, Pay-Masters and Quarter-Masters, not taken from the line, may be admissable into the line in such subaltern ranks, as, by a signed certificate from the field officers of their respective corps, they shall be deemed competent to.

Extract from the Minutes.

CHARLES THOMSON, *Secretary.*

THE QUESTION OF FORAGE LARGELY LEFT TO THE STATE.

In Congress 30 Nov'r 1778.

Resolved, That in all cases where forage is wanted for the troops, and cannot be purchased by the commissaries at reasonable rates, application be made to the executive or legislative authority of the State wherein the forage is required, or to some person or persons properly authorised by them for that purpose, for their interposition and assistance in procuring the necessary supplies:

That it be recommended to the governments of the States, wherein the army or any detachment or part thereof now is or hereafter shall be, to take such measures in aid of the forage masters who shall first use every endeavour to purchase the same, for the procuring sufficient quantities of forage at reasonable rates, as shall in their opinion be effectual and most likely to procure a speedy supply.

Extract from the minutes.

Chas. Thomson, sec'y.*

---

*November 27, 1778, Washington wrote from Fredericksburg to the President of Congress:

Sir, Congress will be pleased to accept my acknowledgments for the communication of the treaties between His Most Christian Majesty and the United States. The resolve respecting the exchange of prisoners has been transmitted to Sir Henry Clinton, and I have appointed commissioners, if he thinks proper, to meet his at Amboy on the 7th of next month.

I have the pleasure to inform Congress, that the whole army, one brigade and the light corps excepted, is now in motion to the places of the respective cantonments for winter-quarters. I have thought it prudent to delay this event awhile, to give time for the convention troops to make some progress in crossing the North River, to prevent a possibility of accident. The third division passes this day; and, if no unexpected inter-

[No. 1951.]

An Assault Case Brought Before the Attorney-General.

Dear Sir, We think it our Duty to inform you of the extream ill Treatment, which Mr. Saml. Hake has lately receiv'd from Mr. Robt. G. Livingston Jr. & his Bro'r Gilb't R. Livingston by their

---

ruption happens, the whole will be over by the 30th instant. When their passage is completed, the remaining troops kept in the field will immediately retire to quarters.

The disposition for winter-quarters is as follows: Nine brigades will be stationed on the west side of Hudson's River, exclusive of the garrison at West Point; one of which, the North Carolina brigade, will be near Smith's Clove for the security of that pass, and as a reinforcement to West Point in case of necessity; another, the Jersey brigade, will be at Elizabethtown, to cover the lower part of Jersey; and the other seven, consisting of the Virginia, Maryland, Delaware, and Pennsylvania troops, will be at Middlebrook. Six brigades will be left on the east side of the river and at West Point; three of which (of the Massachusetts troops) will be stationed for the immediate defence of the Highlands; one at West Point, in addition to the garrison already there; and the other two at Fishkill and the Continental Village. The remaining three brigades, composed of the New Hampshire and Connecticut troops and Hazen's regiment, will be posted in the vicinity of Danbury, for the protection of the country lying along the Sound, to cover our magazines lying on Connecticut River, and to aid the Highlands on any serious movement of the enemy that way.

The park of artillery will be at Pluckemin. The cavalry will be disposed of thus; Bland's regiment at Winchester in Virginia, Baylor's at Frederic or Hagerstown in Maryland, Moylan's at Lancaster in Pennsylvania, and Sheldon's at Durham in Connecticut. Lee's corps will be with that part of the army which is in the Jerseys, acting on the advanced posts. This comprehends the general distribution of the army, except Clinton's brigade of New York troops, Pulaski's corps, and some detached regiments and corps stationed at Albany and at different parts of the frontier, of which Congress have already been particularly advised. General Putnam will command at Danbury, General McDougall in the Highlands, and my own quarters will be in the Jerseys, in the neighbourhood of Middlebrook.

This disposition appeared to me the best calculated to reconcile, as far as possible, these several objects; the protection of the country; the security of the important posts in the Highlands; the safety, discipline, and easy subsistence of the army. To have kept the troops in a collected state would have increased infinitely the expense and difficulty of subsisting them, both with respect to forage and provisions; to have divided them into smaller cantonments would have made it far less practicable to maintain order and discipline among them, and would have put them less in a condition to control and prevent offensive operations on the side of the enemy, or to assemble to take advantage of any favorable opening, which their future situation may offer, should they be obliged to weaken themselves by further detachments, so far as to invite an enterprise against them.

By the estimate of the quartermaster and commissary general, it appears indispensable to have the principal part of the army on the other side of the North River. It was thought impracticable to furnish the necessary supplies of flour for the whole on this side of the river, from the immense difficulty and expense of transportation in the winter season, and from the exhausted state of the country with respect to forage. As this subject has been already fully before Congress, I shall not trouble them with a repetition of the details. In order as much as possible to reduce the demand of forage and facilitate the supplies, I have given directions, when the several divisions arrive at their cantonments, to send away to convenient places, at a distance from them, all the horses not absolutely requisite to carry on the ordinary business of the army.

It is unnecessary to add, that the troops must again have recourse to the expedient of hutting, as they did last year. But, as they are now well clad, and we have had more leisure to make some little preparations for winter-quarters, I hope they will be in a more comfortable situation, than they were in the preceding winter. With the highest respect and esteem, I have the honor to be, &c.

coming to his apartments (at Mrs. Van Allen's) & fastened the Door. They then beat & bruis'd him very much indeed; which he can prove from the most credible witnesses.

Mr. Hake during his stay with us here, have Conducted himself with propriety & very friendly to the States, and we really wish that his Excellency, the Governor would be pleas'd to permit him to continue with us.

We think Mr. Hake's present situation distressing (& agreeable to his request), We recommend in the strongest manner, that you'll instantly be pleased to take the necessary steps to prosecute the Mr. Livingstons with the utmost Severity of the Law, which from their unjustifiable conduct they justly merit, & which we think Mr. Hake is in justice fully entitled to. We are, Sirs, your mo. obt. Ser'ts

David Van Ness
Herman Hoffman.

Red Hook Decemb'r 3d: 1778.

(Copy'd from the original for his Ex'cy the Gov'rs kind perusal.) Egbert Benson Esqr. Att'y General, Poghkeepsie.

[Nos. 1952–1953.]

DISTRESS AND SORROW AT CHERRY VALLEY.

George and James Clinton and Mayor Yates on the Question of Relieving the Sufferers.

Albany 28 Novemb'r 1778.

Sir, I have with me Col. Campbell and Mr. John Moore, Both from Cherry Valley; their Buildings and Effects Destroyed; the wife of the former with four Children and a negro taken prisoners. They have prefered a petition to Genl. Clinton for Relief; many of those Inhabitants who have Saved their Lives have lost every thing else, and now are moved in and about Schonectady in want of Clothing and Subsistence. The Genl. has Given them an order for a weeks provision, that by that Time they may Petition you for further Relief. They Cannot Get a Petition Signed I Suppose, not this Ten Days; and If they Do, I Dont Remember you are vested with any Power to Relieve them—but if any there be, or you be able to Contrive a method for their Relieve, I dare say the Legislature will Confirm it. I foresee a greater Difficulty with those Sufferers then many of the former, their Case being Some what Singular; Chiefly Europeans, have no Relations, but those that lived about them, and are Equal Sufferers with themselves.

It is absolutely Necessary Something be done for the futur that when Such Destruction happens there may be Immediate Relief.

I think the Congress Should Invest the Commander in Each Quarter (be it in what State it will) with proper powers for the purpose & it Should be a Continental Charge for many Reasons. We have no Port, Consequently no goods European or West India but what is at Enormous Prices; by means of the Land Carriage and the manovers of a Parcel of wicked Traders: add to this, that the Congress have Suffered themselves to be Imposd upon, and by Sporting with the Indian affairs have Drawn Down upon this State Death and Destruction. I can write no more; the post waits. Your ob't Hum. S't

Ab'm Yates Jun.

His Ex. George Clinton.

A TECHNICALITY BARS STATE ASSISTANCE FOR CHERRY VALLEY.

Poukeepsie 3d Dec'r 1778.

Sir, I have rec'd your Letter of the 28th Ultimo representing the distressed Situation of the Inhabitants of Cherry Valley & also one from my Brother Genl. Clinton Dated the [28th] on the same Subject. I deplore their unhappy Case & sincerely wish it was in my Power to afford them Relief by placing them at least on the same Footing with the Inhabitants of the German Flatts with Respect to Provision which woud in some Measure aleviate their Distresses. By the inclosed Letter to my Brother which I have left open for your Perusal, you will observe that I was authorized by the Concurrent Resolution of the Senate & Assembly, to supply the Inhabitants of the Flatts while they continued to maintain Fort Dayton, a Post in that Neighbourhood; in Consequence, whereof, I requested Genl. Hand to issue them a proper Supply from the Continental Store, ingaging to pay for the same, if the Measure should not meet the approbation of Congress, to whom he immediately wrote on the subject; but I am not yet informed whether he has received their Answer. You will please to observe that tho the Case of the Inhabitants of Cherry Valley is equally & perhaps more distressing, yet the Resolutions taking up the Case of those of the Flatts as garrisoning & maintaining a Post & it will by no means, therefore, apply to the former. So that in the present Case I am left not only without authority but without Presedent. To advise my Brother to order them supplies of Provission from the public Stores might be leading him into Difficulties & Censure from his Superiors. And by taking upon me to order them a Supply in any other way, I may incur Blame & the Displeasure of the Legislature. I am at the same Time fully of oppinion that some Relief ought to be afforded to those unhappy Sufferers, and if it is not giving you too much Trouble, I coud wish the Members for the County of Albany woud meet & confer upon the most elligible Mode of furnishing them a present Supply of Provisions, to serve till the meeting of the Legislature, & I will endeavour to have it carried into Execution

& as this seems to be the most practicable Mode, trust to their providing for the Expence. I have no News. I am your Most Obed't Serv't

Geo. Clinton.

[To Ab'm Yates Esqr.]

JAMES CLINTON ASKS THE GOVERNOR FOR INSTRUCTIONS.

Albany Nov'r 28th 1778.

Sir, I arrived in this Place the 25th Instant, since which time I have had repeated applications from the Inhabitants for Supplies of cloathing & Provisions for those distressed refugees from Cherry Vally.

As I do not think myself at Liberty to act in this matter untill I receive your Instructions, I have enclosed you a return made me for that Purpose that you may be better able to determine, what is to be done to alleviate the Distresses of these unhappy Sufferers.

I am informed that many of the Inhabitants of the German Flatts, who are not justly entitled to the publick Bounty, avail themselves of the General Calamity, & impose on the charity of the People—to remedy this imposition, I conceive that some Person of Integrity shoud be appointed for the purpose of discriminating between those who are objects of Charity and those who are able to provide for themselves, and make returns accordingly.

In consequence of the enclosed application from Cherry Vally, I have ordered the Commissary at Schanectady to issue one weeks Provision; if this shoud meet with your approbation, you will inform me in line, as soon as convenient, as I shall give no more orders untill I know the Pleasure of the State in the matter. I am your very affectionate

James Clinton.

P. S. The enclosed return from the German Flats contains the number of Persons who draw Provision by order of Genl. Hand.

His Excellency George Clinton Esquire

Governor of the State of New York.

THE VICTIMS AT CHERRY VALLEY.

A genuine account of the slain, and prisoners taken in the action (of the Inhabitents) at Cherry Valley No'br 11th 1778.

Viz: 31 Killed and Barbarous massachred; 33 prisoners Carred off; 38 made prisoners and pirmited to Return.

Prisoners that is Carried off: Colo. Campbell's wife and four Children and a negro Boy; James Moore's wife and three Daughters; James Campbell, Jun'r; James Ramsa, two sons and two Daughters; Will'm McClellan and two Children; Hugh Mitchell's two Children; James Richey's servant Boy and negro man; Robt. Wells's Servant girl and negro man; Mathew Cannan and two Servant Boys; John Scott and two negros; Rev'd Mr. Dunlap's negro wench; Will'm Henderson; a Son of James Leshman.

To the Hounerable Briga'r General Hand, Commander in Cheif of the American forces in the Northern Department:

We, the undernamed Subscribers, at the Request, and in Behalf of the poor Distresed Inhabitents of Cherry Valley, who made their Escape in the Conflagration thereof, on the 11th and 12th of Nov'br 1778, Humbly Sheweth; That the persons and familys whose names in a Schedull is hereunto anexed, By Reason of the Loss and Distruction of their all, is Left in a Dolefull, Lamentable, and Helpless Condition, Destitute (many of them) of meat, money, and Cloathing, Either for Back or Bed.

We, your Memorialists, Humbly pray your Houn'r to take the distresed Condition of these people into your Serious Consideration, and grant Such Supplys of provision, and wood, to those setled in and about Schenactady, as your Houn'r may think fit, and also advise, or devise Some ways and means, in your Houn'rs wisdom, wherby those distresed people may be Supplied with Some Cloathing, to Cover them from the Inclemency of the wether, and your Memorialists Shall Ever hold themselves in duty bound to pray.

Schenactady Nov'br 26th 1778.

> John Moore Quo'm Justice,
> Saml. Campbell, Colo.
> James Willson, Capt.

The following is a List of the persons pointed at in the within Memorial:

Colo. Samuel Campbell's	family	5
Leiut. Colo. Samuel Clyd	Do	10
Cap't James Willson	Do	8
Leiuts. John and Saml. Campbell	Do	8
Adjutant James Cannan	Do	3
Rev'd William Johnston	Do	10
Will'm Dixon	Do	8
Netha'l Hammil	Do	2
Will'm Galt	Do	9
Rev'd Saml. Dunlap	Do	5
Will'm McLellan	Do	4
James Campbell	Do	11
Rich'd Johnston	Do	5

Rebacas Thompson, widdow	Do	6
Will'm Thompson	Do	12
James Scott	Do	6
James Moore	Do	3
James Marr	Do	4
James Lishman	Do	4
Alex'dr McCollom	Do	8
Daniel Ogdon	Do	7
Hugh Mitchell	Do	3
Azaria Holeburt	Do	1
Michal McDearmot	Do	6
Saml. Warfield	Do	4
John Campbell	Do	6
Will'm Cook	Do	4
Saml. Edkins	Do	4
Will'm McConnell	Do	3
James McCollom	Do	4
		173

THE SUFFERERS AT GERMAN FLATS.

A Return of the Refugees, or inhabitants of the German Flatts, that was Burn'd off, and lost their Effects by the Enemy. All above 16 years old, are allow'd one lb. Bread & one lb. Beef; and all under 16 years old, half a lb. of Bread, and half a lb. Beef, pr. Day.

Names of Persons:	above 16 years:	under 16 years:
Henry Herter	5	6
Frederick Bellinger	7	1
Thomas Volmer	3	5

Jacob Weber, Jun'r	3	1
Mcleod Folts	2	1
Marks Ittig	6	5
Joseph Folts	2	5
Christian Rigel	2	4
Frederick Rigel	2	5
Frederick Helmer, Jun'r	2	3
Frederick Dornberger	1	7
Conrod Folts	4	2
Peter Weber	4	3
George Smith	6	2
George Helmer	2	4
George Hills, Sen'r	4	
Eve Frank	1	5
Stephen Frank	2	1
Margaret Pesausie	1	4
Philip Helmer	3	7
Nicholas Herter	6	
Lawrence Herter, Sen'r	3	1
Jacob G. Weber	2	2
George Hills, Jun'r	5	2
Adam Smith	3	4
John Christman, Jun'r	2	3
Ludowick Bersh	2	1
Michael Myer	4	3
John Bellinger	3	1
Jacob Christman	2	5
John Casler	2	4
Jacob Bauman	2	4
John Demuth	3	2

Frederick Herter	5	4
George J. N. Weber	2	
Nicholas Smith	2	3
Adam Bauman	5	2
Frederick Bauman	2	1
William Petry	2	5
George Dochsteder	4	
Mary Myer	4	2
Mary Bell	1	3
Frederick Myer	2	5
Frederick Weber	2	
William Cunningham	2	6
John Smith	2	1
Jacob Bell	2	
Adam Helmer	2	1
Adam Starring, Jun'r	3	1
Elizabeth Helmer	1	8
Jacob Myer	4	6
Joseph Myer	2	5
Christian Ittig	4	6
Jacob Pypher	5	4
John Pesausie	2	2
Augustinus Hess	2	2
Ichabod Bonny	3	3
John Frank	3	5
Frederick Frank	2	4
George Weber	2	1
Frederick Getman, Jun'r	2	1
Henry Miller	5	
Mark Raspell	3	5

William Cline	2	5
Margaret Bersh	1	4
Nicholas Spoon	5	2
Mary Oxner	1	4
Nicholas Christman	2	1
Elizabeth Rankin	1	2
Ludowick & John Campbell	4	3
Rudolph Steale	2	2
Barbary Clapsattle	3	7
Margaret Sharer	1	2
Dorothy Bell	1	2
Ann Schuyler	1	4
Barbara Petry	1	4
Catharine Petry	1	4
William Shoot	2	3
The widow Steinwax	1	4
The widow Iray	1	6
Barbara Cunningham	1	3

Such as have lost Houses & Barns but has some Grain left, and are put on half allowance:

Adam Starring, Sen'r	2	4
Michael Ittick	4	4
George Wents	4	3
John Fox	2	5
Peter Bellinger	4	4
John Osterhout	2	5
Frederick Getman, Sen'r	5	3
Jacob Basehaur	5	3
Tiedrick Steale	6	5

Jacob Folts	4	5
Nicholas H. Weber	2	7
Jacob Krim	3	5
Conrod & Peter Folts	5	5

Such as liv'd distant from Fort Dayton and was oblig'd to leave their habitations all the summer, and has lost part of their Effects and are on half allowance:

George Weber	5	1
John Myer	2	6
Frederick Kast	5	4
Gertrude Kast	1	
Mark Demuth	5	6
Christopher Strobell	3	
Nicholas Weber	2	4
John Davie	2	6
Nicholas Lighthall, Sen'r	2	1
Timothy Frank	2	5
Conrod Fulmer	3	3
Nicholas Lighthall, Jun'r	2	3
John Bellinger	3	6
Peter Flock	2	2
Jacob Broadhack	2	1

Such as are absent at present, but have lost Houses, Barns and most of their effects:

Lawrence Herter, Jun'r	2	3
Nicholas Hills	3	7
Andrew Clapsattle	2	2
William Deygart	7	6
George Nellis	5	1

Sign'd by the Principal Officers and Inhabitants of the German Flatts:

Peter Bellinger, Colo; Frederich Bellinger, Lt. Coll; Henrig Herder Capt; Wm. Petri, Justice, Friederich Gettman, Capt; Adam Helmer, Leut; Frieterich Franck.

―――――

THE GOVERNOR CONFIDENT THE LEGISLATURE WILL ADOPT MEASURES OF AMELIORATION.

Poukeepsie 3d Dec'r 1778.

Dear Sir, I have received your Letter of the 28th Ultimo. Tho I feel for the Distresses of the Inhabitants of Cherry Valley and sincerely wish it was in my Power to afford them Relief I am not authorized to instruct you to supply their wants from the Public Stores, however equitably they may be entitled to this Indulgence. I am sensible their Case is equally hard, & considering the advanced Season of the year in which their Settlement was destroyed, perhaps more so than that of the Inhabitants of the German Flatts, whom the Legislature have by their Resolution (a Copy whereof is inclosed for your Information) authorized me to supply with Provissions, but you will at the same Time observe, that the Reason held out by the Resolution for supplying the Inhabitants of the Flatts, is their garisoning & maintaining Fort Dayton & as it does not apply to those of Cherry Valey, it does not even afford me a Precedent for extending this Indulgence to the latter. It was in Consequence of my Request to Genl. Hand & Promise to defray the Expence, if the Measure shoud be disapproved by Congress, to whom he wrote on the subject, that he has ordered Provisions to be issued to them from the public Stores, and that you may stand on the same Footing with him in continuing these Issues, I now repeat the same Engagements to you. I inclose you also Copy of my Orders to Colo. Bellinger, to prevent the Impositions mentioned in your Letter which I trusted woud have proved an effectual Guard ag't them. If the Contrary however is the Case, as I am entirely Ignorant of Charecter in that Quarter, I must begg you to appoint some Person to this Business, who can be relied on, & I will confirm the appointm't.

The Legislature is to meet the 2d Monday in Jan'y & I have not the least doubt but they will on proper application from the Inhabitants of Cherry Valey which I wish them to make take the Case of these unhappy sufferers into Consideration & grant them suitable Relief. In the Mean Time I have wrote to the Members of the County of Albany for their Oppinion of the best mode of giving them a Temporary Supply, which I am willing the Risque of its being approved by ye Legislature. I am &c.

[G. C.]

[To Gen. James Clinton.]

[No. 1954.]

McDOUGALL AGAIN IN COMMAND AT THE HIGHLANDS.

Governor Clinton Orders Out Three Hundred Militia at His Request.

Peekskill Dec'r 2nd 1778.

My Dear Sir, I was honored with your Favor by Major McDougall. You justly concluded, that I did not intend to ask a promise of you in favor of Colonel Lawrance. I can with great Truth assure you, I had not a wish to obtain a promise from you. Such a Measure is too dishonorable to be proposed, to one in your office, exclusive of the Friendship I bear you.

After traversing the lower part of this State, and part of Connecticut, I am ordered once more by the Commander in chief, to take Charge of the Posts in the Highlands, with Nixon's, Patterson's and Learned's Brigades; and the present Garrison of West Point. The first of these is now hutting, on the Post Road below Mrs. Warren's, the two Latter are not yet come on, from the Eastward. When they arrive, some of them must hut also. With the utmost Dispatch that can be made, it will be the 15th or 20th Instant, before they are covered. Whenever they are, or the Work advanced, I shall send large Parties down to Bedford, North Castle Church and Sing-Sing. His Excellency has called off the Horse and light Troops, to join their respective corps. For these Reasons, I wish you would order three Hundred of the Militia out, for that Service, for fifteen or Twenty Days at furthest, when I shall relieve them, and hope I shall have no further Occasion to call on them, during my Command. Your Favors left at Major Cammel's Continental Village, will reach me. I beg the Favor of a Line from you in answer to this as soon as you can, to govern my Conduct. I am my Dear Sir Your most affectionate Servant

Alex'r McDougall.

His Excellency Governor Clinton.

The Governor Co-operates with McDougall.

Poukeepsie 4th Dec'r 1778.

D'r Sir, I am favoured with your Letter of the 2d Instant and agreable to your Request have orderd out three hundred of the Militia of Genl. Morris's Brigade to serve under you for one Month unless sooner relieved. The Inhabitants of the [Philipse] Purchase, Tarry Town, &ca. are at present much exposed, and the Enemy draw considerable Supplies of Cattle &ca. from those Neighbourhoods. I wish, therefore, that the Militia now ordered out, may be imployed as much as consistent with Safety & the good of the Service to cover those Neighbourhoods. I am in great Haste D'r Sir Your most Obed. Serv't

G. C.

P. S. You'l be pleased to forw'd the inclosed order to Genl. Morris, who I underst'd is at Bedford or in his absence to Coll. Saml. Drake. Genl. McDougal.

[No. 1955.]

COLONEL MALCOM TO BE SUPERSEDED.

He Invites Governor Clinton to Make Him a Call—The Case of Colonel Hay.

Fort Clinton Dec'r 1, 1778.

Sir, When I had the Honor of addressing you yesterday, I knew not or rather did not recollect that the parson's furniture was on board. It is most certainly right that it should be received and I shall with pleasure afford the person who comes to take charge of it, every assistance in my power. I believe Col. Hay's Case is just as your Excellency views it. I am [of] opinion that for the present, it is best to take his salt &c. on shore here for a few days—if it is delivered to him at Haverstraw—it will ruin him. I imagine he has paid or will pay for it & am perswaded he cannot afford the loss. I dare say you will approve of my doing so.

Smith's flag lies about 2 miles below this Garrison, and the other at King's Ferry—but for the conveniency of delivering the parson's Goods, & receiving the familys, I think of ordering her up also & they may go on board at Robinson's. Vandyke nor the others shall not come on shore.

I shall have an officer and a party w'h a whale boat ready, to see both vessells down the River, when your Excellency shall direct it to be done. Col. Hay is not yet come up, but I expect him to-morrow.

In a few days I expect to be relieved from my command. I have no such intimation from the Commander in Chieff but by a Letter from General McDougall & other reports, I imagine it will be the case. I have no regret on this account, only that I imagine that very few will take as much pains to promote the Service as I have done, and if they really would, it would be some time ere they could be properly acquainted with the bussiness to be done. I wish it were possible for your Excellency to ride down or to come down by water, and I woud send a well mann'd barge to Pokepsie. I wish you to see the state of the fort as I leave it, if that turns out to be the case, that at least I may have the credit of whats now done, and I don't want more. I have the Honor to be with due respect Your Excellency's most obed't and very Hbl. ser't

W. Malcom.

His Excellency Governor Clinton.

COLONEL HAY'S CASE LEFT TO COLONEL MALCOM'S DISCRETION.

Poukeepsie 4th Dec'r 1778.

D'r Sir, I am favoured with your Letter of the 1st Instant. I perfectly agree with you in sentiments respecting Colo. Hay's affair & I submit the whole management of it to your Discretion not doubting but it will be conducted in such prudent Manner as not to give Precedent to a Practice which might be injurious to the public Service.

You will receive this from Mr. Davis, who will deliver on Board the Flag, Mr. Bardsly's Furniture & take into his Care Mr. Freligh's, to be delivered at this Place. He is possessed of Lists of each. Mrs. Thom with her Familly & Effects goes down also in Mr. Davis' Boat & as Mrs. Mabit declines going to New York the Flaggs may be sent off as soon without further Delay. If I pos-

sibly can, I will pay you a vissit at the Fort before you leave it.
I am your most Obed't Serv't

G. C.

[To Col. Malcom.]

[No. 1956.]

Colonel Woodhull Determined to Preserve Discipline in His Regiment.

Orange County Decemb'r 2st 1778.

Dear Govenor, Inclosed you have the names of Three of my
Officers with their Charg* stated that I have Laid under an arrest.
I Beg your Excelency would Order a Court Martial To Try them
Immediately. I have had more Troble with my Ridgment for a
few months Past than I Have Had Ever Since the Commencement
of the War. Your Excellency must be Sencible that the Malitia
of this State has been Greatly Harrased Ever Since the Beginning
of the war and of Course must be Extreemly Distressing to the
Poorer Sort of mankind, and if the officers do not use every means
in their Power, it is not Possible to Get them out. Therefore, I
am determined for the future to Lay Every Officer under an arrest
for the Least Disobediance of Orders or who does not use every
means in his Power to Carry them into Execution. I am Determined to Bring them to a Since of their Duty or Resign my Com-
mition and have no further Troble with them. I Received a Letter from Coll. Courtland of the 23 Instant, ordering the malitia to
Menicinck and it appears from your Excellency's order of the
Twenty first of October, that the malitia of Ulster and Orange are
Discharged untill further orders from your Excellency. In Haste,
I am with the utmost esteem, Your Excellency's Very Humb.
Serv't

Jesse Woodhull.

To His Excellency George Clinton Governor of the State of New
York.

---

* Copy of charges not found.—State Historian.

GOVERNOR CLINTON ORDERS A COURT MARTIAL.

Poukeepsie 4th Dec'r 1778.

D'r Sir, I have received your Letter of the 2d Instant enclosing the Charges ag't Capt. Tuthill, Lieuts. Hobart & Horton and agreable to your Request you have herein an Order* appointing a Genl. Court Martial for their Tryal & the Tryal of such other Offenders as may be brought before the Court. You will please to forward the Order to the Presid't, who as he is to appoint the Time & Place for holding the Court, must forward to the different Regts. who are to furnish Members, a Copy of the Order with his Appointm't of Time & Place indorsed thereon.

I highly approve of your Resolution to bring your Regt. to a proper Sense of their Duty, in which you will always meet with my utmost assistance. Genl. Hand, or in his Absence Count Pulaski, commands at Minisinck, & it would be well to consult either of them before the Militia march to that Place, as Col. Cortland's Request may arise from some Misstake & I wish to ease them as much as may be consistent with the Public Safety. I am &c.

[G. C.]

Colo. Woodhull.

[No. 1957.]

McDOUGALL APPREHENSIVE OF AN ATTACK.

A Large Fleet of the Enemy Reported in Tappan Bay—Protecting Both Sides of the River.

Fort Arnold, Dec: 4th 1778.

Sir, I am favour'd with yours of equal date, the Inclosures were delivered to Col. Drake, and your wish respecting the Inhabitants below will be attended to. I came here at noon, to inspect the

----

*Order not found.—STATE HISTORIAN.

state of this post, and to give the necessary Orders for the winter. This moment Col. Hay informs me, there are twenty Sail of large and some small vessels in Tappan bay. Their object must be some stores on the west side of the Ferry. Five hundred Pennsylvanians, now at Peekskill are ordered to cross, and Nixon's Brigade, with all possible dispatch. Learned's is ordered to march to this Ferry. Patterson's to the Village to wait orders. Least any accident should happen the Boats at the Ferry before those Troops can cross, I shall probably order a Detachment from this post. They can always fall back if the Enemy should have any other object, higher up in view. The Troops (those Vessels may contain) would give me no pain, if they were confined to act one side of the river: But as I cant depend on this, I must be prepared for events. I think the Militia on the west side should be collected; ready to march to this post, if the Alarm should be fired. And that on the East side, prepared to move to Fishkill; and there wait orders. I cannot now inform you where yours will find me, as I have dispositions to make. But when this is done, I shall advise you. Three Cannon fired, five minutes after each other will be the signal. I am, Sir, Your hble. serv't

Alex'r McDougall.

7 P. M.

Governor Clinton.

THE MILITIA TO BE HELD IN READINESS.

P. 5 Dec'r 1778.

D'r Sir, I have received yours of yesterday & will order the Militia to hold themselves in Readiness and to march accordingly on Fireing of the alarm Guns. I am your most Obed't Serv't

[G. C.]

Genl. McDougal.

[No. 1958.]

CONFIDENCE IN COLONEL MALCOM.

The Govevnor Regrets He is to be Superseded at West Point—Requests Malcom to Settle the Hay Case.

Poukeepsie 5th Dec'r 1778.

Dear Sir, I am favoured with yours of equal Date. It gives me real Concern to learn that you are likely to be divested of the Command of the Fort ag't which every Reason mentioned in your Letter opperates (in my Opinion) most strongly. I think it will be most adviseable to send the Tories to the Commissioners at this Place at least such of them as it may not be safe to dismiss.

I wrote you this Morning by Mr. Richard Davis who has Bardsly's Furniture & Mrs. Thome & Familly on Board his Boat. He has Orders to receive Mr. Freligh's Effects from on Board the Flagg on his Arival which will be Tomorrow at farthest so that the two Flags may be dismissed without further Delay. I must begg you will compleat the Settlement of Colo. Hay's Affair in such manner as you shall Judge best even tho' you shoud be superceded in Command, there can be no Impropriety in your transacting this Business, as it relates solely to this State & I chuse to intrust it to your Discretion in preference to any other Person. I wish it was in my Power to continue you at the Fort; had Genl. McDougal consulted with me on the Occassion I shoud most certainly have advised it. I am &c.

[G. C.]

[To Col. Malcom.]

23

[No. 1959.]

QUARTERS FOR THE LEGISLATURE.

Inducement Offered by Kingston—The Rate for Board Fixed at Nine Dollars Per Week.

Marbletown Dec'r 5th 1778.

S'r, Inclos'd I Send your Excellency a letter I Rec'd from Mr. Dumond &c. and also a list of the Names of such of the Inhabitants of the town of Kingston, who are willing to board the Members of the Legislature, in case your Excellency should think proper to appoint that place, for the Meeting of the next Legislature. The Town of Hurly is much nearer than Salsbury or Harry Jansen's. Those Gentlemen who chooses to keep Horses can have them well keept and at a Reasonable rate at those places out of town.

I am farther Inform'd that rooms for the Senate and assembly will be provided. What is wanting in my opinion, is a house for your self and family. The lowest paid at Poughkeepsie the last setting (at lest as far as I know) was ten Dollers pr week. Some Gentl'n Paid fourteen. I am S'r with Great Esteem your Most Humble Ser't

Levi Pawling.

[To G. C.]

REPORT OF THE COMMITTEES.

Kingston Dec'r 2, 1778.

Sir, Agreable to our Resolution of yesterday we have taken a Tour among the Inhabitants of this Town respecting the Entertainment of the Legislature at the next Sessions. A List of the Persons who are willing to Board them will be delivered to you

by Mr. Dumond—as to the price from the best calculation we are
able to make, will be nine Dollars p Week. We are, Sir, Your
most Obed't Serv't

John Dumont,

Christ'r Tappen,

Egbert Dumond,

Joseph Gasherie,

D: Wynkoop, Jun.

To The Hon'ble Levi Pawling, Esqr.

[No. 1960.]

THE ENEMY'S FLEET RETIRES TO NEW YORK.

*Merely Off on a Foraging Expedition—McDougall Suggests the
Dismissal of the Five Hundred Militia.*

Peeks Kill Dec'r 6th 1778.

Sir, I am honored with your favor of yesterday. The Enemies
Fleet consisting of 26 saile came up and anchored at Kings-Ferry
at 9 A. M. of the 5th, and Landed 1500 men at 11; but their object being removed, in time, and seeing Nixon's Brigade move
towards them, which crossed in the morning, (within shot,) they
embarked with precipitation. And at 4 P. M. they sett saile and
moved down the river below Tallars Point, and I believe are now
out of sight. There Landed a considerable body at Tarry Town,
the afternoon before. These excursions were for Provisions; as
they are pressed for this Article six men having but the allowance of four. Considering the advanced season; and my present
Force, I think it unnessary now, to detain the common Militia
any longer in suspense. You, therefore, please to order them

dismissed. I am much obliged to you for the ready assistance you afforded me in ordering those out, destined for below, as well as the orders Issued for the others. You may rest assured, I shall not call upon them at any time unnecessarily. My complim'ts to Mrs. Clinton. And believe me to be your affectionate Friend and Humble Servant

Alex'r McDougall.

Gov'r Clinton.

[No. 1961.]

Mr. Bancker Arrives at Goshen with the One Hundred Thousand Dollars Advanced by Congress to New York.

Goshen, Sonday Noon Decemb'r 6th 1778.

Sir, I did myself the honour of addressing your Excellency last Monday when at Philadelphia; I now have the pleasure of Informing your Excellency of our safe Return thus far, and for the quicker Conveyance of the Letters (we received in Philadelphia) to your Excellency &ca. I have thought best to Dispatch One of the Guard by the way of New Windsor, who is the bearer of this. Immidiatly after Dinner shall proceed on to Kingston and Deliver our Charge in the hands of the Treasurer and take his Receipt agreable to our Instructions. The Specie mentioned of in Mr. Duane's Letters being altogether in my own Charge, I shall Deliver the same either to your Excellency or your Order as soon as possible. In the Mean time conclude, with my best Respects to your Excellency and family, and Remain with great Esteem Your Excellency's Most Obed't & Very Humble Serv't

Abr'm B. Bancker.

This accompanies also a Number of the Constitution of our State and 14 of the Treaty of Alliance rece'd from Mr. Lewis.

His Excellency Governor Clinton.

[No. 1962.]

Colonel Malcom Apparently Unwilling to Surrender His Command at West Point.

Fort Clinton, Dec'r 6, 1778.

D'r Sir, I had the Honor to address your excellency by Capt. Neven yesterday. Since that Genl. McDougal is gone to Peeks Kill, the Garrison is reenforced with a few Troops, and at all events I am in no apprehensions for its fate. Whether or not you will think proper to interest yourself in the change of Command that is likely to happen I know not,—Altho' there are some motives which I imagine will incline you to do so, Yet, on the other hand, you woud perhaps risque something on my conduct, by urging the matter to either Congress or Genl. Washington. However, I am sure that the measure is no way connected w'h the public Service, but a cause must be look'd for elsewhere. Genl. McDougal seems to Hesitate, I told him I believed it would not be very agreeable to you & that I imagined you would interest yourself in the matter, He said " he expected so." Our Garrison are highly incensed at the prospect of being sent to Haverstraw to look for Winter Quarters after the excessive fatigue they have done here,

Your militia I am confident would rather Succour me, than any Stranger & they have had a pretty good Specimen of those from the East.

The bussiness recommended in your Excellency's letter by Capt. Davis is Executed, but the flag cannot go down before to-morrow.

Col. Hay is not come yet but expect him every moment.

I shall be exceeding happy to see you here, but beg a day's previous notice. W'h great respect I am Your Excellency's mo. ob. & Very hum'e Serv't

W. Malcom.

[To G. C.]

[No. 1963.]

Tories Abandon Their Wives and Children.

To his Excellency Gorge Clinton, Esqr.

Governor of the State of New York Genl. and Commander in Cheif of all the malitia and Admiral of the Navy of the same.
May it Plas your Excellency,

That where as, John Bates and Ebeneser Wasborn, Both of Fradricksbourgh Precinct, Some months Past absconded and are gone to the Enemy of the United States of America Leaving their wives and a number of Small Children behind who are unable to Soport themselves:

We, the Subscribers, therefore, Beg Leave to acquaint your Excellency, that Considering the Inability of the Families of the S'd Bates and Wasborn's of Soporting themselves, the Scarcity of Grain Occasioned by the Troops Remaining So Long with us, and the Number of Poor we have to Soport at Publick Expence, that it is our humble opinion, that it would be of Geat Servis to the Precinct, if your Excellency in your wisdom, would see fit to Grant a Permit to Zubah Bates and Mary Washborn, wives of the s'd John and Ebeneser, to Pass with their Children within the enemies Lines. as witness our hands at Fradricksbourgh this 7 Day of Dec'br A D 1778.

Mathew Paterson Justice of ye peace; Heman King, Timothy Hatch, Reuben Ferris, Alex'r Kidd Overseers of the Poor.

Granted, on procuring a pass from Com'g Officer of the Department.

[G. C.]

[Numbers 1964, 1966-1967,*]

JOHN JAY ELECTED PRESIDENT OF CONGRESS.

Succeeds Henry Laurens—Promises to Devote His Services to New York—Gouverneur Morris' Tribute.

In Congress Dec. 10, 1778.

Sir, I have the honor to inform you, that this day Congress proceeded to the election of a President, & that the choice has fallen upon the hon'bl John Jay, Esqr.† I am, Sir, Your obed't humble serv't

Chas. Thomson, sec'y.

His Excell'y George Clinton Esqr. Gov'r of State of New York.

---

*For reasons that are obvious, manuscript documents 1966 and 1967 are given precedence in the printed publication over manuscript document 1965.—STATE HISTORIAN.

†Monday December 7. John Jay returned to Congress and presented his credentials which read as follows:

" The people of the State of New-York, by the grace of God free and independent, to all to whom these presents shall come, send greeting.

" Whereas our senate and assembly of our said state did, by their concurrent resolutions of the 21st day of October last, declare that a special occasion did then exist in which the chancellor and judges of the supreme court might be elected delegates to the general Congress, and that of the chancellor and judges, one should be elected a delegate on such special occasion; and also by concurrent resolutions of the 4th day of this inst, month of Nov., did resolve to proceed severally to nominate in the mode prescribed in and by the 30th article of the constitution of this state, of the chancellor and judges of the supreme court, one as a delegate to represent this our state in the Congress of the United States of America, on such special occasion, to continue in office until the first day of March next, and did, thereupon proceed to the said nomination, and did nominate and appoint, in the mode prescribed by the said article, John Jay, Esq. our chief justice of our supreme court of judicature, a delegate to represent this our state in the Congress of the United States of America, on the present special occasion: now therefore, know ye, that, in pursuance of such nomination and appointment, we do, by these presents, commissionate the said John Jay, Esq; a delegate to represent this our state in the Congress of the United States of America, on the present special occasion; and do hereby authorize him to hold and exercise all the powers and authorities to the office or place of delegate belonging, by virtue of the said constitution, and the nomination and appointment aforesaid; to have and to hold the said office or place of delegate upon the present special occasion, unto the said John Jay, Esq; for, and during, and until the first day of March next, and no longer. In testimony whereof, we have caused these our letters to be made patent, and the great seal of this, our state to be hereunto affixed. Witness our trusty and well-beloved, George Clinton, Esq; our governor of our said state of New-York, general and commander in chief of all our militia, and admiral of the navy of the same, this tenth day of Nov. in the third year of our independence, and in the year of our Lord one thousand seven hundred and seventy-eight.

Signed, 　　　　　　　　　　　　　　　　　　　　　　George Clinton,

With the great seal appended, and endorsed.

Passed the secretary's office, by the special command in writing of his excellency, the governor, this 15th of November, 1778.

John Morin Scott, Secretary of State."—From the Journals of Congress.

John Jay's Announcement of the Fact to the Governor.

Philadelphia 10 Dec'r 1778.

Dear Sir, Many unavoidable Delays prevented my arrival here till Sunday evening last.

Yesterday Mr. Laurens resigned the Chair, & this morning Congress were pleased to appoint me to succeed him. This Circumstance was unexpected. Let your public Letters be public ones. I mean that public & private matters should not be mixed in the same Letters.

Commodore Wynkoop's memorial has been presented & committed. You shall have the earliest Intelligence of its Fate.

I have heard, tho not from authority, that the Enemy have quitted the River without having accomplished any thing of Importance. God Grant it may be true. We have no Intelligence worth communicating.

The Season for bringing on the affair of Vermont is not yet arrived, nor can I divine what will be the Issue of it. I can only say that my Endeavors shall not be wanting to bring it to a Termination satisfactory to New York. Be pleased to present my best Respects to Mrs. Clinton & believe that I am very sincerely your Friend & serv't

John Jay.

His Excellency Gov'r Clinton.

Gouverneur Morris Looks for "Good Consequences" by This Promotion.

Phila: 10th Dec'r 1778.

Sir, I have the Pleasure to inform your Excellency that the hon'le John Jay, Esqr. is elevated to the Chair of Congress, which as well from your Friendship for him, as for Reasons of public

Importance will, I am confident, be agreable to you. The weight of his personal Character contributed as much to his Election as the Respect for the State which hath done and suffered so much or the Regard for its Delegates which is not inconsiderable. The Public will I am confident experience many good consequences from the Exchange. I am respectfully Your Excellency's most obedient & humble Servant

Gouv. Morris.

His Exc'y George Clinton, Esqr., Gov'r of the State of N. York Poughkeepsie.

[No. 1965.]

SMUGGLING CATTLE TO THE ENEMY.

Samuel Lyon's Charge Against English Sympathizers in Westchester County.

Horse Neck Dec'br 10th 1778.

Sir, I beg leave to acquaint your Exel'cy that the situation of affairs, are such in the County of Westchester, for want of Guards, that I am reduced to the necessity of quiting my house, and puting myself under the protection of the Guards in this place. This is likewise the fate of every honest friend to his Country in Rye. The consiquence is, that, a number of designing persons under the influence of avaritious & Inimical principles, make a practice, of secretly purchasing fat Catle, and in the night thro woods & bye Places, pass the Guards here, and keep them secreeted untill a convenient opertunity presents, to send them to the Enemy. In this way I am credibly Informed, eight fat oxen and four Cows have lately been sent from the neighbourhood where I should live and a considerable nomber of fat hoggs. There is no doubt this is the case quite across to the North River. In this way the Enemy have a large and ever plentifull supply in New York market. I am confirmed in this by the report of Capt. Olmstead of Col. Enos Regt., on Guard here; who has this week return'd from Valantine's, near Fort Independance, where he had been sent a flag and detained some days, who says he heard and saw while there, two hundred head of Cattle, and a great nomber of Sheep and hoggs pass by there towards New York. This is a harvest for those Infamous Villains, the Cow Thieves, &c., and brings great distress on many of the good Citizens in this quarter of the Country, I would beg leave to hint to your Exelency, that should a party of men, as a patrole under the Command of an active honest man be Employed, I conceive would be of great Importance, and the most likely method to detect the Thieves, I am told Mr. John Haynes proposes to offer himself for that purpose. Whether this, or such other method as your Exelency in your great wisdom shall judge best, I doubt not will soon be adopted. I am, with Great Respect and Esteem, your Exelen'ys most obed't Humble Ser't

                                        Samuel Lyon.
His Exe'lcy Gov'r Clinton.

[Nos. 1966-1967.]*

[No. 1968.]

Colonel Malcom Unhappy at West Point—He Speaks of Tories.

Sir, I send Mr. Hall one of the banished persons—from Vermont—not as a prisoner, he is a good honest man; has been faithfull & I really believe deserves every Trust. He did not like to be left here, nor do I think that he ought to be; he may provide for himself. I pray your Excellency's favor to him.

---

*For the anomalous position of these two documents see page 359, footnote.—STATE HISTORIAN.

Peter & John Angevine are the only Torys that I think is necessary to trouble the Commissioner with. They are base Torys; one of them Peter was with the enemy at the masacre of the Pensyl'a militia at the Crooked Billet* last Spring; they ought to be confined. I hope to see you soon at Poughkeepsie. Things wear such a Complexion here that I am unhappy. The other Torys are discharged. I most respectfully am, D'r Sir, yours most sincerely

W. Malcom.

Fort Clinton Dec'r 10 1778.

[To G. C.]

[No. 1969.]

Albany Citizens Appeal to the Governor in Behalf of the Cherry Valley Sufferers.

Albany Decem'r 12th 1778.

Sir, By the Late Ravages of the Enemy on the Settlement of Chery Vally, many of its Inhabitants having Lost their Provisions, Cloathing, &c. are reduced to the Greatest Distress; and unless a mode is adopted for their present Support, they must inevitably perish. They have petitioned Genl. Clinton for relief, who has Been pleased to order Them provisions for a few Days. We would wish that your Excellency would be pleased to request that the General would continue to furnish these people with Provisions until the next Meeting of the Legislature, who, we have not the least doubt, will approve of the Measure and provide for their farther Support.

---

*The affair at Crooked Billet near Neshaminy, Pa., occurred May 1st, 1778. Owing to the neglect of the American scouts to patrol the roads and leave camp by 2 o'clock in the morning as they were ordered to, the enemy succeeded in completely surrounding the American camp, and surprising the troops that held it. The American loss was upwards of 30 killed and wounded, with 58 missing. The English loss was not reported — STATE HISTORIAN.

We are with every Sentiment of respect Your very Humble Servants

Abr'm Yates, Jun'r, John Tayler, Leonard Gansevoort, Evert Bancker.

His Excellency Governor Clinton.

[No. 1970.]

A Threatening Letter from Four Indian Chiefs.

Decemb'r 13th 1778.

Joseph Brant

Mr. Capt: Sir, It is the Desire of the Seneca Cheifs and other Indians that you will Not in the Least trouble or moliest those People on the Delaware above Econack. The Reason of this your Rables came to Oughquago when we Indians where gone from our place, and you Burned our Houses, which makes us and our Brothers the Seneca Indians angrey, so that we Destroyed men, women, and Children at Chervalle. It is, therefore, the Desier of us Indians that those people Living about Shackaken are our Brothers; we, therefore, Desire that you will Let our brothers live in peace, least you be worst delt with, then your Nighbours the Cheryvalle People was. You may think its a Hard winter will hinder us from Coming to you. I have Big Shouse and can come in a few day to your place. At present my face is another way, But if you Destroy that place, I will set my face again you, for if you hurt my people I shall fell the Strock for the Six Nations fells the Strock that Hurts there Brothers.

Capt. William Johnson, Cheif Mohack; Joseph Ceskwrora, Cheif; Capt. John, Cheif; William George, Cheif.

Copy.

To Cunnell John Cantine Mormeltown.

[No. 1971.]

VIOLATIONS OF THE GATES-BURGOYNE CONVENTION.

Governor Clinton Endeavoring to Secure Evidence for the Use of Congress.

Poukeepsie 14th Dec'r 1778.

Dear Sir, I have lately been favoured by Congress with a few Copies of the Treaties at large between the States and his most Christian Majesty, which I am injoined however not to publish till further Order. I consider myself at Liberty nevertheless to communicate them to my Friends for their Information and I accordingly now inclose you one of the Copies which you will please to return at the Meeting of the Legislature. In the Mean Time you will not suffer it to be Copied.

I am directed by Congress to continue my best Endeavours to procure the fullest Evidence of the Infraction of the Convention of Saraghtoga on the Part of the Enemy. And they are particularly desirous of having a Copy of a Proclamation published by Gov'r Carlton in Canada last Spring, requiring the Prisoners who returned into Canada to join their Regts., as the Convention was rendered void by the Violation of it by Congress.* The Procla-

---

*November 20, 1778, from Fredericksburg, Washington wrote as follows to General Schuyler:

My dear Sir, Congress seem to have a strong desire to undertake an expedition against Canada. The practicability of it depends upon the employment, which the enemy intend to give us on the seaboard next campaign, on their strength in Canada, the state of our resources, and other circumstances, some of which are too much buried in obscurity, others too much in the field of conjecture, to permit us to form any decisive opinion about them at this time. But there is not a moment to spare in preparing for such an event, if hereafter it should be found expedient to undertake it.

In your letter of the 9th ultimo, which you did me the favor of writing upon this subject, you are opposed to an enterprise against Canada by the way of Coos, and assign cogent reasons for not making it a principal dependence. You are also against the route by Oswego; but, as an expedition that way had not been suggested, you do not touch upon the reasons, but recommend the common route by the way of Lake Champlain, and a winter expedition, if the ice will admit of it.

In general, winter campaigns are destructive to troops, and nothing but pressing necessity, and the best state of preparation, can justify them. I fear neither the state of our provisions, the condition of our men, nor the situation of our officers (the distresses of whom, on account of the uncommonly high prices of every necessary of life, are a source of general discontent and indifference to the service), would warrant the undertaking, even if the state of the Lakes, and the force of Canada, should invite *to*

mation is alluded to, I think, in Fry's affidavit, who brought one
of them out of Canada & left it on his way Home in one of the
Eastern States.   I must begg you, therefore, to concert & have

---

the measure. I am clear, also, that neither force nor stratagem can give us a well-
founded hope of a decisive superiority in naval strength upon Lake Champlain, where
the enemy are at present so powerful.

Your scheme for preparing materials for building two large ships upon this lake is
plausible, and, if only one or two were entrusted with the secret, practicable. But
when fifty men are to be consulted, before the measure can be adopted, many of whom
are inattentive to the importance of keeping military manoeuvres secret, and a knowledge of the plans by that means may get to the enemy's emissaries, who are industrious
in acquiring and diligent in communicating every piece of useful information; I say,
when this is the case, I can entertain but little hope of success from a project of this
kind. If, from these considerations, a winter's expedition is found impracticable or
unadvisable; if the conquest of the enemy's fleet on Lake Champlain is not to be accomplished by force nor by stratagem; and if an enterprise by the way of Coos is inadmis-
sible, as a primary object;—

1. What door is left open for an expedition against Canada?

2. How far is there a moral certainty of extending the American arms into that country in the course of next campaign? And,

3. How far short of the entire conquest, and annexation of Canada to the Union,
would give permanent peace and security to the frontiers of these States?

In considering these points, and such others as may hereafter occur, it will be necessary to take the matter up in two points of view; presuming, in the one case, that the
enemy will evacuate the United States; in the other, that they mean to retain New York
and Rhode Island as garrison towns. In discussing them with that freedom and candor,
which I mean to do, you will readily perceive that it is my wish to enter into an
unlimited and confidential correspondence with you on this subject. In addition, then,
to the above queries;

4. Where lie the difficulties of an expedition against Canada by the way of Lake
Ontario?

5. Why did General Amherst take this route, when Lake Champlain was open, free,
and so much more direct, if he did not foresee that some apparent advantages were to
be derived from it?

6. What resources can be drawn from the State of New York towards the support of
an expedition of this kind?

7. At what places would it be necessary to establish posts between Albany and Oswego,
for the support of the communication, and security of convoys? And,

8. How many men will be required at each post for the above purposes, and at
Oswego?

I mean to hazard my thoughts upon a plan of operations for next campaign, if the
enemy should evacuate these States and leave us at liberty; but being unacquainted
with the country, and many other matters essentially necessary to form a right judgment upon so extensive a project, I am sensible that it will be very defective, and shall
consider it as the part of friendship in you, to observe upon every part of my plan with
the utmost freedom.

I have already laid it down as a position, that, unless a winter expedition can be
undertaken with success (opposed to which, in addition to the reasons already assigned,
the want of provisions I find is an almost insuperable bar), or the fleet at St. John's can
by some means or other be destroyed, the door into Canada by way of Lake Champlain
is effectually closed. I am further of opinion, that the distance of land carriage by the
way of Coos for flour and stores is too great to expect, that a sufficient body of troops
can be introduced through that route, to answer *singly* any valuable purpose; and I am
therefore naturally led to turn my thoughts to the route by the way of Oswego, though
difficulties of the same kind, but not in so great a degree, present themselves here, as
on the other Lake.

If I am not mistaken with respect to the water carriage from Schenectady to Oswego,
by the help of finesse and false appearances a pretty large stride may be taken towards
obtaining a naval superiority on Lake Ontario, before the real design would be
unfolded.

carried into Execution such Plans as you shall judge best adapted
to procure the desired Information & Evidence.   I will chearfully
defray the Expence & where Specie is necessary for this Service

The plan I would adopt should be this. By innuendoes and oblique hints, I would endeavour to acquire the mastery of Lake Champlain; and, to give currency to this belief, I would have the saw-mills about Fort Anne and Fort Edward set to work to prepare plank for batteaux, and such kind of armed vessels as may be proper for Lake Ontario. I would go further, and, though it should be inconvenient and expensive, I would build the batteaux, and bring the timber for larger vessels to some place, or places, that might serve to confirm an idea of this kind. A plan of this sort, if well conceived and digested, and executed with secrecy, might, I think, deceive, so far as to draw the attention of the enemy to Lake Champlain, at the expense of Ontario, especially as part of my plan is to advance a respectable body of troops at a proper season to Coos for purposes, which will be mentioned hereafter.

In the spring, when every thing is ripe for execution, and the real design can no longer be concealed, I would advance with the utmost celerity consistent with proper caution to Oswego in the batteaux, which have been provided apparently for Lake Champlain, transporting the armed vessels in pieces to the same place. But here I am to ask, if this is practicable. My knowledge of the water communication from Schenectady to Oswego is not sufficiently accurate to enable me to form a decided opinion upon the possibility of this measure; and, if it is not to be effected, my plan in part fails, and we can only provide the materials under false colors, and depend upon out-building the enemy to obtain the superiority of the Lake. Whether the superiority can be obtained in this manner, I am not well able to determine, though it is very necessary to be known, as it is the corner-stone of the superstructure. Much will depend upon the practicability of the enemy's getting vessels, or materials for vessels, from Lake Champlain or Montreal, to the navigation above La Galette; because I proceed upon the principle, that, if we can deceive them effectually, their whole attention will be drawn to the more interior parts of the country, and of course their ship-carpenters, and materials for ship-building, will be employed in that way.

The foregoing is a summary of my capital movement, to facilitate which, I would, as has been before observed, advance a body of men from Coos. The motions of these should be regulated precisely by those of the main army, establishing posts as they go, for the purpose of retreat, in case of necessity, and to protect convoys, if the main army should be able to penetrate into Canada as far as Montreal. Several advantages will be derived from the advance of a body of troops by the way of Coos. First, strengthening the belief, that we mean to enter by the way of St. John's; secondly, it will serve to distract the enemy in their councils and measures, and either divide their force and render them weak at all points, or, by keeping them collected, expose the interior or exterior part of the country to a successful and fortunate blow from one or the other of these bodies; and it will, in the third place, open a communication for ample supplies of live cattle, if they should be required for troops in Canada.

Upon this plan, it is not only possible, but to be expected, that the enemy, if they should come at the knowledge of our real designs, would oppose their whole naval force to our troops on Lake Ontario, and their land force against those by the way of Coos. In this case I should be glad of solutions to the questions which follow.

9. Is there any practicable route from Johnson's Hall, or any other part of the Mohawk River, or from the upper parts of Hudson's River, to a river emptying itself into the St. Lawrence a little above La Galette, by which we could avoid Lake Ontario, and the armed vessels on those waters, altogether? And if this is not to be effected, and superiority on the lake is despaired of, then I should wish to be informed,

10. Whether Niagara can be approached with an army and the necessary apparatus, by a route, which will avoid this Lake?

11. What will be the distance of the march from Fort Schuyler, the kind of country through which it is to be made, and the difficulties that are to be expected?

12. What will be the advantages and disadvantages of maintaining that post, after possessing it, Canada remaining in the hands of the enemy?

For the more certain reduction of Niagara, and for the peace and safety of the frontiers of Pennsylvania and Virginia, a part of my plan is, to advance a body of troops from Pittsburg by way of the Allegany, Le Boeuf or French Creek, and Presqu' Isle to advance it.   I am with best Respects to Mrs. Tayler, in which

Mrs. Clinton joins me your most Obed't Serv't

[G. C.]

John Tayler Esqr.

P. S.   I have no news worth communicating.

[No. 1972.]

Isaac Goes Makes Complaint Against Certain Tories, and the Governor Replies.

Kinderhook 4th December 1778.

Dear Governor: I Re'd your faver four Days after Date.   I Immadietely atanded on the bisness & have Siezed & Sold to the amout of five hundred pounds Clare of Exspence, & have four barels of flour, one waggon & two horsess on hand (thirty five barels the property of Shepard & others) Sixteen barels two Carts the property of Joseph L. Hobbert who it is Said has maid a Large

---

the above post, if it be practicable; of which I am not certain, as the enemy have armed vessels on Lake Erie, and I am ignorant of the kind of country between Presqu' Isle and Niagara, in case it is to be attempted by a land march. But admitting the impracticability of this, an expedition to Detroit, which Congress meditated last fall, and still have in contemplation, will keep the Indians in that quarter employed, and prevent them from affording succour to the garrison at Niagara. The preparations necessary to the one will answer for the other, while the one to Niagara may be concealed under the idea of going to Detroit.

Although, under the present appearances of things, it is a matter of very great doubt whether we shall be in circumstances to prosecute a project of this kind, I have nevertheless given orders for magazines of provisions to be laid in at Albany and on Connecticut River, from the lower Coos to Number Four, and have ordered the saw-mills about Fort Anne to be set to work, and shall be obliged to you for your advice to Colonel Lewis on this occasion. If it should fall in your way to ascertain with precision the number and strength of the vessels upon Lake Ontario, and down to La Galette, and the force of the garrisons at Niagara and Oswegatchie, I shall thank you, and must beg leave to remind you of the mode you suggested to procure intelligence from Canada in the course of the winter, as it is of infinite importance to be well informed of the strength, expectations, and preparations of the enemy. To receive the account through different channels is also essential, to avoid deception.

I shall be very happy to see you at the head-quarters of the army, in your way to Philadelphia, whenever it happens. Governor Clinton wrote to me that he should be at Albany in the course of a few days. As I have implicit confidence in him, it will be quite agreeable to me, that you should converse largely with him upon the several matters herein contained, and then furnish me with your observations upon my plan, and the most effectual means of carrying it, or some other, into execution, with the necessary preparation to be made during the winter. With the greatest esteem and regard, I remain, dear Sir, &c.

Som of mony by runing wheat & flour out of this State Since the Date of the act; it is my opinion the atty. General ought to be Directed without any Delay to prosocute the said Habbert Lige Ovet & Plummer who have maid it their bisniss to run all thay Could in violtion of the Said act as there is plenity of Evidence to prove it uppon them & will Cause a grat dele of unesniss by many of the good people of this State, if thay are not prosocuted. I have wrote you ons befor this but have had no answer. I wood, therefore, beg the faver of your answer with Such Derection as you Shall Judg nascecary By the furst uppertunity, and I am Your Excelency's most obedent Vary Humble servent

Isaac Goes.

To his Excelency Gorge Clinton Esqr.

THE GOVERNOR FAVORS PROSECUTION.

Poughkeepsie Dec'r 14th 1778.

Sir, I have rec'd your Letter of the 4th Inst. but have not rec'd any other Letter from you on the Subject of the Embargo Law or I should have undoubtedly answered it. I am obliged to you for your Exertions and am clearly of opinion that Joseph L. Hobbert & the others mentioned in your Letter ought to be prosecuted, for which Purpose you'l be pleased to take the necessary Affidavits to be taken & transmitted to me, to the End that the Atty. Genl. may proceed ag't those violators of the Law without Loss of time. I am with great Esteem, Sir Yours &c.

Geo. Clinton.

Isaac Goes Esqr.

24

[No. 1973.]

GOVERNOR CLINTON'S SUGGESTION ACCEPTED.

A Formidable Expedition Planned which Subsequently Culminated with Sullivan's Successful Advance Against the Indians.

Rochester Dec'r 14th 1778.

Dear Sir, I am just return'd from ascorting Brig'r Genl. Edw'd Hand as far as Luning kill on his way to the Minisinks. He has Rec'd orders from his Excellency General Washington, to take the Command of all the Troops on the Fruntiers from this place to Wiomen. Viz: the 2d N. Y. Regt; Pulaske's Legion; Armand's Core; the German & Colo. Hartley's Regts. With this force it is Intended with the approbation of the Commander in Chief, (Should the winter be favourable), to Destroy Chemung and other Indian towns on the Susquehana; (this is at present Secret). I have Received orders to furnish my men if Possible with mittens, Socks, Caps, & Blankets—also one pair of Spare Shoes Pr man— all which I am at a loss to procure. Mittens I hear there are in the State Store. Shall, therefore, be much obliged for an order to Recive as many as I shall want. Shall be glad your Excellency will give me your advice and wether any Dependance can be put on Receiving a Supply of the other articles, in whole or in part. I Shall Receive upwards one Hund'd & fifty pair Shoes from the Supervisors & Mr. John Anthony, which is but little more than 1-3 part wanting. I want 150 Blankets. I have the pleasure to Inform y'r Excel'y that we are Daily Inlisting men. Of Course my Demand for Clothing Encreases. No late news from the westward. The militia at present I think of little Service; about Seventy men Except those at Pienpack will be a Sufficient Quantity to be Disposed of, in the following manner, Viz: 2 off'rs &

25 men at Shandacen; 1 of'r & 10 do at Yough Criplebush; 1 of'r & 12 do at Lunen kill & 2 of'r & 20 do at Mamacotten.

It is probable Genl. Hand will advise Concerning the militia at Pienpack. And also Should the Intended Expidition take place, it may be necessary then, for the time we are absent, to order a Reinforcement of militia which in that Case will be timely applied for. Please to make my best Respects to Mrs. Clinton and believe me to be with great Respect Your Excellency's Obed. Hum'e Ser't

Philip Cortlandt.

His Excellency Governor Clinton.

GOVERNOR CLINTON PROMISES TO CO-OPERATE.

Poukeepsie 22d Dec'r 1778.

Dear Sir, I am favoured with your Letter of the 14th Instant. If the Season shoud be such as to admit of any Enterprize ag't the Enemy, you may rest assured I will render every aid in my Power to promote so desierable an object. How or where to get the Articles wanted to fit your Regt. for this Service I am not able to tell or even advise. There are some Mitts in State Store & you have my Letter inclosed, advising the Commissary to deliver to your order as many as will supply your Regt. with each man a Pair, which I have no [doubt] but he will readilly do. If any of the other Articles mentioned in your Letter are in Store on your apprizing me of it you shall have my order for them.

The inclosed Letter to Colo. Cantine* contains Orders to dispose of the Militia as you have advised which you will please to forward him & oblidge Sir Your Most Obed't Serv't

Geo. Clinton.

Colo. Cortlandt.

---

* Not found.

THE ORDER FOR THE MITTS.

Poukeepsie 22d Nov'r* 1778.

Sir, As you informed me when I last saw you that you had in Store a Quantity of Wollen Mitts purchased for the Use of the Troops is an Article much wanted at this Time by Colo. Cortlandt's Regt. I woud advise you to deliver to his Order as many of them as will supply each Man with one Pair taking a proper Receipt, therefore, & charging the same to the Regt. I am Sir Yours &c.

[G. C.]

Mr. Henry, Com'y of Cloathing for the State of New York.

———

[No. 1974.]

ALARM IN CHARLOTTE COUNTY.

Ebenezer Clark Brings Its Defenceless Condition to the Attention of Governor Clinton.

Charlotte County Dec'r 2d 1778.

Sir, The Descriptive Account which Coll. Webster gives your Excellency of the occurrences in the last alarm, Protracted his Epistle two long to say any thing about the necessity of measures being Concerted for our future safety; he Requests me, therefore, to hint (& also some other Principle Inhabitants) that tho we are Pressed with a Sence of your arduous zeal for the Safety of every Part of the State, yet that the Various avocations of other Parts may so much Press your attention, that we may feel the Severity of Indian & British Cruelty before any Succour can asist us. The People are in general much Perplexed at the Thoughts of Passing another Summer like the last that tho Capt. Barns with his Company have been Reconitreing the Northern Parts, yet they together with all the force in this Department ware not more than

*Apparently a mistake—December is meant.—STATE HISTORIAN.

Sufficient to tell the Inhabitants to run for their lives; the Enemy ware comeing & hardly that for tho the force here might Stop one two or three avenews yet many Remaind open, threw which the Enemy might Come & make New Perth & the ajacent Towns a Catastrophe like Susquahana German Flats &c. &c.

The People are very much alarmd at being Exposed, as the Picture of Destruction on our western Frontiers are fresh in their View & that it would be no Consolation if after next Spring a Paragraph of the Public Papers should hold forth a scene of Burnt Houses, Barns & Perhaps most or all their substance.

If any hopes of forming a Camp above us or other means of Safety Could be devised it would give great quiet to the Inhabitants to know of measures being even in Contemplation, because otherways they would take the Precaution of Transporting their Effects in the winter season in Sleighs into the Interior Parts of the State, & also Famalys which would be attended with Ruinious Consequences to this New Country.

Belive me, Sir, this freedom is not from an Itch for knowledge in warfearing Plans which are necessarily Secrett, but the Effect of anxiety for our Preservation.

That your measures may be Calculated & Sucessfull for Promoteing the Common Good Relieveing the State & Terminate in adorning your name & Famaly is the earnest wish of Your Excellency's most obt. & very Hum'le Serv't

Ebenez'r Clark.

His Excellency Governor Clinton.

GOVERNOR CLINTON INTIMATES PATIENCE.

Poughkeepsie Dec'r 14th 1778.

Sir, I have rec'd your Letter of the 2d Inst. & am sorry to hear of the late Incursions of the Enemy into your quarter & feel for the Distresses of the Inhabitants which may be occasioned thereby. I think it highly probable that offensive Operations will be carried on ag't the Indians & Tories the ensuing Campaign (tho' I am not warranted in this assertion) which if it should be the case, will naturally tend to protect all the frontier Settlements. You may, however, rest assured that my utmost Exertions with the militia & every other means in my Power will be used for your Safety. Yrs. &c.

                                        Geo. Clinton.

Ebenezer Clark Esqr.

[No. 1975.]

Dirck Ten Broeck Furnishes Governor Clinton with Lottery Tickets.

                                    Albany Dec'r 14th 1778.

Sir, I take the Liberty of Transmitting to your Excellency a number of ——— Tickets of the 2nd Class of the United States Lottery; those Tickets that have drawn twenty Dollars in the 1st Class I have reserved for the Proprietors which are renewed of Course, agreeable to the Scheme.

The Lottery will be drawn on the 1st of January next and no Tickets are to be Disposed of after the 31st Inst. I have very lately received the Tickets from the Managers at Philadelphia & now take the earliest Opportunity of conveying them by Expresses thro the State that as many may be disposed of as Possible previous to the Time appointed for Drawing the Lottery. I remain with great esteem Sir Your Humble Servant

                                Dirck Ten Broeck C. L. O.

To His Excellency George Clinton, Esq'r.

[No. 1976.]

*Governor Clinton Guardedly Notifies Colonel Webster that Offensive
Operations will be Taken Against the Enemy in the Spring.*

Poughkeepsie Dec'r 14th 1778.

Sir, Your Letter of the 26th Ultimo,* together with the Proceed'gs of the board of Commissioners of the same Date relative
to the Persons to be removed within the Enemy's Lines I did not
receive until the 11th Inst. As in all probability I shall not be
able to procure an Exchange for the said Persons I hereby inform
you which you'l be pleased to communicate to the board that I do
not intend to detain or confine them for that Purpose.

I am sorry to hear that the Enemy have again made Incursions
into your Country & most sincerely feel for the Distresses which
may [have] been occasioned thereby. As in all probability
offensive operations will be carried on in the Spring ag't those
Disturbers of the Country (which by the Bye I am not warranted to assert) I am in hopes the Inhabitants will thereby be
amply protected ag't any Insults during the course of the next
Summer. I shall, however, in the mean Time use every Exertion
with the militia & other means in my Power for your Safety &
Protection. Yours &c.

Geo. Clinton.

The hon'ble Alex'r Webster Esqr.

———

[No. 1977.]

*Charges Preferred Against Lieutenant Robert Wood, of Hopkins'
Regiment.*

To his Excelencey, George Clinton Esqr. Govoner of the State of
New York &c. May it please your Exelancey; We the Subscrib-

*For Colonel Webster's letter see page 308.

ers Mov'd with Zeal for the Publick Good, Beg leave to lay before your Exelencey our uneasiness upon the account of Lieut. Robt. Wood's* haveing the Command of the New jail in Amena Presinkt; we Judge him not Compatent as to ability for that Importont trust, and we are Dissatisfide with Respect to his Moral Conduct in General; we are likewise dissatisfide upon the Account of his Keeping Strong Drink to Sell by Retail at the sed Jail, whereby he Draws together a Set of Drunken People, as Likewise the Drunkenness insident thareby to the Guards and Prisoners. We are Likewise Dissattisfide with Respect to his Conduct toward Prisoners; upon Several accounts we are likewise Grately Dissattisfide, that for Sum time before the late Escape of the Prisoners out of Said Jail, that he told the Guard, that they need not keep out a Centanil, but that they might all Turn in to Sleep, and when they awok'd, then look out, by which negligence the Prisoners had Opportunity to brake the Jail. We are further Dissattisfide that he Spends so litel of his time at the place of his Charge and in his Absence leaves the Command with a Pitifull Incompetent Serjent.

Wee are with the Utmost Respect your Exelency's most Obedient and humbel Servent,

Signed By, Zebulon Rudd, Samuel King, Ichabod Paine, Robert Hebard, William Barker, Abner Gillett, Elijah Park, Israel Shepherd, James Palmer, Solomon Brown, Jesse Pike, Joseph Adams, Robart Freeman, Elijah Freeman, Richard Shavelear, Gilbert Willett, Isaac Darrow, Amos Parker, Joseph Fowler, Barnabas Paine, Elisha Adams, Abraham Adams, Abraham Adams, un, Rosewell Kinney, Didymus Kinney.

Amena Precinkt Decemb'r 14th 1778.

---

*See page 399.

[No. 1978.]

JACKSON'S REGIMENT ORDERED TO POUGHKEEPSIE.

General McDougall Presents a Discouraging and Demoralizing Condition of Affairs to Governor Clinton.

Fish Kill Dec'r 15th 1778.

My dear Sir, I have been here four days, making arrangements for the winter, and devising expedients to cover the Troops. Altho upwards of an Hundred Tons of Hay, have been delivered out in Nov'r, and a proportionable Quantity for this part of December, near 200 Catle of different Kinds, have been eating their mangers for three days; other are dying. The abuses would shock you. I have not time now to relate particulars. The advanced and inclement season, obliges me to send one regiment of Learnard's Brigade to your Town; they are orderly, and are sent there under the inclosed orders. If their being there, should much income [incommode] civil business, I shall be able to remove them by the first of Feb'y, into the cantonments, now raising in the Con'l village, for a Bay Militia regt., whose time of service will then expire. But I dont wish either of those corps, should know my intention. The sick and convalecence now occupy the Barracks. The totall scarcity of vegatables and the want of Covering for the Troops, constrain me to remove the Convalecence of those belonging to the Corps, with the Commander in chief to Goshen. The Doctors have been there, and report 250 can be well accommodated. I find by Loudon's last paper, General Putnam has a new Correspondent. If you will be so kind as to send me copies of the late examinations taken on the business of the late Flag, his son went with, perhaps I may find an addition to them. My best wishes wait on you and your Household. I am, my dear Sir, Your affectionate Humble Serv't

Alex'r McDougall.

P. S.   The General's last advices to me, were that the Enemy in
New York had taken up 30,000 Tons of shipping.   If this is true,
it looks like his being soon to take an eternal farewell of us.
Governor Clinton.

COLONEL JACKSON'S ORDERS.

Orders for the Commanding Officer of Colo. Commandant
Jackson's regiment.

When ever the regiment has drawn and Cooked its provision,
and delivered its Tents, you will march them to Poughkeepsie.
The Barrack Master is to attend you.   That the Troops or inhabi-
tans may not be incommoded by the formers arriving late at the
Town, you march them from hence by Companies.   If you are retarded on the march, they may be Quartered at night on the road
the D. B. M. G. is instructed to march on that which is best inhabited.   There are nearly Public covering sufficient, to Quarter
the Corps.   The rest will be quartered according to law, in
Houses till you have built Huts, which must be done without a
moment's delay.

That town is the Seat of the legislature which will require all
the room it can afford; besides tranquility is necessary to the
Deliberation of that Body.   For these reasons, and as you will
Soon be called upon for your Quoto of duty on the lines, you will
be very vigilant in Compleating your Hutts, for Officers and Men;
they must all Front to the Southwest, if there is no important in-
conveniency in the Ground to prevent it.   There are Some materials on the Ground, which will greatly assist you in Compleating
the Hutts.   Prevent the men from misappropriating this.   You
will Quarter the men pretty full in the Barracks, till your Hutts
are built.

Let your roll of duty be taken in the Following manner, and it
will give room to the Troops and be productive of many other
advantages, vizt; Let the ajutant take Paper with him, and begin
at one wing of the Quarters, and take down the name of one man
of first room in the wing, then proceed to a second Room & a
third till he has gone thro them all.   Then begin with the first
Room again, take a Second man and Continue in the same order
as at first to take down the men out of all the Quarters Alternately, till all the Sarjeants rank & file are enroled—do the like
with the Officers of equal rank; when the duty is warned, it must
be taken off the Roll in the order it thus stands, which will take it
nearly equal out of each Room.

When you arrive, you will of cource pay your Compliments to
His Excellency the Governor. He is a friend to a Soldier, and
will cheerfully give you every Council and assistance in his Power.
As he is a Brigadier in the Army, you will send him a proper
Guard. If he declines it, you have done your duty; you will
mount a main Guard Consisting of a Subaltern, and thirty; If an
House can be procured in the Town for this purpose, it will tend
to preserve order in it, as your patrols will be near to perform that
duty.

Revellie, Troop retreat and Tatto, will be beat at the usuel
Hours, performed in Garrison duty, and every other of this
nature, regularly performed; you will maintain Strict order and
Discipline in your Quarters; and not Suffer the Persons or property of any inhabitant to be injurd, not insult the one or waste the
other, remembering your Corps were raised for the express purpose of protecting both.

Pay the Utmost attention to the cleanliness of the regiment.
This is absolutely necessary for their Health, and your Honour;

the D. B. M. General is instructed to procure you wood, & Straw, but he will require your assistance in men to furnish you with the Former, and purhaps for the latter, as the Forage of the Country is exhausted.

You cannot rely on public Teams, to do your Carting; you will therefore furnish him with a Sufficient number of Fatigue men, not only to cut wood for daily supply, but to cut a sufficient Quantity in store to serve you till June, in order that it may be brought to your Cantonment, when its good Sleghing; otherwise your men will Suffer often by disappointments, occationed by the badness of the roads; and the uncertainty of getting Teams.

Deep necessary vaults Should be dug, the next day after you arrive; before the Ground Gets more Frozen than it now is; and every other precaution taken to preserve the health of the Corps.

You will receive more particular orders from me, when I get all the Troops Covered.

Colonel Jackson is furnishd with orders for Mechanicks, Tools & such other materials, as are necessary to compleat the Huts.

I have ordered you to be furnished with two Ox Teams. Great Care must be taken of them as they are all the Public ones you can expect to do the Duty till grass. You are no stranger to the extream Scarcity of Forage, and the Cause of it. It will be impossible to supply the necessary Horses for the Public Service with that Article till Grass. Till then the officers of your Corps must content themselves with three Horses, Statedly, viz. one for the Commanding officer, one for the Major one for the adjutent and Q. Master. The other Horses of the Officers entitled to Keep them, must be sent off, to the Distance of thirty miles from your Quarters, where they will be entitled to keeping or money to pay the expence. It is with great reluctance, I am constrained to

Issue any order which will incommode them. But necessity and the Public Service, will plead my apology. I have written to all the Commissaries of purchase in the Neighbourhood to Procure Vegetables for the Troops. You will therefore order a party under a discreet Officer when ever you are quarted to prepare a Pitt or Hole, in a proper soil, well secured against the Frost, to receive what may be sent to your Regt. I am Confident your corps will be among the first that will be well Quartered. I therefore hope they will make a proper use of this advantage, and Conduct orderly in Quarters. If there should be any well Grounded Complaints against; I should be under the disagreeable Necessity of Hutting them all, at a distance from the Inhabitants. You will Please Deliver these orders over [to] your next Senior Officer, when he joins the Regiment. Given at my Quarters Fish Kill 13th Dec'r 1778.

To prevent any irregularrity in the Commissaries accounts you will Please, when a detachment is ordered from your Regt. to be out for more than the Days for which they have drawn Provisions, to cause your Quarter Master to Certify the day to which they have drawn, otherwise they may be disappointed in drawing, as the Com'y will be instructed not to Issue to any detachments, without such a Certificate.

Additional orders.—As the Neighbourhood of Pough Keepsie has been for some time infested with Robbers & Enemies to our Country, who are Disposed to injur us & Dishonour our Cause, if Gov'r Clinton should apply to you for parties at any time to scout the Mountains, you'll Please to order them out—they will follow such Directions as he shall give them.

Alex'r McDougall, M. General.

(Copy)

[No. 1979.]

GOVERNOR CLINTON OBJECTS TO THE PROPOSITION.

Notifies General McDougall that the Billeting of Troops will Interfere with the Work of the Legislature.

Poukeepsie 15th Dec'r 1778.

D'r Sir, Capt. Bancker, D'y B'k Master Genl. informs me, that he has your orders to provide Quarters for Colo. Jackson's Regt. of Continental Troops in this Town & untill they can be hutted to billet them on the Inhabitants. This unexpected Measure gives me real Concern as if carried into Execution it will prevent the sitting of the Legislature who by their adjournment were to have mett at this Place on the 2d Tuesday in next Month. This little Town (now almost the only one left us) is already so full of Refugees as to afford but very Indifferent Accomadation for the Members of Legislature. If to these we must have added the Officers of one Regt. only (and the Sheds at this Place are by no Means fit for their Reception) the Legislature must either give up the Idea of meeting at all or seek for some other less convenient Place. The public Offices of the State are now fixed at this Place. They cannot easilly be removed to another & they must be near the Legislature. The Inhabitants conceive it somewhat strange that while their most valuable Settlements on the Frontiers which would furnish the best of quarters meet with daily Destruction by the Enemy, the Troops seek Quarters in the Centre of the State, & the more so when as Militia they are called upon to Protect those Settlements. There may, however, be good Reasons for this Disposition which would be improper to communicate. For my own Part for the Reasons first mentioned I shoud esteem it inconsistent with the Duty I owe to the State to give Mr. Banker the least Assistance or Continuance in procuring Quarters for these Troops at this Place, unless I am furnished with better Reasons for it than I have yet heard.

Capt. Banker has a genl. Warrant for Impressing the Teems of the Inhabitants to supply the Troops with Fuel & Forrage. Least he shoud proceed to the Execution of it & meet with Difficulty which he certainly will, I think it a Duty to the Friendship I owe you, to assure you that it was not intended by the Law on which the Warrant is founded to give any Genl. officer such authority. It impowers a Genl. Commanding in the State on extraordinary Emergencies only to grant Impress Warrants. The Present are the most ordinary Occasions of the Army & of Course, if at all are to be provided for by the Civil Magistrate. The Forrage Masters assisted by the Civil Magistrate, have already impressed for the use of the Army, all the Forrage the Inhabitants have, leaving them only a very small Supply to bring through the Winter their own Stock, without any to spare their Neighbours, who raise none; this I know to be the Case throughout the greater Part of the State. Woud it not be extreamly hard under the Circumstances to have Teems impressed also to do the Very Business which makes a supply of Forrage necessary for the Army. I am perswaded the People will not submit to it. I am with great Regard Your most Obed. Serv't

Geo. Clinton.

The hon'ble Major Genl. McDougall.

[No. 1980.]

GENERAL McDOUGALL'S MANLY REPLY.

A Comprehensive View of the Condition of the Army and the Country at that Time.

Fish Kill Dec'r 15th 1778. 12 P. M.

Dear Sir, I am unhappily left in this Department, gleaned of almost every comfort for man and Horse; upwards of 200 differ-

ent Cattle, have been for three Days eating their mangers; others
dying for want; altho one Hundred Tons of Hay have been issued
in November last, and a proportionate quantity for what is past
of December, and but very little of it issued to the Brigade encamped in the Vicinity. The Troops are obliged to back wood for
their sick Brethren, about 400 in the Hospitals. These occupy all
the Barracks and other public Buildings fit to receive the Sick
or quarter Troops.

Nixon's Brigade is hutting in the Highlands, but makes but
slow Progress for the want of a sufficient quantity of sorted Tools.
Patterson's at Westpoint, and wants Covering. Learned's has
been directed to be posted above the High Lands, to guard the
Stores and do the Duty at and about this Town. For several Days
during the last bad Weather, they have been in Tents. Two Regiments are still in them.

The severe weather is fast approaching. In this State of the
Troops and the Post, I was reduc'd, and still am, to the utmost
Difficulty to cover them, and to provide them for the Winter;
when I was informed there were public Buildings sufficient to
cover 200 men at Poughkeepsie; Boards near it to aid in covering
the rest, and public Wood Cut on the other side. I, therefore,
determined to send Jackson's, the smallest Regiment there, first
detaching fifty men from it for the Lines, which would reduce it
to 185 now fit for Duty; and it's but thinly Officer'd. They were
ordered therewith; the Instructions inclosed in mine of this afternoon, which will remove the most of the Objections in your favor
of this Day since received. The Officers were so pressing to improve partial Quarters; and willing to make the utmost Exertions
to prevent giving the least public Trouble to the Town.

In short Sir, as it was represented to me, that there were quarters for at least two Hundred men, and when I sent Mr. Banker there to inspect them, I did not conceive that any Difficulty would attend their going there, altho' I knew the State of the Town to be as you represent it, and guarded against it. As to Mr. Banker's press warrant, he was ordered to use it with the utmost Caution, and but in Cases of absolute Necessity. But if the Law does not intend that Warrants should issue when the army is distress'd for Subsistance, it is to them a dead Letter. For I cannot create Means of Subsistance for the Cattle, and if the army has been kept here too long, for the Interest & means of the Country, I am not to blame. I neither command her army or direct her Councils.

I have always understood the Farmers prefer hiring their Teams for a short Distance than to be pinched in their Forage. And I can assure you, no means shall be left unessayed by me, to lessen the Number of public Cattle near the River, however ungracious it may be for me, to reform the abuses or Neglects of others. This Regiment carries with it two Ox Teams, which I believe will be sufficient for their Duty.

As to the billetting or quartering the Troops, in Houses, I meant no more than bare House Room for them a few Days. And if such of the Inhabitants as can spare it, according to Law, will not chearfully give it, when officers and Soldiers are expos'd to the most violent Storms of Rain & snow, they do not deserve to be free.

This State would not support the whole army during the Winter, which constrained the Commander in chief to remove nine Brigades to Jersey. He has left three here, with the Expectation that they would be sufficient to defend these Posts for the winter, without disturbing the Repose of his Troops in their Quarters.

25

I think they will be sufficient for the purpose, altho I have sent that Regiment to your Town for the Reasons already assigned. 'Tis not improbable he meditates an attack on New-York in the winter, if Circumstances permit.

I lament the Condition of our Frontiers. But you must be sensible I cannot order the Disposition of the Troops; nor would it have been prudent in the Course of the Campaign, to have removed more of the army from the Sea Frontiers. I confess I feel a little mortifyed, that my Countrymen should even have apprehensions, that I could take any wanton or unnecessary Measures to incommode, or distress them. No such Charge has been made against me, by Strangers thro' whom Troops under my orders have marched. But this is the dear price, we, General Officers, pay for our Honors.

Connecticut won't have us but in the Hour of Danger.

New York is reluctant we should have any Repose.

New Jersey complain they have had too much of us.

Where, my Dear Sir, are we to go?

Can I defend the Highlands and the Rear Frontiers at the same Time?

These are some of the brave men who aided in rescuing the Northern Frontiers from the Enemy. They are Strangers too. So far as I have learned their Character they are pretty orderly. They, therefore, merit some attention and Indulgence. I beg you to give them what is in your power. Sooner than they should interrupt the Deliberations of the Legislature, I will remove them to the most dreary valley in the Highlands, altho they, and I, should share the fate of their unfortunate Brethren last Winter, at the Valley Forge. I have much to do here, and little to do it with. My Condition is not much better, than the Israelites in

Egypt, who were ordered to make Brick without Straw. But I am determined it's the last Winter I shall be imprisoned in the Highlands to be a Drudge for others. I am, Dear Sir, Your humble Servant

                    Alex'r McDougall, M. General.

P. S. If the Troops both officers and men are not totally out of the Houses before the Meeting of the Legislature I will remove this Corps before they meet.

His Excellency Gov'r Clinton.

[No. 1981.]

GOVERNOR CLINTON ON THE GENERAL PROPOSITION.

Sensible of General McDougall's Situation—New York's Suffering Greater than that of any Other State.

                    Poukeepsie 15th Dec'r 8 P. M. 1778.

D'r Sir, I am this Moment favoured with your two Letters* of this Day's Date. I am very Sensible of the many Difficulties you meet with in the Execution of your Present Command & I am perswaded you will not believe that I wish to increase them. I need not tell you that this State has suffered more by the Enemy than any other on the Continent, and being the principal Seat of the War, the Inhabitants have of Course experienced as much Injury from our own army, which under some former Commands was not a little. They have hitherto chearfully submitted to their Fate & I believe I may safely venture to say they will yet as chearfully exert themselves to accomodate & render the Soldiery comfortable as any.

The acts of the Legislature for Billetting the Troops Impressing Forage & Teams & for supplying the army with Provisions are the highest & best Evidence of this Spirit. I am far from sup-

---

*See page 430, for General McDougall's answer to this letter.—STATE HISTORIAN.

posing the Quartering a proportionate Number of Troops in this Town (were it not for the Reasons mentioned in my last Letter) woud be any ways peculiarly disagreable to the Inhabitants, provided they were regularly supplied with Fuel, so that their Fencing & Timber (which on the Banks of the River is of the utmost Importance as the Loss of them is irreparable) might be preserved; But this fatal Experience has taught us will not be the Case & whether it arises from its Impracticabillity or the Remissness of the Quarter Master, the Injury is equal to the Proprietor & is an argum't ag't Troops being Quartered in such a Situation but from absolute necessity. Your orders are, as I expected they woud be, well calculated to prevent abuses of every kind & discover a proper attention to the Conveniency of the Legislature.

I agree with you that the Farmers ought well afford to give the Service of their Teems by a fixed Rotation of Duty to the public to save their Forrage. I advised the Measure last Winter myself, conceiving it to be not only for their Interest but a great saving to the public; But, Sir, remember that at this early day every Dint of Forrage, except a scanty allowance, barely sufficient to bring the Farmers' Stock alive through the Winter, is already Impressed. If under these Circumstances, their Teems are charged with double Labour through the Winter, will they be in order to perform Spring labour besides, if this Duty is to be performed by them? The Impresses will be more equitably executed under the Direction of a Civil Officer than by Quarter Masters, to whose Indiscretion, Negligence & Mismanagement, great part of our present Distresses may fairly be imputed. I meant not however to blame, but to prevent you from incurring any, when I gave you my Sentiments on this Subject, as I doubted your being possessed of the Law.

The Sheds here will not contain all the Troops. The Barrack Master tells me about thirty are for the present billetted on the Inhabitants. If these might be ordered to the Gaol in Amenia Precinct, they might be well accomaded there & serve in the Interim as a guard to the Prisoners. This & the Officers confining themselves for Quarters to the Houses South of the Town, might, perhaps, prevent the necessity of Hutting any of them, which Cannot easilly be done. I have not rec'd a single Affidavit on the Subject you allude to; if any were taken the Officer omitted sending them or woud with pleasure furnish you with them, as I have not the least Objection to the Business for which they are wanted. I am in great Haste, D'r Sir, Your most obed't

Geo: Clinton.

The hon'ble Major Genl. McDougall.

[No. 1982.]

Abraham Yates and the Fugitives from Cherry Valley.

Albany December 15th 1778.

Sir, Yours of the third Instant I have received; by the Enclosed you will See the method we have taken (to Call the members together I conceived would be attended with Difficulties) and how far it is Effected; I keep the original Copy with me to Lay hold of any members, that may Chance to Come to Town, to get them to Sign; a Copy is Sent to the members of Tryon County for them also to address you on the Same Subject to give it more Weight. I was Just now with Genl. Clinton and Shew'd him the Letter; he Says that there is People Complaining also from Cobles Kill, Some of which are in Equal Distress with those of Chery Valley: this we did not advert to. Should you think to take a ride up here and it will Suit you, you are welcome to a Bed with Your obt. Humble Servant

Ab'm Yates Jun.

19th. P. S. I have been Confused with the Expectation of the Post. I Send this, which I Intended to send by the Post with Myer, who Delivered me yours with the Printed Treaties with France for which I thank you.

His Ex. George Clinton, Esq'r.

[No. 1983.]

Massachusetts Board of War Ask Leave to Export Flour from New York Over Land.

Gentlemen, Major Shepherd who will have the honor to deliver you this, is employ'd by the Board of War to purchase Flour for the use of this State. As that article is extreamly wanted, & the danger of importing it by water very great; We are to request your Excellency & Honors to grant Major Shepherd permission to transport the same by land from your State to this unmolested.

We have the Honor to be, with great Respect Gentlemen Your most Obed't & Very h'ble Serv'ts

By Order of the Board,

John Browne President pr. tem.

War Office Boston Dec'r 15th, 1778.

His Excellency George Clinton Esq.

The Hon'ble Senate & House of Assembly for the State of New York.

[No. 1984.]

Governor Clinton Through Robert Benson Instructs Colonel Budd in the Method of Drawing Ammunition.

Sir, As part of the Regt. I command are called out into actual Service, and no Ammunition being provided for them by Colo. Thomas, I beg you wou'd please to inform me where I can be supply'd, some of the Regt. are in want of Arms, shou'd be glad to know wheather they can be supply'd with any, and where. I am Sir Your most Obed't Hum'e Serv't

Gilb't Budd, L. Colo.

Bedford Decem'r 14th 1778.

To His Excell'y George Clinton Esqr. Poughkeepsie.

Poughkeepsie Dec'r 16th 1778.

S'r, His Excellency directs me to inform you that the ammunition cannot be drawn out of the public Store but agreably to the militia Law, which directs the Colo. or Command'g Officer of a Regt. to draw an Order on the Commissioner of Military Stores of the State in favor of the Quarter Master of the Regt. for as much ammunition as by a Return of the Regt. may appear to be necessarily required; which Order is to be presented to the Governor who backs it with his warrant. The Quarter Master is then entitled to receive it by paying such price therefor as shall be settled by the commissioner, Colo. Jno. Lasher at the Wallkill. There are no arms in Store neither do I know how you can get supplied but by Purchase. Yrs. &c.

Robt. Benson.

Colo. Budd.

[No. 1985.]

INFRACTIONS OF THE SARATOGA CONVENTION.

Congress Appropriates One Thousand Dollars in Specie to Further Discoveries.

Philad. 2d Decem'r 1778.

Sir, I deliver'd Congress the Depositions your Excellency charged me with, respecting the Breach of the Convention of Saraghtoga by that part of Genl. Burgoine's army which was permitted to return into Canada. It is the desire of Congress that this perfidious proceedure may be exposed in the fullest Light, and they, therefore, request that your Excellency will endeavour to procure further Evidence, and, if possible, one of General Carlton's proclamations or orders requiring those Troops to join their respective Corpses.

One thousand Dollars in Specie are now delivered to Mr. Bancker for the purpose of making the necessary discoveries, to be employd in such manner as your Excellency shall be pleased to direct; when it is expended you will be pleased to remit the account to the Treasury board that you may be properly discharged. I did not think it necessary to send the Cont. money directed to be paid into your Hands, for the above purpose. It therefore, waits your disposal in the Treasury. I have the Honour to be with the greatest Respect Sir Your Excellency's most Obedient humble Servant

Jas. Duane.

His Excellency the Governour of New York.

MR. DUANE'S FAMILY WELL.

Poukeepsie [17th December 1778.]

Sir, I am favoured with your Letter of the 2d Instant. You may venture, Sir, to assure Congress that the Specie forwarded by Mr. Banker shall be faithfully expended in procuring further Evidence of the Infraction of the Convention of Saraghtoga, but as the Passage into Canada is at present impracticable & will continue so, untill the Lakes are sufficiently Froze some Considerable Time will of Course elapse before any Thing can be obtained from that Quarter.

I had the Honor of forwarding your Letter to Mrs. Duane by a safe Conveyance, & I have some Reason to expect her Commands to you before this is dispatched, but Least this should not be the Case, I am happy in being able to inform you that your Familly &

Friends at the Manor were in Health a few Days since. I have the Honor to be with great Regard & Esteem Sir Your most Obed't Serv't

G. C.

The Hon'ble James Duane Esqr.

[No. 1986.]

The New York Forage Law Well Executed.

Poukeepsie Dec'r 17th 1778.

Sir, My last to your Excellency was dated the 6th November since which I have been honored with the Receipt of your Dispatches of the 16th of that Month & 2d Instant.

For the Information of Congress I herewith inclose your Excellency an Act of the Legislature of this State passed as early as the 2d of April last for supplying the Army with Forrage &ca. by which you will please to observe the Commissary is enabled to take from the Inhabitants whatever they are possessed of more than is actually necessary for the Subsistence of their respective Stocks & I may safely venture to assure your Excellency that the Law has been very faithfully executed as far forth as the Civil Magistrate is concerned. I have the honor to be with most perfect Esteem & Respect Your Most Obed't Serv't

Geo. Clinton.

His Excellency Henry Laurens Esqr. Presid't &c.

[No. 1987.]

ONE HUNDRED THOUSAND DOLLARS ARRIVE SAFELY.

*So the Governor Notifies New York's Delegates in Congress—
Settlement of the Vermont Affair.*

Poukeepsie 17th Dec'r 1778.

Gentlemen, I have been honored with your Letter of the 1st Instant with the several Papers accompanying it. Mr. Banker

I am well informed is safely arived at the Treasury of this State with the Cash with which he was charged, but as on his way thither he forwarded your Dispatches to me, from Goshen. I have not yet received his Report or the Treasurer's Receipt for the Money.

I am particularly oblidged to you for the Communication of the Treaties of amity & Commerce with his most Christian Majesty, as the perusal of them cannot fail of affording the highest Sattisfaction to your Constituents, seeing they are in every Respect as liberal & Beneficial to the United States as coud be reasonably expected & fully Answer the Idea we had formed of them. The Injunction of Congress respecting them shall be strictly observed.

I am happy to learn that the Vermont Business is at lenghth likely to meet the Attention of Congress & in Confidence that this will be the Case, I now inclose & forward you by Express, sundry Papers, which I am lead to believe, may be of some Service on the Occassion, as besides disclosing the Designs of the usurped Government of Vermont. They afford such Evidence of Disentions & Heats prevailing among their Leaders as may convince Congress that the present is the most favourable Crisis for the Interposition of their Authority & by an explicit Disaprobation of the Conduct of those turbulent People determine a Controversy, which if suffered to continue much longer, may occassion the Spilling of Blood & be attended with other most Serious Consequences.

The inclosed affidavit of Mr. Zedekiah Stone & Copy of Hilkiah Grout, Esqr's Letter, respecting the Declaration of Colo. Allen in Assembly (if his Word deserves Credit) discover the share of Confidence you are to place in your New Hampshire Brethern.

Since my last no new Depredations have been committed on the Frontiers. You have doubtless been informed that about the Time of the Destruction of Cherry Valley many of the settlements on the Borders of Lake Champlain experienced a simular Fate. It is to be hoped that the Season may prevent the Enemy from attempting any Thing Capital ag't us before the opening of the Spring. If, however, the Contrary shoud be the Case, the present Force imployed in the Frontier Service, tho very considerable, is not sufficient to afford the different Settlements protection owing to the great Extent of Country to be guarded. If any Opperations are likely to take Place in the Execution of which the particular Aid of the State may be required, I wish if consistent, I may have Timely notice, that the proper preparatory Measures may be taken at the next Meeting of the Legislature. I am, Gentlemen, with the highest Respect & Esteem Your most Obed't Serv't

[G. C.]

P. S. If Congress are already possessed of Copies of the papers inclosed*

[To Delegates in Congress.]

[No. 1988.]

IRA ALLEN'S VERMONT ADDRESS.

His Arguments to Establish Vermont as an Independent Commonwealth.

Poughkeepsie Dec'r 17th 1778.

Gentlemen, Since sealing my Dispatches of this Date I have been favored with the enclosed Publication of Ira Allen, Treasurer of the pretended State of Vermont, Copies of which are now

---

*Rest of sentence marked through with pen.

circulating thro' the different Towns on the Grants. This Paper you'l be pleased to observe is calculated to incourage the Inhabitants in their revolt from this State & to persist in their Plan of forming a separate Government, and offers the Silence of Congress after so many repeated Applications for their Interposition as conclusive Evidence of their Acquiecence in the Measure. I am &c.

G. Clinton.

The hon'ble the Delegates of New York.

———·———

THE ADDRESS.

To the Inhabitants of the State of VERMONT.

Gentlemen,

Whereas the General Assembly of this State did appoint me to wait on the Honorable Meshech Weare, Esq; President of the Council of the State of New-Hampshire, with a Letter from his Excellency Thomas Chittenden, Esq; and another from Col. Ethan Allen, &c. And, whereas, several of the Members of the Honorable Council and Assembly of this State, desired me to write to them (on my return from New-Hampshire) the state of affairs relative to the Union with sixteen Towns east of Connecticut-River and this State: I, therefore, beg leave to state the following as a short state of the matter, viz:

When I arrived at Exeter found the General Assembly then sitting, delivered said Letters to the President, who, after examining the same in Council, sent them to the House for their inspection: the said Letters were again read and largely discoursed on, and a Committee appointed from both Houses to answer the same—I being then present besides having many other conferences with the Members of both Houses, found that they were unanimous for maintaining Inviolable their Jurisdiction to the East Banks of Connecticut-River, but that they had no disposition to interfere with the State of Vermont in its first described Limits, which will more fully appear by their Resolution in the affair of Mr. Hovey, and an Extract of President Weare's Letter to Col. Ethan Allen, which are as follows, viz:

State of New-Hampshire, " In the House of Representatives, Nov. 10th, 1778.

"According to the Vote of the House of this day, the Honorable Council and House being met in the Assembly Chamber, the Honorable Meshech Weare, Esq; in the Chair, proceeded to take under Consideration the Petition of Nathaniel Hovey, preferred to the Honorable Committee of Safety of this State on the 24th of September last, and the further transactions thereon—and upon consideration of the same, came to the following Resolutions and reported, that Two Hundred Pounds be Granted to the said Hovey, out of the Treasury, by order of the President, for his present necessities, to be by him accounted for; and that the persons named as Rioters in his complaint and Petition, together with Nehemiah Estabrook of Lebanon, be notified to attend the hearing of said Petition before the General Assembly if sitting, or Committee of Safety of this State in the recess, on the second Thursday of December next, and that the Secretary be directed to issue proper notice to the said persons; and that Capt. Samuel Atkinson, of Boscowen, be directed to Notify them accordingly, which Report was read and accepted."

Sent up for concurrence.
John Dudley, Speaker, Pro. Tem.

A Copy Examined by E. Thompson, Sec'ry.

As you have been so full and explicit in your own sentiments, I trust the Body of your People will be of the same opinion, as I am sure every sensible person will; notwithstanding blind designs of some uneasy and never to be contented men, whose Views must certainly be more detrimental to you than they possibly can be to New-Hampshire.—Whatever may be determined by Congress relative to the acknowledgment of your Independence will be freely acquiesced in by this State.

I find by enquiring into the situation of the Grants (so called) east of Connecticut-River, that the Towns in the County of Chester are almost Unanimously Represented in the General Assembly of New-Hampshire—and that about twelve Towns in the County of Grafton are also Represented in the Assembly of New-Hampshire—and that in the sixteen Towns in connexion with this State by said Union, there is a large minority in opposition to said Union.

Amongst the arguments made use of by New-Hampshire to support their Claim to Connecticut-River are the following, viz.

That by the determination of the Court of Great-Britain in establishing Provinces in North America, said Lands were included in the Jurisdiction of New-Hampshire, and, in consequence of that, many Charters for Towns was Granted by the Governor of said Province with all the Priviledges and Immunities that any other Towns in said Province did enjoy, which they held under the crown untill the Revolution, at which time circular Letters was sent to the several Towns thro' that Province, to choose Members to form a Congress to transact the political business of the State; at which time several of those Towns now in Union with this State sent Members. About a year after a second Congress was chosen, and some of said Towns sent Members. Said Congress then established a plan of Government which was to remain in force untill the exigencies of the State would admit of more leasure time to form another, which plan or Constitution said State has ever since and now remain to be governed by. Since the depreciation of Money, an additional pay has been given by the State of New-Hampshire to the Militia of said State, in addition to their Continental pay when in such service; which pay has been chearfully received by the Militia of said Towns.

Thus Gentlemen I have given you a short state of facts, agreeable to the best information I can get, by which you will observe that the State of New-Hampshire are willing that the State of Vermont should be a State in its first discribed limits west of Connecticut-River.

I have also to observe, that by several authentick accounts lately received from the Honorable Continental Congress, that the Delegates are willing that the State of Vermont should be a State within its first discribed limits, (the Delegates of New-York excepted,) which fully appears from that Honorable Body's not passing any Resolves against any of the proceedings of the State of Vermont since its first formation, altho' often requested by New-York.

Having met with several printed papers published by order of those gentlemen that withdrew from the General Assembly of this State, at their Session in October last: But as I did not design this Letter for an answer thereto, shall make but few remarks thereon.

In the course of which papers there is a request to all the Towns on the Grants on both sides of the River, whether united with the State of Vermont or not, to send members to form a Convention to consult and agree upon measures whereby we may all be united together, by being and remaining a distinct State, on such foundation that we may be admitted into Confederation with the United States of America, and under their protection, &c.

A very large part of the Towns on the Grants west of the Mason Line, and east of Connecticut-River, are Represented in the General Assembly of New-Hampshire, and consequently they are Represented in Congress: therefore, they cannot withdraw from New-Hampshire, and connect with any other body politick, and present themselves to Congress to be taken into Consideration with the United States, for they are already taken into Consideration by the way of New-Hampshire—The way them Towns could act, were they to send members to said Convention, would be to act on the latter clause of the Warrant, which is to claim the antient Jurisdiction of the Government of New-Hampshire, and in that way defend ourselves against the pretended right of Jurisdiction of any other State, and thereby become one entire State according to the extent of New-Hampshire Province as it stood before the Decree in 1764 took place—But whether that is the design of the Convention or not I leave the canded reader to determine.

I appeal to every person's own conscience in the State of Vermont, whether, when the Inhabitants on the west and east sides of the Green Mountain, first connected together to become one body politick, they did it under a view that the Grants east of Connecticut-River would join them, and if it had not been for that, they would not have joined in said plan.

All those that did unite together in one body politick to form a State west of Connecticut-River, will, I doubt not, on due consideration, pursue that desirable object; (if any difficulties should arise so as unhappily to seperate those Towns east of Connecticut-

River from this State) for in that view of the case we should then enjoy all we first expected; and, as the Constitution of this State is so happily calculated to preserve inviolable the rights of the people; and, as in it there is ample provision made for the propagation of the gospel, together with proper Seminaries and Schools of learning which are among the greatest blessings God in his wisdom ever bestowed on the fallen race of man.

By what has been already elucidated, it appears that the State of Vermont is in favor with the United States of America; therefore, if the people in said State are, and continue steadfast to maintain the same, they will without doubt support the Independence of said State, as long as the United States do theirs.

Since the choice appears to be in the brest of the good people of this State, whether they will be governed by the agreeable Constitution they have made, or lay that aside and seek for connections with a neighbouring State which is some in debt, and whose known plen of representation is by numbers, so that it would take five or six of our new Towns to send one member, and when we consider that those infant plantations have gone thro' numberless fatigues and expences to defend their just rights from the arbitrary power of New York; and since this present contest, we have been a frontier to three neighbouring States, our inhabitants have been obliged to flee before their enemy, our Soldiery often called forth by alarums, who have fought and bled nobly in the field for the defence of their country—Is there not a much greater probability that we should be considered, for those extraordinary difficulties, by the Honorable, the Grand Council of America, in defraying the expence of this unnatural war, than by the legislature of any State, whose private interest would be nearer connected with ours.

I doubt not, but every reasonable person will, on due deliberation determine that it is best, wisest, and cheapest for the good people of this State, to steadily pursue their plan of government, which will transmit to posterity the blessings of a free State.

I am, Gentlemen, with due respect, Your most Obedient, Humble Servant,

                                                              Ira Allen.

Dresden, November 27th, 1778.

N. B. The Laws of the State is come to hand, and will be ready for Sale in a short time.

[No. 1989.]

Mr. Currie Requests Payment for Sugar Supplied to Troops.

Hopewell [N. J.] Dec. 17th 1778.

Sir, Mr. John Murray of Potts Grove, & State of Pensylvania, for whom I forwarded some Casks of Loaf Sugar to New Windsor, & which remaind there at the time the Enemy continued up the River last year, in July last, gave me a certificate, which he gott from Colo. Taylor to receive payment for 21 Loaves Sugar, belonging to said Murray, & which he says, your Excellency had directed him to give out at Head Quarters then at New Windsor; and as the Greatest part of it has been given out, at your Excellency's, & Genl. James Clinton's, Head Quarters, I beg leave to recomend the bearer hereof, & Nephew to Mr. Murray, to your Excellency, & that you will be pleasd to direct him where,

& from whom payment for said Sugar, is to be obtain'd. I am
with perfect esteem Your Excellency's mo. obed't & mo. hbl.
Ser't

                                                Arch'd Currie.
His Excellency Gov'r Clinton.

[No. 1990.]

Lieutenant Wood Vindicated.

To His Excellency George Clenton Esqr. Governor Capt. General
   of the state of N. York & V. Admiral of the Navy of the same.
   The Petition of Robt. Wood* officer of the New Goal, Amenia
Precinct P. of N. Y. humbly Sheweth, That for and in Consideration of a Complaint made to the Hon'ble the Com'ssrs Respecting my Conduct, I have by the advice of the subscribers, taken
this method to Vindicate my Charactor, against the aspertions,
of a Party who, thus Endeavours to revenge themselves by Vio-
lating my Charactor without a Cause—yea matters, too Effemi-
nate, to Incert Notwithstanding, I shall Chearfully submit to
be examined by men of Veracity & judgment on this Occation,
having always a Contiance Void of offence, towards those Concerned in this Goal, which the most sponcible G. men in this
Precinct will maintain; it is true that on my Return from
Pougheapsie finding some of the Prisoners gone, I examined
the rest with some Severity, by which I learned pritty nigh the
Course they had taken, which is the only time I ever offered
the least Insult to any of them. The underwritten Gent. are
all witness to this & indeed to every part of my Conduct, since
I have taken the Command at this Goal, & their voice I am
willing to abide by, as this paper was wrote at their Request

------
*See page 375.

and, therefore, if I have done Ought amiss in My Duty, I am willing to be Corrected, & on the other hand if I am wrongfully Impeached, I shall hope no less than the offenders to be brought to justice; my fidelity I ever more Endeavoured to shew in the most Conspicuous mann'r I am Capable of, will your Excellency therefore agreeable to your known abbilitys, Consider your Petitioner as much abused by the Complaints affore Recited, owing to private malace or to ans'r some lawless Ends of their own, & not for the Interest of the Country, as I always Endeavour to Conduct my affairs agreeable to my Charactor or the business with which I am Intrusted.

Amenia Precinct December 18 1778.   Robt. Wood, Lt.

We whose Names are under written, have Duly Considered the nature of the Complaint, as we are informed against Lieut. Wood do recomend him as a Gen't who Endeavours to Conduct, as becomes a man of his station or Charactor; being all Wittness to the mode in which he Discharges the Duties Incombent on him Viz.

Roswell Hopkins, Job Mead, Lewis De Lavergne, Justus Knapp, William ———, John Atherton, Ebenezer Park, Noah Hopkins, Nathan Spicer, Simeon Cook, William Chamberlain, Colbe Chamberlain, Joseph De Lavergne, Robrt Williamson, John Kase, Ebzer Mayo, Elnathan Knapp, Thomas Smith, Absolem Early, Justis Knapp Ens.

We the Subscribers Do hereby Recomend and Praise and very much approve of, the Conduct of Lieut. Robert Wood towards the Prisoners in the New Goals, and are very Sorry to hear that a Petition by Some Designing men with Selfish views is Carried in against him, for we are very Sure that the Command of the guard Could not be given to a more firm, active, and Brave Officer, and that when the Prisoners broke Goal he Pursued them thro the Storms & Snow at the Expence of his health, and Considerable money out of his own pocket, and Succeeded Beyond our Expectations in taking three of the worst Villains about 30 miles off. We Desire this may be Delivered to his Excellency the Governour with Lieut. Wood's Petition.

Roswell Hopkins, Job Mead, Justus Knapp, Jonathan Allerton, Rufus Herrick, Stephen Herrick, Jun'r, Samuel Waters, John Denton, James Bedell, Edmond Perlee, Samuel Herrick, Elnathan Tyler, William Wicks, John Drake, Stephen Reynolds, Jacob Reynolds, Stephen Herrick, John McNeill, Benjamin Herrick, Justus Willson, William Reynolds, James Reynolds, Joseph Smith, Rufus Herick, Jun'r, Isaik Golden, Roger Southerland.

Amenia Dec'r 18th 1778.

[No. 1991.]

Governor Clinton Writes Washington in Behalf of James McDowell, Whose Barn was Burned by Captive British Troops.

Poukeepsie 18th Dec'r 1778.

Dear Sir, At the Request of Mr. James McDowell of Little Britain, in this State, whose Barn was destroyed by some of the British Convention Troops quartered in it on their late Route, I take the Liberty of Troubling your Excellency with the inclosed Affidavits & Letter* of Stephen Ray A. D. Q. M. on that Subject and to request that your Excellency will be pleased to order him payment for the Damages he has thereby sustained, if it can consistently be done, & if not, that you will be pleased to refer his Case to the Congress for their Direction. It appears

*Affidavit and letter not found.—State Historian.

from the Affidavits, that the Barn was burnt with Design which
is confirmed by other concurring Circumstances, as well as Mc-
Dowell's own Relation, who is a very honnest Man.   It also appears from Mr. Ray's Letter, that it was the Intention of the
public to Compensate Individuals for the Injuries they might
receive by these Troops, and that this has been the Case in the
whole Course of their March, with respect to Fencing & less
Capital Injuries, & as the present is such as will ruin this Man
if he alone is to sustain it, there are strongest Reasons for his
being Compensated by the public.   I am, Sir, with the most
perfect Esteem & Respect Your most Obed't Serv't

[G. C.]

His Excellency Genl. Washington.

[No. 1992.]

CORRUPTION IN STAFF DEPARTMENTS.

*Governor Clinton Indicates to Gouverneur Morris the Possibilities
for a Dishonest Commissary and Quartermaster.*

Poukeepsie 18th Dec'r 1778.

Sir, I have received your favour of 1st Inst't, & am happy in
having at lenghth been able to relieve you from a Troublesome
Charge, with which you have long been burthened.   Mr. Banker
is safely arrived at the Treasury with the Money.   It is with
Pleasure I am now able to assure you, that the Loan proves
very agreable to your Constituents as, I am perswaded, this will
be esteemed the best Compensation for the Trouble you have
had in obtaining it.

I wish I coud transmit you the Act (alluded to in my last
Letter) making a more suitable Allowance for the Delegates, with
the other Acts of the Legislature of this State, for, as many of
them are founded on the Recommendations of Congress particu-

larly those for supplying the Army with Provissions Forage &c.
for forwarding Military Operations, they might be serviceable,
but this, Sir, is not in my Power, as, owing to the Negligence of
some of our Public Officers, I have not yet received Copies, even
of those passed the first Session or of. the Minutes of either
House. I will take the earliest Opportunity of communicating
to the Auditor, your Desire of having your Account made out,
contained in your Letter with the Memorandums respecting it,
and to the Legislature when they meet, your acknowledgment.
The Sense you entertain of the Provission they have made for
their Delegates—this will, however, be done with a degree of
Caution as considering the Depreciation of our Money I much
doubt its being Competent.

Sensible of the necessity of having our public accounts adjusted & settled, I earnestly recommended to the Legislature at
the opening of the present Session that the proper Measures
shoud be taken for this Purpose & they accordingly appointed a
Committee to Examine & prepare the Accounts, who are now
imployed in that Service & I have some Reason to hope at their
next Meeting, they will adopt some proper & more permanent
Mode for conducting this Business.

Some short Time since I received the Letters of the Committee
of Congress for superintending the Commissary & Quarter Master's Department (of which I observe you are one) of the 11th
Ultimo, inclosing a Copy of their Appointment. This I request,
you will be pleased to signify to your Colleagues & assure the
Committee that the Matters recommended shall be faithfully
attended to. At the same Time please to observe that as the
acquiring a Knowledge of the Resources of the State is a Measure, which (at the Instance of his Excellency Genl. Washington)

was submitted to the Legislature at their last Meeting and yet remains under their Consideration, I cannot therefore with Propriety enter on the Execution of that Business till I have their Authority. I am happy, however, that this little Delay cannot be attended with any ill Consequences, as the Commissary's by two Acts of this State, the one passed in April last & the other the present Session have it in their Power to secure for the Use of the Army all the Flour, Grain & Forrage in the State saving only a Competentcy for Consumption of the Inhabitants & their Stock.

I entertain a good Oppinion of the Gentlemen at the Head of the Commissaries & Quarter Master's Departments; but there are undoubtedly many Abuses practised by their Deputies which call for Salutary Laws & Regulations [to] prevent & correct. The Allowance made them for their Services being by Commission on the Cash they expend, affords them the strongest Temptation to enhance the Prices of the Articles they Purchase, a Sin with which they are charged in every Quarter of the Country. This Practice tends greatly to increase the public Expence, creates an artificial Scarcity, & what is still worse, affects the Credit of our Money which is already so reduced as to occassion apprehensions of the most alarming Nature. Another very Capital Abuse arises from the Deputies being concerned in Trade. They have Agents informally appointed in every Part of the State, who Purchase up large Quantities of Flour & Grain, of which no Regular Returns, & of Course no immediate Entries, are made in the Commissary Book. If the Articles purchased by these Agents rise, as Flour did this year in one Month from £3-4- to £8-10-, they are converted to the Purposes of Trade & sold for the Benefit of the Parties concerned. If they continue the same or fall, they are delivered into the public Magazine & the Purchasser of Course intitled to his Commissions. This is a safe Trade by which I believe many of them have this year alone made enormous sums of Money, while the army is starving for want of bread. You will readily perceive that positive Evidence of these Abuses is not easilly procured. I hope, nevertheless, to be able to furnish you with such strong Presumptive Evidence of these Facts as may be of public Service. In the Mean Time I am, Sir, Your Most Obed't Serv't

[G. C.]

[To Gouverneur Morris.]

[No. 1993.]

Proposition to Negotiate an Exchange of a British Officer and an American Quartermaster.

Dear Sir, Coll. Hay proposes endeavouring to negociate an Exchange, between one of his Quarter masters a prisoner in New York, and Lieut. Drummond of the British army, Provided it meets with your approbation; he is the Person mentiond to me in Coll. Gordon's letter, of whom I Spoke to you. Should you not have any objections to the Exchange it will be of Infinite Service to a young man in Distress, and much oblidge D'r Sir Your Excellency's Most Obed't Serv't

John Tayler.

Albany 18th Dec'r 1778.
Gov'r Clinton.

[No. 1994.]

John Jay Asks for all the Maps and Papers in the Vermont Case.

Philadelphia 19th Dec'r 1778.

Dear Sir, It would give me Pleasure if the Business of Congress did not engross so much of my Time, as that I might daily devote an Hour or two to my Friends. Unfortunately however for me, and I may add for the Public, so it is, that altho the greater Part of our Time is spent in Council, our Dispatch is not proportionate to the Exigency of our affairs, and we experience the Inconvenience of those Delays which invariably attend the Deliberations of public assemblies, assemblies in which men do not always speake to inform themselves or others.

I am happy, however, to inform you that the principal object of my appointment will probably be obtained and I have some Reason to flatter myself that New York will be the better for my coming here. Time however is necessary to prepare for the Introduction of the Business. To precipitate might be to ruin it, and tho I am extremely desirous of returning as soon as possible, my Inclinations shall yield to the public good.

The maps & Papers relative to our Boundaries, which if I remember right, are in the Hands of Mr. R. Yates, together with Copies of all such Letters to Congress &c. as respect Vermont, ought to be sent us without Delay by some trusty messenger. I wish to appear with our whole Strength. My Respects to Mrs. Clinton. I am, dear Sir, your Friend & Serv't

John Jay.

His Excellency Gov'r Clinton.

[No. 1995.]

John Nicoll Writes in Regard to Timber.

New Windsor Dec'r ye 21th 1778.

D'r Governor, By Capt. Bedlow, I send you the accounts Long due to the Neady People of this Place, which Capt. Machin Had in his hands & wass to have Rec'd the money, But Did Not, Returning of them to me when he joined His Redgm't. As youre Excellency is No Stranger to the Destruction made in this Neighbourhod, By taking all of the Best of the Timber for the obstruction of the River, &c. for which Not one farthing hass ever Been Paid, Neither Hass the Timber ever Been Prised, Beg youre Excellency to appoint such Honest men for that Business as are

Proper judges & freeholders in oure Country, & have had No Timber Cut of theire Lands, Foure of their Number I just take the Liberty of mentioning Mr. Cornwill Sands, Amos Mills, Samuel Arthor, & Joseph Wood, None of which have suffered, by having any Timber Cut, Beg as it is in youre Excellency's Power that you would have justice Done, I should have waited on you but it is Not in my Power, ourely called on, all this Part filled with sick soldiers, & my self Not well, I give Mrs. Clinton & youre self much joy for our young Governor. My family is in Common Helth; my wife joines me in Love to youre self Mrs. Clinton Mrs. Topper & family, & am youre Excellency's Very Humble Serv't

John Nicoll.

To George Clinton Esqr. Governor of the State of New York &c. &c. at Poughkeepsy.

GOVERNOR CLINTON'S SUGGESTIONS.

Pokepsie Dec'r 29" 1778.

Sir, I have rec'd your Letter of the 21st Inst. with accounts for work done at the Frizes. The Command of that whole Department being vested in Genl. Putnam previous to your appointm't, he is of Course the proper Person to grant warrants for the sums due on Debts contracted & Expenditures made in the Business since the Time of your being employed. You have already received some Money in Consequence of Genl. Putnam's warr't to discharge those accts. & I was in Hopes that you had taken Care to have repaid yourself what you had expended; whatever remains due must doubtless be drawn in the same way. Genl. Putnam is now at Reading near W. Chester in the State of Connecticut.

A large Quantity of Timber, the Property of diff't Persons, has (I am sensible) been used in the works without a previous ap-

praizement. This should have been made either by the Quarter
Mr. Genl. or yourself. As it has not been done, if you will draw
up a Representation of the Matter, I will lay it before the Legislature at their next sitting, who will probably adopt some proper
method for satisfying the owners of the Timber. Mrs. Clinton
joins in Compliments to Mrs. Nicoll with Sir, &c.

[G. C.]

[To John Nicoll.]

[No. 1996.]

*Jacob Cuyler Writes to Governor Clinton in Regard to Commissary
Abuses.*

Albany December 21st 1778.

Sir, Inclosed I transmit your Excellency the appointments of
sundry Persons for the Execution of a Certain Law of the Lagislature Passed on the 31st of October last.

Col. Lush will deliver you this letter, who has been kind enough
to promise me to Return the Inclosed as soon as your Excellency
has Confirmed the same. It is necessary this should be done as
soon as Posible. Notwithstanding the law, I am informed many
persons are so lost to the wellfare of their Country, that they are
Endeavouring to Ingross all the new Crops, many of whom I am
told are buying for hard money. If the Evil is not soon Prevent
the Consequences must be fatal. I am with respect your Excellencies most Obdt. serv't

Jacob Cuyler, D. C. G. P.

His Excellency George Clinton.

THE GOVERNOR'S REPLY.

D'r Sir, I am directed by his Excellency to acknowlege the
Receipt of your Letters of the 21st & 28th* Inst. and agreable
to Promise I now return your several appointments approved of.

---

*See page 429.

I mentioned to his Excellency the Case of Marignon and he is of opinion that as the permit was granted and the Flour purchased for the special Purpose of supplying the French Fleet to which use it cannot now be applied it ought not to be removed out of the state if wanted by the army. If it is taken however it will be proper to pay Monsieur Marignon the Purchase money & his reasonable Expences. His Excellency nevertheless will not pretend to give any orders respecting it but leaves you to act agreable to what you may conceive to be your Duty on this occasion.

With my best Respects to Mrs. Cuyler & Family I am Sir Yours &c.

G. C.

Dec'r 30 1778.

[To Jacob Cuyler.]

[No. 1997.]

Oliver DeLancey Asks Permission to Visit His Mother.

Poughkeepsie Dec'r 23d 1778.

S'r, The bearer Mr. Oliver Delancey, was sent up from the Enemy's Lines by our army early last Spring & has been kept as a Prisoner on Parole ever since. He now applies for permission to go down to Westchester to return again, on a visit to his mother, who he says is sick. I inclose you a Letter & other Papers from Genl. Parsons* on the Subject & beg leave to submit the expediency of granting Mr. Delancey's request to your Determination. I am &c.

Geo. Clinton.

Major Genl. McDougall.

*Letter and paper not found.—STATE HISTORIAN.

[Nos. 1998, 1999, 2000, 2001.]

EXCHANGING CHERRY VALLEY PRISONERS.

The Pathetic Letter of Colonel William Harper—Severe Criticism of the Tryon County Militia—Correspondence on the Subject.

A memorandum of the popell Killed wounded and Taken prisener, and the buldings consumed at Cheryvaly, ye 11 Nov'r 1778, with ane account of the priseners, which the Enimi sent back on the 13th, two dayes after the action:

The Names of the heads of Famelies and how many Kiled of each Famely.	Kiled	How many yat priseners white & black	prisenors sent back	houses burned	Barns Burned	Mills and Smiths Shops	wounded
Mr. Wells	13	1 wh made { 2		2	1	1	
Mr. Dunlap, his wife	3	1 nagro 1		2	1	Smith Shop 1	
Mr. Moore, his wife & daughters		4	4	1	1		
Mr. Dickson, his wife	1			1	1		
Mr. Johnston's mother	1						
Mr. McCland him selfe & childering		3		1	1		
Mr. Ramsey hs childering		4		1	1		
Mr. Ramsey	2	son nagers 3	1	1	1		himselfe 1
Mr. Scot, wife, 1 nagor	5	childering 3	5	1	1		
Mr. Mitchell wife child'r		nagor 2		1			
Mr. Willson		nagor 1					
Mr. Ritche his white sr		nagro 2					
Mr. Lishman		son 1	3				
Mr. Man			4				
Mr. Henderson him selfe		sa. 3 1					
Mr. Cannon wife 1 himselfe		negr 6	5	2	2		
Coln. Cambple his wife child'r		1	8	2	1		
Mr. Camble his son	4		2	1	1		
Mr. Bacon			1				
Mr. Shankland			3				
Mr. Hubard wife child'r				1	1		
Mr. Slaghlen							
Mrs. Bagnell hur husband now in Abany gall a enemy		mnester					
Mr. McCollom			5	1	1		
Mr. Johnston			5	1	1		

| | | | | | himself 1 | |
| | | | | | fuling ? | |
	33	34	45	32	32	3	2
Mr. McCollom				2	1		
Mr. Campble				1	1		
Mr. Campble				1	1		
Mr. McKillop, a grand Tory whos son was in action with the enemy				1	1		
Coln Cloyd				2	1		
Mr. Gallt				2	1		
Mr. Hamell				1	1		
Mr. Tompson					1		
Mrs. Tompson					1		
Mr Forster, a reputed Tory					1		
Mr. McConell				1	1		
Mr. Fargnson				1	1		
Mr. Warfield				1	1		
Mr. White					1		
Mr. McCollom					1		

This return difers a litell from the furst on beter information the Return of the Contenentall Troupes I Received from the adjetent.

Colnol	Kiled Rank and file.	wounded wounded	Taken					mising	
			Luten Coln	Luten	Insine	Surgans mate	Sargant	Ranck and File	Totall.
1	10	1	1	1	1	1	1	13	30

COLONEL HARPER'S LETTER.

Sir: I send you enclosed a leter from Walter Butler which he sent in by one of the priseners that he sent back. I see it with 1 other to Mrs. Wall. I thought Mager Whiting hade forwarded them till this instant that the inclosed came to hand; the other I understand is in the hand of the man that broght it. I shall send for it as sune as posable, and forward it to you, as I consave the exchange of Inhabitints, is more properly your provence then Genarell Schilers [Schuyler] but your Exselency is best Judg of that mater, and I am shuer you will do every thing in your power to releave our distresed frinds from wors then Divels.

Sir, you will see by the Return the number & Quality of the Priseners, Butler Epects a number equal to those he has sent back, but I must Inform you that a considarable part of them are Toryes, or strongly suspected, and such as oght to be sent back to him agane.

But, Sir, as wee have sent away considarable numbers of thare women & childering already, and severall of note amongest them, parhaps thay oght to be considered as exchanged, but if that shuld not be thoght proper wee have yat anugh to exchange for more than I hope will ever fall in to thare Barbours hands.

Sir, Mrs. Moore is my sister and Duty and natuer binds me to intret hur exchange and hur three daghters, whoo are all women grone, for whome my hart trembels, Least thay wors then Brutes shul treat them with wors then Death.

Liekwise Mr Cannen & his daghter, Coln. Campble's wife and hur for small childring.

I was informed by several of the prisenners that Butler sade he would keepe Mrs. Campble & Mrs. Moore & thare Childering till Mrs. Butler, Mrs. Wall, hur nese and his other frinds are exchanged for them.

I would, tharefore, pray that Mrs. Butler, Mrs. Wall, Mrs. Strachan, Mrs. Clement, Mrs. Harkemer & as many of thier families, as will be eaquell to Mrs. More and hur 3 childering and Mrs. Campble and hur 4 Childring, may be exchanged for them; and, thare is a old Scotch man at Johns Town, McDonald, father to Colaghe, whoo might be exchanged for Mr. Cannon, and thare is Ephram Marsh & Hector Sutherland, & a number of other Toryes in Albany Gall [gaol] whoo might be exchanged for the other men, as the Ramseyes & Hendurson; and for the Ms. Ramseys & the other women, thar is Mrs. McGrear, Mrs. Crafort, 4 Mrs. McDonalds, Mrs. Picken with thar famelys, and Mrs. Hufee and a grate number more, if nead be, &, Sir, as wee are informed that Brant & Butler are yat in our nibourhud at Scenaveses, which doth not exsead 25 miles from Chery Valy; if your Exselancy shuld think proper to treat with them on ane exchange, I think the leters may be convayed with out any grat difucalty; and if it ware sune dun, I do not doubt but it might prevent the priseners being sent to Neagaro [Niagara] as I am fully of opinion that thay are yat at Chenanggo and Chughnut and the other Inden towns on the Siscohanno. Since the setellment caled Coile was destroyed, which hapend a fue days after Chery Valy, the popel on the uper parts of the Mohock River, are moveing of very fast & the report of Brant & Butler lying so near at hand has struck the popell with such Teror that in a short time if thare is not a very Considarable Boddy of trupes sent, I doubt if thar is left a smoking hous above Sconackendy.

And as for our molittie [militia] thay are becum so yousles, that it is ondly puting the Cuntry to cost to call them out on duty two days after Cheryvaly was distred.   Coln. Kuck [Klock] arived thare, thogh not exsading twenty fills distant warmed himselfe, and turned about, marched back without afording the distressed inhabitents the least asistence or releafe, even to bury the Ded or to colect the small remanes of thier Catell or goods; returning to the Mohock River he met with Coln. Fisher, who procaded to the Fort & thogh at that very time the priseners arived, which the enemy sent back, and informed us that Brant & Butler did propose to send back the rest of the women and Childering the next day; the wether being very bad and the distressed popell intreating that he would send out a party to meet them, if thay shuld be dismised and helpe them back, and likewise to help colect the Dead and bury them, and to colect the small remanes of thier property, but thay culd not be prevaled one so much as one man, and wee had much ado to gate the wagons that came with them, to carry of sum of the most distresed popell that ever Ies behald, with out fode, without clothing, without even a shilter to cover them from the wether, which at that time was very distresing; and had not the Contenental trupes ben much moor humane then our nibours, thare must undoubtedly many of the Distresed have perished.

Sir, it is with regrate, I give you such information, but I think I am in duty bound to tel you the sitawation that wee are in, and hope you may devise sum way to secuer the small part of this cuntry yate in our hands; it is truly shocking to see the destructtion of grane & catell & the distres of women & Childering in thease parts, and the dradfull apprehensions that the popell are under. I am, Sir, your most obadint and Humble Sarvent

William Harper.

Mohock Destrict Tryon County 2 De'r 1778.

To his Exselancy Gorge Clinton.

GOVERNOR CLINTON PROMISES TO DO ALL IN HIS POWER.

Poughkeepsie Dec'r 23d 1778.

Sir, I this Day rec'd your Letter of the 2d Inst. with that of Walter Butler* enclosed. I feel most sensibly for the Sufferings of the unfortunate Inhabitants of Cherry Valley & particularly for those who are in the hands of a Savage Enemy. As my Residence renders it impracticable for me to execute the Business, I have requested of Genl. Schuyler (to whom I have sent Butler's Letter) in conjunction with my brother Genl. Clinton, to take such steps as may be most likely to bring ab't an Exchange of our Cherry Valley friends, & as I have referred the matter altogether to them, I doubt not that they will do every Thing in their Power to effect the desired Exchange. Be assured, Sir, that I shall upon every Occasion contribute all in my Power for the Protection & Comfort of the Inhabitants on the frontiers of this State. I am with great Respect & Esteem, S'r, yours &c.

Geo. Clinton.

Wm. Harper, Esqr. Tryon County.

---

*Not found.

The Governor Writes to the Albany Commissioners.

Poughkeepsie Dec'r 23d 1778.

Gent., In consequence of an application in behalf of the unfortunate Inhabitants of Cherry Valley who are Captives with the Enemy, I have requested Genl. Schuyler in conjunction with Genl. Clinton, to take such measures as will be likely to effect an Exchange; and as you are best acquainted with the Characters of such as it would be most proper to offer in exchange, I have to request of you to give your Aid in this necessary Business. I am &c.

Geo Clinton.

Commiss'rs for detect'g Conspiracies &c. Albany.

Also to James Clinton.

Poughkeepsie Dec'r 23d '78.

D'r Sir, The enclosed is a Copy of an open Letter transmitted to me by Mr. Wm. Harper. I have forwarded the original to Genl. Schuyler & have requested of him in conjunction with yourself to take such steps as you shall judge most likely to effect an Exchange of the Prisoners taken by the Enemy at Cherry Valley. I beg therefore that you will as soon as possible wait on the Genl. for his advice & Assistance in this Business. I have also addressed a Letter to the Commissioners in Albany to afford you every aid in their Power as from the nature of their office they may be able to point out the proper Objects to be offered in exchange. I am &c.

Geo. Clinton.

Genl. Jas. Clinton.

AND TO GENERAL SCHUYLER.

Poughkeepsie Dec'r 23d 1778.

Dear Sir, I this Day rec'd the enclosed Paper in a Letter from Mr. Wm. Harper of Tryon County. The Reason he offers for sending it to me is, that it respects the Exchange of State Prisoners which he supposed properly to lie with me. I am anxiously concerned for an Exchange of those unhappy sufferers who are in the hands of the Savages. I have taken the Liberty to Request that you will be pleased in conjunction with my Brother (to whom I have also written on the occasion) to take such measures as you shall think most likely to effect this desirable end. Whatever you may determine on will meet my ready concurrence. I would not wish however to have offered in exchange any who stand indicted for Crimes in the Courts of Justice. I enclose you an extract from Mr Harper's Letter to me on this Subject. I am &c.

[G. C.]

The hon'ble Major Genl. Schuyler.

[No. 2002.]

THE ONEIDAS THREATENED.

Colonel Van Dyck Reports the Result of an Indian Conference—Fort Schuyler on Short Allowance.

Fort Schuyler, Decem'r 23d 1778.

D'r General,* On Saturday Last I was Informed that Peter Johnson (an Indian belonging to the Six Nations) was at Oneidas, Endeavouring to Perswade that friendly tribe to forsake our Interest & Join the Infernal Enimies of these states. I Imediately Detached on Officer with a Party of men with orders to Proceed to Oneida & if Possible to make him a Prisoner & Con-

---

* See page 437.

27

vey him to this place, also to Enquire more Particularly into his Business; the party Returned the Next Evening & Reported that he was gone before they arrived at the Castle, that the Chiefs of the Oneidas would be here the Next Day, Yesterday they Came in and after I had opened the matter they made a speech which I have Inclosed for your Information.

A Party of about seventeen Indians who have fled from Ochquago have made application to me for Provisions; they say Genl. Schuyler has Promised they should Draw Provisions at this place. I have put them off untill I have your Directions in what manner to proceed with them.

The garrison is Reduced to 15 Days allowance of Salt Provisions; the fresh Beef is gone and as the Indians are more or Less Daily at the garrison, they take of considerable Quantities. I, therefore, Request a suply may be forwarded to this place as soon as Possible. I am &c.

Cornelius Van Dyck.

[To Gen. James Clinton.]

Fort Schuyler Decem'r 23d 1778.

Priest Peter Informs that a few Days since, an Indian known by the name of William Johnson, was at Oneida; he Profesed to be sent by the Quiyogas with a message in writing to the Oneidas, which was further Confirmed by Eight strings of black wampum Painted with vermillion.

In the message, the Quiyogas mentioned to the Oneidas the near Connection and Intimate friendship which for a Long time had subsisted between their Tribes, and also the Relation which the Oneidas stood in to the Six Nations as head of the Confederacy. They Exprésed their sorrow that the Oneidas had separated themselves from the Confederacy and Joined its Enemies, by which means they had Exposed themselves to the severe Resentment of the other tribes, but that they, (the Quiyogas) had hitherto Protected them from Insult. That the Conduct of the Oneidas in Carrying Information to the Americans of all the measures of the Six Nations had proved them to be so Notoriously Disaffected to the Confederacy that it was neither their Interest nor Indeed in their Power to protect them any Longer. They Desired the Oneidas to Reflect on the Consequences of their Seperation & to Reunite with their antient friends & allies in a vigorous opposition against the Common Enemy of the Confederacy. But, if they would not be Perswaded to take an active part against the Common Enemy, they hope that they would at Least Strictly Observe those Solem promises of Neutrality which they had Repeatedly made to the Six Nations. At the same time they asured them, that if they would not Comply with either of those Requests, that they should not see another spring in peace, but that this winter should Determine their fate.

The Oneidas Replyed, that the affair was of great Importance and must be Deliberated upon by the whole tribe; that Several of their people were not Returned from Hunting and that an answer must be Defered untill their arrival.

Joseph, a French man, Informs that an Onondago Indian told him that the Bateauxs with Provisions Designed for this post had not been able to Reach this in the fall, & Consequently a Large Quantity of Provisions had been stored upon the Mohawk River, which the Six Nations had Determined to Possess themselves of this winter, and also that they had Resolved Intirely to Cut of the Communication between this and the Settlement below, that their people were gone to Niagara but as soon as they Returned they should undertake the Enterprize.

[January — 1779.]

Dear Sir, I have rec'd your Letter of the 30th Ult. inclos'g the accounts from Fort Schuyler of the Indians Conference, which I presume you have also forwarded to his Excellency Genl. Washington & Congress, if you have not I think it will yet be proper to do it.

Some Regulations will probably be made by the Legislature (who are to meet by their own adjournment next Tuesday) for supplying with Provisions the distressed Inhabitants of Cherry Valley. In the mean Time I think you cannot incur Censure for having relieved them & I am perswaded the State will repay the Continent, if insisted on, rather than that you shoud be in the least Injured. I am &c.

[G. C.]

[To Gen. James Clinton.]

—————

[No. 2003.]

BREACHES OF THE SARATOGA COVENANT.

Affidavits of John Martin and Lemuel Roberts Demonstrating the Truth of the Charges Against the British.

Albany, Dec'r 24th 1778.

Sir, I do myself the Honor to inclose you the Affidavits of Martin & Roberts two persons who have been prisoners in Canada.

Mr. Taylor, who is at present out of Town, hinted to me, last Week, that from some Conversation that had passed between your Excellency and him, he had Reason to conclude that the Necessity of collecting any further Testimony respecting the Saratoga Conventionists was superceded. If I am rightly informed several other persons residing on the Grants are capable of corroborating the material parts of Roberts' Information, and altho' Measures have long since been taken to induce them to come down, they have hitherto proved ineffectual.

Should you, Sir, be of opinion that it would tend to promote the Views of Congress Mr. Swart and myself will repair to that part of the Country for the purpose of taking their Depositions.

We should have done this before, but several of the persons returned from Canada being hunting remote from their Habitations we thought best to defer it till we should receive Intimation of their Return. This will probably be in a few Days. We shall wait your Excellency's Directions on the occasion. I am very respectfully Your Excellency's most obedient Servant

J. Lansing Jun'r.

His Excellency Gov'r Clinton.

DEPOSITION OF JOHN MARTIN.

Albany County ss. John Martin of Schenectady in the County of Albany and State of New York being duly sworn on the holy Evangelists of Almighty God, deposeth and saith, that he was taken prisoner by a party of Seneca Indians on the second Day of August in the year of our Lord one thousand seven hundred and seventy seven, and was by the said Indians carried to the Seneca Country. That this Deponent in attempting to make his Escape from the said Indians was retaken by a party of Rangers in the British Service and carried by them to Quebec by the way of Niagara and Montreal. That this Deponent remained in the province of Quebec as a prisoner from the seventeenth Day of December in the year above mentioned, to the twenty seventh Day of May last, on which last mentioned Day he embarked on Board the ship Maria for Halifax, from whence he was sent by a Flag Ship to Boston in the State of Massachusetts Bay. That during this Deponents Captivity as aforesaid, in the province of Quebec, as well as while he was on Board the said Ship Maria, he had frequent opportunities of conversing with the Inhabitants of the said province and the Mariners of the said Ship. That this Deponent has repeatedly heard during the Time aforesaid, from several of the said Inhabitants & Mariners, that the Canadians and others who had been in the Service of the King of Great Britain previous to the Convention made at Saratoga, between Generals Gates and Burgoyne & had, in Consequence of that Convention, been permitted to return to Canada, had generally taken up Arms against the United States of America after their Return to Canada and subsequent to the said Convention, and farther this Deponent saith not.

John Martin.

Sworn to before me this XIVth Day of Nov'r MDCCLXXVIII.
   Chris'r Yates Justice of the Peace.

DEPOSITION OF LEMUEL ROBERDS.

Albany County ss. Lemuel Roberts of Bennington, in the State of New York, Farmer, being duly sworn on the holy Evangelists of Almighty God, deposeth and saith, that this Deponent was on the twenty ninth Day of January last taken prisoner by a Detachment of McLean's Regiment of Emigrants near Missisque Bay and carried under different Escorts, to the City of Quebec. That upon this Deponent's Arrival at Quebec, he was confined in the provoost Guard, where he remained two Days. That he was then removed to the Island of Orleans. That this Deponent after having been detained about ten or twelve Days, effected an Escape from the said Island, and was retaken near Point-aux-Tremble by a certain Qr. Master Wooster and five Canadians, who this Deponent was informed by them were detached from Point-aux-Tremble by Captain Ephraim Jones, for the purpose of intercepting this Deponent and those who accompanied him. That this Deponent was also informed that the said Wooster was one of the persons who were permitted to return to Canada, in Consequence of the Convention of Saratoga made between Generals Gates & Burgoyne. That upon this Deponent's being retaken as aforesaid he was carried to Point-aux-Tremble at which place he was informed that the said Ephraim Jones commanded. That this Deponent with Samuel Rice and James Hill, two other prisoners who had accompanied him in attempting his Escape were brought before the said Ephraim Jones, who after insulting this Deponent with much abusive Language, directed him, together with the other prisoners, to be conveyed to Quebec. That the said Wooster and the Canadians who took this Deponent & the others guarded them to that place accompanied by the said Ephraim Jones. That upon this Deponent's Arrival at Quebec he was examined by the Lieutenant Governor of Quebec, in the presence of the said Ephraim Jones. That the said Lieutenant Governor after examining this Deponent respecting the Situation of American Affairs, remanded him to the provoost Guard, where this Deponent and the other prisoners taken as aforesaid, were confined three Weeks. That this Deponent was well acquainted with the said Ephraim Jones, previous to the Commencement of the present War. That this Deponent saw and conversed with the said Ephraim Jones at Saratoga, at the Time of the Convention aforesaid and accompanied him as part of a Guard to the said Conventionists as far as the Half-Way Brook on their Way to the province of Quebec. That this Deponent some Time in or about the Month of June last, was carried on Board the Transport Ship Maria, then lying in the River St. Lawrence opposite to the Town of Quebec. That this Deponent in attempting another Escape was taken by some of the St. Francois Indians, and by them carried to Montreal. That from the latter place shortly after his Arrival he found Means to get out of the provoost-Guard, where he was confined, and eloped to Castleton. That while this Deponent was at Montreal a certain Dunham Jones, who this Deponent was informed and believes, had also been included in the said Convention and who acted as Lieutenant in Jessup's Corps committed one of the Soldiers of the said Regiment to the Guard, and that the said Dunham Jones, told the said Soldier in this Deponent's Hearing that he would be obliged to join and do Duty with his Regiment at Sorrel, which the said Dunham Jones said composed part of the Garrison of that place. That in or about the Month of August last this Deponent, while he was detained on Board of the Transport Ship Maria, observing a Number of Boats filled with Men going up the River St. Lawrence, enquired of the Mariners on Board the said Vessel who they were and for what place destined. That upon such Enquiry this Deponent was informed by the said Mariners that the Men in the Boats were part of the Saratoga Conventionists, who were ordered to join the Forces stationed above that place and take Arms against the Rebels, by which this Deponent understood they meant the Inhabitants of the United States.

That during this Deponent's Confinement at Montreal, a certain Mr. Jones, who acted in the Capacity of provoost Marshal at that place, acquainted this Deponent that as the Convention had been violated by the Americans, the Governor of Canada had issued a proclamation directing the Conventionists who had returned to the province of Quebec, in Conformity to the said Convention, to join their respective Corps & to do Duty therewith against the United States. That this Deponent frequently heard his Guards mention, during his Captivity that the Troops who were permitted to go to Canada by the said Convention had subsequent to it, taken Arms under pretence of the said Convention being infracted by the said States.

Lemuel Roberds.

Sworn before me the 24th Day of Dec'r 1778.
Saml. Stringer Justice.

GOVERNOR CLINTON'S VIEWS.

Sir, I have rec'd your Letter of the 24" Ult. with the Inclosures, and think the Enemy's Infraction of the Convention of Saraghtoga so sufficiently supported as to the particular Facts contained in those affidavits, as to render it unnecessary to incur the Expence of a Journey to the Grants to take the Depositions of Persons residing there, further to corrobate the Testimony already obtained. If the Persons you allude to, however, should come down to Albany, as may probably be the Case, you will then receive their Information and transmit it me or perhaps a Gentleman on the spot may be employed able to perform this Service. I wrote to Mr. Tayler lately on this subject, previous to the Receipt of your Letter and would, therefore, have you consult with him as to the most proper measures to be pursued in the further Execution of this Business. I am &c.

[G. C.]

7 Jan'y 1779, Pokepsie,

[To J. Lansing Jr.]

[No. 2004.]

New Hampshire Asks for the Laws of New York Relative to Confiscated Property.

State of New Hampshire Exeter Decem'r 24th 1778.

Sir, I am desired by the Legislature of this State to transmit to your State an Act passed here for preventing the return to this State of certain persons therein named, and of others who have left or shall leave this State or either of the United States of America, and have joined or shall join the Enemies thereof which I accordingly inclose; and am to desire the favor of you to transmit to the Assembly of this State a List of all persons who have left your State and joined the Enemies of the United States, in order that such persons may be prevented from residing in this State.

I shall esteem it a particular favor, Sir, to be informed what measures have been taken in your State respecting the confiscating sequestering or securing the Estates of Absentees or persons who have joined the Enemy. As these are matters of considerable importance and what may be the most proper methods of proceeding therein is now in contemplation here, it will be very acceptable to know what has been done in other States, therefore desire the favor that your Secretary would send me Copies of such Acts or Resolves as have passed in your State relative to these matters.

I have the Honor to be with the highest sentiments or Respect Your most Obedient hum'e Servant

Meshech Weare.

Governor Clinton.

[No. 2005.]

Governor Clinton, the Long Island Whigs and Captain Scudder.

Poukeepsie 25th Dec'r 1778.

Sir, I am favoured with your Letter of the 22d Inst. by Capt. Scudder. I have always believed that the Whiggs on Long Island suffered indiscriminately with the Torries from the Parties, who have from Time to Time been on the Island, owing to the Villainy of some & the Indiscretion of other of them. From a Conviction of this I have not in any Instance gave my Authority to any of these Parties. You may rest assured, Sir, that nothing will be done which may in the least interfere with the orders of the Commander in Chief, but on the contrary, you will meet with every Aid in carrying them into Execution. Capt. Scudder, I have Reason to believe, is a brave honnest Man, his Commission authorizes him to cruise on the Sound only & I doubt not, but he will meet with every Incouragem't from you which can be granted consistent with the good of the public Service. I am, Sir, Your most Obed't & most H. Serv't

[G. C.]

Genl. Putnam.

[No. 2006.]

BILLETING TROOPS ON THE GOVERNOR.

*Captain Nicoll Admits Making an Error—Commissary Stores
to be Forwarded to Poughkeepsie.*

New Burgh, Decem'r 26, 1778.

Dear Governor, I have forwarded your Express as soon as it
came to hand; Deliver'd the Letter to Capt. Nichols myself last
Night at New Windsor, talked to him of the Impropriety of
Billotting troops on your house; he gave me to understand he
had done wrong & promis'd to Remove them this Day or to morrow. Our Post was altogather destitute of forage the 17th inst;
was oblig'd as formerly to turn forage m'r & Comm'y, or lose all
the Cattle at the post; therefore, set out with all the Teams at
the post said Day to do my Endeav'r to keep them alive & the Night
before sent for Mr. Harris & Explain'd our situation for teams;
Desir'd him to have y'r Stores Carried to the Creek the 17th inst.
& at the same time Called Capt. Holdron, Supt. of the ferry, &
gave him orders in writing before Mr. Harris, to attend at the
Creek by the mill at 12 O'Clock; said Day himself with a perriauger & his hands see the Stores put safe & Carefully on Board, &
Immediately proceed to Poughkeepsie & see them Deliver'd safe
to your Excellency.

By getting forage & Vending part of our Oxen did not Return
'till Tuesday the 22d inst. & on my Return found the perriauger
at the Continental Dock with the Stores on board & also met with
Mr. Harris at the Post, when I immediatly Called on Capt. Holdron & Examin'd them both, the Reasons why the Stores had not
been sent as Order'd, when they both gave me to understand
they could not take the Vessel up the Creek on acco't of the tide
being too high, the Vessels being then froze at the Dock; gave

perticular Charge of y'r Cider to Capt. Holdron & the hogs not
being kill'd, sent them back to Mr. Harris in which situation they
now Remain. Yesterday I sent to Col. Hay, inform'd him of the
Quantity & kind of Stores you had here; Requested of him to
know whether or not it was in his power to send them to you
Immediatly (as you much wanted them) if I sent them across
to Fishkill Landing. I Receiv'd his answer last Night; & he informs me they shall be sent on as soon as he hears of their
arrival; shall send them as Quick as this Storm clears up & at
the same time send an Express to Inform him—if it was possible
for me to learn from you, whether or not you wou'd have the
Hogs kill'd here, I should be glad, as I am of Opinion they will
Die on the way. If I dont hear from you in 2 or 3 Days & the
weather Continues severe, I will order them to be kill'd here &
sent on. My best Respects to the family and am, D'r Gov'r Your
most Obt. hum: ser't

And'w Taylor D. Q. M. G.

P. S. Am happy to learn by Thomas that I shall have the
pleasure of seeing you here soon.

[To G. C.]

————

[No. 2007.]

*Samuel Frame's Wife Intercedes for Him—Colonel Cantine Asks to
be Relieved from Frontier Duty.*

Marbletown, 18th Dec'r 1778.

Sir, The Wife of Samuel Frame who is prisoner at Poughkeepsie desired the Favour of me, to inform your Excellency,
that she humbly begs he might be permitted to come Home a
few Weeks; that the Severity of the season as well as the present
Condition she now labours under were very distressing to her.
* * * and no Person to assist her she says. I told her I had

been informed that her Brother Orr had been employed in carrying Letters from New York to the Indians and Tories back of us, which if true, I had great Reason to believe her husband to have been privy to it; That such Conduct forbid me to have any Concern for him, whatever my feelings for her Distresses might be. Whether Frame is guilty of any Crime save Disaffection to the Country the Commissioners probably will know. The Distresses of her and her Family induce me thus far to interceed, if your Excellency should think it adviseable. To permit his coming Home will relieve the Distresses of his Family tho' proscribed to ever so narrow Limits. I should be glad to have your Directions concerning the Hides in the Hands of my Commissary. I can get them tanned for Shares as Customary, or exchange Part of them for tanned Leather. If your Excellency will please to direct what must be done with them I shall Endeavour to get it done immediately. I hope your Excellency will discharge me from (that troublesome Task) the Frontier Service, as I imagine the Dangers are over for this Season, especially in this Quarter of Sir your most Hum'e Ser't

John Cantine.

Geo. Clinton.

Governor Clinton's Reply.

Poughkeepsie Dec'r 26th 1778.

S'r, I have rec'd your Letter of the 18th Inst. & will consult the Commiss'rs on the propriety of permitting Frame to come into your neighbourhood.

The Legislature passed an act to authorize Peter T. Curtenius, Esq. to demand & receive from any Person all such articles belong'g to the State as were necessary for the Use of the 5 Battalions raised under the Direction thereof; he is of course the proper Person to deliver the Hides to, for the purpose of getting Tanned or exchanged for Leather or Shoes.

Previous to the rec't of your Letter I had written my Sentiments to Colo. Cortlandt & yourself respect'g the Dismission of such parts of the militia as should be deemed unnecessary to continue in Service on the Frontiers. I am &c.

Geo. Clinton.

Colo. Cantine.

[No. 6414.]*

A Family Letter from Mrs. James Clinton.

December 26th 1778.

D'r Husband; This is the first opertunity I have had to write to you Since you felt home. I have Recieved But one letter from you Dated November 28th, Thank God I have had my health as well as Common; we have had a good Deal of Sickness Since you left home, But Blessed Be God, we are all alive; your mother has Been poorly for Some time; David has Done no work Since; the too men you left here Behaves very well; my Dear I long to hear from you, But would much Rather See you. I expect you will Come home Soon; your Children are all well and Desires to Be Rememberd to you; my love to Brother Thomas, Capt. Gregg, George Diniston. Mrs. Dinniston is well and lusty. Mrs. Wilson and family are well; we hope to See you all Soon. My Dear I have many things more to write, But must Conclude with my love to you, in hopes to See you Soon. Little Caty is a fine Child; your Brother is well; your mother, Genny and all the family Joines me in love to you. From your loveing and affactionat wife.

Mary Clinton.

---

*From Manuscript Volume XXIV Clinton papers.

If you Can get Sugar there, Bring me Some; there is none here; your Cloath will be Ready when you Come; you mest get lineing and trimings.

[To Gen. James Clinton.]

[No. 2008.]

Commissary Cuyler Asks Permission to Transfer a Heavy Supply of Flour from Claverack Landing to Albany.

Albany 28th Dec'r 1778.

Sir, Coll. Van Ness who purchases for me on the East side of the River in this County, informed me a few days ago, that he had received intelligence, that at Claverack Landing was lying a large quantity of Flour, Suppos'd Eight hundred Barrels, or more, as he was informed belonging to a French Gentleman, who had in Sept. or Oct'r last Obtained your Excellencies Licence, to Carry it out of the State for the use of the Fleet then at Boston, this was the Gentleman who was assisted in his purchases by Mr. Thomas Witbeck, now an Inhabitant of Great Barrington.

I mentioned this matter to Colo. Lush, and that I had reason to believe they would soon remove it across the line, that I had great Occasion for the Flour, if there was any means to detain it, I should be glad to have it purchased and removed to Albany, at which place I was directed to Form a Considerable Magazine of provisions but least it might Slip his Memory, I have thought it my duty to inform your Excellency of this Matter. I am Your Excellencies most Obedient and humble serv't

Jacob Cuyler D. C. G. Purchases.

His Excellency George Clint Esqr.

[No. 2009.]

TO MAKE AN EXAMPLE OF MARAUDERS.

General McDougall Promises to Hang on the Public Roads all of those Captured—Cattle Driven to New York.

Head Quarters Peeks Kill Dec'r 28th 1778.

Sir, Your favor of the 15th Instant* reached me at this place. If it had come into my hands, at Fish Kills, I could not have gratified my inclination in visiting you, as the public Service would not permit it. I sincerely wish to see you, before you are confined by the meeting of the Legislature: If I could leave this, I should make you a Visit. But these posts in general, have been so long without any person, whose particular business it was to superintend the whole, that by the wickedness of some, and the negligence of others, things are in a most deplorable Condition; add to this, the alertness of the Cow and horse thieves. These together, scarce give me time to sleep, but I shall soon put some of them to an eternal one.

It is unquestionable, that the enemy has a plan of our works at West Point. Several Deserters from Robinson's Corps, assert it, and that Serjeant Williams of that regiment, who went from Dutchess County, and frequents Oswego near Fish Kill took it. They say he is now out, with one Bot Knox, of that place. I wish they could be secured.

I have had parties and Guides, in search of them and McKeele, for several days in the mountains but in vain. I understand a reward is offered for the latter, by the Legislature of our State. If so, I wish for the Law it may stimulate the parties to apprehend him and others in the like predicament.

All accounts from the Lines agree in two facts. That a far

---

*See page 387.

greater quantity of Cattle has lately gone into New York, than at any one time, since the enemy got possession of that place: Drove in by all ages and Sexes. And that Emmerick enlists the Cow Boys, for the express purpose of Spies and plunderers, and to give them as he imagines, protection by being inlisted in his Corps. But a few days will convince them, that his promises will not avail them. For I am determined at all hazards, to hang every one of them, on the public roads, that a Court Martial will condemn agreeable to the known Laws of Nations, and every Man belonging to the enemy, who shall be found within our Lines, not publickly in arms, with at least a Sergeant, Corporal and twelve. As to the former Miscreants, they forfeit, their Lives by all Law, Civil and Military. It is necessary to their dark purposes, to enquire particularly for my Guards. If the enemy interrogate them on their position, it cannot be doubted, but they will give them full Information. And what is the Consequence? Why that my guards, hold their Lives at the mercy of the enemy, or they will be butchered as Colonel Baylor's Regiment were?

I have now a choice Collection of those Adventurers. The Court Martial sits to morrow, on them. Among others is the infamous Hobby. I fear he will lead the way, for the dread example. I have now on the Lines, 220 picked men of the regular troops, stationed in four places, under the Command of a Field Officer, Vizt. 60 at, or about Sing Sing Church, the like number southeast of it, three miles, 50 the same distance, on that Route, and the same number near Kings Street.

Mr. Platt is gone down to day, to examine their position, and to endeavor, to get four Serjeants parties, of good men enlisted, as light troops, and guides, to those to the first of May, and I hope the friends of the Cause there will countenance the measure.

This is my present plan for covering the Country. But I have a more efficacious one, in Contemplation, which I shall communicate to you in a few days.

The Militia now on the lines will be dismissed the first of January. I shall however want their assistance, in a few days in different districts, alternately, for their own Security. I wish, therefore, for a general order to the commanding Officers of Corps, in West Chester County, to give me all the assistance in their power, when I call on them. I would chearfully consent to let a party of Jackson's go to Armenia Precinct, but they could not be supplied with provision, without appointing another issuing Commissary, and we have too many thieves of this order already.

Mr. Bostwick informed me forage could easily be provided for two ox teams at Poughkepsie, and there will be sufficient for that small Regiment. The last time I saw the D. B. Master at Fish Kill, I directed him if any of the troops must be quartered in Houses, till their hutts were built, he should put them in those South of the Shedes, which is what you was kind enough to hint in your last.

I am much obliged to you for your intention to guard me against blame. I did not consider yours, as charging with any, but as the apprehensions and opinions of others. In a few days, I shall begin to erect a new Bridge over Croton, about a Mile from its Mouth, to facilitate my Communication with Sing Sing, as well as to shorten the distance ten miles from Kings Ferry, to the Plains. This will be of some advantage to our State, as well as to the Public in General. I am so hurried with Correspondence, that I can only add, that I am, Dear Sir, Your very humble Servant,

Alex'r McDougall.

P. S. If you will favor me with a visit, we can accommodate you, tolerably well. Mrs. McDougal desires her Compliments to Mrs. Clinton, and please to make mine to her.

His Excellency Governor Clinton.

[Nos. 2010-2011.]

AMERICANS NOT PAID FOR PROVISIONS SUPPLIED.

Robert Boyd, Jr., Utters Several Complaints, one Against General Riedesel—Governor Clinton's Reply.

New Windsor, 25th Decem'r 1778.

May it please your Excell'y: Notwithstanding the repeated promises made by Capt. Tappen to me that he would adjust his acc'ts with the Commissary Genl. in order that those persons who has money due and as yet retain'd on his acc't might be enabled to recive satisfaction he has broke through them all, and I am reduced to the necessity of beliveing him a Man intirely void of any regard to his word.

I think it extreamly hard to be perpetually dunn'd on acc't of the public for that I had no Intrest in, save in common with other subjects, therfore, beg your Excellency wou'd devise some mode by which I may be clear'd of it, or the people receive their money.

I am inform'd that Resolves of Congress have been passed for the payment of sums of Money that could not be legaly paid thro' the orderly channel; if so, I can see no reason why it can't be done in the present Instance; therefore, wou'd you be pleased to ex- amine the vouchers, and in doing that, wou'd think proper to give me testimonialls of your approbation of the acc't, either to Genl. Washington, or Congress, or both. I would make a tryal to procure

28

the People their money without the assistance of Mr. Tappen. Col. Bedlow will narrate the particulars relative to your Hogs & Cyder; therefore, I'll say nothing about them least I shou'd dip my pen in gall.

There is a certain Hessian Genl. belonging to the Convention Troops, who came on to Fish [Kill] above two weeks ago, together with his wife, three Children, and a large retinue of servants, in order to follow the Troops; the reasons of his delay I do not know; but after staying more than a week at Col. Hausbrock's, he wanted to engage his winter Quarters there, which being refused he set out yesterday to go over the Walkill, with his whole Family to engage winter Quarters among the High Dutchers; from what I have been inform'd concerning this Gentleman's conversation, since in this neighborhood, I think him a dangerous Man, and its oweing to my strong feelings for my Country, that induces me to give your Excell'y this information; if impertinent I know you'll pardon, when you consider the principle that excites it.

Our kind respects to your Lady & mother, together with Miss Lydia and her two young Misses; we wish you all a happy new year; while in the Interim I am, with the greatest respect, your Excell'ys most obed't & very Hum'e Servant.

Robt. Boyd, Jun'r.

His Excell'y George Clinton, Esq'r. Governour of the State of New York.

The Governor Declares "Hoggs are a Misschevious Animal."

Poukeepsie 29th Dec'r 1778.

Dear Sir, I am this Moment favored with yours of the 25th Inst. by Capt. Bedlow. I have never seen any Resolves of Congress for the Purpose alluded to in your Letter & I have the best

Reason to conclude if any such existed I shoud have been officially notified of it especially as it is a Subject on which I have more than once wrote. I conceive myself extreamly ill-used by the Detention of the Money due to my Neighbours, for the Provission they afforded us at a Time when out Little Army coud not have existed without their aid, & I feel for you, who being on the Spot must be greatly embarrassed by their Repeated Applications for Payment. Both these Considerations will incline me to take every Measure in my Power to Effect a Settlement of these old accounts. That which appears most likely to be attended with Success, is an Application to Genl. Washington & I have, therefore, addressed a Letter to him on this Subject, as well on the affair of Genl. Reidazel, which I have given to Capt. Bedlow to forward, & for your Sattisfaction, inclose you a Copy which, when you have read you will please to destroy.

I am so accustomed to the ingratitude from those I have served, as not to be in the least surprized at it, to experience it from those from whom I might perhaps formerly have expected better. Hoggs are a Misschevious animal.

When I last had the Pleasure of seeing you, I ment'd to you my Intentions of selling my Farm at N. Windsor, if an Opportunity offered. Every account I receive from your Neighbourhood convince me it is my Interest to do it. I shall, therefore, take the first good Opportunity. The Price of the Mill, I will fix at what you mentioned, to wit £1000, for the half & conclude you will be sattisfied. I am with &c

[G. C.]

[To Robt. Boyd Jr.]

GOVERNOR CLINTON SUGGESTS TO WASHINGTON THE REMOVAL OF
GENERAL RIEDESEL TO SOME OTHER PLACE—BILLS FOR COM-
MISSARY SUPPLIES SHOULD BE PAID.

Pokepsie 29th Dec'r 1778.

D'r Sir, After the Loss of the Forts in the Highlands it became necessary to detach a Part of the army on the West Side of
the river which joined by a Part of the militia were under my
immediate command, the River being the Bounds between the
differ't purchasing Comm'rs, none could be found to supply the
Troops; in consequence we were reduced to the Necessity of taking from the Inhabitants the necessary supply of Flour & Cattle,
wh'ch were del'd to the issuing Com'rs, & who passed their Rec'ts
to the owners; the same Measures were taken by the Qu'r M'rs
to obtain Forage. Diff't applications have been made to have
those acc'ts paid off but hitherto without Effect. The purchas'g
Commissaries upon the new Establish't in this departm't, being
appointed since that Time, esteem it improper to discharge Debts
contracted previous to their com'g into office, and those who have
resigned or have been displaced, will give no Satisfaction to the
Claimants. I have been much embarrassed by repeated applications from the Persons to whom the Money is due, & wrote more
than once to Congress on the Occasion with no Effect. I am,
therefore, obliged to apply to your Excel'y and if no other method
can be adopted for the Settlem't of those acc'ts, to request that
you would be pleased to lay them before Congress & urge their
order for Paym't.

I am just informed that Genl. Rheidesel is now at the Wallkill,
a Settlement about 14 Miles to the West of New Windsor, & proposes taking up his winter Qu'rs in that vicinity in a Part of it
peopled principally by his own Countrymen. This Gentleman's

Conduct & Conversation on his march, has been very exceptionable, if I am rightly informed, & as there are already too many
disaffected Persons in that Neighbourhood, their Number will
probably be increased if a Person lately so high in Command in
the British service (who will consequently carry with him a
dangerous Influence) is permitted to remain among them. I submit, therefore, the Propriety of ordering him to join his Corps,
or of remov'g him to some Place where he will have less Opportunity to do Mischief. I am &c.

[G. C.]

[To Gen. Washington.]

[No. 2012.]

SUBORDINATE JAMES TO COMMANDER GEORGE.

*Exchange of the Cherry Valley Prisoners—Scarcity of Ammunition
in the Albany Department.*

Albany Decem'r 30th 1778.

Dear Sir, Your favour of the 23d Instant* Respecting the Exchange of the Prisoners taken by the Enemy at Cherry Valley has
this Day Come to hand, upon which I Imediately waited on Genl.
Schuyler who Informed me he had Received a Letter from you
on the same head; we propose to meet about it tomorrow morning. I send you Inclosed a Coppy of a Letter which I Received
yesterday from Fort Schuyler† by which you will see that the
Enemy are very Industrious in Trying to Perswade the Oneidas
to take up arms against us. Genl. Schuyler advised me to order
the 17 Ochquago Indians small quantities of Provisions at a
time as they have Joined the Oneidas, which I have Done. I have
Likewise ordered a Large Suply of Provisions to Fort Schuyler,
some of which must have arrived before this time.

---

*See page 410.
†See page 417.

I have been obliged to order the Distressed Inhabitants of Cherry Valley another Weeks Provisions, or at Least some part of them, as I Could not Bear to hear their Complaints without Relieveing them; they are Realy in a Distressed Condition without Provisions or Cloaths.

This Department is almost without Powder and Ball. I have wrote to his Excellency about it, but if there should be Occasion to Call out the Millitia before any arrived, I could not Suply them. Perhaps you Could order some up from below for the present. I am with Respect and Esteem, Sir, Your most Obedient Ser't

James Clinton.

My Compliments to your family.

[To G. C.]

[No. 2013.]

TRIBULATIONS OF A BRIGADIER.

General McDougall to Governor Clinton—Lieutenant-Colonel Weissenfels Resigns.

Peeks Kill, 31st Dec'r 1778.

My dear Sir, Altho I am exceedingly hurried with Correspondence, and other business I cannot finish this evening's work, without writing you a flying scrawl, on thoughts which have occurred to me, and ommited in my former Letters. When the Legislature meets if you find Jackson's regt. incommodes them, I will remove it. But I don't wish they should know this. Since I came here 31 deserters from the Enemy have come in to this Post only, beside what may have gone to those on the Sound. As my Guards are now farther advanced I think, it will greatly increase. Provission is certainly Scarce with the Enemy, bread Especially. This renders it necessary I should take the most decisive measure with the Robers and Cow thieves, as it will tend to increase the Dejection of the British, all those who are not in that wicked predicament.

I have long considered it as a loss and Missfortune to this State, that the Good Mechanicks, and weavers who come from the Enemy have been sent out of it to their neighbours. I have, therefore, given passes lately to those of this Character to work, at five miles distance No. and N. E. from the Fish Kill to New Milford. For the future I shall confine them to Col. Moorhouse's and order them to call on you to report their place of abode; and one of the Gentlemen of your Family can take a memorandum of it, and give them in charge to the officer of the Militia of the district, until you signify your disapprobation of my Plan. At present they can do us no injury from the strength of the Posts, and they may give great aid to the State in weaving &c. shoe makers, Especially, I shall direct to you, As I conclude Major Hatfield or Mr. Anthony con employ them to great advantage to the Public at Large. It is unhappy for this State in one point of view, that the Grand Army continued in it so long; to consume the Forage, but it will however enable it from the great price of Produce to pay Taxes. A good Market for staple is alway an advantage to any Country if they improve it. But it must take a streak of Fat and one of Lean. I fear I shall be obliged to press the Teams of the good people or disband the Army. Two hundred of General Putnam's men flew to their Arms owing to a want of Provission; viz, flour for five days. How it has ended I have not Learnt. Nixon's Brigade has not a week in store; and none comes from the Southard. A great part of the Works from thence now with it, and West Point, is unfit for use and Condemned. I intended whenever they were Hutted, which will be in a few days, to advance it to Croton River, to be ready to cover the country; and in case they were overpowered to fall' Back into the mountains. Learnard's to come down to Nixon's Cantonment. But I am at my witts ends to know how to subsist them in this advantagious Possion.

Lieut. Col. Weisenfels was with me to day. He informs me Col. H. B. Livingston has resigned and he seems feafull, Justice will not be done to him; as he has been twice or thrice superceed in the New-York line. He is now the oldest Lieut. Col. in it, on every construction, that can be rasd; and by the Late Resolves of Congress Confirming the opinion of a full Board of General offi-cers at the Plains. I hope, therefore, he will [not] have any future cause of Complaint. From what I know of him, the three last campaigns, he may be considered as one of the best and most attentive officers in the line of the State. adieu. yrs.

Alex'r McDougall.

[To G. C.]

[No. 2014.]

*Petition from Claverack that Richard Esselstyne be Commissioned as a Justice of the Peace.**

[No. 2015.]

Blank Permit for Mrs. McFarren and Her Daughter to Pass to New York.

(——————)

Permission is hereby given to Mrs. McFarren and her Daughter Miss McArthur, with their Effects consisting of wearing apparel Bedding & Houshold Furniture with provisions for their Pas-sage & a negro Girl, to pass to the City of New York (in return

---

*Omitted.—STATE HISTORIAN.

for Mrs. Mitchel & Effects) in the Sloop ————— with a Flag
under the Direction of Mr. Robert North.

———

[No. 2016.]

*Memorandum of Articles to be Brought from New York City for the
Misses Farger.*

(———————)

Memorandum of Sundrys wanted from New York for Alida
Ann, and Elisabeth Farger—submitted to the consideration of
his Excellency Govener Clinton:

2 P linnen — 2 P Pocket handkerchiefs; 2 P Callicor; 2 P Cal-
limanco with binding; 1 P flannel yellow 1 P binding; 1 doz. P
wemons cotton stockings; Black Satten for 3 Hatts and cloaks
with trimming; 1 P Black India Taffety for aprons & handkerchiefs; 1 doz. P Gloves — 6 P Shoes; 1 P Black ribbon — 1 P
white ribbon; 1 P muslin for aprons handkerchiefs and Caps;
Gause Cat gut and trimmings for Caps; 1 P'r pins 500 white chap-
ple needles; some tape Sewing silk and thread; 3 p'r Good Scis-
ars, 3 good pen knifes; 1 P Cheecks 3 p'r Buckells; 2 yds lawn,
3 yds. cambrick, 12 lbs. Coffee, 3 lbs. Green Tea, 3 Loafs Sugar,
12 lbs. chocolate, 6 lbs. Bohea Tea, 6 qure strong writing paper.

Two Hundred pounds in money.

———

[No. 2017.]

*Instruction to Officers Commanding on the Lines, Relating to
Provisions.*

(———————)

Coppy of a paragraph of the Instructions to the Officer Commanding on the Lines.

"If any persons below the Lines who are friendly to the public
cause, apply to carry down provisions for the Support of their

Families, it is to be granted only in way and manner as directed by the late Proclimation of the Governor, to which you will strictly in all respects conform."

[No. 2018.]

A Statement by Peter Dubois.

(————————)

I under Written, Peter Dubois, of Poughkeepsie in Dutches County, do Certify that in the latter end of 1777, I came to the House of Francis Hegerman at New Hackensack, where I saw John Gee, a prisoner, (taken when the Shipping was at or Near Esopus) and was then on his parrole; and after some Discourse with said John Gee, I told him my Brother Matthew Dubois, his son Matthew, was likewise on parrole from New York, and that my Brother Matthew Dubois, together with his son Matthew, was to do their Endeavor to get Nickles James, a Pilot, Exchanged for said Matthew Dubois, Jun'r. And said John Gee then told me that Nickles James was Exchanged several weeks before he left New England as Witness my hand.

Peter Dubois.

The above discourse was in the presence & hearing of Francis Hegeman & Jeremiah Jones.

[No. 2019.]

ANDREW STEPHENSON'S DEPOSITION.

The Military Situation in Canada—Proof of the Violation of the Saratoga Convention.

(————————)

The Examination of Andrew Stephenson on Oath:

Who Saith that he went from Skeansborough the 15th day of June last, for Crown Point & there was taken on Board of the Carelton an arm'd Vesel, and after Examination by the Capt. of

S'd Vesel about news &c. the deponent was sent to St. Johns,. from which Place he was sent to Montreal where Brigadier General Powels Commands, & was there detaind by Capt. Sherewood, (formerly an Inhabitant of Charlotte County and was Included in the Capitulation) & sent back to St. Johns with the View to have him in his Company. Colonel French, the Commanding officer at St. Johns, Gave a Pass to the deponent to go to Quebeck as he said it was agreeable to Genl. orders.

The deponent further Saith, that there is Eight vesels of war on Lake Champlain, besides Gun boats Contain'g no Troops but Sailors only. That there is about 60 men at Point Ufair, about 500 men at St. Johns, 500 at Island [Isle aux Noix] Orr Called the Emigrant Reigt. Commanded by Col. McLean (who is now gone to England with Gov'r Carlton) that the 33d Reigt. is at Chambelee [Chambly] Consisting of about 500 men, according as was Reported to him, & that there was 1100 at Montreal which he heard was going to the West Indias also a few Hessians at St. Denness, some at Sorrell, Some at the 3 Rivers, & at Quebeck there is a Reigt. of Hessians and one of British Troops besides 1500 Volunteers — that he Seen Sir John Johnson at Quebeck, that Gov'r Carlton took Shiping for England, while the deponent was there about the begining of July—that General Haldiman had Some days before the deponent's arival Came in & Took on him the administration of the Govrnment; that 600 Hessians arived about the Same Time and are Scatterd among the different Reigts. in Canida. That it is the General talk there, that the Country had broke the Capitulation, whereby all the Voluntiers are allowed to Take up arms tho Included in the Capitulation—that he did not See any of them Bearing arms, but was Certainly Inform'd they did—that Such allowance was Pub-

lished in their News Papers—that 500 Indians as he was Inform'd ware at Montreal, Some of whome he Saw & was Inform'd they ware going as a Gaurd to a body of Troops about
150 miles to the west, to a Place Called Bucks Island, at which
Place it was Suposed they ware going to build a Fort & Some
Vesels on Lake Ontario as they had a Number of Sailors artificers &c. with them & as they ware under aprehentsions of an
attack from the United States army that way.

The deponent further Saith, he was Induced to go to Canida
because of a Report of Indians Comeing down & went with the
Sole View to Prevent the distruction of his Famaly & the Inhabitants which he offers to Prove, but when he went up he was
not Permitted to Return as soon as he Expected. That many of
the People who went to Canida Last Year would be anxious to
Return and Seem to be under aprehensions of a French war.
That Major Skean told him to take his Compliments to all the
People of his accquaintance who had taken Protection last year
& tell them to make it up with the Country as well as Possable.

The deponent further Saith that when he Received a Pass
from Genl. Powels to Return, he advised the deponent to wait
the Opertunity of a Scout which would go out about a week or
ten days after, which he declin'd this was the 26th of July Last.

And, further, that when the deponent was at St. Johns on his
Return from Quebeck, he hapned to be in Company with the
aforementioned Capt. Sherwood, who Inform'd him that a Flag
from Genl. Stark at Albany, had arived at Crown Point to the
Comodore, desireing an Exchange of Prisoners & that Sherwood
had Sent a Letter to Col. Peters Requesting that Prisoners they
now had might be Exchanged for Major "French and other
worthy Gentlemen" as he Termd them, as they sufferd Great

Hardship by Imprisonment & severe usuage. That Colonel Peters should accquaint the Governor thereof & if there was not Prisioners that he (viz, Sherwood) would go out & Catch Some if he was Permitted.

A True Copy of the Original Taken & Sworn to before the Commissioners.

———

[No. 2020.]

Dr. John Bard Expresses His Gratitude to Governor Clinton for a Display of Friendship.

[——————]

Sir, Mr. Barns did me the Favour of a Visit a few days ago, and in the office of a Friend acquainted me with a circumstance which I own has given me some shagreen. Mr. Barns did not Expressly mention your Excellency's name, But gave me, notwithstanding, plainly to understand, it was from your Excellency he had his Information, which was, That in the confession of some person, my name was mentioned to my Disadvantage, That the person was not now in being; and that your Excellency had put a stop to it, and in such a manner has made me a debtor to your Excellency's good will. It is Painfull, Sir, to a mind, consious of its own Integrity, to be obliged to defend its self, against false and groundless aspertion.

Every part of the above relations is altogether mysterious and unintelegable to me. There is no part of my conduct, which I would not wish to submitt to your Excellency's knowledg, confident of a Justifycation at the Barr of Justic and candor. That Innosense, Sir, has not allways proved a protection from Injuriees, Especially in Times like these, has been the Just complaint of all ages; and tho I dispise the Efforts of Illiberal, and unmeritted slander, I confess myself, not Indifferent to your Excelencey's and the Publick's good opinion, which I hope I need not assure you I have never Justly Forfitted.

From a Just and Humble sense of my own Political abilities, and a natural aversion I have, to mix in the Busie, Buselling, world; I have chose, and it is my unalterable determination ever to remain, in a Private station. I did once, and only once in my Life, contrary to my desire, concent to a Nomination for a publick Imployment. At the Election I was set aside, & while I rejoyced at my rejection, I Experienced, and Laught, at the Industry, and Political Craft, which was Imployd for that purpose; and which on Former occasions, I often observd, had distroyd the peace, and Injured the Interest of my Best Friends in New York. Since that time, my Farm and Profession, have wholly Imployd me, and I hope not altogether uselessly; from the Exercise of these, I Possess that Tranquility, which I could not Enjoy in any other sphere. My amusements are drawn from Private and social Life; and in these pleaseing moments, I shall always feel an additional pleasure in Governor Clinton's company and be Happy at all times to give your Excellency Every Testimony of my respect and Friendship. I am with the greatest Esteem Your Excellencey's most obedient & most Humble Serv't

John Bard.*

[To G. C.]

[No. 2021.]

Volunteer Company in Charlotte County.

[————————]

A List of The Associate Company In Charlotte County State of New York:

Alex'r McNitt Capt; Alex'r Simson 1st Lieut; Ebenezer Clark, Moses Martin, Ebenezer Russel, John McCollister, John Rowan,

---

*See Volume II, pages 522-523.

John Barnes, John Nisbett, James McNeesh, Lews Williams, James Thomson, James Hamilton, Richard Hoy, William Bell, Andrew McLackry, Daniel Mattison, David Tomb, William Mc-Cay, William Moncrief, David Hanna, Robert Armstrong, Robert Lyttle, John McCarter, William Crookshanks, George Crookshanks, Joseph Cooper, Josiah Parish, Robert Getty, Alex'r Gamble, Ezra Terrill, William Boyd, John Foster, James Ramage, David Hoptkins, Robert Hoptkins, Stephen Rowan, Walter Bell, John Beatty, John Gray, James Rodger, James Stephenson, Patrick Wilson, Joseph Welsh, John Lyttel, Andrew Lyttel, Edward Savage, John Miller, John Moore, Hamilton McCollister, Samuel Williams, Charles Hutchan, Lenord Webb, Norman McLeod.

It is the Desire of This Company to have the Capts. and 1st Lieuts. Commissions as soon as possible; this Company its Expected will Be Much larger, which is the reason we have as yet recommended but one lieut.

We want about 30 Guns; most of us is able and willing to pay for them but Cannot be Supplid here.

This to His Excellency, The Governor.

I do Certify that the above persons was the Choice of the Company for officers in my presence.

Alex'r Webster.

To His Excellency George Clinton, Governor of the State of New York.

[No. 2022.]

*Petition in Behalf of Francis De Boe who was Convicted of Stealing a Sleigh and a Span of Horses.**

---

*Omitted.—STATE HISTORIAN.

[No. 2023.]

A Memorandum Concerning Brant.

[————]

Martin Van Alstyn Jacob Miller and Jacob Merkle went to Adam Young in order to correspond with S'd Adam Young; So they Send to John Clauss and John Shell and Henry Merkel to Joseph Brand, and left Henry Merkel by Brand in order to get intelligence wheter Joseph Brand Should come up with his party or they Should go down, So they got notice to be ready upon a minutes warning.

[No. 2024.]

A BRUTAL ATTACK ON ROBERT MORRIS.

Arthur Lee Acting in a Spirit of Revenge Questions the Management of Our Finances by the European Agents.

[————]

*Mr. Morris's negociations as superintendents of Finances.

His Accounts of Pay to the Army will show that the Army was not fairly treated.

The Manner in which the Bills of Exchange are carried out

---

*This document, No. 2024, has been placed in a wrong position by Mr. Clinton, the editor of the MSS.

The attack on Robert Morris in Congress was inspired by Arthur Lee. May 24, 1782, Robert Morris sent a report to Congress on the condition of the finances. This was followed by a motion, inspired by Lee, and hostile to Morris, for the appointment of a committee to inquire into the authority under which the appropriations of the loans and subsidies in Europe had been consummated. The proposition was beaten, and Mr. Morris was merely called upon to report the general purposes to which those resources had been applied.

Morris, toward the end of May, wrote a long letter in which he refuted in detail each of the charges that were made against him.

In June, every influential member of Congress realized that Morris' enemies were pursuing him with malice, and a malignancy that threatened him with harm. Madison wrote to Edmund Randolph:

"I am persuaded that he (Morris) accepted his office from motives which are honorable and patriotic. I have seen no proofs of malfeasance; I have heard of many charges which were palpably erroneous; I have known others somewhat suspicious vanish on examination; every member in Congress must be sensible of the benefit which has accrued to the public from his administration. No intelligent man out of Congress can be altogether insensible of it. The Court of France has testified its satisfaction at his appointment which I really believe lessened its repugnance to lend us money."—State Historian.

makes the Sum in Dollars much less than it ought to be. The am't drawn for is about 10 Millions of Livres the Difference between 5 5 to the Dollar & 5 8 at which Rate they are carried out is 3 Lires making about 80,000 Dollars.

The Breaking of the Contract with Sands Livingston & Co. cost the United States 60,000 Doll'rs advanced Price on the Ration. Sands Livingston & Co. have obtained a Reward in their favor for 40,000 Doll'rs the whole Loss is 100,000 Doll'rs. That there was Money enough in the Treasury to support the Contract.

The Paying of about 200,000 Doll'rs to Bingham & Ross, both, in all probability, Partners of Morris, when the Army was in the extremest Want, was a Misapplication of the public Money.

Documents may be shown for the above.

Mr. Morris's Negociation of Tobacco sent into New York. The United States were to have rec'd all the advantages of this Measure, but as yet they have rec'd none. The amount so sent in can be ascertained.

Mr. Morris's Negociations as one of the secret Committee of Commerce are more important. In his various Contracts & Connections he was personally interested in more than half the Sum drawn out of the Treasury by the secret Committee which was about two Millions of Dollars.

That after this Sum had been drawn out the secret Com'e was dissolved & another Committee by the Name of the Commercial Committee was appointed. That Mr. Morris kept all the Books & Papers of the secret Committee. That he rec'd in General all the Letters & Correspondencies of our various commercial Agents. That he never gave regular Information to any Body. That the accounts have been kept concealed. That no regular Adjustments have ever been made. That the Deficiencies in accounting for the Money appear astonishingly great, that many of the pretended adjustments are made originally in the Hand writing of R. Morris both as to accounts wherein he is personally interested as well as where he is not.

That these accounts do not only extend to the Monies drawn out of the Treasury of the United States, but to all the Sums obtained in France & expended there for cloathing Warlike Stores &ca. That the Persons employed in this Business in Europe were under the Direction of & corresponded only with the secret Comm'e. That it appears in general that the Letters were rec'd by R. Morris, because they are endorsed on the Back in his hand writing.

That these Accounts extend to the immense Sums paid for freight Disbursements on Vessels, Loss of Vessels & Cargoes, purchasing of Vessels Accounts of purchases or Cargoes in this Country for Exportation, accounts of Sales of the same accounts of Cargoes purchased in Europe, Their arrival & Disposition, all which accounts required the most acurate attention to Business, regular Books & proper adjustment at the Time. The Want of which, has left the Business in such a Situation at this late Period, that it is nearly impossible to Adjust them otherwise than upon Principles of Probability & Conjecture.

That the Monies rec'd by Mr. Morris on Contract & otherwise amounting to about one Million of Dollars, the accounts of them remain yet to be adjusted, & the Vouchers produced in Support of those accounts are not such in general as can be admitted at the Treasury.

That Mr. Morris being placed in a Situation of the highest Confidence & Trust, has altogether failed in the Execution of that Trust. That by Reason of his private extensive Engagements he

has always been interested in keeping concealed the public accounts. That it is almost impossible to suppose that a Man thus
situated could act fairly & uprightly for the public. That he has
not, an Inspection of these particular accounts will readily show.

The accounts that fell into the Department of this Committee
were as follows:

John Langdon—Portsmouth New Hampshire

John Bradford—Boston

D. Tillinghast }
N. & J. Brown } Rhode Island

N. Shaw & T. Mumford—Connecticut

P. Livingston, J. Alsop & F. Lewis—N. York

A. Livingston & Turnbull

Willing, Morris & Co.—John Ross, B. McClereghan, Geo. Meade
& Co, & several others in Philadelphia.

Silas & Barnabas Deane, Connecticut

Livingston Lewis Alsop Morris & Deane

Stephen Steward & Richard Carson, Maryland

Braxton, Jett, Harrison &ca., Virginia

Hews & Smith, Edenton N. Carolina

A. Gillon, Clarkson & Dorsius, Livingston & Clarkson, South
Carolina

Gwinett, Wereat Georgia

O. Pollock, New Orleans

W. Bingham, Martinque

S. Ceronie, Cape Francois

Beaumarchais, Paris

John Ross in Europe

Schwighausen, Nantes

Jon'a Williams, Nantes.

In short all the Monies laid out in Europe for account of the United States amounting to near ten Millions of Livres in the year 1778. If we suppose at a moderate Computation that four Millions of Dollars worth of Articles arrived, original Cost they would be worth 16 Millions of Specie Dollars in this Country.

The Fact is we can scarcely form any Idea of the Value of the Property that fell under the Direction of the secret Committee. The Amount of Money drawn out of the Treasury by no Means shews this. If we examine one Branch of the Exports of the United States which is Tobacco, we find it was current at 100. Livres the hundred. That 25 pr cent Insurance & 25 pr cent freight would have carried it safely there. That if we suppose the Price of Tobacco upon an average at 3 Doll'rs Specie pr hundred. The State of Virginia & Maryland could have furnished annually 50,000 Hhds. which would have cost here one Million & an half of Dollars & would have neated in France 25 Millions of Livres.

We find that the Committee in many Instances gave one half for freight & insured themselves which took off ¾ & for what would bring 100 in France they rec'd generally something less than 25 Livres, so alluring was this Trade to private Speculators that the public never was able to get any advantage from, but on the contrary lost much Money by it. Vessels & Cargoes laid for years till they were rotten or taken by the Enemy because they could not get out.

As there were no Limits to the Power of this Committee over the Treasury of the United States, so they had it more in their Power to good or harm than any other Body of Men in the United States. The Produce of this Country fit for Exportation was plentiful, the Means of conveying it were not wanted. The Money

for a long Time answered as well as Specie afterwards it would
purchase without Difficulty tho at an enhanced Price. The
Farmers General wanted all the Tobacco we could send. We
wanted in Return Arms Ammunition Cannon Cloathing &ca. we
wanted annually as follows—

10,000 Stand of Arms a 30	300,000
50 P's Cannon—say	100,000
50 Tons of Gun Powder—	100,000
30,000 Suits of Cloaths a 35	1,050,000
Tents riging for Vessels &ca.	1,000,000
	2,550,000
Insurance a 25 pr cent	637,500
Freight at 25 pr cent	637,500
	3,825,000

20,000 Hhds. Tobacco a 4 Doll'rs including Commission &ca.
pr ct amount to 800,000 Dollars
20,000 Hhds. of Tobacco in France at 100

per hundred amount to	20,000,000
Deduct for freight & Insurance	10,000,000
	10,000,000
Deduct for Commissions	2,000,000
	8,000,000

Thus it appears that the Funds would have exceeded more that
one half what was wanted. That the Prices of Tobacco were
such or nearly that, & that the Farmers General were desirous of
contracting we shall be able fully to show.

Instead of being supplied with these articles thro this channel.
In one Department vizt. that of the Commissary of military

stores we find 8,000,000 Dollars expended. In the Cloathing Department it is impossible to say how much. The Army was always said to be naked. And yet the United States & Individual States could not have expended less than a Million Doll'rs annually for this Object. I believe very little ever reached them thro the Channel of the secret Comm'e. Considering the very advantageous Situation in which this Committee was placed, I believe we might trace our greatest Misfortunes in Money Matters to them. That if they were not guilty of actual Frauds, they were of such gross Omission in Duty, as to render the salutary Intentions of Congress worse than nugatory. Their extensive connections with Characters that no prudent Merchant would have trusted. Their not only Inattention to settle acc'ts but apparent aversion to it implies that they some of them were too deeply interested.

The characters that appear to be principally concerned are R. Morris, Silas Deane, Benjamin Franklin, Francis Lewis &ca. with their various Connections.

I have stated before that 20,000 Hhds. Tobacco was all that was necessary to have been exported annually to have procured every Thing that we wanted in Europe & to have carried us thro the War & finished it without leaving us a farthing in Debt to that Country, instead of which we now owe to France 34 Millions of Livres & 8 Millions florins about 16 Millions of Livres. These immense Debts might have been avoided. And that they were not may with great Justice be imputed to Morris, Franklin & Deane, all of whom were of the secret Committee. It may be remarked that Mr. Morris at the Head of the secret Committee with the Treasury of the United States at his Command, could not, or would not execute a Contract, nor even try to obtain it for

the United States, with the Farmers General of France, altho
urged to it, & whose particular Line of Duty it was to do it, yet
single & alone he enters into a Contract with them to supply
20,000 Hhds. annually & has endeavored to encrease the annual
am't to 10,000 Hhds. more. Mr. Morris after the year 1776 knew
all the Advantages of a Tobacco Contract. His Brother had let
him fully into the Knowledge of it. This seems to account for
the strange Contract made on acc't of the United States with the
Farmers Genl. putting the Tobacco rather under half its current
Value. It seems to be evident that it was intended that the
United States should have no advantage in the Tobacco Trade &
this in fact happened. They lost a great Deal of Money by it.

[No. 2025.]

Proposals for Goods to be Delivered at Southold, L. I.

We whose names are hereunto subscribed do jointly engage to
& with such persons, as shall furnish & deliver to our order at
Southold on Long Island the merchandize mentioned in the following List, or any part thereof; that we will pay for the same, at
or before the Expiration of six months from the Termination of
the present war between the United States of America and Great
Brittain; that we will allow forty pr Cent advance upon the prime
cost of the Goods in New York, and that we will pay an annual
Interest of Seven p Cent from the Time the Goods shall be ready
to be delivered untill the Principal shall be paid.

Signed: (————) (————)

7000 yds Coarse woollens; 400 Do fine Blue Cloath; 200 Do Do
Scarlet, 200 Do Do white at 12 / Ster p yd. prime Cost; 350 pair

fine woosted Hose 350 Do Linnen a 36 / p Doz; 10,000 yds. Good
Dowlas a 1   0; 2500 Do Do Linnen a 1/9 to 2/ 0; 100 Do Cambrick; 6 Gross Shirt Buttons; 20lb Sewing Thread; 15 Double
Gross Double Gilt plain Buttons; 20lb Scotch Sewing Thread;
200 Beaver Hats; 20 Doz. Kilmernack Caps; 20 Doz. Silk Handkerchiefs.

The above prises are intended to be about the sterling cost in
the year 1774.

Copy.

Mr. (————) is desired to procure any Sum of money not exceeding Ten Thousand Pounds New York Currancy, for which the
best Security in the State of New York will be given with an Interest at 7 p Cent pr annum.

Signed (————) (—————)

Dated

Mr.

MANUSCRIPT VOL. VII.

[No. 2026.]

WALTER BUTLER SCORED.

James Clinton Expresses His Sentiments in the Matter of Exchanging Butler's Mother and Her Family.

Albany Jan'y 1st 1779.

Sir, A letter dated the 12th of November last signed by you and directed to Genl. Schuyler, and which was delivered to John Campbell, is come to hand; as its Contents related to Persons who were Citizens of the State, with which the Military dont interfere, the Letter was not delivered to Brig'r Genl. Hand, who then commanded in this department, but transmitted to His Excellency Governor Clinton, that his Pleasure might be known on its Contents. He has authorized me to make the Exchange you request. I am at a loss to know where to direct to you, but also to what part of the Country the Unhappy Prisoners taken from this State have been carried. I therefore send the Bearers John Campbell and Newkirk, with a Flagg to carry this Letter to any place, where they may learn you are or any other officer who can effect the Exchange in your Absence.

Should the Prisoners be in any of the Indian Villages, and in a Condition to be moved, you will please to send them to the nearest of our Settlements or if you do not chuse to do that, I will send proper Persons to treat and receive them at any place you may appoint.

I am not informed if Mrs. Butler, her Famely and such others as will be given in exchange for those whom you have in Captivity and those you have suffered to return as mentioned in your Letter, woud chuse to move at this inclement Season; if they do, they shall be sent, if not, they may remain untill Spring, and then may either go to Oswega or Canada at their Option.

Shoud the Prisoners taken at Cherry Valley, or any others belonging to this State be at Niagara, it will be impossible for them to return untill Spring, and then I request that they may be sent to Oswego or Fort Schuyler, and that you will send notice of your determination, that Provision may be made accordingly.

Do not flatter yourself, Sir, that your Father's Family have been detained on acc't of any Consequence they were supposed to be of, or that it is determined they shoud be exchanged, in consideration of the Threat contained in your Letter. I shoud hope for the honor of sivilised nations, & the sake of human nature, that the British Officers had exerted themselves in restraining the Barbarities of the Savages; but it is difficult even for the most disinterested mind to believe it, as numerous Instances of Barbarities having been perpetrated where Savages were not present, or if they were, the British force was sufficient to have restrained them, had their been a real desire so to do.

The enormous murders committed at Wyoming and Cherry Valley, wou'd clearly have justified a retaliation, and that your Mother did not fall a Sacrifice to the Resentment of the Survivors of those families who were so barbarously masacred, is owing to the humane Principles, which the Conduct of their Enemies, induces a belief that they are utter Strangers to.

The Flagg will carry their arms with them, that they may furnish themselves with Provisions, shoud what they set out with be expended before they reach any place where they can be supplied.

As Captain Butler may be absent I inclose a Copy of his Letter to Genl. Schuyler.

Copy.   James Clinton.

To Captain Walter Butler or any other British officer to whom it may be handed.

[No. 2027.]

General Parsons' Complaint Concerning the Restriction on Flour.

G[reenw]*ich 2nd Ja'y 1779.

D'r Sir, I have this moment arriv'd here to give some orders respecting the Guards in this Quarter; and to my Surprize I find the Bedford Junto Still refuse to Suffer Flower to come on to this Post—are we to be sacrificed? or is there a fix'd Design to Sacrifice the officers commanding in this Division? The Troops must be withdrawn unless some measures can be taken to furnish Flower here without such constant Interruptions as we have experienced in this Quarter; I know your Excellency incapable of being accessery to these Purposes; but I beleive there never was so many artifices made use of to render it impossible [to]* keep our Guards & do our Duty. I beg your Excellency's Interposition & that such orders may be given as will prevent this Evil.

I rec'd your Excellency's answer respecting Scudder. I beleive him brave & tho't him honest; but must beg your particular Direction in his matter. Y'r Obed't h'e Serv.

Saml. H. Parsons.

To His Excellency Governor Clinton, Poughkeepsie.

---

*MSS. torn.

[No. 2028.]

TROUBLES OF DR. JAMES FALLON.

He Believes the Time has Come to Fix the Limit Between the Qualified Whig and the Unqualified Tory.

Quaker-hill Hosp'l Jan'y 3: 1779.

May it please y'r Excellency, as an officer of the Continental army, ordered to this disagreeable Hill for the superintendance of a number of very sick Soldiers left behind—as an officer and as a citizen, sworn to communicate every thing I apprehend, either in Individuals or confederate bodies, that may incline to infringe the Law of allegiance, or obstruct the civil & military measures we are, under God, so prosperously pursuing—as a man zealous both in my official duty and public fidelity, entrusted with the lives of men, and looked up to for medical aid, natural food and military protection, by the poor, helpless soldiery specially committed to me, in this place, for the above purposes; as all such, I say, I was Just sitting down, to intrude a little on your indulgence and politeness, with a representation of some, among the many grievances which this Hospital of mine hath suffered from, in consequence of the open, unconcealed, notorious antipathy of most of its Inhabitants, called Quakers, and their pretended converts to every thing that could further our success— when I was favoured with a letter from Mr. Lush, an attorney, who, as he informs me, may be addressed to at y'r Excellency's house—on this account, and on account of my present torture from Hemorrhoidal pains, as also, and principally, on account of the close connexion between the subject of his and some parts of that matter I had previously in contemplation to communicate to you; I trust to your excellency's indulgence, if I convey the whole to you, and (in consideration of my Indisposition) take the liberty of referring Mr. Lush to your letter, for what appertains to him.

Mr. Lush writes me: that a certain Wing Kelly, (a Quaker of this neighbourhood,) and one of the many lately given in by Justice Sherman (as he himself told me) to one of the commissioners, as a strongly suspected friend to the Brittish arms & cause; and one, whose known Inimical disposition to our cause, as an harbourer of stragling and unfurloughed soldiers in his house, for a long time to the hurt of the army; as a depreciater of our currency by extortion; as an inveigler of my sick to work for him, out of my Hospital; as a man that is known ever reluctant to hire his Team for public service, except it be forced from him; and finally as one, who, in the mouth of every person in this neighbourhood, that has sworn, is in the catalogue of suspected Tories; as one, I say, who, under all these characters, I was about to mention, with other suspected non-jurors to you, (previous to the receipt of Mr. Lushe's Letter,) hath complained to him, as an attorney at Law, that under a warrant illegally issued by me, a couple of my soldiers impressed his waggon and three horses, for the purpose of removing the very worst cases of this Hospital, immediately, for want of proper medicines &c. to Fishkill and Danbury, and at a time when these poor objects must have perished, if not instantly removed to the places they were sent to; of this I, as sovereign within my own Hospital, was the sufficient, proper and only Judge. The inclosed will convince you, that the impress made on Kelly & Irish's two waggons and teams, for the above purpose, was not wanton; was on such immergency of life & death as even the laws of nature would sanctify and authorise; was really consonant to the practice and long usage of military officers, when on seperate command, and in immergencies where the civil power could not aid them; but has been never known to be brought in contest, by the civil authority, against Persons in my rank, (especially when the civil authority could not supply the public call), who have the supreme guidance of men's diseas, lives and wants, and who are (if I may so express it) generals, governors, Directors, Quartermasters, commissaries, Physicians and Surgeons, within their own Hospitals.

Your Excellency will, in the detail, further find, that, notwithstanding the distress of some of my patients, and notwithstanding the usage of Hospitals, never contended 'till now, (in favour of a strongly suspected Tory, and disqualified citizen); I have, nevertheless called upon the civil power very pressingly, which when, for the want of proper force and a proper constable, it could not supply me, Mr. Sherman, seeing the necessity, and I telling him that in similar distress of life & death every public officer must be supposed to have power, he bid me, as I had a guard, and that the guard had no right to receive his orders, to issue my own, and that he would ever support the necessity and propriety of the impress, and would confess his cooperation in't, in my support, as a civil magistrate.

I am affraid that, by my prolixity (tho' agonizing with pain) I must trespass upon y'r Excellency's patience. I want, as a military officer, sworn to the states, to give government my Testimony (as Quakers call it) of my suspicions against certain persons on Quaker-hill; my verdict of applause in favour of the four whig Quakers, and my account of the difficulties this Hospital met with, from all the non-jurors (the above four excepted,) since the army went away; this will give you a clearer Idea of Kelly's affair, and of the insidious, sly, religious, yet Torified conduct of these fellows; and consequently (as men who pretend a concience in not affirming against the Sovereignty of our Enemy, 'till he gives up the claim himself), should, politically speaking, receive little countenance from any true whig, especially against the very officers who oppose this enemy, for having leant on them in preference to poor whigs, and for having adopted measures to do their duty, tho' wrong perhaps in the form, while not against the spirit of Law, and this should ever be attended to. The Kernel is never to be thrown away for the shell. Formal protection to such Hypocrites confirm them in their resistance to the test. What need they take it, while men in power countenance these? Of this they brag on this Hill, and of their numerous protectors in the different branches of the Legislature. We become stauking-horses for them, to shoot at our friends, from under our own bellies. They laugh at our humanity, and charge it to our fear, and I am of opinion, tho' not in universal acceptation with religionist-Politicians: that political evil shoud, on certain occasions, be born, that political good may derive from it, this has been supported by many great men, whose works have enlarged the land-marks of Human knowledge.

On my arrival here, a few days previous to the march of the army, I (as of the General Hospital) superceded the Head-Doctor of the Flying, who held charge of it before me—the Flying Hospital, ever marching with the army, carried all their medicines, stores, waggons &c. with them; leaving me, and a few Doctors under me, a swad of sick, with little or no means to support them; and my Predecessor gave me the highest discouragement, from the disaffection of the Quakers, and all the half-Quakers they keep in tow, about me. I wanted flour, meat, Hay, corn, Teams and waggons, for the purpose of drawing wood, &c. to the hospital, offering my money in the name of the public, but my money was not to their taste. I wanted Quarters for myself & officers; but could not get them, 'till fairly extorted—no man (bad as the weather was) would freely sell, or draw wood or hire to the sick of the army, because they were of the army, and because I would not give six for one of the public money put into my hands—the sight of one of my poor people's uniform would make a Quaker gnash his teeth; and some of them were abused, for going, perhaps, to buy a little milk to their houses—daily complaints came in to me, for Insults, even within the limits of my Hospital, (where military law, as in a camp, or Garrison, is in force;) but shewed no other resentment, than, perhaps, a few threatning words, politically calculated to terrify.

I was four days without wood or waggon—other supplys of medicines & stores soon reached me from Danbury—in this trying situation I writ to Genl. Green, [Greene] as Q. M. G. to supply the Hospital with two public waggons—he sent me word, that the army had scarce a supply for the Baggage then in motion; but he would order an Impress—the constable alluded to in my letter, one Corbin, got the warrant, impressed the widdow Irish and one Akens's Two Teams & waggons. Genl. Green marched of the same day, and Corbin never informed me of any impress made for the Hospital, 'till a month after. I thought, that as no waggons arrived, according to the General's promise, that he must have neglected his duty and me. Irish & Akins detained their waggons at home, when they found I was a stranger to the Impress—this Irish and her sons are public Tories. My charge, my officers and self were all this time (four days) in sufferance for wood to cut, or waggons to draw it—at length old Mr. Russel, an excellent and open whig, tho' a Quaker, condescended to hire me his waggon & ox-team—with this I was obliged to put up, under many disadvantages, 'till now, that the want of proper medicines for some cases, and stores too, put me

under the necessity of removing the sick to a better neighbourhood, Danbury & Fishkill—to the latter I am bound myself, to
take charge there, 'till relieved from the Eastern department,
and I return back to my own, which is the middle; bad and ill
provided as I was, out of 100 sick, providence took but three of
my people off since I come here, which was far from the case before my arrival; old Ferris, the Quaker, pulpiteer of this place,
old Russel and his son, old Mr. Chace and his family, and Thomas
Worth and his family, are the only Quakers on, or about this
Hill, the public stand indebted to.

These firm men and whigs in the very face of their meeting,
and would be disowned and read out, for their very overt Patriotism, were it not that the former conduct of the rest, (in screening
Robbers, Tories out of New York, as I am told, Deserters of Burgoyne's and our army, in holding private, treatorous conventicles,
treasonable discources &c. &c.) has put them in the power of their
menaced discovery, if ejected, or provoked. These four families
are, in my most scrouplous opinion, such, as must extort from me,
as a public and zealous officer, my testimony with you in their
favour, perhaps, at a future day.

As to the rest, such an old Merith the Father, and his three
sons, Benjamin Akins, Abraham Wing, Wing Kelly, Saml. Wal-
ker, schoolmaster, Saml. Downing, a fellow sheltered here among
them, who goes frequently, as I have been led shrewdly to understand, and secretly too with messages from them, and without
regular leave, with stock, and with horses, &c. within the enemies lines. In short, to exclude him from the oath, he wants to
be rec'd among the Quakers, and has every mark of a suspected
man.

Quaker-hill has been the Rendevouz of such tory vagrants—he

30

will talk of furious whigism, the better to conceal himself; but is a Pandar, as I leave to the tories here—he a keen, crafty fellow, and already a Jesuite, or even a Quaker in cunning. He come out of New-York and Long-Island some time ago, and goes in, it is said, when he pleases. He has no property here, but is sheltered by the Quakers, is a Taylor by trade, and follows every kind of business in the Horse and oxen way—sometimes, he will purchase for us, the better to gloss over his conduct. He looks like a spy, and will, in my opinion, be one day taken up as such.

There is also a Quaker-preacher (whose name I now forget) lately arrived from Rhode-Island, and sheltered here among them. He has gone to Rhode-Island some months ago, clandestinely (as Mr. Russel tells me); tarried there with friends, & no doubt with his English friends for some time, and is Just returned with news to this holy flock on Quaker-hill, where every body is sheltered. I have myself ordered a guard to drag Deserters out of their Houses, and took up three Robbers, who broke Jail near Poukepsiee, and were steering straight to, and anxiously enquiring for any Quaker-house on the Hill. This gave me to suspect them at once. I ordered them to be seized on, and delivered them to an officer and party of men then in pursuit of them. I now recollect, that the above Preacher's name is Lancaster.

Having been obliged, (as I already mentioned to y'r Excellency) with old Mr. Russel's waggon & Team, on the usual hire, I had to send my commissary, to look out for wood. As I had but one waggon, and the place hilly, and the roads bad, and the weather too severe for the sick in a large meeting-house, I was obliged to fall on the nearest, and of course the most convenient spot of wood to the Hospital. Old Merith's offered itself. He is a smooth, civil, sly man; but he knew to say no; his son forbid my wood-cutters; but the distress of the sick was such, that (without calling on the civil power) I cut away, and offered payment on valuation. In this, perhaps, I acted against form; but kept up to the law's spirit, as already noticed. According to the principles of Jurisprudence, every Law has its Epikia, or exception, on immergencies. This proves that there are times, when it will be necessary for the public good, that form must give way to the law's spirit, that private must give way to public Interest, and that the shell is often broken thorough for the Kernel.

After this, I had orders from the army, to send one of my younger Doctors, with certain particular stores to Jersey—in this occasion, the moment of dispatch was not so pressing, as when lately it was necessary for the preservation of about 14 lives, immediately to cart them of to Fishkill and Danbury. I consequently thought myself bound, to call upon the civil power. I applied to Mr. Sherman; he instantly impressed one of the younger Meriths; but co'd not take it without an armed force; he writ me, that from the disaffection of the generality of the Inhabitants on Quaker-hill, he could not raise force enough to send me the waggon & Team; and advised to send my guard for it, as being already impressed for the public service. I, forthwith dispatched a serjant and guard, with strict orders to behave well, and they brought me the waggon &c., thus, did my office put me under the necessity, either of not doing my duty, or disobliging a parcell of envenomed Tories. This, I fancy, rouzed the Quakers (I then having but few soldiers here) to try if they could not beat my convalescents, should the public interest call upon me for any more waggons. I knew nothing of the combination. Irishe's waggon and Team were already impressed for this Hospital, by order of the civil power, at Genl. Green's instance; but not sent. It still lay under the impress, not having done the business it was impressed for, and not having been discharged the public service by me; indeed, as already mentioned, the constable or the magistrate who impressed it, never told me a word of the matter, and Genl. Green could not inform me, he being then gone. Kelly had also a Team and waggon in prime order; and both were Tories upon record, non-Jurors to the state, far from being more than ceremonial Quakers, and ever averse to part with their waggons for public use, but by force. This was evidenced by Kelly's conduct, in my presence, in refusing to hire his horses a few miles, to a Lieutenant, for the purpose of transporting the Robbers I delivered up to him, on a violent snowy day, to one Draper's untill, I understand, he got beat into the bargain. He is a sly, plausible, trifty, deceitfull fellow. He affects to be the Mansfield of the Quakers, I am told, on this Hill. He will (as his character says) go to Law, particularly with military men of our army, for six pence; were he a true Quaker, or a true Christian (not to talk of his political principles) he would have lent his waggon, were he never paid, to save the lives of his poor fellow-creatures, tho' Enemies, which it carried to the Hospital at Fishkill.

These waggons being ready, an opportunity offered for their service. I knew of no others, but the waggons of poor whigs, which were harrassed while the army was here; for the whigs of this neighbourhood were ever ready to oblige the public. Kelly's & Irishe's Teams and waggons were hitherto untouched; but the 10 miles the former was forced to drive his, for the Lieutenant & Robbers. I was about to dissolve this Hospital—necessity drove me to it; for I had about fourteen very ill, and no suitable medicines or stores for them—both were near exhausted.

I expected a supply from Danbury; but the weather prevented its coming. I was without resource—their diseases and consequent emaciation were such, as admitted no time to be lost—in this crisis of distress I sent the Inclosed letter to Mr. Sherman. Mr. Sherman waited on me, and having told me that he could not supply me within the time, he approved of my procuring Kelly's and Irishe's at all events, to save the people's lives, and assured me, that, as a magistrate, he would cover me with the civil power, if called on; in the necessity I was reduced to, I acted as guardedly as I could; more I could not do, nor less; as Mr. Sherman could not help me. He had no constable he could depend on. I ever found him a worthy man and an obliging magistrate. In consequence of his approbation, I thought (for I am no Lawyer by Profession) that I was fully invested. I had no personal Interest in pressing waggons. I acted officially; and think, that, without such permission from him, the necessity would Justify it, even in a medical officer of the continent, far inferior to me, in my post. The usage of military Hospitals, in the middle Department, sanctifies this custom with seniors, both senior Surgeons and senior Physicians & Surgeons.

The Inclosed order was, consequently, given by me to the steward of the Hospital, a civil Lad. He very peacefully took four of Kelly's Horses, and a waggon; one I sent back out of pity to a relation of his, an old woman, who wanted to go a Journey. The waggon directly set out with the sick, to Fishkill, and is hourly expected to return. A certificate has been sent to his house by my commissary, and he will (as I always do) be paid regularly for the service. Irishe's waggon and Team was impressed by the steward & corporal of the guard, at the same time, a mob, however arose, headed by Abraham Wing and Benjamin

Akins, with other Quakers, who made a rescue, and almost killed the steward & corporal, the whole party exclaiming against them, (Wing in particular) as Rebels. However, they restored the Team & waggon to me; and it is gone with more of the sickest sick to Danbury; and Irish too has got a certificate from my comm'y, and will be paid.

Thus far have I obtruded upon y'r Excell'ys patience, with a letter as tedious and torturing ∙to you, as my pain is to me, at this moment. I had not time to digest it, as Mr. Lush requests an answer immediately. Tho', perhaps, positive proof could not be easily produced against all the people given in here, as Tories, or rather Tories in masquerade, that is, of overt acts of Toryism; yet I am convinced, as is every warm & sworn whig about here, that they are, if they dare manifest it, at heart, the very essence & quintessence of Tories; the Evils such men are capable of, to the state, are near, and may be great. Immediate dangers, tho' small, influence the mind with greater force, than distant tho' terrible calamities.

The Quakers in Pennsylvania, as well as here, are cunning enough, in political matters, to evade; but not sensible enough to deceive; possessed with the highest confidence in their Jesuitism for craft, they behave with that morose and sullen carriage, which is ever the result of narrow manners and solitary thinking; like vipers which we have cherished in our bosoms, they could never have strength to sting us, had we not, by the foolish warmth of our caresses, given them vigour and animation. Would to God I had the Legislative and Executive powers of Pennsylvania, Maryland, New-Jersey and this state, (not to remove your Excellency from the Post, which, confessedly, you so worthily fill) intrusted to me, but for six months; I would (as in the three southermost states), or ship every Tory of, with forfeiture of property or have, at least, the allegiance of his tounge, public conduct, and Arm. I would not kill; but I would closely shear of the wool; and the fleece should be divided, at a future day, among the poor, disbanded soldiers, as an attonement for their wounds, heroism and virtue.

Alas! poor Randolph,* he is no more; whose influence brought Virginia to give this example to all the states; and was followed by the two Carolinas and Georgia! Perhaps the loss of such a man, to this rising empire, was greater, than all the profits accruing from the forfeitures which his policy brought to it; but it is the misfortune of Humanity, that we never value true greatness, till after we lose it. We are now perfectly sensible of our own strength, and ought, at once, to fix some conspicuous limit between the qualified citizen, and the unqualified Tory. It really dishartens Whigs, to see these vermin publickly protected in crawling on to a level with them. Whatever may be the reasonings of some states for this forbearance and passivity, their motives, I am confident, were for the good of the subject; but the unanimity which the expulsion of all non-jurors brought to the councels of the southern states, and the flourishing situation they are now arriving to, from their being all, almost, of one Kidney, ought to instruct us here, to the northward, to copy after them— in a word, the genius of the times is great, but irregular. It is to be hoped, that, when we are more accustomed to the great act of governing ourselves, like forward children hushed to rest by their own importunities, the at present convulsed states will, at last, settle into harmony, stability & order; as in mechanics, so in Politics; all bodies continue to waver, 'till their center of gravity is supported.

---

*Peyton Randolph, the American patriot, an influential member of the Virginia House of Burgesses, and president of the first Continental Congress.—STATE HISTORIAN.

The sectary of Quakers, however, of all others, is most in opposition to civil Government; its religious principles, similar to those of Jesuits, sap the foundation of that principal base, on which the great fabric of mutual support, and permanent security, as social, is built. I was ever of opinion (laying aside their Toryism) that the Quakers, as a religious people, ought not to be tolerated in those states; because their religion forbids personal service, taxes, and even defensive war. No constitution should tolerate any religion, that holds it as an essential tenet, that the constitution is not to be defended, nor some of its laws obeyed. Could it tolerate such a religion, it would be a Felo de se. It is the property of this religion ever almost to contract the sphere of the human understanding. It is its spirit, like Popery, ever to favour arbitrary power, and its reproach to make Hypocrites.

Should your Excellency be of opinion, after reading the inclosed papers, and this too prolix letter, that even in my circumstances of distress, and tho' in support of public duty, I did any thing amiss, that injures Kelly or the state, I shall give either that satisfaction you recommend; but, if I then acted wrong, when I had no alternative, but either to let 14 men perish, or strain a point, with the magistrate's approbation, to send them of in Kelly's and Irishe's waggons, to save their lives; I must confess, that I should never attend the sick of the army again in this state, where laws co'd exist to exalt a Tory over a medical officer of Rank, in the necessary discharge of his duty, and in the crisis of peril to the lives of men. I remain, with distinguished respect and esteem Y'r Excellency's most obedient and most humble Serv't

James Fallon Senior Phys'n & Surgeon of the Genl. Hospitals. His Excell'y Gov'r Clinton.

[No. 2029.]

Governor Clinton on the Abuses in the Purchase and Sale of Flour.

Janu'y 4, 1779 Pokeepsie.

Dear Sir,* I have just received your Letter of the 18" ult. with its Inclosure and will cause the Inquiry you request to be made. I have to observe however that it will be difficult to ascertain whether Mr. Hazard belonged to your Department at the Time of the Purchase of the Flour from Colo. Freer. The Deputies & assistants make a Practice of informally appointing agents who purchase in different Parts of the Country large Parcels of Flour of which no immediate Returns are made and of Course they have an opportunity either of applying it to the Purposes of Trade or throwing it into the public Magazines as best suits their Interest and I have good Reason to believe that considerable Quantities of Flour which were contracted for, for your Department were converted to private emolument on the sudden rise of Flour in the Eastern states last summer. Hazard is Brother in Law to the Schencks and I believe was employed to purchase for them. I know he afterwards understook to procure Flour for the French Fleet by which he was laid under strong Temptations and if he has not sinned he has a larger share of virtue than I believe him to be possessed of. I am &c.

[G. C.]

[No. 2030.]

Colonel Udny Hay Asks for Instructions in the Matter of Transporting Flour for Public Use.

Fish Kill 7th Jan. 1779.

Sir, I some time agoe desired Mr. John Else to load some Teams which came for corn with as much flour as they could take above the quantity of corn I coud then spare; in consequence of which

---

* The identity of the person to whom this letter was written is not disclosed by the MSS., but a reference to document 2088 indicates that Jeremiah Wadsworth, Commissary General of Purchases, was the person addressed.—STATE HISTORIAN.

he sent seven barrells as will appear by the duplicate receipt transmitted herewith.

This flour is since seizd (and remains in the hands of Mr. James Reed Amenia Precinct) under pretence there was no permitt with it.

Must beg the favour of your Excellency to inform what method is necessary to take for the recovery of this, and at same time to prevent public flour going to public officers and designd for public use being stopt in future, for it is certainly impossible to apply for a permitt every time we have occasion to send flour to the eastward. I have the Honour to be Your Excellencies most obed't & very humble ser.

Udny Hay.

His Excellency Governor Clinton Poughkeepsy.

[No. 2031.]

Destitute Inhabitants of Cobleskill Appeal to General James Clinton for Assistance.

Schoharie Jan'y 7th 1779.

Dear Sir, We the Inhabitants of Cobus kill being burnt and destroyed Last Summer by the Indians, are Reduced to the most Severe Sufferings. We are destitute of Cloathing, Provisions, and Every Necessary to Support our Destressed Families. The greater part of our Service has been taken up the season past. in guarding the Frontiers of this place, and in that time Drew Provision from the Continent, but now we are unable to purchase one Individual, and without assistance undoubtedly our Famalies must Experience the most Extraordinary Severities for Necessaries of Life; by a Letter from Genl. Ten Broeck Directed to Coll. Wempple in Schanectida, we had a Promise of assistance; he wrote thus; " the Inhabitants of Cobus kill who have Been des-

troyed and have Fled to Schoharie must be Supplied with provision, But as Genl. Starks Conceives that this ought to be Done
by the State, I Shall Represent their Case to his Excellency, the
Governor, and must in the Mean time, Request you to Employ
some Person or Persons to Supply them and keep a Regular account of the same."

This Letter was Dated at Albany, the Sixth Day of June Last,
but Never Came to hand till this Day; neither have we Received
any advantage thereby—and as no person in Civill authority appears to Represent our deplored Situation in order for Relief, we
know of no other Method than to Implore your Gracious assistance if Possible to Succour and Relieve a Distressed People.

If your honour Can Prescribe or Direct any way or means for
help, that we may obtain some Relief, under our present Dificulties, we, your Petitioners, are under Every Necessary obligation
to Return you, our Most Sincere and hearty thanks through Life,
Flattering ourselves that if your honour Pleases to notice or
Inspect in our Behalf, it will Redound much to the advantage
of your Destressed Petitioners, as your Influence will be great
with Every person in power. We understand that the Legislative
Body is to Set this month and a small Detail of our Curcum-
stances from your honour might have great weight with them.
In the mean time hoping to Receive some present assistance from
your goodness, otherwise we undoubtedly Suffer. Sir, with all
Due Respect, we are your humble Servants

Adam Schefer, Jost Schefer, George Werner, Niccles Werner,
Lorence Lawyer, Anna ———, Widdow, Gorg ———, Willem
Sneyter, Johannes Freimeyer, George Schill, Johannes Couch,
Jun.

To James Clinton B. Genl.

[No. 2032.]

*Colonel Malcom Petitions for the Pardon of Sergeant John Ryan
Under Sentence of Death for Robbery.*

Goshen, Jan. 8, 1779.

May it please your Excellency, I presume to sollicite your
Excellency's Clemency to John Ryan,* a serjeant in my Regiment
under sentence for Robbery, although I have nothing to plead
in his behalf but his youth (being but nineteen years of age) and
his former good behaviour in the Regiment. The Soldier who
was concernd with this unhappy fellow in the Robbery, was shot
Dead by our party & from both their former characters I have
reason to believe that he was the principal, at least that he
seduced Ryan to Committ the Crime.

To give some countenance to my request for the life of this
poor fellow, I beg leave to inform your Excellency that Ryan was
one of the Guard which I sent to protect the Inhabitants about
the Clove, of whom a very bad character was given to the soldiers.
That this Robbery never would have been discoverd if I had not
taken much trouble to trace the affair, and at my own Expence
sent a man to Jersey to bring back the man who was robbed,
collected the party & took every method to discover the offender
who was sent to Goshen & deliverd to the civil Law. All of which
your Excellency knows might have been omitted & the crime
unnotticed. For these reasons on account of the man's youth &
good behaviour and as one life hath already been sacrific'd for the
offence, I most Humbly & earnestly beseech your Excellency to
spare the life of this unhappy man, a favor which will be gratefully acknowledged by the Corps and by your Excellency's most
Devoted & very Hble. Serv't.

W. Malcom.

---

* See page 497; also Volume II, pages 684-685.

If there had been time a proper Petition we'd have been presented signed by all the officers, but your Excellency may consider
this as if that had been done. The Court I hope will recommend
the man as an object of mercy on account of his Youth.

[To G. C.]

[No. 2033.]

*Philip Schuyler Advocates the Selection of Jeremiah Van Rensselaer
as Surveyor General.*

Albany January 9th 1779.

Dear Sir, Mr. Jeremiah Van Renselaer has Intreated me to mention to youre Excellency that he wishes the office of Surveyor
General. I have formerly had occassion to enquire Into his
abilities as a Surveyor, and found him well skilled in the Therie
part and as he has been much Engaged In the business I have
no doubt that he equally well versed In the practical. If you have
not any other gentleman In view for that office I shall be much
obliged to you for your Interest In his favor. I am D'r Sir with
Great respect and Esteem Your Excellency's most Obedient Humble Servant

Ph. Schuyler.

His Excellency Gov. Clinton &c.

[No. 2034.]

ABRAHAM YATES DECRIES CORRUPTION.

*Flour Smuggled to the Eastward—Helpless Condition of the
Frontiers.*

Albany 9th January 1779.

Sir, I Sit Down in anxciaty and Concern, in Order to Communicate to you the Distresses the Country is in, and likely to Increase.
It Even gives me pain to Burthen you with the Information, when

I am persuaded you would, but that it is not in your power to rectify it, the Corruption in the traders Joined by the Tories the Quarter masters & Commisaries is So great and Evil Doers So many that they keep Each other in Countenance. I am afraid Congress have Even Some in their Body that have a Share in the Corruption of the times.

The flower, I am Informed, is yet Smuggled to the Eastward by thousands of Barrels. Here (in Albany) I see Every day the Sleighs that used to come in Loaded with grain, Carrying the Flower out of this City up into Tryon, that County having not Sufficient to Supply the few Troops that are among them; the Inhabitants of that County under apprehensions of a visit from the Enemy, and nothing incourages them to Stay on their places then that they are made to believe, that Soon in the Spring an Expedition will be Carried on to the westward; and I have my Fears that the Campain will open with the Destruction of part of that County or Schoharry, and, God Knows where it will End; must it not very Soon Create a famine? It makes my heart bleed to know that it has been in our Power to ward of an Indian war for at Least Some Time Longer, when I apprehend we have gone Rashly into it.

That the Indian affairs have Been mismanaged is more obvious at this Day then heretofore, and whether our Diligates or (as they tell me) the New England Diligates were the occasion of it, will make no Difference When the Country is Laid waste. They acted both against better Information. It was the opinion of Mr. Kirkland and Dean (I have it from the mouth of the former) as well as the Oneides that a board of Commissioners Should be appointed (out of people that Could speak the Indian Language and had some Influence among them) upon the Same plan

that the Indian affairs had been managed Before Sir William
[Johnson] had the Superintending of them. Some Gentl'n from
New England might have been added and if the New England
Diligates meant no more I think they were right. This plan I am
perswaded might have kept off the Indian War, at Least the
Last, if not also the future Season—and I am afraid the measures
we have persued the Last year (it is Said by orders of Congress)
has Even Precipitated matters upon the Present plan. For it is
Said, that the Indians have been made to understand that as
Soon as Ever we got rid of the Enemy on the Sea Coast, we
were to fall on them and Either Knock them in the Head or
lay waste their towns; or unnecessary Information and a very
Impolitick one.

Could Ever the King of England have been more Effectually
Served? was it not acknowledging what the ministerial Emissaries had been Laboring (to little or no purpose) from the
beginning of the Controversy. Was it not like the man whose
hands were tied by his Enemy, Calling out that he would Kill
him as Soon as he Could Get Loose? was it not the Intent of
the Indians to take time by the Forelock and to Destroy our
Settlements before we were ready to Destroy theirs and to what
purpose Could it answer in the Name of Wonder if we were so
minded we Could not Suppose that they Would give the like
warning to us? But Gentlemen who Live at a Distance often
talk over and Even enter into measure the Impropriety and Im-
policy whereof would appear Clearly Were they to Live on the
Frontiers; it is Speculating to the one but Death and Destruction
to the other; we are now brought to this, we must make Peace
with the Indians or Early in the Spring, Carry an army up into
their Country and Destroy them or Else they will Come Down

in the Spring (if they wait so Long) and Destroy our Frontiers; and we must act Candadly with the Frontiers; the Inhabitants, tell them we cannot (if that be the Case) Send Such an army, and to Do for themselves as well as they Can (where will it End) for, to Deceive the People and Suffer them to be Butcherd and Destroyed, as has been Done the Last Season will be an abomination to God; the number already murdered, the Lands Laid waste is Shocking.

This letter was Intended to be sent at the Date but missed the Post. Now I Intended to bring it myself, but I shall not be Down till the Beginning of Next week, and now so good an oppertunity. I Remain your obt. Hu. S't

Ab'm Yates, Jun.

Gov'r Clinton.

Sir Henry Clinton Writes an Entertaining Letter to Sir George Germain.

New York January 11th 1779.

My Lord,

I have the honor to transmit to your Lordship the heads of our intelligence from the Rebel Country divested from the too Sanguine reports of the Zealous friends of His Majesty's Government.

General Washington's Army is hutted and cantooned for the winter; The Troops of the Southern Colonies on the West side of the Hudson's river, those of the New England Government on the East side. Head Quarters are at Middlebrook, and Washington in person at Philadelphia.

The Troops of Genl. Burgoyne's army are probably ere this arrived at their destination near the West Mountain, in the interior part of Virginia: as a proof that we have many friends in the Country, I will mention that thirty men of these Troops were conducted in a body Eighty Miles through the Rebel Cantoonments and brought Safe within our Posts.

Party runs very high amongst the Rebel Leaders, and great discontent is said to prevail in the Army owing to the depreciation of the Currency, which renders the pay insufficient to procure the Common necessaries of Life.

From the Supplies given to the French, the Consumption and waste of Provision, the neglect of Husbandry, and the reluctance with which the Farmers part with their produce for paper, every kind of Sustenance is very dear: and from intercepted Letters of their Commissaries and other Channels of intelligence, we have seen that the Troops in Connecticut are in absolute distress for want of bread. On the other hand Ships are loading with Flour in the Delaware, destined, it is said, for Mons'r D'Estaing's Fleet at Martinico.

Although no certain account has been received, there is reason to give credit to a report of Col. Campbell's Command having landed at Savannah and the Country having Shewn themselves friendly; yet we perceive no movements in the Troops in our Neighbourhood.

The Indians have again visited the Frontier and Surprized at Fort Alden, near Cherry Valley, part of two Regiments, thirty or forty were killed and Sixty taken prisoners, amongst them are the names of Field Officers. Our accounts are from Rebel papers and probably Softened, we therefore imagine they have Suffered a great deal.

The Insurgents of Verdmont under Allen, continue to give umbrage to what is called the New York Governm't.

Four Sail of victuallers are arrived within these fed days, a

31

Seasonable relief to a Spirited Army—which without a Symptom of discontent has lived for several days on indifferent Oaten bread.

General Lee is wounded in a dual, but Slightly.

I have the honor to be, My Lord, Your Lordship's most obedient and most humble Servant,

H. Clinton.*

Right Honourable Lord George Germain &c. &c. &c.

[No. 2035.]

President Jay Forwards Newspapers to Governor Clinton.

Philadelphia 13 Jan'y 1779.

Dear Sir, Since my arrival here, I have done myself the Pleasure of writing you several Letters which I hope have reached you. None of your Favors have of yet come to my Hands. I hope the Business of the Legislature will not deprive you of so much Leisure as to leave none for the gratification of your Friends.

I again send you some news Papers, and should indulge some Remarks on several Publications which must appear interesting to the Public, had I not particular Reasons for postponing them to a future opportunity. Remember the Papers. My best Respects to Mrs. Clinton. I am Dear Sir your most obt. Serv't

John Jay.

His Excellency Gov'r Clinton.

[No. 2036.]

Destitute John Hochnell Asks Leave to Return to England via New York.

John Hochnell left Europe 4 years ago last Christmas; brought a Family consisting of a wife and four & left 3 Children at Home; he settled in the Manor of Rensselaer; he got burn't down last

----

spring and is now in distress and poverty; he left his affairs
in Confusion at Home and has a farm for two lives in England;
requests that he may have leave to return home to settle his
Concerns, dispose of his Effects and Estate, and bring his Children with him; he suggests that going by the way of France,
it would be attended with very great Expence, and, therefore,
prays he may be permitted to go directly to Great Brittain by
the way of New York.

Albany Jan'y 14, 1778.

[No. 2037.]

Raids Into Westchester—Treatment of Deserters and Other Matters.

Jan'y 14 1779.

Dear Sir, I have rec'd your Favors of the 28 & 31" ult. and
should have answered them by your Expresses if I had known
they were to return; the want of an opportunity since has obliged
me to defer writing to you till the present.   I have repeated
accounts of the Enemy's Incursions into W. Chester County
mentioned in your Letters, and as I am convinced the supplies
they draw in this unwarlike Manner will not only tend in some
Measure to distress the Troops under your Command but also
afford the Enemy a temporary supply and prevent the certain
Effects of a scarcity of Provision, I shall with Pleasure render
you every assistance in my Power to second your Endeavors in
preventing those dangerous Practices in future. As conducive
to this End I inclose you an order on the Command'g officer of the
Militia of the County to give you such aid as you may occasionally require. The men called out on this order I expect will
draw their Pay from the Continent in the first Instance as our
Treasury is low in Cash.

I approve of your Resolution of trying by Courts martial the offenders you mention, being persuaded that exemplary Punishment will be attended with salutary Effects & that none will be the subjects of it but those who are the proper objects of martial Law.

As to the Deserters, the new Levies formerly Subjects of this state should I think have passes & be directed to wait on the Commissioners for detecting Conspiracies here, as a step necessary to their future Safety. Your mode for disposing of the Deserters belonging to the British & Foreign Corps, I esteem as proper a one as in our present Circumstances can be adopted. The movement of your Troops to Croton River, is in my opinion, such a special occasion as will warrant your impress'g of Teams for the Purpose of conveying Provisions to your army either previous to their March or after they arrive there. Thus will be justified the Intention & necessity of the movement, tho it might be improper in the ordinary Business, of supplying an army with Fuel when in winter Quarters.

The Legislature will convene at this Place on Tuesday next. If after I have laid the Business of the Session before them I shall have Leisure sufficient, & the Riding is good, I shall do myself the Pleasure of paying you a visit.

If the Members of the Assembly & Senate find themselves incommoded by Jackson's Regiment I shall apprise you of it.

[G. C.]

[To Gen. McDougall.]

[No. 2038.]

President Jay to Governor Clinton Relative to a Barn Burned by Continental Troops.

Philadelphia 15th Jan'y 1779.

Sir, Yesterday your Letter, to His Excellency General Washington covering several Papers relative to the burning a Barn at Little Britain by the Convention Troops, was communicated to Congress by a letter from him.

These Papers were immediately referred to a Committee, and your Excellency may rely on my taking the earliest opportunity of transmitting to you the final Resolutions of Congress on the Subject.

I have the Honor to be with great Respect & Esteem, Your Excellency's Most Obed't & most Hble. Serv't

John Jay, President.

His Excellency Governor Clinton.

[No. 2039.]

Anonymous Communication Concerning Spies.

————— January 15th 1779.

Sir, You may remember that some time ago, that ————— was sent to New York as a Spy by ————— and by

Request, I was knowing to the matter, and did talk with you on the Subject, as you may remember. I now give you the earliest intelligence of his Return by my boy, which I send on purpose. I have been in Company with him this evening, and he informs me, that there is Men up in the Country now, that is employed by Governor Tryon, to set fire to the Barracks at Fish Kills, and at the Highlands, and also at a Store of arms, at some place towards Fredericksburgh, and that a large Bounty is bid to any man to kill you. He informs me that he was applied to, to be one of the men, and that the men for the above purpose came up in Company with him, and that one of them is now concealed on the Manor of Cortland, and that Ogden's Jim and the white man that you have in your Guard, came in Company with him, from the Bridge, and that he had but just left them when they were taken. He can bring out a great many tories, and one particular who is just going to recruit a Company. He has, as he tells me, brought a Letter for ———— and myself, within eight miles of here, but dare not bring it further, till he see me, which I have directed him to bring it this night. The Letter he tells me, is from ———— which I shall upon the Receipt of it, shall send it to you by the first opportunity which I believe I shall come myself, if not will send it. I have had but a short Conversation with him, therefore, shall refer you to him for further Particulars. You are undoubtedly much surprized of his staying so long, but he says he can give sufficient Reason for so doing, for which Reason you will be judge. He says that it is false concerning his driving down Cattle, that no Proof of that kind can come against him. He is afraid to be seen publick as the people will take him up before he can come to you. I cant give you any thing particular more, but should be glad you would write me particular by my boy how to act with him, as he will be with me to morrow night, and any orders from you he will obey. I am uneasy about the Store of Mr. Leek, as I think there is provision in it, and no guard, and I think by his account, that the Stores, and Barrack, and publick Building by Bribes seems to be the object for the winter. I am, Sir, with due respect your most obedient humble Servant.*

[No. 2040.]

Commissary Knapp Requests Governor Clinton to Release Flour that was Seized.

Greenwich 15th January 1779.

Hon. Sir, The authority in the State of New York who have Ever kept me in the dark till Lately for what they Stoped flour I purchased and wanted to deliver to the Troops at this post, they

*See page 501.

Now say 'twas because, Mr. Colt had wrote Mr. Leek that I had not orders from him to purchase, Since Last spring I have not pretended to purchase under him from that time, but by the Rec't from him, I sent your Excelency the other day, pr Maj'r Benedict, Shewn that I had from May Last, purchased by order of Colo. Wadsworth, the Com'y Genl. When Genl. Parsons proposed sending Troops here, I acquainted him of the Circumstances of the affair and that I did not Know but their mout [might] be some dispute about my supplying and Issuing to them, and their being no Issuing Commissary here (but myself who was then Issuing to Colo. Enos's Regiment,) and the Number of Troops so small then that 'twas not worth while to have one sent, on which the Genl. Gave me a military appointment, to supply the Troops at this post, which I Send pr Bearer for your Exelency's Satisfaction; but the Flour, they have stoped and condem'd, and on which they taken and Condem'd Teams, was flour I purchased Last winter, while acting under Colt and bringing here for the use of the Troops. The Bearer Brings a Letter from Genl. Putnam adressed to your Exelencey also one to Colo. Enos, which he Sends for your Ex'ys Perusal, If some meathod cant be fell upon immediately for Flour to come here, this post must be Left. I must beg your Exelency's Interposition and that the Flour stop'd by the authority in your state and the teams be Released.

I have the Hon'r to be Your Exelency's Most Obed't and Verry hum'e Serv't

Israel Knapp, Jun'r.

His Exelency Gov'r Clinton.

[No. 2041.]

Jeremiah Chapman Asks Permission to Remove His Wheat from New York State.

To his Excellency George Clinton Esqr. Governor & Commander in Chief of the State of New York, &c.

The Memorial of Jeremiah Chapman of the Town of Greenwich, in the State of Connecticut, humbly sheweth;

That about two years ago your memorialist sold a small Farm
of Land he was possessed of in s'd Greenwich, with a design to
purchase a larger Farm in the State of New York, but having
been disappointed in purchasing any of the places he had in view,
he was, & still is under the necessity of continuing his family in
s'd Town; but being destitute of land therein, your Memorialist
was obliged to work on shares on a farm at a place Called the
Cross Rivers [Westchester County] in York State afores'd, where
he has raised as his share, about fifty Bushels of wheat which
still remains there in Stack. That your Memorialist, unwilling
to do any thing contrary to the embargo Law of your State hath
endeavoured, by buying & borrowing among his neighbours to
procure bread for his family 'till lately. That he now finds it
absolutely impossible either to support his Family or replace
what he has so borrowed without your Excellency's interposition;
and its an addition to his distress that he has not been able to
sow any Grain this Season.

Your Memorialist, therefore, prays your Excellency to take his
distressed Condition into your wise Consideration, and grant him
a permit to transport his s'd wheat into this Town for the purposes afores'd or in some other way grant your Memorialist relief in the premisses, and he as in duty bound shall ever pray.
Dated at Greenwich January 15th 1779.

Jeremiah Chapman.

We hereby Certify, that the within named Jeremiah Chapman
is a person well known to us as a Steady & firm friend to the
American Cause; and that upon enquiry we believe the facts men-

tioned in the within memorial are truly stated. As witness our hands in Greenwich January 15th 1779.

John Mead, Justice of Peace, David Wood, Justice of Peace; Bezaleel Brown, Benjamin Mead, jr., John Mackay, Selectmen of Greenwich.

To his Excellency Governor Clinton.

[No. 2042.]

Massachusetts Desires the Embargo Raised.

State of Massachusetts Bay. Council Chamber Jan'y 16th 1779.

S'r, We have wrote a Letter to Congress of this Date, praying that they would be pleased to recommend to the Southern States a Suspension of the Embargo, as far as relates to the Exportation of Grain to these Eastern States, We are really in great want & have just Cause to fear an alarming scarcity, unless your State should relieve us in this Respect. Divers causes have Concurred to produce this Scarcity, a severe Drought & a great Blight during the Course of the last Summer, the absence of our Husbandmen in the Time of Tillage, the Consumption of the Convention Troops, more than their Supplys from the British Commissaries, the want of the usual supply to our Seaports, arising from the Embargo, are among these Causes. We are not contriving a Scheme of Profit to our Merchants, but are anxious for a supply of Bread, at a Time when the want of it begins to be felt.

If it is more agreeable to your State to permit the Exportation of it, by your own merchants, & in your own Vessels, we shall be thoroughly Content.

We are not sollicitous for the mode of supply, if we are but

supplied. You will excuse our Earnestness, & believe us to be
ready at all times to reciprocate acts of Benevolence & Friendship with you.

In the Name & behalf of the General Assembly I am S'r Y'r
very Humble Serv't

Jer. Powell, Presid't

Gov'r Clinton.

———

[No. 2043.]

Commissary Cuyler Puts in a Plea for the Army.

Albany January 16th 1779.

Sir, I have to acknowledge the receipt of your Excellency's
letter of the 30th ult. thro: Coll: Lush, your secretary, with its
Inclosures. Your opinion with respect to the Flour of Mons'r
Marignon* is very Just, but haveing at Present no Power to take
It by any authority, I have desired the Propriator thereof not to
have It removed. Whether he will do It or not is uncertain. I
understand there are several quantities of flour in this County
under the same Circumstances as that of Mons'r Marignon, the
whole of which I have the greatest Reason to believe will be sent
away as soon as the sleying will admitt; being thus situated I
must Request your Excellencey will be Pleased to lay this matter
before this Lagislature that some mathod may be speedily
directed to Inable me to Procure the said Flour for the use of
the army, for which purpose, It is Exceedingly much wanted. I
am your Excellencies most Obdt.

Jacob Cuyler, D. C. G. P.

His Excellency George Clinton.

———

*Charles-Rene-Louis, Viscount de Bernard de Marigny, was born in 1730, destined for
the church, but ran away at the age of fourteen; entered the Marines and in 1778
became captain. He participated in seven battles during the war for independence.
At the naval battle at the entrance of Chesapeake Bay, fought on the 16th of March,
1781, he highly distinguished himself. In 1783 he became Viscount, in 1792 Rear Admiral
and vehemently opposed the blood-curdling excesses of the Revolution. He was denounced and only the fall of Robespierre saved his life. He was commissioned Vice
Admiral in 1814 by Louis XVIII, and died in 1816. See page 494.—State Historian.

[Nos. 2044-2045.]

A MUTINOUS SPIRIT REPORTED.

Barrack Master Bannister Demands Straw and Blankets for the Troops—Colonel Jackson's Comment.

Fish Kill Jan'y 17th 1779.

Dear General, I received this morning your favor of yesterday, am obliged to the General, for the Care he takes of us. This Minuit 12 o'Clock this day, I received the inclosed from Major Bannister, which I am sorry to send, it is the first time I have had any Complaint of this Nature. As to the Barrack Master, I have done all I can with him. I believe him to be a dilitory Man, and that he might have got straw, if he had taken pains. I'le wait the General's further orders, on the affair, and at the same time, do all I can to keep orders. I will send for Captain Brown, who is at Poughkepsie, in order, that he may be at Peeks Kill, on Wednesday next, with the Court, and evidences may be ready at that time. These from the General's most humble Servant

M. Jackson Colonel.

(Copy)

To M. General McDougal.*

MAJOR BANNISTER'S COMMUNICATION.

Sir, Our good Men that have suffered every thing, but death, for their country, patiently, and looked unto the Officers humbly petitioning and at last, with tears in their eyes, to my knowledge, for the small part of what is due to them, the necessary Articles of Straw, and Blankets, which the Men know can be got, and they cannot do without, have at last determined, to seek Releif by desperate Means. Sir, by what I have seen, and heard, we shall soon

---

*These two documents no doubt belong to document 2051, page 501.

have no Soldiers, unless those Articles are speedily supplyed. I beleive next Thursday is the longest term, that it is possible to persuade them to any order, or duty, but to seek Redress by force of Arms. This Sir, I represent as facts, and as what must be remydied to prevent Confusion.

I am Sir in haste and much Concern Your very humble Servant

Seth Bannister, M. B.

Sunday Morning Jan'y 17th 1779.

Comm'dt Jackson.

(Copy)

[No. 2046.]

POLICY OF THE INDIANS.

Colonel Van Dyck Reports the Result of a Council Between the Tuscaroras, Oneidas and Onondagas.

Fort Schuyler, Janu'ry 18th 1779.

Sir, Last Evening two Oneidas, and an equal number of the Tuscaroras waited on me here, & informed, that for two days past their Tribes had sat in Council & every Individual desired to declare his final resolution as to the part to be taken in the present seeming crisis of their affairs. At the same time should any chuse to join the enemy, free liberty was given to withdraw from their tribe; that the result of their meeting was an unanimous resolution to stand by each other in defence of their lives and Liberty against any enemy that might be disposed to attack them. That they then proceeded to take into consideration the late message of the Quyugas [Cayugas], to which they unanimously agreed to return the following answer, to wit, That as they had ever behaved themselves in a quiet peaceable manner toward the confedracy, they coud not conceive their conduct was reprehencible by them.

They likewise put them in mind of their long and unwearied efforts to prevent the six nations involving themselves in the calamities of war, and that they had exerted themselves so far, as by their influence to relieve from close confinement some of their people whom the fortune of war had put in the hands their enemies. But that they now utterly dispaired of ever being able to effect a reconciliation between the Confederacy and the United States and that the only hope they now had of them was that some of them woud in time abandon the cause they had imprudently espoused. That they woud never violate their aliance with the American States, and tho they woud not be the agressors or wantonly provoke any tribe to war, yet that they should be henceforth on their guard against any enemy whatsoever.

Seven of the principle Onondaga Chiefs, who have hitherto been considered as neutral, being at the same time at Oneida, on their way to this fort, it was determined to call them in and acquaint them with the above resolution, which was accordingly done by a large black belt of wompom. The Onondagas replied that they were very glad to hear the resolution which their children the Oneidas and Tuscaroras had made. They observed that as the Oneidas who were the head of the Confederacy had committed the Council fire & tree of peace to their care, with a charge to guard them against the approach of any thing which might injure either, or tend to interrupt the harmony of the confederacy, they had, therefore, invariably pursued the path of peace, and tho' they had been desired by the opposite party of their tribe to extinguish the council fire; yet that they had refused, nor coud they consistantly do it whilst the Oneidas retained any hope of accommodating matters in the six nations. But as the heads of the confederacy had now declared themselves so fully upon that subject; they now let go their hold of peace, extinguished the council fire, and sunk the tree of peace in the earth, and were determined to join their children the Oneidas and Tuscaroras to oppose any invader.

The Onondogas have further engaged upon their return home to effect a final seperation in their tribe, and insist that every one shall declare for one side or the other. They now join with the Oneidas in requesting that Troops may be sent for their protection, also that a supply of goods may be furnished at this post for a trade.

The Oneidas seem to place great confidence in the engagements of the Onondogas, and are in high spirits to find such a number of them so friendly disposed. I am with great esteem &c.

Copy.   Cornelius V'n Dyck.*

To the Hon'le Genl. [James] Clinton,

[No. 2047.]

FLOUR FOR THE FRENCH ALLIES.

Private Secretary Lush Denies the Claim of M. Marigny that Governor Clinton has Detained an Invoice for the French Fleet.

Great Barrington J'y 17 1779.

Sir, I expected in vain the other day to convince your Excellency that the certificate which I laid before you two or three days ago implyd that Mons. De Valnais* intended the remainder of the flour which I have bought for the French fleet, for the use of a number of sick and wounded men whom they had left in Boston, being unfit for the voyage. I could go to Boston and bring you a more satisfactory certificate but I had rather to be

---

*See page 528.

*De Vallenays, enlisted as volunteer; brevet captain of cavalry with pay 28th of July, 1777.

ROCHAMBEAU.

free from this last trouble and expence of all those that I have suffered these five months upon account of this business. I am a stranger here and I hope for all that your Excellency will lend a favourable ear to my representations, if they are but reasonable. I would even think that being a well recommended subject of a king with whom you have lately made a treaty of alliance, that quality would give me a title to any favour and protection, which is consistent with the duties of your high employment. I will try to convince you that even, if the flour is not wanted for the use aforesaid, yet it would be some injustice to keep it from going out of the state of New York, unless the com'y general of the army would allow me the same advantage which my counteract with the French fleet could have procured to me; for it was only upon the strength of the said counteract together with that of your permit, that I ventured to lay out so considerable a sum and to run the risk of all event, which I would not have certainly done, if I had thougt that you soon would take the matter in another light. Of the flour that I have bought a part of it went down to the French fleet and the other could not get to them upon account of the difficulty of the transportation, which part lays consequently upon my own hands at my own risk. Now, if your Excellency will not allow me to carry that remainder out, what will be the consequence for me? The comissary will make with me such agreement as he pleases and even will be apt to take the advantage of me because he knows that by your late act, nobody has a right to buy but himself such a large quantity of flour. Will that be the benefit that I had a right to expect after five months of the hardest fatigue and the laying out so considerable sum of money and the reward of having served both my country and these states, since they are so connected that who serves one, serves the other? Would not that even be apt to weaken the trust that I had upon your permit, and to encroach upon one of the articles of the treaty of alliance which secures the property of a subject of the king of France in any place of this continent?

I would not give my opinion upon that matter as a rule, but if your Excellency considers the matter in another view, I beg of your Excellency to write a letter to the commissary general whereby you advise him, if the French consul should not want the flour, to take it for the benefit of the army under the same conditions as the French were to have it. I think that any other agreement would be unjust and I will represent besides to your Excellency that I have bought from Mr. Jacobus De Peyster in Fishkill hundred and fifty nine barrels of flour at the rate of 25 shillings of your money pr hundred and having not that hard money upon hands I gave my obligation for it, expecting to be repaid in the same cash by the French. Now, I think that if the comissary pretends to have that flour, he is to fulfill my engagements towards the said gentleman, or else give me the liberty to transport it whenever I will be able to get hard money for it whereby I will be able to fulfill my promise. I will beg of your Excellency to mention this last to the comissary and to write to him as quick as your business will permit. That is the last favour that will beg of you, he who remains of Your Excellency the most obedient and respectful servant

Charles De Matigny.

To his Excellency Governor George Clinton esquire Poughkeepsie.

COLONEL LUSH'S REPLY.
Jan'y 19" 1779.

Sir, I am directed by his Excellency to inform you that he has not given any orders to Mr. Cuyler* for detaining the Flour

------

*See page 490.

purchased by you for the use of the French Fleet. Mr. Cuyler wrote to his Excellency on the Subject and requested his Directions respecting it. I wrote to Mr. Cuyler in answer to his Letter by order of the Governor that he would not pretend to give any Directions respecting it but left Mr. Cuyler to act agreable to what he might conceive to be his Duty on the Occasion but if upon the whole he should determine to take it advised him to pay the Purchase money & reasonable Expences.

His Excellency conceives that he has no controling Power over Mr. Cuyler and if any of the Purchases for the use of the French Fleet are injured by the Gentlemen in the Commissary's Department under the late act of the Legislature their proper Mode for Redress will be by applications to that Body. I am &c.

[Lush.]

[To Monsieur De Marigny.]

[No. 2048.]

CLEMENCY FOR CRIMINALS.

Sheriff Nicoll of Orange County Intercedes for Prisoners—Governor Clinton's Position.

Goshen Janu'r 17th 1779.

May it please your Excellency, I would Recommend to your Mercey and Clemency Amy Auger as a pure under witted Creater and a propper Object of mercey. She is to be Executed Next Friday unless your Excellency will Suspend the Execution.

Also one Matthew Dolson, Convicted of Felony; what makes In his Faver is, he Delivered himself up to the Court when it was in his power to kept out of the the way or gone to the Enemy and was Convicted by his one Confession, and I beleve Hartily Repents of the Evel he has Don; he has a wife and one Child a woman of a good Charactor and a very honast Family.

32

The other is John Ryan,* a young Lad of Ninteene, a Solder in Coll. Malcom's Redgt. a Hansom well behaved young Fellow and one that Truly Deserves mercey and I dout not but your Excellency will to him bestow it! as to Claudius Smith and Jeames Gordon I shal Take pleashure in seeing them Executed.

I have a Faver to ask of your Excellency, if Consistent, if you should thinck propper to parden any of the above, that a Condition in said pardon mought be, that he should Execute the Rest, as it will be Disagreeable to me to do it and the Incom of my Office will not afford my paying any body Else. I Remain your Excellency Most Obediant Servent

Isaac Nicoll.

To His Excellency George Clinton Esquire.

GOVERNOR CLINTON'S REPLY.

19th Jan'y 1779.

D'r Sir, In a seperate Letter which will be delivered to you by the Bearer you will receive a Reprieve for Amy Augur, & under the present Cover you have a like for Mathew Dollson, which I have been induced to grant from sundry Facts laid before me of an extenuating Nature. It will not be in my Power to Pardon either of the Offenders on Condition of their being Executioners, but you may make any lawful agreement with either of them you think proper, only remember Government is not to be bound by any Promises you may make them & I know you too well to suppose you capable of deceiving them in that manner. I think from what I learn it is likely Dolson will in the End receive a Pardon but of this he ought not to have the least Intimation least it shoud not be the case. I am &c.

[G. C.]

Colo. Nicoll.

---

* See page 476.

[No. 2049.]

SCARCITY OF FLOUR.

Governor Clinton Writes General Putnam and Suggests Methods of Regulation for Distribution.

Jan'y 19" 1779 Pokeepsie.

D'r Sir, I have received your Letter of the 12" Instant* and previous to the Receipt had answered that of the 26th ult.* by what I esteemed a safe Conveyance. I now inclose you a Copy of what I then wrote. It would be needless to remind you of the Difficulties which attended the supplying the army in this state last summer and the Distresses which threatned them for want of Flour and that this did not arise entirely from the negligence of the Commissaries but in a great measure from the Exportation of vast Quantities for the Purposes of private Commerce in which Practice some inferior agents who pretended to be purchasing for the use of the army (there is the greatest Reason to believe) were deeply concerned. To prevent this I determined to give no Permits for the Exportation of Flour out of the State under the Embargo Law but to such Persons as were recommended by the Commissary Genl. or his principal Deputy or agent, who then became answerable for its due application, or if it was inconvenient previously to obtain this, the Permission was granted subject to that Condition. This was the Case with Respect to the Licence given Mr. Knapp who I did not even know to be a regularly appointed deputy, and if [he] had complied with the Conditions which it was his Duty to do, I am persuaded he would not have met with the Difficulties experienced by him in attempting to remove the Flour purchased by him in the State for the use of your army. The last seizure of

*Not found.

Flour at Bedford was made at the Instance of Commissary Leake which is the more remarkable if it was really intended for the use of the army. I wrote to the Justice who acted on the occasion, but what Effect my Letter has had, is yet unknown to me and I despair of its hav'g any, as I am not invested by Law with any controuling Power over his Proceedings.

I have the greatest Desire of giving that Part of the army which is under your Command every aid in my Power, and you may rest assured that all applications made to me by the Comm'rs agreable to the above Restrictions will be chearfully attended to; but, Sir, it is a Fact if I may credit the Complaints constantly made to me from every Quarter that Flour has become a scarce article. Mr. Cuyler the Comm'y at Albany writes me that he will not be able to lay in the necessary Magazines for that Departm't. Genl. McDougal acquaints me that he will be obliged to quit the Post he now occupies for want of supplies; and you also complain. Every method has been tried by the Legislature to supply the Troops with Flour; for this Purpose the Comm'rs by Law are empowered to seize all the Crops of year 1777 & the years preceding with such as had been purchased by Traders of the present Crop. But all will prove ineffectual unless Commerce in that article can be stopped; this induces me to believe it is for the Interest of the army to give licences for Exportation under the Checks above mentioned & not otherwise, and I flatter myself of your earliest assistance in opposing a Trade which if countenanced must end in our Ruin. I am &c.

[G. C.]

[To Gen. Putnam.]

P. S. I have rec'd a Letter from Mr. Knapp on the Subject of the Seizure by Mr. Leake but esteem it unnecessary to write to him as this Letter contains all I can say in the matter.

[No. 2050.]

Certificate and List of Booty Taken on the Western Frontier by a Scouting Party.

January ye 19th 1779.

These is to Sartify to all Parsons whom it may Concarn that Jacob Seman hath been in the sarvis on the frontears in Company with me, a scouting, By the orders of Coll. Newcark and hav Taken a Large Bootey* from the Enemy which was devided between the scout by me.

Bezaleel Tyler, Capt., James Little, Esqr. John Wood, Capt., John Little, Capt., David Horton und.

I callicoe Gown, 1 cotton mantle, 1 apron, 1 sheet, 1 pillow case, 1 gauze Handerchief, 1 pr. worsted mittans, I womans Housewife, 4 pewter spoons, 1 pr. mens shoes & buckles, 1 paper pins, 1 bunch calimass, a pair sadlebaggs.

[No. 2051.]

TRIBULATIONS OF A GENERAL OFFICER.

General McDougall Writes at Length to Governor Clinton—Without a Dollar, Deserters and Troublesome Militia—His Plan for Regulating Commissary Supplies.

Head Quarters Peekskill Janr'y 20th 1779.

My dear Sir, Your Favor of the 3rd came duly to Hand. It would long ere now have been acknowleged, but the pressing public Business prevented. I have done a great deal of Business in the Course of my Life; but at no Period, have I been so hard pushed. But I thank God, I am able to do as much as at any Period of it. My call on your Militia, in ordinary cases, will only be on the disaffected, to handle the ax and Spade. If the Com-

---

*See page 519.—STATE HISTORIAN.

mander in chief sends me Money, I shall discharge all their Demands. But you will be surprized to be informed, that I am left
here, without a single Dollar, and the Debts of the grand army,
have gleaned all that was in the Quarter & Forage Departments,
when it left the State. I have borrowed of my Neighbours, as
far as they could lend, to supply both these Lines; and to pay
Deserters, and now, if one Hundred, would save me, the army
and State from Destruction, I cannot command it. The Commander in chief is not uninformed of my condition in this article,
or the general State of the Post. I have written him Line, on
Line on this Subject.

The Spirit of Desertion still continues with the Enemy. Five
came up last Night. These make thirty two since January. As
all but those who have a strong Desire for Pensylvania, are
sent to you, your wants in Domesticks can be supplied at your
own Election.

My Left advanced, is rather exposed, as the Detachments from
Major General Putnam, cannot be prevailed upon, to quit the
Paradise of Saw-Pitts, as if all South of it, was Tophet. To
remedy this, I have wrote to the General for 240 of his Division
to be under the command of Lieut. Colonel Burr, who commands
from my Division.

Your whig Militia below have as great an Itch for plundering,
as the Cow Boys; but if they dont conform to my Orders, I will
flog them, or give them over, to the civil authority to be prosecuted as thieves and Robbers. And if they stir out, but with my
officers, I shall take no Notice of them, if Sir Henry Clinton
treats them, as I shall his Cow and Horse Thieves. Many of
them I know, are brave, and have just Cause to be sore by the
Robberies and plundering of the Tories. But if they want Re-

dress, they must get Letters or Orders of Reprisals from you, and when these are satisfied to cease, otherwise all their Disorders, will be placed to Colonel Burr's account and mine, and besides debauch the regular Troops.

It is unquestionable the Enemy is hard pressed for Bread. The Cork Fleet can bring but little Supply of that Article; even if they should arrive in this extreme Weather, which I think from my Knowledge of the Sea, is very problematical. In this Extremity, it would seem as if our pretended whigs are cooperating with the Enemy, to put this army and Major General Putnam's, in the same deplorable condition. The Particulars of these Machinations, Time will not permit to enumerate. From the Returns I have had from the several commissaries, there is no certainty of Support for the army on the East Side of Hudson's, more than a Fortnight, unless arbitrary Measures are, pursued. In this State of things, the army is discontented on account of their Pay, Blankets. and other articles due to them, a Specimen of which you will see in the Inclosure No. 1 and 2.* There is yet no public Bruite; but if their general Court, does not redress their Complaints, God only knows what the Consequence will be. They have sent home committees from the officers and privates, to represent their Grievances. It is at all Events my Duty, to prevent any cause of complaint on the Subject of Provision, and such Articles as the Country can furnish. I am sensible the Inhabitants near the army, want their Straw but one Sleigh Load from every respectable Farmer will make no great Difference, and tend to quiet those poor Lads, who are very sore, reflecting on their Sufferings and the insufficiency of their Pay.

May I beg the Favor of you, to write a circular Letter to the

---

* See page 491 for the explanation of these inclosures.

Justices, or other Friends of the country, to use their Influence, to cause that quantity to be brought into Fishkill, or Pough-keepsie, as the snow now favors the Transportation. I find no other means will effect it. The Troops of the whole Division, are now doing the duty of Horses, in drawing wood and other Necessaries to their respective Cantonments. Colonel Poor's Regiment on Fatigue at Kings Ferry, have been two Days without flour, notwithstanding every Precaution in my power was taken to prevent it. Its too dangerous an Experiment, to risque such Suffering for the future, considering the various Causes of discontent in the army. No Flour is to be expected from the Southward. If the present Artifices of the Jobbers and Tories in concealing their Produce, are suffered to pass thro' the ordinary Course of Law, in this County to punish them; the army will be obliged to disband, or remove to Jersey, unless I act arbitrary in many Cases, where Necessity requires it, for the Preservation of this State, and the common Cause. To lose the flattering Prospect, of weakening the Enemy's Force, more by Desertion, than have been taken in any Battle, since the Contest, without the Loss of one man of our army, is not to be dispensed with; or to suffer the lower Part of this State, to be burnt and the Enemy to take Possession of these Posts, is too humiliating, to hesitate a Moment what Alternative I must make. There is now in this County alone, Flour and Wheat enough to serve this army till Spring, besides an ample Supply for the Inhabitants. But it cannot be procured by the ordinary Course of Law. Whenever I depart from it, I shall always have Vouchers to satisfy the good People of the State, of the Necessity; and risque the Consequences of my Conduct to their Wisdom and Discernment.

If I had not sent Parties to the Mills east of this, the Division in twenty Days would be disbanded for want of Bread.

The Enemy's Strength on York and Long Islands, is 10,780 strong at the lowest Calculation, exclusive of Delancy's Brigade, Horse and Artillery, besides, the Garrisons of Staten Island and Powles Hook.* Of this I can convince you, when I have the Pleasure of your Visit, and that the Enemy intend to remain in the United States another Campaign, unless the French Fleet in Europe, gains a decisive victory over the British, which is not very probable. Every Intelligence that can be relied on, mark his Intention to remain in the United States.

The Inclosure No. 3 a Letter of General Tryon's, to a person whom I shall name to you, shews the Spirit of the high Servants of the devoted Britains, and No. 4† will inform you of the vile and desperate arts, which they practise. These are communicated in Confidence.

---

*The appended statistics will show the strength of the British forces in America from 1774, with the salaried list of officers, and lists of the dead, prisoners, deserters, the distribution of Sir William Howe's forces, with the monthly return of July 1, 1777, containing a list of the regiments with the names of their commanding officers compiled by the State Historian from the Parliamentary Register:

†See page 485.

Account of Men lost and disabled in his Majesty's Land Service, including two Battalions of Marines and Foreign Troops in British Pay, by Death, Captivity, Desertion, Wounds, or Sickness, in North America, since November 1, 1774, distinguishing each Year, Corps and Service.

Years	Service	Corps	Dead	Prisoners	Deserted	Discharg'd disabled by wounds or length of service
From Nov. 1, 1774,	Under General Gage	British	31		47	16
1775,	Under Gens. Gage and Howe	Ditto	781		115	249
1776,	Under Sir William Howe	{ British	869	967	192	619
		German	65	981	No return	No return
	Under Sir Guy Carleton	{ British	200	48	68	36
		German	176	15	282	490
	Under Sir William Howe	{ British	1202	357		
		German	No return	89		
1777,	Under Sir Guy Carleton	{ British	81	5	No return	No return
		German	58		20	29
	Under General Burgoyne	{ British	385	59	2	
		German	18			

N. B. By convention, British and German 3500 prisoners.

Establishment of General and General Staff Officers, with their respective Pay and Appointments in North America, for the Year 1774.

	£.	Per Diem. s.	d.
General and commander in chief	10	0	0
Two aids de camp to ditto, each 10s.	1	0	0
Secretary to ditto	0	10	0
Two brigadiers general, each 1£. 10s	3	0	0
Three majors of brigade, each 10s.	1	10	0
Deputy quarter-master general	0	10	0
Two assistants to ditto, each 5s.	0	10	0
Deputy adjutant general	0	10	0
Commissary of the musters	0	10	0
Two deputy ditto, each 5s.	0	10	0
Barrack-master general	1	0	0
Judge advocate	0	10	0
Commissary of the stores	1	0	0
Surgeon to the hospitals	0	10	0
Provost marshal	0	2	6
Commanding Officers at the following Posts, viz.			
Fort George	0	7	6
Niagara	0	7	6
Detroit	0	7	6
Ticonderago	0	5	0
Oswegatchie	0	5	0
Michillimachinac	0	5	0
Barrack Masters at the following Forts, viz.			
Forts George, Miller, and the communication to Albany	0	4	0
Niagara, Schlosser, Erie, and the communication to Presqu' Isle	0	4	0

Communication to Philadelphia	0	4	0
Ticonderago	0	4	0
Detroit and Michillimachinac	0	4	0
Cumberland and Nova Scotia	0	4	0
Chartres, Kaskaskias, Illinois country	0	4	0
Oswegatchie	0	4	0
Total	25	2	0

N. B.   Like establishment for the year 1775.

Distribution of His Majesty's troops, British and Foreign for the Campaign, 1777.

(In Sir Wm. Howe's (secret) of 2d April.)

Pensylvania	11,000
Town of York and Island	3,200
Paulus Hook	300
Staten Island	1,200
Rhode Island	2,400
	18,100

N. B.   Prisoners with the rebels, sick artillery and cavalry not included.

Also a corps of Provincials, consisting of 3000 effectives, under the command of his Excellency Governor Tryon.

Monthly Return of the following Corps of His Majesty's Forces in North-America, under the Command of General the Hon. Sir William Howe. July 1, 1777.

Regiments	Battalions	Companies	Dates of Returns	COLONELS.
16th Light Dragoons		6 troops	1st July 1777.	Lieutenant General Burgoyne,
17th ditto		6 ditto	Ditto,	Major General George Preston,
Foot guards	two		Ditto,	Commanded by Brigadier Gen. Edw. Mathew,
4th Foot		10	Ditto,	Lieutenant Gen. Right Hon. Hugh, Earl Percy,
5th do		10	Ditto,	Lieutenant General Studholme Hodgson,
7th do		10	Ditto,	Major General Richard Prescott,
10th do		10	Ditto,	Lieutenant General Edward Sandford,
15th do		10	Ditto,	Major Gen. Right Hon. Rd., Earl Cavan,
16th do		10	1st April 1777	Major General James Gisborne,
17th do		10	1st July 1777,	Lieutenant Gen. Honnorable Rob. Monkton,
22d do		10	Ditto,	Lieutenant Gen. Honourable Thomas Gage,
23d do		10	Ditto,	General Honourable Sir William Howe,
26th do		10	Ditto,	Major General Lord Adam Gordon,
27th do		10	Ditto,	Major General Eyre Massey,
28th do		10	Ditto,	Major General Charles Gray,
33d do		10	Ditto,	Lieut. Gen. Rt. Hon. Charles Earl Cornwallis,
35th do		10	Ditto,	Major General Henry Campbell,
37th do		10	Ditto,	Major General Sir Eyre Coote,
38th do		10	Ditto,	Major General Robert Pigot,
40th do		10	Ditto,	Colonel Sir Robert Hamilton, Baronet,
42d do		10	Ditto,	General Lord John Murray,
43d do		10	Ditto,	Lieutenant General Hon. George Carey,
44th do		12	Ditto,	General James Abercromby,
45th do		10	Ditto,	Lieutenant General William Haviland,
46th do		10	Ditto,	Major General Honourable John Vaughan,
49th do		10	Ditto,	Major General Hon. Alexander Maitland,
52d do		10	Ditto,	Lieutenant General John Clavering,
54th do		10	Ditto,	Major General Marisco Frederick,
55th do		10	Ditto,	Major General James Grant,
57th do		10	Ditto,	Lieutenant General Sir John Irwin,
60th do	{ second, third, fourth }	3, 9, 10	1st April 1777,	Major General James Robertson,
			Ditto,	Colonel John Dalling,
			Ditto,	Brigadier General Augustine Prevost,
63d do		10	1st July 1777,	Major General Francis Grant,
64th do		10	Ditto,	Major General John Pomeroy,
71st do	two { first, second }	20	Ditto,	Major General Simon Fraser,
Marines	second	10	Ditto,	
Royal Fl. Americans		6	Ditto,	Lieut. Colonel Joseph Gorham, Commandant
Royal Hd. Emigrants		10	Ditto,	Lieut. Colonel Allen McLean, Commandant

The total English force in America on that date, under Sir William Howe, was 2076. Under the head "Prisoners with the Rebels" appears: Serjeants, 51; Drummers and Fifers 31; Rank and File 1211.

I have written to the Commander in chief, for one thousand Spanish dollars; when I receive it, a Proclamation will issue, offering a Reward of one Hundred for him, (G. Tryon) Colonel Robinson, and Colonel Emerick, to any Non Commissioned Officers or Soldiers, who shall deliver either to the officer commanding my advanced Posts. The present Scarcity of Bread, favors my Design. To give the Proclamation the fullest and most general Efficacy, I must promise to procure a Pardon, to the Subjects of this State, if any shall be of the Number, who shall execute that good Service. Can you by the Constitution, enable me to do it? Will the Legislature by a short act for a limited Time enable me? They may rest assured, it will not be abused. No Time is to be lost, if its to be attempted. And the Prospect is too favorable to be lost. And the Enemy dare not keep any of his Centeries at Night, without the Redoubts. From the Solicitude of the Enemy to get a Plan of our Works at this late Season, the Number of Spies he has out, and other concurring circumstances, it is abundantly clear to me, he intends to disturb these Posts early, which he can do by water without waiting for Grass. He knows the State of our Supplies, from whence they are drawn, as well as we do; and the Cause of the principal Part of the army, going to Jersey. If that Event takes place, it will be impossible for Flour, to come on from Elk, before, to support the Grand Army on its movement, to Hudson's River. Provision therefore should be made for such Event. If the Exportation of Flour, is not immediately stopt, except for the army, at Providence and the Corps at Danbury, and those under the most circumspect Regulations, there will not be Subsistance, left for those three Brigades till the next Crop comes in.

There is a compleat System formed, by the Enemy to get Flour from this State. The numerous agents, who have hard money in plenty, who have never had any great quantity of any, evince this. The Channel is via Stanford and Norwork, &c. where Cargoes are shipped, as Supplies for New London, Martha's Vineyard and Nantucket. When they get into the Sound, some are taken by Collusion, others are sent from two last mentioned to New York.

Robert Murray is on Long Island, with a Store of Goods, which makes one Link of the Chain. A few Days will put Materials in my Possession, which will develope the whole Scheme. Such is the vast quantity of hard money on the Eastern Borders of this State, and this County in particular, that neither the Commissaries, or those who want Wheat or flour for their own Use, can purchase any, altho' vast Quantities of both are continually going out of the State. Whatever price these offer, those outbid them, either in Continental Money, hard, Molasses or salt. And some of those, have the Impudence to assert, they are employed by the public. This high Sale of the Staple, would be very advantagious to the State, if the supporting the army of our inveterate Enemy, and the disbanding our own, was not the inevitable Consequence. To prevent so capital a Catastrophry, I have thought of the following Plan, which I beg Leave to suggest to your Consideration:

All former Permits for Exportation to be cancelled, by a certain Day. The principal Commissary of Issues of the army for the present, to certify, by every Team, that the Flour is for the army out of this State at Providence, or Danbury as the Case may be, or is intended for it. And the Certificate to be valid but for as many Days, as are necessary to carry the Load out of this State. No Flour to be exported, for any Purpose, after a Day you shall appoint, but on your Permits in pursuance of the following Regulation. A Circular Letter to be written to the officers commanding those armies, to certify to you, the quantity which they will want per Day, or Month. This to be divided, into as many Permits, as the Loads, in which it must be carried out. And two or more Routes mentioned, by Proclamation, in which the Flour in question, for the public Service is to go out; and a person placed on to each, to receive and cancel the Permits.

This plan or some other like it, would supply the army out of the State, and prevent the abuse which is universally made of large Permits, to Persons who obtain them, for public and private use, and are prostituted to the vilest purposes. It is not sufficient, in the present State of the army, that there is wheat and Flour enough in the State, for its Support. It must be collected in Season, while the Sledding and Roads are good, otherwise the want of Forage, and the Condition which public and private Cattle will be in, the latter part of Winter and Spring, will be as fatal to us as if there was not a single grain of one, or pound of the other, in the State. The officers and men of those Troops, however orderly, are very sore at the Merchants and Farmers of their own State, starving their Families. And altho they both submit now to the Drudgery of Brutes, the want of provision, will increase the Discontent, and burst into a Flame, which cannot be quenched. Once the Cord of Discipline is broke, it will not be easily if ever united. The Consequence to this State is obvious. In a few Days, I shall transmit you an Extract of the Rations, daily issued at the different Posts, and what Flour is purchased. I beg Leave to inclose you, a printed copy* of my orders for the Lines. They are the best I could devise. If the

---

* Not found.

Legislature will take up the Subject, and mend those, to answer the objects I shall be very happy. The Deserters Subjects of this State will be sent up as you desire. But it often happens, I am obliged to detain some of them, for stool Pigeons.

From the Length of this Epistle, you would naturally conclude I had much Leisure. but I can assure you, I have had fifty Interruptions, since I began. I am therefore obliged to send it to you very incorrect, and with many imperfections. I am my Dear Sir Your affectionate Friend and very humble Servant,

Alex'r McDougall.

Governor Clinton.

[No. 2052.]

Lieutenant-Colonel Weissenfels Solicits Promotion to the Rank of Colonel.

Rochester Jan'r 17t 1779.

Sir, I have Experienced the high favour of my Country When I wass apointed to a Post of Honor, (which ofice I flatter myself has to the best of my abilietys been held by me, to the advancement of Militairy Discipline, and to the full Execution of the trust Reposed in me) but as there is yet Room left, for a further advance by the Resignation of Col. H. B. Livingston,* I beg leave to adress my self to your Excellency, if you and the Honorable Consel of Apointment, schould think me a proper object, to fill that Vacancy that I may be apointed.

As by the arrangement of this State, and by a Resolution of a Board of General officers, (of which I herewith inclose a Copia) I humble Supose I have a Rigth to.

Your Excellency will Pardon me, When I intrude on your more material Concerns of Government, with this my humble Request,

---

* Weissenfels failed to obtain this promotion.—STATE HISTORIAN.

for nothing Could be more Conducive to my hapines, then to Continue in the Service of my Country. I am with the greatest Respect Your Excellency's Most Obiedient Most humble Servant

Fred: Weissenfels.

His Exellency George Clinton, Esqr, Poughkepsy.

Governor Clinton's Reply.

Pokeepsie, Jan'y 20" 1779.

Sir, I have rec'd your Letter of the 17" Inst. with its Inclosure. I have yet rec'd no official Notice of the Resignation of Colo. Livingston; as soon as it is transmitted to me I will lay it before the Council of Appointment from whom I have not the least Doubt you will meet with the strictest Justice in respect to your Rank. I am &c.

[G. C.]

[To Lieut. Col. Weissenfels.]

[No. 2053.]

A Compliment to John Jay from His Colleagues.

Phila. 21st Jan'y 1779.

Sir, We have to address your Excellency on a Subject which is honorable to our Constitutuents and of great use to the United States. Our worthy Colleague Mr. Jay since his Elevation to the Chair by filling it with Dignity and Impartiality, hath given such general Satisfaction that we are by no means singular in our Regret that we are so soon to be deprived of his abilities in that important Office. We are not ignorant of the Benefits which the State would derive from his Presence and Services on the Bench of Justice and in the Council of Revision. We therefore shall make no Request. Permit us Sir thro your Excellency to assure the Legislature that should they think proper to extend his appointment to the End of the year* it will be agreable to the several Members of Congress and particularly so to Your Excellency's most obedient & humble Servants

Fra's Lewis
Gouv'r Morris.

P. S. Having prepared the above Letter and shewn it to Mr. Duane, he declined signing it, unless he could previously know whether Mr. Jay approved of it, which (having sounded him on the Subject before) I ventured to assure him that I believed he did not. Tho from motives of Delicacy as your Excellency will easily perceive a Communication of the Letter would have been improper. Mr. Floyd also declined the Signing of it, tho he approvd of the Contents but observed that he did not like to dictate a Conduct to his Constituents. I thought it material to say this much lest it should seem extraordinary that the Letter was only signed by Mr. Lewis and myself.

I am respectfully Your Excellency's obed't & humble Serv't

Gouv'r Morris.

[To G. C.]

[No. 2054.]

The Massachusetts Council Ask Leave to Purchase 3,000 Barrels of Flour for Boston.

State of Massachusetts Bay. Council Chamber, Boston, January 21st 1779.

Sir, The Inhabitants of the Town of Boston, having represented to this Court, that by Reason of the long Embargo on Provisions in the Southern States, the many Captures of the Enemy, & the Operation of an Act of your Assembly prohibiting the exportation

of Flour & Grain, which altho calculated on the Principles of true
Policy, Patriotism & humanity, for restraining Monopoly & providing for the Army, contributes to render the supply of those Articles so very partial, as to threaten all the Miseries consequent on a
total Want of Bread, in this populous City, unless speedily prevented by a Suspension of said Prohibition, so far at least as to
allow the Exportation of about three Thousand Barrels of Flour
for their present Necessities.

Anxious to prevent such complicated Distress, we most earnestly recommend to your Sympathy & good Offices, this unhappy
People, who may be relieved by being permitted to purchase &
transport the Quantities of Flour & Grain aforesaid into this
State.

The Agents for whom we would solicit this Permission will
bear Letters Sign'd by John Rowe or Isaac Smith Esqrs., or other
the Chairman of a respectable Committee appointed by their
Fellow Citizens to effect this Supply.

Fully confiding in your Benevolence, in facilitating their Ex-
ertions for the Relief of their Constituents, We are, With due
Respect, Your Excellency's Most Obed't hble. Servants In the
Name & behalf of the General Assembly

                                        Jer. Powell, Presid't.
His Excell'y Gov'r Clinton.

[No. 2055.]

Governor Clinton Through His Secretary Writes a Circular Letter
Bearing on the Subject of Impressing Sleds.

                                        Jan'y 23d [1779].

Sir, I inclose you by the Gov'r's Direction, a Number of Letters for the Justices of such Precincts as you think will best be
able to supply you with a sufficient Number of Sleds for public

Service. If you should find it necessary to call upon more for their assistance you will transmit me the Number of Copies requisite and they will be signed by his Excellency. The inclosed Letters you'l please to direct and seal before they are delivered. I am &c.

Colo. Hay.

THE GOVERNOR'S LETTER.

Pokeepsie Jan'y 23 1779.

Sir, I am informed by Colo. Hay D'y Qu'r M'r Genl. that the public service thro his Department suffers exceedingly by the Difficulty of obtaining Teams when wanted. At the same Time he acquaints me that this Difficulty might be obviated and the Inhabitants of the state not so frequently called upon as they are at present for their Horses and Carriages if while the snow is on the Ground proper Exertions were made use of for a few Days only to supply him with a sufficient Number of sleds by which means magazines may be laid in before the opening of the spring & military operations be greatly facilitated. Let me therefore intreat you to give him every aid which the Law will warrant and particularly to oblige the unwilling who have hitherto evaded their Duty to bear a Part of the Burthen. I am &c.

[No. 6415.]*

Brother Charles Clinton Writes to General James in Regard to a Dispute Over the Sale of a Farm.

Hanover, January the 25th 1779.

Dear Brother, I expected to have wrote to you by your wife and to have seen George Denniston after my Return from Pough-

---

*From Volume XXIV, Clinton MSS.

keepsie, but was disappointed through the Neglect of my Servants not informing me of the message she had sent me about ther going Tuesday morning, and my coming Home only the night before about midnight. My Brother George, advised me to write to you to request you would give your Evidence before a Justice of the Peace of what you know concerning the Dispute between David Mulford and me relating to our agreement about the Currency he was to pay me for my Farm, or how you apprehended that matter; as also my Objections to receiving any other than the Old Currency, vizt. Gold or Silver, and old York and Jersey Bills, at the Time the Writings were executing between us, when he was to make the first Payment; and whether he denyed at that Time he was to pay me the Price of my Farm in the old Currency; or what Part thereof did he acknowledge he was to pay me in the above Currency? And whether he did not promise or agree upon my complying to accept of the Currency he tendered me in the first Payment, that he would pay me all the other Payments in the Currency above mentioned? And what you understood to be the Reasons I accepted the first Payment in the Currency he then tendered me? These Questions, or whatever you or George Denniston can recollect (As perhaps you may be able to assist each others Memories of what passed on this Subject when you were both present) I hope you will strictly attend to. It was for this Reason I wanted to see George Denniston after I had advised with my Brother George upon the Subject. If you can recollect he acknowledged that our agreement was, when you was about drawing the Articles of agreement, that he was to pay me in the different Currencys mentioned or in the Old money, or that I mentioned it before you and he acceded to it, it would prove the Intention of the Agreement. This I hope you will immediatly communicate to George Denniston. You may perhaps recollect a Circumstance that perhaps may be material, after Mulford first talked to me about buying the Farm; namely, that I called you aside into your new Parlour, and told you I intended to make him pay me the Price of it in the Old Currency. I remember it perfectly well with what you replyed. Your Evidence when taken as above, you will be pleased to transmit, inclosed in a Letter to me under Cover, directed to my Brother George as soon as possible, if a safe and more direct Opportunity should not offer. Your Family is well. No News here. If you have any, please to communicate it. I am your affectionate Brother.

Char's Clinton.

Brigadier General James Clinton.

[No. 2056.]

Colonel Malcom Attacks Dram Shops.

Haverstraw Jan. 26th 1779.

D'r Sir, It is my duty to report to your Excellency that almost everyhouse in this neighbourhood is a dramshop, & the consequence is likely to be the ruin of the troops. When they are under such temptations they will drink, & when their money is out they will Rob or steal. I know not what, or whether a military officer has any authority to correct such abuses, nor do I know what Laws the state hath made concerning them, but I am sure if there are none as yet it is time to sett about it. So many of them are the source of many of the evils that prevail in the country & the morals of the inhabitants as well as soldiery are corrupted thereby. I pray your Excellency will be pleased to inform me what I can do in the present case.

By accident I mett with the inclosed paper,* it serves to shew what kind of trade your officers are following on the Frontiers about Minisinck. I put a catalogue of the articles which they call Booty on the back of the certificate, which was given to procure the goods from a person who had stopt them as stolen. Our officers are anxious to know the fate of their application to the Legislature. I have the Honor to be with great Respect Your Excellency's much oblidged and very hum'e Servant.

W. Malcom.

[To G. C.]

[No. 2057.]

Massachusetts War Office Asks Governor Clinton for 100 Barrels of Flour for the State of Massachusetts.

War Office, Boston, 27th Jan'y 1779.

Sir, The Board of War have contracted with Mr. Joseph Ketchum who will have the honor to deliver you this, for one Hundred Barrels of Flour for the use of this State. As that Article is extremely wanted, and the danger of importing it by water very great, we are to request your Excellency to grant permission to transport the same from your State to this unmolested.

We have the honor to be with very great respect Your Excellency's most obed't & very humble Servants.

By order of the Board.

John Browne, President p temp.

His Exc'y George Clinton Esqr.

[No. 2058.]

General McDougall Building a Log Prison for Culprits and Spies.

Head Quarters Pecks Kill January 27th 1779.

My Dear Sir, I have a thousand things to say to you, which must be reserved to a tete a tete. The tory Culprits and Spies

---

*See page 501.

increase greatly on my Hands, and before the opening of a Campaign, their Number will be very considerable. I am, therefore, building a Log Prison, to secure them.

Poughkeepsie is so far from the Lines, and many of the West Chester People find it difficult, to get Security, which induce me to wish a Board of Commissioners would be constituted here, or at Crumpond. By the York Papers, I find Brigadier Leslie commands on Staten Island. He must have a considerable Number of British with him, in addition to those I mentioned to you. Delancy's Brigade is certainly on Long Island.

Brave as your Militia are, in the lower Part of West Chester, there are great Rogues among them, Thieves and Robbers, as Mr. Barkley will inform you. I wish you would Court Martial them. I am, my Dear Sir Your Humble Servant

Alex'r McDougall.

His Excellency Governor Clinton.

[No. 6416.]*

Mr. DeWitt Writes of Family Matters to General James Clinton.

Rochester, ye 27 January 1779.

Dear Brother, Having an oppertunity to Send you these Few Lines can inform you that I, family and all Friends are at Present in Tolarable Health, Thanks be to God; we have had a Troublesome Time last Summer as you without Doubt have heard; continuelly Expected to be attacted by the Savages and their Bloody Associates but have been preserved by Him who governs all. My Son Simeon, has been home a fitnight but is returned to Ringwood where he will keep his winter Quarters; he Likes the Business Midling well. I am informed that Sister Polly is gone up to Albany and is I Expect about this Time there. I beg the favour if you possible can to call on Coll. Morgan Lewis, or his Clerk, Mr. Tuenis Vanvechten, at his office in Albany. Desire him to give you a Copy or Abstract of the Ac't of the Committee of Rochester which I left with him September Last and Send the Same with Polly. She may Leave the Same with my Daughter Anne who Lives near the New Paltz. I will be very glad if you can do it, as I can't pay out the Money before I have a Copy of said acc't, and will prevent a Journey to Albany which is Expensive. I have wrote Several times for a Copy of the acc't and aways proved Abortive; and if you wife is Gone before this comes to hand be pleased to Send the same with another Safe hand to Dirck Wynkoop, Esqr. at Kingston. With my Respects to you and Sister, I Remain your Affectionate &c.

A. D'Witt.

P. S. a few Lines from you will be agreeable to me.

James Clinton, Brig. Gen., Albany.

[No. 2059.]

Walter King, Wounded at Fort Montgomery, Petitions for Relief.

To his Excellency George Clinton Esquire Governor of the State of New York, General and Commander in Chief of all the Militia and admiral of the Navy of the Same.

The Petition of Walter King, of Orange Town, in the County of Orange.

Most Humbly Sheweth, That on the Sixth Day of October Anno Domini One thousand Seven Hundred and Seventy Seven, your Petitioner was and for some time had been in the service of this State, as a private in a Company of Militia then commanded by Captain Humphrys of Ulster County.

That on the said Sixth day of October, your Petitioner was at

the Forts in the Highlands, where the said Company was Stationed for the defence of the same; that in the attack which the
Enemy on that day made on the said Forts, your Petitioner received a wound thro' the Body with a musket ball, which wound is
Still running and no prospect of being healed.

That your Petitioner after having received the said wound, with
difficulty made his Escape from the enemy and got to a House
in the Highlands, where he lay for about Seven weeks without
being in a proper Condition to be moved, much less to attend your
Excellency when Sent for.

And that your Petitioner has not received any pay for his loss
of time nor had any other assistance from the publick, during
the time he has been wounded, and Conceiving it but Equitable
that those who in the publick Service are rendered unable to Support themselves, should be assisted by the publick.

Your Petitioner therefore humbly prays, that your Excellency
will take his Case into Consideration, and endeavour to procure
him such relief and assistance as to your Excellency shall seem
Just and Equitable.

And your Petitioner Shall ever Pray &c. &c. &c.

                                        Walter King.
Orange Town January ye 28th 1779.

THE LEGISLATURE REASSEMBLES.

*Governor Clinton Transmits Recent Congressional Legislation and
Emphasizes the Serious Condition General McDougall's Army
is In.*

*Gentlemen of the Legislature,

I take the earliest Opportunity afforded me, of laying before
you the Resolutions of Congress, of the 2d Instant, on the Sub-

ject of Finance, among other Matters, calling upon the different States for their respective Quota's of Fifteen Millions of Dollars in the present Year, and of Six Millions of Dollars annually, for eighteen Years thereafter, as a Fund for sinking the Loans and Emissions of these United States, to the thirty-first Day of December 1778, inclusive; with their Resolutions of the 5th Instant, fixing the said Quotas—As the Objects of these Resolutions are to prevent the Necessity of further Emissions of Paper Money, to restore the Credit of the Paper Currency, and ultimately to discharge the public Debts, it is of the first Importance, that proper Measures be speedily taken, for effectually carrying them into Execution—You will also herewith receive an Act of Congress, of the 26th of September last, for organizing the public Treasury, among other Resolutions, recommending to the several States to enact Laws for the taking of such Persons, and also to seize the Property of Persons, who, being indebted to the United States, shall neglect or refuse to pay the same—And an Act of the first Instant, recommending to the several States, to adopt such measures, as may be effectual for detecting Persons employed in making counterfeit Bills, or passing the same, knowing them to be such.

Geo. Clinton.

Poughkeepsie, January 28, 1779.

---

*Gentlemen of the Legislature,

It affords me particular Pleasure, to have it in my Power to transmit you Copies of the Treaties of Amity and Commerce, and of Alliance eventual and defensive, between his Most Christian Majesty and these United States. As they are evidently founded on Principles equally beneficial to both Countries, and evince the

---

*From Journals of the Legislature.

Justice as well as good Policy of our great and generous Ally, they cannot fail of affording your Constituents the highest Satisfaction.

With this Message will also be delivered to you, merely for your Information, several Acts of Congress, of the 26th August, 1776, and 25th September, 1778, and of the 24th November, 1778; and also a Copy of a printed Pamphlet, entitled, "Extracts from the Journal of the House of Representatives of the State of Vermont," with Copies of several other Papers respecting the disaffected Subjects in the North-Eastern Parts of this State.

Geo. Clinton.

Poughkeepsie, January 28, 1779.

---

*Gentlemen of the Legislature,

I herewith submit to your Consideration, Copies of three Letters dated the 11th of November, from a Committee of Congress, appointed to superintend the Commissary's and Quarter-Master's Departments, requesting the Aid of the Legislature in correcting Abuses committed in those Departments, and for punishing the Offenders; and for enabling Congress to acquire a Knowledge of the Resources of this State, with Respect to Supplies for the Army; and also a Letter of the 20th Instant, from Colonel Udny Hay, Deputy-Quarter-Master-General, at Fish-Kill, representing the Difficulties he experiences in the Execution of his Office, and the consequent Distresses of the Soldiery. Permit me to add, Gentlemen, That from the best Information I have been able to obtain, the Division of the Army under the Command of Major-General M'Dougal, (on which our present Security against the Incursions of the Enemy depends) subsists upon a precarious Supply of Provisions daily procured for them, and there is the

---

*From Journals of the Legislature.

greatest Reason to fear they will be obliged to abandon their present Posts, and retire into the interior Parts of the Country. The present Difficulties under which the Army labours (you will observe) is imputed, by the Quarter-Master-General, to the Want of the necessary Number of Teams, for the Transportation of Provision to the Camp, and for other Services, owing in a great Measure, to Defects in the Law for regulating Impresses. I would, therefore, recommend the making of such Amendments in that Law, for enlarging the Powers vested in the ordinary Magistrate, as to render it more adequate to the Purposes for which it was intended.

Poughkeepsie, January 28, 1779.

Geo. Clinton.

[No. 2060.]

Congress Makes Provision for Payment for Certain Commissary Stores on Governor Clinton's Certification.

In Congress, January 30th, 1779.

A letter of 29th from General Washington was read, with an extract of a letter from Governor Clinton enclosed, representing "that after the loss of the Forts in the Highlands a part of the army was detached on the west side of the river which joined by a part of the militia were under his command; that the river being the bounds between the different purchasing commissaries, none could be found to supply the Troops, in consequence whereof, he was reduced to the necessity of taking from the inhabitants the necessary supplies of flour and cattle which were delivered to the issuing commissaries who passed their receipts to the owners; that similar measures were taken by the quarter masters to obtain forage; that different applications have been made to have these accounts settled and paid but without effect" Whereupon,

RESOLVED, That, the quarter master and Commissary General be authorized & directed to pay such of the said accounts as are certified by Governor G. Clinton.

Extract from the Minutes.

Chas. Thomson sec'y.

[No. 2061.]

Monthly Return of Colonel Snyder's Regiment for January, 1779.

A Return of the first Regiment in Ulster County Commanded by Coll. Johannis Snyder as Returned to the Said Coll. by the Severall Commanding officers of the Companys of Said Regiment To witt.

Capts. Names & N.	N. of the Subaltron officers.	Non Commis'd officers.	Rank & file.	the amount of the Companys Including officers.
Capt. Silvester Salisbury	1	3	4	43	51
Capt. Tobias Vanbeuren	1	2	8	34	45
Capt. Evart Bogardus	1	2	8	23	34
Capt. Jan L D witt	1	3	8	33	45
Capt. Hendrick Schoonmaker	1	1	8	41	51
Capt. Mattys Ded rick	1	2	8	40	51
Capt. Jeremiah Snyder	1	3	8	32	44
Capt. Philip Swart	1	3	8	41	53
Liut. Simon Lafever	1	1	8	43	53
	9	20	68	330	427

The amount of the Regiment Noncommissioned officers and Privates is 398 men.

Joh's Snyder, Coll.

Bever Kill 1779 Ja'ry 30th.

[No. 2062.]

John Jay Writes Governor Clinton of the Battle Between the French and English at St. Lucia, W. I., and of d'Estaing's Defeat.

Philadelphia 31 Jan'y 1779.

Dear Sir, Whatever may be the Reasons or Causes which have hitherto prevented my recieving any Letters from you: I shall continue running you in Debt, in full Confidence of your ability, and Expectation of your future Inclination, to ballance the account.

There are Letters in Town, tho not to Congress, from Persons of Reputation in Martinique which give the following Information vizt: that a British Fleet under Commodore Hotham with a Body of Troops had made a Descent on the Island of St. Lucia and without opposition taken possession of it; that not long after, Count D'Estaing endeavoured to Retake it; that the Batteries at the mouth of the Harbour prevented his Fleet, tho of superior Force from annoying that of the Enemy; that he landed a considerable Body of Troops and attempted to carry the Fort by assault, that he was repulsed with Loss & retired from the Island; that one ship of war out of six sent to reinforce him from Toulon, had arrived, the Rest were daily expected; that Admiral Byron had not yet appeared; that the Count had been very succesful in making Prizes; that the Goals and public Buildings in Martinique were full of British Prisoners.

As to the operations in Georgia, I can give you no further Information, and indeed not quite so much as you will find in the enclosed News Papers.

Be pleased to make my Compliments to Mrs. Clinton & other Friends at Poughkeepsie. I am Dear Sir Your Friend & hble. Serv't

John Jay.

His Excellency Gov'r Clinton.

[No. 2063.]

JAMES CLINTON FORWARDS LETTERS.

A Fort Building at German Flats—Rations Supplied to the Sufferers from Indian Raids—Exchange of Prisoners.

Head Quarters Albany Jan'y 31st 1779.

Dear Sir, In consequence of the Instructions contained in your Excellency's Letter of the 23d Ulto. relative to the exchange proposed by Capt'n Butler; Genl. Schuyler & myself concluded to dispatch Colonel John Campbell and a certain Jacob Newkirk as a Flag, with a Letter to Niagara, or any other place where they might hear Butler was—a Copy of which Letter,* together with the report made by Col. Campbell on his Return I inclose for your Excellency's Information.

I have also enclosed a Copy a Letter † from Fort Schuyler containing the Resolutions of the Oneidas, Tuscaroras & Onondagas at whose request, (with the advice of Congress) I have ordered a fort to be built at the Oneida Castle, where I expect a considerable Body of them will shortly be collected.

I hope the Legislater will take into consideration the Situation of the distressed Inhabitants of Cherry Valley. Applications have been so numerous from that Quarter that I have been obliged to furnish them (one hundred & fifty) with four weeks Provision, tho' I had no other authority for it, than the necessity of the Sufferers. I shoud be glad to have the Sense of the Assembly on that Subject.

By a return made by Col. Bellinger of the Inhabitants of German Flatts who are fed by the publick's Bounty, I find that there are one hundred & fifty two males & one hundred and sixty females upwards of sixteen years old, who draw full Rations, and three hundred & sixty five males & females under sixteen years old who draw half rations. This I mention for your Information as they still maintain Fort Dayton. I am with Esteem your Excell'ys humb'e Serv't,

James Clinton.

[To G. C.]

---

* See page 457.
† See pages 492 and 494.

[No. 2064.]

Lieutenant-Colonel de Roussi Makes a Request for a Vacant Colonelcy.

May it Please your Excellency,

Sir, I have been Informed this morning by an Express, that Colonel Henry B. Livingston's resignation was accepted in Congress the 13th Instant, and by the Said, the Command* of the 4th N. York Regiment is Devolved, upon me, unless your Excellency should be pleased to order it otherwais, on account of some pretentions that the other Lieut. Colonels of this state, have, by the arrangement of the Committee of Convention. But, as By Brevets, I have the Command of them in the Line of the army, I hope your Excellency will be kind enough to accord me his Protection, that the mistakes of that aboved named arrangem't may be rectified according to Ranks, and for further Satisfaction, I here Inclose (for your Excellency's Perusal) a Resolve of Congress, who confirms me my former Rank, and by which, a Board of Genl. officers Last winter in Valley Forge, give me Rank upon all the Lt. Cols. of the army, as none were found of an older Date. I have wrote already, to his Excellency the President of Congress about the same above purpose, which I hope you will not find amiss, as I expect the whole will be Left to your Excellency's Discretion. I am with Respect Your most obt. serv't,

    Pierre Regnier De Roussi, Lt. Col. 4th N. York Regt.

Fort Plank, Cunnogeharry January 31st, 1779.

His Excellency Governor George Clinton.

GOVERNOR CLINTON'S REPLY.

                Febry. 14" 1779.

Sir, I have rec'd your Letter of the 31st ultimo. Since the organizing of the Government there has been no Power vested in any Body to make appointments in the Continental Battalions.

---

*This officer failed to secure the coveted promotion.—STATE HISTORIAN.

The Legislature have now a Bill under their Consideration refering this Power to the Council of Appointment and I have
written to Congress for the arrangement made by their Committee of the 5 Continental Battalions. As soon as this Bill
shall become a Law and those Papers are received the Council
will proceed to the appointment of an officer to command Colo.
H. B. Livingston's Regiment, in doing of which I have not the
least Doubt they will observe the strictest Justice. I am &c.

[G. C.]

[To Lt. Col. De Roussi.]

[No. 2065.]

*Petition from Orange County for Pardon of Thomas Delamare.**

[No. 2066.]

*Petition from Orange County for Pardon of James Ryan.**

[No. 2067.]

*Petition from Orange County for Pardon of Mathew Dolson.**

[No. 2068.]

*Extract from a Letter of C. Stewart, Commissary of Issues, Relative
to Commissary Magazines in Connecticut.*

(————)

Extract of a Letter from C. Stewart Esq. Com'y Genl. of Issues.

His excellency Genl. Washington has mentioned to me, as
proper places for the principal magazines in Connecticut, Two,
Three or more of the following, viz. Litchfield, Sharon, Canaan,
Cambridge, Hartford & Simsbury, if any other are better adapted
in the Opinion of Genl. Putnam, his excellency will readily agree

*Omitted.

to them, On this Subject you will Consult Genl. Putnam and Inform me his Opinion. To Genl. Putnam also I must refer you solely, for the position of the magazines in the state of New York; he knows that Contry so well, that his Opinion will be Quite agreable to his Excellency.

[No. 2069.]

James Monell Willing to Resort to Extreme Measures in Order to Procure Supplies.

(————————)

Sir, Coll. Hay's instructions to me is to apply to your Excelency for an impress warant when ever I find aney of the inhabitants attempting to frustrate the Designs of the act of legislator in regard of Supplying the troops with provisions.

There is Sundry of the inhabitants that hes been assessed to deliver Beef that has attempted to deliver the porest Cattle in their flocks, which Cattle I have refused, and Can get no other without your Excelency warant.

There is a gentleman in my district, who informs me he has a Quantity of wheat Consel'd in his mill belonging to a dissaffected person. I pray for your Excellency authority to Seize it if youl please to grant it pray Send it by the Baror. I am Sir your Excellency's most obed't Hbbl. Ser't

Jas. Monell, Agent.

Gov'r Clinton.

[No. 2070.]

George Clinton Writes to Francis Lewis on the Deterioration of our Currency.

Feb'y 1st 1779.

Dear Sir, I have been favored with your Letter of the 31st Dec'r. I sincerely wish the Modes proposed by Congress for raising the Credit of our Currency may be attended with the desired Effects & if seconded with spirit by the Legislatures of the different States they will I hope at least prevent a further Depreciation. Ours is now sitting and are at present employed in the Business of Taxation. A Confiscation Bill is also before them—with other Bills of less Consequence as yet only known by their Titles.

I thank you for the Compliments of the Season and if not too late with Pleasure return them being &c.

[G. C.]

[To Francis Lewis.]

[No. 6417.]*

DU SIMITIERE WRITES TO GOVERNOR CLINTON.

Desirous of Adding His Portrait to the Collection He is Making of Distinguished Americans.

Sir, I have to acknowledge the favour of your Excellency's letter of the 8th December last & to return you my thanks for the honour you have done me, it would afford me the highest Satisfaction could I have it in my power to do Some thing to deserve the attention & the continuation of your Excellency's respectable correspondance, and I beg leave to assure your Excellency, that I Shall neglect nothing to make my Self deserving it, in Some measure.

It has been for want of opportunity that I have delayed writing So long. A person call'd on me the first day of the year, as from your Excellency desiring Some new publications; as it was but a verbal message & not particular, I was at a loss to give a proper answer & that person going away, as he Said immediately I had not time to procure Some thing new to Send you, but new

I cannot call it with propriety being almost a year old, yet they are the last that have found their way hither; I mean three numbers of the London Magazine for Jan'y, Feb'y & March 1778, which I take the Liberty to inclose, wishing they may be acceptable to your Excellency.

As I am persuaded that your Excellency See our news papers So you must be well inform'd of all the particulars of the unlucky & untimely dispute which has Subsisted for these two last months; therefore, Shall Say nothing further on the Subject.

I Shall now Say a few words relating to Painting, & acquaint your Excellency that a little more than two years ago, I formed the plan of having the pictures of the American chiefs & other most eminent personnages of this country in my collection, I begun it with your late worthy friend Mr. Philip Livingston, the likenesses are in profil done in black lead pencil, in imitation or to Serve for a large medal; my plan was interrupted for a considerable time; however, I added to it Since, General Gates, Gen. Mifflin, Gen. Arnold, who all very obligingly Sat for it; afterwards when the Ennemy was here, I copied a Striking likeness of Gen. Howe done by an officer of his army, and Capt. Montresor Sat for me also, but turn'd of a different Side, and yesterday by the favour of Mr. President Jay, I had the great Satisfaction of taking a good likeness of the great & amiable General Washington, who condescended to come with the President to my house, and Sat there three quarts of an hour, being all the time he could Spare, as it was the last day of his Stay in Town; and I have the pleasure to assure that it is approved by all who have Seen it. I have Several more in Expectation, but it is difficult for these Gentlemen, So much immers'd in public affairs, to find leisure Sufficient for that purpose. How happy Should I be to

be able to entertain your Excellency with the Sight of the Said
pictures and Several other curiosities relative to the times, which
my perseverance in their pursuit procures me now and then; but
with much less Success than if my circumstances afforded me
to visit the different States & renew my old & form new acquaintances; but I must rest Satisfied to my fate, and Submit.

I have had no answer from Col. Lamb to the letter I took the
liberty to inclose in mine to your Excellency, but I make no
Doubt it has come Safe to his hands.

I am in hope to have the honour to address your Excellency
another letter Soon, expecting Some thing which I Shall take
the liberty to Send, and Shall conclude at present with my assurances of the greatest respect. I have the honour to be Your
Excellency's most obedient & most Humble Servant

Du Simitiere.*

Philadelphia Feb'y 2d 1779.

His Excellency, Governor Clinton.

[No. 2071.]

*George Clinton Writes to Gouverneur Morris in Regard to Pending
Legislation at Albany.*

Feb'y 2d 1779.

Dear Sir, I wrote you on the 10" ult.† in answer to your Letters prior to that Date since which I have had the Pleasure of
rec'g yours of the 10" & 13". Mr. Yates has not yet favored me
with an answer to my Letter respecting the Papers & Maps respect'g our Boundaries. You may depend upon their being forwarded to you the moment they are rec'd. A sufficient Number of

---

* Pierre Eugene du Simitiere, a Swiss artist, was born in Geneva, and died in Philadelphia October 17, 1784. He became famous as a collector of curiosities. His heads
of thirteen notable Americans, which he painted, were published in a quarto volume in
London, a year before his death. His collection of Revolutionary manuscripts, data and
broadsides is deposited in the Philadelphia library.—STATE HISTORIAN.

† Not found.

the members of both Houses to form a Legislature did not meet
until the 27" so that they are only entering upon Business. A Tax
& Confiscation Bill have been read in the Assembly and are in
some Forwardness.

The Genl.* I am informed has announced this to be a Session
of Politics & has introduced the Scene by moving for a Bill in the
Senate for regulating the Council of Revision founded on Doubts
which I suppose never existed except in his own Mind whether a
Lieut. Gov'r a Presdt. of Senate administering the Govern't are
by the Constitution Members of the Council of Revision and
whether the Members of the Council of Revision are amenable
to the Laws of the Land for Mal or corrupt Conduct &c. in that
Capacity as Gov'r Chancellor &c. with a Clause for obliging the
Council to publish their Minutes as well past as future. You
will readily perceive that the Intent of this Law is to hold up
the Council of Revision to the Public in an obnoxious Point of
view as having been guilty of Malconduct concealed from the
Public sufficient to justify this Measure.

The Chancellor has not yet appeared or either of the Judges
so that I am deprived of their aid in warding off a wicked fac-
tious Measure which might perhaps be more easily defeated now
than at a later Period. I flatter myself however the present attempt
will prove abortive. The People of this State warmly interest
themselves in the political Controversy between Mr. Deane &
the Lees and without knowing more than the Gazettes inform
them pretty generally espouse the Cause of the former.

I send you our late Papers tho they are scarcely worth your
Perusal. The Farmer I know not. The language as well as
sentiment will discover to you the author of the real Farmer.

---

* General John Morin Scott, one of the Senators from the Southern district.—STATE
HISTORIAN.

Your Brothers are here & well. I have mentioned them your Desire that they should write to you frequently & am &c.

[G. C.]

Mr. McKesson who is just arrived from Albany informs me that Judge Yates has not the Papers & Maps. That they are not in his McKesson's Office nor can he tell where they are.

[To Gouverneur Morris.]

[No. 2072.]

Governor Clinton Intimates that Jeremiah Van Rensselaer will be Appointed Surveyor-General.

Poughkeepsie 2d Feb'y 1779.

D'r Sir, I do not believe the Appointment of a Surveyor Genl. will be made during the present Session as until the Mode of granting unapropriated Lands is pointed out & the proper Regulations made by the Legislature that Officer is not essentially necessary and the Time of the Council will be fully employed in appointing of such as are immediately so. You may rest assured, however, that if this Business is taken up by the Council, Mr. Rensslaer* shall be proposed with every advantage due to the Character you give him. I am &c.

[G. C.]

[To Gen. Schuyler.]

[No. 2073.]

The Governor Writes William Floyd briefly on Legislative Matters.

Feb'y 2d 1779.

Dear Sir, I have received your Letters of the 2 & 5 January and thank you for the Intelligence they contain. We have nothing here worth communicating. The Legislature were to have

---

*Van Rensselaer failed to obtain this appointment, which eventually went to General Schuyler.—STATE HISTORIAN.

met by their own adjournment on the 2d Tuesday in January, after the usual Delays they made Houses on the 27" ulto. A Taxation and Confiscation Bill have been brought in, in the Assembly, several other Bills are in earlier stages not yet officially known to me. You will oblige me by a Continuance of your Correspondence and I am Sir &c.

[G. C.]

[To Wm. Floyd.]

[No. 2074.]

William Floyd Writes to the Governor Concerning Count d'Estaing's St. Lucia Affair and Congressional Matters.

Philadelphia Feb. 2d 1779.

S'r, Inclosed I Send you a News papers which Contains the Chief of the News that is here, Except by a vessel Just arrived from Martinique in 13 days, and another at Baltimore in 10 days we are Informed, that the Count D'Estaing, Cruising in the West Indies in Expectation of meeting with the English, which went from New York last fall, unluckily mist of them; they went directly to St. Lucia and took that place, the Count Soon getting notice thereof went there; when he arrived, he found their Ships Covered with Such Strong Batteries that he did not think it proper to Risk his own to attack them, But Concluded to attack them by Land, for which purpose Landed his Troops, what number is uncertain; Some Say 5, 6, or more thousand men. The Count being apprehensive that Admiral Byron might arrive there with his fleet and be too Strong for him, which precipitated him to attack them by Storming their Stronghold, he was Repulsed with very Considerable Loss, Some Say near 1500 men; he Returned with the Remainder of his men and Ships to Martinique and is now Joyned by 6 Capitol Ships from France, and it is Said with Several Thousand men; this augmentation of his navy will make him Superior to Byron, and Enable him to Strike the Enemy where he pleases, without being under a necessity of makeing any Rash attempts.

The application you made to General Washington Sometime Since, with Respect to the Demands on the Commissary and Quarter master, and which they did not think them Selves authorised to pay, he laid before Congress, and they thereupon Resolved that the Commissary and Quartermaster be directed to pay all Such of those accounts as your Excellency Should Judge proper.*

I am Sorry as well as Grieved, that I am not able to Inform you that Something is done in that Important affair of Vermont.

There has nothing Important to our State, that has lately passed in Congress, the Grand Business which has for a Consider-able time taken up their attention and is not yet finished, is the arranging and Recruiting our army.

When any thing of Importance happens here I Shall do my Self the pleasure to Inform you. In the mean time I am S'r your most humble Serv't

Wm. Floyd.

His Excellency George Clinton Esquire.

[No. 2075.]

Governor Clinton Acknowledges Official Communications from John Jay.

Pokeepsie Feb'y 2d 1779.

Sir, I have rec'd your Excellency's several Letters of the 2d* 10"† 15§ & 22d† Jan'y and have now to inform you that the Papers they inclosed which required the attention of the Legis-

---

*See page 526.
†Not found.
§See page 484.

lature are submitted to their Consideration. I have the Honor
to be &c.

[G. C.]

[To John Jay, President of Congress.]

[No. 2076.]

Mr. Duer Resigns His Seat in Congress.

Pokeepsie Feb'y 2d 1779.

D'r Sir, I have rec'd your Favor of the 3d ult. and have wrote
to Judge Yates for the Maps & Papers you mention. These I
shall transmit you the moment I receive them as I would wish to
avoid every Cause of Delay at a Period which appears the most
proper & favorable for finally settling our Disputes with the Inhabitants of the Grants.

I have received from Congress their several Resolutions on
the Subject of Finance and have laid them before the Legislature,
and as a Tax Bill is now before them, I flatter myself it will be
so calculated as best to answer and execute in this State the
Intentions of Congress. If the Measures adopted shoud appreciate our Paper Currency ever so little, or even prevent a farther
Depreciation of it, in either Case I agree with you in your
Speculations on the Subject, but if they are inadequate & the
War continues another Campaign, the great Increase of our
necessary public Expenditures and the consequent further Depreciation of the Paper Money will, I fear, render it more difficult
to apply a suitable Remedy & the Consequences more fatal than
sudden appreciation of our Money to its nominal original Value.

My Regard for Mr. Duer as well as Justice will induce me to
do every Thing in my Power to make him happy. His Letters
notifying his Desire to resign his Seat in Congress were addressed

(and very properly) to the President of the Senate & Speaker of the Assembly. I coud not therefore consistently have said any Thing to the Legislature officially on the Subject, & indeed I conceived it needless, being informed at the Time that the Speaker was directed by the Assembly to acknowledge, the Receipt of Mr. Duer's Letter, the Sense they entertained of his Zeal for the Cause of his Country & his Exertions in its Favour. This I believe was done informally to avoid a Precedent which they did not wish to establish. I will remind the Speaker of this, least it may have slipped his Memory, & with Pleasure forward his Commands to Mr. Duer. I omit writing to Mr. Duer least he may have left Phil. before this reaches you. If not, Please to offer my best Respects to him & believe to be with great Respect &c.

[G. C.]

[To James Duane Esq.]

[No. 2077.]

THE GOVERNOR WRITES TO McDOUGALL.

Recognizes the Difficulties of His Position—Warns Him Against Tryon's Plots.

Poukeepsie 3d Feb'y 1779.

Dear Sir, Your Favour of the 23th [20th]* Ultimo came to Hand some Days ago. I am sensible from your Situation & nature of your Command affords you little Liessure & that you are perplexed with a variety of Impertinent Applications which add greatly to your Troubles. I am perswaded whatever Measures you may be oblidged to take out of the ordinary Line for supplying your Army will be calculated for the good of the public Service & warranted by such Evident Necessity & so conducted as to prevent any reasonable Cause of Complaints to the well

---

*See page 501 et seq.

disposed Inhabitants, & I may venture to say you will find the
Legislature as well as the Executive Authority of the State disposed to put the most favourable Constructions on your Conduct
& to render you every Assistance which they can consistently
grant.

Immediately on the Meeting of the Legislature, I submitted to
their Consideration a Representation of the Difficulties & Distresses under which the army labour for want of Provision &c.
In Consequence of which they came to certain Resolutions which
you will herewith receive in an official Letter of equal Date. A
Bill is also before them for ammending the Law for regulating
Impresses by which I am in hopes it will be rendered so effectual
& adequate for the Purpose for which it was intended as to have
the Qu'r Masters without a reasonable Excuse shoud the Wants
of the Army in future proceed from that Department.

The Accts. from New York in your Last Letter ought to put
you on your Guard. I have not a doubt but Tryon is sufficiently
wicked to Execute the Dark Work of Assassination.

The Troops stationed at this Place have behaved in the most
orderly manner & have thereby made themselves very agreable
to the Inhabitants, & having by indefatigable Industry repaired
their Barracks & laid in an ample Supply of Firewood their Quarters is become very comfortable & are therefore extreamly loath
to leave them. There is 4 Months pay now due to them and on
receiving orders to march to Fishkill they gave in decent Representation of their Case to their Major requesting their pay previous to their being oblidged to march but at the same disavowing every Idea of Mutiny. The Major who appears to be a Gentleman & good officer waited upon me last Night to advise on this
Occassion (determined however to compell their march at all

Events). We both agreed that Reluctance to leave their present Quarters Influenced them more than the Want of Pay. I, therefore, desired to ease their Minds on that Score by informing them that I woud write to you on the Subject & if they coud be spared from the Field they shoud ocuppy their present Quarters in preferrence to any other Regt. which I request may be the Case. I am my D'r Sir Yours Sincerely

[G. C.]

Genl. McDougal.

[No. 2078.]

COMMISSARY COLT TO GOVERNOR CLINTON.

Farmers Refuse to Sell their Produce for the Army—Abuses in the Commissary Department—Necessity for Storing Supplies.

Danbury Feb'y 4, 1779.

May it please your Excellency, From the most exact & thorough examination into the State of the public Stores, find we are in an alarming Situation respecting Flour; very little is purchased, more than is deliverd to the Magazines, & but few of the posts supplied for more than 20 Days. My assistants generally assured me that the Farmers refused to sell their new wheat (at the limeted price,) or Flour & yet its necessary that a large Quantity should be immediatly secured, that it may be seasonably transported to the various posts, before the roads become impassable. On this account I was induced to direct my assistants in your State to give Eight Doll's p bush. for good wheat, & Nine pound p ct. for Flour. I hope this will enable them to secure such Quantities as will support the Troops untill we can receive some assistance from the Southard. If, however, I should be mistaken in my oppinion & the Farmers still refuse to sell their produce, in hopes of extorting a higher price, or hard Money,

therefor must request the further aid and assistance of the Legislature of your State, to enable me to feed the Army.   Genl. Mc-
Dougall has assured me he will lay the state of Provisions &c.
before your Excellency, & give me every aid in his power.   He
has stoped a Quantity of Flour passing out of the State, part of it
belonging to Hillhouse.   I have directed Maj. Strang, whom I have
appointed an asst. for the Mannor of Cortland, to be very vigilant
in securing all the wheat & Flour in that Quarter & preventing its
being run out of the State; hope he will be able to make a considerable supply.   I find Mr. Hilhouse has imployd a set of Jobbers
to purchase wheat & Flour for him & that they have raised the
price of those articles greatly; he, one Darrow, & the private Jobbers, have cleared W't Chester County of the greater part of the
old wheat.   I am told that one Christopher Green has exported
large Quantities of wheat & Flour, which he engaged to supply
the Troops with in State Rode Island, & that a Capt. Woodard
had a permit for 400 bush. wheat, which he was to deliver to the
Com'y at the Eastward.   I must request the favour of yr. Excellency to know the truth of these reports, as Mr. Green has deliv'd
but a very little share of his Flour to the Com'y, & that at the
highest price in our late distress at Providence.   Woodward has
deli'd none.   I wish to know whether Mr. Hez. Johnson has had a
permit for about 40 bbs. since the one obtaind for the refugees
from Susquehannah.

Your Excellency will please to remember that you promised to
send me an account of Maj. Schenk's conduct respecting the re-
selling of public Flour.

I am with much Respect, your Excellency's most obd. hum.
Serv.

Peter Colt.

His Excellency Jas. (?) Clinton Esquire.

P. S. I have enquired into the report of Kaen's having sent
400 bbs. damaged Meat to W't Point; find he has not deliverd a
barel of his meat yet. Mr. Fitch assures me that Meat, about
200 bbs. is old Carolina pork recv'd from the Southard last summer. I have directd Mr. Schenk to get Kaen's, Coxe's & Waring's
Meat repacked by a Sworn Cooper before it is removed & to dismiss them from the Service.

I am informed that a report is propagated in your state, that
out of 17,000 bbs. of Flour reported to be on hand last June, belonging to the Army, not more than 3000 bar's has been delv'd &
that the Com's have sold the residue &c. But I can assure your
Excellency, that this Story is false & groundless; they reported
about 15,000 bbs. on hand last June, upwards of 13,000 have been
delv'd, the others were resold by the Farmers & Millers for want
of Mony to pay for the same. I am &c.

P. Colt.

[No. 2079.]

Rhode Island Depends Upon New York for Bread Stuffs.

Feb'y 4, 1779.

Sir, I have been honored with your Letter of the 11th ulto.,
have laid it before the Legislature now sitting and shall take
the earliest Opportunity of acquainting you with the Result of
their Deliberations on the Subject. If your Request is not complied with by the Legislature, I can venture to assure you that
influenced as they really are by Inclination to relieve the Distresses of the Inhabitants of the neighbouring States, the only
Reason that can operate with them for continuing the Embargo
Law will arise from a Desire of preventing the ruinous Consequences of disbanding the Troops (cantoned in this State) merely

35

for the want of Provisions of which they receive daily Complaints.

[G. C.]

[To Gov. William Greene, of Rhode Island.]

———

[Nos. 2080–2081.]

TO SUPPLY THE ARMY WITH BREAD.

Governor Clinton Forwards a Resolution of the Legislature and a Circular Letter to the Proper Persons.

Feb'y 4, 1779.

D'r Sir, The Legislature to obviate the Difficulties experienced in supplying the army at present & to excite the Commissaries to lay up Magazines for future Contingencies have come to the inclosed Resolutions. I transmit you several Letters left open for your Inspection which you will please to direct to the Commissaries supplying your Division. If you should esteem it necessary to have their Number increased you will of Course, if impowered, appoint such additional Number of proper Persons for the Duty & I will approve the appointments & am &c.

[G. C.]

Wm. McDougal of this Place, Archibald Currey of Hopewel & Benj'n Thusten of Goshen are ment'd to me as suitable Persons to assist the Commissaries but whether they woud accept an appointm't or not I am ignorant, & Joseph Genks of Charlotte Precinct in this County. The latter is recommended by Judge Platt & I have reason to believe will accept.

[To Gen. McDougall.]

———

THE CIRCULAR LETTER.

Feb'y 4 1779.

Sir, The many Complaints received of the Difficulties experienced in supplying the Troops cantoned in this State & its vicinity with Bread & the laying in Magazines for the ensuing Campaign have induced the Legislature to pass the inclosed Resolutions. I have therefore to request your most spirited Exertions for having them properly carried into Execution. If it shall hereafter be found that the Army is not duely supplied & sufficient Magazines laid in & the Commissaries have not exerted themselves in taking the Advantages afforded by the Laws of this State enacted for that Purpose all the ill Consequences resulting from the Neglect will with Justice be attributed to the Officers in that Department.

I am also to recommend that such an additional Number of diligent and honest Persons (as assistant Commissaries) as shall be sufficient for carrying into effectual Execution the present Intention of the Legislature be appointed if this is not already the Case and I shall chearfully give my approbation. I am &c.

[G. C.]

You will observe by the inclosed Resolution that the depositing of Money in the Hands of Millers (who can give proper Security) for purchasing wheat & Flour for public uses is particularly recommended & I have Reason to believe that large Quantities may be obtained in this way.

(Copies to Mr. Cuyler, Mr. Van Ness, Mr. Reed.)

[No. 2082.]

McDOUGALL NOT CREDULOUS.

Folly in Believing the Enemy will Evacuate the United States— Georgia in the Hands of the British.

Head Qu'rs Peeks Kill Feb'y 6th 1779, 7 P. M.

My dear Sir, I have this moment received the Paper which accompanies this. It will inform you, that Georgia is in Possession of the Enemy. America is asleep, & dreaming the Enemy will evacuate the United States. She, or two many of her silly sons, imagine the struggle is at an end,* but I wish we may not have to repent our shameful credulity & supineness. When you have perused it, please to send it Immediatly to Mr. Holt, I have sent it by express for the Public information.

My Jail will be compleat to morrow. And a fine one it is. It will secure without a Centery, fifty of the strongest Horse thieves in the Country. What keeps the Commission or Commissioners for detecting Conspiracies? My Compliments to your Lady, and the Gentlemen of my acquaintance of both Houses. I am my dear Sir Your affectionate Humble Servant

Alex'r McDougall.

Gov'r Clinton.

P. S. I beg Mr. Holt to return me the Paper by some safe hand whenever he has done with it.

GOVERNOR CLINTON'S REPLY.

Febry. 9, 1779.

D'r Sir, I am to thank you for your Favor of the 6" Inst. and the New York Paper it inclosed which I have disposed of agreable to your Request. I am at a Loss to determine why a Board

---

*February 7.—Yesterday being the anniversary of forming the alliance between France and the United States, the honorable the Congress at Philadelphia gave a public entertainment to his Excellency the Minister Plenipotentiary of his Most Christian Majesty, at which the following toasts were drank, under the discharge of cannon:

1. May the alliance between France and the United States be perpetual. 2. The United States. 3. His Most Christian Majesty. 4. The Queen of France. 5. His Most Catholic Majesty. 6. The Princes of the House of Bourbon. 7. Success to the allied arms. 8. General Washington and the army. 9. The friends of liberty in every part of the world. 10. May the new constellation rise to the zenith. 11. May the American stripes bring Great Britain to reason. 12. The memory of the patriots who have nobly fallen in defence of the liberty and independence of America. 13. A safe and honorable peace.

The cheerfulness which existed in the company upon the happy occasion of their being assembled was not to be exceeded, and a thousand brilliancies, alluding to the alliance, were uttered. There can be no doubt but that every true American and every true Frenchman will contribute his efforts to preserve that connection which is formed by the alliance, and which is so necessary to the happiness and aggrandizement of both nations. Their mutual interests dictate such a conduct in the strongest and most affectionate terms. The principles of the alliance are founded in true policy and equal justice; and it is highly probable that mankind will have cause to rejoice in this union which has taken place between two nations; the one the most puissant in the old, and the other the most powerful in the new world.—New Jersey Gazette, February 17, 1779.

of Comm'rs has not yet convened in the County of West Chester.
I gave orders for that Purpose a considerable Time ago, and know
not to what Cause to attribute the neglect unless to the Meeting
of the Legislature of which many of them are Members. I shall
however repeat my orders. I perfectly agree with you that the
general Expectation of the Enemy's intend'g to leave the Continent has done more Damage than their arms since that Idea
took Place. I wish this Deception may cease and our Exertions
reduce our Expectations to a Certainty. I am &c.

[G. C.]

[To Gen. McDougall.]

The Legislature Takes Action on the Clandestine Shipment of Flour.
*Gentlemen of the Legislature,

I herewith transmit you an Act of the Legislature of the State
of New-Hampshire, for preventing the Return to that State, of
certain Persons therein named, and of others who have left or
shall leave that State, or any of the United States of America,
and have joined, or shall join the Enemies thereof; and also a
Letter from the Honorable Jeremiah Powel, Esq; President of the
General Assembly of the State of Massachusetts-Bay, which I
received Yesterday, representing the Distresses that the Inhabitants of the Town of Boston are likely to experience, from the
Scarcity of Wheat and Flour, and requesting Permission to export Three Thousand Barrels of Flour from this State, for their
immediate Relief.

Geo. Clinton.

Poughkeepsie February 8, 1779.

The House resolved itself into a Committee of the whole House,
on his Excellency the Governor's Message, of the 8th Instant, and

*From Journals of the Legislature.

after some Time spent therein, Mr. Speaker resumed the Chair,
and Mr. Hoffman reported, That the said Committee had directed
him to report a Resolution, which being read, was agreed to by
the House.

And thereupon, Resolved, That in the Year 1777, the Northern
Frontier of this State, from Ticonderoga to within a few Miles
of the City of Albany, was by the Invasion of the Enemy, and the
Military Operations on the Part of these States to repel them,
laid Waste, and the Farmers not only prevented from gathering
in their Harvest, but also from putting Seed in the Ground for a
Crop the following Year; and that the Inhabitants in that Quarter
must, until the ensuing Harvest, procure their Wheat and Flour
from the other Parts of the State. That in the same Year, in
Consequence of the Loss of the Forts in the Highlands, the Enemy
from the Southward, invaded and penetrated into the most interior Parts of the State; and the Inhabitants from every Quarter
were called forth in its Defence, and necessitated to omit the
Cultivation of their Farms, in the Height of Seed Time—That,
during the Course of the last Year, several valuable Settlements
to the Westward, and from whence considerable Supplies of
Wheat usually obtained, have been destroyed—That this State,
having, since the opening of the Campaign in 1776, been the principal Seat of War; great Part of it, though not within the Power
of the Enemy, hath lain uncultivated; and the Farmers have been
incessantly called from the Cultivation of their Lands, either to
serve in the Militia, or to assist with their Cattle in transporting
Stores and Provisions for the Army—That the Troops and Prisoners, in this State and the Eastern States, have hitherto been
almost entirely supplied with, and still expect, their Flour from
this State—That, notwithstanding the Prohibition, great Quanti-

ties of Flour have been clandestinely carried out of the State, and
either exported or conveyed to the Enemy.—That until the late
Resolution of Congress for preventing it, Wheat was purchased
for Forage, and, while the Grand Army lay at the White-Plains,
consumed at the Rate of upwards of One Thousand Bushels per
Day; and at the other Posts, in the like Proportion.   That in many
Instances, the disaffected, to prevent us from obtaining a Supply
from them, have neglected to sow their usual Quantity of Grain—
That the Crops of the last Harvest, were generally slender, estimated at not above five Eighths of the ordinary Product—That
the Legislature are not informed of a competent Magazine of
Flour, provided in any Part of the State for the Army—That the
Supplies intended for the Troops in the Southern Department of
the State, are so extremely deficient, that we have Reason to fear,
the Posts in the Highlands and Westchester County, will be
abandoned, unless a speedy Supply of Flour is obtained—That
altho' no exact Account hath been taken of the Wheat and Flour
in the State, yet from every Information, there is Reason to conclude, that there is not more than a Sufficiency for the Subsistence
of the Inhabitants, and the Army—That tho' many of these Facts
are alarming, and as such ought undoubtedly to remain a Secret,
and concealed from the Enemy; yet that the Legislature, find
themselves constrained to communicate them in Confidence to
certain Persons, in whom they can confide, and who have applied
for Permission to export Flour, to convince them, that, consistent
with a due Regard to the Preservation of the Army, and the
Safety of the Common Cause, the Legislature cannot comply with
their Request—That no Flour or Wheat ought to be exported out
of the State, except for the immediate Purpose of the War, and
that the Prohibition on Exportation, doth not proceed from

partial or selfish Considerations, but was originally laid, and is still continued, from its absolute Necessity, and solely with a View to prevent the Enemy from receiving Supplies, and to preserve the Means of Subsistence for those Troops, on whom (under God) the Freedom and Independence of these States, so essentially depends—That more effectually to answer these Purposes, the Legislature have entirely precluded all Persons from purchasing, except for the Consumption of their respective Families, or for the Use of the Army—That these Regulations are very prejudicial to the private Interests of the Inhabitants of this State, as they are thereby deprived of the Opportunity of carrying their Produce to the highest Market, and consequently compelled to sell it at an under Rate—That the Feelings of the Legislature, for the Distresses of their Brethern in the Eastern States, can only be equalled by their Wishes to relieve them—That whenever the Legislature shall be informed, that proper Magazines are provided for the Army, and that a Surplus remains beyond the necessary Quantity, for the Support and Maintenance of the Inhabitants of the State; out of that Surplus, Permission will be freely granted to export any Provisions that may be necessary for the Support of their Fellow Citizens in the other States; and that the Legislature will deem themselves extremely happy, that an Opportunity will then be afforded, of contributing to their relief.

[No. 2083.]

JOHN JAY WRITES GOVERNOR CLINTON.

And Offers Suggestions Touching the Necessity of Supplying Rhode Island with Provisions.

Philadelphia 8th Feb'y 1779.

Dear Sir, Inclosed in a Letter of this day you will receive from me an Act of Congress requesting Connecticut & New York to afford a Supply of Provisions to the Inhabitants of the State of Rhode-Island* who are said to be in great distress for want of Bread.

This is a Subject which in my Opinion is to be treated with great delicacy. New York has credit for her Exertions to supply the army & the exhausted State of her resources is known. It is nevertheless hoped that she may be able to give some Releif to her starving Sister, & every motive of humanity & policy will advise it if practicable. Care however ought to be taken of our own Inhabitants, and the Releif, if afforded, should be so regulated as to prevent that amazing Exportation, & intolerable Rise in the price of Provision, which would follow an incautious tho' partial Refusal of the Embargo. Nor would it, I think, be wise to go into any measures in consequence of this recommendation without having previously consulted with the Commissary General, as well as with Connecticut; with the former, on the State of his Magazines, with the latter on the Subject of a joint plan. Unless there be an overplus to be spared from the Necessities of the army, & the Consumption of the Inhabitants all ought to be retained. If there be an Overplus in both States, would it be amiss for the Commissary to purchase & collect it at the Expence of Rhode-Island, & let the Government of that State cause it to be transported, and provide for its due distribution. The Poor of that State will otherwise be at the mercy of Engrossers, and, like the wretched Egyptians, under the vicegerency of Joseph, be obliged to give their hand for corn. I am, Dear Sir, Your Friend & Servant

John Jay.

His Excellency Gov'r Clinton.

---

*See Governor Clinton to legislature, February 18, page 580.

[No. 2084.]

CLINTON WRITES TO JAY ON LOCAL MATTERS.

Tax Bill Expected to Raise One Million Dollars—Fears the Destruction of Valuable Papers Respecting the State's Boundaries.

Poukeepsie 9th Feb'y 1779.

Dear Sir, It is with particular Pleasure I now transmit you a Commission continuing your Appointment* as a Delegate in Congress untill thirty Days after the next Meeting of the Legislature.

I was favoured with your obliging Letter of the 31st Jan'y† yesterday; when you receive my different Letters which the Bearer is charged with I flatter myself you will consider our Accounts settled up to this Date, I have not indeed made as punctual Payments as I coud have wished. This I begg you to impute to what I assure is the true Cause the Want of Opportunity of Conveyance, the present being the only one I have been able to Command since the Date of my first Letter. You omitted inclosing the Papers refered to in your last so that I am not favoured with the public Accounts from Georgia. Robertson's New York Paper of the 4th Instant says that the whole State is in the Enemy's Possession, their Government fully established & a Free Trade opened; and that the Carolinas are likely soon to follow the Example of their Brethren in Georgia in shaking off the Tyranny of Congress & once more enjoying the sweets of Peace under a Free Government. No mention is made in this Paper of their Successes in the West Indies. I woud fain Hope your Accounts from St. Lucia by Way of Martinique are groundless.

Our Tax Bill is yet with the Assembly. It was agreed to & ordered to be ingrossed on Saturday last. The Tax proposed is

---

*See page 514.
† See page 527 et seq.

to be 1 / on Real Estate estimated at its value in 1775 & 6d in the Pound on personal at its present Value; this would yield at least 1,000,000 of Dollars. I have Reason to fear it will meet with strong Opposition in Senate. Yesterday's Paper which you have inclosed will leave you without a Doubt who the author of the Piece under the signature of Real Farmer is, & you will be able to judge what Part he will take on the present Bill. The Bill respecting the Council of Revission has been read the second Time & Committed where I hope it will rest.

I have not yet been able to find the Papers & Maps respecting the Boundaries of this State. I fear they were distroyed at Kingston.

Mrs. Clinton beggs to return her most respectful Complim'ts to you. I am my Dear Sir Yours Sincerely

G. C.

His Excellency John Jay Esqr.

[No. 2085.]

NECESSITY OF PROTECTING OUR FRONTIERS.

Governor Clinton to Delegates in Congress—Blank Letters of Marque and Reprisal.

Poughkeepsie, 9th Feb'y 1779.

Gent., The frequent depredations of the enemy upon our frontier, during the last fall, have excited the most serious alarms amongst the inhabitants of the Western & Northern parts of Ulster, Albany, & Tryon Counties & many of them are desirous of removing, unless I can assure them that such posts will be taken, or such offensive measures pursued, as will tend to protect them. I find myself exceedingly embarrassed by their applications on this subject. To defend them by a militia harrassed as ours are, will be impossible. To encourage them to stay will be to make myself in some measure chargeable with the evils that may fall upon them in consequence of such incouragement; to advise them to break up their settlements, only increases the evil for frontiers & defenceless frontiers will still remain, till Hudson's river becomes our western boundary. In this situation I can only apply to you to know whether Congress mean to take any strong posts to the westward, or to pursue any offensive measures ag't the savages. If they do, I may by general assurances, induce the inhabitants to remain on their farms. If otherwise, common humanity dictates the propriety of removing them in time.

As the proceedings of the Com: of Arangement have not been transmitted to me, few of our officers hold the rank assigned them by such arrangement. Nor indeed any other which they consider as conclusive, so that dissatisfaction frequently arrises on this hand. I must, therefore, beg the favor of you to transmit me the rank roll as far as relates to our batt'ns, together with blank commissions for the officers & any special resolutions that Congress may have passed for filling them up. I could likewise wish to have some Lettres of marque & reprizal, as some of the subjects of this State who are desirous of engaging in privatiers, may find it difficult to give the necessary security in Connecticut where they are not known.

[G. C.]

[To New York Delegates in Congress.]

———

[No. 2086.]

PROGRESS OF THE TAX BILL.

Passes the Assembly Successfully, but its Fate in the Senate Dubious.

Poughkeepsie, 9th Feb'y 1779.

Sir, On the 3d Instant I did myself the Pleasure of writing you a few Lines which I put under Cover with Dispatches to the

President from whom you will receive it. I was favoured yesterday with your Letter of the 21st Ultimo by Mr. Lawrence. In my last I mentioned that a Tax Bill was before the Assembly; it has since passed through its different Stages in that House & on Saturday was agreed to & ordered to be ingrossd. I sincerely wish I had Reason to believe it coud meet the Approbation of Senate; this I despair of being the Case as some Gentlemen in that House are opposed to the Measure. It imposes a Tax of 1/ in the Pound on Landed Property estimating the Value as in the year 1775 & 6d on Personal at its present Value which would yield at least one Million of Dollars & that is sufficient to pay our present Quota to the Public & defray various Contingent Expences for the Ensuing year.

The Letters which I had the Honor of receiving from your Committee for superintending the Commissary's & Quarter Master's Department were among the first Matters which I recommended to the Consideration of the Legislature. They were early taken up in both Houses and several Bills ordered to be brought in in Consequence, thereof, to wit. For preventing Monoply & Engrossing; To prevent the distilling of Spirits from Grain & Cyder & to prevent Abuses in the Departments of Commissary Quarter Master & Forage Master in this State. As soon as these become Laws they shall be transmitted to you. The Committee who was appointed to collect Evidence of the Abuses committed in these Departments have not yet made their Report. The Moment it comes to Hand & I have right to expect it Hourly a Copy with the Proofs accompanying it shall be forwarded to the Committee. I shall wait with Impatience for more favourable Accounts from Georgia. I am with great Regard Your most Obed't Serv't

G. C.

Gov'r Morris Esqr.

[No. 2087.]

A General Press Warrant.

Febry. 10" 1779.

Sir, To relieve the present Necessities of the army I inclose you a general Press warrant to continue in Force for 21 Days by which Time I hope their wants may be fully supplied. I need not request that you will use it so as best to answer the End intended with the least possible Inconvenience to the Subject. Let me intreat that the Persons employed in the Service be such as have not rendered themselves obnoxious to the Inhabitants by past Controversies.

[G. C.]

[To Udny Hay D. Q. M. G.]

[No. 2088.]

Commissary General Wadsworth Offers Governor Clinton a bit of Patronage.

Camp Raritan, Feb'y 10, 1779.

Dear Sir, I have but just returned to camp after a considerable term of absence or I should have sooner noticed your obliging favor of the 4th ultimo. I must again express my thanks to your Excellency for your readiness to promote the interest of my department.

The inclosed resolution of Congress is sent to your Excellency for your sentiments with respect to the most eligible mode of settling the accounts to which that refers. I have taken the liberty to inclose a letter to Paul Schenck a purchasing comisary in your neighborhood directing him to take measures for the settlement. But if your Excellency has a preference for any person to execute this piece of business it will be equally agreable to me that such a person should be employed; and if he can be furnished with cash from the treasury or in any other way, such sums as are required for the purpose shall be immediately replaced & the person transacting the affair suitably rewarded. And should your Excellency appoint a man to do this service, the letter to Mr. Schenck need not be delivered to him. I have the honor to be with much esteem Your Excellency's most Obt. Serv't

Jere'h Wadsworth, Com. Gen. P's.

His Excellency Governor Clinton.

[No. 2089.]

Colonel Hay Acknowledges Receipt of Governor Clinton's Impress Warrant Letter.

Fish Kill 11th Feb. 1779.

Sir, I am honored with your Excellency's of 9th inst. enclosing an impress warrant for twenty one days; the orders and observations given, and containd therein shall be punctually obeyd and my Conduct regulated accordingly. I am with the utmost respect Sir Your Excellency's most obed't & very humble Se't

Udny Hay.

His Excellency Governour Clinton.

[No. 2090.]

Colonel Gansevoort Makes a Requisition for Clothing.

Albany 11th February 1779.

A Return of Cloathing at present wanting for the 3d N. York Regt.—185 Shirts; 193 Blankets; 467 pr. Shoes; 467 pr. overalls; 149 pr. Hose

Signed

Peter Gansevoort, Colo. 3 N. York Regiment

Sir, Deliver for the use of Colo. Gansevoort's Regt. to Capt. Tiebout Cloathing agreable to the within Return or such Proportion thereof as your present Supply will afford doing equal Justice to the other 4 Regiments. Given at Pokeepsie Febry. 14 1779.

Geo. Clinton Gov.

To Mr. Henry Com'y Cloathing &c.

[No. 2091.]

Again the Question of Flour for the French Fleet.

Pokeepsie 11th Febry. 1779.

Sir, The Legislature have had under their Consideration the Case of Monsieur De Matigny and are of opinion that the Flour purchased by him under his former Permit and still remaining unexported is now necessary for the use of the sick & wounded subjects of his most Christian majesty left at Boston by the Count D'Estaing, and that the same ought not to be seized & detained. I have accordingly given Permission for the Exportation of it of which I have thought it proper to give you Notice. I am &c.

[G. C.]

[To Jacob Cuyler, Deputy Commissary General of Purchases.]

[No. 2092.]

Returns of Fourth Regiment, Westchester Militia, under Major Crane.

Cortlands Manor Feb. 12th 1779.

a Regimental Return of the Fourth Regment of militia Westchester County Commanded by Thadeus Crane Esqr.

		Total.
Capt'ns	5	5
Leuts	10	10
Ensigns	5	5
Sergts.	20	20

The Earl of Chatham.

		Total.
Corp'ls	20	20
Drum & fife	8	8
Rank & file	252	252
Firelocks	240	240
Baynots	180	180
Catoch Box	220	220
Rouns	2133	2133
Blankits	150	150
Knapsacks	141	141

[No. 2093.]

Deputy Commissary Cuyler Writes on the All-absorbing Topic.

Albany Fabruary 13th 1779.

Sir, Inclosed I transmitt your Excellency the appointment of Zecheriah Garnrick who has since removed to the Northard, which at the Time of my application for him I was Ignorant off, indeed he says the situation of his family requiers his attention to his farm, and as Colonel Peter Van Ness, A. C. of Purchases is Exceedingly desirous to have another person to Superintend that busyness, I have made an appointment for David Van Ness, Ju'r, which I inclose for your Excellencies Confirmation, he is the bearer hereof. Some of my purchasers Complain that many of the farmers are not willing to sell their wheat for Continental Currency, such as is not seizable by the law, and which the army will stand in Great need off, I wish the lagislature would Propose some Exspidient to oblidge them to Part with It, for the use of the army if they concive It Proper. The Accounts from the Commissary General at Philadelphia are alarming; he Informs me that the article of flour requires our utmost attention, that the supplies from the Southard are by no means Equal to what he Exspected. I hope the Lagislature have Taken into

36

their Consideration the flour that is Still in this state under the Permitts for the use of the French fleet. I am your Excellencies most obdt. humble serv't

Jacob Cuyler, D. C. G. P.

His Excellency George Clinton Esqr. Poughkeepsie.

[No. 2094.]

Petition from Mamakating for a Force to Protect the Frontier.

To his Excellency George Clinton Esqr. Governor of the State of New York, General of all the Militia, and admiral of the Navy of the Same.

The Humble Petition of a number of the Inhabitants of the western frontiers of Ulster County, at and near Mamicotting, Sheweth, that your Petitioners Conceive themselves in a danger-our Situation; Partly from the Repeated threatnings of our Dis-affected Neighbours, who have heretofore taken part with and joined our Savage Enemies, and Partly by the wide Extention of near Thirty Miles (between Peenpeck and Nipennaugh) having no Guard, also the Season fast advancing when (if Providence Prevent not) plundering Parties may be expected, for fear of which, great Numbers are Preparing to remove their Families and Effects, which Removal if once begun (we Conceive) will be of Fatal Consequences. We therefore make no Doubt, but your Excellency upon Consideration of our Situation (If it appears Consistant with the Public good) will grant us some Speedy Re-lief, and your Petitioners as in Duty Bound, will ever Pray.

John Crage, James Huey, Manuel Gunsales, Jun'r, Jacobus Devins, Isaac Roosa, Joseph Crawford, Johannes Masten, John McCreery, Thos. Oliver, David Oliver, James Gillespy, Robert Milliken, John Gillespy, David Gillespy, Adam Ritenbergh,

Abraham Calwall, Thomas Shaw, William Bell, James Tucker, Robert McCreery, Abraham Swart, John Swart, Hendricus Rosacrans, William Cross, John Coulter, Donald Ross, Peter Simpson, Tomkins Odell, William Harlow, Daniel Woodworth, William Stephens, Solomon Wheat, Samuel Patterson, Archibald McBride, Jeremiah Fitzgerald, John Newkirk, Jacob Roosa, Philip Vankuren, Stephen Hoakham, Solomon Terwilliger.

Feb 13th 1779.

[No. 2095.]

THE VERMONT DISPUTE.

Micah Townsend Offers Several Sensible Suggestions on the Questions at Issue.

Brattleboro' Febry. 14th 1779.

May it please your Excellency, Last Week word was sent from the lower part of Gloucester County, by some Friends to the Rights of New York, and Delivered to me, that the People in that County were much divided, and many of them wavering in their Sentiments; some owning allegiance to Vermont, some to New York, (of which there was a Majority in the Town of Norwich) and many chusing to be under the Protection and Government of New Hampshire: That the offers of New York were not understood by the common People, the first Proclamation having never reached them; and that it would probably be attended with great advantage to the State to publish some thing and disperse among them in their present Situation.

I have also to inform your Excellency that some time past Capt. Clay, one of our Judges, went to Exeter, where the Legislature of New Hampshire meets, and at the time of their Session, in Company with Lieut. Governor Marsh and Colo. Olcott, (a Copy of a Letter from the latter to Mr. Clay I formerly sent you). Their Business can as yet only be guess'd at, 'though I think with great Probability of Certainty, from Messrs. Marsh and Olcott being the principal Promoters of our intended Union with New Hampshire: add to this that an assemblyman of that State acquainted a Neighbour of mine that their Legislature was determined to lay Claim to the Grants: But whether they have passed a formal Resolve for that Purpose, or the assemblyman concluded so from the General Conversation of the Members, I could not learn.

Colo. Bellows, also one of their Legislature, when I waited upon him for the Records of this County, (which he very readily delivered to me) expressed his wishes that we might be in one State. I give this Information, Sir, not merely for the sake of writing you the News, but that our State may be on their Guard against such an Event, and take the most prudent and timely measures to render it ineffectual. If the Legislature views the Country to be of the same Importance which I do, they will not be sparing of either Trouble or Expence to preserve it. But if they are inattentive to it, I much fear it will become an addition of Strength to those whom, next to Great Britain, we have most reason to dread.

I should judge it necessary that a large number of States of the Titles of New York and New Hampshire to the Lands, should be dispersed among the Inhabitants, to prevent their being imposed upon by the latter: That the arguments for a new State should be answered, and in short that it be shewn to be our Duty to yield our allegiance to New York. Among others I think it

would be necessary to notice this argument, which tho' not mentioned in the Publications of either of the Allen's, is a prevailing
opinion among the advocates for a new State; vizt. that the
Grants were erected into a seperate Government, by the King of
Great Britain, before the Declaration of Independence; and that
Major Skeene was appointed Governor thereof: this if true, would
be material in their Favor. If any thing is published, it may be
necessary perhaps to see a Performance of Colo. Allen's, which I
am informed appeared in Hartford News Paper No. 732, upon the
Subject.

Should the Legislature be sitting when this comes to hand,
wish, Sir, you would mention to some of the principal Members,
the expediency of appointing a Committee, near Poughkeepsie,
to transact, in the Recess of the Legislature, such Business relative to this Controversy, as will not admit of being deferred until
their usual times of sitting.

There has not, since my Return from Poughkeepsie, been any
Dispute, which I have heard of, between those who are, and those
who are not, in allegiance to New York, but every thing has
(owing I suppose to their Division) been as quiet as could be
wished; insomuch that it is generally thought an Election can be
held in many Towns here in April, without making the least Disturbance; and there is, in the opinion of all the Friends of New
York, with whom I have conversed upon the Subject, as great
Necessity to the full, for a Representation during the Existence of
these internal Disputes, as after the settlement of them: If you
should think it for the best, sir, be pleased to give the Clerk of
the Senate Directions to inform our Sheriff, whether a Senator is
to be elected in this District. A Letter would be most likely to
come safe, if under Cover to me.

In my last, which I understand your Excellency has received, I requested Mr. Lush might write me, about the latter End of last Month, what Congress had done, or whether they were like to do any thing, in the Business upon which Judge Jay was sent. I have not yet received a Line from him, and am, with many others, extremely anxious to know whether we are like to be in a fourteenth state.

The Legislature of Vermont are now sitting at Bennington. I am your most Obedient Humble Serv't

Micah Townsend.

His Excellency Governor Clinton.

[No. 2096.]

Colonel Hay Reports to Governor Clinton the Indifference of Judge Umphrey to Assist Him.

Fish Kill 14th Feb. 1779.

Sir, It grieves me to trouble your Excellency so often on the same subject, when I am certain your mind must be agitated by other matters of much importance.

The principal design of this is to request your influence with the Senate and Assembly to hurry on the bill, which I now hear is before them, for procuring teams with more ease and expedition; this is the eight day since I requested Justice Umphrey's assistance and begd he would procure me ten Waggons; not a single one has appeard. A party of twenty Soldiers goes out tomorrow morning under the sanction of your Excellency's impress warrant, to bring in twenty from that Precinct by way of punishment, but so bad are the roads at present, they must not only be a long time before they can compleat this business, but such fatigue naturally disgusts the Soldier at the service, and cools his ardour for the more Glorious tasks of Honour, which it is our security he should with eagerness pursue. I send you my second to Col. Umphreys as a proof of the different trials I make to obtain Carriages rather than make use of military force.

There is but one regiment now at Fish Kill, the other dutys for which will be so severe I shall scarce be able to procure a man from them for the impress business however urgent the occasion. I have the Honour to be with the utmost respect, Your Excellency's most obed't & very humble Se't

Udny Hay.

P. S. Permitt me to mention to your Excellency that if we do not gett out the number of Carriages wanted now, we shall be under the necessity of calling upon the Farmer in his seed time, which I have ever been aiming to prevent, as it must be attended with a certain degree of danger and may with total ruin to the Country.

His Excellency Governor Clinton Poughkeepsie.

COLONEL HAY TO MR. UMPHREY.

Fish Kill 11th Feb'y 1779.

Sir, I wrote you on Saturday last for ten Teams to be imployed in public Service at this Post for Six Days. Justice Storm was Kind enough to promise the latter Should be delivered you by himself, which I dare Say he did; The Necessity of having an Immediate Supply of Carriages for doing the public Business, is Such, that his excellency the Governor has thought proper to grant me his Genl. Impress warrant for twenty one Days from 9th Inst. notwithstanding, which I would willingly avoid making use of the Military Force on this Occasion, if it can be avoided and

therefore hope you will Send me in the ten Waggons immediately.
I am Sir Your most obe'd Serv't

Udny Hay.

(a Copy)

[To Mr. Umphrey.]

[No. 2097.]

TO SEIZE BRITISH VESSELS ON LAKE ONTARIO.

Governor Clinton Submits a Project to James Clinton—The Legislature Indemnifies the Military for Aiding the Cherry Valley Sufferers.

Pokeepsie 15" Febry. 1779.

D'r Sir, I have received your Favor of the 31st Inst.* The Legislature have passed Resolutions indemnifying the Command'g Officer at Albany for the supplies afforded by him to the distressed Inhabitants of Cherry Valley and making some future Provision for them. I am much pleased with the Determination of the Oneidas, Tuscaroras and Onondagas and the establishing a Post in the Oneida Country as I promise myself it will be a great means of giving security to our Frontiers.

I don't see we can do anything farther with Butler relative to the Exchange until we receive his answer or the situation of things will render it practicable to pass with safety to the Place where he is stationed.

Last Fall a short Time before Gansevoort's Regt. was relieved from Fort Schuyler a Proposal was made to me for taking the Enemy's vessells on Lake Ontario. The Officers who offered themselves for the Enterprize were Lieut. Staats & McClellan who were to be accompanied by a few Privates and some faithful Indians. As the Enemy's vessels were then thinly manned I imagine

---

* See page 528.

it might have been easily effected, and had not the season been so far advanced and the Regiment ordered down I should have given every Encouragement for furthering the attempt. The Opening of the Lakes in the Spring will probably afford as favorable an Opportunity and could it then be effected greater advantages would result from it, as we should then have the Command of that Lake and of Consequence an easier access to the Seneca Country. I wish, therefore, you would turn your attention to this Object. I need not mention to you that it ought to be kept a profound Secret. I would, therefore, have you consult General Schuyler only on the subject. If Officers equally acquainted with the Country and willing to undertake the Business can be found in Van Schaack's it may be proper to employ them to prevent Discontent.

Your Family was well last week. I am &c.

[To Gen. James Clinton.]

[G. C.]

[No. 2098.]

Massachusetts Makes Acknowledgment for Flour Privileges.

State of Massachusetts Bay.

Council Chamber Boston February 15th, 1779.

Sir, We wrote to your State, a few Days since, informing of our Application to Congress relative to the Embargo, the Scarcity of provisions with us (more especially of Grain) together with the Causes thereof, and earnestly requesting that friendly Aid & Assistance herein, which we trust the sister states will be ever ready to grant to the mutual Comfort and advantage of each other. We have since directed the Board of War of this State to Import Grain or Flour from your State, provided we may be permitted so to do; which favor, if we may be so happy as to obtain, we shall feel peculiar Obligation at this Time, and be ready on our part, at all Times, to reciprocal Acts of Friendship and Benevolence.   And we flatter ourselves that the late Conduct of this State in a similar Case, will be a Sufficient Apology for our present application.

In the name & in Behalf of the General Court, I am, with great Esteem, Sir, Your most Obed't Hble. Serv't

Jer. Powell, Presid't.

His Excell'y George Clinton Esqr, Governor of the State New York.

[No. 2099.]

Proceedings of a General Court Martial at Goshen, for Three Commissioned Officers and One Private.

Proceedings of a general Court martial, appointed by the President to be held at the Court house in Goshen, in the County of Orange, on Monday the 15th day of February 1779, agreable to General orders of the 4th of December 1778.

At which day for want of a sufficient number of members adjourned to Tuesday 16th Feb'y.

Tuesday Feb'y 16th the Court met agreable to adjournment when the following members appearing were sworn.

Colonel John Hathorn President.

Major John Popino	Lieut't John Dunning
Capt. Samuel Jones	Lieut't John McDowall
Capt. Samuel Watkins	Lieut't Eliud Tryon.
Capt. John Little	Lieut't Richard Bailis
Capt. David Sweezee	Lieut't Benjamin Moore jun'r
Capt. Isaiah Veal	Lieut't Samuel Webb

Balthazer De Haert Judge advocate.

General orders read.

Capt. Tuthell of Coll. Woodhull's regt. of Orange County militia charged with disobedience of orders and a shamefull neglect of duty in not marching with his classes to Minisink when ordered into actual; being called pleads not guilty.

The Court proceeds to the trial of Capt. Tuthell. Col. Elihu Marvin being sworn, says, that in Col. Woodhull's absence, he received the Governor's orders to send a fourth part of the militia to Minisink, in consequence of which he ordered the Captains & subaltern officers of his regiment to meet; they accordingly met and Capt. Tuthell agreed to go a month; he then ordered each Capt. to send his men to Chester the Thursday following to march under the command of the said Capt. Tuthell to Minisink. That he saw Capt. Tuthell the said Thursday at Chester and ordered him to march to Goshen, and if but few men appeared to tarry there that night; that the Friday following Capt. Tuthell sent for ammunition which was sent him; that the Sunday following Capt. Tuthell came to him told him he was too unwell to go forward and that but a few men had joined him who he sent with a lieut't upon which he ordered the Capt. to stay 'till after a Court martial should sit for the trial of the delinquents which he ordered him to attend and take the men who should be ordered to go with him; that the Court martial sat the next day but Capt. Tuthell did not attend; he further says that Capt. Tuthell sent his son the day after the Court martial to inform him that he was not able to march and that he then sent Capt. Tuthell word that he should not march 'till able to take the command of his men.

Ques. did you expect that Capt. Tuthell would march from Goshen, the morning after he got there, without any further order.

Col. Marvin, yes.

Thomas McGuire being sworn says, that Capt. Tuthell set off from Goshen to march with his men to Minisink that an hour or two after he returned very unwell with a flux, that he stayed all night at his house and the next day went home very ill.

Capt. Tuthell in his defence says, that his indisposition obliged him to return, which he had proved by Mr. McGuire, and that he continued very ill the whole month.

The Court having taken the cause into consideration are of opinion that Capt. Tuthell is not guilty of either of the said charges and do acquit him thereof. By Order of the Court

John Hathorn President.

and then the Court adjourned 'till to morrow morning 8 o'clock.

Wednesday the 17th Feb'y the Court met agreable to adjournment, and proceeded to the trial of Ensign Smith.

Ensign Joseph Smith of Capt. Sweezee's company in Col. Allison's regiment charged by Coll. Newkirk for hiring a private to do his duty and leaving the ground in his absence, being called, pleads not guilty.

Capt. Samuel Jones being sworn says that Ensign Smith came to him while he had the command at Pinpack told him that he had business which made it necessary he should be at home that he had agreed with a private to do his duty if he could be accepted and requested him to accept the said private in his stead to do duty as a private and he further says that he referred the said Ensign and his case to the Officer who came to relieve him and that the said Ensign Smith appeared to him to be unwell.

Lieut. Samuel Knap being sworn says that (after he had releived Capt. Jones and had the command at Pinpack in the absence of Col. Newkirk), Ensign Smith applied to him to let him return home and offered to leave a private in his stead that Smith complained of being unwell, that he accepted of the private to do the duty and gave Smith leave to return home which when Col. Newkirk came to Pinpack he seemed satisfied with and allowed the said private to do the duty of an Ensign which he continued to do till his time expired; he further says that he thinks the Private did Ensign's duty before Col. Newkirk came to Pinpack but that the said private was namd in the payroll only as a private.

Lieut. John McDowall being sworn says, that when he went to Pinpack Lieut. Knap had the command, Joseph Smith Jun'r the substitute of Ensign Smith did the duty of an Ensign which he mentioned to Coll. Newkirk who appeared to be entirely ignorant of it but said the said private would answer as a man on the ground and that the ensign in his opinion had done wrong and deserved to be arrested; he further says, that the Coll. suffered the said private to assume the Character of an officer notwithstanding but said he should not draw Ensign's pay.

The Court taking the Cause of the said Ensign Smith into consideration are of opinion that he is guilty of the charge of hireing a private to do his duty and that he pay a fine of fifty dollars. By order of the Court

John Hathorn President.

Lieut. Hubbard of Col. Woodhull's regiment charged with disobedience of orders and a shameful neglect of duty in not marching with his classes to Minisink when ordered into actual service, being called pleads not guilty.

Col. Elihu Marvin being sworn, says that sometime last October he gave orders to the officers of Col. Woodhull's regiment to meet, at which meeting Lieut't Hubbard agreed with the other officers for a certain sum of money to go to Minisink and stay a month; that a few days after the men marched Lieut't Hubbard came to him and told him that he had not received the money he had agreed for, and asked his opinion of going upon which the witness ordered him to march and some days after hearing that he was not gone sent Lieut't Conklin to order him to march tho' he beleived that he did not march; he further says that he accepted of Lieut't Hubbard as a substitute for an other Lieutenant and accordingly gave him orders to march.

Lieut't Hubbard in his defence, says, that tho' he had agreed to go to Minisink he never rec'd the money he had agreed for and was ordered by Capt. Tuthell to return home 'till he was paid and a little after some people had the small pox in his house which prevented his going to Minisink.

The Court martial taking the cause of the said Lieut't Hubbard into consideration

are of the opinion that he is guilty of the disobedience of orders and a shameful neglect of duty in not marching with his classes to Minisink when ordered into actual service wherewith he is charged and do adjudge that he be suspended from doing the duty
of an officer for the space of six months. By order of the Court

John Hathorn President.

and then the Court adjourned 'till to morrow morning at 8 o'clock.

Thursday the 18th Feb'y the Court met agreable to adjournment.

James Stringham private soldier of Capt. Watkins's Company in Colo. McClaughery's
regiment charged for desertion from the said Company 19th Dec'r 1776 when in actual
service and going to the enemy being called to the bar confesses the charge and prays
that Capt. Veal and Capt. Watkins may be examined as to his character.

Capt. Isaiah Veal being sworn saith that he has known the prisoner from his infancy
and that except his going to the enemy he seemed always willing to do his duty as a
soldier.

[No. 2100.]

The Governor Dreads the Fate of Our Frontier Settlements.

Feb'y 15 1779.

Dear Sir,* I should have answered your Letter of the 5" of
January before but waited to hear from you further (on the subject alluded to) by Mr. Taylor, whose non attendance on the
Legislature this session has deprived you of the safe Conveyance
you expected. I did intend when I had last the Pleasure of seeing Genl. Washington to have been at Albany in a few Days.
Business of a public Nature however prevented my leaving Home
and I have now less Prospect than I had at that Time of carrying
my Intention into Execution. I should be exceedingly happy if
the Enterprize you mention is to be against the Enemy to the
westward as without some offensive operations in that Quarter I
dread the Fate of our Frontier settlements the ensuing season.

Our Representation at present in Congress is rather more
ample than I could wish as all the members elected (except yourself) are attending so that no Inconvenience now can arise from
your being absent; perhaps the Business with which you are intrusted may be compleated in Time to relieve one or two of your
Brethern. There can be no necessity of making a new appointment. I am &c.

[G. C.]

---

*The identity of the person to whom Governor Clinton addressed this letter is not
disclosed by the correspondence.—STATE HISTORIAN.

[No. 2101.]

Mainly in Regard to Mr. Furman a Prisoner in New York.

Head Quarters Raritan Feb'y 5th 1779.*

Dear Sir, Your favour by Mrs. Spicer, did not reach me till a few days since. What became of the Lady I cannot say, as she did not deliver your Letter, nor made any application relative to her son.

Mr. Furman's peculiar situation and unparrelled Sufferings,† engaged my attention early last Summer. I demanded him in Exchange from the Enemy, at several different periods, his not being taken in arms was a singular objection, not properly coming with my Line; however from my repeated applications which were some times joined by Threats of retaliation, the Enemy were at length prevailed on at the instance & Security of some Friend in New York, to Release him from the Provost and indulge him with the Liberty of the City. I am told soon after his enlarg-

---

* This document is out of place. It should follow document No. 2081.

† February 4.—It is painful to repeat the indubitable accounts we are continually receiving, of the cruel and inhuman treatment of the subjects of these States from the Britons in New York and other places. They who hear our countrymen, who have been so unfortunate as to fall into the hands of those unrelenting tyrants, relate the sad story of their captivity, the insults they have received, and the slow, cool, systematic manner in which great numbers of those who could not be prevailed on to enter their service, have been murdered, must have hearts of stone not to melt with pity for the sufferers, and burn with indignation at their tormentors. As we have daily fresh instances to prove the truth of such a representation, public justice requires that repeated public mention should be made of them. A cartel vessel lately carried about one hundred and thirty American prisoners from the prison ships in New York to New London, in Connecticut. Such was the condition in which these poor creatures were put on board the cartel, that in that short run, sixteen died on board; upwards of sixty, when they were landed, were scarcely able to move, and the remainder greatly emaciated and enfeebled; and many who continue alive, are never likely to recover their former health. The greatest inhumanity was experienced by the prisoners in a ship of which one Nelson, a Scotchman, had the superintendence. Upwards of three hundred American prisoners were confined at a time on board this ship. There was but one small fireplace allowed to cook the food of such a number. The allowance of the prisoners was, moreover, frequently delayed, insomuch that in the short days of November and December, it was not begun to be delivered out till eleven o'clock in the forenoon, so that the whole could not be served till three o'clock. At sunset the fire was ordered to be quenched; no plea for the many sick, from their absolute necessity, the shortness of the time, and the smallness of the hearth, was allowed to avail. The known consequence was, some had not their food dressed at all; many were obliged to eat it half raw. On board this ship, no flour, oatmeal, and things of like nature, suited to the condition of infirm people, were allowed to the many sick; nothing but ship bread, beef and pork. This

ment, he took to himself a Wife and is now following his usual occupation of carriage making, his being upon those Terms precludes him an Exchange and an Elopement would involve his benefactor. I am, sir, with great respect & Esteem Your most Obt. & most Hum. Serv't

Jno. Beatty, Com. Gen. Pris'rs.

Gov. George Clinton.

[No. 2102.]

CAPTAIN WILLIAM HARPER ATTACKS KLOCK.

He Declares the Colonel is Inefficient and that Leniency to Tories is Responsible for Much of the Suffering in the Mohawk Valley.

Mohock Destrict Tryon County 16th Febr. 1779.

Sir, When I had the honer to resave your Faver of 23 Dec'r I was then lying sick at Schoharry & have ever since ben confined to my rome or I had ben before this in Poghkipse with a quantity of sulfer, the produce of our manufacturer which I think wants nohing but a sufisant number of furneses and peace to Carry it on.

---

is the account given by a number of prisoners, who are credible persons; and this is but a part of their sufferings; so that the excuse made by the enemy, that the prisoners were emaciated, and died by a contagious sickness, which no one could prevent, is futile. It requires no great sagacity to know, that crowding people together without fresh air, and feeding, or rather starving them in such a manner as the prisoners have been must unavoidably produce a contagion. Nor is it want of candor to suppose, that many of our enemies saw with pleasure this contagion, which might have been so easily prevented, among the prisoners who could not be persuaded to enter their service. Some of them, no doubt, thought they acted in all this with the true spirit of the British Parliament, who began hostilities against America by shutting up the port of Boston interdicting the fishery and those branches of trade that were deemed necessary to our subsistence; and when some members objected to the cruelty of such acts, some well-known friends to the ministry had the face to ring in the ears of others, Starvation, starvation to the rebels—starvation is the only thing that will bring them to their senses! In short, the inhumanity of the Britons, from the beginning of this war, and through every stage of it, is without a parallel in the annals of any civilized nation. These things ought never to be forgotten, though some would fain wink them out of sight. We are not, indeed, to resolve never to make peace with our enemies, but never to make a peace that will leave it in their power to act over again their intolerable oppressions and cruelties. We can never secure ourselves against this, but by maintaining, at all adventures, the sovereignty and independence of these States. Nothing but this can effectually prevent the present generation from enduring the severest punishment for their noble resistance to the tyranny of Britain, nor our posterity from groaning throughout all generations under the most abject and cruel bondage.—New Hampshire Gazette, February 9, 1779.

Saterday last, Mr. James Den, the Inden Intarpreter, on his way to Albany caled to see me, and informed that the Tuesday before, he came from Onido, whare he see a Inden, a tru frind, whoo was dyrectly from Nigara, whoo Informed him that thare was at that place one of the Anodogo cheafs, which was taken prisener at Fort Schilor at the time that Sant Ledger retreted from that place, and was sent prisener to Albany, but after ward set at liberty; this Inden Consaved a plan to Suprise Fort Schiler, which he communicated to the Infamous Colon. Butler, who perswaded him that it could not be dun by Indens, but if he would go aganst the Inhabitents he might have grate sucksess; to which he agreed and was rasing men for that purpos when he came from Nigaro to make a desent on the frontears very sune; Mr. Den thinks it is likly wee may gat intiligance of thare aproch before thay rach the Inhabitents. I have taken the methouds I thoght most prudant to inform the pepell not to aleram them to much by informing the Filde offecers & magestrats.

But, Sir, I do ashuer you, thare is littell to be Expected from the Exertions of our offecers or molitti, for at the time that Chery Valy was destroyed Colon. Kluck with the molitti of the upper part of the County did not arive at that place till two dayes after the dede was dun, thogh he had, as I have ben often informed, promesed Genarall Hand that he would send to that place fore hundred men sum dayes before the Enimy arived, and when he did arive thare, he did not stay above two or three howers, notwithstanding the surviving Inhabitents ware in the grates destress and the Ded not buryed & the Enimy not retiered above six or seven miles from the setelment. The Same Day Colon. Fisher arived at Chery Valy with his Ridgment & a small suply of provisons it being so near night, that he could not march of, he in-camped thare but intimated that he would march of the next morning, on which Colon. Cloyd and Sundry of the Inhabitents requested me as a magestrate to go to Coln. Fisher & demand that he shuld stay & asist in burying the Ded & send a party of his men with a party of the Continentell Tropes to meat a party of the priseners and asist in, as wee had information by sum of the priseners that had cum back, that Brant and Butler Did prommis to send back the rest of the women & Childring, and likewise to asist in moving the Distressed Inhabitents to the Mohock River, which I did that eavening, & the next morning agane I presed on him & his offecers, but notwithstanding all the arguments that could be yoused thay could not be prevaled on to stay to aford the least asistence, thogh I did declare that I would reporte the mater to your Exselency Exsept the wagons that Broght the provisons did carry sum fue of the retched popell away.

But thay did march of that morning.

Sir, you may see from this acount (and I doubt not but many of the same kind have cum to you) what dependence is to be put in our molitti; the privets despise the officers & reproch them to thare faces with thar misconduct. Numbers of the Inhabitents have ben moveing down throw this wholl winter and you may rely on it that Every honast frind in the County will move as sune as there is Grase for the Cattell, if they are not abliged to fly before; but thare is a nother thing I belive wee have rason to fear; it is well known that thare is yat a grat many pepell in theas parts that are unfrindly, and many that are of doubtfull carractours, & likewise thare is grat quantityes of stock & grane in thare hands; now, if theas popell shuld make thar peace and Joyn the Enimy this fruntear might becum moore trublesum; then wee are aware of thare is yat Grane & stock anugh in this County to suport

Indens & Toryes anugh to vex the United States parhaps as much as a larg army could do on the sea cost, espesally if a considarable reinforcement should arive in the spring.

Thare is another surcumstance that Discuriges the frinds & of which thay loudly complane, that is, almost Every Tory that is taken and commited, thogh his gilt be ever so grat & glaring, he is either set at liberty & to imbrace the first opportunity to cut our throts or sufered to make his Escape, and thay do go and join our enemy agane. Sir, it is imposable to discribe or for you to conseave, the Distres & the confusion that this part of the Contry is in, exsept you ware a spectater of it. As to the Destructtion of the Garman Flats it may be atributed to what it will. But, Sir, you know that this County was exemt from the draft to fill up the Ridgments of this State and ware to rase two cumpanyes of Rangers, and when & how many of them was rased I nead not say, but this I can say, that many of them ware a grate part of thare time at home instead of being on duty and the forth part of the molitte which you ordered to be in actuall sarvice, you doubtles have hard how that was exsecuted, & Colon. Pelinger & parhaps the grater part of the Inhabitents of the Garman Flats, can inform that thay did repeatedly call on Colon. Kluck to send them asistence to no purpous.

Colon. Harper at that Time went from Schoharry to the Garman Flats to ingage such of the Inhabitent & Indens as ware willing to go on the then intended Expadition, whare he found the sittuation of that place truly Destresing; the popell could not go to thare worke but at the peral of thier lives by rason of the frequant Incursions of the Enimy on thier satellments.

Colon. Pelinger & Esqr. Harkemer & sundry of the prinsipell of the Inhabitents did ingage Colon. Harper to go [to] Colon. Kluck

37

& Inform him of thar situwation, and pres him in the strongest termes to send them asistence, which he did, & told him that the lives & fortuens of them Popell depended on his exertions, likewise his one Carracttuer; Colon. Kluck promesed to send them ameadaute ade; of this my brother informed me the next day, and Colon. Pelinger has since informed me that notwithstanding all the applycations, thare was not above twenty five or thirty men sent to them & thay stayed a very short time with them. Indead, sir, it is the common saying among the Popell hear, that wee might as well have a old woman at the Head of our molitti; but thay are exsadingly surprised that instead of being caled to ane acount for so many blunders & neglects to find him mad Colon. Comandant.

It is true it is Defucalt to find capable men in thes parts but I dont doubt a exampell or two might even make Ignorant men more atentive to thare duty, for the want of which I beleve wee have sufered very much; wee have ben in grate expecttation of a expadition against the Indens in the spring, but Mr. Wills Caled to see me on his return from Pokipse & informs me that thare is no sartanty of any such thing.

I am, Sir, with the gratest respect your most obadent and very humble sarvent

William Harper.

To his Exselensy Gorge Clenton.

[No. 2103.]

General McDougall Makes a Request on Governor Clinton for Several Orders.

Head Quarters Peeks Kill February 16th 1779.

My Dear Sir, I was favoured in due time, with your several favours by Mr. Barclay. Time and the warm season obliges me to wave all Forms; I am Collecting all the Regular Troops. I wish for an order, on Colonel Ludington, for a good Ensign and twenty men, to guard a Valuable number of Artillery waggons and other Carriages, made and making at Fredericksburgh, and for all his men, who have not appeared in Arms; the like for the latter on Colonel Hay, A Subaltern and thirty of Colonel Brinkerhoffs, good men to guard the Barracks and Stores at Fish Kill, where are all the Spears of the State? I wish for an unlimited order for them. What I get will be paid for? I beg the Militia near these posts and West Chester, may be in the most perfect Readiness to march, on the shortest notice: and provided with ammunition, which I much fear is not the case. Some of the Villains who broke out of your gaol, are now under Examination; one of them is a spy of Tryon's; if the proof is full, I shall not trouble a Court martial with him. I am in the greatest haste Your affectionate Servant

Governor Clinton.   Alex'r McDougall.

GOVERNOR CLINTON'S REPLY.

Febry. 16" 1779.

Sir, I have rec'd your Favor of today's Date and inclose general orders agreeable [to] your request. You'l be pleased to transmit Copies to Colo. Ludington & Colo. Brinkerhoof and such other command'g officers of Regts. as reside in the vicinity of your Quarters.

As to the Delinquents, I do not conceive that I can with Propriety issue the orders you request, especially as some of the offenders may have been already punished by Courts Martial, but I have no objection to your writing to the Colonels, and I dare say they will upon application do what you request of me. Your

Letter by Major Strang is also rec'd and shall be duly attended
to. Whenever you get a New York Paper you can spare, I shall
be obliged by the Loan of it & will return it if required.

[G. C.]

[To Gen. McDougall.]

---

*Governor Clinton Submits an Act of Congress Relating to Flour for
Rhode Island to the Legislature.*

*Gentlemen of the Legislature,

I submit to your Consideration a Resolution† of Congress, of the
8th Instant, directing the President to write to the Governors of
the States of Connecticut and New-York, requesting them to
afford such Supplies of Flour and Provisions, for the distressed
Inhabitants of the State of Rhode-Island and Providence Plantations, as their Necessities call for, so far as their Circumstances
will admit, and under such Regulations as may best Answer the
End proposed; with a Copy of his Excellency the President's
Letter on the subject.

Geo. Clinton.

Poughkeepsie, February 18, 1779.

[No. 2104.]

TO COOPERATE WITH WASHINGTON.

*Our Delegates in Congress Suggest that Clinton Advise with the
Commander-in-chief on Certain Matters.*

Philadelphia 19th Febry. 1779.

Sir, We beg Leave to acknowledge the Receipt of your Excellency's Dispatches of the 9th Instant by Barclay.

---

*From Journals of the Legislature.
†*Resolved,* That the president write to the governors of the states of Connecticut and
New-York, requesting them to afford such supplies of flour and other provisions for
the distressed inhabitants of the state of Rhode-Island and Providence Plantations as
their necessities call for, so far as circumstances will admit, and under such regulations as may best answer the end proposed.

We lament the frequent Ravages of the western frontier. They have been severely felt both by our own State and Pensylvania; and we are called upon by every motive to be vigorous in the necessary Preparations for punishing our Enemies and protecting our Citizens. The Commander in Chief has spent some time in this City in Conference with a Committee of Congress. No pains have been spared to impress him with a strong Idea of the absolute necessity of attention to these great objects. The operations which will be most effectual are submitted to his Judgement, and every Department is placed under his immediate Superintendance. With him, therefore, we wish your Excellency to correspond. We know that he has great Confidence in you and that your Solicitations and advice will have a proper weight.

General Schuyler also stands high in his opinion; & we are fully persuaded that any Plan which you & he suggest, or Requisition which you make, will meet with all possible attention. These are as fortunate Circumstances for our Frontiers as coud be wished, and we are persuaded they will be embraced. If any Obstructions arise, or any thing you may deem essential is omitted (which we have not the least Room to apprehend) we shall stand ready to support your Representations with the utmost Diligence and Zeal.

The arrangement of the army with respect to the relative Rank of the officers is not yet entirely compleated. This Defect, which has given room for dissatisfaction, is chiefly to be ascribed to the Committees' having left Congress before the arrangement was matured for a Report. It is however handed over to the Commander in Chief who is directed to finish it, the principles having been established by Congress. You will, therefore, be pleased to apply to him for Information; his own Anxiety on so interesting a Subject to the whole army will not brook Delay.

The Letters of marque and Reprizal are forwarded by this Conveyance agreeable to your Excellency's Request.

Preparations are making by Congress for the ensuing Campaign. The Intelligence from Europe is not sufficiently decisive to Justify the least Relaxation, tho they are by no means discouraging.

We shall be happy to hear that the acts of Congress respecting Finances & Taxes meet with the approbation and firm support of our Legislature. Congress in this and all other Measures of Importance have decided with an uncommon degree of unanimity. We sincerely wish the same Harmony may ever continue and prevail in the great Council of the United States, and be extended to every Branch of the Confederacy. We have the Honour to be with the highest Respect Sir Your Excellency's most Obedient humble Servants

              Jas. Duane, John Jay, Wm. Floyd, Fra. Lewis.
[To G. C.]

[No. 2105.]

The Case of Dr. Anthony and Captain Scudder.

Sir, The Bearer Dr. Anthony, a Refugee from L. Island, and, I have Reason to believe, well attached to the American Cause, waits upon your Excellency in Consequence of an Order from the maritime Court of Connecticut refering to your Excellency a Controversy between Dr. Anthony & Capt. Scudder, Commander of a small Privateer, relative to a seizure made on L. Island by Capt. Scudder, of a Quantity of Dry Goods the Property of Dr. Anthony. Capt. Scudder had a Commission under this State to cruize on the waters of the Sound and neither his Commission nor Instructions impowered him to carry on any

Enterprize on Land & he was particularly cautioned not to plunder & distress the Inhabitants of L. Island.

[To Gen. Washington.]   [G. C.]

———

[No. 2106.]

CORRESPONDENCE WITH MEMBERS OF CONGRESS.

Francis Lewis Reports Closer Relations on the Part of France Carrying a Strong Moral Effect.

Phila. 20th Febry. 1779.

Dear Sir, I have been honoured with your letter of the 1st Instant.

You will undoubtedly ere this reaches you hear the current bruit of the present time, i. e. that Congress are possessed of great news received from Europe but for reasons of State, think it improper at this time to be devulged; this has raised the curiosity of the public to know what the mighty Secret is. As a member of Congress I am enjoined to Secrecy, but think myself at liberty to communicate to your Excellency (in confidence) that Mons'r Gerrard has given Congress such intelligence as will put our affairs upon a more respectable footing than ever, but then it will be necessary that we exert ourselves in our military appearances, but above all in our unanimity, for the only hope Britain has now left, is to divide us.

The Rumor has this good effect, that Engrossers & monopolizers are at a stand, many offer goods for Sale, but few choose to buy, so that goods fall in price, and our money appreciate; the Express waiting obliges me to conclude Your Excellency's most Obed't Humble Servant

Fra. Lewis.

His Excellency Geo. Clinton Esqr.

[No. 2107.]

William Floyd Writes of Financial Matters.

Philadelphia Feb. 20th 1779.

S'r, The money which I Rec'd as of our Treasurer for the purpose of Bearing my Expences here, happened to be mostly of the two Emitions which were put out of Circulation about the time I arrived here. Some of it I have Changed, the Rest I cannot, without a Loss of ten per Cent. and God knows I am not in Circumstances to put it on Interest; therefore, I Enclose it to your Excellency, and Beg you would Desire Mr. Benson to give it to the Treasurer that he may make a memorandum on the back of my Receipt; there is 568 Doll's.

I Shall be under a Necessity (Contrary to my Inclination), to get from the Continental Treasury Some money on the Credit of our State to Bear my Expences.

Our necessary Expence here is far beyond any thing I had an Idea of.

As I Doubt not, you will be well Informed of Every thing that is passing at this place by my Brother Delegates, I Shall at this time, only Enclose a paper of this day's date and Conclude with Saying that I am with the Greatest Respect S'r your most obed't and humble Serv't

Wm. Floyd.

To his Excellency George Clynton.

[No. 2108.]

Gouverneur Morris Urges the Enactment of a Tax Law—Maps and Papers Relating to Vermont.

Phila. 20 Feb'y 1779.

D'r Sir, I pray you to accept my acknowlegements for your Favors of the 2d & 9th Instant, being much ingaged in Business and in very ill Health I cannot dilate. Let me only observe that my Colleagues were very unfortunate in that they did not mention to me more early their application for the Papers &ca. relative to the pretended State of Vermont. Most, if not all of them, some maps excepted, are in my Possession. I am sorry to learn from you that the Tax Bill will not probably go through. To delay this beneficial measure is almost madness. Inequity must happen in a Tax of any kind. I can raise solid objections against that you mention. So perhaps can others, and so may any man of Genius against any Thing. For God's Sake tax & leave to a future Period, the equitable adjustment of these things. Let me be remembered to all Friends & believe me Yours

Gouv. Morris.

His Excellency Gov'r Clinton.

[No. 2109.]

"THE GOOD NEWS FROM EUROPE."

Francis Lewis Declares it is Withheld from the Public for State Reasons—Necessity for a Respectable Army in the Field.

Phila. 24th Febry. 1779.

Dear Sir, I had the honor of writing to you on the 20th Instant acknowledging the receipt of your favor of the 1st.

I now embrace this opportunity of transmitting you a Pamphlet entitled, " Considerations on the Mode, & Terms of a Treaty of Pease with America," together with the papers lately published here; We have also news of a private nature from Europe, such, as is in no wise disagreeable to Congress, but for reasons of State is not thought proper as yet to be divulged, but will be published in due season.

It will be absolutely necessary that we exert ourselves in bringing a respectable army into the field the ensuing Campaign, as in all probability it may be the last, As to the transactions in the W. Indies I must beg leave to reffer you to the printed papers herewith. The British Troops are in possession of Georgia but we are in hopes of their being soon dispossessed.

The Public, being apprised of some good news received by Congress, tho' not transpired, has already caused great confusion among Engrossers, & Speculators, who are now offering their Hoards for sale, but few incline to purchase; this has occasioned the fall of Goods, & consequently the appreciation of our money. I am with great respect Dear Sir Your very Humble Servant

F. Lewis.

His Excellency Geo. Clinton, Esquire.

[No. 2110.]

John Copp Reports the Approach of Two Parties of the Enemy from the West.

Fort Van Dyck, Feby. 24 1779.

Dear Cap'n, " The bearer Nicholass will acquaint you with the news just now brought in by a scout, which informs of the approach of two parties of the enemy one of thirty men, the other of an hundred. The Indian who brought the news is the bearer of this, for particulars I must refer you to him."

John Copp.

[No. 2111.]

Returns of Colonel Klock's Battalion of Tryon County Militia.

A Return of the Second Battalion of Tryon County Militia Commanded by Colo. Jacob Klock Feb'y 24th 1779.

	Colo.	Lieut. Colo.	Majors	Adjudant	Quar. Mas.	Colo. Clerke	Captains	Lieut.	Ensigns	Sergeants Major	Sergeants	Corporals	Drum'rs & Phif'rs	Privates	Total
Colo.	1														
Lieut. Colo.		1													
Majors			0												
Adjudants				1											
Quarter Masters					1										
Colo. Clerk						1									
Captains							7								
Lieuten'ts								7							
Ensigns									5						
Sergeants Major										1					
Sergeants											24				
Corporals												25			
Drummers & Phifers													3		
Privates														181	
Total															258

Jacob Klock, Col.

[No. 2112.]

THE MURDER OF JOHN CLARK.

Sheriff Nicoll of Orange County Furnishes Governor Clinton with an Account.

Goshen Febr. 24th 1779.

Dear S'r, Inclosed I Send your Excellency a True Acct. of the proceadings Realitive to the Murder of John Clark, If Consistent I hope your Excellency will Order the Court Immedietly to Set on James Smith and James Fluwelling, as I am a Fraid when the weather Gets warm and the Leaves Out, there will be many Murders Committed and Uppon some of Our principal peopal. I am your Excellency Moste Obediant and Humble S'r

Isaac Nicoll.

To His Excellency the Governor.

Goshen Feb'y 24 1779.

A Representation of the Conduct of Richard Smith, Son of the late Claudius, & Six others unknown last Saturday Night at John Clark's Between Stirling & Warwick:

They came to the House of s'd Clark, knocked & were admitted; one pulled out a watch & said it is about 12 O'Clock & by one Clark, " you shall be a dead man; " Clark inquired why they would take his life; they answered " you have killed two Tories & wounded a third," mentioned the Name of the one he had wounded. Clark replied, " I never killed a man in my life, but I believe I did wound the man you mention & I was then under the command of my proper officer & therefore did my Duty." They said with oaths & imprecations used by such miscreants, that he had been very busy &c. &c. &c. & therefore they were determined to hang him; & to comfort his wife who appeared much affected, they told her they intended to be the death of all the leading men of those parts. They drank very freely of sundry sorts of Liquor, of which there were three Barrels in the house, filled their Bottles & stove the Casks; took 3 Bushels of salt & strewed upon the Ground so as it could not be collected: filled Bags with Meat, Bread, Meal & many other things, took about £200 in Cash & gave Miss Clark a Paper written as follows Viz:

" A Warning to the Rebels:

" You are hereby forbid at your peril to hang no more Friends to Government as you did Claudius Smith.

" You are warned likewise to use James Smith, James Flawelling & Wm. Cole well and ease them of their Irons, for we are determined to hang six for one, for the Blood of the innocent cries aloud for vengeance; your noted Friend, Capt. Williams & his Crew of Robbers & Murderers we have got in our Provoe, & the Blood of Claudius shall be repaid; there is particular Companies of us that belongs to Col. Butler's army, Indians as well as white men, & particularly Numbers from N. York that is resolved to be revenged on you for your cruelty & Murders. We are to remind you that you are the beginners & agressors, for by your cruel oppressions & bloody actions drive us to it. This is the first & we are determined to pursue it on your Heads & Leaders to the last till the whole of you is Massacred. Dated New York Feb'y 1779."

They then took Clarke to an out House near his dwelling House, & some said they would hang him, other said they had better shoot him, & while they were disputing which they should do, Richard Smith shot him through the Breast, Clark fell on his Face & lay as dead; they took of his Shoes, which being done he nimbly got up & ran to his House, while running they discharged two Guns at him, lodged the contents of one in his shoulder & left him. Having returned to his wife he informed her as above, particularly that Smith shot him & not long after died.

They then went to one Gideon Maces, drank some Liquor; took some Cash from one Hall a Traveller, which they again returned, threatening him, alleging that he made & sold salt to the Rebels.

After this went in to the Mountains.

The above is as near a Representation of Facts as I have bin able to Get.

Isaac Nicoll.

[No. 2113.]

COMMISSARY SUPPLIES FOR THE TROOPS.

The Legislature Called Upon to Appoint Disbursing Officers in whom Confidence can be Placed.

Hartford Feb'y 27 1779.

May it please y'r Excellency, Considering the heavy complaints & censures that are made against those employed in the Com-

missary Department in the State of N. York, & the evil Consequences arrising to the public from that Quarter, Colo. Wadsworth Com'y General, has determined to apply to the Legislature
of your State, to take up the Matter, & appoint such Persons,
& so many, as they shall judge necessary, to transact the Business; & in whom they can confide. The difficulties & Embar-
rassments attending this Business are so many, in the present
Situation of our Country & its Currency, that its not only necessary that the persons employd to feed the army should be honest Men, & acquainted with Business: but that they should also
have the entire Confidence of the people amongst whom they live.
The Com'y General has directed me to point out to your Excellency my Limits in your State, & request the Favour of you to
consult with the other branches of the Legislature, & appoint
such Men as you can rely on assistant Com's of purchases therein.

My Limits begin at the North west corner of the State Connecticut, & run from thence to Hudson's River, on an East & west
line, & down by the River to York Island. My present purchasers are David Van Ness, Esq. of Redhook, Capt. James Reed
of Amenia, Mr. Paul Schenk, of Poughkepsey, Maj. Henry Schenk,
Fishkill, Maj. Jos. Strang, of Cortland's Mannor, lately appointed,
& Mr. Philip Leak, of Bedford. As those Gentlemen are well
known to the Legislature of your State, I need make no observations on the propriety of continuing or dismissing them the
service.

By the Resolutions of Congress, regulating our Department,
herewith sent you, your Excellency will see the necessity of the
Persons whom you shall appoint Com's, having certain limits
appointed them for the sphere of their purchases, of their taking
the office Oath, & giving in Bonds with 2 sureties for their faithfull discharge of their office.

As several of my people are so disgusted at the severe censure shown out against them, that they have requested a dismission; this Business will require your earliest attention. As soon as you have fixed on the Men, must request your Excellency to make me a Return of their Names, places of abode, & the Limits assigned them, that I may furnish them with Blank Bonds, & such Instructions, and forms, as will enable them to keep their accounts in a similar Manner with my other purchasers. They will also want an immediate supply of Money without which, little can be effected. I expect a large sum in the course of the week, & shall pay immediate attention to their wants.

I have only to add, that Flour is wanted for the Troops at the Eastward; that there is not exceeding 400 ba's in the Magazines at & near Boston, that the several posts of Springfield, Rutland & Wooster are nearly out. The Troops in State Rode Island not furnished with more Flour than to last them till May, fear not so long. The Troops at N. London under Command of Genl. Parsons are worse supplied. General Putnam's Troops & Genl. McDougall's expect to be fed by my purchases. These various demands will amount to 2,500 bar's p Month, and is liable to be increased by the calling out of the Militia on alarms &c. at the above Rate it will take 15,000 bar's Flour to feed the Men now in my department for Six Months. No common Exertions will secure that Quantity. I should not suppose that Dutches & W't Chester would furnish a much larger Quantity; & if it is not immediately secured for the army, private persons, compelld by Hunger, will run it out of the State & send it Eastward.

The Express, J. Stevens, will wait your Excellency's orders.

I am with the greatest Respect, your most obdient hum. Servant

Peter Colt, D. C'y P's East Depart'n

P. S. Some further provision should be made to hinder the exportation of Flour, & some way fallen upon of having each permit, even to the com'y cancelled & returnd to you; think no Flour should be sent out but by gangs of Teams under command of a faithful Conductor; this would prevent great part of the present Inequity, of the Farmers taking advantage of the Teams coming to Sharon with public Flour, & passing the Line in company with them.

His Excellency Geo. Clinton Esquire.

[No. 2114.]

COMMISSARY COLT WRITES CONFIDENTIALLY.

His Private Opinion of the Capabilities of Several of His Subordinates.

Feb'y 27 1779.

Private.

Sir, I wrote your Excellency of this Date, respecting the Business of my Department, which suppose will be communicated to ye General Assembly; shall now, in Confidence, give you my oppinion of the propriety of displacing some of the people hitherto employd by me in Business; and of continuing others. I must begin by observing, that in the summer of '76 I was sent into your State to purchase Flour by order of Col. Trumbull; whilst there, the army retreated from N. York & lost considerable Flour, it became necessary to have regular & large supplies from your State. I applied to the Convention, then siting at Fishkills, for their advice & assistance. They took up the Matter & appointd a Com'e to confer with me on the subject. By their advice I employd Maj. Schenk & gave him the Money I had on hand to prosecute the Business, and returnd home. Colo. Trumbull employd him ever afterwards whilst he continued in the Dept.; when he

resignd & I was appointed Dep'y Com'y Gen. I gave Maj. Schenk
an appointment again; this was in Nov'r 77 & I never heard any
Complaint against him till lately. By his request, I appointed his
Brother Paul, knowing him to be acquaintd with Business & of
good Connections; however I find that both of those Gen'n have
incurred the displeasure & lost the confidence of their Country
Men; on which account they ought to be displaced. Maj. Schenk
has recommended Mr. Isaac Kershow, & Mr. Paul Schenk, his
Brother Peter, to take their districts. But I am not sufficiently
acquainted with either of their Characters to judge of the propriety of giving them an appointment. D. V. Ness Esq. was first
employd by J. Canfield Esq. of Sharon. He secured upwards of
5,000 bar's Flour last spring for the army in his small district.
Mr. Canfield assured me that Maj. V. Ness was the most industrious Man in that Quarter, & could command more of the produce
than any Man he knew; he has purchased upward of 3,000 bar's
Flour since Oct'r for me. As to his Honesty & Integrity, you can
form a better oppinion, than I am able to do upon my short acquaintance with him. I suppose him the fitest person in that
Quarter to be imployd; but as I am so much a Stranger to the
Gentlemen of that part of the Country, shall chearfully submit his
Fate to your determination. Capt. Reed was first imployd thro
my procurement in 76. Col. Trumbull gave him an excellent
Character when he quited the Business & I again appointd him.
I am fully satisfied with his Conduct in the department & believe
he is the best Man in that Quarter; cant but wish he might be
continued. He has exerted himself to the utmost & believe there
would have been no complaint of his Flour's falling short last
summer, had I been enabled to have furnished him with Money
to make good his contracts: But as it was out of my power to

furnish the Money seasonably, the Farmers went to the Mills &
took away the Flour & sold it to the Eastern people. I have no
reason to think Capt. Reed connived at those practices, but believe
he secured as much of his contracts as he could. However if you
judge that he is not fit for the Business, or that a better Man than
him can be found in his District; believe Capt. Reed will cheerfully quit the service. Mr. Phil. Leak was introduced to me in
Nov'r 77, by John Lloyd, Esq. by Papers which he shewd me. I
saw he was entrusted by the convention with state Business, and
as I knew of no other person in that Quarter, employd him; tho he
has procured me considerable supplies from time to time, and on
as reasonable Terms as any Person in that Quarter, yet I cant
but wish some more active Man was appointd in his Room. He
is very ignorant of accounts, is not a person of great abilities, or
Resolution; & does not seem possessed of sufficient might & Importance with the Community to conduct public Business in that
Quarter to advantage. He suffers himself to be abused by people
in such a Manner as renders him, in some Measure, contemptable,
and I fear he has not taken such care of his saltd Meat, as will
prevent all damage. I have heard a Maj'r Lockwood mentioned
as a suitable Person to be imployd in that district, but have no
personal acquaintance with him.

On my Return from Poughkepsey I appointd Maj. Jos. Strang
of Crompond an assistant, and yesterday I recv'd a Letter from
General McDougall, informing me, that he had employd Maj.
Jon't Griffing Tomkins* of Fraderecksburgh to purchase in that
Quarter. He assures me that Mr. Tomkins may be depended on
for his Zeal & attachment, as those two last Gentlemen are so

---

*Major Jonathan Griffin Tompkins was one of the conspicuously loyal Americans of
Westchester. He was the father of Daniel D. Tompkins, the "War Governor" of New
York, during the second war with Great Britain.—STATE HISTORIAN.

lately appointed hope there will appear no necessity of altering them.

Under the present situation of Business perhaps it would be prudent to form another district between Maj. Tomkins's & Capt. Reed. Maj. Talman lives on the great Road by which much Flour is said to be run out of your State; perhaps it might be well to appoint him to purchase. The State of our Magazines is such as requires your spediest attention to this Business. The scarcity of Bread Corn at the Eastward is truly alarming & whilst it bears such a price there, persons will not be wanting who will run all hazards in supplying them. The sooner the Grain is secured for the army the better, as the price will certainly rise much higher than we have ever given. I anf sensible this application is giving your Excellency much trouble; but I dont know how it can be avoided. I shall take it as a particular favour of your Excellency, to acquaint me of any Malpractices of any of my people, or any complaints that may be made against me personally. Being concious of my own Integrity, flatter myself I shall always be able to convince you that I have honestly if not successfully conducted public Business & no longer would I continue in it, than I can support the Character of an honest Servant of the public. I have the honour to be your most respectful hum'e Servant

Peter Colt.

P. S. You will consider this as a private Letter wrote your Excellency in perfect Confidence of its not being made public.
His Excellency Geo. Clinton Esq.

Governor Clinton's Reply.

Pokeepsie 4th March 1779.

Sir, I have but a Moment to answer your Confidential Letter of the 17th Ultimo. The Persons you wish to continue in Office I believe are as proper as any their Charecters being for aught I know unexceptionable. I do not think either of the Persons recommended by the Messrs. Schenck the most suitable. If Melancton Smith Esqr. coud be prevailed upon to accept he woud be the most suitable Person to supply one of those Vacancies. I am Sir Your Most Obed. Serv.

[G. C.]

Peter Colt Esqr.

[No. 2115.]

Bread and Flour in the Several State Stores.

Acct. of Bread & Flour on Hand in the Several Stores in the State of N. York, the first Day of March 1779.

			Bbls. Bread	Bbls. Flour
Nathaniel Stevens A. C. of Issues		Fishkill	7	11
John Else	Do	Do Landing	6½	51
James Hamilton	Do	New Burgh	¼	2½
Simon Phillips	Do	Kings Ferry	76	10
James Forsyth	Do	Continental Village	3	61
Total			92¾	135½

I hereby Certify that the above acct. is agreeable to the Returns of the Issuing Commissaries.

John Fitch, D. C. G. Issues.

Fishkill March 8th 1779.

N. B.   About 400 bbls. Flour at West Point on Hand.

[No. 2116.]

Returns of Colonel Duboys' Regiment Commanded by Capt. Rosekrans.

Return of the Regiment of Foot in the service of the United States Commanded by Colonel Lewis Dubois.
New Windsor 1st of March 1778.*

	Colonel	Lieut. Colonel	Major	Captains	1st Lieutenants	2d Lieutenants	Ensigns	Chaplin	Pay Master	Adjutant	Qu'r Master	Surgeon	Serg's Mate	Serjt. Major	Qr. Mas'r Serjeant	D. & Fife Majors	Serjeants	Drum & Fifes	Privates fit for Duty present	Sick Present	Sick absent	on Command	on Forlough	Total	Serjeants (Wanting)	D. & File (Wanting)	Privates (Wanting)	Inlisted	Dead	Deserted	Discharged	Joind
Capt. Rosekrans				1	1		1										2	1	15	2	4	3	4	28								1
Capt. Hutchings				1	1		1										2	2	19		1			20						1	2	
Capt. Stewart				1													2		18		6	8	2	26								
Capt. Bevier				1													4	2	42	1		2	2	51								
Capt. Godwin				1	1												2	1	18		2	9	3	22						1		
Capt. Lee				1	1		2										2	1	35	1	2			50				1				
Capt. Hamtramck				1	3	3	3									2	3	1	6		4	7	11	9								
Capt. Johnson				1		4											3		9					31								
Prisoner at N. York		1	1								1	1	1	1	1																	
Total		1	1	8	6	7	5			1	1	1	1	1	1	2	29	13	162	4	19	29	23	331	3	3	309	1		1	2	1

Colonel absent one 1st Lieut. on Command one Ensign & Chaplin absent one 1st Lieut. one 2d Lieut. & Two Ensigns Vacant.

Jas. Rosekrans Capt.
& Com'd Officer s'd Regt.

* The original editor of the MSS. placed this document in 1779; the endorsement on the document is 1778. To determine the correct date, a letter was addressed by the present editor to Gen. F. C. Ainsworth, U. S. A., Chief of the Record and Pension Office, Washington, D. C., who replied under date of Nov. 15, 1900: "It is shown by the records of this office that the 5th New York Regiment, Revolutionary war, commanded by Colonel Lewis Duboys, was stationed, on March 1, 1778, at New Windsor, and on March 1, 1779, at Schoharry." This establishes the date on the return as 1778.—STATE HISTORIAN.

[No. 2117.]

A Brief Letter from John Jay.

Philadelphia 1st March 1779.

Dear Sir, Altho I have no Important Intelligence to communicate, or Leisure to write long Letters, yet cannot omit this opportunity of sending to you the news Papers, and telling you I am well.

A vessel with a valuable Cargo is just arrived at Baltimore. Whether she brings any & what advices from France I am yet uninformed.

My next will be more particular. My best Respects to Mrs. Clinton. I am dear Sir Your Friend & Serv't

John Jay.

Gov'r Clinton.

———

[No. 2118.]

STRENGTH OF THE BRITISH.

General McDougall Furnishes Governor Clinton with a Detailed Estimate of the Enemy's Forces in New York City and Vicinity.

Head Quarters Pecks Kill March 1st 1779.

Sir, It has been the misfortune of this Country, that it has been amused at every Period of the Dispute, with Great Britain, with some object, to take its attention from the ultimate one. Today Reconciliation; tomorrow, the Interference of France, is to terminate the Dispute, and give peace to America. And not long since, the Enemy was to have evacuated New York, and by the credulous, it's believed the Force of the Enemy is very inconsiderable. Now 'tis said, Spain's acceding to the Independancy is to effect it. This is the Tub of the Day, to divert the whales.

It is a necessary Part of my Duty to be informed of the Strength of the Enemy. I have used every possible means to accomplish it. The Result you have inclosed. It speaks for itself. I hope this night to write you more fully. I am, Sir, Your humble Servant,

Alex'r McDougall.

P. S. Since this was wrote a Picquet from Colonel Putnam's Regiment posted on Tallar's Point has taken eleven of the Galley men who landed with a view of taking off Stock. Among the Number is the Master, two Marines, seven Sailors and their Pilot, (one Bice from the Neighbourhood of Poughkeepsie).

His Excellency Governor Clinton.

The Corps on the other Side, have been compared with the official Letters and paragraphs, in the Enemies Papers; relative to the embarkation and arrival of the Troops at Barbadoes &ca. and Georgia, but neither of those, are among these. It is certain there are 14 Companies of Light Infantry at South Hampton, and its very seldom, that the Battalion is sent on remote Service, from its flank Companies. I recollect but one Instance in all my reading. Sensible Deserters, Serjeants and Corporals from the Brittish, were confident as to the Cantonments on York, Staten and Long Islands. And the Hessian privates were equally so, as to Regiments of that Nation. The York Calendar, containing a List of them, was read to them repeatedly and questioned particularly where all these Corps were, at the Time of their respective examinations. The Positions of the New Levies, are ascertained on as unquestionable Evidence. The 16th Regiment of Light Dragoons, have been draughted into the 17th, and the officers sent to England. The former is the reason of the present

Strength of the 17th. The seventeenth of Foot, altho' cut to Pieces at Princetown, has had large draughts from the reduced Regiments. A Corporal of it, who detailed the Duty deserted, and was very minutely examined at my Quarters. He appeared to be a sober intelligent Fellow. The 57th is by the concurrent examination of Sixty Deserters, the strongest in America. The Compliment of the Grenadiers, is always compleat, by a standing general order. The Strength of the Corps in General, has been ascertained by Questioning the Serjeants, Corporals and sensible privates on the strength of their own Companies, and whether their Regiment was reputed to be stronger or weaker than another with which it was compared? The Hessian Regiments except the Grenadiers and Life Guards, consist of five Companies and when they first came out were an Hundred and twenty strong Rank and File, now they are from 60 to 80. If it be considered, that the Enemy have but in few Instances, been compelled to make long marches, that they have had the best care taken of them in their Hospitals, well provided with Cloaths, Linnen and acids, that he received frequent recruits from Europe, and several of the Brittish regiments, were reduced to fill others up, no Question remains on my mind of the Truth of this Estimate.

Alex'r McDougall.

Estimate of the Enemy's Strength & Position in New-York and its dependencies collected & collated from the Examination of the most sensible Deserters, British, Hessian & New-Levies & Sensible Friends of America taken by M. General McDougall at his Quarters at sundry Times 'till 16th Day of February 1779.

Corps	Strength	Cantonments
Horse:		
British—17th light Dragoons	300	Long Island.
New ⎰ Lord Cathcart's Legion;	50	Do Do.
Levies ⎱ Emerick's	30	New York Island.
	380	
Infantry:		
British Brigade of Guards	1500	City of New York.
Grenadiers 14th Comp's	700	Jamaica L. Island.
Light Infantry 14 Do	700	South Hampton Do.
7th	265	Harlem on N. Y. Island.
17	410	Near F. Washington Do.
23	350	City of New-York.
26	310	Staten-Island.
33	300	Bedford, L. Island.
37	300	
Highlanders 42 two Battalions	750	Bedford, L. Island.
44	300	Laurel Hill, opposite F. W. York Island
45	350	
57	450	At & near F. W. York Island.
63	320	Bloomingdall, Do.
64	300	Long Island.
	7305	
Hessian 1 Batt'l Chasseurs	350	Flushing, Do.
Grenadiers 3 Batt'l	840	City of New York.
1 Life Guards	350	Near Kings Bridge N. Y. Island.
Hereditary 3d Princes	350	Brookline L. Island.
Prince 4 Charles	350	Do Do.
6 Donops	300	Near F. Washington N. Y. Island.
7 Losbergs	350	7 Mile Stone Do.
8 Kniphausens	350	Along N. River Do.
9 Trumbacks	350	Barracks near F. W. Do.
10th Murbacks	350	Harlem Do.
	3940	
New Levies, Cathcart's Legion	100	Long-Island.
Lord Rawson's, or Irish Volunteers	350	Bowery, N. Y. Island.
Robinson's	150	Harlem, Do.
Sincoe's Rangers	250	Long Island.
Ludlow's Batt'n De Lancey's Brigade	150	Loylds Neck, Do.
Barton's Do Skinner's Do	250	Cuckolds Town, Staten Island.
Buskirk's Do	200	Staten-Island.
Emerick's Chasseurs	90	This Side Kings-Bridge.
	1540	
	13,165	

[No. 2119.]

*General McDougall's Instructions to Captain Merely on the Flour
Question.*

(Copy)

Sir, You will so dispose of your parties on, the most public
Roads of Communication on the Eastern Borders of this state,
from Sharron to the West Bounds of New Millford, as to prevent
all Flour from going out of the state, unless with a Copy of the

inclosed Certificate, & persons having such permits, you will suffer them to pass the Line, with Flour, but they are to return the permits, and you are to transmit them to me, once every two weeks. If any Flour is taken going without such permits, you will seize it, the Horses, Cart & Oxen, & apply to a Justice of Peace, who will dispose of it according to Law. You will apply to James Reed, Esq. A. C. P. Armenia Precinct, who will inform you of the most proper, Roads & places to post your men on. _

You will be particularly attentive, that there be no waste of Forage, as it is extreamely scarse & absolutely necessary, for the support of Cattle, which must draw supplies for the army.

You will maintain the strictest order, and discipline among your men, and not suffer the persons or properties of any Inhabitant to be insulted or injured.

Given at Head Quarters Pecks Kill this 2d Day of March 1779. Capt'n Merely.

———

[No. 2120.]

SCHUYLER AND OUR EXPOSED FRONTIERS.

Apprehension that the Inhabitants will Abandon them unless Proper Protection is Afforded.

Albany March 2d 1779.

Dear Sir, A few days ago I was honored with yours of the 2d & 15" ult. It had really slipt my memory to give you the Information I promised in mine of the 5" Instant. At that time Genl. Washington had ordered me to direct the preparations for an Expedition Into Canada by the way of Ontario;* that rout was

* From headquarters, Middlebrook, Washington, on February 11th wrote to General Schuyler:

Dear Sir, It was not till the 5th instant, I returned to this place. While in Philadelphia what between Congress and a special committee of that body I was furnished with ample employment. I had few moments of relaxation, and could do little more than barely acknowledge the receipt of your obliging favors of the 27th of December

preffered to any other, not only because It was thought Impracticable to gain a Naval Superiority on Lake Champlain and that a penetration by Coos with a large army was deemed Impossible, but because when the army should arrive at Oswego, If such Circumstances turned up that It should be thought unadvisable to proceed to Canada, the army might be Employed In the reduction of Niagara. This design was laid aside from a consideration of the situation of our affairs on the Sea coast and an apprehension that there would be a deficiency of provisions for the Support of

and the 1st and 2d of January Ulto. Even now I find it impossible to be as explicit and comprehensive as I could wish in this letter, my common business having run so much behind hand, during my absence from the army, but as the season is advancing, and no time to be lost, which can be employed in preparing for such operations as our circumstances will allow us to adopt for the ensuing campaign, I shall thank you for your opinion and aid in the several objects of this letter. Some of them were contained in my last, however, I shall repeat them again for fear of a miscarriage.

1st. What number of men do you conceive necessary for an expedition against the hostile tribes of the Six Nations and the force which it is probable they will bring to their aid?

2d. What part of the Indian Settlement should be considered as the central point to which all the force of the expedition from the different quarters, should be directed where a junction of the whole should take place?

3d. Whether any and if so, what artillery will be necessary? And what stores most proper for such an expedition and the quantities of each?

4th. The best route to approach their settlements? Three different routes have been suggested. The 1st by the way of Fort Schuyler, the Oneida lake, and Cayuga or Seneca river. The second by a land march wholly from fort Schuyler, the difficulties of which are variously stated; some making the passage through the country easy, others representing it as the reverse. The 3d by a portage from the Mohawk river, to the East branch of the Susquehannah & down this to a branch made use of by the Indians in their invasion of our frontiers. The advisability of the second will depend in a great measure on the kind of country to be passed through, and that of the first and last upon the goodness and extent of the water carriage. For this will serve only in part; and requiring horses and pack saddles for the performance of the rest, it then becomes a question which is to be preferred in point of economy—time and other circumstances—That wholly by land, or that composed of both land and water portage.

5th. In case the 3d or last route should be preferred, what is the distance of transporting batteaux from the Mohawk river to the Susquehannah, and the physical or natural obstructions? This should be fully scrutinized. Indeed every foot of the route if possible should be described, and the difficulties and the distances from place to place minutely ascertained.

I could wish a similar critical examination of each of the other routes. This would be attended with other advantages, besides those arising to the expedition from a comparative view. The same attention given to each avenue by which the country is accessible must distract the enemy, and may produce a confusion and irresolution in their measures for defence.

6th. The route being fixed on, what time (making a reasonable allowance for unforeseen delays) will it require to penetrate to the heart of the Indian country or to the principal object or point of the expedition.

If a water transportation is to be used either in whole or in part, what inconveniences or obstructions may be expected from the state of the rivers at the season in which the expedition should be executed? And if pack horses are to be employed, and their chief support to be grass, when should the operations commence? Further it is in-so large an army as was Intended to be Employed.   It was, however, resolved that an Expedition should be prosecuted against the hostile tribes of the Six nations and preparations are making for that purpose; however, on some Suggestions of mine It has been thought prudent not to lay wholly aside the first object but to prepare In such a manner, as to take advantage of any favorable Events that may arise either to go Into Canada or attempt the reduction of Niagara.

---

dispensably necessary to ascertain the precise moment for the movement of the main body that diversions from different points may be exactly timed for co-operation.

7th. What distance is it from the Seneca towns to fort Pitt? What kind of a country between? And the land and water transportation?

8th. Is it essentially necessary to have slight stockade forts erected as the Army advances, for the benefit of convoys, and the security of a retreat in case of misfortune? Or, is it, that the good to be expected from *such* works, would be more than overbalanced by the delays occasioned in erecting them, the diminution of strength which the army would suffer in small garrisons—and the advantages which the enemy may derive from the slowness of our movements with the knowledge of our designs. Or what is the proper medium?

9th. Will it do to have the provisions to follow after the army, in case there are no forts constructed, or must the whole stock accompany the army from its first movement?

10th. When ought the troops to rendezvous and where And how long is it probable they will be engaged in this expedition?

11th. At what places should magazines be formed, and when, and for how many days?

12th. How many batteaux will be wanted for this expedition? or are those on hand of the proper kind and sufficient in number?

If we are to build more, no time should be lost. It should be set about immediately and the requisite number completed as soon as possible.

13. What precautions are to be devised to alarm the enemy in Canada, thereby to prevent the troops in that country coming to Ontario to the aid of the Indian nations?

To these many questions would occur, if I had more leisure to pursue the subject: But your time and good judgment will taken in every other consideration of policy or importance. When you have committed your thoughts and enquiries on this occasion you will be pleased to transmit them by some trusty conveyance.

It will be necessary, immediately to employ proper persons unacquainted with each other's business to mix with the hostile Indians that the most unequivocal information may be gained of their strength & sentiments, their intentions and what ideas they may have acquired of our design. We should also learn what support or assistance they expect in case our intended expedition should be known to them; or what precautions they are taking to oppose our operations.

The Indians in friendship with us, may be sent on this purpose. The half tories also if they can be engaged, and will leave pledges as a security for their fidelity might prove very useful instruments. Similar investigations should be carried into Canada, and the garrison at Niagara.

I shall likewise depend on your exertions in having the different routes to the object of the expedition critically explored both by Indians and others, so that a complete knowledge of distances, natural difficulties and the face and nature of the country may be precisely obtained.

I must beg the use of your manuscripts a little longer. Some of them I think interesting. I shall keep them till I find a safe hand to intrust them to or till I have the pleasure of seeing you at Camp. I am, &c.

The Enterprize against the Indians will secure the western frontiers unless the Enemy should attempt their destruction before the troops reach that Quarter, which I apprehend will be the case and have therefore Intreated that the troops may come up the soonest possible. Our Northern frontiers will however remain much Exposed, and from accounts which I have a few days ago received from Canada there is Every reason to believe that the Enemy mean to attack our frontiers In Every quarter. It is certain that a large body of Indians are Expected at Montreal In the beginning of May.

Two Companies of Gansevoort's are marched To Lake George to take post there and repair the Fort &c. It is highly necessary that troops should be stationed at Skensborough and others at the Junction of the North branch of Hudson's river with the Sackendaga branch, but where to procure them is the difficulty. There are none here, and unless these places are occupied the Inhabitants if I may Judge from the apprehensions they labour under, will abandon their Habitations at Least, as far down as Saratoga on the west side of Hudson's river and to Cambridge on the East side. Is It not possible for the Legislature to raise two hundred men for the protection of the Northern frontiers? What the Consequence will be of abandoning so many settlements are too obvious to Dwell upon.

I have been so severely shaken by a ten days fit of the Gout in my stomach that I am quite a Skeleton. It has however left me and hope soon to recover strength.

Mrs. Schuyler Joins me In compliments to Mrs. Clinton. I am Dear Sir with great Esteem & affection Your Excellency's most obedient Hum. Serv.

                                         Ph: Schuyler.
His Ex'l Gov. Clinton.

[No. 2121.]

Mr. Constable of Schenectady Given His Citizenship.

Phila. 2d March 1779.

Sir, Mr. Constable, a Son of Doctor Constable of Schenectady, left this Country in the year 1773 and went to England on private Business. The war prevented his Return for some considerable Time but finally as the Continuance of it took away the Prospect of being able speedily to revisit America he same out to this City in the winter of 1777. Upon the Evacuation he remained and hath taken the oath of allegiance. At present he wishes to be placed in a Situation to visit the state of New York with Propriety and become an Inhabitant and subject. Having never done any act prejudicial to the Interests of the United States I am led to imagine that no objection can lie to this measure. But I pray your Excellency to write me fully on this Subject and to point out the steps which may be necessary for him to take which will much oblige Your most obedient & humble Servant

Gouv. Morris.

His Excellency George Clinton Esqr. Governor of the State of New York.

———

GOVERNOR CLINTON'S REPLY.

Poukeepsie 22d March 1779.

Sir, From the Account you give of Mr. Constable I do not conceive there can be any reasonable Objection to his vissiting Schenectady & becoming a Subject of this State. It will be adviseable for him to bring with him a certificate of his having taken the Oath of Allegiance to the State of Pensylvania & such other Evidence of his Friendship to the Cause of America as he may be able to procure. After all his Reception in the Town Schenectady will depend on the Political Characters of his Father & Friends there if they are on the Right Side it cannot fail of being Friendly. I am with great Regard Yours &c.

[G. C.]

Gov'r Morris Esqr.

· [No. 6418.]*

The Swiss Painter du Simitiere Sends Governor Clinton a List of Books Found in Philadelphia.

Sir, I did myself the honour to write to your Excellency on the 2d ult. & to inclose three London Magazine of Jan'y, Feb'y, & March last year, being the latest I could procure, I hope my letter has come Safe to hands; I had Sent it with Gen. Arnold whom I understood was going your way, but upon his Sudden return here, I enquired of him about the letter & he informed me that all the letters he had for the northward had been forwarded without delay, I Shall be glad to hear of its reception.

Two Political pieces having been lately published here I do my Self the pleasure to Send them to your Excellency & hope I'll have the merit of being the first to communicate them to you, I wish that I might Know what would be most agreeable to Send you and to inform you of, and I would do my best to contribute to your information or amusement.

There is a Catalogue of books handed about here in MSS. which makes Some noise; it is very lengthy & many of the characters would be quite unknown to your Excellency. I have, therefore, Selected a few which I inclose as a Specimen of the whole for your perusal.

I mentioned in my last that I had the honour to have Gen. Washington to Sit for his likeness for my collection, and I have

---

*From Volume XXIV Clinton MSS.

added to it Since, Mr. President Jay, Mr. Silas Deane, Mrs. Henry Drayton & Charles Thomson, all very much approved of. I expect to have a few more capital characters Soon, which will enrich the collection Still more. As to my other collections I have them arranged in the house I now live in, much better than I ever had them before and I am dayly adding Some new Subjects to them.

It will give me a very great Satisfaction to hear from your Excellency Soon and in that hope I have the honour to Subscribe my Self with respect Your Excellency's most Obedient & most humble Servant

Du Simitiere.

Philad'a March 2d 1779.

His Excellency Governor Clinton.

Extract of a Catalogue of Books for Sale in Philadelphia. February 1779.

Duelling improved, a Scurvy edition, bound in asses skin—by John Penn N. Carol.

The widow bewitch'd or what think ye of the Congress now—by Mrs. Fergusson,

The inflexible Captive or plain English, a true Story well told— by Gen. Thomson,

Callipoedia or Theory in practice, a winter's night amusement— by Mrs. Francis, to which is added; a Sensible & risible appendix in Sheets—by a British officer.

The Persecuted Chief, or the modern Sejanus an old book—by Gen. Lee,

Chesterfield burlesqued, or a clumsy attempt at Politeness—by Dr. Cutting, to which is added the Eunuch, an imitation of Terence & Coleman, by the same.

The Babler, a romance 22 vol. an old edition & much out of request—by Miss Fanny Clifton.

Frisky a la mode, a Comedy Second hand & worse for the wear— by the widow Shaw.

The Belle in Despair, a ballad, tune, Babes in the wood, an old copy—by Miss Nancy Clifton,

The man in the moon, or the history of Crazy John in Latin—by Col. John Parke,

The hunted Chief or the back biting Junto—a comedy—by Gen. Arnold,

The Debauched new-light man—a Physical Case—by Maj. Edwards.

The Secret History & Intrigues of Gen. Howe, worse for the wear—by Miss Franks.

Nicotiana or who would have thought it, a humbug—by Maj. Franks.

[No. 2122.]

Commissary Flint, George Clinton and the Commissary Department.

Camp Rariton March 3: 1779.

Sir, Your Excellency's favor of the 3d instant to Colo. Wadsworth was delivered to me last evening. He is now at Hartford. I have sent him a copy of your letter and he will immediatly attend to the several matters you require.

We consider ourselves under strong obligations to your Excellency and the legislature of your state for your great attention to the interest of our department. I am very respectfully Your Excellency's most obt. & h'e Ser't

Royal Flint A. C. G.

His Exc'y Gov. Clinton.

[No. 2123.]

Captain Hallett Prefers Charges Against Lieutenant-Colonel Holdridge.

Head Quarters Pecks Kill March 3rd 1779.

Sir, This will be delivered to you by James Hallett, late a virtuous Pilot in New York. He was in the Service of our Congress and behaved faithfully. He now goes up to enter a Complaint against Lieut. Colonel Holdridge for misconduct in your Government, and to procure a Commission to cruize on the Sound. He is, as far as I know, an honest sober man, and am persuaded he will obey any orders and Restrictions you may think proper to lay him under. The Evidence of his Complaint is inclosed. I have the Honor to be Your humble Servant

Alex'r McDougall.

P. S. I have been inform'd this Day, that the Enemy have paid Horse Neck a second Visit.

His Excellency Governor Clinton.

[No. 2124.]

Governor Clinton Requests Commissary General Wadsworth to Furnish Him with a Monthly Report of Prices for Grain.

Pokeepsie 3d March 1779.

D'r Sir, I have rec'd your Letter of the 10" ult. inclos'g the Resolution of Congress of the 10" Jan'y, but have not delivered the Letter under Direction to Mr. Paul Schenck as I am informed he resigned his office in your Departm't last Fall. I shall have no objection to any Person you may appoint near to this Place or Fish Kill for paying off the accounts agreable to the above Resolution tho' I wo'd not wish that Mr. Henry Schenck might be the Person. Many applications have been already made to me by the People who have Claims under this Resolution.

The Legislature for Relief of the army and to enable the Commissary to lay in sufficient Supplies for the ensuing Campaign, have now under their Consideration an act empowering the Person administring the Government for the Time being, to appoint Persons for seizing & collect'g all the superfluous Grain in the state for the use of the army & delivering it over to the Comm'y of Purchases; they are induced to this measure from a Deficiency in your magazines in this State, which they impute to the Laws not being spiritedly carried into Execution by your assistants. If this Bill becomes a Law I will transmit you a Copy that measures may be taken so as to prevent any Derangement thereby in your Department.

You will oblige me by furnishing me at present & monthly hereafter with the current Prices given for Flour & Grain for the use of the army in the States of Connecticut & New Jersey. I am convinced there can be no other effectual mode devised for preventing the Practice of exporting our Produce into the neighbouring States for the Purposes of Trade than to destroy the Temptation by placing the Prices in the different States upon a more equal Footing than they are at present.

[To Col. Wadsworth.]   [G. C.]

[No. 2125.]

CLINTON APPEALS TO WASHINGTON

For Assistance in Protecting the Frontiers—Suggests that Marinus Willett be Detailed to Command.

Pokeepsie 3d March 1779.

Dear Sir,* Altho' there have been no Hostilities committed by the Enemy during the winter on the western Frontier of this

---

*For Washington's reply see page 619.

state the Inhabitants particularly of Tryon County are so strongly impressed with apprehensions of Danger on the Opening of the Spring, that many of them have already [removed] and I am informed, that most of them will speedily rémove into the interior Parts of the Country, unless they can have reason to expect more perfect Protection than we were able to afford them last year. Within a few weeks I have received repeated applications from them on this Subject intimating their Intentions to abandon their settlements, unless I could assure them that such Measures would be pursued as would render them secure; & as I am sensible that nothing short of spirited offensive operations ag't the Savages can effect this, I find myself particularly embarrassed. If I am much longer silent they will remove, and to encourage them to continue, might in the Event be cruel. I would, therefore, wish if offensive operations are really intended in that Quarter, that I might have such Intimation of it as would enable me to give general assurances to the Inhabitants to induce them to continue on their Farms, which considering the present general scarcity of Bread will be a Capital Object, as that County is one of the principal Granneries of this State. I am also induced to make this application to your Excellency at present, as our Legislature is now sitting, and discover a Disposition to enable me to call out a Body of men for the ensuing season to cooperate with the Cont. Troops your Excellency may destine for this Service. I am advised that Lt. Colo. Willett who has an Influence among the People of Tryon County from his Exertions at Fort Schuyler when invested by St. Leger, might be serviceably employed in arranging the militia there for a few Months, and I would be glad to have it in my Power to call him to that Service if I should esteem it necessary, & this I presume might be done with't injur'g his Regt. as it is completely officered. I will be much obliged to you for any late Intelligence which you are at Liberty to communicate.

[G. C.]

P. S. I omitted mention'g that if we raise any Number of Men we shall be at a Loss to arm them fit for the Field, unless we can be supplied by the Public, the arms to be returned when the Service expires.

[To Gen. Washington.]

[No. 2126.]

George Clinton's Answer to the Petition from Tryon County for Protection.

3d March 1779.

Gentlemen, I have received your Representation of the 23d ult. and shall lay it before the Legislature who have now under Consideration the measures to be pursued for Defence of the Frontiers. I have already wrote to the Delegates from this state in Congress representing in the strongest Terms the Necessity of affording you Protection & will also address a Letter to his Excellency Genl. Washington on the same subject. Whatever may be the Event of these applications you may depend upon every aid in my own Power for your Defence & security. I am &c.

[G. C.]

[To Jacob Klock and others, Tryon County.]

[No. 2127.]

The New Act of the Legislature to Provide an Immediate Supply of Flour for the Army.

March 4" 1779.

Sir, I have rec'd yours of the 24" & 27" and deferred answering your first Letter as the Legislature were then employed in passing an act for giving an immediate supply of Flour to the army. I now inclose a Copy of this Law to Colo. Wadsworth if he sh'd not be at Hartford you will open his Letters, read them, transcribe the act, and forward the Letter with its Inclosure to the Colo. I am &c.

[G. C.]

[To Peter Colt, Esq.]

[No. 2128.]

Governor Clinton Satisfied with the Commissary Department as at Present Constituted.

Pokeepsie 4th March 1779.

D'r Sir, I was favored by the Receipt of your Letter of the 28" ult. yesterday, having just sent off by Express to Head Quarters an answer to yours of the 10" I inclose a Copy. I also transmit you a Copy of the act of the Legislature mentioned in it.

I am convinced that the Legislature of this State place the highest Confidence in the Head of the Commissary's Department and do not consider him as deserving the least Censure for the Deficiencies in the present supplies for the army; they at the same cannot believe that the Exertions of some of the assistants in putting their late Law into Execution have been such as might have been wished. I would not be serious of taking upon myself the appointment of any officers in your Department without conversing with you personally on the Subject; indeed I conceive very few alterations are at present necessary perhaps an addition of one or two active men may be proper. I am

[G. C.]

[To Col. Wadsworth.]

[No. 2129.]

PREPARING FOR THE SULLIVAN EXPEDITION.

Washington's Views on the Composition of the Troops to Undertake It.

Head Quarters 4th March 1779.

Dear Sir, The President of Congress has transmitted me your Excellency's letter to the delegates of New York,* representing the calamitous situation of the northwestern frontier of that State, accompanied by a similar application from the Pennsilvania Assembly, and a Resolve of the 25th directing me to take the most effectual measures for the protection of the inhabitants and chastisement of the Indians.

The Resolve has been in some measure anticipated by my previous dispositions for carrying on offensive operations against the hostile tribes of Savages. It has always been my intention to communicate this matter to your Excellency in confidence, and I take occasion from your letter abovementioned to inform you that preparations have some time since been making, and they

---

*From headquarters, March 3, Washington had written to Governor Clinton and president Reed of Pennsylvania as follows:

Sir, The president of Congress has transmitted me the Instructions of the Assembly of your State to their Delegates, founded on a representation of the distresses of your western frontiers—and farther the opinion of a Committee of the House on the subject of their defence—together with the two Resolves made in consequence.

I am, therefore, to inform Your Excellency that offensive operations against the hostile tribes of Indians have been meditated and determined upon some time since—that preparations have been making for that purpose—and will be carried into execution at a proper season if no unexpected event takes place, and the situation of affairs on the Seaboard will justify the undertaking—But the profoundest secrecy was judged necessary to the success of such an Enterprise for the following obvious reasons—That immediately upon the discovery of our design the Savages would either put themselves in condition to make head against us, by a reunion of all their force, and that of their allies, strengthened besides by succors from Canada,—or elude the expedition altogether—which might be done at the expence only of a temporary evacuation of forests which we could not possess—and the destruction of a few settlements, which they might speedily reestablish.

Tho' this matter is less under the veil of secrecy than was originally intended— Your Excellency will see the propriety of using such precautions as still remain in our power—to prevent its being divulged—and of covering such preparations as might tend to announce it—with the most specious disguise that the enemy's attention may not be awakened to our real object.

With respect to the force to be employed on this occasion—it is scarcely necessary

will be conducted to the point of execution at a proper season, if no unexpected accident prevents, and the situation of affairs on the maritime frontier justifies the undertaking.

The greatest secrecy is necessary to the success of such an enterprise, for the following obvious reasons; that immediately upon the discovery of our design, the Savages would either put themselves in condition to make head against us, by a reunion of all their force and that of their allies, strengthened besides by succours from Canada, or elude the expedition altogether, which might be done at the expence of a temporary evacuation of forests which we could not possess, and the destruction of a few settlements, which they might speedily re-establish.

I begin to apprehend this matter is less under the veil of secrecy than was originally intended, but your Excellency will see the propriety of using every precaution to prevent its being divulgated and of covering such preparations as might announce it, with the most specious disguise.

With respect to the force to be employed on this occasion, it

---

to observe that the detaching a considerable number of Continental Troops on such a remote expedition would too much expose the country adjacent to the body of the enemy's Army.

There must, therefore, be efficacious assistance derived from the States whose frontiers are obnoxious to the inroads of the barbarians—and for this I intended at the proper time to make application—Your Excellency will be pleased to acquaint me what force yours in particular can furnish in addition to the five Companies voted by Congress—when you think those Companies or the major part of them will probably be raised—What proportion of the levies of your State might be drawn from those inhabitants who have been driven from the frontier—And what previous measures can be taken to engage them without giving an alarm—This Class of people besides the advantages of knowledge of the Country, and the particular motives with which they are animated—will be most likely to furnish the troops best calculated for this service.

They should be Corps of active Rangers, who are at the same time expert marksmen and accustomed to the irregular kind of wood-fighting practiced by the Indians. Men of this description embodied under proper officers would be infinitely preferable to a superior number of Militia unacquainted with this species of war and who would exhaust the magazines of Ammunition and Provision—without rendering any effectual service.

It will be a very necessary attention to avoid the danger of short inlistments—their service should be limited only by the expedition or a term amply competent to it—otherwise we shall be exposed to the ill-consequences of having their engagements expire at an interesting perhaps a critical juncture. I have the honor to be, etc.,

is scarce necessary to observe, that the detaching a considerable number of Continental Troops, on such a remote expedition would too much expose the Country adjacent to the Enemy's main body. There must, therefore, be efficacious assistance derived from the States whose frontiers are obnoxious to the inroads of the barbarians and for this, I intended at a proper time to make application. Your Excellency will be pleased to acquaint me what force yours in particular can furnish, what proportion can be drawn from the inhabitants who have been driven from the frontier, and what previous measures can be taken to engage them without giving an alarm. This Class of people besides the advantages of knowlege of the Country, and the particular motives with which they are animated, are most likely to furnish the troops best qualified for the service, which should be Corps of active Rangers, who are at the same time expert marksmen and accustomed to the irregular kind of woodfighting practiced by the Indians. Men of this description embodied under proper officers would be infinitely preferable to a superior number of militia unacquainted with this species of War, and who would exhaust the magazines of amunition and provision without rendering any effectual service.

It will be a very necessary attention to avoid the danger of short enlistments, the service should be limited only by the expedition, or a term amply competent to it, otherwise we may be exposed to having their engagements expire at some interesting or perhaps critical juncture.

I have only to add that I shall be happy to have the advantage of any sentiments or advice your Excellency may be pleased to communicate relative to this expedition.

I have the honor to be with great regard and Esteem Your Excellency's most obed't Serv't

Go. Washington.*

His Excellency Governor Clinton.

*For Clinton's reply see page 646.

P. S.　In your Excellency's Letter to the Delegates, you mention that you have not received the arrangement of the Troops of your State.　It was transmitted me among the rest by the Board of War, and I sent it to Brigadier General James Clinton; inclosed in a letter of the 22d ulto. to Brigadier Genl. James Clinton desiring him to report to me any subsequent alterations that may have happened, and to return the arrangement to me, for completion, Congress having by a Resolve of the 4th Feby. vested me with powers for that purpose.　Commissions will finally be issued from the board of War.　If your Excellency can hasten the termination of this business by affording any light or assistance it will be rendering a very great service.

[No. 2130.]

Sheriff Nicoll Regards Captain Fletcher Mathews as an Exceedingly Bad Man.

Goshen March 5th 1779.

Dear Governor, I Receved your Faver and should with Pleashure a Took the Conducting of the Flag but I have had a Survear Turn of the Reumatism which Renders me not able to Purform the Jurney.　I Understand by Mr. Wisenor that Capt. Fletcher Mathews and Thomas Bull are to be Removed to Albany; if so I am Glad, for I Look on Mathews to be an Exceding Bad man and that he is willing to Do all the hurt he Can, and this I am Confident of, that as long as he Stays in Goshen he never will Try for an Exchange Nor his Friends; and his being a Prisoner to me has Rendered the Office more Disagreeable than any thing Else, as he and Famaly are Continually Teasing of me to Shew him Faver, which is Disagreeable to me; one of his Daughtors has Laid at the Point of Death this Some Days, and by a Request of his wife and my wife I have Purmitted him to go and See his

Daughtor, which I hope you will parden me for. I am with Sin-
cear Reguard Your Excellency's most Obedient Humble S'r

Isaac Nicoll.

His Excellency George Clinton.

[No. 2131.]

ENCOURAGING NEWS FROM EUROPE.

*Washington Willing to Detail Colonel Willett, Provided James
Clinton Thinks He can be Spared.*

Head Quarters 6th March '79.

Dear Sir, The annexed letter written previous to the receipt of
your Excellency's favor of the 3d inst.* will serve as an answer
to the principal part of its contents.

The Intelligence I have to communicate to your Excellency, I
apprehend is no more than will have already been transmitted by
the Delegates of your State. It is in brief as follows: That the
King of Spain has declared he will not be an unconcerned Spec-
tator of the depredations committed on the property of his Ally.
That the King of Naples and Scicily has honored the American
Flag, and ordered his ports to be opened to our Commerce; that
the City of Amsterdam has prepared a form of a Treaty with
America, to be proposed to the States General. That the Empress
of Russia has positively refused to enter into any subsidiary
Treaty with Great Britain and has motived her refusal in terms
breathing a generous regard to the rights of mankind.

I am exceedingly sorry to find that in the present State of our
magazines, I cannot give your Excellency any encouragement to
expect a supply of Arms from thence, for the Levies of your State.

If your Excellency is of opinion that Lt. Col. Willett can be
serviceable in the way you mention, and General J. Clinton thinks

---

* See page 611.

he may be spared from the Regiment, I shall readily consent to his absence.

I am with the greatest respect and esteem Dear Sir Your most obed't serv't

G. Washington.

His Excellency Governor Clinton.

[No. 2132.]

Alarming Indian Rumors.

Extract of a letter from General Schuyler dated Albany 4th March 1779.

*"A party of the enemy have been as high up as Tyonderoga, & carried off some inhabitants and a number of cattle, and it is said that a body of them have taken post at Tyonderoga. I do not beleive it, but have ordered (as Genl. Clinton is absent for a few days) that an officer should be dispatched with a party from fort George to reconnoitre that place."

March 7th.

Last night Colonel Van Schaick read me letters from Cap'n Graham, who commands at Fort Schuyler and Capt. Cop at Oneida. They have received intelligence that a large body of Indians and tories are actually collecting at Niagara and the Seneca Towns, immediately to attack Oneida and from thence proceed down the Mohawk river. That the Cayugas have removed their frontiers to the Senecas.

*This information of the 4th of March I am informed by a person from Bennington who left that place a few days ago is premature.

[No. 2133.]

The Hallett-Holdridge Imbroglio. .

D'r Sir, In Consequence of a Complaint made to me by James Hallett an Inhabitant of this State ag't Lt. Colo. Holdridge I inclose your Excellency Copies of two affidavits taken on the Subject not doubting that your Excellency if you can interfere give such orders respecting the Matter as will ensure to the Party complaining the Justice to which he is entitled. I am &c.

[G. C.]

March 7" 1779.

[To Gen. Washington.]

[No. 2134.]

William Tryon's Orders to the Queens County Exempts for Coast Guard Duty.

Copy of a Letter from His Excellency, Gov'r Tryon, to Colo. Hamilton.

Fire Post, Kings Bridge 7th March 1779.

Sir, As the armed Ships in the South Bay, are a sufficient Security from any insult of the Enemy on the South Side of Long-Island, & as the whale Boats from the Connecticutt Coast, are continually committing depredations on the North Side, the Duty of the Militia must be directed to that Quarter; & whereas the hireing of Gaurds has been found not only an indulgence to the Inhabitants, but the most effectual method to Gaurd the necessary Posts, I do hereby order, that all Persons in Queens County do bear a proportion of the expence of such Duty, according to the Value of their Estates Real or Personal, although exempted from Militia Duty by Age or Office.   I am y'r Ob't Serv't

Signd Wm. Tryon, Gov'r.

To Colo: Arch'd Hamilton &c. &c. &ca. Queens County Militia.

Colo. Hamilton Orders Major Kissam to put the above Orders in force immediately, in his District.

Signd Arch'd Hamilton, Colo. Command't Queens County Militia.

New Town 9th March 1779.

Gent'n, Colo. Hamilton, Orders that the Troop, & Company's, under your respective Commands be duly warned of a General Review the first Week in April next, the day &ca. that may be fixed on, you will be timely inform'd off.

As they have long since been orderd to equip fully it is expected they will appear so, & with their arms &ca. in good Order, as Delinquents will be noticed & punished for their neglect of propper attention to Orders.

Jas. Long, Adjt. Queens County Militia.

Capt'ns Israel Young—at Cold-Spring; Daniel Youngs,—at Oyster Bay; Jarvis Coles—at Musquito-Cove; Thomas Van Wyck,—at East-Woods; & Abraham Van Wyck, at Woolvara-Hollow.

[No. 2135.]

COMMISSARY REED FAVORS A GENERAL SEIZURE.

Urges General McDougall to Use His Influence with Governor Clinton to Secure that End.

Armenia 8th March 1779.

Sir, I received your Favors of the 28th of Febuary advising me to send on the Vegetables promis'd last Winter also of the 100 Certificates & troop of Horse, in answer to which I did all in my power to purchase Vegetables, after receiving your orders for that purpose, and expected sledding to transport them to Fish Kill, but have had very little since, so found that I must loose a great part of them by Frost &c. when I agreed with the People to take them again with some little Loss, which makes it out of my Power to send any. I am well suited with the Permits you sent, hope they will answer a good End; also with the Horse, but could wish there had been more, as there is one capital Road in this Quarter, left unguarded, which is the Road leading from Dover to Kent and New Millford, where great abuses have been committed by those abandoned Jobbers and Tories, to whose account we may charge many Disadvantages we now labour under. If you could spare 4 or 5 more to guard that Road, I should hope soon to see Matters in a better Situation about Bread. You seem surpris'd at our not being able to feed the Division at Danbury & Peekskill. You must remember we have 10,000 men to supply at the Eastward, including Artificers, sick &c which takes off the Chief of my Flour. I have lately sent about 500 Barrels to Danbury, and am continually sending to the Eastward, and am doing all in my power to lay up magazines for Summer, but think it will be out of my Power to lay up such Supplies as to bring Harvest, unless the Legislature will make some provision for seizing the new Crops, and that immediately, as the Tories and those worse than the Tories (the Jobbers) are hiding their Flour in Barns, out Houses and in the Woods untill they can get it over the Line. They will call it all new wheat to prevent my seizing it, which makes the Business go on very heavy. However am determined to do all in my power, but have neither Honor, Profit, nor pleasure in View, as great Part I get is by fighting which makes the people curse me. Our Legislature and General Officers dont do much better, which I take unkind, as I am positive I have done all in my power to supply the army on the best Terms my weak Capacity would admit of. I am Sir Your humble servant

(Copy)   James Reid A. C. P.

P. S. Since writing the above, I am told a Number of Waggons have cross'd the Line to Connecticut loaded with Flour in a by

Road, so that I find there is no stopping that practice unless the means is taken away which will be to seize all the Wheat & Flour.

Pray, Sir, use your Influence with the Governor to have that done immediately, or we never can feed the army with Bread. Yours,

J. R.

(Copy)

[To Gen. McDougall.]

[No. 2136.]

George Clinton Refers John Jay to Mr. Sands for Legislative News.

[March 8, 1779.]

Dear Sir, The Legislature being about to adjourn I am so pressed with Business in the Councils of Revision & Appointment and the ordinary Duties of my office that I have barely Time to acknowledge the Receipt of your Letters of the 3d & 9" ulto. For news, I must refer you to the inclosed Papers and to the Bearer Mr. Sands, who as he has had an opportunity of attending the two Houses the greatest Part of the Session, will be able to give you a satisfactory acc't of the Debates and Proceedings. Be Pleased to offer an apoligy to Mr. Duane & Mr. Morris for my not writing to them by this Conveyance & believe me &c.

[G. C.]

You've inclosed Mr. Stewart's Rec't for [   ] Dollars.

[To John Jay Esq.]

[No. 2137.]

General Schuyler Apprehensive of an Indian Raid on the Frontiers.

Extract of a letter from General Schuyler dated Albany 8 March 1779.

The Indians now with me have no doubt from every account they have had, but that the enemy intend very soon to attack the frontiers with a very considerable force. They think necessity will oblige them to it, to obtain a supply of provisions, which they are already in great want of. Should they succeed in this they will be in a situation to make a better stand than they otherwise would be. If, therefore, it is possible to send up more troops immediately for the protection of the settlements on the Mohawk river, I think it would be prudent to do it.

[No. 2138.]

Returns of Colonel Bellinger's Regiment.

A Return of the Regiment of Militia of German Flatts, and Kingsland Districts, in the County of Tryon, and State of New York.

March the 10th 1779.

Field, and Staff Officers.

Peter Bellinger, Colonel   George Demuth, Adjutant

Frederick Bellinger, Lieut. Col. Rudolph Stailey, Qr. Master

William Petry, Surgeon.

No. of Companies	Captains	Lieuts.	Ensigns	Serj-ants	Corporals	Privates
1st Company		1	1	4	4	31
2nd do	1	2	1	4	4	36
3rd do	1	1	1	4	4	21
4th do	1	2				17
5th do		2		4	4	12
6th do	1	1	1	3	3	16
7th do		1	1			5
	4	10	5	19	19	138

The reason of there being no Captain to the first Company is, there was no Commission sent up for Michael Ittig. And the Capt. of the 7th Comp'y, Henry Eckler, is gone out of this District, to Conajoharie, and some of that Comp'y is kill'd, and taken Prisoners, and most of the rest is gone out of the District. There

40

was no Commission came up for the 5th Company, which is commanded at present, by one of the Lieutenants, Henry Huber.

Peter Bellinger, Colo.

[No. 2139.]

Returns of Colonel A. Hawkes Hay's Regiment.

A Return of Colo. A. Hawkes Hay's Regiment of Militia on the South Side of Orange County, for his Excellency Gov'r Clinton.

Colonel	Lt. Colonel	Majors	Captains	Lieutenants	Adjutant	Ensigns	Quar. Master	Surgeon	Q. M. Serjt	Sergt. Major	Serjants	Corporals	Drum & Fifes	Rank & File	Total
1	1	2	7	14	1	7	1	1	1	1	30	28	14	350	459

The above is a true Return of the Regiment according to the Captains' Returns. March 10th 1779.

A. Hawkes Hay.

[No. 2140.]

McDougall's Plan for Capturing Tryon.

Head Quarters Pecks Kill 10th March 1779.

Sir, The Commander in chief, has enabled me by hard money, to carry into Execution, my Design of offering a Reward, for General Tryon and others. I beg you to try, the Legislature, without Delay, whether they will pass a short Law, to enable me to pardon the Non-Commissioned officers and privates of the New Levies, to induce them, to aid in that salutary work. I think they cannot hesitate, on the Policy and Propriety of the measure.

I beg a Line from you on this Subject, on the Prospect of the Success of the application. I am Sir Your humble Servant

Alex'r McDougall.*

Governor Clinton.

---

*For Governor Clinton's reply see page 644.

[No. 2141.]

Associated Exempts at Goshen, Orange County.

His Excellency George Clinton Esqr. Governor in and over the State of New York and the Territories thereunto belonging &c. &c. &c.

11th March 1779.

Sir, Pardon the Brevity with which I apologize to address your Excellency; the knowledge I have of your Goodness causes the presumption. I embrace the present Opportunity of remiting to your Excellency a List of the persons who are nominated under my Circumspection in Quality of Military Order of Exempts, should do myself the Pleasure to present the Same to your Excellency before now, if I could handsomely accomplish my designs as the association was not complete, nor have they as yet answered my sanguine Expectation relative to their association. Agreeable to the Militia-act, the persons mentioned in the Return met and nominated the officers that should superintend. It happened that I was appointed Capt'n, Jonathan Bailey 1st Lut. Jacob Duning 2d Lieuten't, Will'm Thompson Ensign. Since the Time of appointment, Mr. Jacob Dunning met with a great Misfortune in losing the Use of his right Hand, which unhappily renders him incapable of officiating or serving in a Marshal Capacity. I beg Leave to subscribe myself with due Respect, Sir, Your Excellency's most ob't servant,

Jno. Wood.

———

Orange County ss; We the Subscribers, being under the age of fifty five years, who have held civil or military Commissions and have not been re-appointed to our respective Ranks of Office, or being between the ages of fifty and fifty five years, do hereby

Severally ingage, that we will respectively on all Occasions, obey the orders of our respective Commanding Officers, and will in Cases of Invasion or Incursions of the enemy or Insurrection, march to repel the enemy or suppress such Insurrection in the Like manner as the enrolled militia are Compelled to do, So as that we Shall not when called out in Detachments be annexed to any other Regiment or Company or be under the Immediate Command of any other than our own Officers.

John Wood, Jacob Duning, Jonathan Bayley, Nathaniel Roe, George H. Jackson, Samll. Carpenter, Wm. W. Thompson, Ephraim Marston, Antony Yelderton, William Barker, Joshua Davis, Kadmiel Moore, John Davis, Phinehas Case, James Butler, Coe Gale, Joseph Wood, John Denton, Joseph Grommon, Jonathan Thompson, John Brunson, Gilbert Vail, James Sawyer, James Knap, Israel Wells, Jacob Arnut, Richard Gale, Daniel Everett, Jr.

Goshen Sept. 1st 1778.

GOVERNOR CLINTON'S RESPONSE.

March 15, 1779.

Sir, I have rec'd your Letter of the 11" Inst. inclos'g an Association of Exempts. By the Militia Law, the associators should recommend the Officers to command the Company; 'till this is done the Council of Appointment are not by Law authorized to appoint the Officers & it will be best to have it done as quick as possible. I am &c.

[G. C.]

[To Capt. Jno. Wood.]

[No. 2142.]

Returns of Colonel Jesse Woodhull's Regiment.

Return of the State of Colo. Jesse Woodhull's Regm't of Orange County, Dated at Bloom'g Grove, March 12, 1779.

COMPANIES	Colonel	Lt. Colo'l	Major	Captains	Lieutenants	Ensigns	Adjut't	Qr. Master	Surgeon	Clerk	Serjants	Corporals	Drum & fife	Rank & File	Total
	1	1	1				1	1	1	1					
Capt'n Smith's Company				1	2	1					3	4		30	41
Capt'n Vanduzer's Do				1	2	1					4	4		33	45
Lieut. Brewster's Do					2	1					4	4		49	60
Capt. Conklin's Do				1	2	1					4	3	1	18	30
Lieut. Seely's Do					2	1					4	4		24	35
Capt'n Pain's Do				1	2	1					3	2		22	31
Capt'n Buck's Do				1	2	1					4	4		35	47
Capt. Slut's Do				1	2	1					4	2		10	20
Capt. Woodhull's Lt. Horse Do				1	1	1					4	4		38	49
	1	1	1	7	17	9	1	1	1	1	34	31	1	259	358

I do Hereby Certify that This is a Just and True Return of the State of my Redgment from the Returns that have been made to me.

Jesse Woodhull, Coll.

[No. 2143.]

Captain Edsall's Company of Orange County Exempts.

A Return of Captain Benjamin Edsall's Company of ascociated Exempts of Orange County.

13th March 1779.

	C	Sub.	Serj.	C	D & f	Priv.
1 Captain	1					
Subalterns		3				
Serjents						
Corporals						
Drum & fife						
Privates						37
Total	1	3				37

[No. 2144.]

McDOUGALL FORCED TO ACT AS A DESPOT.

Insists Upon Radical Treatment for Enemies and Traitors—The Militia Proposition.

Head Quarters Pecks Kill 14th March 1779.

Sir, The Spies and Agents I have out, among the Tories. inform me, the Enemy intend paying me a Visit, when the time of Service, of the Nine months men expire. This will be about the first of April, when my strength will be diminished, one Thousand Rank and File. Near five hundred are already gone. When that Day arrives, I shall be left almost with the Name of Corps. The Vicinity of this place, has been almost laid Waste by our own and the Enemy's army. To encourage the Inhabitants, to persue their Agriculture, as well as from a principle of Justice, many Thousand Rails have been cut by the short Levies, which have been delivered to the poorest and most distressed, and where it wou'd best promote the publick service. The Terms on which those Rails were Cut, have lessened my strength. It is with extreame Reluctance, I call for any of the militia, more especially, as Flour is scant, but the protection of the Good people of this state, and the common safety demand it. I must, therefore, request when the next Relief is sent from Colo. Brinckerhoof's Regiment, that it consist of a Captain and fifty Rank and file. Capt'n Haight in the Highlands, who commands a Company of Colo. Ludington's, has done no public duty himself or his company. I wish for an express order, for his Company to fatigue and mend Roads.

We ought now to convince these miscreants, America is their master. They will be well paid, and used, as well all the Detachments called out, if they behave tolerably well. The Season is now advanced, and its time we shou'd be determined, on the disposition of the militia in Case of an alarm. It may be dangerous to the state, and the public service, for me to be obliged to wait your Orders, for those in my Vicinity, on that event; three Days at least may be lost if not more. I, therefore, submit it to your Consideration, whether it will not be expedient I shou'd have your unlimitted Orders for the call of the Militia, of West-Chester and the lower part of Orange Counties? For the above Reasons, I beg you to advise me, how you intend to dispose of those of the upper part of Orange Ulster and Dutchess Counties? Will it not be necessary, that particular inspection be made, into the arms and Amunition of Orange & Ulster least their neglect when Fort-Montgomery was attacked shou'd be repeated. Such is the state of many important matters in the neighbourhood of these posts, that I have been obliged to act the Despot in several instances: The particulars of which shall communicate in a few Days.

When I had the honor of Commanding Here in 1776 and 1777 I earnestly recommended it to the Convention, to raise a Troop of strong Horse, and to burn the Hutts on the mountains, the Harbours and hiding places of Tories spies and Robbers. No Notice hath been taken of either. The Consequence has been, that Emerick's Troop of Horse have been recruited every spring, with the best Horses of our Country, and the Inhabitants robed of their Horses and many Families exceedingly distressed. The audacity of those Villains, is daily increasing, and will be more so when the Leaf gets on the Trees. I had, therefore, determined, when first I came here, to take some decisive measures with the Consealors, of those miscreants, when that period shou'd arrive. But I find them so alert, and doing so much prejudice, to the State and the service, that no time must be lost, or we shall scarse have a Horse to draw a Waggon or an artillery piece, when the Campaign

Opens. The Night before last, three Continental Horses and several private Ones, were taken from Salem. All the American Army, disposed in Guards, in the Covered and Rockey Country of this State, will not totally prevent the mischief, and far less will the small Corps of the Army under my Command effect it. As its my wish in all Cases, where the Civil authority can give a remedy, to apply to them for it, I am constrained now for the safety of the state, and the advancement of the Common Cause, to request your aid and Council, and that of the Legislature, if its not adjourned, to Stop the progress of a practice so advantageous to the Enemy and injurious to America. I shou'd have done this some time ago, but was informed, a Petition from many of the Inhabitants on the same subject, had been presented to the Legislature. Before the Leaf gets on the Tree, I shall be compelled to take some effectual and decesive measures, if the Civil authority does not do it. I cannot pasively See, the Enemy's Light Horse recruited, out of this state. When all the Horses it can spare, will be absolutely necessary for its own safety. It is a hard Condition, for me to be placed in, to be obliged for the security of this state, and the general security, to act as a Despot and then, to be subject to the Caprice and calumny of the times. I hope my Countrymen, will take the Honor to themselves, and not Compell the military to do acts, which will come with a better Grace, from a Watchfull Legislature. On Friday next three Villains will be executed at the Plains, one for attempting to Seize an Inhabitant, to Carry him to the Enemy; the other Two as spies.

I will pledge myself to America, that the means in my power, shall be exerted for the discharge of the Trust committed to me. But if those, who are immediately intrusted, will not give their aid, their Constituents must take the Consequence.

Have the Legislature passed a Law, to enable a Court of Inquiry to call Civil Witnesses before them to detect frauds? You have no doubt heard, of the murder of one of Colo. Putnam's Men by the Horse Theives.

I am, Sir, Your very Humble Servant

Alex'r McDougall.[*]

[To G. C.]

[No. 2145.]

Robert R. Livingston Fears the Tories May again Prove Troublesome.

Manor of Livingston 14th March 1778[9].

Dear Sir, Mr. Duane by sending down an express affords me an opportunity of enquiring of your Excellency if you have rec'd any late intelligence of importance as we have various reports circulating here of a treaty &c. said to come from Mr. Morris. If, as I suppose, they are nothing more than the lie of the day I sh'd wish to have it in my power to contradict them. It is possible that I may have Letters from the southerd; sh'd this be the case I must give your Excellency the trouble of forwarding them by this express. I hope Mr. Morris has taken his seat in Senate; his refusal will be an essential injury both to the publick & himself. I hope this has been hinted to him if he has any doubts about the matter.

What cheafly induces me to trouble your Excellency at this time is the apprehention I am under of the Tories becoming troublesome again in the Manor. I have observed strong symtoms of this among some that I have conversed with. The Committee & majestrates are very desirous of having a small corps of rangers under an Ensign who sh'd be at the command of the

---

[*]For Governor Clinton's reply see page 644.

majestrates & stationed where they sh'd think proper, perhaps a sergeant with twelve men would be sufficient, together with an order to a part of the Claverack militia to march on the first alarm into the Manor. It is much easier to prevent an insurrection than to suppress it.

These fellow have some very intelligent Leader, who will probably profit from their past mistakes.

When the river opens I think it would be unsafe to suffer the two men who went to New York last fall with the enimy & returned the latter end of the winter, to remain at home, as it is more than probable that they are agents of the enimy. As your Excellency is empowered to make such drafts as you think necessary & are furnished with a vote of credit for that purpose, I think you may direct Jacob Power to raise the men, for four months or such other time as you shall think adviseable. If your Excellency has any papers that are no longer new to you I sh'd be glad to see them. I am, Dear Sir, with great esteem & respect Your Most Ob't Hum: Serv't

Robt. R. Livingston.

His Excellency Gov'r Clinton &c. &c. &c. Poughkeepsie.

[private.]

[No. 2146.]

Returns of Colonel Fisher's Regiment.

A General Return of Colo. Frederick Fisher's Batt'n of Tryon County M[ilitia] in the Mohawk Districk in the State of New York.

March 15th 1779.

Companies	Commission'd Officers						Staff Officers						Non Commission'd & Rank & File					
	Colo	Lieut. Colo.	Major	Captains	Lieuts	Ensigns	Chaplin	P. Master	Adjt	Q. Master.	Surgeon	Surgeon Mate	Serjt. Major.	Qr. Master Serjent	Serjents	Corporals	Drummers & Fifers.	Rank & File
1st	1	1	1	1	2	1		1	1				1		2	2	2	22
2nd				1	2	1									3	2		29
3rd				1	2	1									2	2	1	15
4th				1	2	1									2	2		17
5th				1	2	1									2	2		20
6th				1	2	1									2	2		20
7th				1	2	1									2	2		16
8th				1	2	1									2	2		15
9th				1	2	1									4	4	2	40
10th				1	2	1									4	4	1	31
Total	1	1	1	10	20	10			1	1				1	25	24	6	225

Fred'k Fisher, Colo.

[No. 2147.]

Governor Clinton Tenders the Command of One of the New Frontier Regiments to Colonel Willett.

Pokeepsie 15 March 1779.

D'r Sir,* I have Reason to believe that you could do essential Service to the State by taking the Command of one of the Regt. of militia which is to be embodied for the Defence of the western Frontiers, as I am informed the Inhabitants of Tryon County who are most exposed, place the highest Confidence in your Zeal and military abilities and their Losses in the action of Harkimer have deprived them of the best Officers in their respective Regts. Presuming that such a Command wo'd be in no wise disagreable to you, I have wrote to Genl. Washington for the Purpose, and have his Consent, provided Genl. James Clinton should think that you can at present be spared from your Regt. for this Service.

---

*For Colonel Willett's answer see page 656.

I have, therefore, to request, if it is agreable to yourself, that you will consult Genl. Jas. Clinton on this Subject, and acquaint me with the Result; that if you determine & the Genl. consent to your accepting this Command, I may have you appointed & furnish you with the necessary orders. You will please to observe, that I have two Regts. to raise for Defence of the Frontiers; each will be commanded by a Lieut. Colo. & officered nearly agreable to the new arrangement & to continue in Service 'till 1st Jan'y. If there are any officers left out in the new arrange't, or other Persons which you wo'd incline to have with you, you will return their Names & the Rank in which they qualified to serve that I may propose them to the Council for their appointment. I am &c.

[G. C.]

[To Lt. Col. Marinus Willett.]

[No. 2148.]

Washington Orders a System of Beacon Signals in the Highlands.

Head Quarters Middlebrook 15th March 1779.

Dear Sir, The 1st April ensuing, the times of about 1000 of the troops under the command of General McDougall will expire. These returning home will leave the Highland posts in a state much weaker than is proper for them to experience in the approaching season. I shall endeavour to replace them as far as in my power. But in addition to what I may be able to do, it will be expedient to fall upon some plan, by which the posts may receive succor from the neighbouring militia at a moment's warning.

Sensible of the inconveniences of calling this body out upon every occasion, I wish to avoid it on the present till it becomes absolutely necessary. I have, therefore, to request that a convention of signals may be agreed to between General McDougall and your Excellency, by which means notice may be immediately communicated, of the enemies approach, and beacons fired at proper places, as signals for the militia to assemble to his support.

While this mode provides for the defence of the posts, it excludes as much as possible all unnecessary expence, and trouble to the militia.

I have written to General McDougall on this subject, and am, D Sir, Your Excellency's most obt. serv't,

Go. Washington.*

His Excellency Governor Clinton.

P. S.   16 March 1779.

Since writing the above I have received the inclosed intelligence* from General Schuyler, relative to a design against your frontier. One of the letters which the General refers to has not come to hand; but you will be able to judge from the transmitted accounts, and the known policy and circumstances of the enemy, what degree of confidence is to be given to the supposed incursion.

As there can be no addition of regular force ordered at present, to that now on the frontier, without disconcerting other measures, it will be necessary to take into consideration the best means to reinforce it with militia, (should you think the information sufficiently authentic). Or in case this cannot be accomplished, to withdraw to the interior country, the stock and provisions which seem the principal object with the enemy.

The total troops at the different posts along the frontier amount to 2012 men exclusive of Courtlandt's Regim't; These with a

*See pages 620 and 624.

reinforcement of militia, might at least give the inhabitants a security, till more efficacious measures can be pursued at the proper season.

The provision or stock, at all events should not be suffered to fall into their hands, if it can be removed, or protected; and I make no doubt of such precautions on your part, as may appear adequate to this end. I am &c.

Go. Washington.

[No. 2149.]

A CRITICAL SITUATION.

Commissary Colt and the Flour Supply—Gloomy Prospect in Rhode Island and Massachusetts, and for Gates' and Sullivan's Troops.

March 16 1779.

May it please your Excellency, The daily application of my assistants, bringing in their acc's for settlement, prevents my applying in person for your further advice on the Measures necessary to be taken for securing the wheat & Flour, in your State, for the use of the Army. I have, therefore, with the approbation of the Commissary General, prevailed on my Friend, James Lockwood, Esq., to wait on your Excellency, on this occasion.

It will not only be a particular favour to Col. Wadsworth (I would add to me also, could I flatter myself that would be a further Inducment) but an essential piece of Service to the United States, if you could direct Mr. Lockwood to such persons to succeed the 2 Mr. Schenks & Mr. Leak as would fill their posts with Satisfaction to the army & public. I am aware this may subject your Excellency to some small Inconvenience. But my not being acquainted with the persons who would answer the purpose in those Districts, makes this application necessary. You will en-

join that secrecy on Mr. Lockwood which you may think proper
respecting the Reason for having the Schenks displaced.

It will be necessary for Mr. Lockwood to have a return of those
persons whom you have appointed (as far as it respects my limits)
to Seize the wheat & Flour which the owners refuse to sell.

I am obliged, in Duty to the public, to assure your Excellency
that the State of the public Magazines, in the State Rode Island
& Massachusetts, affords the most gloomy prospect to those who
are employed in subsisting the Troops in those Departments;
there is not exceeding 400 bar's Flour at the various deposits in
the latter, and not exceeding ten days Bread for the Troops now
on duty in the former. I have reason to fear they have not even
that. If any extraordinary embarassments should be thrown in
the way of supplying Sharon Magazine, from whence alone I can
draw any supplies for the Eastern post, the Troops under command of General Gates and General Sullivan must disband. I
am with great respect, your Excellency's most obd. hum'e Serv't

Peter Colt.

His Excellency Governour Clinton.

[No. 2150.]

*Commissary General Wadsworth Sustains Colonel Colt—Distressing
Scarcity of Flour.*

Hartford, March 16th 1779.

Dear Sir, Your favours of the 3d & 4th Instant shou'd have
been sooner attended too had I been able to have furnished the
money to pay the acc'ts ordered to be paid by Congress. I have
just now returned from New London where I have had the most
convincing proofs of the real scarcity of Flour, the Inhabitants
totally destitute, the Garrison nearly out, the Continental Frigate

unable to go to Sea for want of Bread, and the Troops at Providence supplied from hand to mouth, and in great Danger of being entirely out. The wise & timely Law of your State gives me hopes. If this and other States will pass Simelar Laws and Execute them, there is yet hopes of supplying our Troops. I cannot think the private demands of any State ought to be preferr'd to the demands of the Continent.

It is impossible for me to wait on your Excellency in Person. Mr. Colt is also engag'd in setling some important acc'ts, which forbids his waiting on you. Major Lockwood has consented to go into your State and will wait on your Excellency. I beg leave to recommend him to your notice. He will receive some Instructions from Mr. Colt and will, with your approbation, make some new appointments and do such other Business as may be necessary to be done in Mr. Colt's District, in all which he will be governed by your advise.

It gives me great Satisfaction that the Legislature of the State of New York are satisfyed with my proceedings, and the Spiritted Vigorous measures entered into by them for furnishing the army with Flour have induced me to try a little longer to hold an office which I had determined to Quit. I will not say I am left unsupported by every other State, and, I am not sure Congress have forgot they have a C— G— but the Vigor and attention of your State gives me fresh hopes. Major Lockwood brings money for the Settlement of the acc'ts above mentioned. I have the Honor to be, Your Excellency's most obedient Humb. serv't

Jere'h Wadsworth, Com. Gen. Pur.

His Excell'y Governor Clinton.

RICHARD LORD HOWE, ADMIRAL.

[No. 2151.]

Lynde Lord Urges the Settlement of His Account for Keeping Prisoners.

Litchfield 16th March 1779.

May it please your Excellency, I herewith send an account against the State of New York, for sundry Expenditures for Prisoners sent from your State to our gaol, in the year 1776, and as this is the third time I have sent the account, and rec'd no remittance as yet, must beg your Excellency's attention to the affair, and that you will direct and order that the acco't may be paid, as it has been long due, and the money greatly depreciated: Your Excellency may se by a rec't herewith sent, that at the time the money was due to me, I had Sixty eight pounds ten shillings New York money in my hands, belonging to your State, which I have since put into your Treasury, with Expectation my acco't would have been paid without any further trouble or Expence. And, as the amount of my acco't is mostly for board and supplying your Prisoners while sick and under my care, must intreat your Excellency to give me a permit to bring wheat or flower out of your state to the amount of my acco't, for the use of my own Family. I am your Excellency's most obedient Humble Serv't,

Lynde Lord.

His Excellency Gov'r Clinton.

[No. 2152.]

COMPENSATION FOR STATE OFFICERS.

The Legislature Defeats a Bill of Attainder—Governor Clinton Opposes the Bill.

Poukeepsie 17th March 1779.

My Dear Sir, I have only a Moment to write you, tho' there are many Matters which I wish to communicate. The Legislature

41

adjourned yesterday Morning having enacted 27 Laws. I inclose you an Extract of the Titles specifying the Purposes for which they are intended. A Bill of Attainder also passed both Houses but was losst in the Senate on Objections made to it by the Council of Revision. It attainted upwards of 300 Persons ipso facto of High Treason, so far as to work a Forfeiture of their Estates. I have not Time to give you a particular description of this Bill. It was in my Opinion neither founded on Justice or warranted by sound Policy or the Spirit of the Constitution.

The Legislature have raised the Allowance to our Delegates to 12 Dollars p'r Day. If I recollect right, this Allowance is to take place as from Octob'r last. It was on the Motion of Genl. Scott who proposed 15 Dollars. A Letter I rec'd from Colo. Floyd mentioning the Insufficiency of the late Allowance which I communicated to some of the Members, some say occasioned this rise, others impute it to a Chance intended in the Delegation. The Chief Justice & Chancellor's Sallary are raised to £400 p'r an; the other Civil Officers nearly in the same Proportion; Judges travelling Expences 10 Dollars p'r Day. The Members Wages are fixed at 4 & the Clerks 6 Dollars p'r Day. Mr. Inches waiting, I am &c.

[G. C.]

[To John Jay Esq.]

[No. 2153.]

Washington Notifies McDougall that the Enemy on Staten Island Are in Motion.

Head Quarters Middle Brook March 17th 1779.

Sir,* I receiv'd intelligence last night, that the Enemy on Staten Island are in motion with more than usual demonstration and

---

*See page 664—McDougall to George Clinton.

parade. This may intend an incursion into the Jerseys, or it may be meant to cover an Expedition elsewhere possibly against the posts under your Command. I, therefore, think it necessary to communicate to you the Intelligence I have receiv'd to put you upon your Guard & that you may accelerate the succours pointed out in my Letter of yesterday.

Shou'd you get information that the Enemy have made a movement this way in force, I wou'd recommend it to you in concurrence with General Putnam to march as large a Body of Troops as can be spared towards Kings-Bridge to give an Alarm there and create a diversion in our favor but this must be done with so much Caution as not to endanger the Important posts under your Command. I am D'r Sir Your most Obed't servant

Copy. Go. Washington.

P. S. You will forward the inclosed to General Putnam, who is directed to give the most immediate succor shou'd the Effort be directed up the North River.

[To Gen. McDougall.]

[No. 2154.]

Massachusetts Looks to New York for Breadstuffs.

Poughpeekse March 17 1779.

May it please your Excellency, The Committe of both Houses appointed to hear and consider our application in behalf of the State of Massachusetts Bay for a supply of Flour, having desired us to inform them what supplys had beene made by Connecticut to Rhode Island and Massachusetts, we would request your Excellency to inform those Gentlemen that upon an application made to Connecticut for a supply, liberty was given to Rhode Island to purchas 7000 bushells of grain, but was denied to our

State upon a misinformation that we had a supply by water, and
upon our arrival at Connecticut no body of Men being seting that
had authority to permit the transportation of grain from that
State we could gain no Licence, therefor, but our Mr. Inches ventured to lodge £2000 with a Mr. Church, at Hartford, if possible,
to be vested in Indian corn & rye, upon the encouragement rec'd
from Governor Trumbull that permission would be given to carry
out the same, the information concerning the supply to Rhode
Island we rec'd from Governor Trumbull, & haveing stated it as
nearly as we can recollect, we remain very respectfully your Excellency's most Humble Servants, &c.,

    Nathaniel Gorham, Ebenezer Wales, Henderson Inches.
To His Excellency Geo. Clinton Esqr. Governor of the State of
    New York.

[No. 2155.]

McDougall's Jurisdiction Over the Militia.

Pokeepsie March 18 1779.

Dear Sir, I am favored with your Letter of the 14".* In Case
of any movement of the Enemy which wo'd render the aid of the
militia necessary it is the Duty of the immediate commanding
officers to call out their respective Corps to oppose the Enemy,
and the militia Law warrants this without waiting my Orders,
but least there should be any Doubt upon the Subject I now inclose you an Order to the Militia of Westchester & the lower End
of Orange for the above Purpose. This Order also directs Coll.
Com'dt Swarthoudt to releive the Detachment of Brinckerhoof's
Regt., with a Capt's Command, & Colo. Ludington to furnish you
with a Proportion of his Regiment which when in Service you

------

*See page 630.

can detach & imploy as you shall judge best, tho' I shoud esteem
it improper in me to order them out for the Express Purpose of
repairing the Roads. I leave it to you to forward Copies of these
orders to the officers concerned. The militia of Ulster, Dutchess
& the upper End of Orange, have positive Orders to hold themselves in the most perfect Readiness for the Field, and I have
Reason to believe from the warrants I have given on the State
Commissary of Military Stores, that they are provided with ammunition; they are but badly armed but we have it not in our
Power to remedy this Defect. In Case of an alarm, they are to be
governed by my orders of the 5" Dec'r last a Copy of which I then
transmitted you. The Legislature is adjourned; they have done
Nothing respecting the Robbers and Horse Thieves, tho' it was a
Matter I had much at Heart. Neither have they passed a Law
(as I had Reason to believe they would) enabling Courts martial
to command the Testimony of civil witnesses. I inclose you a
Copy of a Resolution which was entered into by the assembly &
offered to the Senate for their Concurrence, but was there rejected
in Consequence of a violent Opposition made to it by Genl. Scott
upon what Principles and for what Reasons I am not informed.
This must suffice for an answer to your Letter* on that Subject of
the 10th Inst. I am in great Haste &c.

[G. C.]†

[To Gen. McDougall.]

The wives & Families of two Persons of the name of Barrack
who early join'd the Enemy have requested Permission to go to
New York§ as they possess good Farms (which may be useful to

---

* See page 626.

† For McDougall's reply see page 664.

§ March 18.—Yesterday, the anniversary of Saint Patrick, the tutelar saint of Ireland,
was celebrated in New York by the natives of that kingdom, with their accustomed
hilarity. The volunteers of Ireland, preceded by their band of music, marched into
the city, and formed before the house of their colonel, Lord Rawdon, who put himself at their head, and, after paying his compliments to his Excellency General Knyp-

our Refugees), I have no Objection to their going provided you think it proper they will go by Land or water as you may determine; please to favor me with your answer on this subject. I flatter myself I shall be able to command the attendance of such witnesses as you may want on the Court of Inquiry notwithstand'g there is no express Law for the Purpose.

[No. 2156.]

CLINTON TO WASHINGTON.

Defence of the Frontier—Two New Military Posts to be Erected on the Susquehanna.

Poukeepsie 18th March 1779.

Dear Sir, I have had the Honor of receiving your Excellency's Letters of the 4th* & 6th Instant and am happy in being thereby enabled to give such general Assurances of Protection to the Frontier Inhabitants as I have reason to hope will prevent their deserting their Settlements. This your Excellency may be assured will be done with the utmost Regard to that Secrecy which is necessary to secure Success in Offensive Opperations & therefore the greatest Care will be taken not to give them the most remote Idea of any such Intention.

The Legislature before they adjourned, empowered me to im-

---

hausen, and to General Jones, accompanied them to the Bowery, where a dinner was provided, consisting of five hundred covers. After the men were seated, and had proceeded to the enjoyment of a noble banquet, the officers returned to town, and dined with his lordship. The soldierly appearance of the men, their order of march, hand in hand, being all natives of Ireland, had a striking effect.

This single battalion, though only formed a few months ago, marched four hundred *strapping fellows*, neither influenced by Yankee or Ague; a number, perhaps, equal to all the recruits forced into the rebel army in the same space of time, which shows how easily troops may be formed on this continent, from the people who have been seduced into America, and spurn at the treason and tyranny of the Congress, providing proper measures are followed, and they are headed by men of their choice. And, also, that such men, however long they may have remained in the haunts of hypocrisy, cunning, and disaffection, being naturally gallant and loyal, crowd with ardor to stand forth in the cause of their king, of their country, and of real, honest, general liberty, whenever an opportunity offers.—New York Gazette, March 22, 1779.

*See page 615.

body 1,000 Men for the Defence of the Northern & Western
Frontier or such other Service as I should judge proper to employ
them in. This was the most they conceived the State (under its
present distressed Situation) was able to raise & the greater Part
of them were entered to join the Troops to be imployed in defensive Opperations ag't the Savages. Since the rising of the Legislature, I have received the Resolve of Congress for filling up the
Continental Battalions & this will put me under the Necessity
of taking at least one half of these Levies for the Purpose, as it
would be impracticable to convene the Legislature in Season to
make any new Provission for that Service even tho our Circumstances woud admit of it.

I do not imagine we shall be able to derive any considerable
Force from the Inhabitants whose Settlements have been destroyed. Their Losses & Consequent Distresses are so great that
it requires their utmost Industry to support their Families &
their Persons; the Army, considering the depreciated State of our
Money woud not be competent for this Purpose & the most of
their young Men are already ingaged in the Continental Battallions. Some, however, from a desire to revenge their Losses,
will at all events ingage & the Neighbourhoods that have been
less distressed, will furnish a considerable Proportion who being
as well acquainted with the Country will be equally serviceable.

In order to deceive the Enemy into a Belief that we intend acting on the Defensive only, I submit to your Excellency the Propriety of erecting one or two small Posts on the nearest navigable
Waters of the Susquehanah; they woud not only answer the above
Purpose, but serve also as a security to the Settlements, & of
Course induce the Militia to ingage in the Service with greater
alacrity. I am not sufficiently acquainted with the Country to

determine with certainty the particular Places best calculated for such Posts, but from the general Idea I have of the Country, I am lead to believe that Unida [Unadilla] & where the Susquehanah empties out of the Lakes, West of Cherry Valley, woud be the most elligible. These Posts might be maintaind by Militia, at least while the other Troops were imployed in Offensive opperations.

I have the Honor to be with the highest Esteem & Respect, Your Excellency's Most &c.,

Geo. Clinton.

His Excellency Genl. Washington.

Signals of Alarm.

Poughkeepsie March 18th 1779.

General Orders.

The signal of Alarm being fixd by the orders of the Hon'ble Major Gen'l McDougal on the 19th Feb'y last are as follows viz.

When five Topsail Vessels appear Coming up of the Enemy three Cannon will be fired at Kings Ferry five Minutes after each other, and if ten Vessells appear four Cannon will be fired at the same Distance of Time: and in this Manner if a greater Number of ships appear, that is one Gun for every five that shall exceed that Number. These signals will be Answered by the firing of the heaviest Cannon at West Point in the same Manner—It is his Excellency the Governor's Orders that the same be Communicated to the officers of the respective Regiments of Militia of the Counties of Dutchess Ulster and Orange, who are strictly chargd to see their Men are properly provided with Arms and Ammunition and held in the most perfect Readiness; And that upon the Alarms being given Col. Commandant Swartwout's Brigade will immediately March to Fishkill, and there wait further Orders, and the Regiments of Ulster and Orange (the western Frontier Companies who are to attend to the Protection of the Frontier Settlements excepted) to the Post at West Point.

As the Signal Guns may not be heard but by the Regiments. most Contiguous to the Posts the officers of these Regiments are to Communicate it by express to the other Regiments on their Respective Sides of the River.

This is to be Considered as a standing order until revoked; And as the Safety of the Country greatly depends on the spirited Exertions of the Militia to Reinforce the Continental Troops and strengthen the different Posts on sudden Emergencies it is expected that these orders will be most faithfully complied with.

By order of his Excellency Governor Clinton,

Rob't Benson, A. D. C.*

Capt'n Abraham Schenck, Rumbouts Precinct Dutchess County.

[No. 2157.]

Returns of Captain Thomas Jansen's Company.

Shawangonk, March 18th 1779.

Sir, I was this day served with a copy of General Orders from your Excellency by Col. Hardenbergh dated March the 1st 1779, to make a return of the Corps of Associated Exempts under my command to your Excellency by the 15th Instant which is expired.

I am with due respect your most Humble Ser't

Thomas Jansen Jun'r

a Return of the Associated Exemts under my Command (Vizt.)

Capt'n	Leuts.	Ensign	Serj'ant	Corporals	Privates
1	2	—	4	4	16

*This document belongs to the Collection of Revolutionary relics at Washington's headquarters, Newburgh, N. Y.—STATE HISTORIAN.

The above is a full and perfect return of the said Associates given under my Hand this 18th Day of March 1779.

Thomas Jansen Jun'r Capt.

[No. 2158.]

Governor Clinton Approves Commissary Accounts.

New Windsor Oct'r [   ] 1777.

The United States of America To Sundries—Dr.

Vouchers:

No. 1	To Thos. Belknap for two Bullocks as pr voucher	£70	0	0
	Silas Wood for one Steer as pr ditto	17	0	0
	Wm. Nicolls for one Cow pr do	11	0	0
2	Ebenezer Woodhull for twenty Bullocks pr do	815	0	0
3	Nathan Smith for ten Cows pr do	150	0	0
4	State of N. York for ten Cows pr do	170	0	0
5	James Gage for two Steers pr do	23	0	0
6	George Denniston for 331 lb. of Beef at 10d	13	15	10
7	Jonathan Belknap for five Steers			
	& one Cow pr do	120	0	0
8	Wm. Rider for one Cow pr do	20	0	0
9	Jacob Wiggins for one Steer pr do	20	0	0
10	David Belknap for two Oxen pr do	65	0	0
11	John Mains for one Steer pr do	20	0	0
12	Hezekiah White for one Cow pr do	20	0	0
13	Samuel Clark for Provisions pr do	21	0	2
14	Colo. Jonathan Hasbrouck for			
	Provisions pr do	30	0	0
15	Jonathan Belknap for Services pr do	20	0	0
16	Abel Belknap for Flour &c pr do	326	6	1

17	George Hains for Flour &c	pr do	910 15	9
18	James Jackson's Store for six			
	bbls. Flour	pr do	27 2	6

£2870 0 4

To Robert Boyd, Jun'r, for his Trouble and
Expences for procuring Provisions for the
Troops under the Command of His Excell'y Genl.
George Clinton agreable to his Order and the
acc't hereunto annexed

17 14 6

£2941 14 10

Agreable to a Resolve of the hon'ble the Congress of the 30th
Jan'y last, I hereby certify that I have inspected the above accounts & carefully compared the same with the different
Vouchers & issuing Commissaries Receipts thereunto annexed,
& that I find the several Charges therein amounting in the whole
to Two thousand nine hundred & forty one Pounds fourteen shillings & ten Pence to be justly due.

Given at Poughkeepsie this 19th March 1779.

Geo. Clinton, Gov'r.

To the Com'y Genl. or either of his Deputies.

[No. 2159.]

Claverack Exempts.

Peter Loop, David Genness, Ab'm Vosburgh, Henry Miller,
Wm. H. Philip, Jurra A. Smith, Tobias Legget, Jacob Carter,
Wm. Reese, Peter Hogeboom, Corl's S. Muller Capt., John
T'Brook, Stephen Hogeboom, Peter A. Fonda Lieut., Mathise Hal-
lenbeck, Gerrit Hendrick, Joh's Holsepple, Peter Hogeboom,

Jun'r, Jeremiah De Lamater, Gabrial Esselstine, Lawrance Conyn Ens, Wm. Van Ness, Jun'r, Bar. V Valkenburgh, John Bay, Samuel J. T'Brook, Joh's Kells, Joh's Schorm, Hendrick Clopper, Richard Blamly, Joh's Shult, Lukes Witbeck, Philip Bautle, David Bonestel, Bastian Loop, Andries Cole, James At-water.

Company of Exempts in Claverack. March 19th 1779.

[No. 2160.]

Governor Clinton Notifies His Brother, the General, of the Threatened Indian Outbreak on the Frontier.

Pokeepsie 20" March 1779.

Dear Brother, Last Night I rec'd a Letter from Genl. Washington in which he expresses some apprehensions founded upon Intelligence from Genl. Schuyler that an attack is meditated by the Savages ag't the Frontiers of the State. I have transmitted Copies of this Letter & its Inclosures to Genl. Ten Broeck & requested him to consult you & Genl. Schuyler upon the Propriety of ordering out such a Proportion of his Brigade as may be deemed necessary to reinforce the Continental Troops & to enable them, as far as may be practicable, to protect & defend the Inhabitants on the western Frontier & to prevent the Enemy from drawing Supplies from thence. I could wish Colo. Willett might be permitted (if he will consent) to take the Command of whatever militia might be ordered out for this Purpose.

Colo. Lush will deliver this, who is directed to assist in making the necessary arrangements for this Purpose. I am &c.

Geo: Clinton.

Brig'r Genl. [James] Clinton.*

---

*For James Clinton's reply see page 663.

[No. 2161.]

For the Relief of the Frontier Sufferers.

Pokeepsie March 20 1779.

Sir, It is impossible for me to appropriate the Monies granted by the Legislature for the use of the Inhabitants of the Frontiers distressed by the Incursions of the Enemy without being possessed of a List of such as are intended to be relieved by the Law for that Purpose made. You will, therefore, be pleased to obtain from the respective Neighbourhoods of Lackawack & Pienpack, with the utmost Dispatch, exact Returns of the Persons within the above Description, who are incapable of gaining a Livelihood and transmit me the same immediately after your Receipt of them. You will also be so obliging as to recommend such Person willing to undertake this Charitable Office, as you think best qualified, for distributing the Money to the different Sufferers or supplying them with Provission. Your Complyance with the above Request will greatly oblidge D'r Sir Your most Obed't Serv't

[G. C.]

I have no news to be relied on worth communicating.

[To Judge Pawling.]

[No. 2162.]

Return of Brigadier General Ten Broeck's Command at Albany.

A Return of the Militia in the City and County of Albany commanded by Abraham Ten Broeck Brigadier General. Albany 20th March 1779.

Regiments	Field			Commissioned				Staff						Non Commissioned							Privates																Total
	Colonel	Lieut. Colonel	Major	Captains	1 Lieutenants	2d Lieutenants	Ensigns	Chaplains	Adjutants	Quarter Masters	Pay Master	Surgeons	Surgeons Mate	Serjeant Major	Qr. Master Serjeant	Serjeants	Corporals	Drum Major	Fife major	Drummers and Fiffers	Privates	Having M:n in the Continental Service	In Quarter Masters Department	In Commissarys d partment	Batteaumen	Held Commissions under Congress	Held Commissions before the Revolution	Exemps	Millers	Ferrymen	Engaged in Service	Reformadors	Unfit for duty	Exemps between 50 & 51	Rank & File	
Collo. Jacob Lansing	1	1	2	6	15	5	5	1	1	1				1		18				4	211	60	13	8	20	10	6	78	3	3	70	24	40	35	192	308
Collo. Abraham Wemple	1	1	2	8	6	6	2		1	1						22	24			6	30		84				33	18	3	3	61		22			374
Collo. Jacobus V: Schonhoven	1	1	2	6	7		6			1						24	22			8	264	29				32					5					
Collo. Kilian Van Rensselaer	1	1	2	6	11		5									24	16			10	360															
Collo. Peter Van Ness	1	1	2	3	11	6	5		1	1						19				7	276														338	483
Collo. Abraham J V: Alstyne	1	1	2	6	27		6		1	1						24	36			15	199		12	6		1	10				65				202	293
Collo. Philip P: Schuyler	1	1	1	6	12	5	6		1	1						36					238															321
Collo. William B: Whiting	1	1	2	9	15	5	5		1	1	1					18	26			7	309															532
Collo. Peter V: oman	1	1	2	6	6		4		1	1						26	16			3	219															250
Collo. Peter Yates	1	1	2	6			4		1	1						20	21			7	215	10						85							267	410
Collo. Stephen J: Schuyler	1	1	1	5					1	1						23																			256	286
Collo. Henry Quackenboss	1																																			

[No. 2163.]

ORGANIZING THE MILITIA.

Clinton Notifies Washington of Arrangements Made to Repel an Attack of the Enemy—Reduction of the Infantry Quota.

Poughkeepsie 21st March 1779.

Dear Sir, In consequence of your Excellency's Letter of the 15th Instant,* I have ordered General Ten Broeck of Albany, to confer with Generals Schuyler and Clinton on the matters contained in it, and to call out such proportion of the militia of that and Tryon County as they may on such Conference esteem necessary, to cover the western Frontier and thereby prevent the Enemy drawing supplies from thence. Similar Orders are dispatched to the militia in the vicinity of Col. Cortland's Regiment.

Previous to the Receipt of your Excellency's Letter, I had (at the Request of General McDougall) so far placed the militia of Westchester County and the southern part of Orange under his Direction as to enable him to call the whole of them to his immediate assistance, in case any movement of the Enemy should render it necessary and the militia of Ulster Dutchess & the northern part of Orange are under Orders to hold themselves in the most perfect readiness to march on the Signal of alarm (fixed by Genl. McDougall's Orders & communicated to them) being given; Those of Ulster & Orange (the frontier Companies excepted) to strengthen the Post at West Point & those of Dutchess to rendesvouz at Fishkill & there wait for further Orders. This appears to me the best disposition that can be made at present.

I observe by a Resolve of Congress of the 9th Inst. transmitted me by the President, that the Infantry of the United

---
* See page 636.

States for the next Campaign is to consist of 80 Battalions; whence I conclude the sixteen additional Regiments are to be reduced. If this is the Case, I beg leave to remind your Excellency that Colo. Warner's & a considerable part of Colo. Malcomb's were raised in this State, as [and] if they are to be annexed to other Regiments, those of this State appear to me to have the most equitable Claim, especially to such of them as were Inhabitants of this State. I have the Honor, to be &c. &c.

Geo: Clinton.

His Excell'cy Genl. Washington.

[No. 2164.]

COLONEL WILLETT DECLINES.

Because He Ranks Colonel Regnier de Roussi who has Been Promoted Over Him to the Command of a Continental Regiment.

Albany March 22d 1779.

Dear Governor, Your letter of the 15th Instant* did not come to my hands untill yesterday, too late for me to answer by the Post. Permit me to thank you for the honor you do me in thinking that this State would receive essential Service by my taking the Command of one of the Militia Regiments to be embodied for the defence of the Western Frontiers. This consideration would go far towards Inducing me to accept of this Command, tho in itself it may not appear desirable. There is, however, a dificulty which I am not at present able to Surmount, nor do I expect it can be removed so as to enable me to Comply with your proposal. The bear Idea of being Lt. Col. Com'dt of a Regiment of Militia, while Lt. Col. Regnier, who stands much lower in the N. York Line than I do, is Commandant of a Continental Regt. in the same State is attended with very dissagreable Sensations.

---

*See Clinton to Willett, page 635.

By the advice of Genll. James Clinton I am going to see Col. Wisenfelts, (who is not only in Justice, but by the most express Laws of Congress Intitled to the Command of that Regt., unless an Interposition is made by the State) in order to know his mind upon the Subject of Colonel Regnier's appointment. When I purpose, likewise by the advice of Genll. Clinton to ride round to pay your Excellency a Visit at Poughkeepsie, so that in a few days I hope to have the pleasure of seeing you, but least I should not be with you in time I have thought it best to write you a few lines for fear the business might be retarded on my account.

I have from what appeared to me Sufficient Foundation, expected Col. Wisenfelts would have the Command of Col. Livingston's Regt., and that I would have been the Candidate for the next Vacancie. By the arrangement from the Board of War, Col. Regnier* is placed to the Command of that Regt. General Washington has directed Genll. James Clinton, that if any objections lay against that arrangement they are to be made with the return of it as soon as may be, in order for procuring the Commissions, after the Issuing of which no Claims will be admissable. Against the Promotion of Col. Regnier I purpose to object, nor can I see how I can except of any appointment in the Interim.

I think it also necessary to inform you, that if the Promotion of Col. Regnier is confirmed, it is my Intention to retire to some business where I may have an opportunity of freeing myself from such dissagreable embarrasements as I unfortunatly Labour under at present. I am Sir Your most Obedient & Very Humble Serv't,

Marinus Willett.

Governor Clinton.

---

*This officer's name appears as Pierre Regnier and as Pierre Regnier de Roussi.— STATE HISTORIAN.

42

[No. 2165.]

Governor Clinton and Francis Lewis Interchange Views.

Phila. 13th March 1779.

Dear Sir, I was this day favored with your letter of the 6th Instant by Mr. Sands. You do me honor in requesting a continuance of my correspondence, which I shall with the greatest pleasure Cultivate.

By this conveyance I transmit you the latest public newspapers which contains everything of consequence, except one favorable account, which I am not as yet at liberty to devulge, when that restraint is recinded by Congress, you shall have the earliest intillegence, from him who has the honor to subscribe himself with the utmost Regard & Esteem, Your Excellency's most Obedient Humble Servant

Fra' Lewis.

His Excellency Geo. Clinton Esqr.

Poughkeepsie March 22d 1779.

D'r Sir, I have rec'd your favor of the 13th Inst. with the News Papers inclos'd for which I return you Thanks. Altho' I would wish for a continuance of your favors, yet you will readily perceive that from our diff't situations, I have it not in my Power in return, to send you any but the common occurrences of our State. Our Legislature after having passed ab't 26 Laws, the Titles of which I have transmitted to your Presid't, & in one of which they have raised the Delegates allowance to 12 Dollars, have adjourned to meet at Kingston on the 1st Tuesday in June next. The Confiscation Bill which originated in the Assembly, was returned by the Council of Revision w'th Objections; that House on reconsideration resolved it to be a Law notwithstanding; but on being sent to the Senate it fell through by not being approved of by two thirds of the members then present. Our People are very impatient to know the Important Intelligence which remains a Secret in Congress. I wish it may not so transpire as that when communicated to them they should not view it in that important light it deserves.

I enclose you Hobbs last Paper and remain D'r Sir &c. &c.

Geo. Clinton.

The hon'ble Francis Lewis Esqr.

[No. 2166.]

*Act of Congress as to the Clothing Department.**

IN CONGRESS,

March 23, 1779.

ORDINANCE for regulating the Cloathing Department for the Armies of the United States.

There shall be a cloathier general, a sub or state cloathier for each state, and a regimental cloathier.

The cloathier general is to be subject to the orders of the board of war and commander in chief. He is to furnish estimates of the supplies wanted for the army; to apply to the commander in chief and board of war for assistance therein; to make returns of such estimates to them respectively; to receive all supplies imported from abroad, and purchased in the country by continental agents; to superintend the distribution thereof to the state cloathiers; to settle accounts with them at least every six months; to keep regular accounts of all the cloathing he shall receive, as well as of the distribution thereof among the state cloathiers; and to transmit his accounts twice in every year to the board of treasury, and settle them in the chamber of accounts when required; and generally to take care, on the one hand, that justice is done to the public, and on the other, that the army receive whatever shall be allowed to them in a regular, direct and seasonable manner; and at the same time, so to act between the continent and each particular state, that equal and impartial justice may be done on all sides.

The SUB or STATE CLOATHIER.

A sub or state cloathier is to be appointed by each state respectively, to reside with or near the army, or such detachment thereof in which the troops of the said state may be, as the commander in chief shall direct, the better to know and supply their wants. The state appointing him is to be answerable for his conduct. In case of neglect or misbehaviour, he is to be displaced by the commander in chief, and his successor to be appointed by the state to which he belonged. He is to receive from the cloathier general the proportion of cloathing assigned for the troops of his state, out of the public cloathing imported or purchased by continental agents; and from the state for which he is appointed, all the cloathing which may at continental expence be purchased in such state; of the latter, their quality and price; he shall transmit exact accounts to the cloathier general, and when required, submit the several articles to the inspection of the cloathier general, or any person for that purpose deputed by him: he is to issue all cloathing supplied as aforesaid to the regimental cloathiers, on returns signed by the commanding officers of regiments: he is to keep exact returns with each regiment, inspect those of the regimental cloathiers, see that the articles

---

*See page 701 and foot note.

delivered them are duly issued to the troops, and that all the cloathing procured at continental expence, above the allowance made by Congress, drawn by non-commissioned officers and privates is charged to them, and credited to the pay-roll; and that the commissioned officers receive what is credited to them, and no more: he is to keep exact accounts with the cloathier general in behalf of the publick, charging the United States only with what is allowed to the officers and men. Whenever the troops of any state shall have received their proportion of cloathing from the continental stores, the supplies purchased at continental expence by the state to which they belong, or from both, and there shall remain a surplus which may be wanted for other troops not fully supplied, the sub cloathier possessed thereof is to deliver over the surplus to such other state cloathier as the cloathier general shall direct, taking duplicate invoices and receipts from the state cloathier to whom they shall be transferred, one sett of which he is to deposit with the cloathier general, and the other to retain as his own voucher: the cloathier general on his part making proper entries in his accounts, to do justice to all concerned.

When from a deficiency in the public stores, the troops of any states shall not have received their allowance of cloathing, the state cloathier is without delay to represent their wants, particularly enumerated in return for that purpose, to the executive authority of the state to which he belongs, requesting a speedy and adequate supply.

And in case a state, at its own expence, shall give, and deposite with him, any cloathing, for the more comfortable subsistence of its quota of troops, in addition to the allowance made by Congress, he is strictly to pursue the directions of such state, as well with respect to the distribution, as the vouchers for the delivery, and the manner and time of settling his accounts; transmitting once in every six months a copy of such accounts to the cloathier general, and as often, and whenever required, to the state in which he belongs.

The REGIMENTAL CLOATHIER.

The office of regimental cloathier shall always be executed by the regimental paymaster.

He is to be furnished by captains or officers commanding companies with returns, specifying the mens names and the particular wants of each; these he is to digest into a regimental return, which, being signed by the officer commanding the regiment, and countersigned by himself, with a receipt upon it of the supplies delivered to the regiment, is to be lodged with the state cloathier, and become to him a voucher for the delivery in his settlement with the cloathier general.

He is to keep an account with each officer and soldier for every article delivered, taking a receipt from them, as his voucher for the delivery: He is to credit them for the continental allowance, and to charge them for every thing they receive, making stoppages in the monthly pay-rolls for whatever they may fall in debt to the public beyond the allowance.

And to prevent in future unequal distribution of cloathing either to the officers or soldiers, and the confusion and complaints which have heretofore been occasioned by irregular applications from commanding officers of regiments to public agents in different posts, it is hereby strictly enjoined on those agents, the cloathier general, and the sub or state-cloathier, to issue no cloathing on any pretence whatsoever, but in the manner before prescribed; nor shall any article be credited to either of them on settlement of their accounts, which is not so issued and vouched.

And whereas discretionary changes of the uniforms of regiments have proved inconvenient and expensive; the commander in chief is therefore hereby authorised and directed, according to the circumstances of supplies of cloathing, to fix and prescribe the uniform, as well with regard to the colour and facings, as the cut or fashion of the cloaths, to be worn by the troops of the respective states and regiments, which shall, as far as possible, be complied with by all purchasing agents employed by Congress, as well as particular states, by the cloathier general, sub or state cloathiers and regimental cloathiers, and all officers and soldiers in the armies of the United States. And when materials can be purchased instead of ready made cloaths, it shall always be preferred, in order that they may be made up by the taylors of the several regiments, to save expence and prevent the disadvantages which the soldiers frequently suffer from their unfitness: and instead of breeches, woolen overalls for the winter, and linen for the summer, are to be substituted.

Extract from the Minutes,

Charles Thomson, Secretary.

[No. 2167.]

HANDICAPPED BY TORIES AND JOBBERS.

Commissary Reed Reports Progress to Governor Clinton on the Flour
Question—The Governor's Reply.

Amenia March 23d 1779.

Sir, Since I left Poughkeepsie I have been Closely attending to your advise, which was to Raise the Price to Ten Dollars for Wheat and so in Proportion for Flour, and Purchase all I Could & Seize what Ever I found in the hands of Jobbers which Plan I have been Pursuing Every Day since, Untill I have got Nearly through my whole District, & with Tollerable Success.

I have Purchas'd & Seiz'd, Since I have been Pursuing the last Plan, as much Wheat as will make ten or Twelve Hundred Bar's Flour, Including what I Bo't in Flour,—S'r, I find two Sets People that will not Sell their Crops of New Wheat one is the Toreys, who Insist on hard money, the other is those worse than the Toreys, (the Jobbers) who are not only Keeping back their own, but assisting the Torys to Run theirs over the line or hide it in Barns, out houses and in the Woods, of which Several large Quantities has Come to my Knowledge already; but it is out of my Power to Secure the Same, Unless Some Person were appointed in this Quarter to Seize the New Crops, which I must beg might be Done Soon, or we Shall not be able to feed the army two months longer.

I would beg leave to Recommend to your Excellency, some Persons who I think would answer that Purpose in my District, which are Colo. Wm. Barker & Mr. Danl. Shepherd and to be Under the Inspection and Direction of Judge Paine. I Should like to Pay them for their Trouble out of my Commissions &

Recieve the Wheat into Common Stock for the Public, as keeping that Wheat Separate at the Same mills where I have other Public Wheat will be attended with Some Difficulty. I Could also wish either Esquire Lawrence or Capt. Hartwell, Could be appointed in the Neighbourhood of Spencers as Great abuses are Commited in that Quarter. I am Sir your Humb'e Sev't

James Reed A. C. P.

Governor Clinton.

GOVERNOR CLINTON'S REPLY.

Poughkeepsie March 23d 1779.

Sir, I have this moment rec'd your Letter of the 23d Inst. I have sent out expresses for six members of the Legislature to meet me without Delay for the purpose of appointing proper Persons to carry the Law into execution & fixing the Prices of Flour & wheat. As I have not been able to learn what are the Prices in Connecticut, I must request of you to procure & send me an acc't of them [if] possible by Express. Without this we shall not be able to proceed in the Business with any Degree of certainty. I am &c.

Geo. Clinton.

Mr. Jas. Reed A. C. P.

P. S. You will please to observe that the Law directs that the Price of Flour & Wheat to be seized by it, is to be fixed at the averaged Prices in Connecticut & New Jersey.

[No. 2168.]

Returns of Colonel Hardenbergh's Regiment.

A Return of Colo. Johannes Hardenbergh Ju'r his Regement of Militia (agreeable to Genl. Orders,) Taken from the several

Returns, from the Commanding officers of Companies of said Regement, & of the Field & Staff as it Now Stand, March 23, 1779.

Officers Names.	Officers Present											None Commissioned Officers.			Rank & file.		
	Commissioned officers						Staff										
	Colo.	Lt. Colo.	Maj'r	Capts.	Lieuts.	Ensigns	Adjt.	Qr. Master	Sergt. Maj'r	Q. M. Sergt.	Surgion.	Sergts.	Corpls.	Dr's & fifes	Fitt for duty	On command	Totle.
Field & Staff	1	1	1				1	1	1	1	1						
Capt. Jacob Wood				1	2	1						4	4		48		56
Capt. John Gillespy				1	2	1						4	4	2	43	3	56
Capt. Math Jansen				1	2	1						4	4	2	50	3	63
Capt. Clark's Comp'y					1	1						4	4		50		58
Capt. Will'm Cross				1	2	1						3	2	1	41	3	50
Capt. Jacob Conklin				1	2	1						4	3	1	28	2	38
Capt. Arthur Smith				1	1							4	4		30		38
Capt. David Ostrander				1	2	1						4	4		31	3	42
Capt. Corn's Masten				1	2	1						4	4	2	40	3	53
Capt. Robison				1	2	1						4	2	1	36	2	45
Capt. Stephen Case				1	2	1						4	4		32		40
Totle	1	1	1	10	20	10	1	1	1	1	1	43	39	9	429	19	539

Pr Joh's Hardenbergh, Ju'r, Colo.

To His Excellency, Geo. Clinton.

[No. 2169.]

James Clinton, the Western Frontier and Colonel Willett.

Albany March 24th 1779.

Dear Sir, Your favour* was handed me yesterday by Col. Lush. In consequence of your request contained in it, I waited on Genl. Schuyler in company with Gen. Ten Broeck, who were of opinion, that as the present Season was rather unfavourable for an immediate attack, and as the militia of this State hath been very much harrassed, it was most prudent to order, that that Part of the militia which are nearest the Object of the Enemy's attention, shou'd keep themselves in readiness to act on the shortest notice; and that two hundred Men from Livingston's Mannor who

---

* See page 652.

have done the least Duty, shou'd hold themselves in readiness to march on the shortest notice of the Enemy's movements, which we expect can be easily discouvered, as Genl. Schuyler hath engaged a number of friendly Indians, who are actually employed on that Business.

I shou'd be pleased if Col. Willet wou'd take the Command of any Body of Militia that may be raised for the Defence of the Frontiers of this State: but I fear that unless the Dispute between Lt. Cols. Weisenfels and Regnier, in which he conceives himself interested, shoud be decided in favour of the former, we shall lose his Services altogather, and if otherwise, it is more than likely Regnier will resign, who is a valuable Officer.

An unfortunate affair happened a few days past at Fort George. Twenty three men of a Detatchment of Col. Gansevort's Regt. commanded by Capt'n Aorsen, deserted to the Enemy; the Party which had been sent in pursuit of them, overtook one who had fallen behind, and brought him back. I am with great Esteem, Dear Sir, Your most obedient hum. Se't,

James Clinton.

P. S. I have lately stoped issuing Provision to the Inhabitants of Cherry Valley & doubt they will suffer.

Governor Clinton.

[No. 2170.]
LOATH TO CALL ON THE MILITIA.
General McDougall Also Compelled to Stop Furloughs—Dismal Prospects from His Point of View.

Head Quarters Pecks Kill March 24th 1779.

My Dear Sir, Your Favor of the 18th* has come to Hand. I am informed my Friend Governor Clinton likes short Letters.

*See page 644.

He will in future have them so. The order of the 5th of December respecting the Disposition of your militia on the west Side, in Case of alarm has not reached me. By the inclos'd Copy of a Letter from the Commander in chief* you will be inform'd of what is in Contemplation. Advices from New York correspond; as do those this Day received from General Putnam. It seems the Enemy has detained his Privateers for some Expedition, and I am persuaded New London is the Object.

We have several Frigates, and other arm'd Vessels there; and I am not without some Suspicion that the Enemy have received Intelligence of there being provisions and Stores in that Town. I have orders to enlist the Troops at these Posts during the war, which I fear will be longer than is imagined. It goes on but slowly as I am obliged from the State of my Force to stop Furloughs. If I could get three or four hundred good militia to aid the Garrison at West-Point for two months, I am confident all the Troops would be reinlisted. Could this be done? I am very loth to call on the Militia, but I fear at any Rate some must aid us, as the lines take so many of our best and pick'd men. There have been more than three Hundred Rank and File there for two months past.

I am astonish'd at General Scott's Conduct, nor can I conceive on what Ground he could oppose a measure, which had a fixed and determined Object. But I hope the Business will go on notwithstanding his opposition.

Captain Gilbert Deane is in the Plan I mentioned to you some Time ago for obtaining Intelligence. Mention his Name also to the attorney General.

I always imagined this Country was in a bad state. But since

*See page 642.

I plann'd this Business, I find it infinitely more than I conceived. The twentieth man in it is not a real Friend to the Country.

If Serjeant Williams of Robinson's Regiment should be apprehended, for God sake dont let the villian escape. I shall send for him the moment I am advis'd he is secured. I have many things to say to you of the Fruits of my new System, which I cannot put to paper. If the Enemy is not routed from New York, we shall ultimately be ruined, if he carries on only a defensive war, unless we quit all Trade and Navigation. I am my, Dear Sir, in Haste Your Humble servant,

Alex'r McDougall.*

P. S.   I beg to know, whether there are any more spears which can be had for the Redoubts? If so, where I can have them? Since I began this, advice is brought me from the Lines of General Clinton's non appearance in New York. He is gone on Long Island. Was the Flag sloop detained from this state, in New York returned?

His Excellency Governor Clinton.

[No. 2171.]

McDougall Apprehensive for the Highland Forts.

†Head Quarters Peekskill May 25th 1779.

Dear Sir, By late intelligence received by the Commander in chief and myself from New York, I have reason to conclude that the Enemy have in contemplation some secret Expedition; and there is great reason to suppose his Design is against these Posts. The Commander in chief is so perswaded of it, that he has ordered me to call in all the out Posts. If an attack should be made on West Point I am afraid, in spight of all my Exer-

---

*For Governor Clinton's reply see page 671.

†This document was wrongly placed by the original editor of the MSS. It should follow Document No. 2316.

tions since I have been at this Post, that a sufficient Quantity of Provissions has not been got in. I must therefore intreat your assistance to the Deputy Quarter Master General, with respect to his collecting, in the Country, the Teams necessary for the transporting Provission to that Post; and the carrying off the superfluous Stores should the Enemy come up in great Force. I make no doubt you will excuse this application as upon such an Event the utmost Exertions are necessary. I am with much Esteem D'r sir Your obedient servant

Alex'r McDougall.

His Excellency Governor Clinton.

[No. 2172.]

In Relation to a Pass.

25th March 1779.

I have no objection, to any persons going to New York, you may think proper to permit. B. Genl. Huntington applies to me, for leave for Stephen Curry wife to go in to see her relation, in order I beleive, to get some thing from them. If you give her a permit, I will let her pass.

Alex'r McDougall.

His Excellency Governor Clinton, Poughkeepsie.

Colonel Hay will please to forward this by a safe opportunity.

R. S. McDougall, A. D. Camp.

[No. 2173.]

Governor Clinton Adopts Plans to Protect the Frontier.

*Sir, In consequence of your Letter of yesterday just now received I have issued a General Impress warrant to enable the

---

*This document was wrongly placed by the original editor of the MSS. It should follow Document No. 2318.

Qu'r Mr. Genl. to convey to the different Posts sufficient supplies of Provision, and you may rely upon every other Exertion in my Power to forward this Business. This is the third General Impress warr't I have granted for this service and it is to be lamented that upon every fresh alarm the same want of Provisions still remains.

I inclose you an Extract of a Letter from Colo. Pawling with some intelligence from the westward which as it seems to correspond with other Reports and also with the accounts contained in your Letter may be true. I have therefore ordered the Regiments of Colo. Cantine & Colo. Snyder of Ulster and Genl. Ten Broeck's Brigade of Albany County in Case of an alarm to march to and cover the Frontier, the Rest of the Militia to strengthen the Posts under your Command. I am &c.

May 26 1779.   [G. C.]

[To Gen. McDougall.]

[No. 2174.]

Jonathan G. Tompkins Accepts as an Assistant Commissary.

Paulings Precinct March 25th 1779.

May it please your Excellency, I have now the pleasure to inform you that I have happily succeeded in engaging Mr. Tompkins as Henry Schenck's Successor & he has agreed to go to Poughkeepsie next Monday, I shall also desire Maj'r Strang to go with him, to meet Messrs. Smith & Reed & Settle their respective districts. I shall desire them to apply to your Excellency, in case they disagree, to fix their Limits for them. I have the honor to be your Excellency's most obed't very humble Serv't

Jas. Lockwood.

His Excellency Governor Clinton.

[No. 2175.]

JELLES FONDA OFFERS SUGGESTIONS.

Necessity of Forming the Militia on New Lines—Tryon County in a State of Uncertainty.

Caughnawaga 26 March 1779.

Hon'ble Sir, I have Just received your Esteemed favor of the 15th Inst. and notes the Contents. The map you mention does not fully Comprehend a draft of Tryon County, but the map you mean, I believe Doct'r Stephen McCrea Purchased at Vandue and I think Contains, what you Immagined in mine. I have wrote to Mr. John Taylor of Albany to go and view Mr. McCrea's map, and if it answers your directions to purchase it for you; but should he not Succeed, you may have mine if you think proper.

I hope that there is a Return sent to you of all the militia Regiments before now, and am glad to here that this County is to be put in a posture of defence, which God knows is much wanted, and I think is in great Danger from our Inveterate Enemys, from the Northward, Westerd, and Southerd, and here living the utmost frontiers of the State. Our people here are much affraid, occationed by the Barbaritys Committed last summer in this County by the Indians and Torys; and now, Numbers of Familys are prepareing to move downward, which may be prevented by our geting a Reinforcement of men sent to us soon. I could wish that there were orders sent up to this County for to have at least 500 able bodyd men of the militia to be always in Readyness at a moments warning with Eight Days Provisions &c., that when the Enemy would Invade any part of our County, that those men were ready to follow them, but not to have things carried on as formerly has been, to have the militia to get together when the Enemy was amongst us, murdering, burning, and Plundering, and before they got to the place wanted, the Enemy was gon out of reach with their Booty; we have upwards of 300 Disafected familys back of us, mostly tenants of Sir John Johnson & Colo. Buttler's, where the Enemy frequently comes to from Canada and other places. Our Mohawk Indians that left us, are now with them and are now our worst Enemys, and am much affraid will bring partys through that way to distroy and plunder us. There has been 3 of them home a few days ago, and have taken Eight of the Disafected People with them to Canada; if there was a Scouting party ordered to Sacondaga of about 50 men, it would Cut off the Communication between the Enemy and those Disaffected familys and be a great safe guard to us. I have wrote to General Clinton, Concerning having a Blockhouse built at Sacondaga, and a Scouting party kept there Constantly but as yet have not Received his answer. I have no Indian Curiosities at present, as the upper Nation Indians dos not come this way as usual; all I had I have disposed of, if you Inform me what kind you want, I may perhaps get some made for you. I am with Respect, Sir, your most Obdt. Humble Serv't

                                             Jelles Fonda.
His Exellency Georg Clinton, Esqr.

[No. 2176.]

Ruinous Prices for the Necessaries of Life.

                              Amenia March 27th 1779.

Sir, I Recvd. your Favour of the 24th Instant, Requesting me to advise your Excellency by Express what are the General Price given in Connecticut for Produce, in answer to which, one of my Neighbours has this Moment Returnd from Hartford, also a Gentleman who lives at Hartford has been with me a few Hours ago, from whom I can learn that Wheat has Sold from 20 to 25 Dolls. p Bus'l, in Sharon; and Salisbury from 12 to 15 Dolls. mostly the Latter, Doct'r Shepherd of Sharon has been with me this Day and Says he has been Offerd 16 Dolls. p Bus'l for 20 Bus'ls this morning; at Boston flour has Rais'd to 100 Dolls. p C wt. I am Told by a Purchasing Com'sy Near Litchfield, that for some time he had Bo't Beef at 40 Dolls. p Hund. but that he must Raise to 50 for the Future, which is as Nearly a true State of the Prices as I am able to Collect at Present. I am S'r your Humb. Serv't

James Reed, A. C. P.

Governor Clinton.

[No. 2177.]

PREPARING TO PROTECT THE FRONTIERS.

Governor Clinton Directs General McDougall to Call Upon the Militia if Necessary—Opposes Trusting Women with Passes.

Poukeepsie 27th March 1779.

Dear Sir, I was favoured with yours of the 24th* late last Evening. Your Informant was misstaken with respect to my Dislike of long Letters; you may be assured I shall never be displeased at the Lenghth of yours, provided I may be permitted to give Concise Answers & this will not be an unreasonable Indulgence when it is considered that I have seldom any News to communicate & you are in the way of obtaining the earliest & most important Intelligence which I shall always be much obliged to you for.

I perfectly agree with you as to the Designs of the Enemy being ag't New London, but that this ought not however to divert us from a proper Attention to the safety of the Posts in the High-

---

* See page 664.

lands. I now inclose you the Order aluded to on my last, which I thought had been transmitted to you before, with an Order of the 18th Instant giving the Militia your new Signal of Alarm & for inforcing my former Order; from these you will fully learn the Disposition made of the Militia of the State who are so situated as to be able on a sudden Emergency to assist you & I trust you will approve of it.

I am now making the necessary Preparations for drafting the Militia to fill up our five Continental Battallions & raise a small Body of men for the Defence of our Northern & Western Frontiers agreable to a Law passed at the late meeting of the Legislature. 'Till this Business is compleated it will be extreamly inconvenient if not impracticable to draw out any Part of the Militia for any other Service unless from the lower End of Orange & West Chester County which will be exempted from the proposed Draft as well in Consideration of the Aid which you may require of them being in your Vicinity as of their exposed Situation. These being by my late Orders placed under your immediate Direction you can call for or such Proportion of them as the Service & Safety of the Country may require. I am perswaded you will make the Duty as easy to them as possible.

When I have the Pleasure of seeing you I will explain the Reasons of Genl. Scott's Conduct on a late Occassion. In the mean Time I think it necessary to inform you that I did not think proper to acquaint either House with the Object you had in View, lest it should get abroad & mar the Business.

I will mention Capt. Deane to the Atty. Genl. in a manner that will render him safe. I have not been able to obtain the least Intelligence of Williams since Jaycock was taken. I am informed his Parents live about 6 Miles from Albany & I have wrote to the

Com'rs at that Place respecting him. If there are any more Spears belonging to the State they may be had by applying to Colo. Lasher at Wallkill. There has been no Flagg Sloop detained by the Enemy that I know of, except one which went down last Fall, was a year under the Direction of one Brooks who joined the Enemy as they say, & I believe to be true. The Sloop however as it was not his Property ought to have been returned.

I woud not be understood from what I have said that if there is an absolute Necessity for Militia, they cannot be had; in such Case they must be drawn out however inconvenient.

I cannot think of permitting Mrs. Currey or any other Person to go into New York & Return but on the most urgent Occassion, as if I yield to one Application it brings on a hundred others & gives me infinite Trouble, besides it is at best a Dangerous Practice. The Women who sollicit to go down to continue there, will wait on you one of these Days; it will be best to change the drivers who may go down with them & put trusty Hands in their room. I am with great Regard Yours Sincerely,

Geo. Clinton.

[To Gen. McDougall.]

[No. 6419.]*

Governor Clinton Promises to Add a Few Curiosities to du Simitiere's Collection.

Poukeepsie 27th March 1779.

Sir, I have to thank you for your obliging Favours of the 2d Feb'y & 2d Instant & for the Magazines & Pamphlets which accompanied them. Ousted of our Metropolis & cut off as we are of all Intercourse with Foreign States, we are intirely beholden to our Neighbours for Litterary Productions & News, except such as are merely domestic; under these Circumstances I feel myself particularly oblidged to you for your early & Friendly Communications & I shall be happy when it is in my Power to make suitable Return.

I am not without hopes of being soon able to present you with a few Curriosities worthy of a Place in your Collection, as my Friends in Tryon County have promised to procure me some of those, which belonged to the late Sir William Johnson, which tho' well worth preserving are wantonly scattered abroad, many of them losst, & others in the Hands of Clowns who know not their Value. I am perswaded you will esteem this a Sin not far short of Sacralege & that too much Pains cant be taken to correct it. I had formerly collected a few Articles, which I esteemed as valuable as the Rust of American Antiquity could make them, which I promised myself the Pleasure of transmitting you, but on the unfortunate Loss of the Posts in the Highlands these were sent with my Books Papers & other Personal Property to Kingston & with them shared in the General Conflagration of that Place.

I am much pleased with the Addition you have made to your Paintings. The Profile of our American Hero will be in future Ages esteemed an inestimable Jewel. I am, Sir, with great Regard Your most Obed't Serv't

[G. C.]

[To Mr. Du Simitiere.]

[No. 2178.]

List of Cherry Valley Sufferers.

A List of the Inhabitants of Cherry Valley the number in family and number in Each family that is not able to Support them Selves viz.

Taken by James Scott & James Rickey Mar. 27th 1779.

	Number in Family	Not able to Support them Selves
Jeramiah Bakon	8	4
Nath·niel Hamel	4	1
Will'm Dickson	9	3
Wil iam Galt	9	7
James Scott	6	5
James Willson	8	6
Will'm Thompson	13	9
Wiᵈdow Rebeckah Thompson	6	3
Will'm McᶜoᵔᵔᵔMcCoᵔnal	3	2
Jaᵔᵔes Moor 4 prisnors¸	7	3
Col Sam. Campbᵉll 6 prisn's		1
Rev'd Wm Johnston	9	4
James Cᵔmᵔbeil	8	6
Thᵔmᵔs Ramsᵉy	2	1
Will'm McCleᵔon 3 prisoners	6	3
Jonathan Ogdᵔn	8	4
James Mars	4	2
John McCollom	1	1
Alexᵔ McCollom	10	6
Daniel McCollom	7	4
Wm. Haᵔl	1	1
Wiᵔow Wiᵔlson	1	1
Col. Sam Clyde	10	5
Widow Henderson	2	1
Rev'ᵈ Sam. Dunlope	2	1

[No. 2179.]

Commissary Leek Makes a Requisition for More Flour.

Bedford, 30th March 1779.

Dear S'r, The permit your Excellency gave me for transporting One Hundred Barrels Flour to Northwalk and Horseneck for the Use of the Troop there, Is out and the Troops at those Posts have no Other Resourse for Bread at Present.

I have, therefore, to Beg your Excellency would Grant a Permit for the other Hundred Barrels and I Belive that will be as Much as I Can Procure, Exclusive of What I must Send on to the Lines in this County, as many of our Principal Farmers Seem Determined not to Sell their Last Crops untill they are Compell'd to By Law.

Your Compliance will Oblige the Publick and Your Excellencies Very Humble Servant,

Philip Leek, A. C. P.

Governor Clinton.

[No. 2180.]

*Commissary Leek Requests Egbert Benson to Intercede in His Behalf
with Governor Clinton.*

Bedford 30th March 1779.

S'r, I am directed by Colo. Colt D. C. G. of Purchases to
Supply the Troops at Horseneck and Northwalk with Flour and
I have had a Permit to Carry one Hundred Barrels out of this
State and Have Compleated the Same,   I have, Therefore, to Beg
the Favour that you and one other Gentleman of the Assembly
(Whom I Wish you to Name to the Bierer) Will Request his
Excellency to Grant me a Permit for one Hundred Barrels to
Be Transported to the Places affore Mention'd as they Cannot
Procure Flour from any other Quarter.

Your Compliance Will Greatly oblige your Humble Servant

Philip Leek, A. C. P.

Egbert Benson, Esqr.

———

[No. 2181.]

Drafts to be Made from the Militia.

Poukeepsie 30th March 1779.

Sir, The Legislature were adjourned (to the 1st Tuesday in June
next) some Days before I had the Honor of receiving your Excellency's Letter of the 12th covering the Act of Congress of the
10th Instant for recruiting the Army.   I am happy, however, in
being able to inform your Excellency that the Legislature impressed with the Necessity of compleating the Battallions raised
under the Direction of this State had at their late meeting in
some Measure anticipated the Intentions of Congress by directing
Drafts to be made from the Militia for this Purpose to continue
in Service till the 1st of Jan'y next.   The most vigorous Exer-

tions will be made to carry the Intentions of the Legislature into speedy & effectual Execution.   I am Sir &c.

[G. C.]

Since writing the above I am honored with your Excellency's Letter of the 22d Instant inclosing the Proclamation of Congress of the 20th Inst. recommend'g to the several States to appoint the first Tuesday in May next to be a Day of Humiliation Fast'g & Prayer.

[To John Jay Esq.]

———

[No. 2182.]

Governor Clinton Authorized to Procure an Immediate Supply of Flour.

At a Meeting of his Excellency the Governor and several Members of the Legislature at Poughkeepsie on the 31st Day of March 1778 pursuant to " an Act for procuring an immediate Supply of Flour for the Army."

Present.

His Excellency Governor Clinton

John Morin Scott   Zephaniah Platt

Esqrs. Members of Senate

Dirck Brinckerhoff   Samuel Dodge

Jacobus Swartwout   Egbert Benson

Robert Van Renselaer   William Boerom

Esqrs. Members of Assembly.

His Excellency the Governor opened to the Gentlemen present the occasion of the present meeting and produced to them such Evidence as induced them to be and they are accordingly unanimously of Opinion that an Emergency does now exist which renders it necessary that the aforementioned act be carried into immediate execution. His said Excellency by and with the advice and Consent of the said members having estimated the Prices of Flour, meal, and wheat to be taken for public use by virtue of the said Act as near as may be at the average of the Prices in the States of New Jersey & Connecticut does hereby, by and with such advice and Consent as aforesaid, ascertain and determine the same for the purpose of carrying the said Act into Execution at the following Rates vizt.

Good Flour and well bolted meal respectively at sixteen Pounds per hundred weight; and wheat at sixteen Dollars per bushel. In Testimony whereof as well his said Excellency the Governor as the said members have hereunto subscribed their names the Day & year above written.

Geo: Clinton, Jno: Morin Scott, Zepha. Platt, Dirck Brinckerhoff, Jacob's Swartwout, Robt. V'n Rensselaer, Saml. Dodge, William Boerum, Egb't Benson.

[No. 2183.]

Returns of Colonel Swartwout's Brigade.

Return of Colo. Command't Swartwout's Brigade Dutchess County Militia.

Regts.	Colos.	Lieut. Cols.	Majors.	Capts.	1st Lieuts.	2d Lieuts.	Ensigns.	Adjut'ts	Qr. Mr.	Sergeants	Corporals	Drums & fifes	Privates	Total	Exempts	
Roswell Hopkins	1	1	2	8	8	8	9	1	1	36	35	12	486	608		44
Colo. Freer's	1		1	8	6	5	6	1	1	33	31	10	391	493		38
Colo. Brinckerhoff	1	1	1	6	7	6	7	1	1	27	28	4	401	501		38
Morris Graham	1	1	2	9	9	8	2	1	1	36	33	10	504	615	25	45 mistake to much 10
Henry Luddington	1	1	2	6	6	5	4			24		6	398	455		38
Jas. Van Debergh	1	1	1	5	5	5	5	1	1	20	20	5	323	395	28	28 make 13 to much
Jno. Fields	1	1	1	6	6	6	6	1	1	24	24	3	313	398		28
	7	6	9	48	47	43	37	6	6	199	171	50	2816	3460		254

The above is formed from Colo. Com't Swartwout's Return of 9th April 1779 nearly agreeing w'th former Returns of the Regts. Except Colo. Vandebergh's which is corrected by Colo. Humphrey's last Return of that Regt. & except Colo. Fields which is taken from his Return of 7th March 1778.

[No. 2184.]

Returns of men to be raised from Gen. Ten Broeck's brigade as part of the 1000 men for the defence of the frontiers.
Return of Brigadier General Ten Broeck's Brigade of Militia in the City & County of Albany.

Regts.	Colos.	Colos.	Lieut. Colos.	Majors	Capts.	1st Lieuts.	2 Lieuts.	Ensigns	Adjuts.	Qr. Masters	Sergeants	Corporals	Drummers	Fifers	Privates	Total	Persons who have hired men in Cont'l army	
1st	Jacob Lansing, Jun'r	1	1	2	5	6	6	3	1	1	17				248	293	64	18
2	Ab'm Wemple	1	1	2	8	8	8	5	1	1		2			367	402		28
3	Phil. P. Schuyler	1	1	2	5	6	5	6	1	1	14	7	7	1	302	330		26
4	Kil. V. Rensselaer	1	1	2	7	7	6	4	1	1	11	10	5	2	358	416	16	30
5	G. V. Denbergh	1	1	2	5	5	5	5	1	1	16	14	2	6	280	283		22
6	Step. J. Schuyler	1	1	2	6	5	6	4	1	1	24	24	6	3	225	284		22
7	Ab'm V. Alstyne	1	1	2	6	5	5	5	1	1	21	17	4		206	289	28	20
8	Robt. V. Reusselaer	1	1	2	6	6	6	6	1	1	24	24	6	6	254	326		31
9	Peter Van Ness	1	1	2	5	6	6	5	1	1					317	406		17
10	A. Van Bergen	1	1	2	10	10	9	10	1	1	40	40	10	10	194	220		45
11	P. R. Livingston	1	1	2	6	6	7	6	1	1					439	584		28
12	Jac's V. Schoonhoven	1	1	2	7	7	7	7	1	1			5		327	357		17
13	Jno. McCrea	1	1	2	5	5	4	5	1	1	17	14			185	219		17
14	Joh's Knickerbacker	1	1	1	5	5	5	5	1	1	16	15			234	289		
15th	Peter Vroman	1	1	1	5	5	5	5	1	1					151	213		
16th	Vacant	1	1															
17th	Wm. B. Whiting	1	1	2	9	9	9	9	1	1	36	36	8	7	403	532	65	36
18	L. Van Woert	1	1	2	6	6	6	6	1	1	24	24	6	6	165	255		17
																5698		412
	Ulster Tryon Charlotte & North End of Orange Unbrigaded Regts	17	16	33	106	106	102	91	17	17	260	227	59	41	4605	5878	173	
		8	12	10	89	94	83	92	12	11	361	347	40	27	3223	4508	53	
	Swarthoudt's Brigade	7	6	9	48	47	43	37	6	6	199	171	25	25	2816	3483		
		32	34	52	243	247	228	220	35	34	820	745	124	93	10644	13869	226 deduct Error	
																13689		
																23 deduct Error		
																13666		

N. B. This Return is made from Genl. Ten Broeck Return of 19th Feb'y 1778 except as to Colo. Whiting's Regt. which is taken from the Genl's Brigade Return of 7th March 1779.

Colo. McCrea's Return is made from a Note made by Genl. Ten Broeck at the foot of Colo. McCrea's Return of Officers to the Council of Appointm't. And Colo. V. Woert's Return is taken from the Genl's Letter of Feb'y 1778.

[No. 2185.]

*Petition of Andrew Layton and Others for Pardon.**

[No. 2186.]

Dragoons and Citizens Quarrel Over Flour.

(Copy)   Armenia 1 April 1779.

Dear Sir, Capt'n Mackle† this morning informs me a part of his Dragoons are taken and put under Guard at Sheron for taking some wheat & bringing it back, after it had Crost the Line into Sharon in Connecticut, which mistep has caused a very great Fire to be kindled between the two states, altho' I beleive the Dragoons are not so much to blame as the Inhabitants. But I cannot conceive they will be of any great service for the future unless a greater number as the People in Salsbury have come over in mobs to our state of 30 or 40 men under arms & Carry out whatever they please, notwithstanding the Guards. Unless you or our Governor will take up the matter & Quell those Tumults I fear there will be Blood shed. Capt'n Mackle begs your advice in the affair. I am D'r S'r Your Hum. Ser.

                                    James Reed, A. D. P.

Copy.

General McDougall.

[No. 2187.]

Captain Merely Reports to General McDougall that His Men Are Gaoled for Stopping Flour.

                                    Oblong 1 April 1779.

General, I have this moment receiv'd news that One of my Guards is taken prisoners that was Stationed at Mr. Johnson's,

---

* Omitted.
† See page 687.

one mile & an half from Sharron, One serjt. One Corporal & four Privates, & those six men are to be carried to Litchfield Goal, and its reported that they intend to have me there too if they can get me, because all the Connecticut people are against those Orders for to stop Flour or Grain; they will not beleive that you have any right to give such orders; they will not be bound to the military Law or Orders. Likewise I am imformed of Esqr. Lawrence, that one major Stodder, is to raise One hundred men & to kill every one that has Orders to stop Flour.

But these six men what are taken Prisoners now is done by Esqr. Canfield in Sheron but to do with them I don't know.

I have informed Commissary Reed of it—what has happened; he will give more particulars of it. I am very sorry to trouble you in that Case but I am obliged to it because my men is in riske to lose their Lives if no other method is taken, they Transport Flour thro' the Guards by force of their arms.

Here inclossed two Permits according to your Orders. I am Your most Obedient and humble servant

Copy.   Charles Merely, Capt'n.

N. B. You will excuse Ill spelling. I am in great hurry to send the Express to your Honour.

Alex. McDougall, Major General.*

[No. 2188.]†

Relating to the sale of goods belonging to Samuel Hake, confiscated under an act of the Legislature, and sold in detail by Peter Tappen and John Ferris, at Poughkeepsie May 12, 1779, under authority of the Legislature.

----

* See pages 681 and 687.
† Omitted.

[No. 2189.]

List of Sufferers on the Ulster Frontier Entitled to Bounty.

Peenpeck 1st April 1779.

Hon'd Sir, The 30th Ult. I received yours of the 26th of the same of the Donation intended to those your Letter Describes. Having endeavoured to inform myself of the unfortunates, which comes under that Denomination, from the Strictest Scrutiny of Circumstances I find the following comes under that Description; Viz

John Wallace—in family 4.

Jonathan Pass—in family 6.

Mathew Trewilliger—in fam'y.

Petrus Gumaer—in family 5.

Abraham Venauker—in family 9.

Abel Sprege—in family 8.

Widow Barber—in family 6.

These persons are wholly and severally Distress't by the enemy—and wholy unable to get their livelyhood and must be Supported by Some way—for which I'm happy to find this offered.

Caleb Chase—in family 6.

Bezaleel Tyler Sen'r—in family 5.

Jossiah Parks—in family 6.

Sarah Cuddeback—in family 5.

John Williams—in family 3.

Rebeca Croom—in family 3.

Sir, Agreeable to your request I have the Good Intentions of Jacob Rutsen Dewitt to serve his Disstress't neighbours by Distributing such Charitable Donations as may be appointed for this Settlement.

I must for the further good of these unhappy Sufferers beg the favour of you to Lay out such monies so appointed in Bread Grain in your parts—As it's not to be gotten in our Quarter; For such has been the Destruction in our Setlement that many of us (not herin retturn'd) will find it very hard to make out till harvest.

As it is not to be gotten from those arround us that has not been Destroy'd—such Source being Supply to the troops in this Quarter, I would beg the Acceptance of my hearty thanks (oppertunly) to the Hon'd Legeslature for the Condesending Condesederation of the unfortunate and am Hon'd Sir, Your most Obeid't & very Hum'e Sevt.

Benj'm Depuy.

P. S. By authentic intelegence from Sisquenna we have the following: The enemy attack't the Inhabitants, who fled to the Fort took one man prisoner, 137 head of Cattle & 70 Horses. Colo. Butler Sallied out of the Fort with a party at which the enemy made off. We hourly expect further particulars from that Quarter.

To Levi Pauling Colo., Marbletown.

A list of such persons who have been Distressed by The Incursions of the Enemy, now liveing in Rochester.

Children

Catharine Graham	5	⎫ Husbands all Kill'd
Helena Tack	4	⎬ Very poor and nothing to Support themselves & Children.
Margeret Miller	2	⎭
Maria Baker	3	her husband Taken prisoner In the same Condition as above.
The Widdow Cole		Lost all she had Excepting her land.
John Mullen		⎫ Lost their Crops and Very poor.
Cornelius Chambers		⎭
Eliza Hoornbeek		⎫ Hoornbeek's house & barn burnt Clarwater's barn burnt, and their Crops Lost.
Abraham Clarwater		⎭

I Recommend Capt. Benjaman Kortreght and Andries A. De Witt as persons willing to Distribute the money &c.

Levi Pawling.

[No. 2190.]

Francis Lewis Reports the Loss of British Transports at Egg Harbor and Fisher's Island.

Phil'a 3d April 1779.

Dear Sir, I have been favoured with your letter of the 22d ultimo, with the Inclosed Newspapers for which I return you my thanks.

On the 1st Instant Congress Resolved that the 1000 Men draughted out of the Militia of our state for the defence of the frontiers, should be on Continental pay & rations.

By the last storm a Transport ship was drove on shore near Egg Harbour with about 200 British Troops, from Hallifax for N'w York of which only 44 saved their lives & are now prisioners in this City.

By advices from New York we are informed, that the enemy's troops in Georgia are very Sickly, & through the same Channell, that in the West Indies Genl. Grant has been beat by the French, and We received advice yesterday from Head Quarters, that 14 Sail of British Transports were totally lost on Fisher's Island in the sound by the late Storm, by which means their expedition (supposed) against New London is rendered abortive.

The Express waiting obliges me to conclude with assuring you that I am with profound respect Your Obedient Humble Servant.

Fra' Lewis.

His Excellency Geo. Clinton Esqr.

[No. 2191.]

Commissions for Commissary Agents Under the Act of the Legislature.

By his Excellency George Clinton Esquire Governor of the State of New York General and Commander in Chief of all the militia and admiral of the navy of the same.

To Henry Wyckoff Esquire—Greeting:

Whereas by an Act of the Legislature of the said State, entitled " An act for procuring an immediate supply of Flour for the army," it is declared that it shall be lawful for the Person administring the Government of the said State for the Time being by writing under his Hand from Time to Time, to appoint such and so many diligent honest Inhabitants of the said State to procure flour for the Army as he shall think proper and from Time to Time in his discretion, to supercede such appointments, and that the said Persons so to be appointed shall be vested with all the Powers and authorities granted by one other act of the said Legislature entitled, "An Act more effectually to provide supplies of Flour meal and wheat for the Army " passed the thirty first Day of October last, to the Commiss'y Genl. of Purchases his Deputies or Assiss'ts.

And whereas, it is by the said first above mentioned act, further declared, that it shall be lawful for the said Persons administring the Government of the said State for the Time being, by and with the advice and Consent of six members of the Legislature, whenever he shall conceive the Emergency to require it, to authorize the several Persons whom he shall so from Time to Time appoint, to seize all or any Part of the Flour meal or wheat in the said State for the use of the army, with such further Powers, and under such Restrictions and Regulations as are in the said act mentioned; and also that the said Person administring the Government of the said State for the Time being by and with such advice and Consent as aforesaid be authorized to ascertain and determine the Price which shall be given for the Flour, meal, or wheat so to be taken as last aforesaid, to be estimated as near as may be, at the average of the Prices in the States of New Jersey and Connecticut.

And whereas, his said Excellency the Governor with six members of the Legislature on the 31st Day of March last by writing under their Respective Hands, did declare it as their Opinion that an Emergency exists, which renders it necessary that the said last mentioned Act should be carried into immediate Execution; and his said Excellency, the Governor, by and with the Advice and Consent of the said Six members of the Legislature, did thereupon pursuant to the Directions of the said last mentioned act, ascertain & determine the Prices of Flour, meal and wheat to be taken, by virtue of the said last mentioned act, as near as may be at the average of the Prices in the States of New Jersey and Connecticut, at the following Rates vizt. "Good Flour and well bolted meal respectively at Sixteen Pounds per hundred weight; and wheat at Sixteen Dollars per bushel:"

Now, therefore, by virtue of the Power and authority in me vested, as aforesaid, reposing Confidence in your Diligence and Honesty, I do by these Presents, appoint you the said Henry Wykoff, to procure Flour within this State for the Army, with all the Powers & Authorities granted by the said act, entitled " an act more effectually to provide supplies of Flour meal & wheat for the Army " to the Com'y Genl. of Purchases, his Deputies, or Assis'ts, and by Virtue of the Power and authority in me vested, as aforesaid, by the said act, entitled " an act for procuring an Immediate Supply of Flour for the army," I do further by these Presents authorize you, the said Henry Wykoff, besides the Flour, Meal & Wheat subject to seizure by the said act, entitled " An Act more effectually to provide Supplies of Flour meal & wheat for the army " to seize, at the Prices and Rates above ascertained and determined, all other Flour Meal and Wheat, within the County of Dutchess in this State, for the use of the said Army beyond what shall be necessary for the Subsistence of the respective Families of the Proprietors thereof, to be estimated at the rate particularly mentioned & expressed, in the said Act for procuring an immediate Supply of Flour for the army; and the same to deliver to the Commissary General or his Deputies or Agents, they paying for the same the Prices ascertained & determined as aforesaid, together with such satisfaction for Services and incidental Charges as by the said last mentioned act is directed; governing yourself in the Execution of the Powers hereby vested in you, agreeable to the Directions of the said two acts of the Legislature respectively. Given under my Hand at Poughkeepsie in the County of Dutchess this third Day of April 1779.

" Dr. of Appointment to Henry Wykoff to execute the Act for procuring an immediate supply of Flour for the Army. The like to Eben'r Purdy of Westchester, Walter Livingston, Robt. Van Rensselaer for Albany County, Jno. Haring, Orange County, Isaac Stoutenbergh for Albany & Ulster, Dirck Wynkoop, Danl. Graham & James Hunter for Ulster, Benj. Tusten, for Orange, Henry Oothout, for Albany, Herman Hoffman, Dutchess."

[No. 2192.]

Returns of Colonel Van Bergen's Regiment.

Return of Colo. Anthony Van Bergen's Reg'mt of militia.

Coxseghkie 3rd April 1779.

Companies	Commission'd Off'rs						Staff Officers		Non Com'd Officers			
	Collo.	Lt. Collo.	Majors	Capt'n	Lieut.	Ensign	Adjutant	Qr. Master	Serjts.	Corporels	Drums&fives	Privates
Fie'd Officers.	1	1	2	. . . .	. . . .	. .	1	1	. . . . .	. . . . .	. . . . . .	. . . . .
Capt John A. Witbeck.	. . . .	. . . .	. . .	1	2	. . . .	. . . . . .	. . . . . .	4	4	. . . . . .	60
Capt. Mynd't Van Schaick.	. . . .	. . . .	. . .	1	2	1	. . . . . .	. . . . . .	4	4	2	50
Capt. Abel's Comp'y.	. . . .	. . . .	. . .	. . . .	2	1	. . . . . .	. . . . . .	1	2	. . . . . .	30
Capt. Thom's Hoghtaling.	. . . .	. . . .	. . .	. . . .	. . . .	1	. . . . . .	. . . . . .	3	4	. . . . . .	36
Capt. Benj'm C. Dubois.	. .	. . . .	. . . .	1	1	1	. . . . . .	. . . . . .	4	. . . . . .	. . . . . .	40
	1	1	2	3	7	4	1	1	16	14	2	216

The Above Return is the pres't State of my Reg'mt, Together with the former Exampts & the persons between the ages of fifty & fifty five—Being the 11th Reg'mt in Genl. Ten Broeck's Brigade.

Anthony Van Bergen, Collo.

[No. 2193.]

THE ENEMIES IN THE REAR.

General McDougall Calls Attention to the Trials Imposed Upon Him for Obeying Orders and Enforcing the Laws.

Head Quarters Pecks Kill April 3rd 1779.

Sir,

I forgot to warn you, in my former Letters, to take Care of yourself. Be assured, you are one of those Victims, to be destroyed by any means. To prevent the abuses, which large Permits have created; and to enable the public, to judge what Provision go to the Eastward, as for the Continent, I have been obliged to open, a Custom House Office. The Guards may be impos'd on, by Permits from the civil authority, if they serve for more than one Team. The Supplies for the army are so alarming, that no pains should be left unessayed, to defeat the arts of the Jobbers. The Consequence to this State will be very awfull, if the Enemy should operate in it, before the next Crop comes in. It is, to prevent this, I have taken the Liberty, to order the Guards to stop all Grain and Flour, which have not printed Permits of the Tenor inclos'd. These I have sent for your use. The army is now served with one quarter of a pound of flour less, than last Campaign. The object of those measures I am persuaded, require no apology to you.

You will be inform'd by the Inclosures, contained in the Letters,* which accompany this, the means practis'd by our Neighbours, to defeat those measures, and the salutary Laws of this State, calculated for their own Security, as well as the United States in general. I wish you to write to Governor Trumbull, on this Subject; and give Mr. Reed and the Captain of Dragoons all the advice and assistance you can. Please to seal the Letters for the other Persons, when you have perused them. Divine civil, or military Law, is not in this Day regarded. God only knows, what will be the Consequence. It has a dangerous and baneful aspect, for the Ruin of America. The Enemy and the Line, of our own army, takes up but very little of my Time, compared with what is engross'd by internal Enemies, and pretended Whigs. Indeed, Sir, it is a Task, which I cannot long support, unless the civil authority and Congress will do their own Duty. The most virtuous man in America, cannot expect the army to exist, under

---

* See page 681 et seq.

present Circumstances, to be made Scape Goats of, to bear the Iniquities of the Country, to support them in Ease and Liberty, and to lay a foundation for Riches and opulence for America, subject at the same Time, to the civil Prosecution of every vile Jobber, who is seeking his own Interest, at the Expence of the public's, cannot much longer be born to support even those miscreants. The Confiscation of the Flour, &c., will never restrain the Wicked, from the violation of Laws so important in their Nature. A soldier receives thirty nine Lashes, for absenting himself without Leave; and yet a Citizen, not better born than him shall pass without any Corporal punishment, altho he shall do his utmost to starve that very Soldier.

Inclos'd I send you an Extract of Intelligence the person from whom it is received may be relied on. If the act of Parliament, alluded to is pass'd, they may raise as many Catholicks in Ireland, as Britain can support. I want exceedingly to converse two or three Hours with you, and Mr. Benson, on Subjects of great moment respecting the present and future Security of this state. But I find it next to impossible to leave this. Every moment I can spare from my quarters, is necessary to view and direct the Works. I am, Sir, In great Haste Your humble servant

Alex'r McDougall.*

His Excellency Governor Clinton.

[No. 2194.]

THE DEFENCE OF NEW YORK'S FRONTIER.

President Jay Furnishes Governor Clinton with a Copy of the Act of Congress.

Philadelphia 4th April 1779.

Sir, Herewith enclosed is a Copy of an Act of Congress of the 1st Inst., respecting the Body of men ordered by the State of New York to be raised for the Defence of their Frontiers.

---

*For Governor Clinton's answer, see page 692.

I have the Honor to be with great Respect and Esteem Your Excellency's Most Obedient Serv't

John Jay Presid't.

His Excellency Governor Clinton.

———

Whereas the delegates of the state of New-York have represented to Congress, that the legislature of that state taking into consideration the ravages committed by the Indians last fall, and the distresses occasioned thereby to a great number of families as well as the state at large; and that the said legislature considering the extreme difficulty and expense of covering an extensive frontier by posts against future incursions, have turned their attention to a western expedition against the Senecas, &c. as the cheapest and more eligible mode of securing the frontiers, and that they have empowered their governor to raise 1000 men by drafts from the militia for the defence of the frontiers:

Resolved, That Congress do approve of the spirited exertions of the said legislature, and the measures by them adopted to facilitate such enterprise: that the militia so to be raised shall be allowed continental pay and rations during their continuance in the said service; and that the commander in cheif be immediately informed of the said levy, and be directed to give orders for their pay and subsistence accordingly.

———

[No. 2195.]

Governor Clinton's Instructions to One of the New Commissary Commissioners.

Poughkeepsie April 5th 1779.

Sir, Relying on your Zeal & Readiness to promote the public Service I take the Liberty to send you the enclosed appointment which I must intreat you to accept. I also inclose you a Copy of

the last Act of the Legislature referred to in the appointm't the
other you'l find among the late printed Laws. I am informed considerable quantities of Flour has been lately purchased up at
Verplanck's & other mills in your neighbourhood for the Purpose
of Commerce. It is absolutely necessary that all the flour &
wheat you can lay your hands on, should be immediately seized
for the use of the army. I doubt not but you will exert yourself
in the execution of this Business. I am with great Regard, Your
most Obed't Serv't,

[G. C.]

[To Major Ebenezer Purdy, of Westchester.]*

[No. 2196.]

His Instructions to Walter Livingston.

Poukeepsie 6th April 1779.

Sir, Relying on your zeal & Readiness to promote the public
Service I take the Liberty of inclosing you an Appointment impowering you to seize Wheat, Flour & Meal in the County of
Albany, for the Use of the Army, with a Copy of the Act on which
the Appointment is founded. The other Act referred to, you
will find among the late Printed Laws of this State. You will
please to observ᷎. that I am directed by the inclosed Act, out of
the Wheat, Flour & Meal to be procured to retain for the Use
of the Militia &c., Eight thousand Bushells of Wheat, or a proportional Quantity of Flour. I have, therefore, to request &
pursuant to the said Act do hereby direct you out of the Quantity
you may procure, to deposit in some safe Place or Places in the
Manor of Livingston, a proportional Quantity of Flour, to one
thousand Bushells of Wheat, there to remain untill you receive

my further Orders respecting the same, any Thing contained in your Appointment herewith transmitted to you to the Contrary notwithstanding. I am Sir Your Most Obed't Serv't

G. C.

Walter Livingston, Esqr.

[No. 2197.]

REPUDIATES A GUARD.

Governor Clinton Declares it Is Inconvenient to Keep One—What Is Expected of the New Commissary Commissioners.

Poukeepsie 6th Apl. 1779.

Dear Sir, I have but a Moment to answer yours* of the 3d Instant. The Letters it inclosed I immediately sealed and forwarded by your Express. I am surprized to hear of the attempts made by the People of Connecticut to violate the Laws of this State, in taking Flour out of it by armed Force, as I have not been informed by the Civil Magistrates residing near the Line have been silent on this Subject tho they are expressly charged to see to the faithful Execution of the Embargo Law. Colo. Robert Renselaer & Colo. Brown of the Massachusetts Bay have Permission in Consequence of the advice of a Committee of the Legislature appointed for the Purpose, to export out of this State one Thousand Barrels of Flour for the use of the Inhabitants of Massachusets Bay. It will be impossible to furnish them with your printed Permits, & will be, therefore, necessary that your Officer on the Line be instructed, to suffer this Quantity to pass his Guard. They are both sworn not to export a greater Quantity.

I inclose you an Appointment to Major Purdy† to seize all the Wheat & Flour in West Chester County for the Use of the Army

---

* See page 687.
† See pages 686 and 690.

with a Copy of the act for warranting the Appointment, which
when you have perused, you will please to seal up & forward to
him. There are fifteen other active Persons & of the most reput-
able Charecters appointed in different Parts of the State for the
same Purpose, so that I am in hopes we shall soon have the whole
Collected & delivered over to the Different Commissaries, nor
do I despair of finding a Competent Supply for the Army, untill
the new Crops come in, if we can for a few Weeks prevent any
being run out of the State.

I must trust to Providence for my own personal Safety ag't
any Secret Attempt of the Enemy, as it is not convenient to keep
a Guard. I am in great Haste, Dear Sir, Yours Sincerely

Geo: Clinton.

I have just received the enclosed affidavits of some of the Inhabit'ts of the lower part of Orange County complain'g of Wm.
Simmons in the Commiss'y of Forage Department. I must beg
you to cause an Enquiry to be made into this matter.
Genl. McDougal.

[No. 2198.]

MAGISTRATE GROUT IN DURESS.

*Micah Townsend Brings the Matter with the Papers in the Case to
the Attention of Governor Clinton.*

Brattleborough April 7th 1779.

May it please your Excellency, In my last, with the view of
shewing that the State of New Hampshire had it under Contemplation to revive its ancient Claim west of Connecticut River,
I mentioned Judge Clay's going in Company with Lieut. Governor
Marsh & Colo. Olcott to Exeter: This Information I received in
such a manner that I thought there was no doubt of the Fact;
But having since seen Mr. Clay, Justice to his Character, obliges

me to mention his acquainting me, he went upon his private Business only, and that not in the Company of the above named Persons, but with three of the New Hampshire General Court, one of whose Names was Marsh; and that he is opposed to that Court's reviving their Claim but he has good reason to suppose they will.

The inferior Court of the County opposite to us (as I have been informed by several Persons of Credit who have seen the Letters and Notifications for Town Meetings) have written to the several Towns in their County to instruct their Deputies with respect to claiming the Grants west of the River, and some of them have instructed in favor of the Claim. How this will terminate I know not, but many are of Opinion that the eastern Part of the State will oppose it for the same reason that the western desire it, vizt., that it will occasion a Removal of the Seat of Government. I shall go to No. 4* next Week, and as Hampshire General Court is now sitting, or has lately adjourned, suppose I shall then be able to inform your Excellency of the Intentions of that Court.

The inclosed Letter from Justice Grout came to hand soon after I had sent my last. Should have forwarded it sooner, but was in hopes to have seen him first, or have received the Papers he mentions.

The Officers of Vermont have lately made a Draft, in which they have not spared those who deny their authority. Judge Clay is one of the Persons drafted. Whether they will proceed so far as to distrain for Fines I know not, but expect it will make a Disturbance if they do. This Draft, the orders say, is made by the advice of Genl. James Clinton.

*Charlestown, New Hampshire.

I inclose a Pamphlet, a Passage in which will corroberate an affidavit I formerly transmitted your Excellency, and will serve to set the Characters of either Colo. Allen or some Members of Congress in their true light. It also contains a Copy of a Letter from President Weare, which may be of Use in a Contention with New Hampshire. The signers of the Performance acted as part of a Committee appointed by the Legislature of Vermont, tho they now dissent from them unless they keep up their Claim East of Connecticut River.

Those who adhere to the Interest of New York here, will this Month elect Representatives; and if the Sheriff should seasonably get word from the Clerk of the Senate, will vote for a Senator, if there is any to be chosen in this District.

It appears very strange to me, and those with whom I converse, that Congress have not yet interfered in a matter which so greatly affects the Confederation, and has so immediate a Tendency to disturb the Peace and Unity of the States, as the present Revolt. I cannot but think that Justice to this, and the Precedent it will make for the refractory Subjects of other States, will at length induce that honorable Body to interpose; and yet they delay their Interposition so long without apparent Reasons, that they appear indirectly to countenance Vermont, —who, by being in Possession of the Powers of Government, must gain Strength, and Consequence the longer they are let alone. I have not the least doubt but Judge Jay and the other Delegates from New York, will do what can be done to induce Congress to recommend to the revolted Subjects to return to their Duty. If they are unsuccessful at Philadelphia, it only remains for the Legislature to determine whether they will give us up, or keep us at all Events, and protect the Persons & Property of those who continue their faithful Subjects. This is bringing the matter to a Crisis, but if Congress will not interfere, the sooner in my Opinion these Points are settled the better, as the Country increases very rapidly, and those who now become Settlers generally do it under the Notion of being in a fourteenth State.

Mr. Lush's Letter, inclosing some Copies of the Election act, came very seasonably; for which and the Promise of future Intelligence respecting Vermont, I am much obliged both to your Excellency and Mr. Lush. I am Your most Obedient Serv't

Micah Townsend.

His Exc'y Governor Clinton.

Hilkiah Grout's Statement to Micah Townsend.

S'r, Last weak on Tuesday morning, I set out from home with a gentleman from the State of New Hampshire, who had a case Depending in the Superiour Court at Exeter, in Said State of considerable consequence and Depended altogether upon evidences from Otercrick [Otter Creek] and to have them taken by known Athority for Vermont athority has been Refus'd in their court. It was agreed that I should go to the westerly part of this county and there remain whilst he should go into the Crick and Bring the People out to me to be sworn; on Wednesday eve they came out and were sworn; about two o'clock the same night the house was surrounded By seaven men, armed with guns, sword Bayonets, and entered the Room where I Lodged, and made me their prisoner, and carried me to Rutland (and shew me no abuse except it was in surly Look), before one Capt. Brownson Belonging to Colo. Warner Rigement, who command a post their, to answer to a complaint of two of the Inhabitants, complaining that Hilkiah Grout and his associates, were planing something verry enemical to the United States of America. A court of enquirery was immediately call'd and I was Brought to treat and Dis-[charged;] I was then taken with a warr't from one of their Justises, complaining that the said Grout had been officiateing as a Justice of the peace without the approbation of there Freemen, &c; after holding me a prisoner two days, they made out to prove that I had administered the oath to five men; the Judgment of court was, that I should find sureties for my appearance Before their Sup [reme] court to be holden in Rutland next June, or be commited to close goal. I gave bond, and am now at home and have neither been whipt nor Insulted; the New Hamshire gent. whome I went to assist was taken as a prisoner and Brought to tryal. Judgment was that he pay five pound fine, and thre pound cost of court for Introduceing an unconstitutional Justice into the state of Vermont. The copyes of the whole will be brought to me By a friend as soon as they can be made out and then you may expect to see me at Brattleborough. I am but this minit come home and Mr. Whipple the Bearer now waits. I am S'r your most Humble Serv't.

Hilkiah Grout.

To Mr. Micah Townsen, Esqr.

February ye 21 1779.

THE COURT MARTIAL PROCEEDINGS.

Fort Ranger, Feby. 18 1779.

Gerreson orders.

A Court martial of Enquery to set att twelve oclock this Day to Examen and here the Evidence for and aganst Such Prisonors as shall be Brought Before them, whereof Capt. Thomas Lee is Pre'dt—members, Lt. Marin, Lt. Mott, Ensign Beach, Ensign Bruesh.

By order of Ged'n Brownson, Capt., the Court being met, and Duly sworn, Proced to try Melkiah Grout; the Prisinors being brougt before the Court Pleads not Guilty; the Court after hearing the Evidence for and against the Prisiners it is the opinion of the Court that the Crime is not suported.

pr Thomas Lee, Pr'dt.

The above Judgment is aproved of by Commanding officer and orders the Prisiner to be set at Librty.

Pr Ged. Brownson, Capt. Comdt.

TESTIMONY HOSTILE TO GROUT.

The Evidence of Reuben Squires, in a case Depending Between the freemen of the State of Vermont and Helkiah Grout, viz., that on the 17th day of Instant February Mr. William Oliver, Intredused Helkiah Grout Recommending him in Caracter of Justice of the Peace unto Said Reuben Squires, Desireing Said Squires's wife and Daughter to give their Evidence before said Grout consarning a certain Peace of Holland Cloath.

The Evidence of Charles Button: Charles Button of Lawfull age, under oth testafyes and says, that in the Evening of the Seventeenth Instant, upon the Desire of Mr. William Oliver, he the s'd Button went to the house of Lemuel White in Shrewsbury, and gave his affidafit conserning a case depending Between said Oliver and one West before Helkiah Grout, who took the said Button's affidafit and administred an oth to him with several others in caracter of Justice of the Peace.

The Evidence of Abel Spencer: Abel Spencer of Lawfull age under oth testifyes and Declairs, that he also took his oth before Helkiah Grout, acting in the caracter of Justice of the Peace, and that he saw him, the said Grout, administer oths to a number of others at the same place and time that Charles Button Evidence Refers to.

The Evidence of Lemuel White: Lemuel White of Lawfull age under oth Testifys and Declairs to the same, that Charles Button and Abel Spencer testafyed to or to the same purpose.

Rutland, Feby. ye 19: 1779. These are a trew and Just Coppy of the Evidences of Reuben Squires, Charles Button, Abel Spencer and Lemuel White as taken under oth.

Before me   Benj'n Whipple, Justice.

THE WARRANT FOR GROUT'S ARREST.

State of Vermont, County of Bennington ss.

To the Sheriff of the County of Bennington his Depute of Either of the Constabels of the town of Rutland Greeting.

In the Name of the Free men of the State of Vermont you are hereby authorized to take and in safe custody keep Helkiah Grout a transient Person who pretends to officiate in this State in the character of Justice of the Peace, not haveing athority Derived from the free men of this State, as Stipulated by Constitution: and as soon as conveniently may be, bring him before me, the subscriber, at the house of William Robarts, in Rutland, to answer for his said conduct aganst the Peace and Dignity of this State.

Given under my hand. Rutland, Feby. ye 18th 1779 in the third year of Amarican Independenc and secont of the State of Vermont.

Benj'n Whipple, Justice Peace.

a trew coppy—attest—B. Whipple.

GROUT PLACED UNDER BONDS TO APPEAR IN COURT.

Rutland Feby. ye 19th 1779—At a court held before Benj'n Whipple, Justice of the Peace, Helkiah Grout is convicted of acting in the caracter of Justice of the Peace contrary to the

Constitution of this state. Said Grout is ordered by this court to
procure Bonds of one thousand Pounds Lawfull money for his
appearance at the next superiour court, to be held within this
State at Rutland, on the second Thursday in June next for Trial
or in Defalt to be commited untill then.

Benj'n Whipple, Justice Peace.

a Trew coppy —attest— B. Whipple.

Mem. Mr. Grout wants Gov'r Clinton's advice in what manner
to conduct himself—Whether the State will protect him—If
Court fines him whether to pay ye Fine or Go to Goal—Will not
ye State allow Counsel to Mr. Grout—Get something from ye
Gov'r to show Mr. Grout is a Magistrate.

[No. 2199.]

List of Distressed Families in Mohawk District.

Memorandom the Distressed famelys in Tryon County, Mohok
District 1779 Apl. 7 Day.

Gotfret Shonn in His famely	9
John Potman's wedo [widow]	1
John Rese, wife	2
Harmanes Salesberry, Do	4
George Kugs	7
Yebler Alger	5
Joseph Schot,	7
The wedo Cetcham,	5
Andres Bowman,	5
Charels Morenes wedo,	3
Hendrick Kelly,	5
Rachel Hansen,	6
Totel	59

The above Persons have mostly all Lost the Personal Property.
(On back of document)   ·   *

Sir: I have Packed two hodsed of oats and have had them
Cupered in good order to Send Down—one hodsed No. 1 Contanes
18 Schepl and No. 2 Contanes 23 Verry Large, in all 41—now
there is about two Schepl over—your was gone and Mr. Snell
nor my wife Cant tell wot is become of them.

[No. 2200.]

John Jay Transmits Two Acts of Congress to George Clinton.

Philadelphia 7th April 1779.

Sir, Herewith enclosed are Copies of two Acts of Congress—
one of the *23rd Ult., for regulating the cloathing Department,
the other of the †5th Inst., providing for the Pay of the Officers
employed in it.

You will perceive that the first refers the appointment of the
Sub, or State-Cloathiers to the different States, & that the Second
leaves their Salaries to be ascertained & paid by the States appointing them.

Such has long been the deranged State of this Department, &
such is the importance of immediately carrying the present System into Execution, that Congress hope it will meet with the
earliest attention.

---

* See page 659.

† Resolved, That until the further order of Congress the clothier-general have a
salary of 5000 dollars per annum.

Whereas the duties of the sub or state-clothiers who are to be appointed according to
the late regulations of the clothier's department will be very unequal, the quota of battalions of the several states differing:

Resolved, That each state determine and pay the salary proper for its clothier, and
that each state-clothier shall be allowed two rations and forage for one horse per day
during the time he is in actual service with the army, and going to and returning from
the same:

That the regimental-clothiers have an allowance of 30 dollars per month in addition
to their present appointment:

That the clothier-general be authorized to employ one clerk, who shall receive the
same allowance as the clerks of the auditors of the army.

I have the Honor to be with great Respect your Excellency's Most Obedient Serv't

John Jay, Presid't.

His Excellency Governor Clinton.

[No. 2201.]

WAR AGAINST THE ONONDAGAS.

A Secret Expedition Sent to Attack their Castle—Failure of a Flag to Niagara.

Albany April 8th 1779.

Dear Brother,* Yours of the 1st Instant came safe to hand; in consequence of its contents, I have ordered John Storms of Duboys's Regiment, and a certain Nelson of the Train to attend immediately as Witnesses against Jaycocks.

Inclosed I send you a copy of the return of the Flag, which was sent to Niagara in pursuance of your Directions. I consulted Genl. Schuyler on the Propriety of sending a Duplicate of the Inclosures to Congress, but he is of opinion, that it woud come best from you, as we acted immediately under your orders.

The repeated applications that are daily and hourly made to me by the distrissed Famelies from the Frontiers, for Provision, and the feelings of Humanity, have induced me, I believe, to exceed the Bounds of my authority in relieveing their Wants, which are truly melancholy. I shoud be glad to have your directions in a matter of such moment. If the assembly have made Provision for them, no time is to be lost, in the distribution of it—if they have not, the dreadfull consequence will be that they, or many of them must inevitably perish.

A detatchment of five hundred Men commanded by Col. V. Schaick and Willet, are just marched, with a View of surprising and destroying the Onondaga Castle,† and of making as many

---

*For Governor Clinton's reply, see page 711.

†April 24.—This afternoon, the detachment sent out last Monday [April 19th] on an expedition against the Indians at Onondaga, returned to Fort Schuyler. The following account of it is given by a writer in the New York Packet:—" An enterprise against the

Prisoners as possible. The Plan has the Sanction of His Excellency, and if properly conducted, I think cannot fail of Success; as Secrecy is absolutely necessary, no Individual hath the least Intimation of it except the Officers commanding the Party, and

Onondaga settlements of the Indians having been projected and approved of by his Excellency General Washington, and the direction of it committed to Brigadier-General James Clinton, commanding in the northern department, he, on the seventh of April, issued his orders, and gave the execution of them to Colonel Van Schaack, commander of the 1st battalion of New York Continental troops, appointing as second and third in command Lieutenant-Colonel Willet and Major Cochran, of the 3d New York battalion, all officers of approved courage and abilities. The detachment for the service consisted of six companies of New York, one of Pennsylvania, one of Massachusetts troops, and one of riflemen, amounting, in the whole, to five hundred and four rank and file, and fifty-one officers.

"Fort Schuyler being appointed the place of rendezvous, from thence, early on Monday morning, the nineteenth of April, the whole party began their march, provision for eight days having been previously sent off in twenty-nine batteaux into Wood Creek.

"After a march of twenty-two miles, the troops arrived about three o'clock in the evening at the old Scow Place, but the boats having much farther to come, did not arrive till ten o'clock. As soon as the boats arrived, the whole of the troops embarked, and, upon entering the lake, were much impeded by a cold head wind.

"At eight o'clock in the morning of the twentieth, the troops halted at Pisser's Bay till all the boats came up, and then proceeded to the Onondaga landing, opposite to old Fort Brewerton, which they reached at three o'clock in the afternoon. From thence, after leaving all their boats with a proper guard, they marched eight or nine miles on their way to the Onondaga settlement, and, not being able to continue their march in the dark, lay on their arms all night, without fire.

"Very early on the twenty-first they proceeded to the Salt Lake, an arm of which (two hundred yards over, and four feet deep) they forded, with their pouches hung to their fixed bayonets, and advanced to the Onondaga Creek, where Captain Graham took prisoner an Onondaga warrior. The creek not being fordable, the troops crossed it on a log, and as soon as they were over, the utmost endeavors were used to surround the settlements, but as they extended eight miles, besides some scattered habitations lying back of the castles, it was impossible; and on the opposite side of the creek, though our troops entered their first settlement wholly undiscovered by them, they soon discovered some of our advanced parties, and took the alarm in all their settlements. The colonel, however, ordered different routes to be taken by different parties, in order to surround as many of their settlements as possible at the same time; but the Indians fled precipitately to the woods, not taking any thing with them. Our troops took thirty-three Indians and one white man prisoners, and killed twelve Indians. The whole of their settlements, consisting of about fifty houses, with a large quantity of corn and beans, were burnt, a number of fine horses, and every other kind of stock were killed. About one hundred guns, some of which were rifles, were among the plunder, the whole of which, after the men were loaded with as much as they could carry, was destroyed, with a considerable quantity of ammunition; one swivel, taken at the council house, had the trunnions broken off, and was otherwise much damaged, and, in fine, the destruction of all their settlements was complete.

"After this, the troops began to march on their return, recrossed the creek, and forded the arm of the lake, on the side of which they encamped on a good ground. They had only been once interrupted by a small party of Indians, who fired upon them from the opposite side of the creek, but were soon beaten back by Lieutenant Evans' riflemen, who killed one of them.

"On the twenty-second the troops marched to the landing, embarked in good order, and rowed to Seven Mile Island; on the twenty-third crossed the lake, and landed two miles up Wood Creek. On Saturday, the twenty-fourth, at twelve o'clock, the whole detachment returned in safety to Fort Schuyler, having been out five days and a half."— New Jersey Gazette, May 12, 1779.

those whose duty intitled them to know it.   I am, Dear Brother,
Yours affectionately

James Clinton.

Gov'r Clinton.

———

COLONEL CAMPBELL REPORTS THE FAILURE OF HIS MISSION.

Report of Col. John Campbell of Cherry Valley, on his return
from Connesaraga.

Whith the dispatches I received from Generals Schuyler and
Clinton I proceeded in company with Jacob Newkerk to the
Oneida Castle, after requesting a Guide to pilot me to Niagara;
the Chiefs called a Council, in which it was determined, that it
was impossible for us to proceed, as there was a Council then
sitting at Keuga [Cayuga] who were unacquainted with the
nature of a Flag, and, therefore, might treat us as Enemies.
Nevertheless, being deeply concerned in the Business I was on,
I ventured to proceed as far Connesaraga; after making the same
demand there, the Chiefs called a Council, and determined as the
Oneidas had done, alledging that they cou'd not be answerable
to the American Chiefs, for any misfortune that might befall us,
that they woud very justly incur the Displeasure of their
Brothers, the Americans, if they permitted us to proceed, when
they knew the Consequences that woud ensue—they therefore insisted on us to return, promising that they woud forward the
Letters to Captain Butler, with more Expedition & safety than
if we went ourselves.

In Consequence of which I thought it best to return.

signed,   John Campbell.

Copy.

[No. 2202.]

Returns of Dutchess Brigade under Colonel Swartwout.

A Return of the Brigade of Militia of the County of Dutches, Commanded by Colo. Comdt. Jacobus Swartwout. agreeable to the Returns of the Commanding Officers of the Several Regiments of said Brigade.

REGTS.	Field — Colo.	Lt. Colo	Major	Officers Commiss'd — Captains	1st Lieuts.	2d Do.	Ensign	Staff — Adjutant	Q. Master	Non Comm'ss'd — Serjeants	Corporals	Drum's	Fifers	Rank & file	Exempts by having Certificates for hired men in the army	Exempts having borne Commissions	Exempts above 50 years of age
Colo. Roswell Hopkins' Regt.	1	1	2	8	8	8	9	1	1	36	35	6	6	486			
Colo. John Frear Do	1		1	8	8	5	6	1	1	32	31	5	5	391			
Colo. Abr'm Brinckerhoff	1		1	6	7	6	7	1	1	17	28	4		401			
Colo. Morris Graham	1	1	2	9	9	8	2	1	1	36	33	8	2	504	25		
Colo. Henry Luddenton	1		1	6	6	5	4			24		6		398	28	18	76
Colo. James V. D. Burgh	1	1	1	5										358			
Total	6	4	9	42	36	32	28	4	4	155	127	29	13	2,588			

N. B: Colo. Field's Return is not Come; therefore Could not Enter it.

Colo. Van Der Burgh's Rank & file, Includes the Subalterns & Serjts. of his Regt.

The Exempts by Certificates are made no Return of Only of 2 Regts.

By Order of Jacobus Swartwout, Colo. Comdt.

Hend'k Wyckoff, B: M:

Fishkill, April 9th, 1779.

45

A Return of the Associated Exempts in the Brigade of Militia of Dutches, Commanded by Colo. Comdt. Jacobus Swartwout, agreeable to the Returns of the several Capts. Commanding said Companies.

COMPANIES	OFFICERS						Rank File
	COMMISSIONED				NON COM'D		
	Capts.	1st Lieut.	2nd Do.	Ensign	Serjts.	Corp's	Privates
Capt. Abr'm Schenck	1	1	1		2	2	31
Capt. Wm. Leonard's	1	1	1		2	2	28
Capt. Rufus Herrick's	1	1	1	1			42
Total	3	3	3	1	4	4	101

N. B: Capt. Elias Van Buntschoten's and Capt. Isaac Bloom's Returns are not Come; therefore Could not Enter them.

By Order of Colo. Comdt. Jacobus Swartwout.

Hend'k Wyckoff, B: M:

Fishkill April 9th 1779.

His Excellency, Gov'r Clinton.

[No. 2203.]

Governor Clinton Indulgent in the Case of Mrs. Cregier.

Poughkeepsie April 9th 1779.

Sir; Mr. Harpur applied to me in behalf of Mrs. Cregier for permission for her to go to New York for the Purpose of conveying
a Child thither, which she took to nurse several years ago &
which is now become burthensome to her. As Dr. Bruce who engaged in behalf of its father, to pay her for keeping it, is there,
she intends leaving the Child with him. Altho' I had determined
not to give Permission to any Person to go into New York, with
an Intent to return, yet in consequence of Mrs. Cregier's Private
as well as political Character I submit it to your Consideration
whether good Purposes might not be affected (in procuring Intelligence) by granting her request. If you approve of the
measure I have no Objection to her being permitted to go. I have
directed her to attend you with this Letter & wait your Directions
on the subject. I am &c.

Geo: Clinton.

Genl. McDougall.

[No. 2204.]

Richard Harison, Tory, Makes an Appeal in Behalf of His Family.

N. York 9 April 1779.

Sir; Having obtained Permission from General Jones to remove
my Family & Effects to this Place by a Vessel now going up the
River with a Flag, I cannot entertain a Doubt of your not only
allowing, but forwarding that measure. To accumulate Distresses
upon those, whom for Reasons of mere Policy, it has been thought
proper to banish under the circumstances in which we were,
would be such a Violation of Humanity as I cannot in Justice,

think you capable of. On the contrary, I shall want no Inducement to suppose that you will chearfully promote, what may indeed conduce to the private Happiness of an Individual, but can
have no Influence as to what regards the Public. Actuated by
these Sentiments, I beg Leave to request that the inclosed Letters
may be forwarded to my Family, with such further Instructions
as you may thing proper; & permit me (in confidence that those
Sentiments are well founded) to subscribe myself with all due
Respect, Sir, Your most humble & obedient Servant

Rich: Harison.

Gov'r Clinton.

[No. 2205.]

Peter Colt Reforms His Opinion of Mr. Leek.

Hartford Apr. 10: 1779.

Sir, On Mr. Lockwood's return, I had, from his representation,
given over the thoughts, at this Time, of removing Mr. Leak. I
have never been able to discover any knavery in his dealings.
My objection to him is a want of that determined Spirit & resolution which seems necessary to insure success in Business at this
Critical Juncture. I am a Stranger to Capt. Townsend's place
of abode; however, will enquire him out, & if possible engage him
in the service. If not shall continue Mr. Leak.

Your Excellency will please to accept my acknowledgments for
your kind & ready attention to the Business of my Department,
I cant but flatter myself that the late alterations in the Officers
of the Dept., in your State, will advance the public service. I
shall endeavour to support those Gentlemen with Cash. I
am with due Esteem, Your Excel'y most obd. Ser.

Peter Colt.

His Excellency Gov'r Clinton.

[No 2206.]

FOR THE AID OF THE FRONTIER SUFFERERS.

Governor Clinton Calls Major Lush's Attention to the Necessity of Prompt Action.

Poukeepsie 11th March [April] **1779.**

Dear Sir,* I expected before this to have heard from you & to have received thro you as well Genl. Ten Broeck's Return, as a Return of the Persons in the County of Albany & Tryon, who are objects of the Law for granting three Thousand Pounds for the Relief & Support of those who have had their Possessions destroyed by the Enemy & are incapable to support themselves. The Want of the former only occassions a Delay in raising the Men for the Defence of the Frontiers of the State, which may be attended with fatal Consequences & Subject both Genl. Tenbroeck & me to much Consern.

I suspect that the procuring the other Return may be attend with more Trouble & Delay than I at first apprehended. I have, therefore, thought it most adviseable to attempt a Distribution of the Money without it. And, for this Purpose, I desire you will borrow of your County Treasury, or of Jacob Cuyler, Esqr., D. C. Genl., of Purchases, twenty two hundred & fifty Pounds & deposit it in the Hands of such Person or persons as shall be recommended to you by Genl. Tenbroeck & the Members of Senate & Assembly for the County of Albany, residing in the City, to be distributed agreable to the Directions of the Law to those in the County of Albany & Tryon who are the proper Objects of it taking proper Receipts.

If you obtain the Money from your Treasurer, I will replace a like Sum in the State Treasury, which will save him the Trouble

---

* See page 724 for Major Lush's reply.

of conveying it thither. If from Mr. Cuyler, I will repay it to his order in Favour of his Deputy at Kingston. I begg you to pay particular & early Attention to this Business & let me hear from you by the first Opportunity. I am &c.

Geo: Clinton.

Major Fonda informs me Doct'r McCrea has a Map of the State or Part of it which I wish you to endeavour to procure for me. To Major Lush.

[No. 2207.]

ARRANGING FOR THE EXCHANGE OF PRISONERS.

Governor Clinton Submits the Proposition of Walter Butler to the New York Delegates in Congress.

Poughkeepsie, 11th April 1779.

Gentlemen, Soon after the desolation of the Settlement of Cherry Valley by the Savages under the Command of Brandt & Butler, some of the Inhabitants who were captured by the Enemy at that Place were released & permitted to return home on Parole. They brought with them written proposals made by young Butler & directed to Genl. Schuyler for an exchange of the Inhabitants of this State who were Prisoners with the Savages, for Butler's mother, & other disaffected Persons in our Possession. In Consequence of which, I requested Brig'r Genl. Clinton then commanding at Albany, to confer with Genl. Schuyler on the Subject & to pursue the most proper measures to effect so desirable an object. I now enclose you a Copy of a Letter from Butler in answer to one addressed to him by Genl. Clinton on that Subject with the Papers referred to in it. You will please to observe that the proposals now made, are more extensive than those first stated, and as in the exchange now offered, continental officers & soldiers &

Your's most truly

Cornwallis

Inhabitants of other States are comprehended, I am not authorized to agree to the present Proposals. An insolent Expression
in Butler's Letter prevents my laying it (officially) before Congress. But as the Releasements of the unhappy Subjects of this
State who experience the most distressing Captivity with the
Savages, is a matter I have much at heart, I have taken the
liberty of addressing you on this occasion in hopes you may be
able to fall on some mode of obtaining such genl. Directions from
Congress on this Subject as will enable us to accomplish this
Business without taking any public notice of Butler's impertinent
Epistle. I am &c. &c.

Geo: Clinton.

The hon'ble the Delegates from the State of New York in Congress.

[No. 2208.]

Governor Clinton Believes the Legislative Appropriation for the
Frontier Sufferers Inadequate.

Poukeepsie 11th April 1779.

Dear Brother, I am favoured with your Letter* of the 8th Instant. The Papers it inclosed respecting an Exchange of Prisoners taken on the Western Frontier shall be transmitted to Congress by the first Conveyance for their Consideration & further
Direction. The Legislature at their last Meeting granted three
thousand Pounds for the Relief of the distressed Families on the
Western Frontiers. This Sum when distributed among the Number who are rendered by the Depredations of the Savages in-
capble of supporting themselves, will be found very incompetent.
The Law granting it is not yet printed & I am not possessed of a
Copy of it, neither have I been able to obtain Returns from the
different Districts which have been destroyed, of the Number of

---
*See page 702.

the Inhabitants of each which are the Objects of the Law, and have, therefore, not been able to make a proper Distribution of the Money. Major Lush is now in Albany & to prevent further Delay, I have directed him to borrow from the County Treasury, twenty two hundred & fifty Pounds & to deposit the same in the Hands of such Person or Persons as shall be recommended by Genl. Ten Broeck & the Members of Senate & Assembly for the County of Albany, residing in the city, to be expended in Support of the unhappy Sufferers in the County of Albany & Tryon agreable to the Direction of the Law. I cannot pretend to advise you further to exceed your Authority in supplying them with Provision from the Public Stores, least you shoud incurr Blame. I wish Success to the Detachment you mention as having marched, & am Yours Sincerely,

Geo: Clinton.

The hon'ble Brig'r Genl. Clinton.*

[No. 2209.]

Petition in Behalf of Sundry Convicts, viz. Andrew Layton, Peter Lansing, Jacobus Kidney and Samuel Johnston.†

[No. 2210.]

EXPERIENCES OF VATHER AND RODINGBURG.

Judge William Harper Sends their Depositions to Governor Clinton.

Mohock destrict, Tryon County, 12 Aprl. 1779.

Sir; I inclose to you the Deposisonens of Abart Vather and Androus Rodingburg, Both my near nibours, who ware taken prisener by the Enimy yesterday in the afternune; Samawell Kenady is likewise my near nibour's son he with—Longs and the young man from Sconackendy are carryed of. I knew nothing

---

*For James Clinton's answer, see page 735.
†Omitted.

of the mater till mr. Vather returned this morning, thogh the afare hapened on the farm that Jockapie and Rodingburg pased by my Doer within fore minets after he was relased,   As Sune as I hard of it, I sent for him and Examened him and my Brother Dispatched a later Express to the Genarall at Albany; my Brother is Gon to Johnstown with a party of young men in hopes to gate a party of Contanentals to Join him and pursue them; if Rodingburg had informed us last night wee might have got before them, but Vathers ascaping will undoubtedly hasten them. Colnoll Williet naraly mised being taken as he pased that way but a short time before my Nibours ware taken.

I was informd by a offecer from Johnstown, thare was one Hans Helmer, a Tory taken yesterday, by one Solleman Wodward, a true whig in Johnstons bush; this Helmere was taken in the party that was taken back of Ball Town, going to the Enimy in Seventy seven, and is now a solder in Sir John Johnston's Ridgment, and is home on his perole; he sayes Sir John is made a brigader Genarall, and that this part of the cuntry will be cut of this Spring; thare is severall partyes of Toryes gone to Canady latly from theas parts, and severall Toryes and Tory women have advised thier frinds to take care of thare selves, as thar will be a party of five or Six hundred from Canady as sune as the wods and waters are pasable. The fue tru whigs amongst us, are intierly discureged and dar not medel with the Toryes, as almost everry one that has ben taken up by the sivel or millatery athoraty, has ben set at liberty or have made thier ascape out of Gale [gaol] and wee are so thretened by sum of the Commsoners of Conspiresies, and others prosecuted for seasing thar property, so that all most the wholl of the popell that have ben tru to the Caus, cry out that the Toryes are protected & the whigs are

oprest. Sir, I know many that have ben astemad Enemies to the
Cuntry ever since the contest began, and have ben sent to the
Commisoners at Albany, and have bin set at Liberty, or on thare
perole, without ever caling for any evidence aganst them, and,
sir, the popell are very uneasey at Justice, or rither unjustice as
thay call it, being huger mugered so, and thay exposeed to thare
enimies over agane when thay Exasperateed and protected.

Sir, I wroght you sum time ago, that I was of opinon that thare
would not be one whig living on the Mohock Rever above Sconackendy by the first of May, and I am prety shuer it will be so;
as to my selfe and all the whigs that are in my nibourhude must
move dyrectly. It is a grate pitty thate thes Rever shuld be
vackaated for the whate [wheat] hath not ben known to luck so
well at this time of the year as it now doeth.

Thare was three Indens went to Sacondago sum dayes ago; we
are all convins thay ware spies and parhaps in this party that
tuck the priseners. Mager Fundew tells me that thay Had Mr.
Hanry Glen's pas as frinds, and that he essued provisen to them
and orders to Draw more at Johnstown, all go unmolested & pro-
tacted amongst us Toryes and Indens and in the very hants whare
wee expect and whar the Enemy do cum.

Sir, I am harttily Sorry that I have not more agrable Subjects
to [write] you on but beleve me, Sir, a sincer Frind to my Cuntry
and your Sincer frind and harty well wisher.

William Harper.

To his Exselency Georg Clenton.

DEPOSITION OF ALBERT H. VATHER.

The Deposesition of Alburt H. Vather, Living in the Mohock
district, Tryon county, Taken before me, Wm. Harper Esqr.
April 12, 1779.

The Deponant saeth that Sunday, ye 11 instant, about son a howr high in the after nune, he left his hows at Fort Johnston to go to the hows of Coln. Closs, whare Wm. Harper, Esqr., and Coln. Harper dwels, about one mill distante from Fort Johnston, to hear what nues, as he expected that Coln. Harper was cum Albany; that he went along the publick rod about one thurd of the way, till he came to a bruck whare he see severall Indens runing towards him, naked with thier guns in thier hands; thay layed hold of him and tuck the handcurch from his nack, and the buckells out of his knes & Shues, & then convayed to the rest of thier party, who Lay at a small distance from the rode. When he came to the rest of the party, he found Andres Roding-burg, Samawell Kenady a sartan Mr. Longs that lives at the Nos & a yong man that Lived with Andro McFarland, of Sconackendy, all priseners; from thence thay moved up the hill a small distance whare thay halted & eate sum vitells.

The Deponant saeth, he knew one of the Indens named Peter, haveing but one hand who belongs to Fort Hunter, and two white men that ware with them, John Rotch and Barnet Wem-pell; thate one of the white men asked him, the Deponant, whare he lived, and how many men was at his hows, and how many Guns he had, and if he did kepe Taveron, and that thay inquired who lived in Coln. Closses hows that Sml. Kenady told them Esqr. Harper & Coln. Harper, but that Coln. Harper was not at home then; thay inquired how many men was at the hows; Sad Kenady told them that Esqr. Harper and two boys; thay Likewise ast how many guns thay hade in the hows; to which he answered Eaght or nine; whiche he the Deponant thinkes prevented them from atemting any thing farther; from thence thay Set out in to the wods, and he, Vather, did not See Rodingburg after that;

thay martched about three miles till thay got in to a thick ham-
lock wood, whare thay kindeled a fier about darke, & about bad
time thay Pinyoned him and the rest of the prisoners, and gave
him the Deponant, his Grate Cote, to kiver him, which thay had
taken from him when thay furst tuck him prisenner and thay mad
him Ly down between the two white men Rotch and Wempell.
The Deponant farther Saeth that he inquired of sad Wempell
whare thay came from, & how many thay ware, to which he
answered from Canady and thate thay ware sprad all over.

And the Deponant [saith] that the Enimy asked him if he had
hard of any partyes of Indens on the fruntears, and whether
thare was not ane Expaditison going on aganst Canady last winter, and whether he, the Deponant, had not a Commison among
the Rebles; and farther that one of the white men told him that
the Indens belonged to Fort Hunter and that the Capts. name
is John; & he farther Saeth, about midnight as he suposeth, finding that the enimy ware all aslepe, he got up very softly and
moved very sloly for sum distance, and then got of his pinyon
and ascaped as fast as the darkness of the night would parmit,
and arived at home this morning, and farther Saeth not.

Sworn befor me   Wm. Harper Justice.

TESTIMONY OF ANDREAS RODINGBURG.

The Examenation of Andres Rodingburg* taken before William Harper one of the Justices for Tryon County: Sad Rodingburg, was at Albany bush the 11 instant; that on his return
home as his hors was Drinking in the Bruck between Fort Johnston and the Hows of Colonall Closs [Claus] he was taken pres-
oner; that Albart Vather, Samawell Kenady, a young man from
Sconackendy, and a man from the Nose or thare about, was

_____

*See page 735.

prisoners at the same time; the party Consisted of ten Indens and two white men; one of the white men was John Rotch and the other Barnet Wempell; thay inquired whoo Lived in Coln. Closses hows, and if thay war at home, and how thay war armed; the party was Commanded by Catreans John of Fort Hunter; thar was also one Peter a Inden, with one hand; after John the Inden, who Commanded the party, had thretened sad Rodingburg with his hatchet over his hade to kepe the mater sacret for three or for dayes thar to, he let him go.

Swor before me this 12 of Aprile, 1779.

Wm. Harper, Justice.

[No. 2211.]

Commissary Cuyler Urges the Seizure of Wheat in Albany County.

Albany 12th April 1779.

Sir: I have reason to believe from good information, that Several persons in Tryon County and some at Schoharie, are Still possessed of some new wheat, and who are endeavouring to hold it privately after all our application; they are in Expectation I understand to Sell for hard money, which perhaps they may now soon have an opportunity to those who are buying for Col. Robert Van Renselear, who I understand, has got a permit to purchase a Certain quantity; if he gives hard money, those who buy for the army cannot pretend to buy any till he is supplied. I under-stand, Sir, that the legislature have passed a law at their last Session, by which your Excellency with the advice of some of its members, can grant warrants to impress wheat and flour of the growth of 1778. I could wish that proper persons were ap-pointed for the purpose. The Service stands in great need of it. If proper persons were appointed for Tryon County & Schoharie, I am in hopes they wou'd procure a Supply for the troops Cantoned in that Country, which otherwise must be brought from the lower Part of this County, at a great Expence &c. I am, Sir, with respect your most obt. Servant

Jacob Cuyler, D. C. G. P.

His Excellency George Clinton.

———

[No. 2212.]

Governor Clinton Permits Sheriff Nicoll to Show Leniency to Thomas Bull, a Sick Prisoner.

Goshen April 13th 1779.

May it please your Excellency; Mrs. Bull wife of Thomas Bull, Requested of Me for Liberty for her husband, to take a Rume In the Township of Goshen, as he is in a pure State of helth, the Goal Much Crouded and the Blody Flux amongst the prisoners. I let hur know, that without an order from your Excellency, I Could not give any such Liberty; last Night She Caled again, and Let me know that She had wated on your Excellency and that you Told hur that if I thought it Necessary, you would Grant that Liberty. I Can Certyfy that Mr. Bull is in a Pure State of health and has bin Confined to his bed a Considerable part of the Time Since he has bin Confined heare, and that it tis and oncumfortable place for any Sick person to be in.

Since Matthew Dolson has made those Discoveryes in Newboroug precienct, I have not Confined him in Goal but in a house. I Should be glad to know your Excellency pleashure Conserning him and Ryan under Sentance of Death. Mrs. Mathews has had a Sevear Turn of the Blody Flux in Goal and hur Husband now has it. I am, Your Excellency Most Obediant Humble Servent.

Isaac Nicoll.

To George Clinton Esqr. Governor of the State of New York &c.

Poughkeepsie 15th Apl. 1779.

Sir, If there is an Infectious Distemper in Goal that renders it necessary (to prevent it spreading among the Prisoners) to confine Bull in some other Place in Town, I have no Objection to it, provided you will be answerable for his safety & Conduct, but as an Indulgence of this Kind may prevent his endeavouring to have himself Exchanged is not to be continued longer than the State of Goal renders it absolutely necessary.

When your next Court of Oyer & Terminer sits you will have my final orders respecting Ryan & Dolson. I am with great Regard yours

[G. C.]

Colo. Nicoll.

[No. 2213.]

Clothing Accounts.

Philadelphia April 13th 1779.

Sir, I am directed by the Honourable Board of War to transmit to your Excellency the enclosed Resolve* of Congress, and to de-

---

* " The board of war having represented that application has been made to the board for arrearages of clothing due to two regiments for the year 1777, and that other regiments in the service have similar demands, which ought to be adjusted and paid with all the dispatch compatible with the prevention of frauds to the United States:

Resolved, That a proper person be forthwith appointed and commissioned to settle and pay all accounts of arrearages of clothing due to the troops of these states for the year 1777:

That this commissioner be authorized to call on the clothier-general and his deputies, for immediate and exact returns of all clothing by them issued for the year 1777, shewing at what times, to whom, and for whose use the same was issued; which returns the clothier-general and his deputies are directed to make accordingly. The clothiers in the several states are also desired to make to the said commissioner similar returns of all the clothing by them issued for that year, on account of the United States; and the governments of the states respectively are requested to give the orders and assistance necessary for this end. And all officers of the army who have received clothing for the troops, either of any continental or state clothier, or by purchase or impressment, are directed to render to the commissioner aforesaid a return of the same, and account with him for their due application:

That the commander in chief, and officers commanding at any separate posts, do forthwith cause the captains and officers commanding companies, in the troops under their immediate commands, to make out the accounts of their respective companies, specifying the names of the claimants still in the service, where they are, what they have received, and what is still due; these points in cases of doubt to be ascertained by a particular enquiry of the officers, non-commissioned officers and privates of each company. The accounts thus formed and ascertained, shall be delivered to the regi-

sire you to give the necessary orders to the Clothiers and other Persons in the State of New York, who have supplyd Cloathing to any of the Continental Troops for the [year] 1777, on account of the United States, that they make Returns of the same, according to the Resolve.

Have also to request that the Returns may be sent to me at Camp, directed to the Care of Royal Flint Esqr. Assistant Commissary General at Head Quarters.

Permit me with all due submission to urge, that the Returns may be forwarded with all possible dispatch, as the Payment of arrearages due to the Troops, on Cloathing Bounty acct., for the

mental pay-masters, who shall draw them into a general one, and settle the same with the commissioner aforesaid, and the commissioner shall certify the sums due on such accounts, and to whom; whereupon warrants shall be issued for payment, in like manner as for the monthly pay of the troops:

That the said regimental pay-masters pay the arrearages aforesaid to the non-commissioned officers and soldiers themselves, or their representatives, to whom they are due; and account with the commissioner aforesaid for the monies they received for that use, producing the receipts of the non-commissioned officers and soldiers, or their representatives, as vouchers. And if upon such accounting, there shall appear to be monies in any pay-master's hands, received for non-commissioned officers and soldiers who afterwards died or deserted, the said commissioner shall certify the same to the pay-master-general, or his deputy at the post where the regiment of such pay-master is stationed, to whom he shall pay over all such monies remaining in his hands:

That all non-commissioned officers and soldiers entitled to the continental bounty of clothing, who served in the year 1777, but are not now in the service, and their representatives in case of death, shall also receive the arrearages due for such clothing: provided they produce or transmit to the commissioner aforesaid accounts thereof, properly authenticated by the certificates of the officers under whom they immediately served or other sufficient evidence. And the said commissioner, being satisfied therewith, shall certify the sums due on those accounts; whereupon warrants shall issue as aforesaid for payment:

That as in the course of this enquiry it may appear, that the clothing issued to divers non-commissioned officers and soldiers for the year 1777, exceeds the bounty allowed by Congress, the regimental pay-masters shall enter the names of such in two separate rolls, for the inspection of the commissioner aforesaid, who shall transmit one of them to the pay-master-general, or his deputy at the post where the regiments may happen to be, and the other to the commanding-officers of the regiments to which such non-commissioned officers and soldiers belong, who shall thereupon be put under stoppages by order of such commanding-officers, to the amount of the surplusages of the allowed bounty; for which the regimental pay-masters shall account with the pay-master-general or his deputy aforesaid, upon every application for the regiment's monthly pay:

That the said commissioner be permitted to employ one or more clerk or clerks, to assist him in executing the commission aforesaid, as the business shall require:

That the said commissioner be allowed, while in actual service, the same pay and subsistence as an auditor of the army; and that he be appointed by and accountable to the board of war, and continue in office so long only as they shall think proper; and that his clerk, if the board of war shall deem it to be necessary he should be allowed one, have the same pay and subsistence as is granted to a clerk of an auditor of accounts in the army."

year 1777, too long delay'd already, must be tottally Suspended, untill the Returns in Question can be Collected. I am, Sir, your very obedient Servant,

Ralph Pomeroy, Commissioner of Cloathing Accounts.

His Excellency Governor Clinton.

[No. 2214.]

Lists of Sufferers in Tryon County.

Return of the Distressed Inhabitants who have sufred By the Enemy the Last Summar in Conejohere Destrect, in the County of Tryon, and State of New York.

Chirry Valley.

HEADS OF FAMELES	Nomber in Eich famely
Rev'nd Saml. Dunlap,	2
Saml. Campbell, Coll.	2
Saml. Clyde,	11
Nathenel Hamel,	4
Jarimiah Backen,	8
Asariah Holobord,	1
William Dixon,	9
William Galt,	9
James Scott,	6
James Willson,	8
Samuel Ferguson,	1
Saml. Warfield,	3
Jane McClellen,	6
John Campbell, Jun'r,	9
James Ramsey,	3
Thomas Ramsey,	2
James Campbell,	9

HEADS OF FAMELES	Nomber in Eich famely
John Campbell, Sen'r,	6
Daniel Ogden,	7
Rev'nd William Johnston,	10
James Moor,	3
James McCollom,	3
William McConnal,	3
William Thompson,	12
John Foster,	6
Abegill Winston,	4
Alex'dr McCollom,	8
Hugh Mitchal,	3
John Thompson,	6
Total	164

Saml. Clyde, Lt. Coll.

Canejohery, Aprl. ye 13th 1779.

The above Menchonad Persons heve Lost all there houses, Barns, Green Cattel, Cloos, and mony Except John Campbell, Jun'r., who got all his Stock Seved.

Return of Springfield, that was Destroyed By the Enemy Last Summer, in Conejohere Destrict, Tryon County Aprl. ye 13 1779.

HEADS OF FAMELES	Nomb'r in Eich famely
George Canouts,	8
Isaec Coller,	5
William Staneel,	9
George Mayer,	5
Conrad Picket,	10
Herrey Bratt,	7
Devett Teygert,	4

HEADS OF FAMELES	Nomb'r in Eich famely
Adolph Wallrat,	4
Isaec Quack,	4
John Spallsbere,	6
Josiah Heeth,	5
Henery Deygert,	5
George Bush,	4
the wedo Davis,	4
Total	80

Return of Woonded Men in Canejohery Destrect that is not abel to help them Seilves.

Capt'n James Scott, Jacob Right, Beral Sparkes, John Picket.

The above Menchoned Inhabitants of Springfield Lost all there Personal Property, Except there Clothing; there Buldings was all Burnt, and there Cattel allmos Drove of, and there Green and hay, they were not abel to Cutt.

[No. 2215.]

Johannes Ball Recommended to Distribute the Relief for the Cobleskill Sufferers.

Schoharry April 14th 1779.

D'r Sir, I Rec'd your Letter of 30th of March desiring a Return of the sufferers at Cobus Kill, which I have made as near as possible. I thought it unnecessary to remark the wounded, as there were only three & those not in the Least Disabled. You Likewise Mentiond that I was to recommend a Proper person to Distribute the Donation among the Respective Inhabitants. I, therefore, Recommend Mr. Johannes Ball, who, I think, a proper &

Judicious person for that purpose. The Return here Inclos'd is an Exact Return of the Sufferers. I am D'r sir, with Respect, Your very Hum'e Serv't

Peter Vroman.

Stephen Lush Esqr. A. D. C. to Gov'r Clinton.

[No. 2216.]

THE ORIGINAL SIXTEEN TO ONE.

Major Lush Replies to His Chief in Regard to the Distribution of Supplies Among the Frontier Sufferers.

Albany 15th April 1779.

Much respected Sir, Immediately upon the Receipt of your Excellency's Letter of the 11th Instant* (dated by Mistake the 11th March) I waited upon Genl. Ten Broeck and he has this Morning sent off by Express his general Return.

I wrote a few Days ago to Colo. Benson by Mr. Ab'm P. Lott informing him that I had by Letters requested of Colos. Bellinger, Fisher & Clyde of Tryon, & Colo. Vrooman of Schohary, Returns of the Persons, objects of the Law granting three thousand Pounds for the Relief of the Sufferers on the Frontiers, incapable of gaining a Livelihood. I have not yet received the answers of those Gentlemen but daily expect them.

Agreable to your Excellency's Directions† I applied to the County Treasurer for £2250 for the above Purposes; he informed me all the Money in his Treasury was of the two Emissions called out of Circulation by Congress. I then waited upon Mr. Cuyler who has agreed to supply me with the Money. This Morning I consulted with Genl. Ten Broeck, Mr. Yates, Mr. Taylor & Mr. Gansevoort as to the Persons most proper for distributing it;

---

*See page 709.
† For Governor Clinton's reply, see page 731.

they recommended Colo. Vrooman of Schoharry for Cobus Kill, but think it adviseable to wait for his Return, and they further advised me to write to Major Fonda & request him to consult with the other Members of Tryon County as to the Persons most proper to be appointed for this Business. I have accordingly wrote to him on the Subject & pressed his earliest attention and immediate answer. As the Sum to be distributed will support the sufferers but a short Space of Time, Gen. Ten Broeck and the Other Gentlemen are of Opinion it ought to be divided among them according to their respective wants, but wish to know whether the Persons who garrison Fort Planck (and their Families) and who agreable to Resolutions of both Houses still draw Provisions from the Continental Stores, are included within the act.

As soon as I draw the Money from Mr. Cuyler I shall write to your Excellency.

Doct'r McCrea informs me that he has given the Map mentioned in your Excellency's Letter to Colo. Hay, D'y Qu'r Mr. Genl. Fish Kill; that it was drawn by Guy Johnson and he thinks the western Parts of this State are laid down from actual Surveys.

A few days ago a scout consisting of two Indians & 6 whites from Canada, took off five of the Inhabitants of Tryon County living near Johnstown; one of them made his Escape and says there are more scouts out upon the same Errand. Lt. Colo. Willett passed this Place on his way to Fort Schuyler but about twenty Minutes before the Inhabitants were taken off.

I would wish to apologize to your Excellency for the Marks of Haste appearing in this Letter. The Express who carries it goes off Tomorrow morning early.

Perhaps it may not be improper to mention to your Excellency, that the People murmur and blame our Legislature at the raising the Price of Flour to sixteen Pounds; the Farmers I am informed in Consequence of it have made the Difference between Hard Money & Continental as 16 to one—16 Dollars or one for a Bushel of wheat. Taxes are nevertheless paid with great Reluctance; and if Congress had not called the two Emissions out of Circulation I imagine the Collectors would have found it difficult to perform the Duties of their Office.

With my best Respects to Mrs. Clinton & Family, I am, Sir, with the highest Deference and Esteem, Your Excellency's most obed't ser't,

Stephen Lush.

His Excellency Governor Clinton.

[No. 2217.]

Jelles Fonda Calls for Troops to Protect Tryon County from Another Indian Foray.

Tryon County at Cachnewago 15th Apl. 1779.

Honned Sir, I Sapose you have Before this Been Informed that the Enemy, Indians and Toryes, have Killed two men and Taken four Preseners at Sacondago, about Eighteen miles to the norward of me; and also Tuck five Preseners Below fort Johnson Last Sunday nune; theay had, By wat we Can lern, about Sixty men who was Divided in three Partys; this is wat I Expected, as I have wrote to you Sum thime ago, and By the Deferent accounts I have, theay will Continue and Breack up all [the] Settlements in Tryon County if not Prevented.

For God Sake, Do all you Can to Send our Trupes up to our Relefe; we Sertenly live in Danger. The molise [militia] have Been in arms Sence last Sunday and are yet; the Enemy Come from Caneda, Sum By the way of Crown Pinte and Sum all the way True the woods so. I Remane, with my Kinde wishes for you, Your most Humble Serv't,

Jelles Fonda.

To George Clinton, Esqr. Governer.*

[No. 2218.]

ABRAHAM BININGER'S ACCUSATION.

In Effect that the Commissioners of Sequestration have Robbed Him—A List of Goods Stolen.

To his Excelency Govenor Clenton Esqr.

The petition of Abraham Bininger, freeholder of Cambden, humbly shued, That your petitioner is from Switzerland, Canton Zurich, Setteld here on the Land of Mr. Jeames Duane, Esqr., of N. York. I have to the best of my knowlege Tow Sons fighting under Genl. Washington's Banner, if alive, and one Son near Three years, Clarke in Canada. I never was in the Enemies Camp, or any way assistded them yet. Left John Barns, Capt. Allex'dr McNute, of New Perth, and Ensen John McLong of Cambrige, have Robed me at diferent Times of Goods worth near Three hundert poud, in Day Time with an Armed Scout. Your petitinor, aged 60 years, my wife about 57, is now destitud of ouer Children, and Robt of ouer property, have bin nigh 2 year, in very Great distress, unable to persue the said Robers at Law, McLong and McNute, aforesaid being Commess's of Conspiraceys. May it, therefore, please your Excelency, who is by Nature and high Office, the defender of the Injurd and oppresed, to direct your petitinor how to be Relivt, and send such advice by the worthy Lt. Colonel Blare. It will be a Great act of Charity and Compasion, don to your distitude and humble petitinor.

Abraham Bininger.

Cambden Apil 16, 1779.

---

*For Governor Clinton's reply, see page 759.

The inclost is a List of Goods taken from me, and now the said
Robers and there party detain my property, and threaten to drive
all dos [those] they have robt, in to the Enemis Lins, under the
predended Name of Torys, to prevent ouer pursuing them at Law.

The Articles Stolen.

Charlotte County Cambden.

1777 in the Month of July.   Abraham Bininger had the following heads of Cattle taken from him, by Order of Capt. Joseph
M'Craken and by order of Generall Schouylor as the told me:

Viz: A yok of young Stiers in there 4th year; Two hifers 2
years old. The 12 of Sept. the same year Leftanad Jn. Barns,
Jeames More his Son Jeames, one Ramage, old Alex'r M'Nite
and his Son, young Rowin a weafer, from New Perth, Ensign
John M'Long and Wealls, from Cambridge with some more of
there Companians took the folloing Goods after the had, in my
absence, broke oppen a good Doble Lock of the House door, then
a Jest well Lockt, a Jest of Trawers well Lockt. The Robt me of
the following goods; the told me the had leave of Gen. Starks:

Mens Clothing, A good brod Cloth cotte, collor Bown, ditto a
weastcott, blow; a new pr. of Blush breeches, Black, ditto a Good
pr. buck Skin Breech; a whit corded Jacked good, a Stript blue
and white weastcotte, good, a pr. of Jake Trowsers, Three Nak-
laces, good.   Tow pr. of thread Stokins.

Close the took from my Tow Sons: a suite of Brod Cloth cotte
w't cotte and Breeches, collor Brown, ditto a blue Brod Cloth
cotte Good, a new beaver hate, 2 Sumer w't cotts good, ditto a
w't cotte read stript, A new pr. of Leader Breeches, a darke brown
Jacked new, a new Linnen Jacked, Tow pr. of good Stokins, a
New pr. of wousted Stokins, a good pr. of Shoes ditto Three Neck-
laces.

Womans aparell belonging to my wife: A Russel damaske new rapper, a Short chinze Gowne, good, a doble Sattin Bonnet new, a Vealwoud hud, ditto a Silk Cloke, Tow pr. of Cloves, a black Barcalona Hangertshif most new, ditto a Gaws hangertshif, ditto 2 read and whit ditto a new Backed Hang't.

Linnen Shirts and other valluable things.

Three holand shirts Good, ditto a new holland shirt, ditto 6 other Good Shirts, Three fine hol'd Shifts, good, a Jake apron, a pr. of new hol'd Shietes, wich we La^id by for ouer Burials, ditto 6 other Shiets, a Large fringe dyaper Table Cloth in one pise, ditto a smaller Table Cloth, a pr. of Cotten Mens Stokins ribt, a pr. of locked slive Bottens, 4 yards of read and whit spoted Camlot new, 4 yds. of new Cros bard Camlot, a pise of Brown Brod Cloth, An Eivery Fanne, a large Green Curtain, 4 breaths bound with yeallow, a read damask Needl book, silk, ditto a damask Bocked Book, ash Collor, ditto a read Leather backed Book, a Tine Box with 5 or 6 hund'rd Needles, a Scane of Sowing Thread w't about ¼ lb., about a lb. of Stoking yarn, difrent Collor, 2 yards of Flannel new, a ¼ lb. of English wosted Black, about Six Shillings in Coppers, Tow new pr. of Sissars, ditto 2 pr. of old Sissars, 4 penn knifs, a Quire of wrinting paper, a parscell of Taps and Bindings, 2 Snuf Boxes, 6 Rows of pins, ditto more of different sorts, Nine yards of new Flax Linnen cut out for Shifts, a Brass kittle, a Copper Sasband, 2 Quart Bassons, a porringer, a pewter dis, a Tinn pane, one Case knif, 2 Clasp knifs, a pewter Tea pot, Nine Silver Tea Spoons, 2 lb. of hard Sope, a Large Rose planked, a Gold Ring taken of off my wifs finger by one Backer of Erlington, a Good Cow about Six year old, a yrd. of Tow Linnen new, a hocoback towell a yd. and half long, ditto some coars Towels, one Eyvry Comb, ditto 2 Coars Combs, a New billow

Case, ditto Three more Billow Casses, Good, a pr. of womans Cotten Stokins good, 6 or 8 Ribbunds, 2 point Botts Tinne, a Tinne Tonnel, a phisik Book, a Farriers Book, a Sermon Book, a wash Line about 8 or 10 fadom Long, 4 or 5 lb. of Bakken, 4 Cheeses whait about 12 or 14 lb., a Sampel or marking Cloth about a foot Square, there was much Labour bestowd on it, a side of a round pinn Coushen Needle work.

Tottal valled at that Time by an Impartial Gentleman £267-16-10.

———

[No. 2219.]

Returns of Captain Israel Young's Troop of Horse, of the Enemy's Militia, on Long Island.

A Return of Capt. Israel Youngs Troop of Horse, Apriel ye 16 day 1779.

Capt. Israel Youngs, ⎫ Philip Youngs, Clark ⎫
Left. Townsin Hulett, ⎪ Penn Weekes, Ser.   ⎪ Belt Swivel &
Cor. Eldred Van Wyck, ⎬ John Walters, Ser.   ⎬ Cut lash
Qur't William McCoon, ⎪ Vanaely Robers, Ser. ⎪
                      ⎭ William Wright, Ser. ⎭

Nethaniel Weekes,   Carbine, Belts, Swivel, & Cutlash.
Isaac Wood,
Thomas Place,
John Williams,   doto   doto   doto   doto
Benjamin Burdsel,   doto   doto   doto
Isaac Robenson,
Stephen Hendrickson,
Zebuland Doty,
William Hopkins,
John Jones,

Daniel Lotten,	doto	doto	doto
John Hawhurst, Miller,			
John Wright,	doto	doto	doto
George Dryee,			doto
Isaac Burr,	all wontred, Rob by the Rebels		
Isaac Smith,	doto	doto	doto
Hulcutt Dryee,			
Adom Lefford,	doto	doto	doto
Jeams Lefford,			
Titus Lefford,	doto	doto	doto
Daniel Veluanson,			
Jeams Place,	doto	doto	doto	doto
Samuel Burdsell,			
Lemuel Weekes.			

[No. 2220.]

*Petitions for the Pardon of William Jaycocks.**

[No. 2221.]

The Governor Sends Directions to Major Lush Relative to Supplies for Frontier Sufferers and the Prices of Breadstuffs.

Poughkeepsie 17th April 1779.

Dear Sir: Your Letter of the 15th Instant† has this Moment come to Hand. I waited till the 13th for Genl. Ten Broeck's return but conceiving no Consideration coud Justify a further Delay in raising the Men intended for the Defence of the Frontiers, I ventured to fix the Quotas the different Corps are to furnish from such Returns as I had rec'd & my Orders are accord-

---

* Omitted.
† See page 724

ingly issued. I have now, therefore, only to desire that while you continue in Albany you will afford Genl. Ten Broeck such assistance as you can with Conveniency to [in] expediting the Levies in his Brigade.

It is impossible for me to give any Directions more particular than those contained in the Law as to the distribution of the Money granted for the Relief of the Frontier Inhabitants whose Property has been destroyed by the Enemy. It is clear that those who are supplied with Provissions by the Public (if this is to be continued to them) are not the Objects of the Law. The sum granted I know is very inadequate. It must, therefore, be well husbanded & no Part of it be given to any Person who can by any Means subsist without it. This is the best Rule the Persons appointed to this Business can govern themselves by.

I am sensible the High Price of Wheat & Flour will be severely felt by many Individuals & it will of Course occassion them to murmur. However, if they coud be fully informed of the Reasons that induced the fixing of the present Prices of those Articles I am perswaded they woud not condemn but approve the measure. The Common Price of Wheat in Connecticut Jersey & in every other State to the Southward [is] at least 20 Dollars pr. Bushel & Flour in Proportion; at Boston Flour sells at £40 lawful pr. Ct. This afforded so strong a Temptation to smuggle & run their necessary Articles out of our State where they did not sell at half the Price, notwithstanding the Embargo Law & Guards sent to different Passes by Genl. McDougal to inforce it. This Business was carried on with such Success that I am morally certain, the army in this State & to the Eastward must have, in a very short Time disbanded for want of Bread & a Famine happened among the Inhabitants. The Temptation by raising the Price to what it is & it is now 4 Doll's beneath what the Law directs, to wit the Average of the Prices of N. Jersey & Connecticut, has destroyed the Temptation & put & [an] End to the exporting of it out of the State, & in all probabillity will prevent the Price raising higher, which I am sure it woud had the present Prices not been fixed.   Mrs. Clinton joins in Complim'ts to your Mother &c.   I am yours Sincerely,

[G. C.]

[To Stephen Lush.]

[No. 2222.]

GOVERNOR CLINTON POWERLESS.

Unwilling to Advise Frontier Inhabitants—Advises Colonel William Harper to Bring Charges Against the Commissioners of Conspiracies.

Poughkeepsie April 17th 1779.

Sir, I have received your Letters of the 16th Feb'y* last & 12th Instant† the former I should have answered before this Time had a convenient opportunity offered & as it treated principally on the Subject of Sulpher, concerning which I am not authorized to give any particular Directions, I conceived the Delay more immaterial.

I am exceedingly sorry to hear of the Distresses of the Inhabitants in your Quarter & of the Danger they Experience from the Enemy.   It is impossible for me to advise them whether it will be safe to continue on their Farms or whether they had better remove their families to the interior part of the County.   I may, however, venture to assure you that such measures will be taken as to protect them ag't the Incursions of the Enemy in Force, but in this Case they may remain in some Measure exposed to the

---

*See page 574.
†See page 712.

Depredations of small Parties from whom you apprehend most Danger. If I should advise the Inhabitants not to remove & they shoud thereby be influenced to continue on the Frontiers, & the measures intended for their Defence prove unsuccessful or inadequate & they meet with any Calamity the Reflection would be very disagreable. I have issued my orders pursu't to act of the Legislature for raising a body of men from the militia for the Defence of the Frontiers to continue in Service until the first of Jan'y, which I doubt not will be executed without Delay. If I could have procured the Returns of the militia in Season, this Business might have already been compleated & the Frontiers of Course in a greater state of safety than at present.

I am extreamly unhappy to learn from you that the Conduct of the Commissioners towards the Disafected is such as to create Suspicions in the Whiggs & give Confidence to the Tories. Does not their releasing those that are apprehended & sent before them, arise from a Neglect in furnishing the Com'rs with the proper Evidence of their Charecters & Crimes. If this shoud be the Case they may not merrit Consern, & I woud recommend, therefore, that this Circumstance be inquired into & that whatever Charges may after such Inquiry appear to be well founded ag't the Com'rs or either of them, shoud be reduced to particulars & with the Evidence to support them transmitted to the Council of Appointment. I am, Sir, with great Respect & Regard your most Obed't Serv't

[G. C.]

[To Wm. Harper.]

[No. 2223.]

General James Clinton Suggests a Company of Rangers to Scout the Schoharie Valley.

Albany, April 15th 1779.

Dear Brother, Your favour of the 11th Instant* in answer to mine of the 8th Came safe to hand, I Send you Inclosed a Coppy of an Examination of Andrew Rodinburgh† which is all the News here at present Excepting several Roberies being Committed by the Tories on the Whiggs between this place and Schoharrie; the Commissioners of Conspiracy was adviseing with me what method they should take to put a stop to it. A Company of Rangers would be of service to Range that Country, and as there is several noted Tories there, I think they ought to be Removed Either to the Enemy or of the Frontiers; they send for your advice.

If Doct'r Tappen has bought any thing for me, I wish he would send it up the first good Opportunity, Particularly the Hat and Cloth for my Coat which I want very much. I am Yours, Affectionately

James Clinton.

His Excellency George Clinton, Esqr., Governor of the State of New York, &c.

———

GOVERNOR CLINTON'S REPLY.

Poukeepsie 17th April 1779.

Dear Brother, I am this Moment favoured with your Letter of the 15th Instant. A Copy of the Affidavit & Account it contained were transmitted me by Mr. Harper & received before your Letter came to Hand. I am surprized that the Com'rs for detecting Conspiracies &c. shoud hezitate a Moment on the Prop-

* See page 711.
† See page 716.

riety of removing & confining the disafected Persons who reside on the Western Frontiers. Their Powers are perfectly competent for this Purpose. The very design of their Appointment is to secure the State ag't the Intrigues & Plotts of the disafected in Cases where the ordinary Magistrate coud not with propriety interfere. I have had frequent Complaints from the good Subjects of the Frontier Settlements that many Persons notoriously disafected were suffered to continue among them. That they furnished the Enemy with Provissions & Intelligence & notwithstanding when apprehended & sent down to the Com'rs, were by them released & permitted some on giving the most Triffling Security for their future good Behavior to Return Home. To this they impute in some Measure the Distresses they have experienced from the Savages & Tories who have joined them. You will please to inform the Com'rs, that it is my Oppinion, that they should not suffer any Person of whom there is just Grounds for Suspicion to go at large in or near the Frontier Settlements as they [will] be able to do greater Injury there than in any other Part of the State. I have not one Word of News. Yours &c.

[G. C.]

[To Gen. James Clinton.]

——————

[No. 2224.]

President Jay Sends George Clinton Two Acts of Congress, Relating to Persons Going Within the Enemy's Lines, and to the Export of Flour.

Philadelphia 18th April 1779.

Sir, You will receive herewith inclosed Copies of two Acts of Congress of the 14th Inst.—one* to prevent Persons going within

—————————————————

*Whereas Congress on the 21st day of August last did resolve, that when any persons are desirous of going within the enemy's lines, they shall apply to the executive powers of the state to which they belong, and if the said executive powers approve the motives and characters of the persons applying, and shall be of opinion, especially at so critical

the Enemy's Lines unless authorized in the manner mentioned in
it; The other* on the Subject of permitting Persons, under the
direction of the Board of war of Massachusetts-Bay, (if authorized
by that State) to export Grain and Flour &ca.

I have the Honor to be With Respect & Esteem Your Excellency's Most Obed't Servant

His Excellency Governor Clinton.

John Jay, Presid't.

[No. 2225.]

William Jaycocks' Self-Sacrificing Relatives.

To his Excellency George Clinton Esqr. Governor &c. of the
state of New York.

May it please your Excellency, Wee, Simon Van Kleeck, and
Cicely his wife, Simon Leroy and Wyntje his wife, Matthew Van
Keuren, Jun'r, and Ann his wife, Peter Lossing and Mary his
wife, James Deering & Geertrey his wife, which wives are All
sisters of William Jaycocks† now under sentence of Death, Humbly beg leave to crave your Excellency's pardon, for him, on
account of his youth and on account of his Declarations when
he came home, of his desire and Intention to surrender himself,

---

conjunctures as the present, that no danger will ensue by granting such permission,
that they recommend them to the officer commanding the troops next to the enemy, who
upon such recommendation may at his discretion permit the persons to go in.

For the better execution of the said resolution,

Resolved, That any officer who shall permit a person to go within the enemy's lines,
without such recommendation or the orders of the commander in chief or the commander of a separate department, and shall thereof be duly convicted before a court-
martial, shall thereby forfeit his commission.

*It being represented to Congress that the general assembly of the state of Massa-
chusetts-Bay, have authorized and directed the board of war of the said state to purchase flour and grain for the use of the inhabitants thereof, who are greatly distressed
by the want of bread:

Resolved, That it be and hereby is recommended to the executive powers of the states
of Virginia, Maryland, Delaware, Pennsylvania, New-Jersey and New-York, to permit
the exportation of such flour and grain as has been or may be purchased within the
said states respectively, under the direction of the said board of war if authorized as
aforesaid.

†See page 740 et seq.

47

to the mercy of his Country, and that the principal evidence against him is far from being credible and are so well satisfied and convinced of his intention of behaving in future as a good subject, that if your Excellency shall vouchsafe to grant our request wee are willing to be bound, to the full value of our estates, for his good behavior during the war, or for so long a time, as shall be tho't proper and that he shall be confined to this precinct, or even within the bounds and limits of his farm, wee are your Excellency's most Obedient and most humble Servants

Simon Van Kleeck, Siseeley Van Kleeck, Simon Leroy, Wyntje Leroy, Matthew Van Keuren, Jun'r, Hanna Van Keuren, Peter Losing, Mary Losing, James Dearin, Gitry Dearin, Bengemen his X mark Jacocks, Isaac P. Lauson, Andress Lawsen.

April 19th 1779.

[No. 2226.]

STEUBEN'S IDEAS OF THE MILITIA.

Submits His System of Organization to Governor Clinton for His Judgment.

Sir; The reason which has determined Swizzerland as well as other Republiks of Europe to place their Security in a militia capable of Supporting their Independency, is the want of the necessary means to maintain a Standing army. This reason hath a much greater weight in the United States, where it would be impossible to keep up armies numerous enough to defend so extensive a Country from every Hostile invasion; Especially when the naval force of our Enemies is so much Superior to ours.

It is then in our militias that we must find the real Strength, which we are to oppose to that of Great Britain; and these are indeed the most respectable forces, which consist of brave Citizens who animated by the noblest motives, defend their country and their Liberty. Our Business is then, now to find out the means of rendering that militia capable to supply the Want of a well regulated standing army, at least as much as lies in our Power.

These means should be Simple uniformity in the formation, in the march, and in the motions of the Troops, and the keeping them together in order, are the most Essential points.

In the Composition of the first part of the regulations which have been just published; I have established general principles as easy and convenient for our Regiments of militia as for the Continental army, putting aside the manual Exercise which I look on in Some part as superfluous. The rest may be introduced without the least difficulty, and the greatest advantage will result, when a Body of militia will join the army, as well as when it will act Separately.

I am induced by this reason to address a copy of these regulations to your Excellency, and Submit them to your Judgment, and in case you are of opinion that these Rules, actually introduced in our army may Serve for the militia of your state. I have not only engaged with the Continental Board of war, to keep copies of them in readiness for the Legislatures of the Several States who will demand them, but I expect only your orders to request of the Commander in Chief, to Send you an officer capable of introducing them and giving the necessary Explanations. I have the honor to be With great Respect, Sir Your Excellency's Most Obedient and very Humble Servant.

Steuben, Maj. General.

Philadelphia April 20th 1779.

His Excellency G. Clinton Esq're Gov'r of New York.

[Nos. 2227, 2228, 2229.]

THE JAYCOCKS CASE.

The Culprit Appeals for a Respite—The Governor Refuses to Interfere—Correspondence with the Reverend Isaak Rysdyk.

To his Excellency George Clinton, Esqr., Governor and Comm'dr In Chief of the State of New York.

The Petition of Will'm Jaycock, Sheweth, That your Languishing Prison'r, most Humbly begs of your Excellency to take his unhapy condition into your mature Consideration, and give him a respite of time for a Week or ten days; for I think that the time that was Allow'd me by the Judge, is two Short, for I am not Reconsiled within my Self that I am yet fit to Leave this world. And I hope, that I may repent of All my transactions that I have Commited in this Transitory Life, in hopes that I may true a thorough Repentance be received into eternal Joy and permanent felicity in the next. Your Excellency, granting as Above Begs As in Duty bound your Petition'r shall ever pray.

Will'm Jaycocks.

Poughkeepsie April 20th 1779.

THE REVEREND MR. RYSDYK'S APPEAL.

May it please yr. Excellency.

S'r, I have been very earnestly entreated by James Livingston, Esq., & ye friends of Mr. Jacocks, one of the prisoners condemned, to attend him during these awful moments in his preparation for another world, and would have complyed with their reasonable Request with all Readiness, but having been hindered to day in the performance of this pastoral duty, as will be ye case doubtless also to morrow by insourmountable Obstacles in my family, I cannot but heartily join with the friends of Mr. Jacocks, that the Execution, if it be any ways convenient with the Circumstances of the Law, might be deferred for a few days, that there may be Sufficient time & opportunity to give this wretched youth, who Seems to be very desirous to have some intercourse at large with ministers about his eternal concerns; when together with the minister of Poghkeepsie, I wo'd be willing & very desirous to attend him in this necessary & holy Employment to the utmost of my power.

Your Excellency will doubtless thereby, greatly oblige a number of Respectable parsons, & among them more particularly Your Excellencies most humble & most obedient Servant

Isaak Rysdyk.

New Hakkensak April 21, 1779.

For his Excellency Governor G. Clinton Esq.

GOVERNOR CLINTON DECLINES TO INTERFERE.

Rev'd Sir, I feel extreamly unhappy in not being able to comply with your Request in Favour of the Criminal Jaycocks & it woud add greatly to my Concern on this Occassion if from the Reports I have had from those who have vissited him in his Confinement, I had the least Reason to believe he is affected with a due Sense of his Guilt or discovered the most distant Desire of imploying the short Time left him in preparing for the great & Important Change which he is so shortly to undergo, but this I am assured by those who have attended him & in whom I can place the highest Confidence is not the Case. I informed Mr. James Livingston on the Day Jacocks was convicted, that I was fully convinced of his Guilt & that he was not to expect a Pardon. I repeated this to his Friends on their first Application in his Favour & advised them to mention it to the Prisoner, that he may not be diverted by false Hopes from the Necessary Preparation for Death. If they have not done this they have neglected their

Duty. I am sorry to add that I have Reason to suspect, that the Prisoner & his Friends are not influenced by the good Motives mentioned in your Letter in craving a respite at this late Hour, but that their Design favour an Escape, or that some other Event may take Place, which will prevent the Execution of the Sentence, to prevent which is indispensable Duty & Guards consisting of the Inhabitants of this Place are for this Purpose kept at the gaol every Night. I cannot think of continuing that Burthen upon them any longer than is absolutely necessary. Believe me, Sir, it will give me Pleasure at all Times to serve you & that I am with the greatest Respect & Esteem

[G. C.]

[To Rev. Isaak Rysdyk.]

THE REVEREND MR. RYSDYK RECONCILED TO THE GOVERNOR'S VERDICT.

N. Hackensack 21 April 1779.

S'r, Your Excellencies kind Condescension in acquainting me with the reasons, why a Respite should not be granted to the Criminal Jacocks, inspires me with the warmest Acknowledgments, & dictates the few Lines, wherewith I am troubling y'r Excellency another Time. Indeed I ventured to write a few lines to y'r Excellency this morning in favour of this unhappy youth, only with a view, to enjoy the Opportunity together with my Brother in the Gospel, ye Rev'd Mr. Freligh, to visit a Soul, perhaps panting after Salvation, & only in want of sufficient Instructions & Directions towards the Accomplishment of these great and desirable Events. But now, fully acquiescing in your Excellencies Letter (as I cannot be spared from home to morrow morning, and there is a Minister in the place:) I leave & commend this wretched Criminal to a mercifull God; whom, if He would Seeck for him earnestly, he will find infinitely more propitious to him, than either a Governor or Minister or indeed even his best friends & Relatives can be Supposed to be. I am with deep Respect, S'r, Your Excellencies most humble & most Obedient Servant,

Isaak Rysdyk.

For his Excellency Governor Clinton.

[No. 2230.]

The Frontiers Unprotected, Lackaway Burned, Colonel Malcom's Regiment Consolidated and He Is to Leave the Service.

Minisink Apl. 21 1779.

D'r Governor, To morrow the troops all leave this place for Easton,—So the Frontiers are unprotected and the inhabitants are in great distress; about 40 Savages burnt Lackaway & houses within 13 miles of the River last Saturday. I think it my duty to give your Excellency this notice.

My Regiment is now incorporated with Spencer's; all my Officers except 2, or 3, leave the Service, and that being the case, I shall do so too, I expect to be home in 2 or three weeks; another such corps cannot be raised soon, but we are not to blame. My best Respects to Mrs. Clinton, Mrs. Tappen and to my old friend Genl. Scott, and be assured that I am very Sincerely, D'r Governor, Your much oblidg'd and very hb. Servant

W. Malcom.

His Excellency Governor Clinton at Poughkeepsie.

[No. 2231.]

Governor Clinton Drops a Hint to His Brother James.

Poukeepsie 21st Apl. 1779.

Dear Brother, By a Letter I have this Moment received from a Gentleman in Cumberland County, I am informed a Draft is ordered by the Authority of the pretended State of Vermont of the Inhabitants on the Grants, for the Defence of their Frontiers, which is extended without Distinction to the Inhabitants well affected to this State; and to give Weight to these Orders, it is said they are founded on your Advice. I think it necessary to inform you of this, as it will discover to you the Necessity of continuing to act with the utmost Caution with those designing & Turbulent People & to avoid giving them even the Shadow of Encouragem't in the Exercise of their undue Authority. I am &c.

G. C.

G. Jas. Clinton.

[No. 2232.]

New York Soldiers in the Invalid Corps.

War Office 22nd April 1779.

Sir; The return, of which the inclosed is a copy, has been filed in this Office, agreeably to the resolution of the 15th of March last; and I am now directed to transmit a Copy thereof, to your Excellency, that the State over which you preside, may receive credit for the quota of troops contained in it. I have the honour to be, with high respect Your Excellency's very Obed: Serv.

P. Scull, Secry.

His Excellency Gov'r Clinton.

A Return of Officers and men now in the Regiment of Invalids, raised in the State of New York, not formerly belonging to the Regiments of that State, but to be allowed as Part of the Contingent thereof, agreeable to the Order of Congress of the 15th March.

Names.	Rank.	State.	Counties.	Towns.
James Macgraw,	Private	N. York	Dutchess	Æsopus
Barney Wimple,	Do	Do	Albany	
Will'm Serjeant,	Do	Do		New York

(Signed)   Lewis Nicola, Col. Inv.

War Office 22d April 1779.

The foregoing list contains a true copy of a return made by Col. Nicola, & filed in this office.

P. Scull, Secry.

A Return of Officers and Men formerly in the New York Line now in the Regiment of Invalids.

Names.	Rank.	States.	Counties.	Town.
John Douherty,	Private	New York	Fort George	
John McKimm,	Ditto	Ditto	Orange	

Sign'd   Lewis Nicola, Col. Inv.

War Office, 22 April 1779.

The foregoing is an exact copy of a return made by Col. Nicola & filed in this office.

P. Scull, Secry.

[No. 2233.]

DELINQUENCY OF PEACE OFFICERS.

A Report that the Enemy Contemplate an Attack on the Highland Forts.

Head Quarters Peckskill, April 22nd, 1779.

Sir, The Enemy for six Days past has closed up the Communication with the Country. Some important movement is in Contemplation. He has a great Number of small Vessels ready for some Enterprize.

A sensible Negro who waited on Colonel Emerick has deserted

to us, and informs me he heared a Conversation pass at Dinner between him and Governor Tryon and other Officers of the making Laws in New York to cut the Chain, and a quantity of match being prepared to set fire to Houses. In this State of matters, the Garrison of West Point has not four Days salted Provision. The Justices will not do their Duty to enable Colonel Hay to bring in the Provision. The public Teams are utterly unable to do it.

As the supreme Executive of this state, I think it my Duty to inform you of the Danger which threatens it.

I have in vain since I came to these Posts endeavoured to supply the Forts with Provisions; But neither Justices or Constables will do their Duty and they seem indifferent about the Consequences. The Law of the State for impressing Teams, as its construed give no aid to the public Service, but when the Enemy is at our Beards. I have, therefore, sent Colonel Hay to you for Advice. I am, Sir, Your humble Servant,

Alex'r McDougall.

His Excellency Governor Clinton.

[No. 2234.]

RUDOLPH SHOEMAKER DENOUNCED.

A Delegation from German Flats Lays the Facts Before Governor Clinton.

Fort Dayton, Aprill the 22d 1779.

Sir; We, the Inhabitants of German Flats, greatly distressed do lay their complaints before your Excellency,* hoping your natural affection towards true and faithful Subjects will give us redress; we have here Several unworthy neighbours, amongst whom is one Rudolph Shoemaker, who Signed for the first, that

---

* For Governor Clinton's reply, see page 760.

infamous paper at Johns Town and ever Since being infected
with that poison, he never has done any good to ouer Cause;
the Deserters or as we comunly call Toris, have been treated by
them before their departure to the Enemies, and when the militia
being on their march towards fort Shuyler with General Herkemer, a Number of the militia being hided there by S'd Shoe-
makers in the Bush by wich plott two of his Son-in-laws have
been; and, if one of that Plott came to the House of Shoemaker,
they have been piloted by their youngest Son to their place of
rendevous; and when they suspected that they be Discovered,
they have been warned to leave the place; this plott was to join
Buttler, after this the pretended flag of Truce put up their Quarters by him and at the Same time Peter Weber heard S'd Shoemaker Say, it would be the best to lay down the arms, and we
could get Protection by Buttler; whereupon Peter Weber replied,
" what then if the Yankees does come upe here;" Shoemaker
made answer " then I will fight in my House as long as I am
alife;" further about the Same time, Jacob Mayer made oath
on the holy Evangelist that he heard S'd Shoemaker say, when
he spoke to him that it was dangerous Time the Indians might
come and cut of the River. Shoemaker answered " no, a flag of
truce will come the first, and if we consent to their will they
will leave us peaceably;" whereupon Jacob Mayer replied " what
then if the Yankees does come upe here;" he answered "they have
their hands full down below & we Should not have taken upe
arms aginst the King, we would have lifed peaceably"; & at the
Same time Andreas Weber heard of S'd Shoemaker, that it had
been a bade thing that the peoples did Sign & Swear the oath
of allegiance; further Georg Weber after being duly Sworn
deposed, that he heard S'd Shoemaker Say, about the Same time,

" I am the only Justice that is here for the King," and Weber
asking him what Buttler with his party would do if they would
take the Inhabitants along, he answered " no General St. Ledger
would send him an order & form for to qualify the peoples " then
he Saith, " I am the Justice where they mus Swear by;" then
Weber replied " what will be done afterwards;" then Shoemaker
answered " General St. Ledger would send five hunderd Indians
and them they have been Sworn are to go with them and give
them assistance to take the Yankees at that time posted at fort
Dayton;" whereupon Weber replied " this five hundred Indians
might not be Sufficient;" upon this Shoemaker answered " ———
——— ——— we have Soon got them if we go with them, and
we ought to fight against them;" whereupon Weber replied
agin " Supose they do take the fort and the Garrison and a part
of the grand arme would come upe here;" then Shoemaker Saide
" if all this would miscarry then he would go up to St. Ledger
and leave all his Things behind."

Complaints have been made to the Commissioners of Conspiracy
about Saide Shoemaker, and that he did life on a verry dangereous
Place where the Enemies had their passage, but they never entered ouer County for to bring those disaffected persons to Justice; upon this the peopels being enraged Since they Sustained
Such great a looss by the Enemies and Suffering unaccounttably
they tooked his Hay, pease, oats, wheat and all Such articuls, and
Some other Things from him; now this Transaction of the peopels
is not justifiable by law, though it has been Comitted not out of
malice or Rogerie, they can deliver an inventarie thereof, to the
Comissioners if it Should be required, and they will delivered it
to the public when demanded by the least farthing; for this he
went to law with the peopel and they have been Sued for tres-

pass; now, we pray your Excellency to bring this man to Justice, and if possibly could be done that he might have his Trial at Pewkapsie; if this famely Shall be Sufferred there, treacherie can be comitted by them continually, and if he is brought to due Trial, this will prevent other mischiefs on both Sides; wherefore, we pray that your Excellency will give us redress in ouer Grievances, for wich we remain your Excellencies most obdt. Hble. Serv'ts

Henrig Herter, Nicolaus Weber, Jacob Mayer, John Bellinger, Wm. Petry.

[No. 2235.]

Commissary Commissioner Graham Reports Progress.

New Paltz, ye 23d April 1779.

Sir, In consequence of the appontment your Excelency Sent me for the procuring Flour &c., I have procured a Quantity of Wheat unmanufactored, and no mills nearer than the Green Kills for that purpose, If it must be Transported to that place for grinding, perhaps it may be proper to Store it there, as it can be mutch Easier Taken frome thence, Either to the Highlands or to the Fronteers, Your Excelency will pleas to Signify your Pleasure to me in this Matter, which Shall be Strictly Observed by your very Humble Ser't

Danl. Graham.

To his Excelency.

Poukeepsie 23d Apl. 1779.

Sir, I have received your Letter of this Date & approve of your Proposal of having the Wheat you have procured for the use of the Army, ground & stored at the Green Kill Mills. I am with great Regard Your Most Obed. Serv't

Geo. Clinton.

Daniel Graham.

[No. 2236.]

Colonel Udny Hay Writes Despondently.

Fish Kill 23d April 1779.

Sir; It is with real grief of heart I now wait on your Excellency to beg your assistance in procuring the Necessary Number of Waggons for the Support of the army in this State. Though I have tried every possible method which I could devise, since the new Law for Impressing Teams, they have all proved Ineffectual. I now produce to your Excellency, a return of every Waggon we have had Since 23d March, a Number Inadequate to the purposes they were Intended to have Served. I must likewise beg your Excellency's attention to the Copys of Some of the letters I have wrote the justices, in which I have beged their advice and assistance in the most humble manner, but have not yet been favour'd with an answer in Writing from any one of them that tended to give me the least Satisfaction.

I have attended in the Strictest manner to the Law of the State in hopes by Such a Conduct I Should Concilate the affections of the People to the Service, but all in vain.

I yesterday apply'd to the General for Orders from whom I bring a Letter to you on the Subject, and now beg your Excellency's particular Instructions which I will Implicitly Obey.

The Number of Teams which has ever readly been Turned out from Rumbout Precinct, is a Convincing proff either of its being Oppressed above measure or that the justices of the Other Precincts have, in an unpardonable degree, Neglected their Duty. I am with due respect, Sir, your most Obt. Serv't

Udny Hay.

His Excellency Governour Clinton.

[No. 2237.]

THE DEFENCE OF THE NORTHERN FRONTIER.

Captain Stockwell Selected to Command a Company—Governor Clinton's Directions.

Poughkeepsie 24th April 1779.

Dear Sir, By a Letter I have this Moment received from his Excellency Genl. Washington, I am informed that it is determined that the Force which is to move by the Way of the Mohawk River upon the intended Expedition, shall rendevouz at Canojohare by the 12th of May, & that this will occassion the calling off the Detachments of Genl. James Clinton's Brigade which are now at Saraghtoga, Lake George & some other Places upon our Northern Frontier; & Warner's Regt., only, will remain in that Quarter, and as by your letter to his Excellency of the 3d Instant, you express apprehensions which I believe to be well founded, that the Northern Frontier will be exposed while we are acting to the Westward except a greater Force is kep up in that Quarter, I, therefore, take the Liberty to inform you, that of the 1000 Men directed to be raised for the Defence of the Northern & Western Frontiers of this State, Charlotte County is to furnish 27 Men, & I have this Day ordered Genl. Ten Broeck out of those to be raised in his Brigade to detach 73 to join those of Charlotte County for the Defence of the Northern Frontier; Capt. Levi Stockwell, late Lieut. of Col. Gansevoort's to command this Company.

It is some Time since my orders for raising these Men have been in the Hands of the different Officers, & if they exert themselves, they may be completed in Season for this Service; at least the Proportion of them ordered from Genl. Ten Broeck's Brigade. I have, therefore, to request, you will use your Influence with Genl. Ten Broeck & his Officers to expedite this Business, as it is the only means in my Power at present of affording any Security to the Northern Frontiers, except what may be expected from the Militia of that Part of the Country, which tho they are under orders to hold themselves in perfect Readiness, are but Weak, and I fear not much to be depended on.

I wish Genl. Ten Broeck to appoint a Lieut. for this Company, whose Appointment will be confirmed by the Council of Appointment, and that the men first raised in his Brigade be taken for this Service & march immediately. You are much better acquainted with the Country than I am, & of Course better able to determine on the Posts this Body of Men ought to occupy, so as to afford the greatest Security to the Frontier Settlements. You will, therefore, be good enough to give the necessary Orders to Capt. Stockwell, of which I will be oblidged to you for a Copy, as well for your Sentiments with respect to what aditional Number of Men, if any, will be necessary for the Northern Frontiers & what Passes will be most necessary to guard to the Westward, taking into Consideration our intended Operations in that Quarter, with which I am not sufficiently acquainted to be able to form a proper Judgment on this Subject. A great Part of the 1000 Men ordered to be raised for the Defence of the Frontier Service, are in Consequence of a Requisition of Congress, to be applied to the filling up the five Continental Battallions raised under the Direction of this State, so that the Number I will have remaining under my Controul will be but small. I am, D'r Sir, with great Regard & Esteem your Most Obed't Serv't

[G. C.]

Genl. Schuyler.

Captain Stockwell Notified of His Appointment—His Orders.

Poughkeepsie 24th April 1779.

Sir; You are appointed a Capt. of a Company of the Levies ordered to be raised for the Defence of the Frontiers of this State & your Commission as soon as made out will be forwarded to you by the first conven't oppertunity. You will, therefore, take the Command of those raised from the militia of Charlotte County which together with 73 men I have ordered from those first raised from Genl. Ten Broeck's Brigade will form your Company. You will receive & obey Genl. Schuyler's directions as to the Posts you are to occupy, & the Duties you are to perform, for the security of the frontier Settlements until you receive my Orders to the contrary. You will draw Provisions & such other articles as you may be entitled to from the nearest continental Stores. Mr. Boggs is appointed one of your Lieuten'ts, the other will join you with the men from Genl. Ten Broeck's Brigade. And as the nature of this Service & the Safety of the Frontiers require the greatest Exertions I expect the utmost diligence & vigilence on your Part. I am &c.

Geo: Clinton.

Capt. Levi Stockwell.

Colonel Webster Urged to "Greater Exertion" by Governor Clinton.

April 24th 1779.

Sir; As the Detachments from Genl. Clinton's Brigade, now stationed for the Defence of the northern frontiers will soon be ordered from thence, I have directed Capt. Levi Stockwell, who is appointed to the Command of a Company of the Levies to be raised from the militia, purs't to the late act of the Legislature, to take Charge of those to be raised from your Regt., which together with 73 I have ordered from those first raised in Genl. Ten Broeck's Brigade, will form his Company. I have requested Genl. Schuyler to give him such advice & Direction as to the Posts most proper to be occupied & other Duties, as he may judge best for the genl. Safety & Security of the Northern frontier Settlements. As on a Requisition from Congress within the Time limited by the act, I am under the necessity of disposing of the greater Part of the men to be raised, in filling up the five cont'l Battalions of this State, I shall have but a small force left for the Defence of the frontiers, and as Capt. Stockwell's Company will probably be all that can be spared for the defence of the northern Frontiers, the greater Exertions will be necessary from your Regt., and I expect, therefore, that you & your Officers will use your utmost endeavors in holding it in the most perfect Readiness to join Capt. Stockwell in repelling any Incursions of the Enemy. I am &c.

Geo. Clinton.

Colo. Webster.

[No. 2238.]

Ulster County Troopers Pay a Complimentary Tribute to Captain Salisbury.

Kingston April 24th 1779.

The Petition of the Troopers in the north Part of Ulster County to his Excellency Governor Clinton humbly sheweth;

As a mutual attachment and good Understanding between Officers and their men are an Essential Part of the many Requisites which are necessary to ensure victory to our arms and Freedom to our Country, And, Whereas, Capt. Sylvester Salis-

bury, (between whom and your Petitioners there subsisted the
greatest Harmony and Confidence), has resigned his Commission,
and that solely, because he was to be under the Command of a
man whom he deems unworthy of the Rank he holds;

We, the Subscribers, Beseech your Excellency, either to annex
the Troop to some other Regiment, or put them under the Command of some superior Officer, and re-appoint Captain Sylvester
Salisbury to the Command of the Troop. Should this be the
Case, your Petitioners beg leave to assure your Excellency, that
their Services shall, as they have heretofore been, Free, Chearful,
& Ready. And your Petitioners &c. shall ever Pray &c.

Adam Woolfven, Abraham Keater, Roeloff Eltenge, Christian
Dull, Moses Pattison, Tjerck Low, Petrus Winne, Junier, Henry
P. Freligh, John Dewitt, Jr., John A. D. Witt, John E. Schoon-
maker, Peter C. Brinck, Edward Osterhoud, Hendryck Turck,
John Turck, John Freligh, Benjemin Velten, John J. Chrispel,
Benjamin Winne, John De Witt, Jun., John Brink, Jun., Baltus
Kiffer, Peter Van Leuven, Christian Fero, Marten Hommel, jr.,
Hermanus Hommel, Abraham Hoffman.

[No. 2239.]

*Clinton Reports His Dispositions to Washington—Drafts from the
Militia—Troops for the Frontier.*

Poughkeepsie 25th April 1779.

Dear Sir; I have had the Honor of receiving your Excellency's
Letters of the 9th & 17th Instant. In Consequence of the latter,
I have ordered 100 Men to the Northern Frontier to relieve the
Detachments of Genl. James Clinton's Brigade now in that
Quarter. The Officer who commands these Men is ordered to
observe such Directions as he shall receive from Genl. Schuyler

(to whom I have written on the Subject) as from his Knowledge
of the Country he will be able to make the best Disposition of
this small Force. The Militia in that Quarter have also my
Orders to hold themselves in the most perfect readiness, but it
being a new Country they are weak & having been once in the
Power of the Enemy under Genl. Burgoine are not much to be
depended on.

I formerly mentioned to your Excellency, that I imagined this
State might be able to raise one thousand Men for the Frontier
Service. The Legislature soon after, accordingly provided for
the embodying of that Number by drafts from the Militia; but at
the same time directed that a Proportion of them shoud be applied towards filling up the Continental Battallions, raised under
the Direction of this State, if a Requisition for this Purpose
shoud be made by Congress. The Militia Officers are now imployed in making the Drafts in their respective Regiments & I
have Reason to believe they will soon be compleated the greater
Part by volluntary Inlistments. Those who are to join the Continental Regiments will be immediately delivered over to them.
The Remainder which will be upwards of four hundred, & commanded by a Lieut. Col. & Major, I will order to join the Troops
now on the Frontiers, & to such other Passes as are best calculated to cover the Country from the Incursions of the Enemy,
until I shall hear further from your Excellency. You will
readilly perceive, Sir, that without knowing the Rendevouz of the
different Parties who are to [be] imployed in the operations to
the westward & the Routes they are respectively to take, it will
be impossible for me to make the proper Dispositions of the Force
that may be left in their absence, for the protection of the
Frontier Settlements, as some Parts will be rendered perfectly

secure by the movements of our Troops whilst others will be more exposed. Your Excellency's orders, therefore, on this Subject will be necessary. I am with the greatest respect, & Esteem, D'r Sir, your most Obed't & very Humble Serv't

Geo: Clinton.

Since writing the above I received a Letter from Genl. Ten Broeck* with the enclosed Copy of a Letter from Mr. Fonda.† The disagreeable Intelligence it contains will I fear, greatly retard the raising of the Drafts from the militia as it will disconcert the measures taken for that purpose.

His Excellency Genl. Washington.

[No. 2240.]

Recommendations for Commissary Commissioners for the Schoharie District and Tryon County.

Albany April 26th 1779.

Much respected Sir; Agreable to your Excellency's Request I have inquired of Mr. Cuyler who were the most proper Persons for seizing wheat and Flour for the use of the army in the District of Schoharie and in Tryon County, he recommends Volckert J. Veeder, for Tryon and Peter Snyder, Jun'r, for Schoharie and wishes to have their appointments if agreable to your Excellency as soon as may be convenient.

I have received a Set of Returns from Cobus Kill and Tryon County‡ of the Inhabitants in those Parts distressed by the Enemy's Incursions the last Campaign, and in Consequence, thereof, incapable of gaining a Livelihood and shall place the Money for Distribution into the Hands of such Persons as the

* Ten Broeck's letter not found.
† See page 726.
‡ See page 721.

Gentlemen of the Legislature in this City shall recommend. With my best Respects to Mrs. Clinton & Family I am, Sir, with the highest Respect your Excellency's most obed't serv.

Stephen Lush.

His Excellency Gov'r Clinton.

MAJOR LUSH'S LETTER TO JELLES FONDA.

Albany 14th April 1779.

Sir, The Legislature at their last Meeting granted three thousand Pounds for the Relief & Support of such Persons who have had their Possessions destroyed by the Enemy and are incapable to support themselves.

I was directed by his Excellency to enable him to put this Law into Execution to obtain Returns of the sufferers within the above Description in Albany & Tryon Counties, and for this Purpose I wrote to Colos. Klock, Bellinger & Fisher of your County but have not yet been favored with their answers.

Yesterday I rec'd a Letter from his Excellency requesting me (as he supposed I might meet with Difficulty in obtaining the Returns) to deposit £2250 (for the use of the sufferers by the Destruction of Cobus Kill, Cherry Valley, the German Flatts Andrews Town & Springfield now incapable of gaining a Livelihood) into the Hands of such Person or Persons as should be recommended to me by Genl. Ten Broeck and the Members of Senate and Assembly residing in this City.

I have accordingly consulted Genl. Ten Broeck, Mr. Yates, Mr. Taylor and Mr. Gansevoort who have advised me to write to you on the Subject and request that you wo'd consult with Mr. Jacob G. Kesch, Colo. Campbell, Mr. Bell Mr. Waggoner & Major Newkerk members of Senate & Assembly as to the Person or Persons most proper to distribute such Part of the Money as shall be proportioned for the Sufferers (within the Description of the act) in your County, and also to request from you & those Gentlemen a particular Return of them discriminat'g their Situation as exactly as possible as some of the Persons may require less than others to enable them to subsist.

You will also be pleased to consult with the above Gentlemen whether it will be best to divide the Money among the Objects of the Law at once or place it in the Hands of some Person or Persons to purchase Provisions & deliver it out to them as their Necessities may require. You will observe no allowance is granted by the Law to the Persons who are to distribute this Money tho' I am convinced this will not prevent any Gentleman from performing the Service.

As his Excellency is particularly anxious to have this Business perfected & as the Persons intitled to the Money are doubtless in immediate want of it, I would request your answer by the Opportunity directed to the Care of Genl. James Clinton at this Place & am Sir with the highest Esteem & Regard &c.

[Stephen Lush.*]

[To Jelles Fonda.]

[No. 2241.]

Governor Clinton Promises Jelles Fonda Protection Against Indian Incursions.

Poughkeepsie 26th April 1779.

Sir: I have just received your Letter of the 15th Inst.† I am extreamly unhappy in hearing of the present Depredations of the Enemy in your Quarter as well as the future Danger you apprehend.

---

* See page 724.
† See page 726.

The Returns of the militia not being sent to me agreable to Orders early issued for that Purpose in due Season, has occasioned great Delay in rais'g the men for the Defence of the Frontiers. This Business is now, however, in such Train as to give me reason to hope that it will be soon accomplished. About one half of the men to be raised will be disposed of in filling up the five cont'l Battalions of this State; the other half I have ordered to be marched to the frontiers as fast as they are raised. Be assured, Sir, that I shall exert my utmost endeavors in the use of every means for your Protection. I am &c.

[G. C.]

Jellis Fonda, Esqr.

[No. 2241½.]*

Governor Clinton Instructs Colonel Bellinger to Submit His Complaints to the Conspiracy Commissioners.

Poughkeepsie 26th April 1779.

Gentlemen, I have rec'd your Letter of the 22d Instant and am much concerned about the matters you complain of & the more so as I have no authority to give you Relief or any Directions on the Subject & your proper Method is to represent the matter to the Board of Commiss'rs for detect'g Conspiracies, whose Duty it is to have apprehended & confined all such Persons whose going at large may be dangerous to the Safety of the State. I have formerly written to the Commiss'rs at Albany on Complaints from your County of People of suspicious Charecters. I doubt not that on a proper representation made to them they will do what is proper with respect to Shoemaker tho as to any Suits he may have commenced they cant interfere in. I am &c.

G. C.

John Bellinger & others, Tryon County.

---

* This document has been manifestly misplaced by the original editor of the Clinton MSS. It belongs to document 2234, instead of document 2241.—State Historian.

[No. 2242.]

Lieutenant John Smith appointed to the Command of the Levies from the Four Tryon County Regiments.

Lieut. John Smith, of Tryon County, will take the Command of the Levies to be raised for the Defence of the Frontiers from the four Militia Regiments of that County pursuant to his Excellency's, the Governor's Orders, of the 13th Instant. He is to obey the Orders he may receive from the Commanding Officer at Albany, to whom he is to deliver a Copy of this Order, as to the Duties he is to perform, untill he shall receive the Gov'rs Orders, to the Contrary. The Regts., are to furnish the following Quotas of Men to wit: Colo. Clock's 20; Colo. Bellinger's 15; Colo. Fisher's 21; Colo. Cambell's 15; Total 71. Lieut. Smith will use utmost endeavours to have the Men compleated with all possible Expedition, & as soon as this is effected he will Report the same to his Excellency, accompanied with a Muster Roll of the Men, & his Commission will then be sent him. It will be necessary to deliver a Copy of this Order to each of the Commanding Officers of the above Regts.

By Order of his Excellency, 26th Apl. 1779.

[No. 2243.]

James Duane Grieves Over the Extravagance of Living and the Intolerable Burdens of Public Business.

Philad. 27th April 1779.

Sir; We had the Honour of your Excellency's Favour respecting the Exchange of our unfortunate Friends in the Hands of the Enemy. Congress some time since vested the Commander in Chief with full power to settle a general or partial Cartell for the Exchange of Prisoners, leaving the whole transaction to his

Discretion. I have for this Reason, with the approbation of my Colleagues, transmitted your Excellency's Letter and the Enclosures to the Commander in Chief, and requested him to correspond with you on the Subject: & I have no doubt but he will do every thing you wish or recommend.

I congratulate your Excellency on the important Success of our little Squadron; it is a Seasonable Supply for us, & will distress our Enemies. Favourable Reports prevail respecting the Operations to the Southward but they are not sufficiently authenticated to deserve a detail of particulars.

The Extravegance of living here is beyond description and the Burthen of publick business, intollerable. I am for my own part worn down and stand in great need of Relaxation; when our Finances are placed on some Footing, I must beg for your Excellency's Indulgence, the more so, as I am here without Summer Cloaths, and cannot reconcile it to my Feelings to purchase at the immoderate Prices which are current.

I beg leave to refer your Excellency to Mr. Lewis for Information on the State of publick matters, and have the Honour to be, with the highest Respect, Dear Sir, Your Excellency's most Obedient humble Servant,

Jas. Duane.

His Excellency Governour Clinton.

[No. 2244.]

Benjamin Tusten's Heart Clearly not in His Work.

Aprill 27, 1779.

May it Please your Excellency; I receved yours of the 6th Instant and have obser'd the Contents, and find that I am appointed to a business, which at present there is nothing to do. I have had oppertunity within a few Days to Converse with prin-

sable men from Different parts of the County, who informe me
that they are Sertain that there is not any wheet or flower to
Spare in the County; and this I know that grate quantities of
wheat is brought out of Ulster County, for the actual use and
Supply of the Inhabitants of Orange; therefore, I think it will be
to no good purpos to Spend any more time in making inquiry;
however I am Ready to do any thing that Shall be thought best.
From your Excellency's most obe't Humble Servant

Benj. Tusten.

[To. G. C.]

[No. 2245.]

GENERAL McDOUGALL WRITES AT LENGTH.

*Captain Sloo a Villain—In Doubt Whether the Enemy are Going
South or Contemplate an Attack on the Highland Forts.*

Head Quarters, Pecks Kill, 27th April, 1779.

Sir; When the Court-Martial finished with Captain Sloo, there
was not time to make out a second Copy of the Sentence, to be
sent up to Poughkeepsie. The Provost was so full, that it was
necessary to send Sloo up, and Major Platt, wrote Mr. Benson
that the Judge Advocate wou'd send up his Crime. I have since
heard he is going at large; if so, I fear he has made his escape,
as I consider him to be a Villian. I have, however, transmitted
a Mittimus from Colonel Drake, for his Confinement, and as you
are better acquainted with a proceedure of that kind, than I am,
no doubt you will take the necessary steps. I wish to be informed,
when he is secured.

The Enemy have certainly made another Embarkation of
Troops, of about four Thousand Men, and from their fortifying
Laurel Hill, opposite Fort Washington, I conclude those are
going abroad. This Embarkation, I think is destined for South

Carolina. For a Week past, a number of flat bottomed Boats have been ready at the North side of York Island, capable of containing two Thousand men, which have been under marching Orders, design'd for an Excursion up the North River or to Jersey. I think this was designed, to attempt a surprise on Nixon's Brigade, the Troops at Haverstraw, or the Works at Kings-Ferry.

You have not yet favor'd me with a Permit to export some Flour to procure stores for the Campaign; if it has escaped your attention, and you think proper to grant it, please transmit the same to, Sir, Your Humble Servant,

Alex'r McDougall.

His Excellency Governor Clinton.

P. S. Col. Emeric is recruiting his horse from this State; as I expectd, and the theives and Harbourers pass with impunity.

[No. 2246.]

THE DEFENCE OF THE FRONTIERS.

Governor Clinton's Soldierly Instructions to Major Van Benscoten—Non-Commissioned Officers to be Appointed on Merit in Militia Service.

Instructions for Major Van Buntschoten, or other the Command'g Officer of a Regiment of Levies from the militia for the Defence of the northern & western frontiers & such other Services, as shall be directed:

Sir; You will immediately convene the Officers appointed for your Regiment, & for whom Commissions are herewith delivered to you, and assign to them the Regiments of militia in the Counties of Ulster, Dutchess, & Orange which they are respectively to attend, & receive the Levies which may be raised therein, agreable to my Orders of the 13th Instant, a Copy of which you will herewith receive. They will be particularly careful not to receive

Deserters from the Enemy, or our own army for this Service, & that the men they do receive be properly armed & equipped according to Law, and at the same Time to receive from the command'g Officers of the Regiments, Rolls containing the names & descriptions of the men, distinguish'g such as have engaged voluntarily, from those Drafted, into this Service, which they are to return to you, in order that you may be enabled therefrom, to make & transmit to me, a genl. Return as soon as possible. These Officers, are, on the Receipt of the men, immediately to march them to the Posts now occupied on the frontiers of Ulster & Orange Counties, & put themselves for the present, under the direction of the Command'g Officer of those Posts. It will be most convenient that the men raised in Orange County be marched to Pienpack, & those in Dutchess & Ulster to the Posts in the vicinity of Rochester. It will be necessary that the Levies from Dutchess, at least those from the Southern part of the County, be furnished with Provisions for their march; you will, therefore, draw a sufficient supply for them from the Commissary at Fishkill, who (as these Levies by a Resolve of Congress are to be paid & subsisted by the Continent) will issue the same. It may be proper & necessary to mention to you, that, altho' by my Orders of the 13th, 920 men are to be raised for this Service, your Regiment is only to consist of 500 including Officers; the residue are to be applied in filling up the 5 Cont'l Battalions of this State.

Your Regt. is to be composed of the Levies from the Regts. adjoining the northern & western Frontiers, (who it is to be presumed is best adapted to this Service), & of those from the other Regts., who have voluntarilly engaged in this Service.

I have requested Genl. Clinton to appoint Officers from the cont'l Battalions, to receive the Drafts in Genl. Ten Broeck's

Brigade, & Genl. Ten Broeck is directed to nominate four suitable Persons, one as Capt., the other Subalterns to take the Charge of those of his Brigade who are voluntiers. One of the Lieutenants is to march 73 of these men to Charlotte County, (which with the quota raised in that County will form one Company), to be commanded by Capt. Stockwell & to be stationed at such Posts on the Northern Frontiers as Genl. Schuyler shall direct until further Orders. The Capt. & other two Lieuts. to be nominated by Genl. Ten Broeck, are to march the residue of the voluntiers to such Post on the Western frontiers as shall be assigned them by Genl. Clinton.

Lieut. John Smith will take the Charge of the Levies to be raised in Tryon County & join the Troops stationed at Fort Dayton. It will, therefore, be necessary that you collect Returns from these different Detachments, as soon as conveniently may be; as also an account from Genl. Clinton or Genl. Ten Broeck, of the number of men raised in the County of Albany, who are annexed to the continental Battalions, that you may be enabled to deliver over to those Battalions, their full complim't of 500; in doing which, you will take a just proportion of those raised from each Brigade & Regt., in order to prevent any Jealousies or suspicion of Partiality which I would wish you carefully to avoid, as I am informed the Levies prefer being in your Regiment.

The Lieut. Colo., who is to command the Regt. & several other officers are not yet appointed. This has been delayed, by endeavoring to proportion the officers to the diff't parts of the State furnishing the Levies; as soon as this is effected, they will be ordered to join, & the Corps will be properly arranged & formed into Companies.

The most Central Station for yourself will at present be on the frontiers of Ulster County. The non commissioned Officers, are to be appointed in the ordinary way, but it is my wish that preference should be given to those who have been non commissioned Officers in the militia.

As you are to receive your Pay from the Continent, you will make your Returns to the Officer commanding the Department, & be particularly carefull, in having your men mustered & Pay Rolls made out, in due season, & you will likewise make monthly Returns to me; as these Orders are calculated for the command'g Officer of the Corps, you will deliver them over to the Lieut. Colo., as soon as he shall be appointed & join the Regt. I am &c.

Geo. Clinton.

Poughkeepsie April 27th 1779.

If any of the Officers decline serving, it must be reported to the Governor immediately that others may be appointed in their Room.

Major Van Buntschoten.

———

[No. 2247.]

Rochester, Ulster County, Makes a Request that Governor Clinton has Anticipated.

To his Excellency George Clinton Esqr. Governour and Commander in Chief of the State of New York &c.

These Humbly Sheweth, That your Petitioners are informed by Coll. Cortland, that he has received Marching orders from his Excellency Gener'l Washington, and Will March by Munday Next, and Consequently your Petitioners will be left Defenceless, unless Speedly provided for; your Excellencies Petitioners do Humbly Pray, that your Excellency may be Pleased Speedly, as you, in your Wisdom Shall think fit, provide us a Sufficient

Guard, as we are Apprehensive (by information) that the Enemy are out, and your Petitioners much Dread the Consequence of being invaided by a Savage and Merciless Enemy in a defenceless Condition, and Need not inform your Excellency of our Daingerous Situation at this Juncture.

We Shall Ever pray and remain your Humble Petitioners.

A. D Witt, Andries A. De Witt, John Brodhead, Stephen De Witt, John Dewitt, Benjamin Bevier, Johannis Bevier, Jun., Jacob Bevier, Cornelius Bevier, Cornelius Vernooy, Johannis Hoornbeeck, Johannis Vernooy, Nathan Vernooy, John Vanwagenen, Jaobus ――, Moses Depue, Arth Van Wagenen, Jr., Terck Dewitt, Jory Mak, Jacobus Bruyn, Junr., Cornelius Newkerk, John Kittle, And's Bevier, Peter Cantine, Johannis Ge. Hardenberg, Benjamin Kortreght, Benjamen Hoornbeek, Hartman Ennist, Frederick Vandemerk, Derick Hoornbeek, Jacob Tornaer, John Sammon, Jacobus Wynkoop, Johannis Oosterhout, Benymen Oosterhoudt, Cornelus Oosterhout, Henderickus Oosterhoudt, Elisa Hoornbeek, Philip Hoornbeek, Hennery Hoornbeek, Jno. Sleght, Rich. Brodhead, Petrus Schoonmaker, Jacobus Quick, Jr., Johannes Schoonmaker, Benjamin Schoonmaker, Jacobus Schoonmaker, Martinas Schoonmaker, Joacim Schoonmaker, Cornelius Depuy, Jacob Krom, Jonas Hasbroock, Joesep De Puy, Daniel Schoonmaker, Lodewyck Schoonmaker, Jacob Depuy, Benjamen Depuy, Jr., Derick Wesboock, Frederick Wesbroock, Ephraim Depuy, Ephraim Depuy, Jr., Jojachim Depuy, Benyamen Van Wagenen, Jacobus Van Wagenen, Zacharias Rosakrans, Aart Van Wagenen.

Rochester, ye 27 April, 1779.

[No. 2248.]

An Earnest Petition from Saratoga.

The Humble Petition of the Freeholders Inhabitants and residents of the District of Saratoga in the County of Albany;

To His Excellency George Clinton Esqr. Governor and Commander in Chief of the State of New York Capt. Gener'll of the Militia and Vice Admiral of the Same.

Humbly Sheweth, That we, your Excellencies Petitioners, living in Saratoga District have, heretofore, been greatly distressed by the Calamities of war, in so much that even the most able among us have met and still do meet with the greatest Dificulties by our own Industry and every other Honest and Prudent Measures we have been able to adapt, to procure for ourselves and Families the Common and Necessary Supports of Life, and from our present Situation are become the frontiers Inhabitants of a wide and Extended Tract of Country, exposed to the Daily and Hourly Incursions of a numerous and Savage Enemy, by no Means secured with proper Guards, so as to render our habitations either safe or Secure; at present your Excellency has called upon us for a proportion of men to be taken from this Regt., which we humbly Imagine, you would have Exempted had you been properly Informed of our Situation and present Circumstances; these are facts related to your Excellency, which we hope you will take into Serious Consideration, and grant us such Relief in the Premises, as you in your wisdom may Judge right, and your Excellencies petitioners as bound in Duty shall ever pray.

John McCrea, Colonel, Cornelius Van Veghten, Lt. Colo., Daniel Dickinson, 1st maj'r, Jacob Van Schaick, maj'r, Ephraim Woodworth, Capt., John Thompson, Capt., Peter Van Wort, Cpt., John Fish, Hezekiah Dunham, Eben'r Marvin, Thomas Dennis, Cornel-

49

yus P. Van den Brgh, John Davis, Lut, Philip Rogers Ensighn, Iner's Child, Nath'n Shepherd, Dirck Swart, David Archer, Peleg Tripp, John Carthy, John ——, Silvenus Dunham, William Bradshaw, Joseph Seeley, Edward Hissted, Daniel Smith, Josha Whelh, Ezekiel Ensign, Witham Frisbe, Thomas Armstrong, John Ries, Jur., Josiah Benjamin, Titus Andruss, Cyprian Watson, Israel Taylor, Jacob Howard, Ebenezer Andrus, Mathew Patrick, Ebenezer Cobb, John Reis, John Cobb, Daniel Rowland, Joshua Cobb, Samuel McCrea, Elisha Andrus, Solomon Cambell, John Ashton, William Leahy, George Palmer, Elias Palmer, Robert Cambell, Jehiel Parkes, Joab Cook.

Saratoga District April 27th 1779.

[No. 2249.]

JAMES CLINTON AS AN INDIAN HUNTER.

His Modest Allusion to His Great Victory at Onondaga—The Situation in Tryon—A New Post Established.

Albany April 28th 1779.

Dear Brother,* I am just returned from an Excursion up the Mohawk River, in Consequence of an alarm given by a Body of Indians, in number about sixty, from the Seneca Country, who made their appearance at the same time in different Quarters.

One of the Parties attacked the Houses of a certain Mr. Layer, and Cowley, back of Schohary, both whom they took and plundered; at the same time, another Party attacked the House of a certain Captain Richter, back of Stone Raby where he, his Wife, two Boys, and an old man were. Richter and the two Boys being armed, defended themselves and killed the two Indians, but the old man who was unarmed was killed, with a Boy about 17 years

---
*For Governor Clinton's reply, see page 791.

old. Richter's arm was broke, and the other Boy wounded in the Elbow, and the Woman in one of her Legs. Another Party took a man, two Boys & two Horses about five miles West of Fort Plank, but tho' they were closely pursued by Scouts from the Fort, yet they escaped. It is supposed that those on the North side of the River were from Canada as many of them were known to be Mohawks. The alarm was general thro' the whole Country, and I believe in a few days Schanectady woud have been the Frontier of the State, if it had not been for the appearance of the Troops, which I immediately marched up, consisting of that part of Gansevoort's Regt., which was in town, and the Schenactady Militia, amounting in the whole to about two hundred, with which I proceeded as far as Johnstown, where I was joined by a number of the Tryon County Militia who turned out chearfully on the occasion. As the establishing a Post at, or near Sockondoga seemed to be the only method left of restoring the Inhabitants to their former Tranquility, I determined to erect a Block house, on the Road leading to Sir William Johnston's Pleasure House, ten miles from Johnstown, near the Road leading to Mayfield, and gave the necessary orders for that Purpose leaving Col. Gansevoort to see them executed.

I Intend to garisson the Fort with a Detatchment from Col. Duboys's Regiment, as the whole Regiment will shortly move to Johnstown.

In consequence of your Request, I have ordered, proper officers to attend, & receive the Drafts from Genl. Ten Broeck's Brigade, who are now in Town: but the General thinks it best that the respective Colonels should send their Quotas to Albany where they can be received with less danger of Desertion. Letters have been circulated for that Purpose. I coud wish that the most

efectual measures were taken to expedite this necessary duty, as
every Letter from His Excellency indicates a speedy movement.

I have been, and always shall be, very careful in giving the
least shadow of encouragement to the usurped authority of the
pretended State of Vermont; the frequent applications from that
Quarter, for troops induced me to give them the same advice I
had given to other parts of the State in similar Circumstances
with respect to the Enemy, which was, that they shoud have a
number of their militia ready to turn out on the shortest notice,
as it was impossible for me to supply them with troops.

I sincerely congratulate you on the Success of our Onondoga
Expedition, a Copy of the Proceedings of which I send you inclosed.* The Conduct of both Officers and men on this occasion,
cannot be too much admired; it is of too much consequence to be
kept from the public. I have sent it in its original undress and
request that you woud polish it, and commit it to the Press;
when the Prisoners arrive, they shall be sent down to you to
keep. I am, Dear Brother, Yours &c.

                                        James Clinton.
[To G. C.]

                        ————

                    [No. 2250.]
            Colonel Cortlandt Ordered to Minisink.

                                    Rochester April 28, 1779.

Dear Sir, I am Ordered by his Excellency General Washington
to march my Regt. Immediately to Minisinks, and I Suppose will
proceed on with General Hand who is now in Wyomen. I shall
march from this, next Munday and as this Fruntier will then be
Exposed, I take this Early oppertunity of Informing your Excellency that you may give Such Orders as you may think Necessary
for the further Security of the Inhabitants.

———————————————————————————————
*Not found, but see page 702 and accompanying footnote.

I was on my way to Poughpaken and Schohaken when I Rec'd the Genl's Orders, and of Course was under the Necessaty of Returning. I did Intend to have gone down the Delaware by the way of Keshecten, if I had not been prevented. I think that it will not be amiss to Send a party on an Expidition of that Kind, However yr. Excellency may Soon be better Informed, as I have Sent Four men as Spies into that Country and on their Return will Inform you thereof. I Remain with Respect your Hum'e Ser't

Philip Cortlandt.

His Excellency Gov'r Clinton.

GOVERNOR CLINTON PROTECTS THE DISTRICT LEFT UNCOVERED BY COLONEL CORTLANDT'S TRANSFER.

Poukeepsie 29th April 1779.

Dear Sir, I have this Moment rec'd your Favour of yesterday in Consequence of which I have ordered one fourth Part of Colonels Cantine's & Snyder's Regts., to occupy the Posts you now hold, on Monday next, untill I can relieve them by the Levies intended for the Defence of the Frontiers, which are not as yet compleated. I wish you an agreable March & am with great Regard your Most Obed't Serv't,

[G. C.]

Colo. Cortlandt.

[No. 2251.]

A Line of Grievances from the Inhabitants of Lower Orange County.

To Gov'r Clinton:

May it please your Excelencie, We the Civel majestrates, Freeholders & Inhabitants on the South side of the mountains in the County of Orange, beg leave in a most Humble manner to lay some of its Inumerable Grievances before your Excelencie, Hop ing in your Benign Wisdom and Benevolence towards your People you will lend your attention.

With such Confidence, we make bold thus to lay our Grievances before you, We Understand by a Letter from your Excelency in answer to Coll. Hays that your Excelency has given General McDougal authorety to call your militia out from here and Detatch them in what manner seemeth best to him. Sir, many Circumstances has accur'd since the date of that Letter. Several of our good friends have been Robb'd; not Less than Twenty Horses have been Stolen in one night from our best Friends; a Gentleman robb'd near Widdow Sidman's of upwards of Eleven Thousand Pounds, York Currency, (Esqr. Satterley of upwards 2000£ Collected as Tax,) Information is now actually given that no Less than nine Different Scouts of these most atrocious wretches is out this Instant, in and about the mountains boardring [bordering] upon us, and their ready getting to the Enemy in Safty or within their Lines Stands in need of more force then we are able to maintain to defeat them. These and many other such Circumstances Emboldens us to State our Grievances to you, And Whereas, we Humbly Conceive, that your Excellency as our General and Chief Majestrate, is the only recourse from which we may Hope for Relief; And, Whereas, it is well known to Some of the Subscribers, since the abovementioned Robberies, a Number of the good people here, has but one night in three in their Beds, and that without Safety or Comfort, on account of these dangers, and for some prospect of Safety, Padrols are kept on the roads and paths every night.

From these Stated facts we hope your Excelency will Conceive that the men called from here by Order of General McDougal is a real Grievance and actualy renders us more Defenceless.

The many calls of the Inhabetants with their Teams and other things, which the army wants, in passing and Repassing thro this part of the State, takes at least one Sixth part of its Inhabitants Constantly Employ'd in that way; your Excelency will Judge what Strength we can have to defend our Extensive Frontier, besides the above mentioned internal Enemies and many others that Secretly Harbors them. All which we Humbly submit to your Consideration. And beg leave to Subscribe ourselves, your Excelency's most Obedient Servants.

Paul V. d'Voort, Barent V. d'Voort, David Pye, John Coleman, Jacob Cole, John D. Coe, John Coe, Jonah Hallsted, Theunis Cuyper, John Beekman, John Suffern.

April 28 1779.

[No. 2252.]

THE ORANGE COUNTY ROBBERS.

Prisoners to be Held as Hostages—James Clinton's Victory Over the Onondagas.

Poukeepsie 29th April 1779.

Dear Sir, Your Letter of the 27th Instant was handed to me last Night. The Warrant it contained ag't William Sloo I have delivered to Mr. Harper one of the Com'rs. If Colo. Drake had taken the Examination of the Witnesses ag't Sloo, it woud have been much more proper than to have founded his Warrant on the Sentence of the Court Martial; however, I am informed there is not the least Danger of his attempting to Escape.

From the superior Land Force I am informed France has in the West Indies, it appears to me more probable that the last Embarkation at New York is intended as reinforcement for Genl. Grant than for South Carolina. I so entirely forgot your Ap-

plication for a Permit to export a small Quantity of Flour, that I
am inclined to believe that you intended only, as I cannot find a
word about it in your Letters tho I have examined all of a late
Date. Be kind enough to mention in your next, the Number of
Barrels you wish to export & I will endeavour to send you a Permit.

I have just received from our Friend Gov'r Livingston, the
Examination of which I inclose you a Copy of one Cole & other
Robers who have been lately convicted & executed in his State.
These discover, not only the names of the Persons in the different
Gangs of Robers who infest this State, but also those who harbour
& abet them. It is of the utmost Importance that they be immediately apprehended & secured. I have, therefore, taken the liberty
of sending you the enclosed warrant ag't those Persons named in
the Examination who reside in the neighbourhood of Kakiat in
Orange County. As I have Reason to fear that the Execution of
it (if committed to the civil magistrate or the militia) may be
attended with Delay and rendered unsuccessfull, I must request of
you to appoint one of your Officers (whom you shall deem best calculated for the Business) with a proper Detachment to carry the
same into immediate execution. You will please to get Major
Strang to insert his name in the Blanck left in the warrants for
that Purpose, as there is not a suff't number of Commiss'rs here
at pres't to form a quorum.

I have informed Colo. Isaac Nicoll of Orange County who is
charged with the execution of this Business in the Clove & in the
neighbourhood of Sterling Iron Works, that it would be begun
on the So. side of the mountains on the 5th of next month. I
mention this as it is necessary, that both Parties should strike
about the same time to prevent the Persons being alarmed &

making their Escape; indeed it is necessary that this whole Business should be conducted w'th Secrecy. When these fellows are apprehended it might be well to give it out that they are to be kept as Hostages & if any Robberies or murders are committed in future they will be put to Death. It may perhaps defeat Colo. Emerick's recruiting Business. From the Desire I know you have, that these Robbers & Horse Thieves should be apprehended & bro't to punishm't I flatter myself you will excuse the trouble I now give you. Be assured, Sir, that I shall be ever ready to compensate for it by the execution of any matter you may wish to have performed tho' it should be equally out of the line of my Department. I have just been informed by Tom Henderson, who arrived this morn'g from Albany & which is since confirmed by Capt. Tiebout, from the same Place, that the Detachm't which lately marched under Colo. Van Schaick have destroyed the Onandaga Settlement with a quantity of Wheat, Indian Corn, & other Stores, some muskets &c. &c., took 32 Prisoners, killed 17 & are returned without the Loss of a man. I am &c.

Geo. Clinton.

Major Genl. McDougall.

[No. 2253.]

Colonel Cortlandt Reports He has on Hand One Hundred Barrels of Flour More than He Needs.

Kingston April 29, 1779.

Dear Sir; I have acquainted you in a letter of yesterday that my Regiment is ordered from the Fruntier of Rochester, but Forgot to Inform you that the Commissary of Issues for my Regt., has on hand upwards of One Hund'd Barrels of Flower, more than I Shall want, and Some Beef. I therefore, beg you will please to

Inform me by the Return of the bearer, whether the provision will be wanting where it is at Warsink or not; if not I must have it Removed, I Should be glad for the Sake of the Inhabitants that Some of the Draughts Could arrive at the post before I leave it. Since my Return, I find all the Country is allarm'd, but I am persuaded without reason, and it may be Depended on, it will frequently be the Case, untill some Expedition is Carried on into the Country on the Delaware as I have Hinted in the letter I Sent your Excellency. The reasons I make no Doubt, are very obvious without mentioning them, for a few Tories may keep this Fruntier in Continual allarms, and a more timed people some few Excepted I never Saw. The Express is waiting, am your Hum'e Ser't

Philip Cortlandt.

P. S. I Shall, if time will permit, Call on your Excellency before I march.

His Excellency Governor Clinton, Poughkeepsie.

————

COMMISSARY SUPPLIES WILL BE NEEDED FOR THE NEW LEVIES.

Poukeepsie 30th April 1779.

D'r Sir, I wrote you yesterday, by which you will be informed that the Provissions in the Hands of your Commissary will be wanted for the Levies for the Defence of the Frontiers; I hope I shall be able to have part of them on that Service in a few Days; in the Mean Time I have ordered out one fourth of Colo. Snyder's & Cantine's Regts. to occuppy the Posts your Regt. is to leave. I shall be happy to see you, before you march if you find it convenient, & am, Sir, &c.

[G. C.]

[To Col. Cortlandt.]

[No. 2254.]

General Schuyler's Instructions to Captain Stockwell.

Albany April 29th 1779.

Sir,* His Excellency the Governor having requested me to dispose of your Company In such a manner as will best Cover the frontiers against the Incursions of the Enemy, I think It advisable for the present, to Station it at Skensborough, but as Colo: Warner's Regim't is ordered to remove from Fort Edward, and it being necessary to keep that post, you will send an Officer, with two non Commissioned Officers, and twenty five privates to that place. You will Charge the officer to keep small scouts Constantly on the North side of Hudson's river, as far up as the North branch, and to give notice to General Ten Broeck and the nearest Colonels of militia, of the approach of Enemy that may be discovered Specifying If possible their numbers and the rout they may take. You with the remainder of your Company, will proceed without delay to Skensborough, and from thence send small scouts constantly towards Tyconderoga on both sides of the lake with directions, if they should discover any Enemy, to ascertain their numbers as near as may be, and the route they pursue; on receiving Intelligence of any body approaching in such force as to render a reinforcement necessary to your or any other post against which the Enemy may be Supposed to point, you will dispatch the Intelligence to Gen. Ten Broeck at Albany and to the Nearest Colonels of the Militia in the Counties of Albany & Tryon.

Should the movements of the Enemy strongly indicate an attack on you, and their force be such as to render any opposition

---

*This letter belongs to a letter written May 3, 1779, by General Philip Schuyler to Governor Clinton. See page 828.

Ineffectual, you will then, unless you have a prospect of being reinforced before the Enemy can come to your relieve, to retire orderly, to where Fort Ann stood, and watching their Motions. If you find they bend towards Fort Edward, you will reinforce that Garrison. If towards any Settlements more east, you will take such a position as to afford the Greattest possible protection to the Inhabitants. Every Intelligence you receive, you will also Communicate to the Commanding Officer at fort Edward, Fort George & Rutland.

The disgrace of a surprise must be strictly guarded against, and that you may not Experience one, you will be Extremely vigilant and watchful; not suffering your men to strole from the post or be absent on furlough is Indispensibly necessary.

As soon as any more troops can be sent for the protection of the Northern frontiers, that part of your Company now ordered to Fort Edward will join you. I am, Sir, &c.

P. S.

Capt. Levi. Stockwell.

[Copy.]

[No. 2255.]

Governor Clinton's Instructions to Sheriff Nicoll Touching the Orange County Robbers.

Poukeepsie 29th April 1779.

Dear Sir; I have to acknowledge the Receipt of your and the Rev'd Mr. Kerr's Letter of the 16 Instant, and as the Suspicions you entertain of Downing appear to me to be well founded, I will send over a proper Person to sound him and discover his true Charecter, as soon as I can meet with one quallified for this Business. I will possess the Person employed with whatever may be necessary to engage the Confidence of the Master, & induce him to disclose his Business & Designs.   He will be addressed to you for advice & Directions.

A few Days ago I received from Gov'r Livingston, the Examinations of one Cole & others, who were lately convicted for Roberies and executed in New Jersey of which you have Copies inclosed.* You will observe that, by these Examinations, we have been able to discover not only the Persons concerned in the different Roberries which have been of late committed in this County Ulster & Orange; but also the different Persons who harbour & abet them. You will also please to observe, that among other Enterprizes this Banditi have in Meditation, the Court House, your House, & some others in Goshen are to be fired, yourself & Colo. Malcom Plundered.   This I dare say will furnish you the most striking & feeling argument on the propriety of having these Robers & their Harbourers immediately apprehended & secured; & for this Purpose I now inclose you Warrants from the Com'rs of Conspiracies at this Place, in which (for want of a sufficient Number of Members here to form a Board) you will get Mr. Wisener or Moffat to insert his name in the Blank left for that Purpose & then have executed with all possible Dispatch on those who reside in the Clove or at or about the Sterling Iron Works. I have sent simular Warrants to Genl. McDougal, for those mentioned in the Examinations, who reside on the South Side of the Mountains, which I have requested him to have executed by a Detachm't from his Army on the 5th of next Month. If you shoud accomplish your Part of the Business before that Time, it will be absolutely necessary that the Reasons for apprehending these Persons & the Discoveries made by this Examination shoud be kep a profound Secret, least a discovery shoud alarm those as-

---

* Not found.

signed to Genl. McDougal. Indeed the whole Business must be conducted with Secrecy, if you are to expect Success. Colo. Heathorn or the Commanding Officer of any other of the Regts. in your County, to whom you may think proper to apply, will furnish you with a proper Detachment of trusty Men for this Service, on shewing them that Part of this Letter which relates to this particular Business, in the Execution of which I woud advice you to call on Capt. Jno. Wood for his Assistance. The Commissioners will pay the Expence attending it, on the account thereof being rendered to them. I am with great Regard your Most Obed't Serv't

[G. C.]

P. S. It may answer a good Purpose when these People are apprehended, to give it out that they are to be kept as hostages & if any Robberies or murders are committed they will be put to Death.

Colo. Nicoll.

[No. 2256.]

Jelles Fonda Writes Major Lush Relative to the Money for the Frontier Sufferers.

Cachnewago 29th Apl. 1779.

Sir, I Rec'd your Letter of the 14 Instant and note the Contents of it. I am Laid op in my home with a Sore ledg. I have had my Sone in law, Mr. Van Veghten, Round to all the members of the Sennete and asembly in our County, Except Coll. Cambel, who is moved out of it, and he has Shown them your letter, and advised with them all: theay all Say that the Distressed Peple will get Grane Soner and Cheper, then if one man had to Buy it: and agree that John Frey, and John Fonda Shall Be the Persons to Devide the money to those who are Distressed By the Enemy in our County at once; it has not Been in my Power to Precure a Proper Retorn as you mene to have it. I have had Sum Sent to me, which was the Same as has Bene Sent to the Governor Sum thime Past: we have a great many Persons in our County who are Realy obiects of Charity: if I was able to go about I whould get a Proper Retorn. By writing I Can not Sucseed—the Suner the money was Sent the Better. So I Remane your most Humble Serv't

Jelles Fonda.

P. S. I whould Sent Round to the Colls. again But it forty miles Round and then Perhaps whould not Be Rightly onderstoud as to the Retorn Required. J. F.

To Madger Stephen Lush.

[No. 2257.]

Return of flour seized in April for the use of the army by Hendrick Wyckoff.

A return of Flour Seized by Hend'k Wyckoff and Delivered for the use of the Army of the United States in the Month of April 1779.

Time when Seized	Of whom Seized	Where Deposited	Flour				To whom Delivered	At what Price		Total Amount		
			No. Casks	C	Qrs	lb		Flour	Cask Containing the Flour	£	s	d
1779 April 8	Nathaniel Wait, an Inhabitant of Boston	Thos. Storm, Esqr. Barn	9	16	0	17	Jon'n G. Tompkins, Esqr. A. C. P.	£16 pr C	20/ Each	267	8	6¾
— 20	Daniel Outwater, who is gone to the Enemy	Daniel Outwater's House	8	13	3	0	Do Do Do	16 Do	21/ Do	229	12	
	Total Seized		17	29	3	17	Total Amount			£497	0	6¾

N. B. The Flour of Mr. Wait Seized as above was purchased with intent to be Transported out of the State.

Fishkill April 30th 1779.

Errors Excepted

Hend'k Wyckoff

[No. 2258.]

Returns of flour and wheat, purchased from 13th to 30th April, by Hendrick Wyckoff.

A Return of Flour and Wheat Purchased by Hend'k Wyckoff and Delivered for the use of the Army of the United States, from the 13th to the 30th Day of April Included, 1779.

Time when Purchased	Of whom Purchased	Where Deposited.	Flour No. Cask	C	Qrs.	lb	Wheat Bush'l	pecks	Prices of Flour & Wheat	Prices of Flour cask containing the Flour	Total Amount £	s	d	To whom Delivered
1779 April 13	John Swartwout	Daniel Hasbrook's Mill	12	20	0	8	6		£ s 6-8 pr. bus.		38	8		Jonathan G. Tompkins, Esqr. A. C. of Purchase.
13	Samuel Swartwout	Do Do Do				0	10		6-8 Do		64	2	10	Do
16	James Hicks	John Cook's Do	6	10	1	0			16 pr. C	20/ Each	333	6	9	Do
17	Abraham Lent, Jun'r	Abr'm Lent's House	10	10	1	21			16 Do	20/ Do	170	11	5	Do
19	Dominicus Monfoort	John Cook's Mill	11	20	1	4			16 Do	20/ Do	170	16		Do
19	Peter T. Monfoort	Samuel Verplank's Do	10	17			12		16 Do	24/ Do	338	18	6¾	Do
20	Rynier Suydam	Corn's V. Sicklen's Do							6-8 pr. bus.		288	8	6¾	Do
24	Abraham Young	Daniel Hasbrook's Do	10	19	0	10			16 Do	24/ Do	76	12		Do
25	Jacob Brinckerhoff	Jacob Brinckerhoff's Do	33	62	1	14			16 Do	24/ Do	317	7	5	Do
25	Richard Van Wyck	Samuel Verplank's Do	10	17	3	17			16 Do	24/ Do	1087	8	6¾	Do
25	Archibald Currie	Jacob Brinckerhoff's Do					24		6-8 pr. bus.		298	18	6¾	Do
25	Benjamin V. D. Water	Daniel Hasbrook's Do	14	24	1	11		2	6-8 pr. bus.	24/ Do	153	8		Do
26	Robert Brett	Jacob Brinckerhoff's Do					21		6-8 pr. bus.		406	12	5	Do
26	Gabriel Hughson	Samuel Verplank's Do					50		6-8 pr. bus.		137	7		Do
26	John Losee	John Cook's Do	13	22	1	17			16 pr. C	24/ Do	320	12		Do
26	Joseph Jackson	Samuel Verplank's Do	12	22	1	6			16 Do	24/ Do	374		6¾	Do
26	Colo. Jacobus Swartwout	Do Do	17	32	2	19			16 Do	21/ Do	871	5		Do
26	Abraham Duryee	Abr'm Duryee's Barn	30	51	1	14			16 Do	24/ Do	543	2	3½	Do
27	Cornelius Van Sicklen	Corn's V. Sicklen's Mill	16	28	2	8			16 Do	24/ Do	858			Do
27	Jacob Brinckerhoff	Jacob Brinckerhoff's Do	43	82	2	23			16 Do	24/ Do	476	6	10	Do
28	Colo. Abraham Brinckerhoff	Do Do	4	9	0	27			16 Do	24/ Do	1374	17	8¾	Do
28	William Van Wyck	Wm. Van Wyck's Do	5	9	0	2			16 Do	24/ Do	120	13	10	Do
28	Jacob Brinckerhoff	Jacob Brinckerhoff's Do	16	27	3	3			16 Do	24/ Do	150	5	8	Do
30	George Brinckerhoff	Do Do							16 Do	24/ Do	463	12	7	Do
	Total purchased		268	486	0	11	123	2			£8882	10	0¼	

[No. 2259.]

Tryon County Asks for a Special Court of Oyer and Terminer for the Trial of Twelve Conspirators.

Stone Arabia, 30th April 1779.

Sir; We beg leave to acquaint your Excellency that we have lately discovered a most daring Conspiracy formed against the People of this County, and that in Consequence thereof, we have apprehended twelve of the Conspirators, who are charged with Treason and Misprision of Treason; we have taken some of their Examinations & collected some proof, for the particulars of which we refer your Excellency to Capt. Fox, the Bearer.

As the Prison of our County is insufficient to hold Prisoners we have the Prisoners under a military Guard, where we shall keep them untill we have your Excellency's Instructions.

We intreat your Excellency, that as we have a Number of Persons charged with felonious Acts, besides the above Prisoners, you will be pleased to order a special Court of Oyer and Terminer for this County.   We can with the greatest Confidence assure your Excellency, that if a speedy Example is not made of those Miscreants, the well affected Inhabitants of this Place cannot with safety to their Persons or Property remain upon their Farms.   We are Your Excellency's Most Obedient H'ble Servants,

Jacob Klock, Petter Wagner, Peter S. Deygert, Just., Will'm Deygert, Justice, Chris'r P. Yates.

His Excellency Gov'r Clinton.*

[No. 2260.]

A List of Sufferers in Canajoharie District, Entitled to State Relief.

A Return of the Distressed Familys whose Propertys has been Destroyed By the Enemy Last Year and those of Each of said

------

* For Governor Clinton's reply, see page 797.

Familys that is not Able to gain a Livelyhood Canojoharie District Tryon County April 30th 1779.

Heads of Familys.	Number in Each Family.	Number of those in each Fami'y that are not able to Work for a Livelyhood.
The Reverend Samuel Dunlap,	2	1
The Reverend William Johnston,	10	5
Samuel Campbell,	2	1
Samuel Clyde,	11	7
Jeremiah Bakon,	8	4
Nathaniel Hammil,	4	1
William Dickson,	9	4
William Gault,	9	7
James Scott,	6	5
James Wilson,	8	5
Widow Warfield,	3	2
William McConnall,	4	2
John Campbell, Sen'r,	6	1
James Ramsey,	3	2
James Campbell,	9	6
John Campbell, Jun'r,	9	3
Daniel Ogden,	7	3
James Moore,	3	2
James McCollum,	3	2
William McClaallen,	5	4
William Thompson,	12	6
John Foster,	6	2
Widow Winstone,	4	3
Hugh Mitchell,	3	2
Widow Thompson,	6	3
Alexander McCollom,	8	4

Heads of Familys.	Number in each Family.	Number of those in each Family that are not able to Work for a Livelyhood.
Thomas Ramsey,	2	2
George Kinnout,	8	3
Isaac Collier,	5	4
William Stensel,	9	3
George Myer,	5	2
Coonrod Picket,	10	5
Henry Brat,	7	3
David Tygert,	4	2
Adolph Walrod,	4	2
Isaac Quack,	5	3
John Spalsberry,	6	2
Widow Hath,	5	3
Henry Dygart,	5	3
George Bush,	4	2
Widow Davis,	4	3
Perils Sparks,	4	3
John Pickett,	7	4
Jacob Wright,	2	1

Saml. Clyde, Lt. Coll. 3   Total 256   Total 137
To Coll. Fredrek Fisher, Coughnawago.

[No. 2261.]

George Clinton to Colonel Curtenius as to the Clothing Department.

Poughkeepsie 1st May 1779.

Sir, I enclose you Copies of Letter* from the Commiss'r of Cloathing Accounts & an Act of Congress of the 2d March on the

---

*See page 719.

Returns of the battalion un

Weekly Return of the 4th New York Battalion of

May 2nd 1779.	Officers present fit for Duty														
	Field		Commissioned				Staff							Non Co	
Companies	Lieut. Colonel	Major	Captains	Capt. Lieutenants	1st Lieutenants	Ensigns	Chaplain	Adjutant	Pay Master	Qr. Master	Surgeon	Mate	Serjant Major	Qr. Mr. Serjant	Drum Major
Colo Company	1					1					1	1	1	1	
Major's Company					1	1									
Capt. Sacket			1		1										
Capt. Davis			1		1										
Capt. Walker					1	1									
Capt. Smith			1		1										
Capt. Titus			1		1										
Capt. Norton			1												
Capt. Fowler			1		1	1									
Total	1		6		7	4					1	1	1	1	
Officers Sick present															
Vacant						5	1								

Absent officers names	Places where	Reason for	and tim
Major McCracking	Bennington	Not Joind	Months
Capt. Walker	Gen'l Stuben	Aidecamp	
Capt. Smith	present	acting pay Mr.	
Capt. Lieut. Dunscomb	Albany	on Command	
Lieut Elsworth	present	Acting Adjutant	
Lieut. V'n Hovenbergh	Albany	on Command	
Lieut. Barrit	present	Acting Qr. Master	
Serjt. Howel	Poughkeepsie	on Command	
Stephan Buckingham	Drumer New Windsor	Sick	

N. B. One fifer promoted to fife Major.

Peter Elswo

The Amount of the non Commission'd Officers and Privates in the abov
to be left w'th the Treasurer for their Gratuity amount'g 225. Capt. Smit
Return and that the other is a true Return of the Regt.

I Certify Honour the within Returns to be a true state of the Officers,
my Command without fraud to the United States or any Individuals.

Lieutenant Colonel Regnier.

Commanded by Lieut. Colo. P. Regnier, Fort Plank.

ssioned			Rank & File						Wanting to Compleat			Alterrations Since Last Return					Joind		
	Serjants	Drumers & Fifers	Present fit for Duty	Sick Present	Sick Absent	On Command	On Fourlough	Total	Serjants	Drumers & Fifers	Rank & File	Dead	Discharged	Deserted	Sent to the Corps of Invilds	promoted	Serjants	Drumers & Fifers	Rank & File
1	2	1	16					16	1	1	40								
	1	2	19			3		22	2		34								
	2	1	19	3	1	4		27	1	1	29								
	2	2	16	2	1	2		21			35								
	2		23					23	1	2	33								
	1		13			1	1	15	2	1	41								
	1	1	24	4	1	1		30		1	26								
	1	1	10	1				11	2		45								
	2	1	24	1		3		28	1	1	28								
1	14	9	164	11	3	14	1	193	10	7	311								

	2	1	Sick at		2 on his excellency's Guard
			Fishkill	1	1 with Gen'l McDougal
			at Denbury	1	1 with John Francks Late pay Master
			at Albany	1	1 with Capt Dunscomb
bsence				—	4 on Command at Norwalk
				3	5 at Albany
Days					14

P. Regnier, Lt. Col. Comdt.

Adjutant

eturn appears to be five less than the Return made by the Colo. Command't ho made out the last mentioned Return says there is a mistake in this

ncommissioned officers, and Privates of the 4th N. York Regiment, under

P. Regnier, Lt. Col. Comdt.

same Subject. You'l make your Returns to the Commiss'r of Cloathing accordingly. As Congress have made considerable alterations with respect to the business [of] the Cloathing Department I wish to have an Opportunity of conversing with you on the Subject as soon as may be convenient. I am &c.

Geo: Clinton.

Colo. Curtenius.

[No. 2262.]

Commissary Townsend, for Permit to Send 100 Barrels Flour to Troops Outside of the State.

Peeks Kill 1st May 1779.

Sir, I Am Directed by P. Colt, Esqr, D. C. Genl. of Pur's To Apply to your Excellency for Permition To Send flour out of this State, for Supplying the Guards at Horse Neck & Norwalk, & as I am Unacquainted with the Quantity that may be Wanted for that purpose at present, please to Grant a permitt for one hundred Barrels flour & Enclose the Same To me att Bedford. For your Exc'cy Hum'e Serv't

Saml. Townsend A. C. of P. West Chester County.

His Exc'cy George Clinton.

[No. 2264.]

Colonel Curtenius Appeals for the Exemption from Military Service of Matthias Warner.

Wall Kill May 2d 1779.

May it please your Excellency; The bearer hereof Mr. Matthias Warner, a Refugee from the City of New York, has had the misfortune to be drafted in the nine months servise. If he is obliged to go, it will bring Ruin & great distress on his family, for he has no one to take care of his business on the farm (he has hiered) but his son who is a small lad & not capable to do the business & as to hireing a man he is not able; he having expended the greatest part of his money which he brought out of town with him, If your Exellen'y could consistently Exempt him, it would save a good man & his family from great distress.

The plea he has to be exempted, besides what is mentioned above, is that he may be Considederd as being in public servise, for I have hiered part of his House to put the Soldiers Cloathing in, & I think it is necessary that he stay with the cloathing to take care of them. I remain with due respect Your Excellen's most Obed't Serv't

Peter T. Curtenius.

[To G. C.]

[No. 2265.]

Robert Yates Reports that Fifty Depredators are Working the Woods on the West Bank of the Hudson.

Albany May 2d 1779.

Sir: During the sitting of the Court the last Term, William Hooghteeling was tryed and convicted of two Robberies, the one at the house of Teunis Van Slyck, and the other at the house of Michael Halenbeek upon full proof. His execution is ordered on Saturday the eighth instant.

This Felon was apprehended last Sunday morning a few hours after the last Robbery was committed, by a party of Continental Troops.

From the best information, it appears that there are sculking in the woods in this county, on the west side of the River about fifty persons, whose designs are to continue their depredations on the Inhabitants for some time, and afterwards intend to join

the Enemy to the westward, I am, with the greatest respect,
Your Excellency's, most obedient and humble Servant,

Robert Yates.

His Excellency George Clinton Esqr.

———

[No. 2266.]

*Governor Clinton Approves of James Clinton's Expedition up the
Mohawk.*

Poukeepsie, 2d May, 1779.

Dear Brother, I was Favoured with your Letter of the 28th*
Ultimo yesterday Evening, & am extreamly happy to learn that
the Alarm which called you into Tryon County has not been attended with as much Distress & Injury to the Inhabitants as from
the Accounts first transmitted to me, I had reason to apprehend.
As the Security of the Frontier Settlements ag't the Depredations
of a Savage Enemy is an Object of the first Importance, I highly
approve of your establishing a Post at the Pass you mention, &
you may rest assured, that every Exertion will be made on my
Part, to expedite the compleating the Levies for filling up the
Continental Battallions & for the Defense of the Frontiers.

I am perswaded great Advantages will result from the late
fortunate & very Successfull Expedition against Anandaga, & it
cannot fail of reflecting high Honor on those who planned & executed it. I have Reason to hope it will secure our old Colonel that
Promotion to which he is intitelld & which has long been shame-
fully witheld from him. Holt will give the Account of it to the
Public Tomorrow in the best dress [the] Short intervening Time
will admit of. I have no news to communicate but such as the
public Papers afford. I shoud be happy if you coud dispose of the

Prisoners without sending them to me, as I know not where to be able to secure them.　I am yours, Affectionately,

G. C.

Genl. James Clinton.

———

[No. 2267.]

COMPLICATIONS IN VERMONT.

Committees from Nine Towns Oppose the Creation of the New State and Appeal to Governor Clinton.

To his Excellency George Clinton Esqr., Governor of the State of New York, General Commander in Chief of all the Militia, and Admiral of the Navy of the same.*

The Petition of the Committees of the Towns of Hinsdale, Guilford, Brattleborough, Fulham, Putney, Westminster, Rockingham, Springfield & Weathersfield, in Cumberland County, chosen for the Purpose of opposing the pretended State of Vermont, & convened at Brattleborough the 4th May 1779.

Humbly Sheweth; That there being a numerous Party in avowed Opposition to legal Authority, your Petitioners and others have been compelled to submit, though reluctantly, to live without the Benefits arising from a well regulated Government. They have been destitute of the regular means of punishing the most atrocious Offenders, & of compelling the Execution of private Justice.　In short they are, and for a long time have been, in such anarchy that even Committees, where they do exist, are without Power.

In this distracted State your Petitioners have waited, with much Impatience, the Lieusure of the Grand Council of the American Empire, to whose authority alone these deluded Men pretend Submission.　We had no Doubt, as we understood applica-

———
* For Governor Clinton's reply, see page 814.

tion had been made for the Purpose, but Congress would use the first moment they could spare from more important Concerns, to recommend to the revolted Subjects of the State, a return to their allegiance. We were encouraged to expect it, not only as this Revolt established a Precedent which might be dangerous in other States, and as the Continent could derive no assistance of Consequence from the Grants, either in Men or Money, while they remain under a disputed Government; But because the States had confederated for their mutual and General Welfare, and bound themselves to assist each other against all Force offered to, or attacks made upon any of them, on account of Sovereignty, or on any other Pretence whatsoever.

But to our very great Surprize and Concern, Congress have not, as we can learn, done any thing since the year 1776, in a matter of so great moment to the Peace and Harmony of the confederated States.

That the Partizans for a new State have confiscated & sold, and are selling, many valuable real and personal Estates.

That they have attempted repeatedly to exercise judicial and military authority over those who continue loyal to the State of New York; and have very lately had the assurance to take the Cattle of those who refuse to comply with their illegal Orders. They have also assessed, and endeavoured to collect Money from those who do not admit the Validity of their authority, and have been restrained only by force. In some Instances they have intimidated the Subjects of New York State to give up their Property, rather than to contend with them.

They have also made Prisoner of a Magistrate acting under authority of the State of New York, in a matter which no way concerned the Subjects of the pretended State of Vermont, and compelled him to give Bond, in the Penalty of one thousand Pounds lawful Money of New England, Conditioned for his appearance before their superior Court in June next.

In fine from the General Tenor of their Conduct, they now appear determined, at all Events, to enforce Submission to their Government.

That the Subjects of the State of New York here, cannot long endure their present unhappy Situation, and have only the State to which they owe allegiance, to look up to for Succour in this critical and calamitous Hour. The Protection of Individuals and their Property we esteem the principal End of Government: that Protection we have a right to claim in return for our allegiance: And we have besides the solemn Engagement of the Legislature, to concur " in the necessary measures for protecting the loyal Inhabitants of the State, residing in the Counties of Albany, Charlotte, Cumberland, & Gloucester, in their Persons and Estates."

Your Petitioners were in hopes that the disaffected Party would not have reduced them to the disagreable Necessity of applying for Protection during the Continuance of the War with Great Britain; But our present Circumstances loudly demand the speedy and effectual Execution of the Promise made by the Legislature: We shall otherwise be compelled to obey a Government which we view as an Usurpation, and add our Strength to oppose one which we conceive entitled to our dutiful Obedience and Support.

Your Petitioners, therefore, humbly, and in the most urgent & earnest manner, on behalf of themselves and their Constituents, entreat that your Excellency will take immediate and effectual Measures for protecting the loyal Subjects in this part of the State in their Persons and Properties; and to convince the honorable the Congress of the Impropriety of delaying a Publication of their Sentiments in a matter which so nearly concerns the Peace, Welfare, & probably the Lives, of many of their firm adherents. And your Petitioners, as in Duty bound, shall ever pray &c.

By order of the Committees.

Samuel Minott, Chairman.

Brattleborough 4th May 1779.

[No. 2268.]

Essex County, New Jersey, Officers Appeal to Governor Clinton to Procure the Exchange of Captain Joseph Crane.

To his Excellency George Clinton Esquire Governor, Captain General and Commander in Chief in and Over the State of New York and Territories &c.

We, the Subscribers, Inhabitants of the County of Essex, State of New Jersey, Beg Leave to acquaint you, That Capt. Joseph Crane Late of Clarks Town, Was Taken by the Enemy near Tapan Last fall, and we understand is now on Long Island, and has a Great Desire to be Exchang'd and Return home to his Family and be of Further Service to his Country. Therefore, we Humbly Petition your Excellency, that he be Exchanged as Soon as Possible: as he has been an Officer under the Command of his Excellency General Washington & after that, in the militia, during all which Time he has Proved himself to be a faithfull friend to his Country, a Good Officer and a brave Soldier.

And that your Excellency may Live to See our Enemies Intirely Defeated, the Blessing of Peace return, and injoy the Great

Happiness of Governing a Free and Independent People, your Humble Petitioners, as in Duty bound, Shall Ever Pray.

Philip V. Cortlandt, Con'l	Joseph Crane, Lieut.
Isaac Dod, Justice of peace	Jonathan Crane, Ins.
Caleb Dod, Major	George Harrison, Ajut.
Amos Dod, Captain	Jno. Range, Clerk.
Isaac Morrison, Cap.	Samuel Dod, Lieut.
Jed'h Chapman, V. D. M.	Frans Post, Ca't
Samuel Pierson, Capt.	

[May — 1779.]

General Washington Commends Governor Clinton's services.

Head-Quarters, Middlebrook, 3 May, 1779.

Dear Sir, I am honored with your favor of the 25th of last month. The readiness, with which you comply with all my requests in prosecution of the public service, has a claim to my warmest acknowledgments. I am glad to hear of the measures the State has taken for raising a thousand men, and of your expectation that the number would be soon completed. I hope the intelligence from Colonel Cantine will not materially retard the progress of a business, on which the general security of the frontier so much depends.

In a letter I have lately received from Mr. Duane, in behalf of the delegates of New York, he transmitted a packet received from you on the subject of frontier prisoners, under an idea that the general direction of prisoners was in my hands. There is a misconception in this, for I have never had any thing to do with any but military prisoners. The exchange of inhabitants has generally rested with the States to which they belonged. So far as these are concerned, therefore, I consider them out of my province.

With respect to military prisoners, under which description I comprehend all the officers and soldiers of the Continental army, and of the militia when taken in actual service, I shall be ready to concur with your Excellency in exchanging any such as may be in possession of the parties. In this, as to the officers, I must for the present confine myself to those taken on both sides on the frontier, according to the principle of equality of rank. When this is done, if any officers of ours remain in their hands, they must wait, till, in the rotation of exchanges and in the order of capture, it shall come to their turn to be exchanged. I observe by the list, that there are very few on either side. It will be agreeable to me, that such as cannot be exchanged on this plan shall be mutually released on parole. The enemy appear to have no privates of ours in their hands, so that no exchange can take place with regard to them. If they had any, we would very readily exchange; but I have made it a maxim, for obvious reasons, not to confound military prisoners and inhabitants, and consequently not to exchange them for each other. Dear Sir, yours, &c.

[To Governor Clinton.]
                                        [George Washington.]*

[No. 2269.]

Tryon County to Obtain a Special Court of Oyer and Terminer.

                                        4 May [1779].

Gentlemen, I have rec'd your Letter of the 30th Ulto.† A Commission of Oyer & Terminer shall immediately be issued for your County, to try the Criminals who you have been so fortunate as to apprehend, but as the Court is to meet in Orange County

---

* Not in Clinton collection. Taken from Sparks' Washington.
† See page 786.

this month, I do not think it probable the Judges will be able to attend in your County before the beginning of June. As I have no authority to order the Prisoners to be confined out of the County & your gaol being insuffic't to hold them I think the best thing that can be done is to keep them under their pres't Confinem't.

It is essential that you keep a watchful Eye over the Disaffected, for as long they are permitted to go at large, your Secrets will be betrayed & your Safety rendered extreamly dangerous. Yours &c.

Geo: Clinton.

Jacob Klock, Esqr. & others.

[Nos. 2270-2271.]

Another Raid on the Ulster Frontier.

Warwasink, May 4th 1779 4 O'Clock P. M.

Dear Sir, I am Sorry to Inform you that this morning just as I was marching my Regt., from this place I Rec'd an acc't that Several Houses were burnt at the Fantine Kill. I march'd to Intercept the Enemy which I Saw twice, but Could not Surround them, being on a mountain; when I Discovered them, we Exchainged Several long shot with them, but they have made their Escape; they have burnt four Houses (and Killed Six that we have Seen, and it is Supposed have Killed three or fore more of the Inhabitants); they have not hurt any of my men, nor have we Killed any of them, they being affraid to Ingage us; by a woman who they took prisoner and Released, it appears they are about 30 or 40 in number.

As I am under the most pressing orders to march with all Expidition, I send an Express to Inform you of what is happened, that you may give such further orders as you may think proper.

Colo. Cantine is gone to Lagawack, But I do not think above fifty of the men are arrived, which you have ordered, tho they may arrive tomorrow, but I believe not Enough. From y'r Hum'e Ser't

Philip Cortlandt.

His Excellency Governor Clinton.

The Governor Takes Immediate Action.

Newburgh May 5th 1779.

D'r Sir, I have this moment rec'd your favor of yesterd'y. I have ordered out ¼ part of Hardenbergh's & McClaughry's Regt., to join Colo. Cantine & the like proportion of the three northern Regts., of Orange to such Posts on the frontiers of that County as the command'g officers of those Regts., shall judge most Proper. Yrs. &c.

Geo: Clinton.

Colo. Cortlandt.

[No. 2272.]

The Governor Sends Instructions to Colonel Cantine.

New Burgh 5th May 1779.

D'r Sir, In consequence of a Letter which I have this moment received from Colo. Cortlandt I have issued my Orders for the ¼ part of Colo. Hardenbergh's & McClaughry's Regts. immediately to march & put themselves under your command. You will, therefore, make such disposition of them & the force which you already have as to give every possible Security to the frontier Inhabit'ts. Yrs. &c.

Geo: Clinton.

Colo. Cantine.

[No. 2273.]

COLONEL PATERSON SUGGESTS CIVIL WAR.

Unless the People of Vermont Acknowledge the Rights and Privileges of Citizens of New York.

Hinsdale May 5th 1779.

May it please your Excellency;* Some late Conduct of the Vermont Party, tending rapidly towards a civil War, obliges me to give your Excellency early Intelligence of it, and of our Proceedings in Opposition to them. That Party having ordered Capt. James Clay, Lieut. Benjamin Willson, and one Mr. Cummins (all acknowledged Subjects of New York, in Putney) to provide a man to go into Service for a short Space of Time, to guard the Frontiers; the Week before last forcibly took a Cow from Capt. Clay, and another from Mr. Willson, to pay a Person they had hired for them, and the Expences. Last Wednesday was the Day appointed for selling the Cattle, at which time myself & Field officers & a considerable Part of my Regiment met, all unarmed, to prevent the Sale. After vainly endeavouring, with Calmness, to convince them of the Impropriety of this Proceeding, and to perswade them to give up the Cattle, we took Possession of them, the owners drove them off, and every man returned to his Home.

In Fulham, some Persons, Subjects of New York, have lately had their Property taken from them by Direction of the Vermont Officers, and have acquiesced in it, rather than to contend. One other was also threatened with the like Usage; but since our retaking the Cattle in Putney, they have been quiet about it.

In Guilford, a Sum of Money was assessed upon those who were supposed to have done least in the War; the Persons who were to

* For Governor Clinton's reply, see page 814.

collect it, were, upon a Trial, frightened from it by those who oppose Vermont. In Westminster & Rockingham they have drafted some Yorkers; I fear it will not end without a Disturbance, as in those towns the Parties are nearly equal.

Colo. Fletcher, who commands the New State men in this Regiment, hearing that Men were raising to prevent selling the Cattle of Messrs. Clay and Willson, went over to their Council at Arlington, whether for Men or advice I cannot learn. But as Colo. [Ethan] Allen has repeatedly threatened us with his Green Mountain Boys, and some of that Party about here give out that this is only the beginning of the matter, and as they appear resolute to enforce Submission to their authority; many are fearful that what they have already done, has been in Pursuance of a General Plan for subduing all those who are in allegiance to New York.

In this distracted Situation, I would request your Excellency's particular Direction, how far, for the future, to proceed in Defence of the Persons & Property of those under my Command, and what Steps to take, if the Vermonters should attempt by force of arms, to seize the Persons or Property of such as do not acknowledge their authority?

As there is a Probability that Men may be sent from the West Side of the Mountains, to assist those here, I would beg leave to suggest to your Excellency, the Necessity of having the Militia of Albany County held in readiness to attack them, if they should gather with that Design. The Brigadier General of that County, may with ease have early Information of any Plan of the kind, by employing some of the Enemies of Vermont in their Towns, to give him Notice. What the Consequence will be of permitting

51

the Green Mountaineers to come here unmolested, may be easily foretold.

The Legislature having promised to protect the Persons & Property of their loyal Subjects in this part of the State; it has become their general Desire that Measures may be very speedily taken to fulfil that Engagement. And I hope your Excellency will pardon my saying that unless it can be speedily done, I must be under a Necessity of resigning my Commission.

There are near 500 Officers & Men under my Command, who are in general but poorly armed & provided with ammunition. I am not yet prepared to make an exact return to your Excellency, as some of my Captains have not yet returned the State of their Companies to me, & others have done it very informally.

The Field officers, having thought it for the Interest of the State to acquaint your Excellency with our present Situation, have prevailed upon Mr. Townsend to wait upon you. A few Individuals, have advanced his Expences, and agreed to pay for his Time and Horse hire; but as it is the Business of the State upon which he goes, it will be discouraging if he is not paid by the State. I am Your Excellency's most obedient Servant,

Eleaz'r Paterson.

His Excellency Governor Clinton.

[No. 2274.]

Returns of Wheat and Flour Found in Sundry Mills and Purchased by Henry and Paul Schenck.

Acc't of Flour & Wheat found in the Different Mills Purchased by Henry & Paul Schenck:

Time when purch'd
1779   Cask flour
March 6th 10 of Direk Hoogland at 9 £ pr C

6   17 of Obadiah Cooper at 9   Do

23   50 taken of Matthew V. Buntschotin 9 £ pr C   at Van Buntschoten's mill.

25   11¼ Bus. wheat at 8 Doll. pr bushel

29   25 Cask Flour of David Currie at 12 £ pr C

20   16 Do of Joh's Wiltsee at 12 £ pr C at J: Brinckerhoff's Mill

29   40 Do of Samuel Verplank at 12 £ pr C   Samuel Verplanck's Mill

29   28 Do of John Brinckerhoff   12   Do

29   24 Do of John Sickles at 12 £   Do   Corn's V. Sicklen's Mill

    9 Do of Mr. Elsworth at 12 £   Do   at Jno. Cook's Mill

    42 Do of Edward Howard at 9 £ at Thos. Notheway's Mill Beekman's Prec't

---

261 Cask Flour & 11¼ Bushel wheat.
The above is purchased by Henry Schenk.

18 Cask Flour in Daniel Hasbrook's Mill Purchased the Beginning of last Fall by Paul Schenk.

Hend'k Wyckoff.

Fishkill May 5th 1779.

[No. 2275.]

DRAFTS SLOW IN COMING UP.

James Clinton Forwards to the Governor, Lieutenant McClennan's Report of the Oswegatchie Expedition.

Albany, May 7th 1779.

D'r Sir, I am sorry to inform you that the Drafts from Genl. Ten Broeck's Brigade come in so very slow, that I fear they will not arrive before we march, which probably will be attended with some Inconveniencies. They are mustered as fast as they are received, but they are chiefly without arms, and very ill provided with Cloaths.

I woud beg the favour of you to request Col. Duboys to make hast up; he is much wanted; his Character, and his regiment, suffer by his absence, and no Letter from me is sufficient to bring him.

I have enclosed a Copy of Lt. McClennan's Discouveries at Oswegotchee, for your Inspection. With the greatest Esteem I am Yours &c.

James Clinton.

Gov'r Clinton.

McCLENNAN'S REPORT.

Fort Schuyler April 30th 1779.

Honoured Sir, I have the Pleasure to acquaint you that in pursuance of Col. V. Schaick's Orders of the 18th Instant, I left this Place on an Expedition to Oswegotchee, accompanied by Lt. Hardenbergh of the 1st N. Y. Regt., one Sergeant, one Corporal and thirty Privates; as there cou'd be no line of Conduct laid down on an Expedition like this, I suppose, was the reason, why the Col. did not give any written Instructions. However I hope you will have no reason to think, but that we have applyed the Party to the best advantage. On my arrival at Oswegotchee, was the 25th Instant, we sent three Indians to reconeiter the Garisson; in the mean time we discouvered an Indian canoe coming up Black River; we sent another Party after them, who took the canoes, and brought the Indians to us, whom we immediately examined, as you will see by the enclosed. By this time, the Indians we had sent to reconoiter the Garrison returned, & brought three British Prisoners, with them, who told us the same the Indians had done. We then moved with our Party nearer the Garrison; in the mean time our Van took another Prisoner, who told the same as the former. Here we were at a Stand what to do; to surprise the Garrison was impossible; so that after consulting the Indians, we agreed to try to get a party of them out, which we happily efected by making the Indians shew themselves in the Edge of the Woods. They sent a small party out; we then endeavoured to draw them as far as possible, but coud not, the Indians were so warm, that they had scarcely entered the Woods, before they began their firing; the Enemy retired without returning a Shot, leaving two Dead behind them. We pursued within sight of the Fort, but they gave us such a warm fire of artillery and musquetry as obliged us to retreat back to the woods; we then marched seven miles from the Garrison, & then encamped for the night. The next morning one of the Coughnawage Indians acquainted us, that he had a Letter written by the Marquis de la Fayette to the Canadians, in the French Language, dated the 10th December 1778, and that if we thought proper he woud now carry it to Canada; as we were so near, he agreed to leave his Son as an Hostage for his faithful performance; we agreed to send him & gave him these Instructions, that he shoud go to Coughnawago, & hear from his friends what the Enemy were doing in Canada, and if they thought it safe, he might proceed to Montreal, and return by the way of St. John's, taking particular notice of the Strength of the Enemy, to which he readily consented. We then collected what Provisions we coud spare and sent him off. We then made the best of our way to this Place which we reached this day. The Indians have insisted on taking the Prisoners to Oneida, but have promised to return them in a few Days. These, Sir, are the Perticulars of our Rout. I am, Sir, your very humb'e Serv't

Thos McClennan.

Copy.

The Examination of two Onondoga Indians taken Prisoners at Oswegotchee:

Qus'n 1st. How the State of Garrison of Oswegotchee was?

Ans'r. That the Garrison was commanded by Capt. Davis, with one Subaltern and forty men, with four pieces of Cannon.

Qus'n 2d. What news from Canada?

Ans'r. That they had received a Letter from the Comd'r in Chief at Quebeck, informing them, that he coud send them no Troops against the Rebles, this year. But that he intended to

send them a large army the next year, so that they must act only
on the Defensive at present.

Ques'n 3d. In what State the Garrison at Bush Island was?

Answ'r. That the last week he had left that place, and that
they were fortifying themselves. He farther said that the Garrison consisted of a few Regulars and Sir John's Regiment, making in the whole, not more than two hundred men, and that they
had a Disorder among them, of which they died very fast, & that
that and no Reason mad him & some others leave that place. He
farther says, that yesterday, Genl. Haldeman's Aide Camp passed
that Place, with orders to the Commanding Officers of the back
posts.

[No. 2276.]

THE SULLIVAN EXPEDITION.

*Governor Clinton Notifies the General of the Preparations Made by
New York State.*

Poughkeepsie 10th May 1779.

Dear Sir, I am honored with the Receipt of your confidential
Letter of the 29th Ulto. You may rely, Sir, on my affording all
the Assistance in my Power to render the intended Expedition
which you are to have the Honor of commanding, ag't the Indians
of the Six Nations, Successfull. The Legislature of this State
at their last meeting authorized me to raise by Drafts from the
militia 1000 men to be employed in the Defence of the western
Frontiers or such other Services as should be directed. The one
half of these will be applied towards filling up the continental
Battalions raised under the Direction of this State. The Residue
are intended for the Protection of the northern & such of the

western frontier Settlements as will not derive immediate Security by the operations ag't the Six Nations, and every possible
exertion will be made on my Part to have them ready to take
the field in due Season. It is unnecessary to remark that Business of this kind, conducted by militia Officers, is at best not attended with as much Expedition as cou'd be wished; but add to
the Delay which is occasioned by their inactivity & want of
knowlege, the present Service has been much retarded by frequent alarms on the frontiers of Ulster & Orange Counties which
have hitherto deprived the militia of those Counties from paying
the necessary attention to their Duty.

The Legislature have made the most effectual Provision for
enabling the Commissaries to procure an immediate Supply of
Flour for the Army. I flatter myself, therefore, we shall experience no inconvenience for the want of Bread; if a sufficient Quantity of meat is not already provided, it must be had from Connecticut. I am, Dear Sir, yrs. &c.

Geo: Clinton.

The Hon'ble Major Genl. Sullivan.

[No. 2277.]

Isaac Davis Forwards Intangible Rumors.

Kingston May 11th 1779.

These are the Inteligence I Can Give from the Indians after
they Retured from Shandaken; they was to Go to fitch Brandt
with his Company to Come Down this Quarter, Burn & Distroy
where Ever they Come; their first attempt was to Be at Schohery
from Butler; that, they Suposed would Draw the melitia their;
then Brant would Come Down this way to Marbletown, Hurley,
Kingston, Churchland, &c.; a Report I have heard that they want

to Gether all the Tories they Can, for fear if they Should be Beaten of, the Indians Should turn their arms against them. These Informations I have Received from my wife; from who She has it, I Dont know, But the whole to Remain a Secrit.

Isaac Davis.

[To G. C.]?

[No. 2278.]

Stephen Lush's Receipts for funds for the Frontier Sufferers.

Albany May 12th 1779.

Received from Jacob Cuyler, Esqr., for His Excellency Governour Clinton One thousand Eight hundred pound Currency. £1800.   Stephen Lush Secry.

To be repaid to Mr. Cuyler's Order on his Excellency in Favor of Mr. Cuyler's Deputy at Kingston.

S. L.

Rec'd from Jacob Cuyler, Esqr., for his Excellency Gov'r Clinton, two hundred & fifty Pounds N. York Currency. £250.   Stephen Lush, Secry.

Rec'd of Mr. Cuyler 200 Pounds for Gov'r Clinton. May 18th, 1779.

Stephen Lush,
Jacob Cuyler.

[No. 2279.]

John Frey's Receipt for £1800, to Stephen Lush.

Received, from his Excellency Governor Clinton by the Hands of Stephen Lush Esqr. Eighteen hundred Pounds to be distributed by myself and John Fonda, Esqr., among such Persons as have been distressed by the Incursions of the Enemy into Tryon

County and are now incapable of gaining a Livelihood agreable
to an act of the Legislature in such Case made & provided.

John Frey.

Albany May 12" 1779.

[No. 2280.]

*George Clinton Gives Directions for the Distribution of the £1800
Among the Tryon County Sufferers.*

To John Fonda and John Frey Esquires:

Gentlemen: You have in your Hands Eighteen hundred Pounds,
which you will distribute to such Persons now incapable of gaining a Livelihood, as have been distressed by the incursions of the
Enemy into Tryon County, in such Proportion as you think will
best answer the Intentions of the Legislature and tend to the
Relief of the Sufferers. For these Purposes, you will make the
strictest Inquiry as to the Persons & their Circumstances, who
are the Objects of the Law, with the least possible Delay, and
when you distribute the Money, take proper Receipts for the
same, and after the whole Business is completed, transmit them
with an account of your Proceedings to his Excellency, the Governor, to be laid before the Legislature.

May 12, 1779.

[No. 2281.]

CORNERING BREADSTUFFS.

*Mr. Watson as an Inspector Files an Interesting Report with
Governor Clinton.*

Sir: At the request of the Commissary Genl., I have been into
Salisbury, Berkshire-County, & the parts of this State adjacent;
to inquire into the state of the Flower-trade & whether an immediate supply could be procured for the eastern department where
there is a great deficiency.

Upon examination I find that a number of private Purchasers, belonging to each of these States, have, by paying for some, contracting for more, & offering a higher price for all; acquired almost the entire disposal of all the grain & Flower in that quarter; & have in fact run great quantities out of this State into Connecticutt & Massachusetts, notwithstanding all the vigilance & severity that has been used. I am informed that Flower has latly been sold in Sheffield from 20 to £25 L. M. Pr Ctm. In Connecticut, it is £20 pr Ctm when Seized & apprized, by men under Oath, it has been that price. The great distinction between these prices has enabled Private Purchasers to out-bid the Public ones in this State & run their risque, which together with the disaffection occasioned by Seizing has prevented the Commissaries in these parts from procuring the necessary Supplies. Upon this view of the case, I proposed to the Com'y Genl., to make use of these Private Purchasers & take all they had & all they could procure off their hands at their own price, which is 50 Doll'rs pr Ctm.

In this way it appears probable that a very considerable & immediate supply might be obtained, the designs of raising it frustrated, the inconveniences of seizing avoided (& as I immagine) the price eventually lowered & a considerable saving made to the Continent.

The Com'y Genl. has referred me to your Excellency, but since I am so unfortunate as not to find you at home, would request that your instructions might be forwarded to him at Hartford where they will be immediately Rec'd & obeyed By Your Excellency's Obdt. & very Hum'e Ser't

J. Watson.

Poughkeepsie May 12th 1779.

N. B. It is proved that the Flower should be rec'd in this State & the Purchasers have no permitts to transport it out.

[No. 2282.]

Fort Dayton Again Attacked by Indians and Tories.

Albany, May 13th, 1779.

Dear Brother; Inclosed I send you a Copy of a letter from the Commanding Officer at Fort Herkemer, by which you will see that the savages have not yet forgot to thirst for Blood. It appears that Colonel Bellinger was requested to furnish the guides to the Parties who were Ordered to pursue them, which he declined.

I did not conceive that there would be any Occasion for the militia as the Drafts from Tryon County were ordered to Assemble at Fort Dayton under the Command of Lieut. Smith, except those of Colonel Visscher's Regiment which I ordered to the Block house, at Sackendauga as Guides to Colonel Dubois' Regiment.

The Drafts continue to come in but very slow, and those who do come in, are possesed with notions of Joining a Regt., by themselves which occassions much Difficulty.

I have reason to believe they are encouraged by Genl. Ten Broeck, as he informed me that he received a letter from you which seemed to Justify such encouragement.

There are a few Ensigns appointed in the fourth New York Regt., who can not be commissioned without your approbation, which I beg you would give to Colonel Dubois, who will wait on you for the Purpose. I am, D'r Brother, y'r very hum. ser't,

James Clinton.

To His Excellency, Gov'r Clinton, Poughkeepsie.

CAPTAIN DAY'S REPORT.

Fort Herkimer, May 11th, 1779.

Dear Genl., On 10th Inst. the Inhabitants at Fort Dayton was alarmed by the Enemy, on which Occasion I dispatched a Lieut.

and twenty odd men to their assistance, but before the Party had time to get to the fort, the Indians had taken five scalps and one Prisoner, and made their Escape and by the best Intelligence, the party consisted of about twelve or thirteen Indians and three Tories.

The officer that went with the party, desired Colonel Bellinger to send some pilots with him and he would Pursue them, but he declined sending them. I likewise sent an Officer after that, to see if he would send as I thought might be overtaken, But the Colonel still declined sending men, and my men were unacquainted with that part of the Country, therefore, I thought best not to send alone.

On the 10th, likewise, Capt. Graham arrived at this Garrison, which informs us that there had been a Party of Twenty four Indians discovered about ten miles from the Old Indian Castle, but they have not done any Damage in this Quarter as yet. I am, sir, with due Respect and Esteem, your hum. servant,

Luke Day, Capt. Commanding.

Genl Jas. Clinton, Albany.

A true Copy.

[No. 2283.]

Copy of a Pass Signed by the British Lieutenant-General, Jones.

By Lieutenant General Jones, Commandant of New-York:

Permission is given to Thomas Cloudsal, to pass with a Flag of Truce up Hudson's River in the sloop Henry, navigated by Thomas Barker, master, and the two hands named in the margin (Gilbert Conklin, Isaac Burr) for the purpose of carrying out such Persons as have passes, and in return to bring to this City the Family and Effects of Mr. Samuel Mabbit, Mrs. Harrison, Sen'r,

& George Harrison, her Nephew with their Effects.   The Family and Effects of Richard Harrison, Esqr., Mrs. Allan McDonald (of Collachie [Colonie] above Albany) with her Family & Effects, Mrs. Conroy, with her Family & Effects, Mrs. Elizabeth Skadon, with her Family and Effects, Mrs. McGuin, her Family, and Effects, Miss Nancey Asscough, Miss Willemintie Anthony, Mr. George Wood, & Mrs. Bennett with their Effects, and Also the House Hold Furniture of Mr. James Peters.

Given under my Hand & seal in the city of New-York the thirteenth Day of May 1779.

D. Jones Lt. Gen.

By Order of the Commandant John LeRoome, Secr'y. To all whom it may concern. Copy.

Places where the Persons are to be found mentioned in the annexed Flag.

Mr. Mabbit's Family—Nine Partners, Dutchess County.

Richard Harrison's Family,—at Bell Mount, near Goshen, Mrs. Harrison & her Nephew at the same place.

Mrs. Allan McDonald & her Family—At Collachie, above Albany or at Schenectady at Mr. Ellis's.

Mrs. Conroy, the Wife of Patrick Conroy—In Dutchess County.

Mrs. Skadden & her Family—At Campbell Hall, Ulster County.

Miss Nancey Ayscough—At Mr. Richard Langdon's, Murderers Creek.

Miss Willemintie Anthony—At Mr. Nich's W. Anthony's Poughkeepsie—Or John W. Vredenburgh's at Red Hook.

Mrs. McGuin & her Family—The Wife of Daniel McGuin at Mabrough Precinct, Ulster County.

Mr. George Wood & Mrs. Bennet at Nine Partners Dutchess County.

[No. 2284.]

THE VERMONT MATTER.

Governor Clinton Advises Mr. Minott to Act with Firmness and Prudence—Confident that Every Effort will be Made to Secure a Decision from Congress.

Kingston 14th May 1779.

Sir, I am honored with the Receipt of your Petition* together with a Letter from Colo. Paterson† on the Subject of the unhappy Disturbances which still prevail in the North-Eastern Parts of the State.

I have anxiously expected for some time the Determination of Congress upon this important matter and have every Reason to believe it will be favorable to the State of New York. The Business has, however, been deferred, tho' I am confident from no other Cause than that the attention of Congress has hitherto been called to Objects of greater Moment. I shall, notwithstanding, immediately transmit to them, by Congress, your Petition, and urge every argument in my Power to induce them speedily to determine this Controversy and by a seasonable Interposition to prevent if possible, the dreadful Consequences of having Recourse to arms.

As in my former Letters, so in this I forbear to point out the Line of Conduct I could wish the well affected Inhabitants in your Quarter should observe, upon every particular Occasion. I conceive it impossible and, therefore, can only recommend in general, Firmness and Prudence, and in no Instance to acknowledge the Authority of Vermont unless where there is no alternative left between Submission and inevitable Ruin. This appears to me the only proper advice I can give at present, till we are

---

*See page 792.
† See page 800.

favored with the Sentiments of Congress relative to the Dispute or untill we are convinced the Business is designedly procrasti- nated; in either Case as the Legislature have promised, so I have no doubt but that they will afford you Protection, and that effectual measures will be immediately taken for vindicating the Rights of this State, and enforcing a due Submission to legal Government. If, however, any Outrage or Violence, which you may suppose, will produce Blood-shed, should be committed in the Towns continuing in their allegiance to New York, either by the Green Mountain Boys or any Parties who may come under a pretence of carrying into Execution the Laws of Vermont, you will immediately apprise me of it, and you may be assured of all the assistance in my Power, and I trust it will be sufficient for your Safety and Defence; in the meantime, I will myself en- deavour to procure Intelligence, and if I should discover that any attempt will be made by Vermont to reduce you by force of arms, I will instantly issue my Orders to the militia who are properly equipped, and who will be led ag't the Enemies of the State, whoever they may happen to be. From the Information of Mr. Townsend, I perceive that Mr. Grout acquits the Officer who ap- prehended him, from having acted wrong intentionally; should this, however, upon Enquiry appear not to have been the Case, you will please to acquaint me with it and I will immediately have them brought to Justice.

As Mr. Grout is bound in Honor to indemnify the Gentleman who became his Surety, I would recommend that he should ap- pear at the Court agreeable to his Recognisance, and make no other Defence, than merely to deny their Jurisdiction, and as the Injury he may sustain in Consequence must be considered as a Sacrifice to the Common Cause, I might almost venture to assure him that the Legislature will make him proper Compensation. Justice most certain requires it.

I have desired Mr. Townsend to send me an account of his Expences upon this Errand, and I will lay it before the Legislature for Payment.

From the Confidence I have in the Gentlemen who represent this State in Congress, and particularly the Chief Justice, who was elected for the special purpose, I am perswaded, that every means will be used for obtaining the Decision of Congress relative to this Dispute and, therefore, I could ardently wish that the Inhabitants of Vermont would conduct themselves in such manner as to avoid the Necessity of bringing matters to a Crisis, ruinous to them and very injurious to Individuals among us.

You will please to communicate the Contents of this to Col. Paterson. I am, with great Respect, your most obed't Serv't,

Geo: Clinton.

Saml. Minott Esqr.

[No. 2285.]

Samuel Mabbitt Makes an Appeal to Governor Clinton.

New York, May 14th, 1779.

May it Please the Governour; Before I left Home I did myself the Honour of Calling upon thee and Received thy promise that my Family Should be sent to me whenever I applied for them. Such was their Situation last Autumn, owing to the Illness of one of my Children, that it became Impossible for it then to be Removed, but I have not the least doubt that thee will now Permit me to enjoy the pleasure of seeing Persons so dear to me, as I have Obtained a Flag for the purpose of bringing them down, Likewise grant them Equal Indulgence with others in mine and their Situation; upon this occasion I flatter myself that even Exclusive of thy promise I might trust To the Sentiments of Humanity for what will so much Oblidge thy Friend,

Saml. Mabbitt.

P. S. I have sent for my Wife, three Children and a Small apprentice Boy, a Son of my Sister's, who Humbly Intreats thee will permit him to Come.

S. M.

[To G. C.]

[No. 2286.]

The Wheat Situation in Lower Orange County.

Orange-Town, May 15th, 1779.

Sir, I have not been able as yet to purchase more than twenty four Barrels Flour and about two Hundred Bushels Wheat, I find neither room nor necessity of impressing, as the people as far as I can find, have not as much as the law allows for the Support of their Families; yet out of what they have they spare as much or more than Could be expected. Mr. Reynolds has engaged for what I have; he has paid part and promised to pay the remainder in a few days. Mr. John Hooglandt, who is an assistant to Mr. Reynolds, this day Confirmed what I had before heard, to wit, that they would not pay the persons from whom they had taken—* wheat, for such wheat, and Mr. Hooglandt insists that the farmers have no right to expect it.

I also beg leave to mention that I [have]* it from good Authority, that Messrs. Reynolds and Hooglandt have forced away so much wheat from some of the inhabitants as has distressed them. Mr. Hendrick Jos. Blauvelt whose family Consists of six or seven persons had about one Bushel left him.

Mr. Douwe Tallman, who was Stabbed by the Tories last Sunday morning, Died of his wounds on Tuesday last; he wanted but a few weeks of being Ninety years. I am, Sir, Your Very Humble Serv't

John Haring.

To His Excellency, George Clinton, Esq., Governor of the State of New York &c., Poughkeepsie.

---

* MSS. torn.

[No. 2287.]

A Guard Asked for the Frontier of Northern Ulster County.

To His Excellency George Clinton, Esqr., Governor and Comander in Chief of all the Militia of the State of New York and Admiral of the Navy of the same.

The Petition, of the principal well affected Inhabitants of the most northerly part of Ulster County, Humbly Sheweth:

That, whereas, after having Sincerely consider'd our present Situation, we find that we live in a very Dangerous part of this State; many Disaffected Persons among us, and a Savage Enemy Dayly on our weakly Guarded frontiers; and whereas, four young men out of our Nighbourhood, who have lately Engaged in the Eight months Service, are gone off, and Joyned without Doubt the Enemy, they will Discover unto them, our present weak Situation, for the Small Guard at Woodstock is in no State to our Safety; for this minute we are alarmed, and Called out to the Blue mountains, for the Enemies are making their approach on our Quarter, as we Supose, will take their Revange on us, because a few Disaffected Persons have been Sent under Guard to Kingston, out of our Nighbourhood. In any General Alarm, when the militia is Called forth in Defence of this State, the well affected men turn out, and the Disaffected Persons remain at home; as witnesseth the late alarm in every such Case. Our Families and Effects are greatly Exposed, for some of our militia Men are gone to Nepenak, some are at Woodstock, and if more men Should be Continually Called, our Farming Business must be neglected, to the great Loss of this State, and we fear much, if we be not Timely assisted, Shall be obliged to flight, and leave our all to a Savage Enemie.

Therefore, We, the Subscribers, most humbly approach your Excellency with this our humble Petition, imploring your Protection in Sending a Reinforcement of Fifty or Sixty men out of Dutches County, and to Station them at the Blue Mountains, at and near Tobias Wynkoop's, for Such a Guard will be most handy, when Station'd as above said, either to reinforce the present Guard at Woodstock, or assist us in Time of need,

Sir, We do not presume, to prescribe unto your Excellency how to prodect this State, but knowing your Excellency's Mind can not at once be every where, makes us approch you with these presents, not Doubting your aid,

Sir, That Divine Providence may Bless and prolong your Days and give Success to your Endeavours to Suppress our Savage Enemy, we Shall Ever pray.

John Christian Fiero,
Christian Fiero,
Yurry Wm. Regtmeyer,
Jurry Hommel,
Johannes Folck,
Johannes Rechtmeyer,
Ludwigh Roessell,
Christian Fiero, jun'r,
Petrus Backer,
Stephen Fiero,
Christiaen Snyder,
Petrus Myer,
Johannis Persen,
Cornelius Persen,
Matthew Dederick,
Peter Eygener,
Wm. Emerich,
Salomon Schut,
Jacobus Dederick,
Jury William Dederick,
William Falk,
Peter P. Eygener,

Christian Will,
Jeremiah Snyder,
Petrus Emrich,
Benjamin Snyder,
John L. DeWitt, Capt.,
Peter Oosterhoudt, Lu.,
Ephraim Myer,
Cornelius Dewitt,
Abraham Low, J.,
John Langandyck,
Peter T. Myer,
Jacobus Whitaker, jun'r.,
Peter Myer, Jr.,
Jacop Frans,
John Cox, Jun'r.,
Corn'ls Langendyck,
Tunis Myer,
Philip Feltan,
Tunis Ousterhout,
James Winne,
Will'm DeWitt,

May ye 15th 1779.

[No. 2288.]

GEORGE CLINTON PRAISES GENERAL SCHUYLER.

And Trusts Arrangements will be Made that the Delegates in Congress May Relieve One Another in Their Attendance.

Poukeepsie, 15th May, 1779.

Dear Sir, I ought to appoligize for having so long delayed acknowledging your Favour of the 21st of March. Charged with a variety of Important Business at the rising of the Legislature, which required Dispatch & almost daily interrupted by Accounts of the Depredations of the Enemy & the consequent Alarms on the Western Frontier, I have been deprived of the least Leissure for Friendly Correspondence.

It afforded me great Pleasure to learn that Genl. Schuyler was to continue in the Military Line, as his Country might justly expect Important Advantages from his Services, especially in the Prosecution of the intended Operations ag't the Hostile Savage Tribes, for, exclusive of his superior abilities & Experience, his General Knowledge of the Western Country & of the Manners of those People, woud have given him great Advantages in the Command of such an Expedition. But by a Letter I lately had the Honor of receiving from the General, I am informed that his Resignation is since accepted.

I am much oblidged to you for so full a Communication of your Sentiments respecting the Western Boundaries of the State, & the Advantages which we have a Right to expect from the Success of the American Arms in that Quarter, & I must intreat that you will occassionally continue to give me your Thoughts on every other Matter wherein the Honour & Interest of the State may be concerned.

I dare hardiy venture to pronounce what the Sentiments of the

Majority of the People with respect to an Additional Tax. Our last was very high, & I suppose if it had been as faithfully assessed & collected in the other Counties, as it has in this (which I [am] informed however is not the Case) it woud have ammounted to near double the Sum required by Congress. In this County alone it is upwards of £150,000. A majority of the People with whom I have conversed on this Subject & especially the most Sensible, are for repeating the Tax until the Credit of our Paper Currency is restored. Those who object to Taxation alledge, that the Credit of the Money is already too far sunk to be appreciated by any ordinary Means. Every man has become a Financier & of Course we have numberless Plans for paying off our Debts & restoring the Credit of our Money. You have doubtless seen the Real Farmer's Plan, published in Holt's Paper; it had at first many Advocates tho' I believe few at present.

I am very sensible, Sir, that after so long an absence from your Familly in the steady Attention to the Duties of your Office, it is but reasonable that you shoud have the Relaxation you desire. But, as I have not any Directions from the Legislature on the Subject, & as there is no other Delegate whom I can call upon to relieve you, I can only lay your Request before them, which shall be faithfully done as soon as they meet. I flatter myself that they will give such Directions as to obviate in future the Difficulties you now labor under, by fixing the Rotine of Duty, that you may relieve each other at convenient Periods, as well as encrease the present allowance, so as that it may be at least equal to the expence attending the Service. I am, &c.

Geo: Clinton.

The hon'ble James Duane, Esqr.

[Private.]

[No. 2289.]

Major-General McDougall Ordered to Albany to Report to General James Clinton.

Head Quarters Peckskill May 15th 1779.

Sir, I have this moment received Orders from the Commander in chief for the New Levies, which might be collected at these Posts, to proceed to Albany, there take the Orders of Brigadier General James Clinton.

You will, therefore, immediately on Receipt of this, proceed there with the New Levies under your Command; and apply to Colonel Hay, D. Q. M. Genl. at Fishkill for Boats to transport the men and Baggage. I am, sir, Your humble servant

Alex'r McDougall, M. General.

The Officer commanding the New Levies at Fishkill.

[No. 2290.]

Commissary Commissioner James Hunter Makes a Report to Governor Clinton.

Nuburgh, ye 15th May, 1779.

Honored S'r, I Recved you Letter and Appointment to Purchase Wheat and Flour for the Use of the army and Fronteers and Imediately acted Upon it, but with Little Success. I have Collected about the value of one thousand Bushels of wheat, or flouer, that will be Equvelent thereto, but I find Difficulty in getting Casks to Pack it in. The Coopers Insists on having the Price agreable to the price of the Wheat, which I think is rather Extravegant, but have promised them the price that you would Direct me to give. I, therefore, am Desiros that you would be pleased to Regulate the price of the Grinding and Casks, and Let me know as Soon as Convenient, and it will Settle the mater, and prevent Grumbling; there is Several farmours that Choses to

Grind their own Wheat, and as soon as I get their Returns, I will Render you a perticuler acount of the whole of my Proceedings, in the mater.   So I am with all Due Reverance, & Respect, your most Humble Serv't

James Hunter.

To His Exelency George Clinton.

[No. 2291.]

Major Van Benscoten Receives His Orders to March to the Ulster County Frontiers Without Delay.

Poughkeepsie 15th May 1779.

Sir, I am directed by his Excell'cy the Governor to request, that you will march such of the Levies as are in readiness, to the frontiers of Ulster County without the least Delay, those of Orange, had better rendezvous at Pienpack, & those of Ulster & Dutchess at Mamacotting, Shandaken & Laghawagh, at the two latter of which Places there are Posts ordered to be established. Colo. Cantine is possessed of his Excell'cys orders on the Subject.

Dr. John Smedes who is appointed Surgeon to the Regt., will wait on you for medicine, You will, therefore, procure a proper supply for him from the Director of the Hospital at Fishkill who, as the Regt. is to be paid & subsisted by the cont't, will furnish you, therewith.   I am &c.

Robt. Benson.

Major Van Buntschoten.

[No. 2292.]

DEFICIENCY IN TWO REGIMENTS OF LEVIES.

Governor Clinton Threatens to Put Two Colonels in Arrest, Unless the Full Quota is Made.

Rochester, May ye 15th 1779.

Dear Sir; I have this day meet with the Inhabitauts of this town in order to git Carages and tools to Begin the Works at

Lackawack with which they have Cherefully furnished me, the troops at this post at present are as follows Viz.

	men for Eight months:
Colo. Hardenbergh	30
Colo. McClaughree	24
Duches County	26
Cantine	31
tottle	111

out of which, I Have Sent a Lieut. & 26 to Mammacoting, 20 to guard the Stores at Brown in Warwasinck; with ye Remainder I shall march to Lackawack, which will Be on Monday morning; the one forth of my Regiment Except those who Live on the out Skirts of ye frunteers, will Be about fifty men, with which will also march on Said Day to Lackawack; the one forth of Colo. Hardenbergh which when ordered out Consists of 28 men, Colo. McCloughrie's 15 men, who Say they are ordered out for a fortnight. I am with Esteem, Sir, your most obedient Ser't

George Clinton, Esqr.   John Cantine.

GOVERNOR CLINTON'S REPLY.

[May 16, 1779.]

Sir, I have received your Favour of yesterday & observe the Deficiency in the Levies from Colo. McClaghry's & Hardenbergh's Regiment. I, therefore, desire you will immediately send an Officer to demand of those Regiments their full Quota, & if an Immediate Compliance is not made, I will on your Report thereof order the Delinquent Officers in arrest. I have refered a Petition of the Inhabitants of Nepenagh to you with some Directions thereon & am with great Regard your most Obed't Ser.

[G. C.]

Some more of the Levies from this County will march this Day. Mr. DeWitt tells me that a Post might be taken at a Pass not quite so far West as Legeweck more conducive to the Genl. Security. He will wait upon you & explain to you the Spot he means, & his Reasons on the Subject, & if they agree with your own, Colo. Pawling's & Squire Hardenbergh's & other principal Inhabitants, I woud in that Case give it the preference.

[To Col. Cantine.]

[No. 2293.]

Governor Clinton Asks Sir Henry Clinton to Permit the Wives of Captured American Officers to Visit Them in New York.

Poughkeepsie 15th May 1779.

Sir: Mrs. Allison, Mrs. McClaughry, Mrs. Logan & two other Ladies, have my permission to visit their Husbands who are among prisoners taken at Fort Montgomery. I have no reason to doubt but your Excellency on their arrival at your advanced post, will give such directions as will facilitate their design, & secure to them this reasonable & Common Indulgence.

I am induced, however, by their Importunity to trouble your Excellency on this Occasion, as they attended last Summer three weeks at Elizabeth Town, for the like purpose, but from the Situation of affairs at that Time, it was not thought expedient to suffer them to proceed, unless they could consent to continue with their Husbands, which the Situation of their Families would not admit of.

I have only to add, should your Excellency think proper to permit their Husbands or either of them to accompany them on their return to visit their Families, from my personal knowledge of the Gentlemen, I may venture to assure you, they will faithfully comply with such restrictions as they may [be] put under, and punctually return at the time appointed. I have the Honor to be, with due Respect, Your Excellency's Most Obed't Serv't,

[G. C.]

His Excellency, Leut. Genl. Sir Henry Clinton.

The Bearer Mrs. Allisson, wife of Colo. Allisson, has Permission to pass to visit her Husband a Prisoner in New York or on Long Island & to return here again unmollested. Given at Poughkeepsie, this 15th Day of May, 1779.

Mrs. McClaghry, Wife of Colo. McClaghry

Mrs. Logan,   "   Major Logan

Mrs. Halsted,   "   Lieut. Halsted

Mrs. Brewster,   "   Lieut. Brewster

[No. 2294.]

Captain Robert North's Flag of Truce.

By his Excellency, George Clinton, Esqr., Gov'r of the State of New York &c. &c. &c.

Permission is hereby granted to Capt. Robert North to proceed with a flag of Truce to New York in the Sloop ——— navigated by the said Robert North, & the hands mentiond in the margin, for the purpose of conveying thither the wives of Colo. Allison, Colo. McClaughry, Major Logan, Lieut. Halsted & Lieut. Brewster, Prisoners in New York or on Long Island, to visit their Husbands, & Mrs. McMenomy to attend them, together with the following Persons, vizt. Mrs. Byvanck, with her furniture, wearing apparel & Bedding, & a small negro Girl, in exchange for the wife of Uriah Mitchel, now on Long Island with her family & Effects, Elizabeth Duncan, for the Child of Morris Hazard, now with its Grandfather Ab'm Schenck on Long Island, Mrs. McFarren & her Daughter with their furniture, wear'g apparel, & Bedding & a small negro Girl, in exchange for such women in New York or on Long Island, as have Husbands in the Country, & who may incline to come out. Given under my Hand at Poughkeepsie, this 16th Day of May, 1779.

By his Excellency's Command.

Orders for Capt. Robt. North.

Capt. North with the Flag of Truce this Day granted, will be careful that no abuses are committed thro' the Medium of his Flag & on his Return, he is to bring no Person out, but such as shall have the Gov'rs Permission to return, or such others as may be sent out on Exchange; neither is he to suffer to be brought out in his Sloop any Articles of merchandize.

[No. 2295.]

Sheriff Nicoll Vouches for Downing, a Suspect.

Goshen May 16th 1779.

Dear S'r, It Gives me pleashure that the person you Sent Over to Sound Mr. Downing, has Don his duty, affectually, and I now have Reson to thinck Mr. Downing is not the Man we Expected him to be. I yesterday Returned from the New Citty, and Immedietly on my Comming home, Mr. Downing wated on me, and Informed me that there was One Campbell, at McQuier's, which he Supposed to be a Dangerous person and Gave me his Reasons, which makes me beleve him to be an Honesst Man; from your Humble Servant

Isaac Nicoll.

N. B. Mr. Harper Desiered me to let the Bairer have what money he wanted and I have let him have 100 Dolers.

To His Excellencey, George Clinton, Esqr., Governor &c. &c. &c. of the State New York.

[No. 2296.]

CLINTON DEPLORES SCHUYLER'S RESIGNATION.

And Explains Why Military Operations are Hindered in New York State.

Poukeepsie, 16th May, 1779.

Dear Sir; I have received your Letters of the 29th Ultimo & 3d Instant, the latter inclosing the Orders to Capt. Stockwell.* I am much oblidged to you for the Judicious Disposition you have made of the Company under his Command as well as for your Sentiments respecting the other Posts necessary to be occupied for the Security of the Northern Frontier. The Dilatory Time of many of the Militia officers & the Obstructions which the Service unavoidably meets from frequent Alarms on the Western Frontiers, greatly retards the raising of the Levies ordered for filling up the Continental Battallions, & the Defence of the Frontiers as soon they are compleated & the Frontier Settlements rendered more secure by the Opperations of our Army to the Westward, I hope I shall be able to detach a competent Force to the Passes you mention; in the mean Time I have requested my Brother to employ Capt. McKeans Company of Genl. Ten Broeck's Brigade, which shoud consist of near 100 Men & the Levies of Tryon County in that Service.

I shoud have been happy if you coud, consistent with your Honor, have consented to continue in the Military Line, at least the Ensuing Campaign, as I am perswaded the Continent at large & this State in particular, woud have derived Important Advantages from your Services; & more especially the Opperations intended to the Westward to be pursued. The friendly Tender you make me of your Services demands my most greatful Thanks. I

---

* See page 779.

shall always esteem it a Happiness, to have your advice & assistance. I am &c.

Geo: Clinton.

The hon'ble Philip Schuyler Esqr.

[No. 2297.]

DELAYS IN FILLING NEW ORGANIZATIONS.

Schoharie District the Most Exposed—Extirpation of the Savage the Only Guarantee for the Security of the Frontier in the Opinion of Governor Clinton.

Poughkeepsie, 16th May 1779.

Dear Sir, Since my last I have been favoured with your three Letters of the 7th* 8th† & 13th‡ Instant the two first were delivered to me on my Way to Kingston, whither I was called by an Alarm occassioned by the Appearance of about 100 Indians & Tories at Great Shandeacon. They were joined at that Place by 27 Tories, chiefly Hesian Deserters, from the Convention Troops, & soon after disapeared without doing any Misschief. The latter was handed me by Colo. Du Bois yesterday Evening. General Ten Broeck has my most positive Orders to compleat, with all possible Dispatch, the Levies from his Brigade for filling up the Continental Battallions & for the Defence of the Frontiers &c. By the enclosed Copy of a Letter wrote to him by Colo. Benson after I left Home for Kingston, you will learn what Proportion of them are to be annexed to the Continental Battallions. The residue exclusive of the 73 who are ordered to Charlotte County under Capt. Stockwell are to be commanded, until the Regiment is formed, by Capt. McKean & stationed, either at Schohary or on the Frontiers of Tryon & Albany Counties, as you may judge

----

*See page 803.
†Not found.
‡See page 811.

most conducive to the safety of the Frontier Settlements. Tho from the best Accounts, I have been able to collect, I judge Scho- hary to be most exposed, especially while your Troops continue at or near the Place of Rendevouz appointed for them, & even for some short Time after they march from thence.

I inclose you the Account of one Davis* who lives at Little Shandeacon with respect to the Hostile Intentions of the Enemy ag't Schohary & the Settlem'ts of Ulster County. The Levies from the other Counties are in considerable forwardness & I flat- ter myself will be soon compleated. I have ordered those to ren- devouz at Peenpack, Legeweck & Shandeacon (at the two latter of which Places I have ordered posts to be taken & some Works of defence to be erected), a small Part of them having already arived at these Places & others are on their March. The moment they assemble I will order such Part of them as are designed for filling up the Continental Battallions to be detached, & marched to join the respective Regts. The whole Number intended for this Purpose is 500, but making the ordinary allowances for Deficiencies in the Regts., who are to furnish them, Desertions & other Casualties, I much doubt whether they will exceed 400. You will readily perceive the Reason of appointing the Frontiers as their Places of Rendevouz, as the moment they arive there, they serve as a Protection to the County & being on Duty, are more easily kept together & detached to any other Service. I Inclose you the Copy of Letter I have this Day written to Genl. Ten Broeck, on the necessity of expediting the Levies from his Brigade, & of calling the Officers who have neglected their Duty in this Respect to an immediate & Severe Account.

The Excursion to Oswegatje was well conducted & does Mr.

* Not found.

McClelan great Honor; these little Successfull Enterprizes will, I am perswaded, be attended with good Effects, but nothing less than penetrating the Indian Countries with Powerful Armies capable of exterpating the Savages will secure tranquillity to our Frontier Settlements. Before I returned from Kingston, Holt had parted with all his Papers containing the Acc't of the Anandago Expedition, which however was not so perfect as the one which was drawn up & sent to him to publish. My Complim'ts to Mr. & Mrs. Taylor, & Major Popham. Your Family was all well a few Days since. I enclose you Capt. Stockwell's & Lieut. Boggs' Commissions which you will please to forw'd to them.

Yours Affectionately

[G. C.]

The hon'ble Brig'r Genl. Clinton.

[No. 2298.]

Governor Clinton Extends a Favor to a Captive British Half-pay Officer.

Poukeepsie, 16th May, 1779.

Dear Sir, This will be handed to you by Mr. James Grant, a half pay Officer, in the British Service, and who has been a Prisoner on Parole ever since the Commencement of the present Controversy. I am informed that he has strictly complied with it, & [in] all Respects, behaved with the greatest Prudence & Propriety & his general Charecter is that of great Truth & Integrity. He is very desirous of going to New York, where he says, he has private Business of Importance to him to transact (which I believe to be true); he applied to me a year ago for this Indulgence, at a Time when it was not so convenient to grant it & before I was informed of his Charecter & has waited patiently for it ever since. I have now consented to his going, & gave him my Pass on his obtaining your Permission, which I take for granted will not be refused, as an honest Scott merrits a degree of Confidence as well as Indulgence.

I am just returned from Kingston, being called there about Six Days ago by an Alarm on the Western Frontiers. A Party of about 100 Indians & Tories appeared at Great Shandeacon, but were deterred penetrating farther or doing any Misschief. About 27 Tories, chiefly Hessian Deserters belonging to the Convention Troops, were pilotted through the Mountains by the Tories & joined the Enemy at that Place.

I inclose you at the Request of Colo. Hasbrouck a Description of two Negroes which have lately left him, & one of his Neighbours & he has heard are taken up by your Guards. If so, he beggs you will please to forward them by the first Guards coming this Way, & he will chearfully pay any Reasonable Expence attending it.

I have not since your last, been able to meet with two Members of the Legislature together, so as to be able to send you your Flour Permit, but I will do it as soon as Mr. Benson arives at this Place, which expect will be Tomorrow. I am, &c. &c.

[G. C.]

The hon'ble Major Genl. McDougall.

[No. 2299.]

Frontier Sufferers of Albany County.

Received of His Excellency Governor Clinton, by the Hands of Stephen Lush, Esqr., two hundred and fifty Pounds to be distributed among such Persons now in the City of Albany, who have been distressed by the Enemy's Incursions on the western Frontiers and are incapable of gaining a Livelihood.

Gerrit Groesbeck.

Albany May 17" 1779.

[No. 2300.]

For the Cobleskill Sufferers.

Rec'd of his Excellency Gov'r Clinton, by the Hands of Stephen Lush, Esqr., two hundred Pounds to be delivered by me to Mr. Johannes Ball of Schohary, and by him to be distributed to the late Inhabitants of Cobus Kill distressed by the Incursions of the Enemy and now incapable of gaining a Livelihood.

Peter Vroman.

Albany May 18" 1779.

[No. 2301.]

HOLDING UP THE PRICES OF BREAD AND FLOUR.

New England Discriminating Against New York—The Cause and Effect.

Hartford May 9th 1779.

Dear Sir, The Bearer Capt. James Watson is a Gentleman of strict Honor and Integrity; he has at my earnest request, gone into that part of your State bordering on Massachusetts and this State, where I had reason to believe much illicit Trade was carried on in the article of Flour; he has obtained all the information in his power and will communicate it to you, and I will thank you to instruct and advise him. He can also tell you the price Flour sells at in this State, and you will from him obtain such Information as will enable you to know what a medium price is between this State & New Jersey. I have the Honor to be, Your Excellency's Most Humb. Serv't

Jere'h Wadsworth, Com. Gen. P.

His Excel'y Governor Clinton.

53

GOVERNOR CLINTON'S REPLY.

Poukeepsie 18th May 1779.

Dear Sir, I was unfortunately from Home when Capt. Watson was at Poukeepsie. On my Return I rec'd your Letter of the 9th, with one from him, respect'g the Business in which you employed him. The Prices fixed in this State purs't to the Act for procuring an immediate supply of flour for the army, a Copy of which I transmitted you, were 16 Doll's per bush'l for wheat, and 16£ per C for flour; these at the time were supposed to be nearly the average of the Prices in Connecticut & New Jersey and tho' as they are the staple Commodity of the State, it wou'd be its Interest to raise them, equal to the pres't Prices in those States, which Capt. Watson informs me is £20 lawf'l in Connecticut for Flour, I am persuaded, nevertheless, that from the Desire of supplying the army at moderate rates & supporting the Credit of our Currency, it would be a disagreable measure to the People at large &, therefore, will not be done. You will readily perceive, Sir, that while the Prices of flour & wheat in Connecticut & Massachusets Bay are so much higher than in this State, there is the greatest Temptation for running it out of the State, & our greatest exertions will not be able wholly to prevent it, & of course the greatest quantities will be found in the hands of Traders. Whether, therefore, as Mr. Watson proposes, to take it from them at their own Prices (vizt. 50 Doll's pr C) will be best, can only be determined from a knowlege of the present State of our magazines, as in my opinion the measure could only be justified by the necessity there is of obtain'g an immediate Supply.

If the States of Connecticut & Massachusets Bay could be induced to lower the Prices of these articles, making only a proper allowance for transportation, nearly equal to the Prices in this

State, it would facilitate your obtain'g Supplies more effectually than any other measure I can think of, as the Trader would then not be tempted to purchase & the farmer would despair of getting an higher Price than that given by the Commissary, & would be thereby induced to sell to him. Besides, I believe it would enable the Inhabit'ts of the eastern States to derive greater Supplies than they have hitherto done. I am &c.

Geo: Clinton.

Colo. Wadsworth.

[No. 2302.]

The Governor Acknowledges the Receipt of Letters from John Jay.

Poughkeepsie May 18th 1779.

Sir, I have to acknowledge the Rec't of your Excellency's Letters of the 4th* 7th† & 18th§ Ulto. together with the several acts of Congress which they enclosed. Such of them as are to be carried into effect by the Executive authority shall be carefully attended to & I will embrace the earliest opportunity of laying the others before the Legislature. I have the Honor, to be with the most perfect Esteem, & Respect Your Excell'cys most Obed't Serv't

Geo. Clinton.

His Excellency, John Jay, Esqr., Presid't &ca.

[No. 2303.]

THE VERMONT AFFAIR REACHING A CRISIS.

Governor Clinton Places the Responsibility on Congress Should Civil War Ensue.

Poughkeepsie May 18th 1779.

Sir, Inclosed I transmit Copies of several Papers relative to the Disorders which still prevail in the North-Eastern Parts of

---

*See page 689.
†See page 701.
§See page 736.

this State, with a Request that you will please to lay them together with this Letter before Congress.

From these Papers, it evidently appears that matters in that Quarter are fast approaching to a very serious Crisis which nothing but the immediate Interposition of Congress can possibly prevent.

The Legislature have from time to time given the most solemn assurances of Protection to their well-affected Subjects, and relying upon these Promises, the Inhabitants of several Towns have hitherto persevered in their allegiance to this State; they will not I imagine remain much longer content with mere Promises and I daily expect that I shall be obliged to order out a Force for their Defence. The Wisdom of Congress will readily suggest to them what will be the Consequence of submitting the Controversy especially at this Juncture to the Decision of the Sword. It will not, however, I trust be imputed to this State that we have precipitately had recourse to coercive measures. We have anxiously expected the Sentiments of Congress upon this important Business and it was our earnest wish, that, in the mean time, the Inhabitants on the Grants who deny the authority of this State would by a proper conduct on their part have prevented the Necessity of Force, but Justice, the Faith of Government, and the Peace and Safety of Society, will not permit us to continue longer passive Spectators of the Violences committed upon our Fellow Citizens. I am, with the Highest Esteem & Respect, Yours &c.

Geo. Clinton.

His Excell'y John Jay, Esqr., Presid't of Congress.

———

[No. 2304.] *

---

* This document is identical with 2303.—STATE HISTORIAN.

[No. 2305.]

Relative to the Exchange of Prisoners and Removal of Tory Families to New York.

Poukeepsie 19th May 1779.

Sir, I have rec'd yours of the 18th Instant, inclosing a Copy of a Flagg to Thomas Clousdal, granted for the Purpose of carrying to the Enemy the several Persons mentioned in it together with their Effects. I have no Objection to the removal of the Families of such Persons as were removed within the Enemy's Lines, in consequence of the late Test Act, & upon this Principle do consent that the Families of Richard Harrison, (including his Mother), and Samuel Mabett, and also Mrs. Skadden should be permitted to pass to New York, with such of their Effects as consists only in Household Furniture, Bedding, and Wearing Apparel; males capable of bearing Arms however to be excepted. With Respect to the other Persons mentioned in the Flagg, I am extreamly sorry that the Conduct of the Enemy in their late mode of Warfare has made it my Duty to detain them to be exchanged for the Women and Children, which have been carried off in Captivity from our Frontiers. As soon as these are released, and I have Assurances that the Inhumane and unmanly System upon which the War on our Frontiers is carried on, will no longer be pursued, I will readily suffer the Wives and Families of every Person with the Enemy to pass to New York.

You will oblidge me in communicating, by the Return of the Flagg, the Contents of this Letter to the Commanding Officer in New York. I am with much Esteem your most Obed't Serv't

G. C.

The Hon'ble Major Genl. McDougal.

[No. 2306.]

JAMES CLINTON WORRIED.

Apprehensive that Washington's Instructions for the Indian Expedition have Fallen Into the Hands of the Enemy.

Albany May 20th 1779.

Dear Brother,   As Time and Circumstances will not permit me to give you a full and separate account of what I wish you to be informed of, I have sent you Genl. Washington's Packet unsealed, that you may see the disagreeable Condition I am in at present, in consequence of the late unfortunate Miscarriage of His Excellency's Letters, which are of the more importance, as I have reason to believe they contained perticular directions relative to the opperations of the ensuing Campeign, and if they have fall'n into the Enemies Hands, may be attended with the utmost ill Consequences.

By Mr. Dean's Letter of the 16th inst., you will see that the Enemy have intercepted a Letter of a public Nature near the Frontiers of Virginia, which informed them in some instances of our Plan; however, I hope we shall be able to concert measures in such a manner as to prevent them from being very great gainers by the important Discouvery.

The motion of the Drafts is so very slow, that the officers appointed to receive them are almost out of Patience; I do not believe that out of the five hundred we shall be able to get more than one hundred.   Indeed I have some reason to suspect that they are intentionally kept back, that they may be embodied in Regiments by themselves, after we march.   I am, Dear Brother, yours sincerely,

James Clinton, B. G'l.

Gov'r Clinton.

[No. 2307.]

George Clinton Revokes His Action in the Mabbitt Matter, Unless the Effects of Mr. Sands are Shipped from New York.

Poughkeepsie 20th May 1779.

Sir,   Since writing you yesterday on the Subject of the Flag from the Enemy under the direction of Thos. Clousdal, I am informed that Mr. Benj. Sands, late an Inhabitant of Cow Neck on Long Island, who for his attachment to the Cause of America was tried by a Court Martial, constituted by the Enemy & banished with marks of Ignominy without their Lines, is very desirous of obtain'g his family & Effects from thence.   And, as it is unreasonable that the families & Effects of those who were removed under our late test Act should be permitted to be taken in to them unless similar Indulgences are granted to our friends, I am under the necessity of recalling my Consent, expressed in my Letter of yesterday to the removal of the family & Effects of Mr. Saml. Mabbett to New York, until I receive proper assurance that the family of Mr. Sands, with his Effects of equal Value to that of Mr. Mabbett's, will be permitted to come out in Exchange for them; on the Rec't of such assurance, Mr. Mabbett's family & Effects will immediately receive Permission to proceed to New York with the proper Means of Conveyance thither, & as the vessel which will be allowed to take them down, may on its return bring out Mrs. Sands's family & Effects, he will readily consent to pay half of the Expence.   I am &ca.

Geo. Clinton.

The hon'ble Major Genl. McDougall.

[No. 2308.]

John Haring Desires the Release of John Nagel.

Orange Town May 20th 1779.

Sir; Last Monday morning Mr. John Nagel, of Closeter, in Bergen County, was taken prisoner by the Enemy and is now prisoner at Hoboke; they had also taken Mr. Jacob Nagel, but have yesterday permitted him to return home; he says Boskirk sent a Verbal Message by him, that if Teunis Halling could be released, they would release John Nagel; how far this can be Complied with, I cannot pretend to say, but can assure you that Mr. John Nagel, is a warm friend to his Country, and is seventy odd years old; should therefore be glad if any thing Could be done for him. The Bearer, is a son of John Nagel, and is a man you may Confide in; to him I refer you for particulars. Mr. Jacob Nagel is out on parole; he is to return to them in a day or two, when they expect an answer to the above message. I am fearful that this part of the Country will soon be laid waste. I am, Sir, Your Humble Serv't,

John Haring.

General Mac Dougall,

[Nos. 2309-2310.]

CONGRESS AND THE VERMONT AFFAIR.

President Jay Forwards a Set of Resolutions which were Introduced by Gouverneur Morris with an Appropriate Speech.

Philadelphia 22 May 1779.

Dear Sir, I have now the Pleasure of transmitting you a Copy of certain Resolutions moved in Congress this morning respecting the pretended State of Vermont. They were introduced by Mr. Morris with a proper prefatory Speech. On Saturday next the

House will be resolved into a Committee of the whole to take them into Consideration. What may be their Fate is uncertain, tho I am by no means without Hopes of Success. They are temperate & founded on plain Principles. Opposition will hence be more difficult, and their Defence more certain. The Yeas and Nays shall be called on every Question respecting them; and I will furnish you with a minute Detail of the Proceedings of Congress in every stage of the Debates on the Subject. The Delays attending this Business have been unavoidable, and rather unpleasant than prejudicial. It will now be pressed forward, and you may rely on our utmost Exertions and Care.

I now send you some Papers and Journals. My best Respects to Mrs. Clinton. I am, dear Sir, very sincerely yours &c.

John Jay.

His Excellency Gov'r Clinton.

THE RESOLUTIONS.

Whereas divers of the Inhabitants of a certain District of Country, over a particular Part of which the State of New York, and over the Residue of which the State of New Hampshire, at the Time when these United States were Colonies of and subject to the Crown of Great Britain, did exercise Jurisdiction; have under various Pretences refused allegiance thereto, and attempted to constitute themselves into a separate State under the assumed name of the State of Vermont:

Resolved, that the States of New Hampshire, Massachusetts Bay, Rhode Island, Connecticut, New York, New Jersey, Pennsylvania, Delaware, Maryland, Virginia, North Carolina, South Carolina and Georgia, are severally entitled to, and ought to hold and be maintained in the Possession of all the Lands and Territories which appertained of Right to each of them respectively while they were Colonies of and subject to the King of Great Britain.

Resolved, that none of the said States ought, or shall be divested, of any Lands or Territories over which they respectively exercised Jurisdiction at the Time aforesaid, unless by Judgment of Congress in Favor of certain other of the said States, claiming the same or any Part thereof, and prosecuting that Claim in the way prescribed by the articles of Confederation.

Resolved that no Part or District of one or more of the said States shall be permitted to separate therefrom, and become independent thereon, without the express consent and approbation of such State or States respectively.

Resolved that it be recommended to the Inhabitants of the said pretended State of Vermont to return peaceably to their former Jurisdictions, that is to say, those who have separated from the State of New Hampshire to the State of New Hampshire, and those who have separated from the State of New York to the State of New York.

Resolved, that Congress will readily hear, examine and interpose to obtain Redress of, any Grievances, of which the said Inhabitants may have Cause to complain against their said respective States.

Resolved, that nothing in the preceding Resolutions contained, shall be construed to confirm or prejudice the Title of the States of New Hampshire or New York to the Jurisdictions aforesaid, or to exclude or bar any Claims which other States may have thereto or any part thereof.

[No. 2311.]

General James Clinton Receives the Instructions He Feared were Lost.

Albany May 22d 1779.

Dear Brother; I have just time to acknowledge the Receipt of your Letter with the Enclosures. I have forwarded the Commissions to Capt. Stockwell &c. and shoud have informed you of the different Stations of the Drafts now on the Frontiers, but that the Express is just waiting, and Genl. Ten Broeck informs me he hath done it, in some respects, tho' not fully.

The Express which I conceived was losst, hath been received yesterday, by the way of Saratoga, thro' mistake. I am, D'r Brother, yours sincerely,

James Clinton.

Gov'r Clinton.

[No. 2312.]

COLONEL VAN SCHAICK UTTERS A COMPLAINT.

Compelled to Reward Indians Out of His Own Pocket for Making Captures—A Scout to Oswego.

Fort Schuyler May 22 1779.

Sir, Yours of the 17th Inst. I have received by the post. The scout I sent to Oswego returned yesterday; their provisions having got damaged by a heavy rain, oblidged them to come off some days sooner than was intended. The Officer informs me that he has been on the ground at Oswego seven days without making the least discovery of an enemy at or near that place.

The five Oneidas whom I sent with one of my soldiers to Buck Island have returned yesterday; they brought in three Soldiers belonging to Sir John Johnson's Regiment whom they took on the Island, By them, I have been informed that no Reinforcement of men had arrived at Buck Island this spring, but that the remainder of Sir John's Regim't, being seven Companies, was daily expected.

When the soldiers were taken, which was the 15th Instant, there was then on the Island about Six hundred men, and about three hundred Indians; that a body of Troops were coming up the River St. Lawrence this Spring; that besides the four Vessels on the Lake Ontario two large Vessels on the Stocks at Buck Island would be launched in a few days. Butler and Brandt left Buck Island before the Soldiers were taken, in order to Collect the foreign Indians.

I shall be under the necessity for the future to desist from sending any Parties of Indians in order to take prisoners from the enemy, as I have it not in my power to make them any Reward but what comes from my own purse. It seems that my Superiors dont think proper to trust me with the same Powers and Materials with which the former Commanders at this Post were intrusted. Shall, therefore, Content myself with endeavouring to Comply with your Orders, respecting the sending of Scouts to Oswego by Land, a mode foreign to my expectation.

The Indians have promised me to deliver up the prisoners to me in four days. When that is Complied with I shall forward them down to Albany by the first Conveyance. Your Obed't Servant

G. V. Schaick.

To Brig'r Genl. Jas. Clinton.

A true Copy.

[No. 2313.]

Relating to Exchanges.

Head Quarters Pecks Kill May 24th 1779.

Sir, Your Favors of the 19th* and 20th† came to Hand. On Receipt of the first, I gave orders for the Flag to pass to New

---

*See page 837.
†See page 839.

Windsor, or Fish-Kill Landing under proper Guards, to take on Board the Effects of the Families mentioned in your answer. But as Mr. Mabbit's Effects are not to go, for the Reasons you mention, in the 20th, I wish you will cause it to be signified to the Family, in order that the Effects may not be brought down to the Flag.

I sent Captain Hunter in with a Flag to endeavor to get Vantassel, Oakley and Young exchanged, which he has accomplish'd for the two former; and they are come out on Parole, till John Cummins now in Albany Goal, and Lewis Vincent are sent in—the latter was discharged yestarday, but it depends on you whether Vantassel or Cummins shall go in. I wish to have your answer on this Subject as soon as possible. Poor Vantassel has suffered greatly and it's high Time he should be exchanged.

The inclos'd was brought to me three Days ago, with a message from Judge Harring, that Tunis Helling, is a subject of Jersey. He is one of those taken up, on the Precepts of the Commissioners. It lies with you or them whether this Exchange shall take place; of which the Persons interested are very solicitous to be informed. I am, sir, your humble servant

Alex'r McDougall.

His Excellency Governor Clinton.

[No. 2314.]

Colonel Levi Pawling Forwards Rumors and Facts.

Marbletown, May 24th, 1779.

S'r; I was Informed yesterday, in a Private way, that, the Enemy from the westerd, Intended to Come down in a large Body, about the begining of next month, and to meet the Regulars who was to Come up the River at that time.

This Informent tells me that a few Days ago Some white men with two Indians, went to New York, and he thinks they are Returnd; they Cross'd the mountain near Mamacating; he promised me to make a farther Enquiry and let me know; many of the New Levies, (as I understand) are Behind, both in Ulster and Dutches. Albert has wrote to Cols. Hardenbergh and Newkerk to send them forward. The fort at Shendeken is done, (I heard yesterday) but by the means of the late Heavy Rains, little has been done at Lagewack. I am with great Esteem, your Most Hum'e Ser't,

Levi-Pawling.

His Excellency George Clinton, Esqr., Governor &c., Pough-keepsie.

[No. 2315.]

ETHAN ALLEN MAKES A RAID.

Captures New York Militia Officers, Bids Defiance to New York and Declares He Will Establish Vermont by the Sword.

Brattleborough, May ye 25th 1779.

Sir; The Committee of this County who are now met for the purpose of opposing the authority of the State of Vermont, take this oppertunity to inform your Exelency by Express, that Con'l Eathon Alline with a number of Green mountain Boys, made his appearence in this County yesterday, well arm'd & equip't, for the purpose of redusing the Loyal Inhabitents of this County to a Submition to the authority of the State of Vermont, and made prisonars of Con'l Patterson, Liut. Con'l Sargeant and all the Militia officers Exept one, in Brattleborough, with Mr. Townsend and a number of other Persons. They have also taken the Militia officers in Putney and Westminster with others; the number of prisoners we cannot assatain. Con'l Alline Declared that he had five hundred Green mountain Boys with him; we are not able to assatain the number, but belive there is not Quite so many who are come from the west sid of the mountains; they are assisted by a number of the Inhabitants of this County; where they will carey the prisoners we cannot tel.   Con'l Alline treted the People here with the most Insulting language; Assaulted and wounded Several Persons with his sword, without the least provocation, and bids Defiance to the State of New Yorke; declares they will Establish their State by the sword, and fight all who shall at-tempt to oppose them; nothing but the Reluctance the People here have to sheding human Blood, could hinder them from at-tempting to rescue the Prisoners; they had every Insult which the humane mind is able to conceive of, to promp them to it; our Sitiuation is truly criticle and Destressing; we, therefore, most humbly beceech your Exelency to take the most speedy and Effectual mesures for our releaf; otherwise our persons and prop-erties must be at the Desposal of Eathon Alline which is more to be Dreded then Death, with all its Terrors.   Sir, we are with the greatest Esteem, your Exelencies most Obadient humble Ser'ts,

Signed by order of the Committee

Samuel Minott, Chairman.

To his Exelency, George Clinton, Esquire, Governor of the State of New Yorke &c.*

[No. 2316.]

Governor Clinton Invokes the Aid of Westchester Magistrates in Securing Teams for the Army.

Pokeepsie May 25" 1779.

Gentlemen, The Qu'r Mr. Genl. informs me that he has a Quantity of Provisions and other Stores which it is absolutely

*See pages 858 and 859.

necessary to bring in from different Places for the Use of the army, that for the want of Forage and other unavoidable Difficulties he is unable to keep public Teams at present sufficient to answer these and other similar Purposes, and that he finds it impossible [to] procure Carriages from the Country agreable to the act of the Legislature lately made, without uncommon aid from the civil magistrate. I have, therefore, to recommend, that you will use your utmost Exertions in furnishing the Teams necessary for the public Service at this critical Conjuncture, when the least Neglect might be attended by the most fatal Consequences, in preventing the army from being supplied with Provisions, and perhaps forcing them to abandon the Posts they now occupy in the Support of w'ch you are particularly interested.

At a Meeting lately held by the Magistrates of this Ulster and Orange Counties, they adopted a System for carrying this Law into Execution which, as it has been followed by salutary Effects, I would earnestly recommend to you as the most likely Means of accomplishing the Intentions of the Legislature with least Distress to the Inhabitants of wh'ch Colo. Hay will furnish you with a Copy. I am &c.

[G. C.]

[To Justices of the Peace, Westchester County.]

[No. 2317.]

Colonel Udny Hay Asks for an Impress Warrant and the Governor Rebukes Him.

Fish Kill, 26th May, 1 A. M. [1779]

Sir; By a Letter this inst. rec'd from General McDougal, he seems apprehensive there is an attack designd on the Fort; as usual I do not think there is four days Provisions in it; have, therefore, to request a General Press warrant from your Excellency with orders to the militia to assist in enforcing it, if you think the General's present apprehensions are of sufficient importance to make such a measure eligible.

This moment an express goes off to the Q'r Master at Litchfield, requesting in the most pressing terms, that he will immediately send on the salt Provisions now lying there; should he be remiss in complying with this request, upon this occasion had not the Waggons of this State better be sent for a part of it. I am with respect Your Excellency's most obed. Ser't

Udny Hay.

Governour Clinton.

The Governor's Reply.

Sir, I have this Moment rec'd your Letter of Today and now inclose a General Impress Warrant to enable you to convey a Supply of Provisions to the different Posts in the Southern Part [of] this State. It is to be lamented that upon every fresh alarm these Posts are found so exceedingly deficient, not only for the fatal Consequences that may result from the Enemy's attacking them when thus unprovided, but also that the use of General Impress Warrants will defeat the Regulations adopted by the ordinary Magistrate for carrying the Impress Law into Execution. You'l readily perceive that it is out of my Power to order the Teams of this State to convey Provisions from Litchfield.

The Officers both civil and military, you'l observe, are by the Tenor of the warrant directed to assist in executing it. I am &c.

[G. C.]

May 26 1779.

[To Col. Udny Hay.]

54

[No. 2318.]

Governor Clinton's Response to Colonel Levi Pawling's Letter.

May 26" 1779.

Sir, I rec'd your Favor of the 24" Inst. and this Day rec'd a Letter from Genl. McDougal of which I inclose you a Copy. The Intelligence it communicates leads me the more to believe the acc'ts you rec'd from the westward. This has induced me to issue the inclosed Order, Copies of which you will be pleased to forward to Colo. Cantine & Colo. Snyder. I am &c.

[G. C.]

[To Col. Levi Pawling.]

[No. 2319.]

Orders to Colonel Van Rensselaer.

May 24th 1779.

Colo. Rensselaer will immediately proceed to Albany—on his way thither, he will call on the Officers of Colo. Livingston's Regiment & the other Regiments of militia between that & Albany & use every means in his Power with them to collect with all Possible Dispatch, the Levies from the respective Regiments & cause them to be forwarded to Albany or such other Convenient Place of Rendezvous as he shall appoint. He will on his arrival at Albany, assign Officers to receive the Quota from Genl. Ten Broeck's Brigade, & annex such part of them, as are ordered, to fill up the cont'l Battalions to those Regts., the Residue are to be stationed at such Passes on the northern & western frontiers of Albany & Tryon County as Genl. Clinton shall direct. Major Van Buntschoten is ordered to assemble the Levies from Dutchess, Ulster & Orange at the Posts on the frontiers of the two Latter, & as they come in, such part of them as are to be annexed to the cont'l Batt'ns he is to forward without Delay by Detachments to

Albany for that Purpose. Colo. Rensselaer will immediately collect & make out proper Returns of the Levies, designating therein the militia Regt., from which they were raised, & the Places where they are stationed, a Copy of the Orders given to Major V. Buntschoten, together with such farther Orders as may be necessary, will be transmitted to Colo. Renssalaer, as soon as the Levies are collected, & his Regt. is formed, to accomplish which the Colo. will use in the Mean Time, his utmost Influence and exertions with the militia Officers of Albany & Tryon Counties.

R. Benson, A. D. C.

[No. 2320.]

COLONEL CORTLANDT IN THE INDIAN COUNTRY.

Constructing a Road for the Passage of the Artillery for the Sullivan Expedition.

Great Swamp Wilderness, of the Shades of Death 25 Miles from Wyomen, May 26, 1779.

Dear Sir; By an Officer passing to your State have Just time to Inform you of the good Health and Spirits of the Officers and men under my Command, I have in a letter Sent by Lieut. Livingston, Informed you of the nature of the Command I am order'd upon, which is to make a Road to Wyomen, for the transportation of artilery, which is Coming in with Genl. Sullivan and now (as I am Informed) at Easton, together with the Jersie Brigade and hear that Genl. Poor is on his march for this also. I have little to Inform you of. I Just Rec'd a Letter from Genl. Hand who is at Wyomen; things go on well in that Quarter; provisions are Transported up the Susquehana and meet with no obstruction as yet from the Savages, altho Small parties are Very

Frequently Seen near the fort, and have been on the Path from this to Wyomen, but have not as yet attempted any thing to the prejudice of my partie. However, I Expect they will before I have Completed the work; the Danger will be when I advance beyond the Swamp. Shall be Very Happy to Hear from you, and how affairs go with Respect to the Fruntiers I guarded last winter. Please to Direct for me, to the Care of Colo. Hooper, D. Q. M. G., at Easton, who will forward the same; with my best Respects Remain Your Obt. Hum'e Ser't

Philip Cortlandt.

His Excellency Governor Clinton.

[No. 2321.]

George Clinton's Brief Letter to James Clinton.

May 26, 1779.

D'r Brother, I have rec'd yours of the 22d and am happy to find that the Dispatches you thought had miscarried are come to Hand.

I inclose you the latest acc'ts I have rec'd from the Southward & westward. Genl. Ten Broeck will communicate to you the orders I have issued in Consequence, thereof, and I beg you will give him such assistance as may be necessary in making such Disposition of them as will be best calculated to cover the Frontiers. Scohary appears to me in the most immediate Danger.

Major Van Bunschoten has my positive orders to forward without Delay, by Detachments, such Proportion of the Levies from the Southern Counties as are to be annexed to the Continental Battalions, and I have Reason to expect that some of them will arrive at Albany before this reaches you. With my Compliments to Mr. & Mrs. Taylor I am &c.

[G. C.]

[To Gen. James Clinton.]

[No. 2322.]

Soldiers Complain Because of the Sufferings of Their Families.

Johnstown, 27th May, 1779.

Honored Sir, At the request of several of the soldiers of our Regt., have undertaken to inform you of the several complaints made to me by them of the starving condition their Families are in at home; they are receiving letters from them daily, informing of them that unless they are supply'd with provision they unavoidably must suffer; also the thirty pounds allow'd them by the state, they say, they have not received it, neither do they know where to apply for the same, and shou'd be exceedingly glad to know from your Honor where to apply or what meathod to take so as to come at the same. I shou'd not have troubled your Excellency with the matter if it were not on acc't of pacifying the men. I was fearfull a few days ago that they wou'd have mutinied on the same acc't. I prevaild with them to rest easy by promissing them that I wou'd write to you on the subject. Have nothing farther meterial, am and remain Your Most Obt. and Verry Hum. Servant

Jas. Rosekrans.

His Excellency, Geo. Clinton Esqr.

———

[No. 2323.]

Governor Clinton Sends Secret Instructions to Commissary Elmendorph.

May 28th 1779.

Sir, I shall have occasion for Salt Provision and hard Bread for about 600 Men for one Month to be at Marbletown, or some other Place, contiguous to the Frontiers of Ulster County without Delay. You will please to let me know with all possible Dispatch

what Means you have of laying in this small Magazine, & within
what Time it can be completed, and I will transmit you my further
orders on the Subject.   In the Interim you will not unnecessarily
disclose the Contents of this Letter.   I have only to add that his
Excellency Genl. Washington has been previously consulted and
that I act in Consequence of his Directions.   I am &c.

[G. C.]

[To Coenraedt Elmendorph Esq.]

[No. 2324.]

Governor Clinton Makes a Proposition to Lieutenant-General Jones,
the British Commander in New York City.

28th May 1779.

D'r Sir, Last Evening Capt. North, with the Ladies [who]*
lately went to New York with a flag returned to this Place greatly
distr[essed]* at their Disappointment,   My Reason for sending
Mrs. Farren to you before granting the [permit]* was not only
to know whether you had any Objection to [   ]* going, but also
whether it wou'd be proper to s[end]* them in, without previous
notice being given to the Command'g Officer at New York & his
consent obtained.   I have informed her that I had rec'd a Letter
from Genl. Jo[nes]* last winter to that Effect.   I care not how
few Flags [   ]* between us & the Enemy & cou'd wish that they
were conf[ined]* to military matters.   However as some of these
women have parted with all their family necessary's, & the others
are exceedingly anxious to see their Husbands after near two
y[ears]* absence in Captivity, I have been induced to make the
enclosed Proposals [to]* Genl. Jones which you'l be pleased to
[send]* to him.   As I have lately written to S'r Henry Clinton

---

*MSS. torn.

on the above Subject [and not]* as yet been fav'd with an answer, I cannot w'th propriety write a second. Th[is]* with the Importunities of the Ladies will I hope be a suff[icient]* appology for the Trouble I give you. I am &c.

Geo: Clinton.

The hon'ble M. G. McDougall.

———

It is proposed, if agreed to by the Commander Officer at New York, to permit Mrs. McFerron, Miss Nancy McArthur, Mrs. Byvanck, Mrs. Elizabeth Duncan, with two small Negro Girls, and the Furniture, wear'g apparel & bedding of the above Persons, to go into New York in Exchange for the wife of Uriah Mitchel, at Hempstead, on Long Island, her Family & Effects, the Child of Mr. Morris Hazard & his Effects, in the Hands of Ab'm Schenck, Esqr., of Long Island and a negro Girl and the Effects of Jno. Quackenboss now in the Hands of Mr. David Mallishaw in N. York & Mr. Horn at Bloomingdale in N. York. It is also proposed, if agreed to as above, that the wives of Colo. McClaughry, Major Logan, Leut. Halsted & Lieut. Brewster, Officers, Prisoners in N. York or on Long Island, with Mrs. McMennomy to attend them, be permitted by the same Conveyance to visit their Husbands and to return. It might have reasonably been expected that the above Persons who had obtained a Flag to go to New York & actually arrived there, would have been received without previous Notice & Consent, as a Sloop was lately sent out from the City as a Flag for Families in the Country & received, without my insisting on the observance of such Regulation, which it is, however, expected will be complied with in Future.

———

* MSS. torn.

[No. 2325.]

Johannes Ball Renders an Accounting.

Schohary May 29th 1779.

Sir, I have Received your letter and the money which was Raised or granted by our Legislature for the Sufferrers on the western fronteers at Cobis Kill by the Indians and tories, and have given it to them accorting to your orders to the best of my knowlelge. I have Inclosed the Receits of them in my letter.

The beoble are very much oblitge to his Excellency for his kintness. I am, Sir, your most obed. Servend

Johannes Ball.

to his Excellency Govenor Clinton.

Schohary May 29th 1779.

Received of Johannes Ball the Sum of fifty four tollers, being money which is granted to me by the Legislature. Goerge Werner; fifty four tollers Lorence Lawyer; Sixty two tollers Adam Schäfer; forty four tollers George G $\overset{\text{his}}{\text{S}}$ M Shelman; Sixty tollers Johannes Freimeyer; forty four tollers William Snyter; forty Six tollers Nicolas $\overset{\text{his}}{\text{X}}$ Werner; forty four tollers ——— ——— $\overset{\text{mark}}{}$ being Sufferrers on the western fronteers of Jacobes Kill.

Forty Eight tollers Nicolas ———; forty four tollers John Bouck. Being Sufferers on the western fronteers of Jacobes Kill.

———

[No. 2326.]

A British Diversion Up the Hudson River.

Head Quarters Pecks Kill 29th May 1779.

Patrick Rogers says he is a native of Ireland, was a Corporal in Lord Cathcart's Legion, and deserted* this morning in Company with two others of the same Corps.

* See pages 860 and 861.

He Says, that Seventeenth British Regt. of Horse, Lord Cathcart's Legion, Emerick's Corps, The Hessian Yagers, Sincoes the
7th 23d & 63d British Regts. lay on this side the Bridge encamped
from Cortlandt's to Valentine's. That last Evening he carried
Orders from General Kniphausen to Sir William Erskine for the
Troops mentioned to march at 6 o'Clock this morning*. That
he over heard Colonel Emerick read the Orders which mentioned
that all the Troops on this side the Bridge were to march out 18

*May 31.—Day before yesterday, fifteen hundred men, consisting of British and Hes-
sian grenadiers, light infantry, volunteers of Ireland and Yagers, landed on Teller's
Point, eight miles below Peekskill, on the North River, and the following day another
party landed on the west side of the river, where they burnt some houses, and
opened two small batteries, from which they threw shells, and cannonaded Fort de la
Fayette across the river, all day; at the same time two galleys kept up a severe fire on
the fort. They have continued their firing till eleven o'clock to-day. Meanwhile their
army marched from Teller's to Verplanck's Point, on which the fort stands. By a flag
they demanded a surrender; the parley continued two hours, when Captain Armstrong
thought fit to surrender. General McDougall has not yet received a justifiable reason
why the fort was given up.
This little fort was built on purpose to secure King's ferry from the insults of the
enemy's vessels, which frequently interrupted the American boats in crossing. It was
small, and would contain, with conveniency, about a company of men. The redoubt
was strong, and covered a barbette battery, mounting three pieces of cannon. We had
in the barbette a company of artillery; they were all drawn off but a sergeant, a corporal, and twelve privates. In the redoubt were a captain, two subalterns, three ser-
geants, and forty-four rank and file. They had provisions and water sufficient to serve
them thirty days.—New Jersey Gazette, June 9, 1779.
A British officer gives the following account of this affair:—" On Monday morning, the
thirty-first of May, part of the army, under the command of Major-General Vaughan,
landed on the east side of Hudson River, about eight miles below Verplanck's Point.
The corps intended to land on the west side, under his excellency the commander-in-
chief, with Major-General Pattison, proceeded up within three miles of Stony Point,
where they landed, about which time the rebels, who had a block-house and some
unfinished works on a height of that point, commanding the ferry, as well as Fort
la Fayette on the east side of the river, set fire to the block-house, and ran off to the
mountains. That corps, about four o'clock in the afternoon, continued their march
round, and took possession of the heights; during this time the galleys fired some shot
at Fort la Fayette, on the east side of Verplanck's Point; these were returned from the
fort, which was a small but complete work. Artillery was now necessary in order to
expedite the business; his excellency the general ordered Major-General Pattison to
command the troops and carry on the attack. In the night, the artillery for that service, notwithstanding great difficulties from a bad landing place and a very steep preci-
pice, were got up, and batteries completed by five o'clock in the morning, when orders
were given for firing upon the enemy's works; which, notwithstanding the great distance, was soon perceived to be effectual. The galleys and batteries continued the
cannonade about two hours, when the main body, under Major-General Vaughan, having made a detour and approached the fort, the commander-in-chief being there in person, sent orders to General Pattison and the galleys to cease firing, the enemy having
surrendered; they laid down their arms, became prisoners of war, and on Thursday
morning arrived in New York.
" The commodore had, previous to the attack, ordered up the Vulture sloop-of-war
above the fort, with a row-galley, which prevented the enemy's retreat from the fort."—
Gaine's Mercury, June 7, 1779.

miles into the Country with their Tents & Baggage and there encamp.

That the British and Hessian Grenadiers, British Light Infantry & 17th Foot were to march to Williams's Bridge with Tents &ca. and there encamp. That the Hessian Guards and 44 British Regt., & Robinson's Corps, with Capt'n Sandford's independant Troop of Horse were to do the Duty on New York Island. That a serjeant of his own Corps told him he Saw two Brigades Consisting of 6 Regiments embark at New York on the 27" Instant and that they sailed the Day following up to Fort Washington, and that he heard several Guns fired from the ships, and that it was reported they were going to attack some Fort up the River.

[No. 2327.]

Governor Clinton Lays Before Congress Papers on the Vermont Affair.

May 29" 1779.

Sir, You will perceive from the inclosed Papers* that what I have long expected and frequently apprized Congress of, has actually happened. These Papers which need no Comment, I have transmitted to your Excellency by Express, with an earnest Request that you will please immediately to lay it before Congress.

Altho' this matter will scarce admit of a moment's Delay yet as the Legislature are to meet on Tuesday next, I shall defer taking any decisive measures except issuing the necessary orders to the militia to hold themselves in readiness until I can have an Opportunity of obtaining their advice and Direction.

[G. C.]

[To President Jay.]

* See page 846.

[No. 2328.]

CIVIL WAR THREATENED.

Governor Clinton Notifies the New York Delegates in Congress of His Determination to Repel the Vermont Outrage.

May 29, 1779.

Gent'n; I have by the same Conveyance with this, dispatched an Official Letter to the President, covering a Copy of Letter I this moment received from the Chairman of the Committee of Cumberland County to which I must refer you for particulars.

I presume it is unnecessary to inform you that the Vermont Business is now arrived at a Crisis, or to urge any arguments to induce your utmost Exertions in obtaining the Sence of Congress without Delay.

The Legislature will meet on Tuesday next, and in the mean time I shall issue my orders to the militia and make the necessary arrangements for marching to repel this Outrage. I shall also conceive it my Duty to order the 1000 men destined for the Defence of the Frontiers and to compleat the Continental Battalions, except such small Part as are already annexed to those Regiments to march to Brattleborough for the Protection of that and the adjacent Towns unless the Interposition of Congress sh'd render this measure unnecessary. It doubtless will occur to you that the Legislature will be extremely impatient for an Answer from Congress. I must, therefore, request you the moment it is obtained to forward it by a special messenger.

[G. C.]

[To New York Delegates in Congress.]

[No. 2329.]

Major Cochran's Land Grant Application.

May 29" 1779.

Sir, I have rec'd your Petition of the 18" May and as no Land Office is yet established within the State, I shall take the earliest

Opportunity of laying it before the Legislature at their next Meeting (which commences on Tuesday next). Whatever Resolutions they may enter into in Consequence of it, I will immediately transmit you, not doubting that they will pay proper attention at all Times to the Interest and applications of the Gentlemen of the army & am &c.

[G. C.]

[To Major Cochran.]

[Nos. 2330-2331.*]

MOVEMENTS OF THE ENEMY.

General McDougall Forwards an Important Communication from Major Hatfield.

Head-Quarters Pecks Kill 30th May 1779, 12 A. M.

Sir, I received your favor with an inclosure, directed to Lieut. General Jones. Neither time, or the Service will permit my attending to it which you will see by the Inclosures. The Deserter† whose examination is inclosed, came in last night; the other Intelligence came in this morning. The Commander in Chief informs me, the Enemy have been embarking Shells and other military Stores, in New-York, for several Days past. It is certain he is now at the Plains, in very considerable force. Frequent calls of Alarm, on the militia may prevent their turning out when they are wanted. However, in the present State of the Enemy, it is necessary they shou'd be provided with a Week's Provision, and ready to march on the shortest notice. I fear it will be impracticable to remove, all the Stores at Fish-Kill, as the Teams of the Country will be necessary to collect Provision. We must fight for them. There are two Brigades of Good Troops at the Point

---

*This document and the one following have been reversed from the original numbering in the MSS. and consolidated for reasons that will appear obvious.—STATE HISTORIAN.

†See page 856.

two here and Parsons ordered to march to these Posts.   I am in haste Your affectionate humble Servant

                                        Alex'r McDougall.
His Excellency Governor Clinton.

———

MAJOR HATFIELD'S REPORT TO GENERAL McDOUGALL.

South Salem 29th May 1779, 12 o'Clock at night.

Sir, I this moment arrived to this place from Bedford which I left about 10 o'Clock this night being immediately after Intelligence came there of the Enemy's having got to the White Plains. This news was told me by a man who came from near the Head of the Plains who received his Intelligence from one Fisher near that Place who was taken Prisoner by the Enemy's Light Horse a little before Sun Set this Day but made his escape.   This Fisher informed that he heard the Enemy's Drums at that time a little West of the White Plains and was told by the Light Horse their force consisted of 12,000 but from the Intelligence this morning received at Bedford of three Deserters from the Enemy who has (I dare say) informed you respecting their force I think their number is much less.   As I have reason to think from the secret movement of the Enemy that you have not received Intelligence of their arrival at the White-Plains thought it my Duty to give this Information.   An account of this is dispatched to General Parsons.   I am sir yr. Obd. Serv't

                                        Richard Hatfield.
       Copy
Major General McDougall.

———

[No. 2332.]

The New Levies and the Ulster Frontier—Major Van Benscoten's Disposition of His Forces.

                                    Rochester, May 29th, 1779.

May it please your Excellency, On my Journey to Peenpack, I was taken with a great illness, which obliges me to keep my room ever since my return. Having no officers at this place, but the adjutant, makes the Duty very hard to me. Lieut. Wesbrook at Laghawack dus not incline to serve any longer, then to, he is reliev'd by another officer. Please your Excellency, order one Captain, and Subaltern to this place. Lieut. Ostrander, with fifty five Men, have march'd to Albany; at his return I have order'd him to relieve Lieut. McBride, and take Charge of the Levies of Dutchess County, and Lieut. McBride to repair to this place. In pursuance of your Excellencies Orders to me directed, I have taken my Instructions from Coll. Cantine, in fixing the men to Different Posts. They are as follows; Captain Wood with fifty Men, at two posts in Peenpack; Lieut. Pawling with Twenty five Men, at Mama-Catten; Twenty Men of Coll. Cantine's at Lunen Kill; Twenty Men at Nepenack; Fifteen at Wasing; one Sergant, and Twenty Men at the Stores at Brown's; one sergt. and Twelve Men at Van Horn's Mills; Fifty Men at Laghawack; Fifty Men at Shan-Deaken; I am, with great respect, Your Excellencies, most Obed't hum'e Serv't

E. V. Benscoten.

His Excellency Governor Clinton, Poughkeepsie.

GOVERNOR CLINTON'S REPLY.

Poukeepsie 31" May 1779.

Dear Sir, I have rec'd your Letter of the 29" Inst. & am extremely sorry for your Indisposition especially when your Country may require your most active Exertions. Capt. Faulkener has rec'd his Commission and is ordered to join the Levies under your Command; one other Capt., and a Lieut., in Albany County are also commissioned and are to join Colo. Renselaer. These are the only Officers among the many appointed by the Council who have accepted. Colo. Renselaer is appointed to take the Command of one of the Regts., of the Levies but as he is now at Albany and as those Troops will be so distributed along the Frontiers as to render it impossible for two Field Officers to pay the necessary attention to the different Passes to be guarded, and as the Duty will become more burthensome by Detachments from the Militia, being frequently called out, I have thought it necessary also to issue Major Pawling his Commission as Lieut. Colo., which I have not the least Doubt will be agreable to you.

As soon as proper Persons can be found for subalterns I will have them appointed, and you will of Course be enabled to relieve Mr. McBride and order him to the Frontiers.

[G. C.]

[To Major Van Benscoten.]

[No. 2333.]

Captain Stockwell Sends in a Report from Skeenesboro.

Skenesborough, May the 30th 1779.

Sir, I inclose you a Return of what men I have, joined my Company, and a acount of what Regt. from the resons I have not my Full Coto I Cannot tel without it is Neglect of the Colonels. Sir, agreable to my Derection from General Schuyler, I took Post at this place the 6 of May, but with very few men, but Have had more joind sence; my orders was to send one Lieut., and 27 men to fort Edward which I sent 17 but as Duty is very Hard here I should be glad that part of my Company Could join me. Sir, I should be glad to no in what form the pay for my men Can be got, whether by proper pay roles, or abstracks to the Pay master; likwise to no, who is my Colonel that I may Communicate to him. I have wrote General Tenbrock several Times Concerning the men from his breggade. I have Scouts Constantly on both sides of the lake as fair as Crown Pint but Can make no Discoveries as yet; I have no Remarable Currences To inform you of, but Remain Your very humble Ser't

                                    Levi Stockwell.

To His Excellency George Clinton, Esq., Govennor & Commander of the State of New York.

                                    Skenes Borough.

A Return of Capt. Levi Stockwell Company of New Leavise, Rased for the Northly & westly frounttears & acount From whome I have Receivd them.

Cornels

Cornels Yats .... men   13

Cornels Vanwort .... men   14

Cornels McCray .... men   17

Cornels Webster .... men   13

    Total   57

                                    Levi Stockwell, Capt.

[No. 2334.]

Commissary Elmendorph Reports Progress.

                        Kingston 30th May 1779.

Sir, I Last night Receiv'd yours of the 28th. The Stores at Warsinck Have bin Intirely out of Salt provisions, though I Have yesterday Receiv'd 150 Barrels Beef from Albany, part of which may answer your Intended purpose, I Have this morning, Sent an Express to Albany to forward 100 Barrels more, which I think will Be Sufficient with the beef now on hand, if no more Could be Spared there; I understand Mr. Read at Sharon Has a Large Stock On Hand. I think It would be advisable for your Excellency to order 100 Barrels from there to Major Redley's Store;

if the Beef from Albany arrives It may be forwarded from there to any other Post on the River. As for Hard Bread, I Have yet Ninety Barrels and three tierces on hand, and if any more Should be wanted It Can Soon be Baked. I am, Sir, Your most obed't Humb'e Ser't

Coenraedt J. Elmendorph, A. C. P.

To His Excell'cy George Clinton.

[No. 2335.]

Major Albert Pawling Receives His Commission of Li ut nant-Colonel.

May 31" 1779, Pokeepsie.

Dear Sir, Altho' Colo. Renselaer has accepted of his appointm't to the Command of one of the Regt. of Levies, raised for the Frontiers, considering the Duties these Troops will have to perform and that they will be greatly dispersed by Reason of the different Posts to be occupied by them to give Security to the Frontier Settlem'ts, I have thought it necessary to issue your Commission also which I have the Honor now to inclose you. You will please, therefore, to accept of it & for the present take under your Command the Levies now on the Frontiers of Ulster and Orange Counties, with such Detachm'ts of the Militia as may from Time to Time be ordered out for the Defence of the Frontiers of those Counties, not hav'g a Colo. to command them. You will follow the Instructions heretofore given to Major Van Bunschoten, and as I have directed Colo. Renselaer to make me a Return of the Levies at the different Posts, you will furnish him with a Return of those under your more immediate Command. You will please to call upon Colo. Cantine for my orders to him, founded upon Intelligence of the movem'ts of the Enemy rec'd yesterday. I have not the least Doubt but the most friendly understanding will prevail between you & Major Van Bunscho-

55

ten, and that proper attention will be paid to him as a Person in whose Bravery & Conduct I have great Confidence. I am, D'r Sir &c.

[G. C.]

[To Major Albert Pawling.]

[No. 2336.]

Preparations for Meeting the Enemy.

31st May 1779 Pokeepsie.

Sir; I have received your Letter of yesterday with its Inclosures; in Consequence of which I have written Letters to the command'g Officers of the militia of Ulster, Dutchess and Orange (a Copy of which I inclose). The Orders alluded to, designated your Signals of alarm, directed them to hold their different Corps in the most perfect Readiness at a minute's warning; those of Dutchess County to rendezvous at Fishkill and to join the Troops under your immediate Command, those of Ulster & Orange (such Companies excepted as are to guard the Frontiers) to march to West Point. The militia of West Chester by my former Orders on such movement of the Enemy as sh'd render it necessary, were to join your army of which, when you shall judge it requisite, you will please to remind them and give them the necessary Orders.

You'l please to continue to give me the earliest Intelligence of the Enemy's Movements that I may be able to direct such aid as I can afford you to the proper Points. I am &c.

[G. C.]

P. S. With respect to the Proposals directed to Genl. Jones I have only to request that when you are at Leisure & the public Service will admit of it, to forward them as I wo'd be sorry if the People concerned sho'd meet with Disappointment.

[To Gen. McDougall.]

[No. 2337.]

Signals for Alarm.

Whenever the enemy appear in Force on Hudson's River, the Commanding Officer at West Point, will order three of the heaviest Cannon at that Post, to be fired, five Minutes after each other. These will be answered at New-Windsor, by firing the like number, at the above distance. Then three Cannon will also be discharged at the Artillery Park at Fish Kill; at the like intermission.*

[No. 2338.]

Governor Clinton Directs Commissary Elmendorph to Rely on His Own Resources.

Pokeepsie May 31" 1779.

Sir; I have rec'd your Letter of yesterday. I do not think it will be convenient to order any Salt Provision from Mr. Reed as all that he is possessed of will be wanted for the Posts in the Highlands. I have given you the Number of Men and the Space of Time for which they are to be provided; you must make the necessary Calculations and lay in accordingly. I am &c.

[G. C.]

[To Commissary Coenraedt J. Elmendorph.]

[No. 2339.]

FORTY BRITISH SAIL REPORTED.

And the Commissary and Quartermaster Departments More or Less Disconcerted.

Fish Kill 31 May 1779 1 P. M.

Sir, Enclosed is the last intelligence I have rec'd, which I thought it necessary to communicate to your Excellency by ex-

---

* See preceding document.

press. You shall hear from me frequently; if there is any news of consequence arrives. I am w'h respect, Your Excellency's, most obed. Ser't,

Udny Hay.

I am just beginning to move off the stores from this; if lost the damage cannot be repaird this Campaign; that makes me more carefull.

If I mistake not much, there is a pass about three miles below this, where a redoubt may be thrown up in a short time, in which three hundred men w'h half a Doz'n pieces of Artillery (which we have here) would be able to retard the whole Enemy's army a considerable time.

U. Hay.

Governour Clinton.

———

Sir, This moment I have had Intellegence of the enemy; there is forty Sail of Shipping in the river Coming as fast as the wind will drive; its Genl. McDougall's Orders the Stores here are moved Immediately and I have not a team to do it with; if it is in your power to Send any relief for Heaven's Sake let it be Sent without the loss of time. I can make Shift to get away my public accounts and that will be all. While writing this two alarm Guns is fired at Kings Ferry. I am, Sir, Your H'ble Serv't

Danl. Carthy, for John Campbell, A. D. Q. M. G.

Cont'l Village 31st May 1779. (a Copy)

Col. Hay D. Q. M. G.

———

THE GOVERNOR ASKS FOR THE EARLIEST ACCOUNTS OF THE MOVEMENTS OF THE ENEMY.

5 P. M. [May 31, 1779.]

Sir, I have rec'd your Letter of Today containing Intelligence of the Enemy's approach. I sho'd be glad you wo'd continue to

give me the earliest accounts of their future Movements. The
Militia have my Orders to assemble at the Posts on the Firing of
the alarm Guns. I am &c.

[G. C.]

[To Col. Hay.]

[No. 2340.]

THE FORT AT KINGS FERRY ATTACKED.

*Colonel Udny Hay Begs for Teams and Governor Clinton on the
Way Down with Militia.*

Fishkill, May 31th 1779.

Sir; I have Just now been inform'd by Col. Hay that the Enemy
have ben up to Kings Ferry and Attacked the fort and in all
provibility they must have Surrendered and are now on thare
March to Peecks Kill. I am, Sir, your humble Ser't

Udny Hay.

4 O'Clock Afternoon.

Lett me entreat your influence in sending us down Teams immediately.

His Excellency Governour Clinton.

GOVERNOR CLINTON PROMISES ASSISTANCE.

[May 31, 1779.]

Sir, I have been favored with your second Letter of Today, Colo.
Swarthout has my most positive Orders to assist you with all the
Teams in his Brigade. I mean to be down Tomorrow with the
militia and I will direct them to impress all the Teams that can be
obtained. In the mean Time you will highly oblige me by Con-
tinu'g to give every Intelligence you may receive. I am endeavoring to get out the Militia with all possible Dispatch and hope to
take down a very considerable Force. I am &c.

[G. C.]

[To Col. Hay.]

[Nos. 2341-2342.]

THE ENEMY REPORTED IN GREAT FORCE.

General McDougall Anxious for the Stores—Governor Clinton Orders Out Teams and the Militia.

Fish Kill 31 May 1779 8 P. M.

Sir, Matters appear to remain much as by my last this afternoon, I suppose the enclosed* contain more particular accounts than I can give; We have no Horses to remove our Ammunition or Artillery. The Country is really tardy. You may depend on hearing from me whenever any thing happens worth relating. I wish you coud take a view of the ground below this. I am w'h respect, Your Excellency's, most obed't Ser't,

Udny Hay.

Governour Clinton.

———

THE GOVERNOR TO COLONEL HAY.

10 Cl'k night May 31" 1779.

Sir, I have rec'd yours of 8 P. M. inclos'g one from Genl. McDougal; it is dated at 5 P. M. it gives no other acc't than that the Enemy with 35 large vessels and a Number of Flat Bottomed Boats were up as far as Tellar's Point, where they had landed ab't 1500 men and a few at Haverstraw; that they were in great Force and had not then passed Kings Ferry. I have this Evening issued Orders and sent them by Express to the militia, to turn out all their Teams with unarmed Tories as Drivers, and to hurry them down to Fish Kill with the greatest Dispatch, but I imagine they will not be there before Tomorrow afternoon; those ordered by Colo. Swarthout may arrive earlier. You may rely on my best Exertions to assist you, and believe me &c.

[G. C.]

[To Col. Hay.]

---

*See McDougall to Governor Clinton, page following.

GENERAL McDOUGALL REPORTS TO THE GOVERNOR AND ASKS FOR
HIS ADVICE.

Village 31st May 1779 5 P. M.

Sir, I have this moment received your favor of this day. The
enemy have advanced up the River in about thirty five large
vessels, and a great number of flatt Bottomed Boats, as far as
Tallar's Point, where they have landed about 1500 Men, and a few
at Haverstraw. They are in great force, and they have not yet
passed Kings Ferry. Tomorrow I suppose, they will pass, their
force must be very considerable. The Succours of Militia, for
the Point, should be expedited without delay. Considering the
State of the Stores, and other Circumstances on this Side, I am in
doubt about the propriety of taking the Command at West Point.
The duty there is plain, but on this Side very complex. If I am
locked up there, I can be of no Service, but on the Spot. I wish
for your advice on this Subject, when you write again. I am,
My Dear Sir, your humble Servant

Alex'r McDougall.*

His Excellency Governor Clinton.

[No. 2343.]

THE MILITIA ON THE WEST BANK ORDERED OUT.

Governor Clinton Believes the Objective of the Enemy is Fishkill.

Pokeepsie, 10 Cl' Night, May 31" 1779.

Dear Sir, I have just rec'd your Letter dated 5 P. M. I am
using every Exertion in my Power to get the militia of this County
out to Fish Kill to which Place I mean to repair myself Tomorrow.
I have forwarded Orders this morning to the Militia on the west
Side of the River to march to the Forts on the Firing of the alarm
Guns, and as these were distinctly heard at this Place, I have no

---

* These documents have been consolidated for reasons that will appear obvious.—STATE
HISTORIAN.

Doubt but they are now on their march. However, I shall again repeat my Orders and make use of every possible means to expedite their arrival at those Posts.

It is clearly my Opinion every Thing considered, that you ought not to be in the Fort, if you have Officers there in whose valor and Prudence you can place Confidence, for I conceive it is probable that the Destruction of the public Stores at Fish Kill, (which I am informed are very valuable and that their Loss would be irreparable), are as likely to be their Object; however, of this you are best judge. I wish you heartily success, and am,

[G. C.]

[To Gen. McDougall.]

[No. 2344.]

Returns of flour seized by Hend'k. Wyckoff.

A Return of Flour Seized by Hend'k Wyekoff and delivered for the use of the army of the United States in the Month of May 1779.

Time when Seized	Whose Property	Where Deposited	To whom Delivered	Flour				Price of		Total Am't		
				Bbls.	C	Qrs	lb.	Flour pr C	Cask Contain'g the flour.	£	s	d
1779. May 20	Gilbert Purdy gone to the Enemy	Peter Kettletas Mill Rombouts Prec't	Jonathan G. Tompkins Esqr. A. C. P.	7	11	2	19	£16	3 Dol.	195	2	3 ¼

N. B. The above flour I have paid for to Doct'r Theod's Van Wyck, on his Demanding the same, as one of the Commissioners for Sequestration. Also have paid him for the flour Seized of Daniel Outwater— £195 2 3¼
amounting to as above
as pr Return of April Delivered to his Excellency the Gov'r—amounting to 229 12

£424 14 3¼

Total paid to Doct'r Van Wyck

Errors Excepted

Hend'k Wyckoff.

Fishkill May 31st 1779.
His Excellency Gov'r Clinton.

[No. 2345.]

A Return of Flour Purchased by Hend'k Wyckoff.

A Return of Flour and wheat Purchased and Delivered for the use of the army of the United States to Jonathan G. Tompkins Esqr. Asst. Commissary of Purchase, by Hend'k Wyckoff in the month of May 1779.

Time when purchased	Of whom Purchased	Where Deposited	Flour Bbls.	Flour C	Flour Qrs.	Flour lb.	Wheat Bushels	Prices Flour pr C £	Prices Wheat pr Bus'l £ S	Flour Cask Containing the flour Doll's	Total £	Total s	Total d
1779 May 1	Roelof Schenck	Samuel Verplanck's Mill Rombout's Precinct	4				200	16	6.8	3	1280		
2	Philip Sentzenbach	Philip Sentzenbach's House Beekmans Do		6				16			100	16	
3	Isaac Dennis	Isaac Dennis Mills Do					15		6.8		96		
4	Teunis Van Vleckren	Daniel Hasbrook's Mill Rombouts Do	1	2		11				3	34	15	5
5	Joseph Losee	Jacob Brinckerhoff's Mill Do					50		6.8		320		
5	Abraham Losee	Do Do Do					60		6.8		384		
7	John Sickles	Daniel Hasbrook's Mill Do	12	25	2	9		16		3	423	13	8½
	John Wyckoff	Do Do Do	17	29	3	11		16		3	497	19	5
11	Joseph Harris	Jacob Brinckerhoff's Mill Do					27		6.8		172	16	
12	Geysbert Schenck	Samuel Verplanck's Mill Do	22	40	3	13		16		3	680	5	1½
16	Mary Lennenton	Cornelius Van Sicklen's Mill Do	8	13	1	14		16		3	223	12	
20	John McKeeby	Peter Kettletas' Mill Do	30	51	1	2		16		3	856	5	8½
21	Ahasuerus Elsworth	John Cook's Mill Do	9	15	3	18		16		3	265	7	5
24	Adrian Brinckerhoff	Samuel Verplanck's Mill Do	7	13		13		16		3	218	5	1½
27	Matth'w V. Bunschooten	Teunis Van Bunschooten's Mill Do Do	50	85	2	13		16		3	1428		
		Total Purchased	160	283	2	7	352				£6981	15	11

Fishkill May 31st 1779.   Errors Excepted

His Excellency Gov'r Clinton.   Hend'k Wyckoff.

END OF VOLUME IV.